EFFECTIVE PUBLIC RELATIONS

EIGHTH EDITION

Scott M. Cutlip, APR, PRSA Fellow
*Dean Emeritus, Henry W. Grady College of Journalism
and Mass Communication
The University of Georgia*

Allen H. Center, APR, PRSA Fellow
*Distinguished Resident Lecturer
San Diego State University
Vice President of Public Relations (retired),
Motorola, Inc.*

Glen M. Broom, Ph.D.
*Professor, School of Communication
San Diego State University*

*Prentice Hall
Upper Saddle River, New Jersey 07458*

Acquisitions Editor: Leah Johnson
Editorial Assistant: Michele Foresta
Editor-in-Chief: Natalie E. Anderson
Marketing Manager: Shannon Moore
Production Editor: Tara Ruggiero
Permissions Coordinator: Monica Stipanov
Associate Managing Editor: John Roberts
Manufacturing Buyer: Kenneth J. Clinton
Manufacturing Supervisor: Arnold Vila
Manufacturing Manager: Vincent Scelta
Senior Designer: Kevin Kall
Design Manager: Patricia Smythe
Interior Design: Karen Quigley
Photo Research Supervisor: Beth Boyd
Image Permission Supervisor: Kay Dellosa
Photo Researcher: Anthony Arabia
Cover Design: Karen Quigley
Cover Illustration/Photo: Steve Puetzer/Amana America, Inc.
Composition: Rainbow Graphics, LLC

Library of Congress Cataloging-in-Publication Data
Cutlip, Scott M.
   Effective public relations/Scott M. Cutlip, Allen H. Center,
Glen M. Broom.—8th ed.
     p.   cm.
   Includes bibliographical references and index.
   0-13-541211-0 (case)
   1. Public relations.   I. Center, Allen H.   II. Broom, Glen M.
III. Title.
HM263.C78   1999
659.2—dc21   99-21943
                                           CIP

Prentice-Hall International (UK) Limited, London
Prentice-Hall of Australia Pty. Limited, Sydney
Prentice-Hall Canada, Inc., Toronto
Prentice-Hall Hispanoamericana, S.A., Mexico
Prentice-Hall of India Private Limited, New Delhi
Prentice-Hall of Japan, Inc., Tokyo
Pearson Education Asia Pte. Ltd.
Editora Prentice-Hall do Brasil, Ltda., Rio de Janeiro

Printed in the United States of America

10 9 8 7 6 5 4 3

IN LOVING MEMORY
OF ERNA FLADER CUTLIP

BRIEF CONTENTS

CONTENTS

PART II　　　FOUNDATIONS 143

CHAPTER 5　　　ETHICS AND PROFESSIONALISM 143

PREFACE

Scott M. Cutlip

Allen H. Center

Welcome to *Effective Public Relations (EPR)*. You are about to read a book that has a rich and important history. I (Broom) can say that because my senior co-authors practically created an institution when they wrote the first edition in 1952. This edition follows eight previous editions (including a fifth edition and a fifth edition *revised*) giving it a legacy matched by few books in any field.

The eighth edition of *EPR* will complete half a century of defining public relations as a profession, schooling its practitioners, and serving as a reference for those in the calling. For many of those years it was viewed as "the bible of public relations," often referred to as simply "Cutlip and Center." Since the first edition, **Scott M. Cutlip** and **Allen H. Center** have played leading roles in the professionalization of public relations and their revolutionary book made public relations an acceptable subject of academic study. Many of their ideas and ambitions in the first edition still serve as beacons leading public relations practice and study into the new millennium.

The role and function of *EPR* has changed however. No longer can it serve as the comprehensive encyclopedia of public relations—the body of knowledge has outgrown the bounds of a single book. No longer is it the only credible academic textbook or professional reference—many good books now help prepare future practitioners and serve the field. Public relations education and professional preparation have progressed beyond the limits of a single book or course. All the same, *EPR* is the basic reference for the field worldwide. It is the book used by those preparing for accreditation exams, and it is the book most frequently cited in public relations literature.

So what can you learn from the pages of the eighth edition of *EPR?* First, you will learn about the field of public relations, from how to define basic concepts to how the practice is conducted in various settings. Second, you will gain an understanding of the theory, principles, and processes that guide the practice. (Other public relations books and courses now cover in depth such topics as writing and techniques, research and evaluation, and management issues and case studies.) Third, you will learn updated information and examples to help you understand the concepts, models, practices, and issues in contemporary public relations. Each chapter begins with specific learning objectives to help you study and master the material.

This edition contains four parts: part I describes the field and defines basic concepts, describes what practitioners do and their work settings, and identifies influential historical leaders and traces the origins of current practice. Part II introduces the principles and theory that underpin and guide the practice. This part outlines the professional, ethical, legal, and media contexts of public relations. Within the framework of systems theory, chapters also present communication and public opinion theory essential to understanding the function of public relations. Part III applies theory to practice by outlining what is known as the "four-step public relations process." Part IV gives context to the practice by illustrating what public relations does and how it functions in business and industry; government and military; nonprofit organizations, health care, and education; and associations, professional societies, and labor unions.

You also need to know what *EPR* does not do. *EPR* does not trivialize public relations by presenting brief, oversimplified case studies. A few paragraphs cannot provide enough detail and background for you to be able to devise recommended solutions to complex problems. Rather, *EPR* provides the foundation for subsequent courses and books devoted to strategy and tactics for solving public relations problems. In short, although there are many sections that deal with applications in practice, this is not a how-to manual for public relations. One should be wary of how-I-saved-the-day books that claim to show how to succeed in public relations without first providing a foundation derived from the body of knowledge.

This eighth edition contains new data, ideas, examples, and sources from many people who influenced both the substance and style of what you are about to read. More colleagues than I can name here provided valuable reactions and useful suggestions on drafts of chapters. Some were unidentified reviewers who provided feedback on sample chapters. They will recognize how their feedback changed and improved the book. I hope Prentice Hall paid them handsomely for their work. Others either responded to my requests for help or through their own publications made significant contributions to this edition. At the risk of offending those not named, the following deserve special mention: **James E. Grunig, Ph.D.**, University of Maryland, College Park, and his colleagues in the IABC Foundation's *Excellence Project*, which contributed importantly to the theoretical foundation of the practice; **Ray E. Hiebert, Ph.D.**, University of Maryland, College Park, the long-time editor of the field's first scholarly journal, *Public Relations Review*; **Susan J. Henry, Ph.D.**, California State University–Northridge, whose creative historical research and powerful writing produced a series of must-read articles about the life and times of Doris Fleishman and her collaboration with Edward L. Bernays; **Melissa A. Johnson, Ph.D.**, North Carolina State University, who provided detailed feedback on the seventh edition and whose suggestions are reflected in the pages that follow; and **Elizabeth L. Toth, Ph.D., APR**, Syracuse University, Syracuse, New York, editor of the *Journal of Public Relations Research*, which records the body of knowledge that serves as a foundation for this and other books. Among colleagues also deserving credit here are the many authors of other textbooks who keep raising the standards of excellence in books serving our common interest in public relations.

Former and current students form a pipeline of new information and examples. I cannot list all who contributed, but those I most associate with this edition include: **Vicki Hoffman Beck**, Center for Disease Control, Atlanta; **Henry J. DeVries, APR**, Henry DeVries/Communications, San Diego; **Julian Hebron**, Financial Relations Board, Chicago; **Vance Hickin**, Ketchum Worldwide, Washington, DC; **Andrea Lacy**, San Diego Urban League; **Jim McBride**, Kaiser Permanente, San Diego; **Heidi Patterson**, Kreab/Stayer AS, Oslo, Norway; **MaryLee Sachs**, Hill & Knowlton, London; and **Bill Trunpfheller**, Nuffer, Smith, Tucker, Inc., San Diego. In addition, students in my classes suggested changes that made their way into the eighth edition. I want to thank them all and hope that you will be as generous with your suggestions.

Likewise, I cannot list all the practitioners who contributed to this edition. I pretested many of the ideas on them in presentations, in discussions and sometimes heated debates, and over extended lunches and dinners. Several responded to my requests for their help or served unwittingly as respondents to my ideas. I would like to mention a few of them: **Walter G. Barlow**, Research Strategies Corporation, Princeton, New Jersey; **Tom Gable, APR**, The Gable Agency, Inc., San Diego; **Patrick J. Jackson, APR, Fellow**, *pr reporter* newsletter and Jackson, Jackson & Wagner, Exeter, New Hampshire; **Walter K. Lindenmann, Ph.D., APR**, Ketchum Worldwide, New York; **Carol Perusso**, *Los Angeles Times*, Los Angeles; **Lori Lee Ragan, APR**, American Society of Association Executives, Washington, DC; **Kerry Tucker**, Nuffer, Smith, Tucker, Inc., San Diego; **John Woods, Ph.D.**, Chemonics, Washington, DC; and **Darlene Meadors**, Phillips Petroleum Company, Bartlesville, Oklahoma.

Four collaborators made extraordinary contributions to the eighth edition: **William C. Adams, APR, Fellow**, Associate Professor, Florida International University, helped with chapter 14 on business and industry; **Stephanie Casenza, APR**, Communications Officer, Alliance Healthcare Foundation, San Diego, helped revise chapter 16 on nonprofit organizations, health care, and education; **Mark S. Cox, APR**, Director of Public Communications, City of Chesapeake Virginia, helped update chapter 15 on government and politics; and **Kathy R. Fitzpatrick, J.D., APR**, Associate Professor, Southern Methodist University, Dallas, Texas, provided expertise in revising chapter 6 on legal issues.

Prentice Hall editors provided able assistance and firm direction in getting the eighth edition produced: **Gabrielle Dudnyk**, Editor, apparently gave up on trying to get slow-working authors to meet deadlines and returned to graduate school in business. I would like to thank her for her persistence and wish her well in her studies and new career. **Michele Foresta**, Editorial Assistant, provided a steady presence and valuable assistance in pulling all the pieces together toward a finished manuscript. **Leah Johnson**, Senior Editor, caught most of the mistakes and careless wording making the eighth edition more readable than my original manuscript was. Production Editor, **Tara Ruggiero**, skillfully turned all the pieces of the manuscript into the book you have in your hands. In spite of their seemingly unrelenting push to meet deadlines, their not-so-veiled threats about the consequences of my tardiness, and their marks all over my manuscript, I am indebted to them and appreciate their help in producing the eighth edition.

I am forever in debt to my co-authors for giving me the opportunity and the challenge of revising "Cutlip and Center." I am proud to be associated with them and with this book.

I am also grateful for the support of my wife, **Betty**. Often her most important support was serving as role model and setting the pace as she revised the ninth edition of a nursing textbook, published several research articles, and taught students how to help families bring healthy babies into the world. Countless "fun evenings" at the Broom house saw the two of us staring into our computer monitors late into the night. Without her love and support, I could not have found the energy or desire to undertake such a revision.

Nor would I want to do an eighth edition without you, the reader. This book is for you. It introduces you to the challenging and rewarding calling of building organization–public relationships in an era of instantaneous global communication. I hope the pages that follow help you achieve success and satisfaction in your public relations career.

Glen M. Broom
San Diego State University

Glen M. Broom

INTRODUCTION TO CONTEMPORARY PUBLIC RELATIONS

Public relations is the management function that establishes and maintains mutually beneficial relationships between an organization and the publics on whom its success or failure depends.

OBJECTIVES

After studying chapter 1, you should be able to

▼ Write a definition of *public relations* that emphasizes building and maintaining relationships between organizations and their publics.

▼ Distinguish between the public relations and marketing functions of organizations, identifying the *exchange* between provider and customer as the distinguishing characteristic of marketing relationships.

▼ Define and differentiate among related concepts, including *publicity, advertising, press agentry, public affairs, issues management, lobbying, investor relations,* and *development.*

▼ Outline how public relations helps improve organizations and society.

This book is about building and maintaining relationships. Individuals and groups have always entered into relationships with others to satisfy mutual wants and needs. In modern society, however, increased interdependence requires even more complex social, political, and economic interaction. As a result, establishing and maintaining relationships in all levels of social systems have become important areas of scholarly study and professional practice.

For example, *human relations, marriage relations,* and *interpersonal re-*

lations are terms used to describe the study and management of relationships between individuals. At the other extreme, *international relations* deals with relationships among nations, the largest social system. Courses and books are devoted to the study of these relationships, as well as relationships in families, work teams, groups, organizations, and other social entities.

This book is about relationships between organizations and their *publics*—people who are somehow mutually involved or interdependent with these organizations. The term *public relations* refers to the management of organization–public relationships, one of the fastest-growing fields of professional employment.

In everyday conversation and in the media, however, people use *public relations* to refer to many things, paying little attention to concise definitions. For example, some use "it's just public relations" as a pejorative description for what they consider to be an insincere public gesture. Others say something is "good public relations" or "great PR" if it appears in the newspaper or on the evening news, apparently equating public relations with anything that attracts media attention. Still others see public relations as trying to hide the truth or putting a positive spin on bad news. One author even suggests that "the terms PR and *public relations* have become widely accepted shorthand for subterfuge and deception."[1] In short, public relations means different things to different people, and often has negative meanings.

This chapter defines the concept of public relations in terms of a positive organizational management function, discusses its parts and specialized practice, and distinguishes it from other management functions and activities. The definition process begins with a review of how the concept has changed over the years.

EVOLUTION OF THE CONCEPT

Changing views of public relations reflect the evolution of this maturing function in organizations and society. They also indicate the struggle of an emerging profession seeking its own identity as a management function in organizations. Highlights of the evolution illustrate how the concept took on its current meaning. (See chapter 4 for a more detailed analysis.)

Powerful business interests in the early 1900s employed public relations to defend themselves and their monopolies against muckraking journalists and government regulation. The emphasis was on telling their side of the story and on counterattacks designed to influence public opinion and to prevent public policy changes calling for increased regulation of business.

One-way persuasive communication dominated as the United States entered World War I and President Woodrow Wilson created the Committee on Public Information. Headed by George Creel and staffed by young propagandists who would later establish public relations firms, the committee's goal was to unite public opinion behind the war effort through a nationwide propaganda campaign. During those early years, public relations took the form of publicity designed to influence others.

Many still define public relations as merely persuasion. For example, one dictionary defined *public relations* as "*inducing* the public to have understanding for and goodwill" (emphasis added). This definition reflects the writings of Edward L. Bernays—one of the founders of public relations—in his influential book, *The Engineering of Consent* (1955). Even today many practitioners work with managers and clients who see public relations as simply one-way communication to persuade others.

During the several decades following World War II, definitions evolved to include notions of two-way communication and relationships. Definitions included words such as *reciprocal, mutual,* and *between,* indicating a maturing view of the function. This interactive concept appeared in *Webster's Third New International Dictionary's* definition: "The art or science of developing reciprocal understanding and goodwill." The British Institute of Public Relations defined the function as an effort to establish and maintain "mutual understanding between an organization and its publics."

Previous editions of this text also defined public relations as an interactive concept, "the planned effort to influence opinion through good character and responsible performance, based on mutually satisfactory two-way communications." Another influential text during the 1980s emphasized communication in yet another version of this interactive concept, "the management of communication between an organization and its publics."[2]

Yale professor and *Public Opinion Quarterly* founder Harwood L. Childs had introduced an even more advanced concept in the late 1930s. Going against the conventional wisdom, Childs concluded that the essence of public relations "is not the presentation of a point of view, not the art of tempering mental attitudes, nor the development of cordial and profitable relations." Instead, he said the basic function "is to reconcile or adjust in the public interest those aspects of our personal and corporate behavior which have a social significance."[3] In short, Childs said that the function of public relations is to help organizations *adjust* to their environments, a concept of public relations that reemerged many years later as part of contemporary thought.

Organizational adjustment as the outcome for public relations suggests a management-level, policy-influencing role and calls for *corrective action* in addition to *communication.* The International Public Relations Association adopted these elements by including "counseling organization leaders" and implementing "planned programs of action" in its definition of public relations.

In summary, the one-way concept of public relations relies almost entirely on propaganda and persuasive communication, typically in the form of publicity. The two-way concept emphasizes communication exchange, reciprocity, and mutual understanding. An expanded two-way concept includes organizational adjustment, adding counseling management and taking corrective action to the role of public relations. Contemporary practice reflects all of these concepts.

DEFINING THE CONCEPT IN PRACTICE

Describing what public relations does in practice is yet another way to define the function. One of the most persistent efforts to define public relations operationally has been by *Public Relations News,* one of several commercial newsletters serving the field. Notice how this definition describes how public relations operates in organizational settings.

> Public relations is the management function which evaluates public attitudes, identifies the policies and procedures of an individual or an organization with the public interest, and plans and executes a program of action to earn public understanding and acceptance.

Hundreds have written definitions attempting to capture the essence of public relations by listing the major activities that make up the practice. A long-time public relations scholar and professional leader, the late Dr. Rex F. Harlow, collected definitions written between the early 1900s and 1976, identified the major elements in each, and classified the central ideas. He said he would attempt to say what public relations *is,* not say what it *does.* After analyzing 472 definitions, however, he produced a definition that includes both conceptual and operational elements:

> Public Relations is the distinctive management function which helps establish and maintain mutual lines of communication, understanding, acceptance and cooperation between an organization and its publics; involves the management of problems or issues; helps management to keep informed on and responsive to public opinion; defines and emphasizes the responsibility of management to serve the public interest; helps management keep abreast of and effectively utilize change, serving as an early warning system to help anticipate trends; and uses research and sound and ethical communication as its principal tools.[4]

In November 1982, the Public Relations Society of America (PRSA) formally adopted an even longer "Official Statement on Public Relations." The authors, a blue-ribbon panel of PRSA leaders, attempted to provide society members a definition of the field that stressed public relations' contributions to society. In addition to this conceptual aspect of the definition, the panel included activities, results, and knowledge requirements of public relations practice. (See Exhibit 1.1.)

Elements common to many definitions suggest that public relations:

1. Conducts a planned and sustained program as part of an organization's management.

EXHIBIT 1.1

PUBLIC RELATIONS SOCIETY OF AMERICA'S "OFFICIAL STATEMENT OF PUBLIC RELATIONS"

Public relations helps our complex, pluralistic society to reach decisions and function more effectively by contributing to mutual understanding among groups and institutions. It serves to bring private and public policies into harmony.

Public relations serves a wide variety of institutions in society such as businesses, trade unions, government agencies, voluntary associations, foundations, hospitals, schools, colleges, and religious institutions. To achieve their goals, these institutions must develop effective relationships with many different audiences or publics such as employees, members, customers, local communities, shareholders, and other institutions, and with society at large.

The management of institutions need to understand the attitudes and values of their publics in order to achieve institutional goals. The goals themselves are shaped by the external environment. The public relations practitioner acts as a counselor to management and as a mediator, helping to translate private aims into reasonable, publicly acceptable policy and action.

As a management function, public relations encompasses the following:

▼ Anticipating, analyzing, and interpreting public opinion, attitudes, and issues that might impact, for good or ill, the operations and plans of the organization.

▼ Counseling management at all levels in the organization with regard to policy decisions, courses of action, and communication, taking into account their public ramifications and the organization's social or citizenship responsibilities.

▼ Researching, conducting, and evaluating, on a continuing basis, programs of action and communication to achieve the informed public understanding necessary to the success of an organization's aims. These may include marketing, financial, fund raising, employee, community or government relations, and other programs.

▼ Planning and implementing the organization's efforts to influence or change public policy.

▼ Setting objectives, planning, budgeting, recruiting and training staff, developing facilities—in short, managing the resources needed to perform all of the above.

▼ Examples of the knowledge that may be required in the professional practice of public relations include communication arts, psychology, social psychology, sociology, political science, economics, and the principles of management and ethics. Technical knowledge and skills are required for opinion research, public-issues analysis, media relations, direct mail, institutional advertising, publications, film/video productions, special events, speeches, and presentations.

In helping to define and implement policy, the public relations practitioner uses a variety of professional communication skills and plays an integrative role both within the organization and between the organization and the external environment.

Formally adopted by PRSA Assembly, November 6, 1982.

2. Deals with the relationships between an organization and its publics.
3. Monitors awareness, opinions, attitudes, and behavior inside and outside the organization.
4. Analyzes the impact of policies, procedures, and actions on publics.
5. Adjusts those policies, procedures, and actions found to be in conflict with the public interest and organizational survival.
6. Counsels management on the establishment of new policies, procedures, and actions that are mutually beneficial to the organization and its publics.
7. Establishes and maintains two-way communication between the organization and its publics.
8. Produces specific changes in awareness, opinions, attitudes, and behaviors inside and outside the organization.
9. Results in new and/or maintained relationships between an organization and its publics.

The evolution of the concept and the numerous attempts to describe the practice lead to the following definition:

> **Public relations is the management function that establishes and maintains mutually beneficial relationships between an organization and the publics on whom its success or failure depends.**

This conceptual definition positions the many activities and goals in public relations practice as a *management function.* It also identifies building and maintaining *mutually beneficial relationships* between *organizations* and *publics* as the moral and ethical basis of the profession. At the same time, it suggests criteria for determining *what is* and *what is not* part of the function. As one scholar correctly observed, definitions serve at least two purposes: to help us understand the world around us and to argue for a particular world view of how one concept relates to other concepts.[5]

CONFUSION WITH MARKETING

Many people confuse public relations with another management function—marketing. Job openings for "public relations representatives" turn out to be positions as door-to-door sales representatives or telephone solicitors. In some small organizations, the same person does both public relations and marketing, often without distinguishing between the two functions. Because of this confusion, some have concluded that there is no difference between the two.

Confusion also occurs in nonprofit organizations and government where "nonprofit marketing" and "social marketing" refer to building and maintaining relationships with members, patients, donors, and other constituencies. In one such case, a practitioner who worked for a large hospital arrived on a Monday morning to find a new sign on her office door—"Marketing Communication Department." Much to her surprise, management had changed the title of the "Public Relations Department" without telling her! Hospital administration apparently saw no problem with putting a marketing title on the public relations department. After all, in their view, they were not proposing a program change, only a title change.

Those in the practice also add to the confusion. Some public relations practitioners' business cards say that they do "marketing communications" or "marketing support programs." Some public relations firms have "marketing communications" or "marketing public relations" in their titles and on their letterheads. A former principal of one such firm wrote a book describing "marketing public relations" as the practice "that supports the marketing of goods and services."[6]

In fact, many hired into "public relations" jobs spend much of their time supporting marketing, introducing new products and services, publicizing their uses, and promoting aspects of the marketing strategy. For many firms, marketing support pays the bills. As one principal said, "Take away our work in marketing and you take away more than half our business." After considering the public relations versus marketing distinction, the president of another public relations firm observed that if sales is not the mission of public relations, then "75 percent of public relations people are really in marketing."

This happens because public relations practitioners and their clients confuse publicity with public relations, because publicity is what their firm or agency is paid to do, or because they read one of the many books suggesting that public relations is really just a tactic used in marketing, "a promotional mix element concerned with how people feel about issues, products, and individual or corporate personalities."[7] Given widespread confusion even in the practice of public relations, it is not surprising that others assume that the purpose of public relations is promoting goods and services to increase sales—"just like marketing."

If not always clearly defined in practice, public relations and marketing can be distinguished conceptually and their relationship clarified. First, people's wants and needs are fundamental to the concept of marketing. What people want or need gets translated into consumer demand. Second, marketers offer products and services to satisfy the demand. Consumers select the products and services that provide the most utility, value, and satisfaction. Third, the marketer delivers the product or service to the consumer in exchange for something of value. *This transaction distinguishes the marketing function—two parties exchanging something of value.*[8] Marketing can be defined in a form similar to the definition of public relations:

Marketing is the management function that identifies human needs and wants, offers products and services to satisfy those demands, and causes transactions that deliver products and services in exchange for something of value to the provider.

In practice, marketing consists of a coordinated program of research, product design, packaging, pricing, promotion, and distribution. The goal is "to attract and satisfy customers (or clients) on a long-term basis in order to achieve an organization's economic objectives. Its fundamental responsibility is to build and maintain a market for an organization's products or services."[9]

To that end, product publicity supports marketing. Because public relations specialists typically know how to write for the news media and how to work with journalists, marketers call on them to write product publicity and to arrange media coverage of new products. These actions, however, are part of the marketing effort, as they are designed to promote the exchange between an organization and its customers. For example, the public relations firm Hill & Knowlton coached Procter & Gamble nutritionists on how to handle journalists' inquiries about the "fake fat" olestra, during the test marketing of Frito-Lay's Max fat-free potato chips.[10]

Some organizations treat the marketing relationship with customers as only one of many organizational relationships. On their organization charts, marketing is part of the larger public relations function. Other organizations view marketing as the major function, viewing all noncustomer relationships (with employees, investors, neighbors, government, etc.) as necessary only in the context of marketing. In these organizations, public relations is subordinate to and reports to marketing. A few organizations identify "consumer relations" as part of public relations, making the public relations department responsible for nonmarketing concerns of customers and other consumers—such as product use instructions, safety information, complaints, and repair service. In the majority of organizations, however, marketing and public relations are separate management functions with different but complementary goals.

The goals must be complementary because these are the two major management functions that most frequently deal with an organization's many external publics. Marketing typically operates as a *line management* function engaged in turning organization inputs into outputs of value to others. Public relations, on the other hand, operates as a *staff management* function providing counsel and other services to support line functions. In too many organizations, however, neither senior management nor public relations and marketing practitioners clearly distinguish between the two concepts or understand the relationship between the two organizational functions. (More on line versus staff management, and the relationships between public relations and other departments appears in chapter 3.)

In summary, marketing focuses on exchange relationships with customers. The result of the marketing effort is quid pro quo transactions that meet customer demands and achieve organizational economic objectives. In contrast, public relations covers a broad range of relationships and goals with many publics—employees, investors, neighbors, special-interest groups, governments, and many more.

Effective public relations contributes to the marketing effort by maintaining a hospitable social and political environment. For example, a hospital that maintains good relationships with volunteers, nurses, physicians, employers, local government, and community groups will likely enjoy success in the marketing effort to attract patients and referrals for treatment. Likewise, successful marketing and satisfied customers help build and maintain good relations with other publics, such as employees, investors, government regulatory agencies, and community leaders.

Misguided marketing strategies and gimmicks illustrate how these efforts can backfire and create public relations problems. "Joe Camel" may have been an effective marketing tactic for reaching children and teenagers, but it may have been the straw that broke the camel's back for the tobacco industry. Nestlé's successful marketing of its baby formula in developing nations earned it a tarnished reputation around the world when babies died from drinking the polluted water used to mix the formula. Pepsi's marketing promotion promised "Pepsi Stuff" for points collected from Pepsi products, ranging from a T-shirt for 80 points earned to a $24 million Marine Harrier jump-jet fighter for seven million points. The company earned negative press coverage and lost points by claiming the promotional was just a joke and rejected a 21-year-old student's apparently valid fulfillment of the promotion's offer on the Harrier jet.

Clearly, a university's relationships with its students, alumni, staff, faculty, and community groups help determine the success or failure of its marketing effort to attract new students. Likewise, if a bank suffers from employee morale problems and high turnover, from diminished investor confidence and resulting stock price drops, from increased regulatory scrutiny, or from diminished stature and reduced community involvement, then it may have difficulty mounting a successful marketing effort to attract customers. In fact, its public relations problems may become the message broadcast by competing banks in their marketing materials.

To achieve organizational goals, then, organizations must attend to both public relations and marketing. Each makes unique but complementary contributions to building and maintaining the many relationships essential for organizational survival and growth. To ignore one is to risk failure in the other.

PARTS OF THE FUNCTION

Public relations also gets confused with its activities and parts. For example, many think that "publicity" is simply another way of saying "public relations." Publicity is often the most visible part, but seldom the only program strategy. Similarly, "lobbying" is often the most noticeable public relations activity in Washington, DC, and in state capitals. Lobbying typically operates as part of a larger public relations strategy, with the lobbyists reporting to the organization's top public relations executives.

The contemporary meaning and practice of public relations includes all of the following activities and specialties.

Publicity

Much of the news and information in the media originates from public relations sources. Because the sources do not pay for the placement, however, they have little or no control over if the information is used, when it is used, and how it is used. Public relations sources provide what they think is newsworthy information, with the expectation that editors and reporters will use the information. Media decision makers may or may not use the information, based on their judgment of its news value and interest to their audiences. They may use the information as provided, change the original information, or change how it is presented, usually without identifying the source. In the eyes of readers, listeners, or viewers, the medium carrying the information is the source.

Publicity is information from an outside source that is used by the media because the information has news value. It is an *uncontrolled* method of placing messages in the media because the source does not pay the media for placement.

Examples of publicity include a story in the financial section about increased earnings for a major corporation, a columnist's item on the progress of a charity fund-raising campaign, a feature story in the health section announcing the latest scientific findings from a cancer research center, an entertainment calendar listing of the local appearance of your favorite music group, and television news coverage of the new civic center dedication ceremony. Typically, such stories are originated by the corporation's public relations department, the charitable organization's director of donor relations and development, the university medical school's news bureau, the music group's publicist, or the mayor's director of media relations (sometimes called "press secretary").

Print media usually receive a press release, feature story with photographs, or press kit including detailed background information. Broadcast media usually receive a broadcast-style news script, recorded interview, video news release (VNR), or press kit including material suitable for broadcast (see Figure 1.1). To generate publicity, the source must know what information will attract media attention, identify a newsworthy angle and lead, and write and package the information appropriately for each medium. It also helps to have a reputation among journalists as a trustworthy news source.

Newsworthy events also generate publicity by attracting media coverage. Groundbreaking ceremonies, ribbon cuttings, open houses, reunions, dedications, telethons, marathons, ceremonial appointments, honorary degrees, contract and legislation signings, organized protests, press conferences, and other "media events" are designed as "news." Disneyland made news, for example, when the 400 millionth "guest" entered the park. Network news crews covered the President signing environmental legislation as leaders of environmental groups posed with him on the White House lawn. By staging and managing such events, sources attempt to attract media coverage and to gain some control over what is reported. Successful publicity events have real news value; appeal to media gatekeepers; offer photo, video, or sound recording opportunities; and communicate the source's intended message.

In its infancy, public relations was primarily publicity, so it is not surprising that some still confuse publicity with the broader concept of public relations. Even today, public relations in some organizations consists of little more than publicity releases and special events designed to attract media coverage. There is much more to public relations than publicity, however.

FIGURE 1.1   PUBLICITY MATERIALS

Courtesy Nuffer, Smith, Tucker, Inc., San Diego.

Advertising

Whereas the source does not control publicity placement in the media, advertising sponsors can control content, placement, and timing by paying for media advertising time and space. Both publicity and advertising are nonpersonal, mediated communication, but advertising gives the source control over placement.

> **Advertising is information placed in the media by an identified sponsor that pays for the time or space. It is a *controlled* method of placing messages in the media.**

Many associate advertising with marketing—selling goods and services—but it is not limited to that purpose. Other parts of the organization also use this controlled means of placing messages in the mass media for nonmarketing purposes. For example, personnel departments place advertisements in newspaper classified and Sunday business sections to announce job openings. Legal departments place advertisements in "newspapers of record" to conform with public notification requirements, such as when corporations issue new bonds or sell shares, when recalling a defective product, or when complying with a court settlement. For example, Eastman Kodak Company lawyers placed advertisements in newspapers nationally, announcing settlement of the "Kodak Instant Camera" class action lawsuit. The advertisements described settlement terms and provided a return form to be completed by those who purchased instant cameras from Kodak.

Public relations uses advertising to reach audiences other than the customers targeted by marketing. For example, investor relations specialists place advertisements to assure stockholders and financial analysts that the corporation has thwarted a hostile takeover attempt, or to announce a merger, such as when Compaq Computer Corporation merged with Tandem Computers Incorporated. Public affairs at Southwest Airlines used advertising space in daily newspapers to encourage grassroots resistance to a proposed "head tax" on domestic airlines passengers. An areospace company's community relations department places an advertisement announcing its gift to the local symphony, yet not a single member of the intended audience buys the wing assemblies and air frames manufactured by the company. A local charity's public relations committee buys a full-page advertisement to thank contributors to the fund drive for a new homeless center.

Mobil Oil began using "advertorials" on op-ed pages and in magazines in 1970 (see Figure 1.2) "to speak out on a variety of issues designed to reach opinion makers."[11] According to Mobil's then–public relations vice president, Mobil's chairman wanted to make the company's positions on economic and political issues part of public debate. The advertisement did not sell Mobil products. The Minnesota Law Review described such corporate advertising as "a hybrid creature designed to use the means of paid advertising to accomplish the goals of PR." Another example is Toshiba Corporation's advertisements in major newspapers across the nation expressing "its deepest regrets to the American people" and admitting that one of its divisions had violated trade agreements. San Diego Gas and Electric (SDG&E) ran advertisements explaining why its board of directors unanimously voted to merge with Tucson Electric Power Company (TEP) and unanimously rejected SCEcorp's (Southern California Edison) unsolicited takeover. When the TEP merger fell through, SDG&E's advertisements explained why being acquired by SCEcorp would be in the best interest of customers, employees, and the community—until local opposition stopped that merger also. None of the advertisements promoted the consumption of electricity and gas. To the contrary, much like Mobil Oil, SDG&E wanted to express its point of view without having to deal with a sometimes unsympathetic press. Advertising allowed SDG&E to place messages in the media exactly how and when the company wanted. The recent merger of SDG&E's parent company (Enova) and Pacific Enterprises (Southern California Gas) received generally favorable treatment in the media during the review process, so neither company used advertisements to build support for the merger.

Organizations use advertising for public relations purposes when they are not satisfied with what is being said in the media, when they feel that their point of view is not being reported fairly, when they feel that their publics do not understand the issues or are apathetic, or when they are trying to add their voices to a cause. For example, Nike placed advertisements in major newspapers announcing the results of a six-month investigation of its labor

FIGURE 1.2   PUBLIC RELATIONS ADVERTISEMENT

Sanctions:
a fresh wind blowing

Old habits—like imposing economic sanctions on nations whose policies and practices we don't like at the drop of a hat—die hard. We are encouraged that the Administration and Congress are beginning to question the unilateral sanctions habit. While lawmakers are currently focusing on future sanctions, serious consideration should be given to developing a deliberative process for re-evaluating existing sanctions.

Since the end of the Cold War, the popularity and proliferation of sanctions have grown at an alarming rate. Currently, the U.S. has gone it alone, imposing unilateral sanctions on 70 nations, representing two-thirds of the world's population. The President's Export Council estimated sanctions were used 61 times between 1993 and 1996. Sanctions are popular because they appear to be an inexpensive way to express America's indignation or outrage with another country's behavior.

When the U.S. acts alone, sanctions usually fall far short of their goal and frequently produce unintended, adverse consequences. Unilateral sanctions may hobble the very citizens they're intended to help. They lead to lost business opportunities which cost American jobs both at home and abroad. They weaken U.S. trade competitiveness, damage our reputation as a reliable supplier and strain relations with staunch allies. All of this without persuading the sanctioned nation to change.

Policymakers' discomfort with sanctions has been building. Earlier this year, Undersecretary of State, Stuart Eisenstadt, announced the State Department was "reviewing the use of this controversial tool" in an attempt to develop guidelines for considering sanctions. The President has criticized the "automatic" feature of U.S. sanctions laws, noting that they hamstring America's foreign policy flexibility.

Lawmakers from both sides of the aisle are also concerned. Here's what several are saying:

■ "In many cases, unilateral sanctions are well-intentioned, but impotent [creating] the illusion of U.S. action. In the worst cases, [sanctions] actually undermine U.S. interests in the world." Senator Lugar (R).

■ "We need to bring some common sense to our sanctions policy. Sanctions used to be a method of last resort, but they've become a short-sighted reaction used too frequently by Congress." Senator Hagel (R).

■ "We need to be examining more alternatives to sanctions....The engagement with other nations, rather than isolation, is...a direction we need to pursue." Senator Johnson (D).

An 18-member Senate task force has been established to examine the sanctions issue. As it goes about its business, we would hope the Administration and Congress would put on hold any action on future sanctions. Put simply, adding more sanctions while a task force is trying to develop a solution would only exacerbate problems.

As a starting point, the task force should reconsider provisions of the recently tabled Lugar-Hamilton-Crane proposal. It's a common sense approach to sanctions—one that has gained considerable momentum in the Senate. It would establish criteria for using unilateral sanctions, assessing their economic and humanitarian costs and retiring them after two years unless they are re-approved.

The Lugar-Hamilton-Crane approach focuses on the future use of sanctions, but it does not address the troubling problems that existing sanctions have created. Nevertheless it is a good first step toward developing a deliberative, responsible process for economic sanctions.

It shouldn't stop there. The Congress should re-evaluate current sanctions with an eye to eliminating those that put the U.S. at a competitive disadvantage, tarnish our national reputation and unwittingly harm ordinary citizens of sanctioned countries. It's time to put this fresh wind to work.

Mobil The energy to make a difference.

http://www.mobil.com   ©1998 Mobil Corporation

Courtesy Mobil Corporation.

practices overseas. The company chose advertising in an attempt to counter the critical news coverage of "Asian sweat shops" and to deflect attention from being subjected to ridicule by editorial cartoonists, including the Doonesbury cartoon strip.

In the final analysis, given adequate budget, organizations turn to advertising to gain control over content, placement, and timing of public relations messages.

Press Agentry

In *Walking the Tightrope,* the late Hollywood publicist Henry Rogers summarized the essence of press agentry, "When I first started, I was in the publicity business. I was a press agent. Very simply, my job was to get the client's name in the paper."[12] He candidly reported that in 1939 he had lied to the West Coast editor of *Look* magazine about Rita Hayworth's "fabulous" wardrobe. The magazine devoted its cover and 10 pages of photographs to the then relatively unknown actress and her hastily borrowed clothes. Following such attention in a major national magazine, she became the talk of Hollywood, and Columbia Pictures extended her contract. To the extent that mass media coverage confers status, Rita Hayworth's early stardom can be attributed in part to her press agent's lies about the size and worth of her wardrobe.

Press agents attempt to attract public notice more than to build public understanding. Publicity is their major strategy. They base their approach on the agenda-setting theory, which says that the amount of mass media coverage subsequently determines the relative importance of topics and people on the public agenda. In short, the practice can be defined as follows:

> **Press agentry is creating newsworthy stories and events to attract media attention and to gain public notice.**

And the press coverage does not have to be positive, according to some. For example, the Swedish pharmaceutical company Astra AB's announcement that it had fired the head of Astra USA operations and several other U.S. executives received wide media coverage. The fired executives had been charged with "an organized pattern of sexual harassment" and embezzlement. An Astra board member was quoted in the Swedish magazine *Maanadens Affaaerer* as having said of the publicity, "Of course it's not good with sex scandals, but in the United States this has helped us get out Astra's name without having to pay expensive advertising fees."[13] *The New York Times* quoted a spokesperson for Bruno Magli shoes—made famous in the O.J. Simpson trial—as taking a similar view of negative publicity, "It's certainly not the best way to get the name out there, but it's effective. Now we have a bigger audience of people who know about our shoes."[14]

Press agentry plays a major role in record companies, circuses, tourist attractions, motion picture studios, television, concert promotions, and business enterprises headed by "media personalities." Press agentry plays a major role in political campaigns and national political party conventions attempting to build name recognition and attract large audiences through media exposure. Successful press agents gave us the legends of Davy Crockett and Hulk Hogan; promoted the Indianapolis 500 Memorial Day auto race and the Super Bowl into national events; turned Miami Beach and Puerto Vallarta into internationally known resorts; positioned Florida's Disney World and Euro Disney as vacation destinations even before opening days; and made the Batman movie series and each new Disney animated release must-see movies before the editing was completed.

In the candid words of a veteran press agent, "We stoop to anything, but our stuff gets printed." And it can pay off. A musical group's earning power may be as much a tribute to the skill of its press agent to get publicity as to its musical abilities. A career-launching appearance on a popular talk show may reflect the work of a press agent more than the talent of the guest. Likewise, a good press agent can make a new club or restaurant the "in place" even before a single customer experiences the ambiance, food, or entertainment of the place itself.

There are full-time press agents, but most public relations practitioners engage in a little press agentry at some time or another to achieve public notice through publicity. There is more to public relations than press agentry, however. Confusion results when press agents describe what they do as "public relations" or give their agencies more prestigious, if less accurate, titles. Hence, many journalists refer to all public relations practitioners as "flacks," even though *The Associated Press Stylebook* defines "flack" as "slang for *press agent*."

Public Affairs

The armed services, many governmental agencies, and some corporations use the "public affairs" title in place of public relations. In the armed services and governmental agencies, this title is part of a name game dating back to the 1913 Gillett Amendment to an appropriation bill in the House of Representatives. The amendment stipulates that federal agencies cannot spend money for publicity unless specifically authorized by Congress. This legislative hostility was reaffirmed in Public Law 92-351, Section 608(a), enacted July 13, 1972. This law expressly prohibits government spending on "publicity or propaganda purposes designed to support or defeat legislation pending before the Congress."

Neither the 1913 amendment nor the 1972 law refer to public relations. Nevertheless, many federal, state, and local governmental officials apparently confuse publicity with the larger concept of public relations. As a result, governmental agencies typically use other terms to describe building and maintaining relationships with their constituents. It is nothing more than a label switch, however, as thousands of public relations specialists work in government under titles such as "public affairs," "public information," "communications," "constituent relations," and "legislative liaison."

In corporations, "public affairs" typically refers to public relations efforts related to public policy and "corporate citizenship." Corporate public affairs specialists serve as liaisons with governmental units; implement community improvement programs; encourage political activism, campaign contributions, and voting; and volunteer their services in charitable and community development organizations (see Figure 1.3, pg. 16). Hewlett Packard's public affairs department states its mission as to "shape public policy to foster an environment that allows HP to achieve its business objectives."[15] Likewise, public

FIGURE 1.3   PUBLIC AFFAIRS JOB DESCRIPTION

Public Affairs Managers

Times Mirror Cable Television, one of the largest multi-cable systems in the nation, has maintained its commitment to bring quality entertainment and services to the marketplace. This continued demand for excellence coupled with new growth has created 3 additional openings for Public Affairs Managers.

The successful candidates will work with field management to develop and implement broad-based public affairs programs at subsidiary cable TV systems nationwide. Other responsibilities will include insuring franchise compliance, producing press releases and other media, developing and implementing strategies to resolve regulatory problems, and conducting a community relations program. In addition, to be effective in this position, it is crucial that applicants are willing to work in a staff support role.

For this position, we are seeking public policy-oriented individuals with a BA degree and a minimum of 5 years direct hands-on experience in at least 2 of the following: government relations, public relations, community affairs or the cable industry. Grad work and/or a law degree would be a definite plus. Other requirements include: strong oral and written communications skills as well as knowledge of local government and/or public sector regulatory functions.

We are a subsidiary of The Times Mirror Company and offer an attractive compensation and benefits package including free dental insurance and a company paid pension plan. If you are a talented, assertive and skilled professional, we encourage you to explore our career opportunities. For immediate consideration, please send your resume and salary requirements to the **Human Resources Department, Times Mirror Cable Television, P.O. Box 19398, Irvine, CA 92713. (No phone calls please.)**

TIMES MIRROR CABLE TELEVISION

We are an equal opportunity employer and encourage women and minorities to apply.

Courtesy Times Mirror Cable Television.

relations counseling firms use the public affairs label for their lobbying and governmental relations services related to affecting public policy.

A public affairs specialist recently clarified the relationship between public relations and public affairs as follows: "public affairs is the public relations practice that addresses public policy and the publics who influence such policy."[16] A survey of public affairs officers identified their major responsibilities as including (in descending order) federal government affairs, state government affairs, local government affairs, community relations, political action committees, contributions, grass-roots support, and issues management.[17] Forty-three percent of their departments use the title "public affairs." Other commonly used titles include "corporate affairs," "corporate relations," and "external affairs."[18] The practice can be defined as follows:

> **Public affairs is a specialized part of public relations that builds and maintains governmental and local community relations in order to influence public policy.**

Growing interest in public affairs parallels high turnover in government, changes in communication, increasing importance of state and local governments, and a more complex regulatory environment. For example, term limits imposed on elected officials and voter dissatisfaction with those in office have produced unprecedented levels of turnover in all levels of government. Such turnover increases the power of staff members, who may outlast the elected officials they serve, and increases the need to provide information to newly elected officials. The Internet, 24-hour news channels, C-SPAN, and satellite links worldwide give constituencies instant access to events around the globe. Federal budget cuts and decentralization of many governmental programs mean that government relations specialists must also follow programs from Washington, DC, to state capitals and city halls. All of these changes coincide with increased governmental and press scrutiny of those engaged in public affairs work, with rules and regulations constantly changing.[19] In short, public affairs work is occuring in an increasingly complex environment.

Issues Management

Two points capture the essence of issues management: (1) early identification of issues with potential impact on an organization, and (2) a strategic response designed to mitigate or capitalize on their consequences. For example, in the context of public opinion, issues management "attempts to discern trends in public opinion so that an organization can respond to them before they amplify into serious conflict."[20] As part of the public relations function, issues management is defined as follows:

> **Issues management is the proactive process of anticipating, identifying, evaluating, and responding to public policy issues that affect organizations' relationships with their publics.**

When issues management operates in areas of public policy, it is part of public affairs, which in turn is part of the larger public relations function. As originally introduced by public relations consultant W. Howard Chase in 1976, issues management includes identifying issues, analyzing issues, setting priorities, selecting program strategies, implementing programs of action and communication, and evaluating effectiveness. He said the process "aligns corporate principles, policies and practices to the realities of a politicized economy."[21] More recently, Chase has defined issues management as the process of closing the "gap between corporate action and stakeholder expectation."[22] A panel of experts expanded the definition beyond the public relations function.

> Issues management is the management process whose goal is to help preserve markets, reduce risk, create opportunities and manage image as an organizational asset for the benefit of both an organization and its primary stakeholders. This is accomplished by: anticipating, researching and prioritizing issues; assessing the impact of issues on the organization; recommending policies and strategies to minimize risk and seize opportunities, participating and implementing strategy; evaluating program impact.[23]

Even though issues management was originally touted as a new approach that would give practitioners new status, many practitioners do not see it as anything different from what they already do. Others express concern that the term suggests something unlikely and unacceptable because it sets up visions of manipulation—that an organization can "manage" major public issues. Many major corporations, however, have created issues management units, or "task forces," either by establishing specialized sections or by renaming existing sections of the public relations department. They concern themselves with how to respond to public concerns about downsizing and plant closings, globalization and the exportation of jobs, biotechnology (genetic engineering), damage to the ozone layer (greenhouse effect), toxic waste disposal, managed care in health care, an aging population, and corporate influence in politics.

Conceptually, if not always administratively, issues management is part of the public relations function. When viewed merely as persuasive communication to influence public policy, however, it becomes part of tactical decision making, not part of an organization's strategic planning. When concerned with adjusting the organization and building relationships with stakeholders to achieve mutual goals, "public relations and issues management are quite similar and result in similar outcomes."[24]

Lobbying

Lobbying, an even more specialized—and criticized—part of public affairs, attempts to influence legislative and regulatory decisions in government. Even though the U.S. Constitution protects the right to petition the government, some view lobbying as an attempt to manipulate government for selfish ends. Movies and television depicting smoke-filled rooms and payoffs by lobbyists working for powerful corporate and special interests perpetuate this cynical view of lobbying. News stories sometimes report illegal or questionable cash contributions to legislators, lavish fund-raising parties, and hosted weekends at exotic resorts designed to corrupt the democratic process and competitive free enterprise. However, it typically takes the form of open advocacy on matters of public policy.

Lobbying is a specialized part of public relations that builds and maintains relations with government primarily for the purpose of influencing legislation and regulation.

Federal and state laws open most lobbying to public scrutiny by requiring those who petition the government professionally to register and to report income sources and expenses. Registration laws and their enforcement vary from state to state, but all who engage in lobbying the U.S. Congress are required to report their activities and expenditures under the Federal Regulation of Lobbying Act (see chapter 6). In spite of occasional abuse and public rebuke, lobbying remains a legal and accepted way for citizen groups, associations, labor unions, corporations, and other special-interest groups to influence government decision making. Although clearly labeled and monitored at national and state levels, similar lobbying efforts on county and municipal issues often are part of and undifferentiated from public affairs, community relations, or other public relations efforts.

Lobbyists at all levels of government must understand the legislative process, know how government functions, and be acquainted with individual lawmakers and officials. Because such topics are not part of many public relations practitioners' educational preparation or work experience, lobbyists typically have backgrounds as well-connected lawyers, governmental administrators, elected officials' important staff members, or other insiders with good relationships with important governmental decision makers. In fact, critics say that lobbyists "sell" the influence they earned while working for government to special interest groups that want to influence the lobbyists' former colleagues.

The number of lobbyists has increased dramatically in recent years. For example, between 1975 and 1990, the number of lobbyists registered with the U.S. Senate increased from about 3,000 to more than 33,000. About three of every four companies with sales of $100 million or more have staffs engaged in lobbying. One publication lists more than 14,000 people and firms who represent 12,500 domestic and foreign businesses, trade associations, unions, and other advocacy groups.[25]

In Washington, DC, and state capitals, lobbying is closely related to "grassroots lobbying" and "political action." For example, the two sides for and against deregulating America's electric power industry spent $32 million in one year lobbying on Capitol Hill. Additional millions were "poured into research, polling, television advertising and stirring up grass-roots action."[26]

In practice, lobbying must be closely coordinated with other public relations efforts directed to nongovernmental publics. Sophisticated communication attempts to mobilize like-minded constituents so that their voices will be heard by lawmakers and officials in government. Computerized mailing lists, high-speed printers, and software for individualizing letters can produce a flood of mail, phone calls, faxes, and personal visits from constituents. Customized e-mail address lists; news groups, forums, and list servers on the Internet; and "blast" or broadcast faxing provide even faster ways to mobilize constituents.

Getting the folks back home to take up the cause is referred to as "grass-roots lobbying" and is part of many coordinated public relations efforts designed to influence public policy. In some cases, however, responses actually come from "front" groups created to deceive or mislead policy makers regarding public sentiment on the issue at hand. Former U.S. Senator (Texas) and Treasury Secretary Lloyd Bentsen referred to such pseudo-grassroots movements as "Astroturf lobbying." Examples of such front groups include "Citizens for Riverboat Gambling," funded by a gambling organization trying to pass a local referendum, and "Citizens for a Free Kuwait," funded by wealthy Kuwaitis trying to encourage U.S. participation in the Persian Gulf War.[27] Both front organizations were designed to give the appearance of widespread citizen support, when in fact they were created by their sponsors to promote narrow interests.

In its primary roles as credible advocate and reliable source of information, however, lobbying takes the form of information designed to persuade (see Exhibit 1.2). Lobbyists succeed or fail in part based on their traditional public relations skills: their abilities to construct and present convincing communications to government officials, to grassroots constituencies, and to their clients. In addition to those abilities, a sophisticated knowledge of government, legislative process, public policy, and public opinion processes is needed. Stereotypic images of the cigar-chomping insider dispensing stacks of cash no longer apply to most lobbyists and their work:

> Indeed, lobbyists spend substantially more time collecting information from government than they do communicating to it, since sound lobbying strategies, tactics, and positions are highly dependent on a strong base of information.[28]

Lobbying is an outgrowth of our democratic system functioning in a pluralistic society, keeping government open to those affected by proposed legislation and government regulation. In Washington, DC, and state capitals, the role of lobbying and other public affairs efforts will play increasingly important roles in formulating and implementing public policy. The challenge con-

EXHIBIT 1.2

LOBBYISTS

"I personally believe lobbyists have a very useful role. If you want to find out the real information, if you want a breadth of opinion, call the lobbyists who are for it and the lobbyists against it. You'll get an education in a hurry. They'll give you all the best arguments on both sides. I think the system works."

—Sen. James A. McClure (R–ID) from Bernard Asbell, *The Senate Nobody Knows* (1978).

tinues to be how to more effectively regulate campaign finance and lobbying. In the end, however, no law can prevent those determined to abuse or corrupt the right of all citizens to participate in government—to elect or defeat candidates and to petition those in office.

Investor Relations

Also referred to as "IR" and "financial relations," investor relations is another specialized part of public relations in publicly held corporations. Investor relations specialists work to enhance the value of a company's stock and to reduce the cost of capital by increasing shareholder confidence and by making the stock attractive to individual investors, financial analysts, and institutional investors.

> **Investor relations is a specialized part of corporate public relations that builds and maintains mutually beneficial relationships with shareholders and others in the financial community to maximize market value.**

Investor relations specialists keep shareholders informed and loyal to a company in order to maintain a fair valuation of a company's securities. Their work involves tracking market trends, providing information to financial publics, counseling management, and responding to requests for financial information. Annual reports, e-mailed earnings reports, and home pages that detail corporate financial information are the major strategies for disseminating timely information to analysts, investors, and the financial press. Here is an example of how it works to benefit both a company and its investors:

A new biotechnology company has 10 million shares outstanding, with each share selling for $20. The company has a market value of $200 million. Assume that the stock becomes more attractive to institutional investors, financial analysts, and individual investors as they learn more about the company's products, its management, "financials," and plans. If the share price moves to $25, the market value of the company increases to $250 million! Now assume that the company needs $10 million to support expansion or to research promising new products. At $25 a share, it needs to issue only 400,000 new shares, versus 500,000 shares at $20, to raise the $10 million to finance the expansion or research. Not only are investors' holdings worth more, but it takes fewer shares to raise additional capital.

On the other hand, consider what happens to the value of investments and the cost of new capital when a corporation loses shareholder confidence, fails to respond to analysts' concerns about the latest quarterly earnings report, or receives negative coverage in the financial press. The potential impact on market value and cost of new capital for large corporations amounts to millions, even billions, of dollars.[29]

Investor relations specialists must know corporate finance, accounting, Wall Street, international equities trading (the Tokyo Stock Exchange is the world's largest), international business trends, the Securities Exchange Commission and stock exchange financial reporting requirements, business journalism, and much more. "Public relations practitioners who do not have solid

FIGURE 1.4   INVESTOR RELATIONS JOB DESCRIPTION

Finance

INVESTOR RELATIONS

The Titan Corporation, a high-tech San Diego-based NYSE company, is currently seeking a seasoned professional to manage the company's investor relations programs. Reporting to the CEO, the successful candidate must be able to effectively communicate company information to all audiences, including shareholders, brokers, analysts, media and employees. Responsibilities include: liaison to the financial community; preparation of financial press releases; assisting CEO with shareholder and road show meetings; development and distribution of investor materials and company story; review of SEC filings; and maintenance of current shareholder, mailing and fax lists.

The ideal candidate will possess 10 years' direct experience in investor relations and corporate communications, excellent verbal/written communication skills, ability to deal with Board of Directors and Executive Staff, computer skills, and the highest standards of ethics and integrity. MBA preferred.

In return for your expertise, we offer an excellent salary and benefits package, including bonus and stock option programs. To take advantage of this excellent opportunity, please submit resume, including salary history in confidence to: The Titan Corporation, 3033 Science Park Rd., San Diego, CA 92121. Fax (619) 552-9745, Via E-mail to: resumes@titan.com We are an equal opportunity employer.

http://www.titan.com

⊘TITAN

Technology for Changing Times

Courtesy Titan Corporation, San Diego.

training and experience in business, management, and law will apparently be unable to fill even entry level positions in investor relations," according to researchers who studied CEO perceptions of the function.[30]

As a result, investor relations people combine studies in communication with coursework in corporate finance. An MBA degree is sometimes seen as necessary preparation (see Figure 1.4). It also helps to know more than one language, to be widely traveled, and to have studied the rapidly changing international political scene. Corporations and investor relations increasingly deal in a global economy. Because few practitioners have such required knowledge and background in finance and the competition for those who do is great, investor relations is the highest-paid specialty in public relations.

Development

As investor relations helps finance publicly held corporations, so do fund-raising and membership drives provide the financial support needed to operate charitable and nonprofit organizations. Such organizations typically use the title "development" for this aspect of public relations. Nonprofit hospitals, social welfare groups, disease research and service charities, and universities have a "director of development." Organizations that rely on membership fees for some or all of their revenues—museums, zoos, theaters, symphony orchestras, professional societies, unions, trade associations, and citizen-action groups—often have a "director of member services and development."

Development is a specialized part of public relations in private nonprofit organizations that builds and maintains relationships with donors and members for the purposes of securing financial and volunteer support.

Development specialists work for public broadcasting stations, disease prevention and research foundations, community arts groups, youth clubs, and religious organizations. Because these groups depend on donations, membership fees, or a combination of the two, they rely heavily on annual campaigns and special events to call attention to their needs and to solicit public support and contributions.

An annual telethon, 10K run, open house, homecoming, or celebrity auction, however, represents only a small portion of a yearlong program designed to establish and maintain relationships with volunteers, alumni, members, and donors, as well as prospective members and donors. Fund-raising activities and membership services make up part of an overall program to build and maintain relationships with various publics. This makes development a significant part of the larger management function—public relations—in nonprofit organizations.

Confusion of Terms

The terms discussed in the preceding sections all deal with an organization's relationships with specific groups or publics. They are all parts of the broader organizational management function known as public relations. Some organizations divide the function on the basis of internal and external publics. *Internal relations* deals with publics concerned about or involved in the internal workings of the organization, such as employees, families of employees, and volunteers. Relations with publics outside the organization—neighbors, consumers, environmentalists, investors, and so forth—are the responsibility of *external relations.*

Title confusion is further complicated when the total function is given one of many other labels such as *corporate relations, corporate communications, university advancement, hospital relations, public affairs,* and *public information.* Whatever name is used, the basic concept and function of public relations are similar from one organization to the next—large or small, local or global. All effective organizations establish and maintain relationships identified as important to survival and growth. In practice, however, too often employers and clients define public relations narrowly or wrongly by the various tasks they assign to it. In one organization, public relations takes the form of candid, open communication with many publics. In another, it attempts to maintain a silent, low profile. In one organization the purpose can be to provoke controversy and to maintain an adversarial relationship that motivates and activates members. In yet another, public relations tries to reconcile and compromise with an important public; for example, management may attempt to reconcile differences with a labor union.

Likewise, practitioners define public relations every day by the limits of what they do and by what they call "public relations." For example, many do product publicity because that is what they are paid to do under the rubric of public relations. Others see it as "getting ink" or exposure in the mass media, because that is their experience as former journalists now claiming to be public relations practitioners.

Concerned citizens see frequent references to "PR," "public relations," and "flacks" in press coverage of oil spills, industrial toxic waste leaks, political campaign shenanigans, city hall corruption, and so forth. Media coverage seldom associates public relations with positive stories of organizations and their accomplishments. Books such as *PR! A Social History of Spin* and *Toxic Sludge Is Good for You* selectively report post hoc analyses of press agentry and advocacy on behalf of clients and causes later proven to be of questionable merit. There is little market for books that report all the good work done by public relations on behalf of clients and causes judged to be worthy of public support. In other words, it depends on whose side you are on, much as it depends on which side lawyers represent in controversial cases.

In short, most people know public relations by what they see organizations and practitioners do or by what gets reported as having been done in the name of public relations. Few study the concept itself or the roles public relations plays in organizations and society. The challenge to practitioners is to define and perform public relations in ways consistent with the contemporary meaning of this necessary organizational and social function.

TOWARD RECOGNITION AND MATURITY

Some scholars credit public relations for the heightened attention to public accountability and social responsibility among government administrators and business executives (see Exhibit 1.3, pg. 26). Others point to the function's role in making organizations responsive to public interests and to its contribution to the public information system that is essential to a democratic society.

Public relations deserves credit for establishing and sustaining the connection between public support and organizational management's heightened attention to social responsibility and to leadership in personal standards of behavior. As one business leader long ago said, "We know perfectly well that business does not function by divine right, but, like any other part of society, exists with the sanction of the community as a whole. . . . Today's public opinion, though it may appear as light as air, may become tomorrow's legislation for better or worse."[31]

Public relations also helps organizations anticipate and respond to public perceptions and opinions, to new values and lifestyles, to power shifts among the electorate and within legislative bodies, and to other changes in the environment. This contributes to making the democratic process—as well as the social, economic, and political systems—more effective in meeting social needs. Without effective public relations, organizations tend to become insensitive to changes occurring around them and to become dysfunctional as they grow increasingly out of step with their environments.

Public relations also makes information available through the public information system. Practitioners increase public knowledge and understanding by promoting expression and debate in the competitive marketplace of ideas regarding, for example, the need for welfare reform, the causes of ozone depletion, the value of a new public transportation system, the impact of international trade barriers, or the need for blood and organ donations. Public relations serves the public interest by providing a voice in the public forum for every point of view, including the views of those—such as the homeless and powerless—who would not otherwise be heard because of limited media attention.

The practice serves society by mediating conflict and by building the consensual relationships needed to maintain social order. Its social function—its mission—is accomplished when it replaces ignorance, coercion, and intransigence with knowledge, compromise, and adjustment. In other words:

Public relations facilitates adjustment and maintenance in the social systems that provide us with our physical and social needs.

In the final analysis, an organization's relationships are the responsibility of top management. As public relations counselor Henry DeVries rephrased the definition of public relations, "Public relations is the boss's job to build and keep strong bonds with key groups that the organization needs to grow and thrive." Once this concept of public relations is embraced at the top, it spreads and becomes part of an organization's culture.

In the short term, the policies and activities of employers, clients, and practitioners often define the day-to-day practice. The evolution of the concept and the professional calling, however, reflects the changing needs of organizations adjusting to a global, multicultural society. In its advanced form, the function responds to long-term social needs, not to immediate special interests that ignore undesirable side effects and negative consequences for society. As practitioners accept their social responsibility and act accordingly, others will understand and value public relations' contributions to organizations and society.

Public relations professionals who help organizations establish and maintain mutually beneficial relationships perform an essential management function that has an impact on the larger society. They encourage social responsibility in organizations and promote public relations' essential role in maintaining social order. Inherent in this concept of public relations is a moral commitment to harmonious adjustment among interdependent elements of society. That calling motivates the chapters that follow.

THE ROLE OF PUBLIC RELATIONS IN JOHNSON & JOHNSON'S TYLENOL CRISIS

The public relations decisions related to the Tylenol crisis and the product's strong comeback came in two phases.

Phase one was the crisis phase, which began . . . with the grim news of the cyanide poisonings. Because the extent of the contamination was not immediately known, there was grave concern for the safety of the estimated 100 million Americans who were using Tylenol. The first critical public relations decision, taken immediately and with total support from company management, was to cooperate fully with the news media. The press was key to warning the public of the danger.

Later it was realized that no meeting had been called to make that critical decision. The poisonings called for immediate action to protect the consumer, and there wasn't the slightest hesitation about being completely open with the news media. For the same reasons the decision was made to recall two batches of the product and later to withdraw it nationally. During the crisis phase of the Tylenol tragedy, virtually every public relations decision was based on sound, socially responsible business principles, which is when public relations is most effective.

Almost immediately, planning began for phase two, the comeback, and this involved a more detailed and extensive public relations effort that closely followed important marketing decisions and reached out to many audiences. The comeback began officially with a 30-city video press conference via satellite, an innovative approach suggested by Burson-Marsteller, a public relations agency responsible for Tylenol product publicity.

The video conference and all other key decisions were discussed and debated by a seven-member strategy committee formed by Chairman and CEO James E. Burke to deal with the Tylenol crisis. The committee included a public relations executive and met twice daily for six weeks. The decisions it made dealt with every aspect of the problem—from packaging to advertising to appearances on network television. Many required follow-up by the public relations staff at corporate and McNeil Consumer Products Company—the subsidiary that manufacturers Tylenol.

The Tylenol tragedy proved once again that public relations is a business of basics and that the best public relations decisions are closely linked to sound business practices and a responsible corporate philosophy.

—Lawrence G. Foster
Corporate Vice President–Public Relations (retired)
Johnson & Johnson

Courtesy Lawrence G. Foster and reprinted with permission from *Public Relations Journal.*

NOTES

1. Stuart Ewen, *PR! A Social History of Spin* (New York: Basic Books, 1996), viii.
2. James E. Grunig and Todd Hunt, *Managing Public Relations* (New York: Holt, Rinehart and Winston, 1984), 6.
3. Harwood L. Childs, *An Introduction to Public Opinion* (New York: John Wiley and Sons, 1940), 3, 13.

4. Rex F. Harlow, "Building a Public Relations Definition," *Public Relations Review* 2, no. 4 (Winter 1976): 36.

5. Joye C. Gordon, "Interpreting Definitions of Public Relations: Self Assessment and a Symbolic Interactionism-Based Alternative," *Public Relations Review* 23, no. 1 (Spring 1997): 57–66.

6. Thomas L. Harris, *The Marketer's Guide to Public Relations* (New York: John Wiley and Sons, 1991). Examples on the first page of the first chapter illustrate the use of publicity and other sales promotion activities in marketing. This is not a book about public relations. Rather, it describes how public relations practitioners apply their understanding and skills to support marketing.

7. Bruce G. Vanden Bergh and Helen Katz, *Advertising Principles: Choice, Challenge, Change* (Lincolnwood, IL: NTC Business Books, 1999): 537.

8. Philip Kotler, *Marketing Management,* 9th ed. (Upper Saddle River, NJ: Prentice-Hall, 1997), 9–12.

9. Glen M. Broom and Kerry Tucker, "An Essential Double Helix," *Public Relations Journal* 45, no. 11 (November 1989): 39. See also Glen M. Broom, Martha M. Lauzen, and Kerry Tucker, "Public Relations and Marketing: Dividing the Conceptual Domain and Operational Turf," *Public Relations Review* 17, no. 3 (Fall 1991): 219–25.

10. Raju Narisetti, "Anatomy of a Food Fight: The Olestra Debate," *The Wall Street Journal,* July 31, 1996, p B1.

11. Gerri L. Smith and Robert L. Heath, "Moral Appeals in Mobil Oil's Op-Ed Campaign," *Public Relations Review* 16, no. 4 (Winter 1990): 49.

12. Henry C. Rogers, *Walking the Tightrope: The Private Confessions of a Public Relations Man* (New York: William Morrow, 1980), 14.

13. Associated Press, "Astra Exec Fired in Sex, Theft Scandal," *San Diego Union-Tribune,* June 27, 1996, Business Section, p 2.

14. "A Shoe-In for Product Publicity," *Public Relations Tactics,* 4, no. 1 (January 1997), 3.

15. Raymond L. Hoewing, "The State of Public Affairs: A Profession Reinventing Itself," in *Practical Public Affairs in an Era of Change,* ed. Lloyd B. Dennis (Lanham, MD: University of Press of America, 1996), 45.

16. John L. Paluszek, "Editorial Note: Defining Terms," in *Practical Public Affairs,* ed. Dennis, xviii.

17. Hoewing, "The State of Public Affairs," in *Practical Public Affairs,* ed. Dennis, 34.

18. Ibid., 35

19. Margery Kraus, "Government Relations in the 90s and Beyond," in *Practical Public Affairs,* ed. Dennis, 89–100.

20. Priscilla Murphy, "Chaos Theory as a Model for Managing Issues and Crises," *Public Relations Review* 22, no. 2 (Summer 1996): 103.

21. W. Howard Chase, "Public Issue Management: The New Science," *Public Relations Journal* 33, no. 10 (October 1977): 25–26.

22. W. Howard Chase and Teresa Yancey Crane, "Issue Management: Dissolving the Archaic Division between Line and Staff," in *Practical Public Affairs,* ed. Dennis, 130–31.

23. Kerry Tucker and Glen Broom, "Managing Issues Acts as Bridge to Strategic Planning," *Public Relations Journal* 49, no. 11 (November 1993): 38–40.

24. Martha M. Lauzen, "Understanding the Relation between Public Relations and Issues Management," *Journal of Public Relations Research* 9, no. 1 (1997): 80. For a theoretical basis of issues management, see Robert L. Heath, "Corporate Issues Management: Theoretical Underpinnings and Research Foundation," *Public Relations Research Annual* 2 (1990): 29–65.

25. Washington Representatives, 15th ed. (Washington, DC: Columbia Books, 1991).

26. Jim Drinkard (Associated Press), "Lobbyists Play Key Role in Deregulation Power Play," *San Diego Union-Tribune,* April 27, 1997, sec. I, pp. 1, 8.

27. Carol A. Bodensteiner, "Special Interest Group Coalitions: Ethical Standards for Broad-Based Support Efforts," *Public Relations Review,* 23, no. 1 (Spring 1997): 31–46.

28. Charles S. Mack, "Lobbying and Political Action," in *Practical Public Affairs,* ed. Dennis, 105.

29. For detailed analysis of investor relations program impact on stock prices, see Kenneth A. Saban, "Demasking Wall Street's Influence on Stock Prices," *Public Relations Review* 13, no. 3 (Fall 1987): 3–11.

30. Barbara K. Petersen and Hugh J. Martin, "CEO Perceptions of Investor Relations as a Public Relations Function: An Exploratory Study," *Journal of Public Relations Research* 8, no. 3 (1996): 205–6.

31. Quote from former General Electric Company President Ralph J. Cordiner, as reported in Scott M. Cutlip and Allen H. Center, *Effective Public Relations,* 2d ed. (Upper Saddle River, NJ: Prentice-Hall, 1958), 6.

ADDITIONAL SOURCES

Center, Allen H., and Patrick Jackson. *Public Relations Practices: Managerial Case Studies and Problems,* 5th ed. Upper Saddle River, NJ: Prentice-Hall, 1995. Collection of classic case studies illustrating problems and opportunities in managing public relations.

Grunig, James E., ed. *Excellence in Public Relations and Communication Management.* Hillsdale, NJ: Lawrence Erlbaum Associates, 1992. Influential summary of public relations theory and research literature produced with the support of International Association of Business Communicators (IABC) Research Foundation.

Kelly, Kathleen S. *Effective Fund-Raising Management.* Mahwah, NJ: Lawrence Erlbaum Associates, 1997. Introduces history, theory, ethics, legal issues, and techniques of expanding practice of fund raising and development in not-for-profit settings.

Kotler, Philip. *Marketing Management: Analysis, Planning, Implementation, and Control,* 9th ed. Upper Saddle River, NJ: Prentice Hall, 1997. A marketing expert's view of public relations as a marketing tool—"like advertising and sales promotion."

Newsom, Doug, Judy VanSlyke Turk, and Dean Kruckeberg. *This Is PR: The Realities of Public Relations,* 6th ed. Belmont, CA: Wadsworth Publishing Co., 1996. One of several useful introductions to the field.

Toth, Elizabeth L., and Robert L. Heath, eds. *Rhetorical and Critical Approaches to Public Relations.* Hillsdale, NJ: Lawrence Erlbaum Associates, 1992. Discusses public relations as rhetorical dialogue and describes critical theorists' methods for studying public relations.

White, Jon, and Laura Mazur. *Strategic Communications Management: Making Public Relations Work.* Wokingham, UK: Addison-Wesley, 1995. British perspective on rapidly growing public relations practice in Europe.

Wilcox, Dennis L., Phillip H. Ault, and Warren K. Agee. *Public Relations Strategies and Tactics,* 5th ed. New York: HarperCollins College Publishers, 1998. Yet another useful introductory text.

PRACTITIONERS OF PUBLIC RELATIONS

The way to gain a good reputation is to endeavor to be what you desire to appear.

—*Socrates*

OBJECTIVES

After studying chapter 2, you should be able to

▼ Describe practitioners' characteristics and work assignments.

▼ Define the four major roles played by practitioners, discuss the major differences among the roles, and distinguish among them in practice.

▼ List the five criteria for evaluating the professional status of public relations and discuss the extent to which public relations measures up on each of the criteria.

▼ Outline the major requirements for success in public relations, identifying *writing* as the primary requirement for entry to the field and success in the practice.

This chapter discusses the number of public relations practitioners, who they are, what they do, the roles they play, and their professional aspirations. Compared with accounting, law, medicine, and nursing, the relatively young practice of *public relations is an emerging profession*. Unlike the more established professions, public relations does not require a prescribed educational preparation, government-sanctioned qualifying exams, and peer review to assure competent and ethical practice. Nor do its practitioners operate in clearly defined roles recognized as essential for the common good. And because there are no complete official lists, estimates of who and how many practice public relations are based on membership data from the major professional societies and statistics from the U.S. Department of Labor.

NUMBER AND DISTRIBUTION

The number of practitioners continues to increase as organizational, social, economic, and political forces change the role and stature of the public relations practitioners worldwide. For example, a professor in the Netherlands estimates that there are 1.5 million public relations professionals worldwide.[1] *Reed's Worldwide Directory of Public Relations Organizations* reports that approximately 150,000 members belong to 215 public relations associations, societies, clubs, and other groups worldwide.

Different organizational titles and job descriptions, however, make accurate counts difficult even in the United States, let alone worldwide. As noted in chapter 1, what one organization calls "marketing communication" may actually describe a public relations position. What another organization calls a "public relations representative" would be more accurately titled "sales" or "customer service representative." Little agreement on the underlying concept and inconsistent use of titles complicate attempts to count how many really work in public relations.

The U.S. Department of Labor reports public relations employment statistics in its monthly *Employment and Earnings* under the occupational headings "managers: marketing, advertising and public relations" and "public relations specialists." Unfortunately, these categories do not include all who work in the field. For example, public relations managers are counted along with other managers, so separate counts are not available. Artists, graphic designers, photographers, videographers, lobbyists, receptionists, researchers, and other specialists who work in public relations departments and firms may be counted in other categories. As a result, the Labor Department's figures probably include fewer than half of all those working in public relations. Even though the data are incomplete, Table 2.1 clearly illustrates public relations' rapid growth and why *Fortune* magazine rated it among the 20 most rapidly growing industries during the 1990s.[2] And the number of jobs will continue to increase, according to the October 27, 1997, "Best Jobs" issue of *U.S. News & World Report,* with a 55 percent increase by 2006.

Where They Work

Employment opportunities for public relations specialists exist in almost every community but are concentrated in major population centers. For example, the greatest numbers of Public Relations Society of America (PRSA) members are in California, New York, Texas, Ohio, Michigan, Pennsylvania, and Illinois. Washington, DC, however, has the largest PRSA chapter, with al-

TABLE 2.1	PUBLIC RELATIONS EMPLOYMENT	
		Number of "Public Relations Specialists"[a]
	1950	19,000
	1960	31,000
	1970	76,000
	1980	126,000
	1990	162,000
	2000 projected[b]	197,000

[a] U.S. Department of Labor category and statistics from *Employment and Earnings* reports.
[b] Projected total computed using linear regression model.

most 1,000 members. New York is a close second, with almost 920. The Atlanta, Georgia chapter has more than 700 members; the Chicago chapter, 560; Detroit, 500; Denver, Colorado, 480; and Los Angeles, 465.

About 40 percent of practitioners work in business and commercial corporations: manufacturing, financial, industrial, consumer goods, media, utilities, transportation, and entertainment; 27 percent in public relations firms, advertising agencies, and individual consultancies; 14 percent in associations, foundations, and educational institutions; 8 percent in health care: hospitals, medical agencies, and other health services; 6 percent in federal, state, and local government; and 5 percent in charitable, religious, and other nonprofit organizations (see Table 2.2, pg. 32).

The single largest employer for public relations is the federal government. According to the U.S. Office of Personnel Management, 4,400 "public affairs" specialists work under various titles. The total jumps to almost 20,000 in the "information and arts" category, however, when the count includes photographers, writers and editors (not including technical writers and editors), visual information specialists, and others working in public communication for the government.[3] Presumably, this figure includes the 6,567 persons working for the U.S. Information Agency: 3,323 in the United States and 3,244 abroad.[4] However, because the function is often camouflaged to hide it from Congress and the press, reliable figures on the number of public relations specialists in government are not available.

The growing number of public relations firms range in size from an individual counselor (who may use "and Associates") to a large national and international firm with a staff of several hundred. For example, New York–based Burson-Marsteller—the largest firm, with net fees worldwide of $265 million—employs more than 2,100. The second-largest firm—London-based Shandwick, with net fees of almost $160 million—has 1,750 employees worldwide. Each of the next four largest firms—Porter Novelli International, Fleishman-Hillard, Edelman Public Relations Worldwide, and Ketchum Public Relations Worldwide—employs more than 1,000. Burson-Marsteller and Hill &

TABLE 2.2

PUBLIC RELATIONS EMPLOYERS

Organization	Estimated Percentage of Practitioners[a]
Corporations: manufacturing, industrial, consumer goods, financial, insurance media, and entertainment	40
Public relations firms, advertising agencies, marketing communication firms, and individual practitioners	27
Associations, foundations, and educational institutions	14
Health care: hospitals, health maintenance organizations, clinics, home health care agencies, and mental health facilities	8
Government: local, state, and federal	6
Charitable, religious, and social welfare organizations	5

[a] Estimates based on PRSA and IABC membership profiles and descriptive statistics from other surveys of practitioners.

Knowlton, with offices worldwide, both have headquarters in New York. Burson-Marsteller has 350 employees in New York, 135 in Washington, DC, and 100 in Chicago. Hill & Knowlton employs more than 150 in New York, 120 in Washington, DC, and 80 in Los Angeles. Shandwick has more employees in its Minneapolis office—125—than in its London headquarters—100. Fleishman-Hillard, an international firm based in St. Louis, employs 325 in its headquarters office, 115 in Washington, DC, 100 in New York, and 80 in both Kansas City, Missouri, and Los Angeles. The largest firm in Los Angeles—Rogers and Cowan of Shandwick—employs about 100 practitioners.[5]

Several major corporations have 100 or more public relations specialists in headquarters and branch offices. Downsizing during the 1990s greatly reduced the number of large staffs and shifted work (outsourcing) to a growing number of increasingly specialized external firms and individual practitioners. Public relations staffs work in international and national corporate headquarters and in branch offices around the globe. AT&T has 450 public relations specialists, the National Association of Securities Dealers (NASD) employs 45, Owens Corning 30 (down from 42 in 1997), and ITT only 2 (down from about 180 in the mid-1980s).[6] Four out of five practitioners, however, work in departments that have fewer than 10 public relations professionals.[7]

The New Majority: Women

According to 1968 U.S. Department of Labor statistics for the "public relations specialists" occupational category, only 25 percent were women. By the end of 1983, women held more than 50 percent of public relations jobs. In the January 1998 report, 65.7 percent were women.[8]

When the late Rea Smith wrote "Women in Public Relations: What They Have Achieved" in 1968, only one in ten members of PRSA was female.[9] The ratio was one in seven in 1975 when Sondra Gorney concluded that "the walls of the traditional 'man's world' have not tumbled yet."[10] Apparently the walls had tumbled by 1990, when PRSA membership was 54 percent female, and International Association of Business Communicators (IABC) membership was 60 percent female.[11] Current PRSA membership is approximately 60 percent female, and IABC's membership is almost 65 percent female.[12] Surveys of colleges and universities indicate that there are approximately two female students for every male student planning to enter the profession.[13]

EDUCATION AND PREPARATION

More than 92 percent of practitioners are college graduates, including almost 23 percent with some postgraduate studies without a graduate degree completed, 25 percent with master's degrees, and two percent with doctoral degrees.[14] Surveys typically show that practitioners enter the field from many academic majors and work experiences. Approximately 40 percent majored in journalism, with news-editorial graduates outnumbering public relations graduates two to one. English, speech, communication, and business (in that order) follow journalism as college majors of those entering public relations.

Increasingly, however, employers look for specialized public relations degrees and advanced degrees emphasizing research and social science. Professional development programs stress updating skills and career planning. In addition to the more than 300 colleges and universities offering public relations undergraduate and graduate programs, PRSA, IABC, Arthur W. Page Society, and other professional groups sponsor continuing education courses, institutes, seminars, and conferences.

Journalism experience is no longer required preparation for public relations employment. On the other hand, journalistic media experience gives practitioners an understanding of media gatekeepers' values and ways of working. If that experience leads to a "journalist-in-residence" approach, however, public relations will be limited to news dissemination and media relations. Older and more experienced practitioners have typically worked in the media prior to their career in public relations. Fewer than one out of four younger practitioners have worked for newspapers, magazines, radio stations, or television stations before being hired in public relations. More and more employers and public relations managers consider public relations education desirable preparation, making it easier to move directly into the field after graduation. Given the choice, however, employers still value media experience, even if only with the school newspaper or radio station.

Many employers also look for education or experience in a specialized field in addition to public relations. The most difficult positions to fill are those that require specialized preparation and backgrounds such as computer technology, corporate finance, health care, and agriculture. For example, students who combine public relations education with a minor in health care or hospital administration have a clear advantage when applying for hospital public relations openings. Likewise, graduates who minored in computer science while completing their public relations education have a competitive advantage in the world of high-tech public relations.

SALARIES

PRSA reports the highest salaries are paid to practitioners working for management consulting firms, marketing communication firms, financial or insurance companies, and utilities (see Table 2.3). IABC reports salaries by major product or service, showing that the highest paid practitioners worked in petroleum, automotive, metals and mining, communications utility, and aerospace companies.

Many experienced practitioners earn $100,000, $200,000, or more. These practitioners typically work for multibillion-dollar corporations in which the top public relations executives often are corporate officers, either elected or appointed. Officers typically receive stock options, bonus or profit-sharing checks, and lucrative retirement programs in addition to their six-figure salaries. Fringe benefits and perquisites add considerable value to their positions. Employers do not frivolously dispense high salaries or extra benefits, however. Just as when recruiting other top executives, employers must compete for top public relations professionals and managers. For example, Fidelity Investments, Boston, paid more than $500,000 in salary when it hired a new senior vice president to head the public relations function. The compensation package for the top public relations post at Time Warner reportedly totals $1 million.

Competition for management-level talent is so intense that executive search firms (sometimes called "headhunters") are retained to identify, screen, and recruit finalists for top public relations positions. Executive recruiters report that "some top corporate PR posts are now paying $500,000+ and management is having a hard time filling them. Searches go on for a year or more."[15]

Salaries tend to be highest in the Northeast and Middle Atlantic, led by New York and Washington, DC. The West also pays relatively high salaries, with northern California's Silicon Valley leading that part of the country. Salaries in the Midwest and South are below the national median. The U.S. Department of Labor reports that the median weekly salary for full-time wage and salary workers in public relations is $656.[16]

Salary survey results show a pay difference in public relations that deserves special attention: Surveys consistently find that salaries paid to women are below those paid to men. For example, PRSA's most recent salary survey put the gap at $18,350, with the difference tied to age and years of experience. PRSA found that 56 percent of women earn less than $45,000, but only 27 percent of men earn below that salary. At the other end of the salary scale,

TABLE 2.3

SALARIES

	Median
All Respondents (n = 2,405)	**$ 49,073**
By Type of Organization	
Financial / insurance	66,284
Utility	65,609
Public relations counseling firm	64,364
Travel / hotel / entertainment	55,640
Industrials / manufacturing	53,029
Solo practitioner / consultant	51,298
Professional services	50,666
Government	48,928
Health care	47,871
Scientific / technical	47,744
Religious / charitable	42,705
Association / foundation	42,496
Advertising agency	40,426
Education	39,042
Media / communications	37,097
Entry-Level Respondents	**23,030**
By Type of Organization	
Corporations	23,550
Nonprofit organizations	23,210
Public relations firms	21,110
By Region	
West (includes AL and HI)	25,790
Northeast	24,010
South	22,350
Midwest	22,160

Source: Salary Survey of Public Relations Professionals (New York: Public Relations Society of America, 1996), 23–24, 27. (Study conducted for PRSA by Simmons Market Research Bureau.)

29 percent of the men in PRSA—but only 13 percent of the women—earn $75,000 or more.[17]

Researchers have studied the relationship between gender and salary in public relations since at least 1979. One series of studies tracked practitioner salaries from 1979 to 1985 to 1991. Between 1979 and 1985, the salary gap between men and women increased. The results showed that women earned less than men even when they had equal education, professional experience, and tenure in their jobs.[18] That disparity appears to be diminishing, however. When researchers compared 1979 salaries with 1991 salaries and controlled for years of professional experience, role in management, and participation in decision making, salary differences between men and women were not statistically significant.[19] The researchers cautioned, however, that although this one study indicates progress toward gender equity, it does not mean that the glass ceiling has been removed.

There are other positive signs. PRSA and IABC salary surveys conducted during the 1990s found evidence that more women than men received raises and that women received larger percentage raises than did men. Just as in many other fields, however, the overall pattern is that women in public relations make less than do their male counterparts.

WORK ASSIGNMENTS

Some describe public relations work by listing the specialized parts of the function: media relations, investor relations, community relations, employee relations, government relations, and so forth. Such labels do not describe the many activities and diverse assignments in the day-to-day practice, however. The following ten categories summarize what public relations specialists do at work:

1. *Writing and Editing:* Composing print and broadcast news releases, feature stories, newsletters to employees and external stakeholders, correspondence, Web-site and other on-line media messages, shareholder and annual reports, speeches, brochures, film and slide-show scripts, trade publication articles, institutional advertisements, and product and technical collateral materials.
2. *Media Relations and Placement:* Contacting news media, magazines, Sunday supplements, freelance writers, and trade publications with the intent of getting them to publish or broadcast news and features about or originated by an organization. Responding to media requests for information, verification of stories, and access to authoritative sources.
3. *Research:* Gathering information about public opinion, trends, emerging issues, political climate and legislation, media coverage, special-interest groups, and other concerns related to an organization's stakeholders. Searching the Internet, on-line services, and electronic government databases. Designing program research, conducting surveys, and hiring research firms.
4. *Management and Administration:* Programming and planning in collaboration with other managers; determining needs, establishing priorities, defining publics, setting goals and objectives, and developing strategy and tactics. Administering personnel, budget, and program schedules.
5. *Counseling:* Advising top management on the social, political, and regulatory environments; consulting with the management team on how to avoid or respond to crises; and working with key decision makers to devise strategies for managing or responding to critical and sensitive issues.
6. *Special Events:* Arranging and managing news conferences, 10K runs,

conventions, open houses, ribbon cuttings and grand openings, anniversary celebrations, fund-raising events, visiting dignitaries, contests, award programs, and other special observances.

7. *Speaking:* Appearing before groups, coaching others for speaking assignments, and managing a speakers' bureau to provide platforms for the organization before important audiences.

8. *Production:* Creating communications using multimedia knowledge and skills, including art, typography, photography, layout, and computer desktop publishing; audio and video recording and editing; and preparing audiovisual presentations.

9. *Training:* Preparing executives and other designated spokespersons to deal with media and to make other public appearances. Instructing others in the organization to improve writing and communication skills. Helping introduce changes in organizational culture, policy, structure, and process.

10. *Contact:* Serving as liaison with media, community, and other internal and external groups. Listening, negotiating, managing conflict, and reaching agreement as mediator between an organization and its important stakeholders. Meeting and entertaining as host to guests and visitors.

Although last on this list, being "good with people" is often the first thing many associate with public relations. True enough, public relations people often find themselves dealing with people problems and sensitive relationships, but it would be misleading to limit one's view of public relations work to this commonly held stereotype.

The mix of assignments and responsibilities varies greatly from organization to organization, but one task is the common denominator: writing. (Study the job descriptions in Exhibit 2.1.) Writing skills remain a requirement throughout one's career. Daily logs in Exhibits 2.2, 2.3, and 2.4 illustrate the central role of writing in public relations work. To manage their jobs, individual practitioners devise and apply similar strategies and approaches day in and day out. In other words, they develop and play roles.

ROLES

Over time, practitioners adopt patterns of behavior to deal with recurring situations in their work and to accommodate others' expectations of what they should do in their jobs. Four major public relations roles describe much of the practice. At one time or another, however, practitioners play all of these and other roles to varying degrees, even though a dominant role emerges as they go about their day-to-day work and dealings with others.

Communication Technician

Most practitioners enter the field as communication technicians. Entry-level job descriptions typically list communication and journalistic skills as requirements. Communication technicians are hired to write and edit employee

Director–University Relations

Director will report directly to university president and lead program of media relations, publications, electronic media and issues management. Responsible for researching, writing and editing news releases, feature stories, fact sheets and other materials about the university to national news media. Must be hands-on leader with knowledge of strategic management, publication production and new media design.

VICE PRESIDENT
INVESTOR RELATIONS

International pharmaceutical company seeks experienced investor/financial relations executive. New VP reports directly to CEO/president and serves on the exec. committee. VP manages IR web site; maintains institutional, broker and retail investor contacts; coordinates financial reporting; and produces annual reports. Corp./IR communication exp.; and strong analytical, writing and management skills; and working knowledge of SEC disclosure requirements. MBA preferred and prior exp. in pharm./health care necessary.

PUBLIC RELATIONS

Software company seeks PR
writi
article
ade
s
d
e dir
her
r

COORDINATOR—INTERNAL
COMMUNICATIONS

Medical center Communications Division opportunity for leader with 8-10 years significant supervisory experience in organizational communication. Coordinator will supervise internal publications, staff communications and recruiting outreach support. Must have extensive writing, planning, consulting and project management experience. Experience and knowledge of new communication technology required. Master's degree preferred.

public relations account executive

Requires minimum five years experience in tourism / hospitality industry account service, travel writing background and strong media contacts. Fluency in Spanish helpful. Portfolio of results-oriented work and strong reference letters from previous clients required for interview.

COMMUNICATION DIRECTOR

Laser systems company seeks accomplished professional to direct government/community relations and public affairs. You also will direct institutional advertising, environmental communications, customer relations, employee
and plant tours.

Public Relations Director

Health care provider seeks senior manager to plan strategic public relations activities and collaborate with other departments heads to maintain relationships with payors, physicians, area consumers, and employees. Must have top-level media and community contacts.

Director of Campaign Communications

Major charitable foundation seeks pro to direct media relations, special events, donor relations and campaign communications. Requires significant experience in fund raising; proven record of establishing program goals, identifying target publics, and setting specific communication objectives; significant experience managing multimedia communications program; and strong presentation skills. Successful candidate will plan, manage and direct implementation of a $5-million capital campaign. Position reports directly to Executive Director.

EXHIBIT 2.2

DAY IN THE LIFE OF AN ASSISTANT ACCOUNT EXECUTIVE

Heidi Pettersen, Information Assistant
Kreab/Stayer AS (public relations firm)
Oslo, Norway.

I don't think I am alone when I find it hard to describe a "typical day" in a public relations firm. My job as an information assistant in a Norwegian public relations firm is varied, very exciting, and probably similar to a job in a firm in other countries. A major part of my job is assisting the manager in working with his clients, doing everything from writing press releases, letters, and other communication material to assisting with public relations plans, proofreading, and translating. Here is what my typical day is like:

8:30 A.M.	I start work at 8:30 A.M. every morning, grab a cup of tea, and try to get through the major newspapers.
9:00	I join my boss in a client meeting. The company's communication plan is discussed, so I take notes to work on it when we get back to the office.
10:30	We are back in the office and I spend an hour working on our client's communication plan. We are working on their media strategy and I go through some clippings to try to find journalists who might have an interest in our client.
11:30	At 11:30 A.M. every day, all 15 employees in the firm have lunch together. We enjoy a half-hour in each other's company, eating typical Norwegian open-faced sandwiches with fresh bread and all that comes with a Scandinavian "smorgasbord."
Noon	I meet with three coworkers to discuss our name-change arrangement. We will invite clients to a small afternoon event in the office on the day of the name change. We discuss the day's agenda, food and drinks, entertainment, and so forth.
2:00 P.M.	I do the finish work on a press release that is going out today. I make the media list, have it approved, and prepare the distribution. With the help of our receptionist I pack the press releases and get them in the mail.
3:30	My U.S. education provided me with not only knowledge about public relations but also English skills, making me the firm's translator. I spend the last hour at work translating one of our foreign customers' press releases.
4:30	Another day at work is over. Time to go home.

I was lucky in my first job out of school to come to a place with challenges and great learning opportunities. My boss is my mentor, so I feel that I am getting a good understanding of how public relations works in practice. The experience so far has certainly lived up to my expectations and I look forward to many years in this business.

EXHIBIT 2.3

DAY IN THE LIFE OF A PUBLIC RELATIONS DIRECTOR (NONPROFIT ORGANIZATION)

Andrea Lacy, Public Relations Specialist
San Diego Urban League

8:00 A.M. Scan local newspapers for articles relevant to the League. Photocopy and file pertinent articles.

8:30 Review personal calendar to determine upcoming deadlines and tasks.

8:35 Check e-mail and incorporate new tasks into personal calendar.

8:45 Call printing company to arrange delivery of Life Member Reception invitations. Hosted by the League's board of directors and the president and CEO, the reception is an opportunity for contributors to mingle with each other and the organization's department heads.

9:00 Conference call with supervisor and graphic artist to discuss newsletter design and timeline.

9:40 Draft newsletter timeline, send it to supervisor for review, and fax to graphic artist. The newsletter will be distributed to board members and corporate and private contributors, as well as key locations within the community.

10:15 Call League supervisors to request lists needed for research. (A board member who is the

newsletters, to write news releases and feature stories, to develop Web-site content, and to deal with media contacts. Practitioners in this role usually are not present when management defines problems and selects solutions. They are brought in later to produce the communications and implement the program, sometimes without full knowledge of either the original motivation or the intended results. Even though they were not present during the discussions about a new policy or management decision, they are the ones given the job of explaining it to employees and to the press.

Practitioners not only begin their careers in this role but spend much of their time in the technical aspects of communication, as illustrated by the list of work assignments presented in the preceding section and by the job descriptions in Exhibit 2.1. When limited to this role, however, practitioners typically do not participate significantly in management decision making and strategic planning. They complain that they are not part of the management team and that they are "the last to know."

president of a local research firm will survey key publics identified by the public relations plan. The research will be used as a benchmark.) Call research firm to discuss status of lists and future deadlines.

11:05   Gather press releases, letters of correspondence, and photos for newsletter articles. Prepare questions for interviews. Draft short article.

12:30 P.M.   Read weekly business journal and daily business newspaper at lunch.

1:30   Check e-mail and in box for messages and today's mail.

1:45   Return call to graphic artist. She wants to discuss changes to the newsletter timeline. Edit timeline per discussion and send copy to supervisor.

2:20   Receive disk containing one of the lists needed for the research project. Reformat the list and set aside.

2:50   Draft calendar announcement for Life Member Reception and select appropriate media. Prepare envelopes for mail. Send announcement to supervisor for approval.

3:20   Return to newsletter activities. Draft calendar of events and outlines for several articles. Search the National Urban League Web page to gather information for a feature article on the Thurgood Marshall Achievers Society, a group founded in part by the League to increase the number of African American students entering college.

4:55   Send e-mail to supervisor to inform her about the day's activities and any upcoming deadlines.

5:10   Send e-mail to League department heads requesting clerical assistance with handwritten invitation envelopes.

5:20   Note tomorrow's activities on personal calendar. Pick up weekly community periodical from convenience store on the way home.

Expert Prescriber

When practitioners take on the expert role, others see them as the authority on public relations problems and solutions. Top management leaves public relations in the hands of the expert and assumes a relatively passive role. Practitioners operating as expert practitioners define the problem, develop the program, and take full responsibility for its implementation. Other managers may want to keep public relations as the sole responsibility of practitioners so they can get back to business as usual, content that things will be handled by the "PR experts."

The expert prescriber role seduces practitioners because it is personally gratifying to be viewed as the authority on what needs to be done and how it should be done. It seduces employers and clients because they want to feel sure that public relations is being handled by an expert. They also erroneously assume that they will no longer have to be involved once the expert is on the job. Limited participation by key top managers, however, means that

EXHIBIT 2.4

DAY IN THE LIFE OF AN ACCOUNT EXECUTIVE

Julian D. Hebron, Account Executive
Vance P. Hickin, Account Executive
Ketchum Public Relations, Washington, DC

8:30 A.M.	Arrive, check voice and e-mail. Read print edition of *Wall Street Journal.* Scan *Washington Post, ZDNet,* and *Cnet* on-line.
8:45	Prioritize and respond to voice and e-mail from reporters, clients, and colleagues. Draft agenda for client conference call. Read daily clip report containing the day's top-tier print media articles about clients, competitors, and technology and financial issues. Augment conference call agenda with relevant information from the morning's news.
9:30	Join three account team members on client conference call with head of financial risk management division of major consulting firm. Update client on media outreach results, including story placements from the past week and pending interviews with financial publications. Review key messages and discuss fresh story angles to pitch based on regulatory and market landscape.
10:45	Brief new hire joining team responsible for managing multitiered consulting firm account. Explain how the client is split up into several divisions, each developing software systems for individual industry sectors (i.e., telecom, healthcare, financial, etc.) and how Ketchum's account team is split up to service each division.

their relevant knowledge does not get factored into the problem-solving process. Public relations becomes compartmentalized and isolated from the mainstream of the enterprise.

By not participating themselves, managers become dependent on the practitioner any time public relations issues arise. Managers also develop little or no commitment to public relations efforts and do not take responsibility for the success or failure of programs. In effect, other managers in the organization assume an it's-not-my-job stance on public relations matters. They see public relations as a sometimes-necessary job handled by support staff not directly involved in the organization's main line of business.

Whereas the expert prescriber role is called for in crisis situations and periodically throughout any program, in the long run it hinders the diffusion of

11:00	Write communications plan for new product launch of Internet domain name company. Because this existing client's PR objectives and strategies are already known, they are mentioned quickly (slightly tailored for the project) at the beginning of the proposal, and much of the focus is given to results-oriented tactical recommendations. Eat lunch at desk while writing. Submit draft to team leader, revise, and send to client.		client. Draft messages for product launch pitching next week, submit to Internet domain name client for review.
		4:30	New business brainstorm (delayed half hour) with four team members. Review "key needs" e-mail and collect free flow of newsworthy initiatives for Internet service provider. Review and approve template in art department, drop it into presentation, and begin writing program objectives and strategies.
1:30 P.M.	Go for a walk.	5:30	Enter billable time via corporate Intranet. Gather receipts together and fill out expense report. Book plane tickets and hotel accommodations for next week's Internet trade show in Los Angeles.
2:00	Receive and read request for proposal (RFP) from growing regional Internet service provider looking to outsource media relations initiatives. RFP turnaround time set for two days. Meet with art department to brainstorm ideas for PowerPoint template for capabilities presentation. Summarize key needs from RFP and send out e-mail requesting brainstorm session at 4:00.		
		6:30	Make to-do list for next day broken down by consulting client, Internet domain client, and new business project. Pull together relevant reading materials for new hire. Send various voice and e-mail updates to clients and colleagues.
3:30	Follow up calls with financial reporters to confirm interviews for financial risk management	6:45	Leave office.

public relations thinking throughout the organization. It also leads to the greatest dissatisfaction with practitioners, because they are held solely accountable for program results even though they had little or no control over critical parts of the situation and the factors that led to public relations problems in the first place. Top management often responds by simply replacing one expert with another, endlessly searching for someone who can make public relations problems go away without having to make needed changes in organizational policy, products, or procedures.

Communication Facilitator

The communication facilitator role casts practitioners as sensitive listeners and information brokers. Communication facilitators serve as liaisons, interpreters, and mediators between an organization and its publics. They maintain two-way communication and facilitate exchange by removing barriers in relationships and by keeping channels of communication open. The goal is to provide both management and publics the information they need for making decisions of mutual interest.

Practitioners in the communication facilitator role find themselves acting as information sources and the official contacts between organizations and their publics. They referee interactions, establish discussion agendas, summarize and restate views, call for reactions, and help participants diagnose and correct conditions interfering with communication relationships. Communication facilitators occupy boundary-spanning roles and serve as links between organizations and publics. They operate under the assumption that effective two-way communication improves the quality of decisions organizations and publics make about policies, procedures, and actions of mutual interest.

Problem-Solving Facilitator

When practitioners assume the role of problem-solving facilitator, they collaborate with other managers to define and solve problems. They become part of the strategic planning team. Collaboration and consultation begin with the first question and continue until the final program evaluation. Problem-solving practitioners help other managers and the organization apply to public relations the same management step-by-step process used for solving other organizational problems.

Line managers play an essential part in analyzing problem situations, as they are the ones most knowledgeable of and most intimately involved with the organization's policies, products, procedures, and actions. They are also the ones with the power to make needed changes. As a result, they must participate in the evolutionary thinking and strategic planning behind public relations programs. When line managers participate in the public relations strategic planning process, they understand program motivations and objectives, they support strategic and tactical decisions, and they are committed to making the changes and providing the resources needed to achieve program goals.

Problem-solving facilitators get invited to the management team because they have demonstrated their skill and value in helping other managers avoid and solve problems. As a result, public relations thinking is factored into management decision making.[20]

WHAT ROLES RESEARCH TELLS US

Researchers have studied what leads practitioners to play different roles, as well as what happens when they enact different roles in their organizations. Their findings have isolated factors that influence role selection and enactment, salary and career advancement, and participation in organizational decision making. Other scholars have used the role models to describe similarities and differences in the practice internationally.

Technicians versus Managers

Research findings show that practitioners play several roles, but that over time one emerges as the dominant role. For example, in a study of PRSA and IABC members in the United States, 37 percent rated themselves dominant in the expert prescriber role and 37 percent scored communication technician as their dominant role. Another 21 percent scored the problem-solving facilitator role as dominant, and only 5 percent put themselves in the dominant role of communication facilitator.[21]

In a similar study of Canadian Public Relations Society and Canadian IABC members, 42 percent rated themselves in the dominant role of communication technicians, 16 percent as expert prescribers, 15 percent as problem-solving facilitators, and 12 percent as communication facilitators. Fifteen percent weighted two or three roles equally.[22]

Not surprisingly, survey results indicate that practitioners' dominant roles are associated with sex, age, and years of experience (see Table 2.4). For example, comparisons of PRSA and IABC members' dominant roles produce different profiles: Whereas 44 percent of PRSA members practice in the dominant role of expert prescribers, only 27 percent of IABC members operate primarily in that role. On the other hand, 50 percent of IABC members, but only 29 percent of PRSA members, act in the communication technician dominant role.

Role differences also help explain the disparity in men and women's salaries. Women in role studies typically rate communication technician as their dominant role. Men, however, more frequently score the expert prescriber role as dominant than do women. Even after accounting for differ-

TABLE 2.4

ROLE DIFFERENCES

Dominant Role	Percentage of Mean Salary[a]	Years of Full-Time Experience	Years in Current Job	Percentage in Each Dominant Role	
				PRSA	IABC[b]
Expert prescriber	116	16	6.6	43	27
Problem-solving facilitator	104	15	6.5	29	50
Communication facilitator	97	13	6.6	5	4
Communication technician	69	10	4.6	23	19

[a] Salary base of 100 represents average salary. Salary, years of full-time experience, and years in current job from PRSA sample ($n = 458$).

[b] Dominant role data from survey of PRSA members ($n = 207$, 56 percent male respondents) and IABC members ($n = 135$, 62 percent female respondents).

ences in age and years of professional experience, there remain significant differences in the roles played by men and women. Because salaries are clearly associated with dominant roles, the differences in roles played help explain the salary gap (see Table 2.4).[23] In fact, in one follow-up study of public relations roles, the salary gap between men and women was not statistically significant after controlling for differences in manager role scores, professional experience, and participation in decision making.[24]

High scores on the communication technician role tend to stand alone. For the other three roles, however, high scores on one tend to go with high scores on the other two. In other words, practitioners who play the dominant role of expert prescriber, communication facilitator, or problem-solving process facilitator also tend to play the other two roles. High correlations among the three roles suggest that they go together to form a single, complex role that is distinct from the communication technician role. As a result, two major dominant roles occur in practice: *public relations technician* and *public relations manager.*

Public relations technicians are primarily concerned with writing, producing, and disseminating communications, such as press releases, speeches, Web sites, feature stories, and annual reports. They tend to be the creative, artistic, and technically proficient; see themselves as their organization's "wordsmith"; and exhibit little inclination or aptitude for strategic planning and research. For the most part they focus on communications and other activities in the *process.* Those in this dominant role typically make less and are not part of the management inner circle but enjoy high levels of job satisfaction if they remain in the technician role by choice. This role constitutes the traditional core of public relations work—writing news releases and other mediated communications and doing media relations.

The public relations manager role casts practitioners as part of organizational management. This role calls for research skills, an aptitude for strategic thinking, and a tendency to think in terms of the *outcomes* or *impact* of public relations activities. Practitioners in the public relations manager role do not limit their tactics to communications. They use environmental scanning and organizational intelligence, negotiation and coalition building, issues management, program evaluation, and management counseling as public relations tools. Accountability and participation in organizational management earn these practitioners high salaries, as well as high stress and responsibility. Researchers who studied 321 organizations in the United States, Canada, and the United Kingdom, however, found that the major predictor of public relations excellence was the extent to which the organization's top public relations executive was able to enact the manager role versus the technician role.[25]

Environmental Influences

Tables 2.4 and 2.5 illustrate, however, that important distinctions are lost when the three managerial roles are combined. For example, a practitioner's dominant role is a function of an organization's environment. Communica-

ORGANIZATIONAL ENVIRONMENTS AND ROLES		
	Low Threat	**High Threat**
Little Change	Communication technician	Problem-solving facilitator
Much Change	Communication facilitator	Expert prescriber

TABLE 2.5

tion technicians tend to work in organizations with relatively stable, low-threat environments, such as many nonprofit organizations and charities. Communication facilitators predominate in organizations with relatively turbulent settings that pose little threat, such as school districts and some governmental agencies. Problem-solving process facilitators and expert prescribers work in organizations with threatening environments. In relatively stable settings, including some utilities and associations, the problem-solving process facilitator role dominates. Expert prescribers dominate in rapidly changing environments, particularly in public relations firms that specialize in crisis communication and in consumer products companies subject to high levels of competition and government regulation.[26]

In short, the expert prescriber role appears when immediate action is imperative, whereas the problem-solving process facilitator dominant role is preferred when there is time to go through a process of collaboration and joint problem solving. Highly paid problem-solving process facilitators and expert prescribers tend to work for organizations most threatened by competition, government regulation, labor conflicts, and public scrutiny. As the salaries reported in Table 2.3 indicate, these practitioners likely work for marketing communications firms, financial and insurance companies, utilities, and public relations firms. By contrast, lower-paid communication technicians and communication facilitators typically work as promotional publicists for media and advertising agencies or for educational and religious organizations and charities.

Scanning and Evaluation

The various studies of public relations roles have consistently demonstrated the impact of using research to manage the function. In the three-phase study of roles reported previously, practitioners who use all types of research and information gathering were the ones most likely to operate in the management roles. The relationship between research and managerial role also appears in the findings of an international sample of IABC members.[27] Operating in the manager role correlates with the use of scientific, informal, and mixed approaches to research, whereas operating in the technician role does not. Canadian researchers found a similar pattern when they surveyed members of the Canadian Public Relations Society (CPRS) and Canadian members of IABC, but the highest correlations were for communication facilitators. The researchers concluded, "Perhaps communication facilitators require more objective information than the others in order to keep channels of communication open between various parties."[28]

Research shows that all types of information gathering help practitioners move into management roles. The obvious conclusion is that practitioners must be actively gathering information useful in decision making before they are invited to the management table. Furthermore, becoming part of the management team does not happen simply because of years on the job. Rather, how much research practitioners do determines the likelihood that they have a role in management decision making.[29] Moving into the management role, however, "does not immediately ensure that practitioners have the knowledge or expertise to enact the manager role," according to Lauzen and Dozier.[30] Simply put, practitioners long accustomed to operating in the technician role may not be able to make the adjustment to the strategic manager role.

Many factors influence practitioner roles, including education, professional experience, personality, supervision, and organizational culture and environment. Practitioners who understand the causes and consequences of playing different roles can develop strategies for dealing with a variety of situations and with others' views of practitioner roles. This understanding may be particularly important for women because role differences are associated with both salary and participation in management decision making.

THE GLASS CEILING

Studies of women in public relations historically have found both a salary gap and a "glass ceiling" on promotions to management positions. As one researcher put it, there is a "million-dollar penalty for being a woman," noting the effects of male-female salary differences and limited advancement opportunities over the course of a career.[31]

Roles research findings indicate that annual income and participation in management decision making increase when practitioners change from the technician role to one of the managerial roles. These same studies show that changes to the manager roles occur for men more readily than for women. For example, in one study the percentage of practitioners in the technician role decreased significantly and the percentage in the management role increased significantly over a six-year period. Detailed analyses revealed, however, that whereas women tended to remain in the communication technician role, men moved out of that dominant role to one of the management roles. In the first survey, 38 percent of the communication technicians (dominant role) were women; six years later 52 percent of the technicians were women. The role differences mean not only that the salary gap widened but also that during the six years between surveys more men gained access to and participation in management than did women.[32]

Those who study the glass ceiling problem suggest the following strategies:

1. Women aiming for top management must develop career plans and select employers with care and not plan on "being in the right place at the right time." "Women have to get into the game and be as aggressive and determined as any male counterpart."
2. Women must develop management skills: goal setting, analysis, planning, research, program execution, measurement, and evaluation. They must also know how to communicate with managers. As one female manager put it, "I think as time goes on, and this is especially critical for women, communicators are going to have to think like managers, talk like managers, and communicate with other managers."
3. Women must aim higher. One study found that when women are asked to estimate what salary they will be making in 10 years, they project only 60 percent of what men project. Rather than undervalue themselves, they should research salaries in the area and in comparable organizations before accepting an offer. Researchers also found that women may forget to negotiate perks: professional dues, conference expenses, and other benefits in addition to salary.[33]

Research evidence suggests, however, that the field is making progress toward gender equity and breaking the glass ceiling. Women enhance their chances of advancing in public relations management by conducting research—environmental scanning and program evaluation.[34] Unlike earlier findings, a follow-up study of public relations roles found that gender is not a significant factor in moving into the manager dominant role, once the influence of professional experience is taken into account.[35] Deans and directors of journalism and mass communication programs rated public relations as having the best record of hiring, developing, and promoting women among the nine employment areas for graduates.[36] Finally, researchers studying job satisfaction found reason for optimism for gender equity in the public relations workplace:

> The transition of women into the workplace appeared to be moving from the crisis stage of the 1980s into a genuine negotiation stage from which the profession and the workplace will eventually emerge stronger and, perhaps, with a different set of values that combines the best of both.[37]

Much of the credit for progress goes to women in public relations who have struggled to break through the managerial glass ceiling and to feminist scholars who have explicated and documented the process and effects of gender discrimination. Although the glass ceiling and gender discrimination have not been eliminated, as the authors quoted above put it, "Watch for falling glass."

MINORITIES

The 1990 Census counted 167,000 in the public relations workforce, but only 14 percent of them were people of color.[38] U.S. Department of Labor statistics show a marked increase of minorities in the "public relations specialists" category, from slightly more than 3 percent in 1979 to more than 14 percent

Black and of Hispanic origin in 1997.[39] Membership profiles of PRSA and IABC indicate that minorities represent a little more than 7 percent of membership in these two professional societies. These figures do not compare favorably, however, with estimates that minorities represent 25 percent of the U. S. population and are growing as a percentage of the overall population.[40]

Demographic trends and the increasing marketplace power of minorities call for an even greater presence in the years to come, according to public relations scholar Marilyn Kern-Foxworth.[41] Recognition of the importance of building and maintaining relationships with all racial and ethnic segments of the community has increased opportunities for individual practitioners as well as for minority-owned firms. Globalization has also increased demand for skilled practitioners able to bridge cultural and communication gaps.[42] Ketchum Public Relations, based in New York City, opened Ketchum Asociados in Miami to help clients reach Hispanic publics "by assembling a group of seasoned, multilingual and multicultural communications professionals."[43] Kern-Foxworth emphasized the need:

> Many practitioners believe that, in the year 2000, minority professionals in the field will be in the right place at the right time. The information brokering skills of all practitioners will be needed more than ever in the pluralistic society, they say, but minority practitioners may be in particular demand because of their ability to communicate with both segmented and general markets.[44]

Experts point to the growing need for both internal and external public relations directed to minority audiences. Public relations firms and public relations staffs that do not have these staff capabilities will find themselves at a competitive disadvantage. Two scholars assessing the need and opportunities for people of color in public relations concluded that unless the field attracts more minority practitioners, "the public relations profession will continue to encounter difficulties in capitalizing on the multicultural and multinational opportunities described by Kern-Foxworth and others."[45]

However, surveys continue to show that minorities are underrepresented in corporate departments, firms, and other major organizations' public relations staffs. Educational programs in public relations continue to recruit minority students, scholarships and internship programs encourage participation, and employment opportunities reward those who take advantage of them. Minority practitioners with public relations training and skills will continue to be in demand because all organizations need to communicate with the many publics in an increasingly pluralistic society. Ketchum's Raymond Kotcher succinctly summarized the challenge: "The public relations profession should aspire to be representative of the communities served by our companies, clients and organizations across the nation."[46]

PROFESSIONALISM

When practitioners assemble at professional meetings, discussions typically turn to the extent to which public relations qualifies as a profession. The topic of professionalism dominates many conferences. The many publications and newsletters serving the field all address the professionalization of public relations. Concern about professionalism prompted PRSA to require accredited members to complete continuing education in order to maintain their accredited status.

Criteria for assessing the professional status of a field date back to preindustrial England. Sons of wealthy landowners went to either Cambridge or Oxford to receive a liberal arts education before taking exams to enter the practices of law and medicine. Wealth was a prerequisite because professional practice provided little, if any, remuneration.

By the late 1800s the "status professionalism" of England began to give way to "occupational professionalism." Specialized skills and knowledge became the basis for entry, opening the way for the growing middle class. Although being challenged in some fields, many of the values associated with the origins of professions persist today: "personal service, a dislike of competition, advertising and profit, a belief in the principle of payment in order to work rather than working for pay and the superiority of the motive of service."[47]

Many have attempted to define contemporary professions, but no single definition fits all fields. Typically, disagreement results when an occupational group argues for a specific and unique characteristic designed to exclude others. There is general agreement, however, that the following criteria apply to all professions:

1. Requires specialized education to acquire a body of knowledge and skills based on theory developed through research. The practice is based more on unique knowledge than on performance skills.
2. Provides a unique and essential service recognized as such by the community. Practitioners are identified with their profession: "She's a lawyer" or "He's the accountant."
3. Emphasizes public service and social responsibility over private interests. Private economic gain and special interests are subordinate to the public good. There is "nobility of purpose."
4. Gives autonomy to and places responsibility on practitioners. Freedom to decide and act carries with it individual accountability.
5. Enforces codes of ethics and standards of performance through self-governing associations of colleagues. Values are interpreted and enforced by disciplining those who deviate from accepted norms and prescribed behaviors. Professional societies set standards for specialized educational preparation, determine who is admitted into practice, monitor practitioner performance against agreed upon standards, and confer different levels of status on practitioners.

Any discussion of practitioners' educational backgrounds makes it clear that entry into public relations does not require specialized educational preparation. A small percentage of practitioners belong to the major professional associations. An even smaller number are "accredited" or "certified," meaning that they have passed a battery of tests and been judged to be competent practitioners by a panel of their professional peers. No state requires a license to practice public relations. Not only are there varied and often bizarre notions held by others about what constitutes public relations, there is also disagreement within the field.

Frequent examples of self-serving behavior and advocacy on behalf of special interests bring into question the extent to which public service and social responsibility guide the practice. News reports expose "public relations spin doctors" or "damage control specialists" retained by clients charged with unethical or illegal activities. Only a small percentage of practitioners work as truly independent counselors. In fact, most function in staff positions accountable to line management, so autonomy and personal responsibility are not commonly associated with their roles. And because only a small proportion of practitioners belong to strong professional associations, the vast majority are not subject to enforced codes of conduct.

These issues are discussed more fully in chapter 5, but it is obvious that a strict interpretation of the criteria precludes qualifying public relations as a profession. In fact, if required to completely adhere to the standards, few, if any, fields could pass the test. Many practicing public relations, on the other hand, qualify as professionals, on the basis of their commitment to meeting professional standards. Widespread efforts in education and the professional associations advance the calling and professionalize the field. Professionalism is an important concern and goal for those entering the emerging profession of public relations.

REQUIREMENTS FOR SUCCESS

Surveys of top public relations executives show that they think communication skills, knowledge of media and management, problem-solving abilities, motivation, and intellectual curiosity are needed for success (see Exhibit 2.5). Exhibit 2.6, pg. 54, presents Bill Cantor's list of personality traits required for success in public relations. Public relations consultant Richard Long lists five qualities of those on the career "fast track":

1. *Results.* The single most important key to success is a reputation for getting results, being goal oriented. Employers and clients pay for *results,* not *hard work* and *effort.*
2. *Conceptualizing.* Those on the fast track have an ability to focus on the employer's or client's needs. The strong conceptualizer is a "quick study" who is a good listener and thorough note taker.
3. *Human Relations.* Persons on the fast track are team players who balance personal goals with those of the organization. These persons also know how to deal with management, including when they do not agree with the boss.
4. *Style.* The most important style-related trait is a "can-do" attitude. Another is constructive competitiveness. Those on the fast track translate confi-

EXHIBIT 2.5

REQUIREMENTS FOR SUCCESS

Skills

▼ Effective writing
▼ Persuasive speaking

Knowledge

▼ In-depth knowledge of various media
▼ Understanding of management process
▼ Business, financial acumen

Abilities

▼ Problem solver
▼ Decision maker

▼ Deft in handling people, generates confidence
▼ Assumes responsibility

Qualities

▼ Stability and common sense
▼ Drive and enthusiasm
▼ Wide-ranging interests and intellectual curiosity
▼ Good listener
▼ Tolerance for frustration
▼ Style

Courtesy Jo Proctor and reprinted with permission from *Public Relations Journal.*

dence into persuasive advocacy and substantive public relations contributions.

5. *Intangibles.* This quality almost defies description, but charisma, presence, and moxie affect the way other managers evaluate people in public relations. Go to school on the boss. The bottom line with bosses, however, is to find ways to make their jobs easier. Know what your boss expects of you.[48]

Among other traits sought by employers are an understanding of how the business works (whatever a particular organization's business is), skill with computer software and new media technology, being well-read and informed on current events, and having an ability to deal with frustration and to improvise. One trait tops every list, however. *Ability to write is number one by a wide margin.* As one executive put it,

> Too often, clear writing is not stressed sufficiently and the public relations professional goes through his or her career with one hand tied behind. Learn how to write before you start to climb the public relations ladder.[49]

Another said, "If our experience is typical, writing is one of the very weakest areas of most new graduates. That's probably being kind . . . 'appalling' is what's really crossing my mind."[50]

In short, both entry-level employment and long-term career success require the ability to write grammatically correct, easy-to-read, forceful, informative, and persuasive copy for publication and speech.

EXHIBIT 2.6

CANTOR'S TRAITS FOR SUCCESS

1. *Response to tension.* Most successful public relations executives are intense people, although it may not always be evident even to themselves. Often they are at their best under fire, and rather than solving problems by abstract analysis, they will reach practical solutions by direct action.

2. *Individual initiative.* Successful public relations executives will usually take immediate action before a situation becomes blown out of proportion. They usually will not wait for instructions but take the initiative to solve the problem; seek to anticipate and adjust to change; lead the public relations effort.

3. *Curiosity and learning.* The public relations professional should have an inquiring mind, should want to learn everything possible about the product, service, client or organization, and the competition. Because public relations is not an exact science, frequently the public rela-

tions executive must try a number of approaches in order to solve a problem, some of which might not work. If and when they don't work, professionals regard them not as personal blunders but as learning opportunities. They solve problems by persistence and intelligence. They never stop learning.

4. *Energy, drive, and ambition.* Successful public relations people have energy, drive, and ambition. They work rapidly and are not afraid to take a calculated risk. This is a very important element in the personality of public relations executives. Most of the top practitioners are stimulated by the problems to be solved and are willing to work the hours it takes to reach their goals.

5. *Objective thinking.* Public relations executives must be as objective and factual as possible and above all have excellent judgment. They must know what to do

NOTES

1. Anne van der Meiden, Foreword to Milenko D. Djuric, *Public Relations: The Key to a Successful Appearance on the Market* (Belgrade, Yugoslavia: Marketing Research Institute, 1992), 203. The first book written on the state of the emerging profession in Yugoslavia. An overview of the book in English summarizes the seven chapters.

2. James Aley, "Where the Jobs Are," *Fortune* (September 18, 1995): 53–55.

3. U.S. Office of Personnel Management, Office of Workforce Information, *Federal Civilian Workforce Statistics: Occupations of Federal White-Collar and Blue-Collar Workers* (Washington, DC: Government Printing Office, September 30, 1995), 34.

4. U.S. Office of Personnel Management, Statistical Analysis and Services Division, *Federal Civilian Workforce Statistics: Employment and Trends* (Washington, DC: Government Printing Office, August 1997), 37.

5. For data on employee numbers, see current editions of "Jack O'Dwyer's Newsletter" and *O'Dwyer's Directory of Public Relations Firms.*

6. Estimates gleaned from various newsletters, *O'Dwyer's Directory of Corporate Communicators,* and personal communications.

7. *Profile 1997* (San Francisco: International Association of Business Communicators and IABC Research Foundation, 1997), V-4.

and say and when. They must have a sense of timing. They must have a capacity for intense concentration, attention to intricate detail, and keen powers of observation. This is especially critical in counseling.

6. *Flexible attitude.* It is crucial that public relations executives have the ability to see things from someone else's viewpoint, for example, executive management's, a publication editor's, or a hostile audience's.

7. *Service to others.* Most successful public relations executives have a natural desire to help people. Pleasure in the success of others is a major motivation for the service behavior.

8. *Friendliness.* Public relations people generally are perceived as likable, friendly, and genuinely interested in others, rarely as resentful, bitter, or hostile. They develop and maintain a wide range of personal contacts.

9. *Versatility.* Successful public relations executives are often able to perform well in a variety of areas because they have a venturesome spirit and a lively interest in the world at large. The best practitioners are generalists with a specialty. The desire to learn and the ability to focus on varied subjects helps them adjust rapidly to new tasks and multiple client problems and needs.

10. *Lack of self-consciousness.* Successful public relations executives are much less self-conscious than other executives, perhaps because they often function as catalysts. Although some practitioners have large egos, they often are self-effacing, functioning in the background while projecting others into the limelight. This trait is indigenous to the public relations professional.

Courtesy Bill Cantor and reprinted with permission from *Public Relations Journal.*

8. U.S. Department of Labor, Bureau of Labor Statistics, *Employment and Earnings* (Washington, DC: U.S. Government Printing Office, January 1998), 175.
9. Rea W. Smith, "Women in Public Relations," *Public Relations Journal* 24 (October 1968): 26, 27, and 29.
10. Sondra K. Gorney, "Status of Women in Public Relations," *Public Relations Journal* 31 (May 1975): 10–3.
11. David Y. Jacobson and Nicholas J. Tortorello, "Salary Survey," *Public Relations Journal* 46, no. 6 (June 1990): 18–25; and *Profile '89* (San Francisco: International Association of Business Communicators and IABC Research Foundation, 1989).
12. *IABC's Profile '97 Highlights* (San Francisco: International Association of Business Communicators and IABC Research Foundation, 1997).
13. Lee B. Becker and Gerald M. Kosicki, "Annual Survey of Enrollment and Degrees Awarded," *Journalism & Mass Communication Educator* (Autumn 1997): 69.
14. Weighted data based on *Salary Survey of Public Relations Professionals* (New York: Public Relations Society of America, 1996), 69.
15. *O'Dwyer's Newsletter,* August 14, 1996, 8.
16. *Employment and Earnings* (January 1998), 210.
17. *Salary Survey,* 18–9.
18. Glen M. Broom and David M. Dozier, "Advancement for Public Relations Role Models," *Public Relations Review 12,* no. 1 (Spring 1986): 37–56. The research re-

ported here was supported by grants from the Institute (formerly Foundation) for Public Relations Research and Education.

19. David M. Dozier and Glen M. Broom, "Evolution of the Managerial Role in Public Relations Practice," *Journal of Public Relations Research 7,* no. 1 (1995): 17.
20. For the original conceptual definitions of the roles, see Glen M. Broom and George D. Smith, "Testing the Practitioner's Impact on Clients," *Public Relations Review 5,* no. 3 (Fall 1979): 47–59.
21. These previously unreported data were gathered as part of the third roles study, "Evolution of the Managerial Role," conducted by Dozier and Broom (see note 15).
22. Jennie M. Piekos and Edna F. Einsiedel, "Roles and Program Evaluation Techniques Among Canadian Public Relations Practitioners," *Public Relations Research Annual 2* (1990): 95–113.
23. See Glen M. Broom, "A Comparison of Sex Roles in Public Relations," *Public Relations Review 8,* no. 3 (Fall 1982): 17–22; and David M. Dozier (with Larissa A. Grunig and James E. Grunig), *Manager's Guide to Excellence in Public Relations and Communication Management* (Mahwah, NJ: Lawrence Erlbaum Associates, Publishers, 1995): 158–61.
24. David M. Dozier and Glen M. Broom, "Evolution of the Manager Role in Public Relations Practice," *Journal of Public Relations Research 7,* no. 1 (1995): 17.
25. Dozier, *Manager's Guide to Excellence in Public Relations,* 23–37.
26. Lalit Acharya, "Public Relations Environments," *Journalism Quarterly 62,* no. 3 (Autumn 1985): 577–84.
27. David M. Dozier, "The Innovation of Research in Public Relations: Review of a Program of Research," *Public Relations Research Annual 2* (1990): 16–21.
28. Piekos and Einsiedel, "Roles and Program Evaluation Techniques," 109.
29. Glen M. Broom and David M. Dozier, "Advancement for Public Relations Role Models," *Public Relations Review 12,* no. 1 (Spring 1986): 37–56.
30. Martha M. Lauzen and David M. Dozier, "Issues Management Mediation of Linkages Between Environmental Complexity and Management of the Public Relations Function," *Journal of Public Relations Research 6,* no. 3: 180.
31. Carolyn Garret Cline, "Public Relations: The $1 Million Penalty for Being a Woman," in *Women in Mass Communication: Challenging Gender Values,* ed. Pamela J. Creedon (Newbury Park, CA: Sage Publications, 1989), 263–75.
32. Broom and Dozier, "Advancement for Public Relations Role Models," 45–49.
33. Adapted and quoted from Cline, "The $1 Million Penalty for Being a Woman," 272–74.
34. Dozier, "The Innovation of Research in Public Relations," 22.
35. Dozier and Broom, "Evolution of the Manager Role," 16.
36. "The Media and Women Without Apology," *The Freedom Forum Media Studies Journal* (Winter/Spring 1993).
37. Shirley A. Serini, Elizabeth Toth, Donald K. Wright, and Arthur G. Emig, "Watch for Falling Glass . . . Women, Men, and Job Satisfaction in Public Relations: A Preliminary Analysis," *Journal of Public Relations Research 9,* no. 2 (1997): 116.
38. "Detailed Occupation and Other Characteristics from the EEO File of the United States," *1990 Census of the Population Special Report 1–1* (U.S. Bureau of the Census), 3.
39. *Employment and Earnings* (Washington, DC: U.S. Department of Labor, Bureau of Statistics, January 1980 and January 1998): 175.
40. For a discussion of the three major minority publics—African Americans, Asian Americans, and Hispanic Americans—see Linda P. Morton, "Targeting Minority Publics," *Public Relations Quarterly 42,* no. 2 (Summer 1997): 23–27.

41. Marilyn Kern-Foxworth, "Status and Roles of Minority PR Practitioners," *Public Relations Review* 15, no. 3 (Fall 1989): 39–47.

42. Marilyn Kern-Foxworth, "Black, Brown, Red, and Yellow Markets Equal Green Power," *Public Relations Quarterly* 36, no. 1 (Spring 1991): 30.

43. Raymond L. Kotcher, "Diversity in Today's Workplace and Marketplace," *Public Relations Quarterly* 40, no. 1 (Spring 1995): 7.

44. Marilyn Kern-Foxworth, "Minorities 2000: The Shape of Things to Come," *Public Relations Journal* 45, no. 8 (August 1989): 22.

45. Clint C. Wilson II and Félix Gutiérrez, "Public Relations: An Opportunity to Influence the Media," in *Facing Difference: Race, Gender, and Mass Media,* ed. Shirley Biagi and Marilyn Kern-Foxworth (Thousand Oaks, CA: Pine Forge Press, 1997), 168. Previously published in Wilson and Gutiérrez, *Race, Multiculturalism, and the Media: From Mass to Class Communication,* 2nd ed. (Thousand Oaks, CA: Sage Publications, 1995).

46. Kotcher, "Diversity in Today's Workplace and Marketplace," 8.

47. Philip Elliott, *The Sociology of Professions* (London: Macmillan, 1972), 52–3. Useful reference on the origins and evolution of professions.

48. Adapted from a speech by Richard K. Long, LONG-term Solutions, Federal Way, WA. Long formerly served as public relations executive at Dow Chemical Company, Midland, MI, and Weyerhaeuser, Tacoma, WA. Used with permission of the author.

49. From speech to Black Public Relations Society of Greater New York by Kenneth R. Lightcap, managing director, Manning Selvage and Lee, New York, April 17, 1991.

50. James E. Lukaszewski, Chairman, The Lukaszewski Group, Inc., as quoted in Jack Haberstroh, "PR Graduates Don't Measure Up as Writers," *Public Relations Quarterly* 39, no. 4 (Winter 1994–95): 22.

ADDITIONAL SOURCES

Bivins, Thomas H. *Handbook for Public Relations Writing,* 3rd ed. Lincolnwood, IL: NYC Business Books, 1995. Provides an introduction to the wide range of writing assignments in public relations practice.

Center, Allen H., and Patrick Jackson. *Public Relations Practices: Managerial Case Studies and Problems,* 5th ed. Upper Saddle River, NJ: Prentice Hall, 1995. Case studies illustrate how practitioners apply public relations theory and principles.

Creedon, Pamela J., ed. *Women in Mass Communication,* 2nd ed. Newbury Park, CA: Sage, 1993. Essays explore feminist theory and the women's movement in mass communication.

Hon, Linda Childers, Larissa A. Grunig, and David M. Dozier. "Women in Public Relations: Problems and Opportunities." In *Excellence in Public Relations and Communication Management,* edited by James E. Grunig, 419–38. Mahwah, NJ: Lawrence Erlbaum Associates, 1992.

Wilcox, Dennis L., and Lawrence W. Nolte. *Public Relations Writing and Media Techniques,* 3rd ed. New York: Longman, 1997. An effective introduction to and instruction in the day-to-day work assignments in public relations practice.

ORGANIZATIONAL SETTINGS

Public relations people, if they are to be truly respected by management colleagues, must merit "a seat at the management table."
—*The Public Relations Strategist*[1]

OBJECTIVES

After studying chapter 3, you should be able to

▼ Discuss top management's impact on determining the relative importance and role of public relations.

▼ Distinguish between line and staff functions, and explain why public relations is a staff function in most organizations.

▼ Outline major advantages and disadvantages of internal departments and outside counseling firms for serving an organization's public relations needs.

▼ Describe working relationships between the public relations unit and other departments in organizations.

▼ Outline three primary approaches public relations firms use for billing clients.

More than a decade of acquisitions, divestitures, downsizing, globalization, reengineering, and mergers has produced great changes in the structure of corporations. Budget cuts and deficits, taxpayer revolts, and deregulation have led to reorganization, decentralization, and staff cuts in all levels of government. A nationally publicized scandal, embarrassing revelations about executive salaries and benefits, increasing demand for social services, and vigorous competition for funds have forced changes in the missions and fund-raising methods in many nonprofit organizations. Employees at all levels learned to live and work with sometimes contradictory rhetoric saying that their organization was trying to become "lean and mean," that reorganization and retraining meant "empowerment," that layoffs and plant closing were aimed at "right-sizing," and that high overhead and budget cuts had forced "outsourcing." In short, much has changed recently in the organizational contexts of public relations.

Many, if not most, organizations reorganized the public relations function, reduced department staff size, and tried to do more with fewer people. Many shifted part or all of the workload to outside counseling firms and agencies, producing dramatic increases in cash flow and profitability. Small public relations firms merged, bought out others, or affiliated to form regional, national, and international networks. Large national public relations firms became international by opening or acquiring branches outside their headquarters country or by merging with firms in other countries. Large advertising agencies purchased public relations firms, promising clients "one-stop shopping" and "integrated communication."

Practitioners work in these turbulent organizational settings, dealing with both internal and external change. Many work at the highest levels of management, helping chief executive officers (CEOs) manage organizational change. This chapter discusses the origins and place of public relations in organizations, its responsibilities, and its working relationships with other departments.

ORIGINS WITHIN ORGANIZATIONS

Public relations in organizations often can be traced back to unintended and humble beginnings. It can begin with someone simply answering letters from customers or members; with someone writing copy for direct mail, institutional advertising, or the annual report; with someone handling visitors, conducting tours, or arranging the annual meeting; or with someone serving as an organization's ombudsman for employees or neighbors. In other organizations, public relations starts as product and service publicity, as news support for a national advertising campaign, or as a fund-raising or membership drive.

Public relations' creation, however, does not always spring from a welcome opportunity. For example, emergencies or crises such as accidents, product recalls, and layoffs attract public and media attention. If no one on the staff is qualified to deal with the media and to handle public information, the function begins under crisis conditions. Media specialists or outside public relations counsel brought in on a short-term basis to help with the immediate crisis subsequently may be hired or retained on a continuing basis. Long after the emergency or crisis subsides, public relations gets defined and redefined to fit changing missions, new problems and opportunities, and the values and views of a succession of CEOs.

Because so many factors influence how public relations begins in organizations, even some large organizations have small public relations departments. Conversely, some relatively small enterprises employ many practitioners, in some cases supplementing their work with outside counsel. Many departments report directly to the CEO, whereas others report to the top human resources or marketing officer. In a few organizations, public relations reports to the top legal officer. Some organizations retain outside counselors, even though setting up their own internal staff would be logically the more appropriate choice. In others, internal staffers get assignments that could be better handled by outside counsel.

Public relations departments in some organizations have large staffs and generous budgets, even though the original motivations for the function have long been forgotten and their mission is not clearly defined. Departments in other organizations strain to marshal public support, to neutralize well-organized public opposition, or to build new relationships across international borders without either the staff or the funds necessary to achieve program goals.

Such mismatches often represent nothing more than delays in adapting to change. But even practitioners disagree about what is the best structure and place for the function in various types of organizations. As a consequence, each internal public relations department is tailor-made to suit a particular organization and its unique circumstances, particularly the expectations of the CEO.

Establishing a Public Relations Department

The position of public relations on the organization chart and its relationship to top management often can be explained by how the function came into being. For example, top managers in a rapidly growing corporation discover that they have lost touch with employees, and their former face-to-face communications with all employees are no longer possible. The CEO then directs the human resources department to hire a writer-editor to create a weekly news update for the company's intranet and to publish a quarterly employee newsletter. On the basis of the success of the employee communication efforts, top managers soon ask the energetic and ambitious communication specialist to write occasional news releases about employee achievements and corporate successes. Shortly after, the job expands to include duties such as speech writer for the CEO and the corporation's media contact. The communication specialist hires an assistant to handle a growing number of internal and external communication needs.

Because the function expanded beyond its original employee communication origins, top management moves it out of the human resources department and gives it a new title—"Public Relations Department." The new department's manager reports directly to the CEO. Its missions are to improve communication and to build better relationships with all the corporation's major internal and external stakeholders.

As the corporation grows, the public relations department takes on responsibilities for maintaining relationships with investors and financial analysts, government agencies at all levels, community groups, environmental and other special-interest groups, and an increasingly diverse workforce. The public relations manager gets promoted to vice president and appoints managers for each of the specialized areas. In some instances, the new vice president is elected to the executive committee and participates in corporate decision making at the highest level.

From its origin as a low-level communication support function in the human resources department, the role evolved to become an integral part of the management team. To stay on the management team, however, it must contribute to achieving organizational goals and demonstrate accountability through measurable results.

Retaining Outside Counsel

Client relationships with outside counseling firms also can begin in simple and unexpected ways. For example, an organization retains an outside firm (sometimes called an *agency*) to conduct a survey of community public opinion regarding a proposed trash-to-energy recycling plant. After receiving the survey results, client management asks the firm to help interpret the findings "from an outsider's perspective" and to help solve a public opinion problem identified by the survey. Success in the follow-up project leads to a continuing and expanding relationship as the client draws on the full range of the firm's public relations capabilities.

The client pays the firm a monthly retainer fee, ensuring access to outside counsel and covering a set number of hours of service each month. Above and beyond regular counsel and services, the firm takes on special projects such as producing the annual report, designing and creating the organization's home page on the World Wide Web, and special-event planning for the grand opening and dedication of the new facility. The firm bills the client an agreed-upon hourly fee or a fixed fee to cover all costs associated with the additional projects.

The firm's account executive and the internal department's management work as a team to plan and carry out the public relations program. The account executive meets periodically with the client's senior management and public relations staff to discuss plans and to assess progress. The client–firm relationship becomes so close that the firm's account executive sits in on many of the client's internal planning meetings.

Friction sometimes develops, however, when the account executive is not available because of travel and work demands from other clients or, more commonly, when the firm charges for more hours than the client's management anticipates. A hastily called meeting to discuss the invoice reminds both the account executive and internal public relations management that outside counsel is a variable cost and that the outside firm has its own economic goals. The relationship continues but with frequent reminders that clients and outside counselors work from different perspectives. That outsider's perspective was, after all, why the client organization retained the counseling firm in the first place.

PUBLIC RELATIONS STARTS WITH TOP MANAGEMENT

One of the few safe generalizations in public relations is that an organization's public reputation derives in substantial part from the behavior of its senior officials. As those in top management act and speak, so go the interpretations and echoes created by the public relations function. Thus, public relations is inescapably tied, by nature and by necessity, to top management, with public relations staff providing counsel and communication support.

For example, recall how Source Perrier responded when traces of benzene were found in its bottled water. Perrier's top management first suggested that it resulted from a single, isolated cleaning accident and that contaminated bottles were limited to only the few being recalled in North America. The next installment of top management's story came when scientists found benzene-tainted products in Europe. This time management attributed the benzene to a simple problem with the filter system. Finally, red-faced Perrier management announced a worldwide recall. Tests showed that consumers around the world had been drinking contaminated products for months. The media blasted Perrier, questioning management's integrity and raising concern for public safety. Perrier lost and has not regained its former share of the bottled water market.

Likewise, Exxon's CEO did not go to Alaska after the tanker Exxon *Valdez* spilled millions of gallons of crude oil into the environmentally sensitive Prince William Sound. TWA's CEO resigned three months after 230 people lost their lives in the crash of Flight 800. He had been criticized for delaying 13 hours before leaving London to go to the crash site and for not immediately expressing concern about crash victims and their families. Both companies have struggled to regain public confidence and respect.

Johnson & Johnson's handling of the Tylenol tampering crisis, however, stands in stark contrast. Top management put customer safety first, immediately pulling the product off retail shelves and recalling capsules in the United States and abroad. Management took these dramatic steps even though the only known tampering cases were limited to the Chicago area. Media coverage praised the company's socially responsible actions, reported the company's cooperation with federal agencies, and gave full coverage to later announcements of new tamper-resistant packaging.

Similarly, Texaco's CEO quickly apologized when taped recordings were released that exposed senior managers discussing past racial discrimination and the planned destruction of evidence for a civil rights case. He then announced the formation of an independent task force to help the company implement its plan to increase diversity in its employees and management, and among the outside firms hired by Texaco. Unlike the crises at Perrier, Exxon, and TWA, Johnson & Johnson's crisis became a classic case study in crisis communication management and Texaco's embarrassing revelation motivated long-overdue change. In these cases, the CEO set the course and became the public face in responding to the crisis.

Crises potentially involve and affect many stakeholder groups: customers, employees, wholesalers and retailers, consumer action groups, government agencies, stockholders and investment analysts, international media, and concerned citizens around the world. The Perrier case probably contributed to the subsequent series of investigations and media disclosures about the quality and purity of all bottled waters, so even competing brands were affected. Exxon credit card holders cut up and returned their cards, quit buying Exxon products, and even protested the use of single-hull tankers. TWA lost its CEO and media relations director, suffered a major setback in consumer confidence, and had to play down rumors of impending bankruptcy. By contrast, Johnson & Johnson's response positioned it as a leader in safe packaging—forcing competing brands to follow suit, led to Johnson & Johnson's ranking among the most respected corporations, and helped the company retain market share for Tylenol. Texaco's quick apology, immediate corrective actions, and announced long-term strategy for organizational change cut short public criticism and made the company's responses part of the story. Each crisis provides an example of top management's key role in an organization's public relations.

These cases illustrate that public relations credibility starts with management's integrity and socially responsible action. In addition, long-term success in public relations calls for the following from top management:

1. Commitment to and participation in public relations
2. Retention of competent public relations counsel
3. Incorporation of public relations perspectives in policy making
4. Two-way communication with both internal and external publics
5. Coordination of what is done with what is said
6. Clearly defined goals and objectives

The first and continuing task for public relations is to earn and hold support from top management. Johnson & Johnson's former public relations head reports that such support is not easily earned and requires mutual respect:

> Perhaps in more than any other relationship among senior executives in a company, the chemistry that exists between the CEO and the senior public relations executive is most critical. If things are working as they should, the public relations person is given the unique opportunity to become the CEO's "loyal opposition," the one who, behind closed doors, can say, "If you do this, you are making a huge mistake."[2]

Support and understanding develop with time and on the basis of a track record of achievements that contribute to organizational success.

Executives in top management determine long-term goals, set policies, and approve procedures to guide the entire organization. In the process they decide, at least tentatively, on the scope and the place of all office and field management functions. Intentionally or not, they determine the role of each and the relationship each has with the others.

STAFF ROLE

Public relations is one of several staff functions, meaning that it advises and supports line managers who have responsibility and authority to run the organization. Practitioners therefore need to understand the staff role.

The line–staff management model originated in the military but now is used in most large organizations. *Line functions* in industry include the product- and profit-producing functions: engineering, production, and marketing. *Staff functions* include those that advise and assist line executives: finance, legal, human resources (formerly personnel), and public relations. The Meredith publishing and broadcasting corporation makes the staff role explicit in the position title—"Staff Vice President/Director of Public Relations."

Staff support becomes increasingly necessary as an organization increases in size and complexity. Line executives have the authority and responsibility to set policy and to oversee the operations, but they need assistance in the form of plans, advice, support services, and suggestions from staff executives. Staff officers advise top executives and provide support to line officers.[3] Many years ago, a management expert made the distinction rather bluntly: "Specialists are necessary, but 'they should be on tap—not on top.' "[4] In other words, staff officers contribute to the main line of business rather than complete self-contained tasks or produce the organization's end products. As one executive put it,

> In public relations—and I now know that I share this frustration with other staff officers—you're always spending somebody else's money. You're always doing something for them; you're bailing them out, or you're writing a piece for them, or putting out a publication that deals with their subject, not yours. The result is a built-in requirement for an extensive approval process.[5]

Line management and public relations staff should be able to count on each other for support. Management reasonably expects the following from the public relations staff:

1. Loyalty
2. Counsel on the public relations aspects of decisions
3. Skill in articulating principles and in enhancing public understanding of the organization
4. Inspiration to help all members do their best
5. Influence in restraining other members from saying or doing anything detrimental to the organization's welfare
6. Character—honesty, trustworthiness, and discretion

One CEO defines the ideal public relations officer as

Honest, trustworthy, discreet, with solid analytical skills, and a total comprehension and understanding of the core business and the key publics. He or she will have the ability to listen, the ability to counsel, and the ability to help the CEO manage competing priorities. The most important qualities, however, are chemistry, trust, and respect. Without them, it's impossible for the CEO and chief communication officer to establish a productive long-term relationship.[6]

Public relations staff expect the following from line management:

1. Positive public relations leadership
2. Support of approved communication policy
3. Strategic plans embracing all policies and programs
4. Adequate budget to do the job, including funds for adequate public opinion research, analysis, and program evaluation
5. Reasonable availability for consultation and for public appearances

Each also has the right to expect of the other character and performance that will stand public scrutiny and fulfill the organization's social responsibility.

Differences between line and staff management, however, call for different roles in the relationship. Line management determines the ground rules and sets the course. Once all points of view have been aired and debated, the resulting decisions may result from a consensus or from choices made by line management. Both line and staff managers must participate, but final decisions are the province of senior line management. Public relations works within those rules on matters having an impact on the organization's internal and external relationships.

Because managing organizational relationships is an increasingly important and central function, some public relations practitioners advance from staff positions to line management. A few have become CEOs. As the Perrier, Johnson & Johnson, TWA, and Texaco examples make clear, public opinion and public response to an organization's actions may have as much influence on the bottom line as the performance of engineering, research, marketing, manufacturing, and other executives. As a result, public relations executives increasingly participate in making important strategic decisions. Some eventually find themselves chairing these decision-making meetings.

Public relations practitioners typically applaud when public relations executives move into line management but view the reverse with alarm. In a bit of semantic tyranny, the Task Force on the Stature and Role of Public Relations labeled movement into public relations management from other staff or line units as "encroachment," identifying it as a threat to the profession.[7] Their concern centers on who will make public relations program decisions and recommendations and who will be left with the tasks of implementing programs.[8] On the other hand, not all agree that there is an encroachment problem, pointing out that executives who get public relations experience move on to other assignments with a greater understanding of the function.

Line managers often rotate through a variety of assignments before reaching the top. Not many, however, include public relations in their regular rotation of assignments. Public relations experience would add to the credibility of public relations as a management function, demystify the function for other managers, and expand career opportunities for those now viewed as communication technicians with no role in management.[9] In most organizations, however, the demarcation between line and staff management continues to guide decision making.

ROLE IN DECISION MAKING

Traditional and somewhat rigid distinctions between line and staff managers—giving orders versus giving advice—do not always represent their respective roles in decision making. For example, practitioners operating in the expert prescriber role often have power to choose among public relations program alternatives, with line management later endorsing the selections or exercising veto power. Practioners, when in a problem-solving, process facilitator role, often collaborate with line managers to make decisions. Increasingly, practitioners are assuming positions in the policy-setting and decision-making "dominant coalition," a term used to describe those who hold power in organizations.[10]

Proximity and *access* are important factors influencing the role of public relations in management decision making. For example, when faced with bankruptcy, Federated Department Stores expanded their dominant coalition to include Carol Sanger, the vice president of corporate communication, as she explains in an interview:

> They moved the corporate communications function to the 20th floor; the 20th floor is where the senior management offices are located. So we were literally right in the midst of things. . . . It's a very informal communications process. There was an amazing amount of contact that occurred in the hallway. The president would just walk down the hall and come in my office. It is casual in that respect, but really is an important component of the access to the thought process, access to the person, access to judgment calls when they need to be made.[11]

Organizational changes also can enhance or diminish the role of public relations in management. For example, Volvo's CEO, upon appointment at the Sweden-based manufacturer, elevated the senior communication and government relations officers to the top management team. At United Airlines, the establishment of an employee stock option plan led to an expanded role for public relations in corporate decision making. Vice president of corporate communication John Kiker said that since that change, United's CEO and other managers increasingly seek public relations input and counsel before making decisions, rather than "make decisions first, and communicate the decisions afterwards."[12] When Boeing Company acquired McDonnell Douglas Aircraft Company, it restructured its management team, forming an executive council that reports to the chairman's office. The vice president of communications and investor relations and the vice president of ethics report to the council, placing these staff management executives in positions to influence decision making.[13]

In addition, *characteristics of the practitioners* themselves—particularly *personal credibility*—contribute to their inclusion or exclusion from the dominant coalition. Researchers have identified practitioners' lack of broad business experience, passivity, naïveté about organization politics, technical education, gender, and tenure in their organizations as factors contributing to the relatively limited power of public relations in organizations.[14]

Public relations participation in organizational decision making also depends on the extent to which the function conducts various kinds of research. Researchers have called such research "organizational intelligence gathering," "environmental scanning," "scanning for planning," and "formal versus informal research." Regardless of labels, survey results consistently show that when the function engages in various types of research, there is a greater likelihood that public relations staff will be involved in decision making and other management planning activities.[15]

The major determinant of public relations' role in organizational decision making, however, is the degree to which line managers and practitioners themselves view the function as part of the management team. When top management views the function as marginal and outside the main line of business, it remains outside the dominant decision-making coalition. The Excellence Study researchers discovered that CEOs in the top 10 percent of organizations were almost three times more supportive of the public relations function than were CEOs in other organizations. Likewise, top public relations executives in the top 10 percent of organizations in the study rated the dominant coalition as more than three times more supportive than did public relations executives in other organizations.[16]

In organizations in which public relations is seen as communication output only, the function becomes routine and highly structured. Practitioners spend most of their time on "programmed decisions," working primarily as communication technicians issuing weekly news packets, publishing the monthly employee newsletter, and creating other communication materials. Programmed decisions dominate in most organizations in order to free managers and resources to make "nonprogrammed decisions" dealing with the "novel, unstructured, and consequential."[17]

When public relations operates in the realm of programmed decisions, it is seen as part of organizational routine and overhead. When it participates in nonprogrammed decision making, on the other hand, it is seen as playing an important role in achieving organizational goals and contributing to the bottom line. When public relations employs management by objectives (MBO), management by objectives and results (MOR), or management by key results to guide program planning and management, then the focus shifts from producing communications (process) to results and consequences (impact). It also makes public relations more a part of the management team held accountable for achieving organizational goals.

According to Robert Dilenschneider, former president and CEO of Hill

& Knowlton and now chairman of the Dileschneider Group of New York and Chicago, "seven deadly sins in this business" threaten progress in integrating the function:

1. Overpromising, making commitments for things they know they cannot deliver
2. Overmarketing, or overselling the client on the capabilities or expertise of public relations
3. Underservicing (referred to earlier as "bait-and-switch"), listing senior people as part of the account team but using junior staff to do the work
4. Putting the firm's financial results ahead of performance and results for the client
5. Using the quick fix, when public relations takes the form of shortsighted responses to complex problems that require long-lasting solutions (Note: It is easy to fall into the trap of client or management expectations that public relations has the power to fix problems without having to make changes in the organization.)
6. Treating public relations as simply a support function charged with implementing strategies formulated by lawyers, financial officers, and top line managers
7. Violating ethical standards, thereby damaging the function's reputation for ethical conduct and concern for social responsibility[18]

As a management function, public relations is part of an organization's structure and process for adapting to change. Its responsibilities include helping organizations identify, assess, and adjust to their turbulent economic, political, social, and technological environments. In the words of one corporate CEO,

> I believe the public relations field will continue to be pressed by the dynamics of public media and special interest group scrutiny, and the acceleration of global telecommunications technologies. The public relations profession needs to anticipate social, political, and economic issues that have the potential of impacting business plans, instead of being only reactive.[19]

In the final analysis, however, as Pacific Gas and Electric CEO Richard A. Clarke said, "The only way CEOs can get what they need from their public relations advisers is to have them at the table when the policies, strategies, and programs are being hammered out."[20]

THE INTERNAL DEPARTMENT

The internal department is the most common structure for serving the public relations needs of organizations. The unit of specialists within the organization may consist of only one person, as in a small hospital, or a staff of almost 500, as at AT&T. There is probably even more work in public relations in the Department of Defense, but the actual number there remains difficult to determine. A public relations department may be concentrated in the organization's headquarters or scattered among many locations. The department's size, role, and place in the organization chart vary from one organization to the next.

The Department's Advantages

An internal department has at least four factors working in its favor:

1. Team membership
2. Knowledge of the organization
3. Economy to the organization for many ongoing programs
4. Availability to associates

Team membership is the department's greatest advantage over outside counsel. In some organizations the top public relations executive's office is next door to the chief executive's office. As an example of the close working relationship, for years the top public relations executive at Eastman Kodak began most workdays meeting with the CEO.[21] Federated Department Stores moved the public relations function to the twentieth floor where other senior management offices are located because "it's a more complicated, complex, interrelated . . . involvement than ever before."[22]

Frequent contact between the public relations department and top line management is the rule rather than the exception. According to *pr reporter* newsletter, 60 percent of public relations executives meet with their CEOs at least once each week. Such a close working relationship between the public relations department and the CEO builds confidence, trust, and support. It can also position public relations as a key player on the management team.

Knowledge of the organization means an intimate, current knowledge that comes from being an insider. Staff members know the relationships among individuals and departments and are fully aware of the undercurrents of influence and internal politics. They can call on key people to make decisions and avoid those who put personal ambition and expedience above organizational and public interests. They are aware of who can serve as able and articulate spokespersons as opposed to those who become tongue-tied or are media-shy persons who do not perform well on camera.

Occasionally a trusted outside counselor is able to acquire such knowledge, but insiders are in the better position to do so and to apply their knowledge on a continuous basis. Because they are part of the organization, internal departmental staff are able to advise, conciliate, and provide services while taking into account organizational history and culture. They know who and what to avoid, as well as who and what to include.

Economy results from typically lower overhead costs and efficient integration in an organization. When the need for public relations is continuous—and in most organizations it is—then a full-time, permanent staff is typically more cost-effective than outside counsel and services. For example, the marginal costs of the department's space, heat, and light are typically a small portion of overhead costs in a large organization. The outside firm's overhead can be higher than that for an internal department simply because outside firms are typically smaller than the client organizations they serve, so economies of scale are lost.

Start-up costs for projects often are less, because internal staff members already have the necessary background, access, and understanding. Routine aspects of the work, such as weekly news releases, monthly publications, quarterly reports, and so forth, are efficiently handled by those closest to the sources and other departments in the organization. Efficiency contributes to cost-effectiveness.

Availability of staff practitioners has many facets. When things go wrong, practitioners are only a minute away from a face-to-face meeting with the organization's officers. And as deputies, they can be entrusted with delicate matters. For example, if a senior executive defects in a huff, the CEO wants a public relations specialist on the spot who knows the background, understands the dangers of mishandling the news, and has credibility with the news media and other key players.

Availability also means being on call for all other departments, divisions, and operating units. Staff members can be called into meetings on short notice. In some organizations, public relations is decentralized, with specialists assigned to each operating unit. In others, a centralized function operates from headquarters much in the fashion of an outside firm, treating operating units and other departments as clients. The difference, of course, is that the on-site internal staff members are relatively handy for consultation.

The Department's Disadvantages

Team membership can be a problem when a person sacrifices objectivity and perspective in order to be a team player. If people are too loyal, they may be exploited when friendships and collegiality lead to subservience. Availability can cast the function as a catchall if it does not have a clearly defined mission and specified roles.

A *loss of objectivity* can happen ever so slowly and unwittingly as practitioners are subjected to day-to-day pressure and politics in the workplace. In supporting and being supported, they tend to be absorbed and compromised by group views. Their ability to see other points of view gives way to the subjectivity that afflicts those they were hired to counsel. They lose their ability to do the boundary spanning needed to avoid or solve problems in the organization's relationships with others. In effect, practitioners run the risk of becoming part of the problem. After all, they work hard to become part of the management team.

Domination and subservience result when the function becomes co-opted as a group of yes-men and -women. Being team players and helping others is one thing; being diverted from goals, planning, and strategy to run errands for others is another. Practitioners walk a narrow line between rendering professional services that are valuable, helpful, and appreciated and rendering low-level support that is easily replaced. Successfully making this distinction in practice tends to sort out potential staff managers from those who will remain in technical support staff roles. There is much more to it than simply knowing organizational politics or playing the political game. The key is being a team player providing staff support based on public relations knowledge and skills while retaining one's unique role and professionalism. Inaction based on fear of making a career-threatening move or decision renders the function powerless and undermines its role as counselor to top management.

Confused mission and roles can result from being readily available. Practitioners find themselves serving as stand-ins for top executives who make commitments but do not or cannot follow through themselves. For example, a CEO accepts an invitation to serve on a community organization board or committee but finds it difficult to attend the meetings. The practitioner gets a call to attend in the CEO's place. Some would say that this indicates that the CEO trusts the public relations officer to effectively represent the organization. External constituencies are seldom pleased to have a public relations representative instead of the CEO but accept the switch in order to maintain the organization's support and permission to use the CEO's name on the letterhead and in other public communications.

The dilemma of a state bar association public relations director provides an example of confused mission and roles. Among many miscellaneous duties, he was put in charge of the housekeeping staff and was directed to deal with the homeless and others who entered the main reception area to use rest room facilities and to seek refuge from the cold and rain. How did the practitioner get such duties? Being the only nonlawyer at the director level probably did not help, but a vague and open-ended job description made the function vulnerable. The public relations director also was the most available, because other directors were often out of the office conducting programs and providing direct services to members. It became a vicious cycle: The more miscellaneous assignments the director had, the less time he had for the association's public relations efforts and publications. Not surprisingly, the executive director eventually questioned the public relations director's effectiveness and criticized him for missing publication deadlines.

Titles and Reporting Relationships

Titles and positions of departments in organizations vary greatly. *O'Dwyer's Directory of Corporate Communications* lists titles for 5,500 departments in companies, associations, and governmental units. Recent editions of this annual directory show that about 30 percent use "public relations," making it still the most commonly used title. Another 20 percent use "corporate communications" or "communications." Slightly less than 10 percent use "public affairs," and about the same number combine functions in the title "advertising/public relations." Other commonly used titles include "corporate relations" and "public information." Among Fortune 500 companies, however, only one in five use "public relations" titles (alone or in combination with other names), with almost half using "communication" alone or in combination to label the function.

There is no compelling reason to conclude that some other title will replace "public relations." To the contrary, "public relations" has survived almost a century in spite of the many attempts by practitioners themselves to find an alternative, in spite of the occasional taint of malpractice by individual practitioners, and in spite of public relations bashing by the media. Both news media and publics worldwide have come to understand the term and to use it to describe this function in organizations. Switching labels does not change more than 100 years of history.

More significant than the department's title, however, is the top public relations executive's place on the organizational chart and reporting relationship to the CEO. Often public relations is not included in the CEO's decision-making circle, the executive committee. In a corporation, for example, that group typically brings together the CEO, the president (if someone other than the CEO), and the heads of manufacturing, finance, marketing, engineering and R&D, and legal. Too often, public relations joins administration and personnel or human resources functions as outsiders to this decision-making executive group. As a result, external implications of decisions and communication needs are not taken into account when decisions are made.[23]

Even if not included in the decision circle meetings, the top public relations executive typically reports directly to the CEO. Findings from a study of 100 major corporations show that 54 percent of the senior public relations executives report directly to the CEO or president. Ninety-three percent meet with their organization's CEO at least weekly to provide strategic counsel and to participate in planning.[24]

For example, Roy Clason, who left the American Red Cross to assume the new post as vice president of global communications at MasterCard International, reports to the president and CEO. In the Chesapeake, Virginia, municipal government, public relations director Mark Cox reports to the city manager, who in turn reports to the city council, much as a corporate president and CEO reports to the board of directors. The vice president of university relations at the University of Chicago reports directly to the university president, a typical reporting relationship in universities, foundations, and other nonprofit organizations.

Reporting relationships and job functions are included in organization charts and job descriptions. These lay the groundwork for division and specialization of work, communication up and down the chain of command, and acceptance of various functions throughout the organization. Some practitioners, however, become preoccupied with trying to change the charts and edit their job descriptions, as though these, with no other changes, will elevate the public relations function or somehow change how it is performed. As one long-standing opponent of organization charts—the late Clarence Randall, a management innovator when he headed Inland Steel—pointed out,

> To know who is to do what and to establish authority and responsibility within an institution are the basic first principles of a good administration, but this is a far cry from handing down immutable tablets of stone from the mountaintop. . . . It is not the preparation of the organization chart that I condemn, but its abuse: this blowing up its significance to a point where guidance ceases and inhibition sets in.[25]

FIGURE 3.1   LINE AND STAFF ORGANIZATION CHART

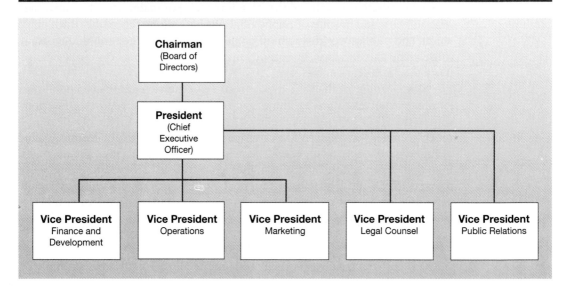

Organization charts are, at best, approximations, but they do help clarify the role and relationships of various functions. Figure 3.1, for example, illustrates how public relations and legal *staff* functions report to the CEO differently than do the *line* managers. Figures 3.2 and 3.3 detail reporting relationships *within* public relations departments at a university and a corporation.

FIGURE 3.2   UNIVERSITY PUBLIC RELATIONS DEPARTMENT

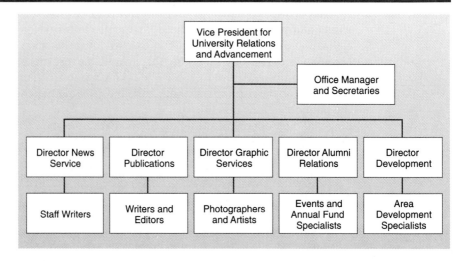

FIGURE 3.3   CORPORATE PUBLIC RELATIONS DEPARTMENT

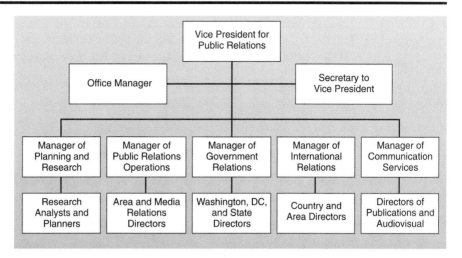

WORKING WITH OTHER DEPARTMENTS

Public relations staff work most closely with the marketing and finance units. They also collaborate with the human resources (or personnel), industrial or employee relations, and legal departments. All these functions overlap with public relations in varying degrees, occasionally leading to unavoidable confusion about or even outright conflict over their respective roles. Disruptive and costly friction occurs particularly in relations with marketing, legal counsel, human resources, and development. To discharge obligations effectively, each function needs the support and cooperation of the others. But with the potential for conflict, practitioners should be aware, alert, and ready to redefine the mission of public relations and to mend fences.

Marketing

As chapter 1 points out, public relations is most often confused with marketing. These two major communication and outreach functions must work in harmony in dealing with an organization's many publics. Conflict usually arises in corporations over which function should be responsible for institutional advertising and product publicity. In nonprofit organizations, the two functions struggle over responsibility for and resources—budget and people—for fund-raising, membership drives, or public education and persuasion campaigns. Confusion often results from differing views of the roles of marketing versus public relations, with marketing specialists typically defining "public relations" as simply publicity or, even more mistakenly, as "journalism." Some holding this view also define any goal-driven strategic plan as "marketing."

Confusion also results from the mistaken notion that advertising is the sole province of marketing. Advertising designed to establish, change, or maintain relationships with key publics (usually by influencing public opinion) should, by its objectives and strategic nature, be supervised by the public relations department. Advertising for public relations purposes—causes and issues, corporate reputation, financial, or special events—may require the advertising department's expertise to produce and place the advertisements, but the outcome sought has more to do with public relations than with selling goods or services, in other words, marketing.

Conversely, publicity about products and services designed to increase sales is clearly directed to achieving marketing outcomes. Because public relations staff members are typically more skilled at writing and placing publicity, they often are enlisted to help publicize new products, product changes, price changes, product recalls, and special promotional activities as part of the marketing effort. Microsoft used national publicity efforts, along with advertising, to help introduce each edition of Windows. Even though it may have had impact on publics other than customers—such as investors, competitors, government regulators—the publicity was designed primarily to support the marketing effort.

Advertising and publicity produced by either public relations or marketing should be coordinated with the other's communications. For example, public relations should not tell environmental groups about the company's commitment to protecting the environment when marketing is running a nationwide sale of "nongreen" products that cause environmental damage. Backlash is an ever-present danger. The growth of articulate protest and consumer groups, widespread use of the Internet globally, investigative and consumer reporting, and government scrutiny all make cooperation between public relations and marketing essential.

Cooperation does not mean co-optation, however. Calls for combining public relations and marketing under the umbrella of "integrated marketing communication" (IMC) typically originate from those working in the marketing function. Their rationale for integration, however, makes clear that the focus is on the marketing relationship with *customers,* and that public relations is viewed simply as another tool in the marketing arsenal:

> All disciplines must work together to win the customer's confidence and loyalty. We may call what we do advertising or public relations or direct marketing or sales or whatever—but to the customer, it's all one thing.[26]

Public relations management consultant Jim Arnold counters this view by pointing out that "maintaining public support for any enterprise requires a broader focus than 'getting and keeping' customers," and that "public relations is an important senior management discipline in its own right, not merely a tool to be stirred into the mix of marketing tricks."[27] He argues that

> Its [public relations's] independence of marketing should be maintained to provide top management with unfiltered counsel and advice across the entire array of stockholders and public, not merely the psychographics and demographics of the IMC data base. And, in fact, many of these audiences—financial analysts,

news media, public officials, and employees come to mind—are often suspicious and mistrustful of "marketing communications" with its emphasis on selling.[28]

Newsletter editor Jack O'Dwyer observes that advertising agencies often form IMC teams in which the public relations specialist's role is reduced to pitching the advertising theme developed for the marketing effort. This subordinates public relations to marketing; as one source advised, "You'd better understand how PR fits into the bigger marketing scheme." The late Philip Lesly saw the focus on marketing tactics and processes as "essentially the product publicity and promotion that were underway in the 1920s, updated for a wider range of media and a more diverse populace."[29]

Competition, even conflict, between these two functions is understandable. Practitioners often compete on parallel career tracks for recognition, job advancement, and budgets. For example, a public relations author published an article with the subtitle "How to Steal Budget from Those Folks in Advertising." In some organizations, marketing and public relations report to the same executive, who is charged with coordinating efforts. Usually, however, they are separate departments, with public relations in a staff relationship to the chief executive officer and marketing in the line management chain of command.

Legal Counsel

The conflict between public relations and legal staffs is an old one. In the days of the muckrakers, corporate executives turned first to their lawyers to fix things. Some still do. One of the founders of public relations, Ivy Lee, felt strongly about this in 1925:

> I have seen more situations which the public ought to understand and which the public would sympathize with, spoiled by the intervention of the lawyer than in any other way. Whenever a lawyer starts to talk to the public, he shuts out the light.[30]

Traditionally, legal and public relations counselors approach situations from different perspectives. Lawyers tend to favor "no comment," pointing out that what you say may come back to haunt you (be used as evidence in court) and reminding that you are not legally obliged to say anything. Public relations practitioners, on the other hand, espouse the virtues of openness, of sharing information as soon as possible, of cooperating with the media, and of responding to people's claims to a right to know. Lawyers are accustomed to getting extensions, to protracting the process in private, and to delaying responses as long as possible. Public relations specialists routinely meet deadlines, recognize media time constraints as real, and respond immediately to media requests.

Public relations practitioners work to build and maintain mutuality and harmony in relationships. If public relations succeeds, then top management assumes that things are going smoothly and that there is no need for counsel. Lawyers, on the other hand, are called on when conflict and discord dominate an organization's relationships. Under conditions of threatened or actual legal action, top management turns to legal counsel for advice and protection. Hence lawyers gain power when organizations face conflict and discord with publics that turn to the courts for redress.

Under more positive conditions, public relations practitioners with good writing skills can help make legal documents more understandable. In doing so, they can save organizations the costs of being misunderstood or of being offensive because of obscure or needlessly harsh language. Cooperation between these two functions can protect the organization legally while at the same time serving the public interest, as when Sentry Insurance led the way in the insurance industry by rewriting policies and literature in plain English. The new policy descriptions meet the test of legal counsel and greatly increase information value to policyholders and prospective customers.

Close cooperation between legal and public relations counsel also is critical during labor contract negotiations, product recalls, layoffs or other sensitive personnel matters, consumer protests or boycotts, and other legally based or explosive situations. Additionally, legal and public relations counsel must be coordinated on such matters as booklets explaining benefits to employees, the legality of advertising or publicity claims, plant security, and disclosure of financial information.[31]

Once a concern primarily in business and industry, close cooperation between legal and public relations counselors now is necessary in most organizations. Examples from various settings illustrate the need: Universities defend themselves both in the courts of justice and public opinion when fraternity hazing deaths, date rapes, or discrimination charges in tenure decisions become national news. The presidents of Stanford, MIT, and other major universities called in both lawyers and public relations specialists when excessive overhead charges on federally funded research projects made headline news.

Executives at Red Cross and other blood banks nationwide consulted both legal and public relations staff when news of contaminated blood activated lawsuits and eroded public confidence in the nation's blood supply. Church leaders consulted both lawyers and public relations practitioners after news reports of a priest admitting to molesting children in a church school program and charges that church funds had been used to support a political cause.

It is often too late, but mayors and city managers call in both lawyers and public relations staff when the evening news leads with reports of out-of-court settlements involving large sums of tax dollars and secrecy agreements about discrimination, sexual harassment, police brutality, or other misconduct on the part of public officials. The Air Force found itself subject to a media trial—including an appearance on *60 Minutes*—long before former First Lieutenant Kelly Flinn faced a court-martial on charges of adultery, fraternization, making a false official statement, and disobeying a superior officer. Certainly the White House used both legal and public relations counsel when Paula Jones charged President Clinton with sexual harassment, as well as throughout the investigations by Independent Counsel Kenneth Starr and the impeachment proceedings in the House of Representatives and Senate.

Increasingly, legal and public relations specialists collaborate when counseling CEOs, and coordinate their responses in courts of law and in courts of public opinion. Additionally, more and more CEOs began their careers as lawyers; one survey of CEOs found that almost one-third had law degrees.[32] As one lawyer advised fellow legal counselors, however, "Make sure you are the lawyer and that public relations is handled by a public relations professional."

Human Resources

The American Society of Personnel Administrators changed its 40-year-old name to the Society for Human Resources Management in 1989. Some predicted that the emerging conflict between public relations and human resources would become a turf war similar to the one public relations and marketing experienced in the 1980s and early 1990s. Lines were blurred and opportunity for friction was high. They still are.

Fundamental problems include: (1) whether human resources' role in strategic planning in personnel matters during downsizing (read "layoffs"), reengineering, mergers, and acquisitions extends to areas outside employee relations; (2) the extent to which communication efforts within the community constitute an extension of the organization–employee relationship; and (3) whether programs directed to the employee public draw more on public relations concepts than on those developed from the traditions of personnel and extended to the new function of human resources. Control of employee communications (not the whole of employee relations) is the most frequent source of conflict between these two functions. Compromise comes when practitioners and human resource specialists realize that internal relationships inevitably reverberate externally.

Surveys of the field indicate the nature of overlapping assignments. Results of the Benchmark 1997 survey indicate that 88 percent of corporate communicators are responsible for employee communication and that this function ranked second in importance only to financial communications–investor relations for achieving corporate goals.[33] Seventy percent of *pr reporter* newsletter's readers report that employee communication is handled by the public relations department, whereas only 22 percent report that employee communication falls under the human resources function. As was the case with respondents to the Benchmark 1997 survey, the newsletter's survey respondents were primarily public relations practitioners.

In contrast, recent surveys conducted by Watson Wyatt Worldwide, a consulting firm that deals primarily with human resources and personnel departments, show a different picture. More than half—53 percent—of the responding companies place employee communication under human resources, whereas only 30 percent put it under public relations. A similar survey conducted by a communication executive search firm found that 20 percent of the responding corporate communicators report to the head of human resources.[34]

Recognizing that the workforce has been and is changing, many organizations have increased efforts to develop their major resource, people. Concerns about employee loyalty and mobility, "virtual organizations," quality-of-life issues, and employee education and training are seen as directly affecting the bottom line.

> Change is now probably the only corporate constant. And if employees are expected to go along with the new programs, who better to collaborate and strategize about workforce changes than human resources and public relations?[35]

Some human resources departments employ organizational development (OD) specialists to help introduce and manage organizational changes, management team building, quality control programs, and leadership development. Confusion and conflict intensifies when internal communications and traditional public relations external communication roles such as community relations and media relations are assigned to human resources or OD specialists.

To help manage change, organizations are reorganizing, restructuring, and reengineering communication units, according to Paul Sanchez at Watson Wyatt Worldwide:

> Many communicators, once identified as part of the human resources or public relations function, are now a separate and distinct communication department, reversing a trend from the late 1980s. As senior management looks for more strategic integrated communication programming, they are finding that other staff agencies often lack the expertise or time to provide the required focus or skills spectrum. This is especially true for the types of broad communication initiatives that organizations must undertake to support organizational change.[36]

Strategic management of human resources and organizational change requires close cooperation and collaboration between public relations and human resources specialists. Otherwise, it is apparent that top management will create new units to conceive and implement internal and external communication strategy to achieve organizational goals.

THE OUTSIDE COUNSELING FIRM

Beginning in the 1980s, many "public relations agencies" changed their titles to "public relations firms." The change reflects an increased emphasis on counseling and strategic planning services, viewed as more professional than the communication tactics produced by press agents and publicity agencies. Another reason for the switch is to position the firm as something different from advertising agencies and other vendors of services working on commissions. Although some still refer to "agencies" in unguarded moments, most in the field prefer to be seen as similar to law firms, management consulting firms, certified public accounting firms, architectural firms, and consulting engineering firms.

Public Relations Firms

The more than 2,300 public relations counseling firms and agencies in the United States range widely in size and scope of service.[37] *O'Dwyer's Directory of Public Relations Firms* provides the most complete listing of U.S. firms by location and specialty, plus 500 in 55 other countries. New York leads all cities in the number of firms, with Chicago and Washington, DC, in a virtual tie for a distant second. The largest New York–based firm—Burson-Marsteller—employs more than 2,100 people worldwide, but worldwide there are uncounted thousands working as independent self-employed counselors. Many work as "_____ and Associates," often meaning, "If I can't handle a project myself, I know other practitioners I can bring in on the project."

In New York, Burson-Marsteller's office employs 350; Ruder Finn, 285; Edelman PR Worldwide, 275; and Ketchum Public Relations and Hill & Knowlton, 150 each. The Chicago office of Edelman Public Relations Worldwide has 210 employees; Shandwick-owned Golin/Harris, 175; Financial Board, 115; and Burson-Marsteller, 100. The Washington, DC, offices of Burson-Marsteller, Hill & Knowlton, Fleishman-Hillard, APCO Associates of GCI Group, Porter Novelli, Ketchum PR, and Ogilvy Public Relations Worldwide each employ 100 to 135. Fleishman-Hillard has 325 employees in its St. Louis headquarters and 75 in the Kansas City office. The Weber Group and Brodeur Porter Novelli each employ 110 in Boston. In Los Angeles, Shandwick's Rogers and Cowan has 95 employees; Hill & Knowlton, 85; and Fleishman-Hillard, 80.

With the growing recognition of the global economy and formation of the 15-nation European Union, the public relations capital has shifted from New York to London. According to London-based *Marketing* magazine, the leading professional publication in London, Shandwick—the second largest public relations firm worldwide, with almost 1,800 employees—has 380 employees in its London office. Hill & Knowlton's London office (see Figure 3.4, pg. 82), with 260 employees, is bigger than its New York headquarters in both size and billings. Countrywide Porter Novelli employs 246 in its London office. The next largest London-based firms specialize in investor relations: Citigate, with 175 employees; Weber Public Relations Worldwide, 148; and Dewe Rogerson, 146.[38] These numbers could increase dramatically in London and other European capitals with the introduction of a common currency and decreased international barriers to commerce.

Phone directories in every major city list firms under "Public Relations" and "Publicity." For example, the London yellow pages directory contains more than 500 listings under "Public Relations Consultancies." (In Europe, *consultancy* is used instead of *firm*.) Another 70 listings appear under "Publicity Consultants." Kohtes & Klewes Kommunikation (Dusseldorf) is Germany's largest public relations consultancy with 165 employees. The two largest U.S.-owned consultancies in Germany are Burson-Marsteller and Edelman PR Worldwide, both in Frankfurt. Shandwick Asia Pacific Ltd. is the largest firm in Hong Kong (350 employees), but most of the largest international firms have offices or affiliates there. The same is true in Japan, where

FIGURE 3.4   **HILL & KNOWLTON'S LONDON OFFICE**

Kyodo Public Relations Co., Ltd., with 100 employees; IR Japan, Inc., with 110 employees; and IPR Shandwick Co. Ltd., with 80 employees, head the growing list of firms.

As their client organizations increasingly operate in the global economy, public relations firms have opened branches, acquired smaller firms, and affiliated with firms in major cities around the globe. Firms use different approaches to globalization, however. For example, many of Shandwick's more than 100 offices use the names and approaches to client services that they had before being acquired by Shandwick. In order to "operate in a diverse world of many cultures," each office is staffed by nationals who know the media and cultures in the area served. Following a similar approach, the loosely affiliated international network of 91 partner firms known as The Worldcom Group, Inc., says it provides "global access, local focus" through 113 offices on six continents.

Burson-Marsteller, Hill & Knowlton, and Fleishman-Hillard, on the other hand, have strong corporate cultures and procedures that guide operations in offices worldwide. Each uses its corporate name worldwide, moves executives among offices, and directs international operations from U.S. headquarters. The firms also tend to start their own offices in countries and build their own businesses rather than acquiring existing firms. Burson-Marsteller founding chairman Harold Burson says that international public relations firms no longer depend solely on U.S. talent, however:

> That is not how it works. In Europe, we have 19 offices—most of them are either first, second or third in size in their country. All are almost totally staffed by local nationals. The fact is, we have barely a half dozen U.S. nationals in all of Europe.
>
> In France, Burson-Marsteller's Paris office is as much a French office as any of our locally owned and managed competitors. Many of our people in France (and elsewhere around the world) worked at other French PR firms before joining us. The same is true in the 35 countries where we have offices.[39]

As markets and economies became global, as global alliances formed, and as global media delivered messages around the world within seconds, public relations and every other aspect of corporate business became global enterprises. As a result, public relations firms in most major cities operate transnationally, either through affiliates or by subcontracting with local firms in other countries. For example, Sumner Rider & Associates, based in New York and Washington, DC, used local firms in Germany, Japan, Mexico, and Italy for a program directed to the automotive industries in those countries. According to SR&A president Peter Rush,

> We demand the same things of firms in other countries that we demand of ourselves—credibility, accountability, expertise, experience, ethics, and, most important, results—although we fully understand that we have to allow them to execute the work in keeping with their cultural norms, especially as they relate to media relations.[40]

Whatever the approach, public relations firms now serve clients with new approaches to communication and sophisticated counsel in a global village.

Standards of practice for public relations firms are more closely monitored and enforced in Europe than in the United States and Asia. More than 200 firms belong to the Public Relations Consultants Association, which requires member consultancies to follow specific guidelines for dealing with the media, clients, and competitors; for conducting investor relations for publicly traded companies; and for enforcing the "Professional Charter" through arbitration and settlement. Strict enforcement forced Ogilvy Adams & Rinehart to withdraw from PRCA when it refused to list all of its clients in the association's confidential "Annual Register" as required in the PRCA Professional Charter. The first such association of firms in the United States was formed in

1998 after 38 founding firms, representing most of the major national and international firms, contributed $200,000 to establish the American Association of Public Relations Firms (AAPRF). Ketchum Public Relations Worldwide CEO David Drobis chaired the task force that surveyed potential members and opened the new headquarters office.

Advertising Agency Ownership

Of the 20 largest firms, 10 are subsidiaries of large advertising agencies. Many were acquired as advertising agencies bought out retiring founders and principals of closely held public relations firms. The trend began in 1978, when Foote, Cone and Belding purchased Carl Byoir and Associates. The largest U.S.-based firms are now owned by advertising agencies: Burson-Marsteller and Cohn & Wolfe by Young & Rubicam, Inc.; Hill & Knowlton, Inc., by J. Walter Thompson Co. (which in turn is owned by London-based WPP Group PLC); and Ketchum Public Relations Worldwide, Porter Novelli International, and Fleishman-Hillard by Omnicom Group Inc.

Those who work in firms owned by large advertising agencies point to greater cooperation between the marketing and public relations functions being served by the "full-service" team, better research provided by the more experienced and sophisticated research departments of advertising agencies, greater communication production resources and capabilities, and better management.

Critics of advertising agency ownership believe that public relations firms lose their independence and clients lose the benefit of the counselor's alternative view in communication planning. They also point to diminished budgets and power for public relations as it inevitably becomes subservient to the marketing-driven budgets and goals of the advertising team. Problems also arise when two strong institutions with different histories and cultures try to perform as a team, especially when historically they were competitors. Even though they are under the umbrella of common ownership, they remain competitors for the client's budget. Because each unit of a large conglomerate is rewarded on the basis of how much business it generates, in effect advertising and public relations units compete for the client's business. Moreover, critics question the value of the offer of one-stop shopping. Few clients use the firms as communication supermarkets. Rather, most large clients prefer to spread their business over several agencies and firms, expanding the range of perspectives and client experiences.

History suggests that forces work against the advertising agency–public relations subsidiary arrangement. Advertising agencies have found it difficult to determine what public relations services to offer, how to organize the function effectively, and how to sustain it apart from the advertising side of the shop, from which it derives the vast majority of dollar billings. The N. W. Ayer advertising agency pioneered in 1920, and the Albert Frank-Guenther Law agency took the next step when it began offering full-fledged public relations and publicity services. In the 1930s, J. Walter Thompson, Young & Rubicam, and Benton & Bowles soon followed. By the mid-1940s, 75 agencies provided publicity service for clients, according to an *Advertising Age* survey.

Specialization

Most firms claim to be "full-service" firms, but some carve out specialized client–service market niches. Although there are many specialties, the most dramatic growth has occurred in Washington, DC, firms that specialize in government relations—lobbying, public affairs, and legislative affairs. Clients retain these firms primarily to participate in the public policy process and to have influence on those who formulate and implement public policy.

Client lists at many such firms also include foreign governments and foreign corporations who follow developments in the U.S. capital and who want their points of view to be considered in the White House, Congress, or federal agencies. The service can be nothing more than putting out news releases about a visiting dignitary or providing updates on legislation of interest to a foreign client. Regardless of the assignment, individuals who represent foreign interests must register with the U.S. Department of Justice. The Foreign Agents Registration Act of 1938 requires registration by any "public relations counsel, publicity agent, information-service employee, or political consultant that acts within the U.S. in the interest of a foreign principal." Globalization and increased international commerce of all kinds suggest that this will continue as a growth area for public relations firms specializing in government relations.

Unfortunately, the Beltway (Washington, DC) set also includes influence-peddling operations that rise and fall with administrations and as the public service–private sector revolving door produces more and more insiders with connections in their former government employers. Commenting on the antics of those who turned government service into profitable public relations and lobbying practices, one editorial writer asked, "Has the murky 'profession' of public relations turned to sleaze?" In fact, for some who abused their positions of public trust, it meant prison time and hefty fines for illegal lobbying. Those exceptions aside, there remains a large and growing need for legitimate public relations counsel on legislative affairs and lobbying in the nation's capital, as well as in every state capital and major city.

Other specialties include agriculture, financial public relations and investor relations, health care, high-tech, sports, and travel and tourism, to name only a few. In *agriculture,* for example, Morgan & Myers (60 employees) in Jefferson, Wisconsin, serves clients such as the American Dairy Association, Asgrow Seed Company, and the National Pork Producers Council (see Figure 3.5, pg. 86). The world's largest *financial* public relations firm, the Financial Relations Board (Chicago, New York, San Francisco, and Sherman Oaks, CA), serves a long list of clients, including Ameritech, Mutual of New York, and Sears, Roebuck & Company. The client list at InterScience (New York) includes *health care, pharmaceutical,* and *biotechnology* organizations such as the American Association of Clinical Endocrinologists, Bristol Myers Squibb, SB Health Services, and the National Institutes of Health. In the *high-tech* setting of Santa Clara, California, Austin, Texas, and Cambridge, Massachusetts, the client list at Cunningham Communication, Inc., includes Cisco Systems, Inc., Hewlett-Packard, IBM, and Motorola, Inc. Alan Taylor Communications, Inc. (New

FIGURE 3.5   **MORGAN & MYERS**

**Moving from one end of the food market
to the other requires skillful navigation.**

Whether your target is at the helm of a tractor
or the head of the kitchen table,
we'll help steer you in the right direction.

**Morgan
&Myers**   *Public
Relations
Counselors*

Phone: *414-674-4026*   ·   **Fax:** *414-674-6670*   ·   **E-mail:** *gmyers@morganmyers.com*

Member
The
WORLDCOM
Group, Inc.

JEFFERSON, WISCONSIN · MILWAUKEE · MINNEAPOLIS · WATERLOO, IOWA

Courtesy Morgan & Myers.

York) specializes in *sports* publicity, special events, and media tours for clients such as General Mills, Nicklaus Golf Equipment, Reebok, and World Ironman Triathlon Corporation. And as a final example of specialization, M. Silver Associates, Inc. (New York) serves *travel* clients American Express, Caesar Park Hotels, Elephant Back Safaris, and the Monaco Tourist Board.

In addition to industry specialization, a few firms provide specialized services to help clients target particular communities. For example, after retailer Eddie Bauer was threatened with a national boycott after a nationally publicized security guard's questionable accusation that a Black customer had shoplifted, the company retained the Black-owned firm Robinson Associates (Washington, DC), for counsel on community relations.

Other consultants and counseling firms such as Daniel H. Baer & Company (Woodland Hills, CA) and Arnold & Truitt (New York) specialize in communication management consulting—conducting public relations audits, assessing client–firm relations, and helping clients select public relations firms. For example, Visa International retained consultant Baer to evaluate its worldwide public relations efforts, resulting in a restructured in-house program. Following a Teamsters Union strike, Yellow Corporation (Overland Park, KS-based freight trucking company) retained Baer to conduct an audit of its internal communication efforts and to recommend improvements. IBM retained the Arnold firm to help evaluate proposals from firms being considered by the computer manufacturer. (See Exhibit 3.1 for guidelines for selecting a firm.)

Reasons for Retaining Outside Counsel

Chester Burger, longtime consultant to the public relations industry, lists six reasons why organizations retain firms:

1. Management has not previously conducted a formal public relations program and lacks experience in organizing one.
2. Headquarters may be located far from communications and financial centers.
3. The firm has a wide range of up-to-date contacts.
4. An outside firm can provide the services of experienced executives and creative specialists who would be unwilling to move to other cities or whose salaries a single organization could not afford.
5. An organization with its own public relations department may need highly specialized services that it cannot afford or does not need on a full-time, continuous basis.
6. Crucial policy matters require the independent judgment of an outsider.

As an example, GTE Diversified Products retained Hill & Knowlton to help plan and conduct the global public relations program for its joint venture with Siemens A.G., Germany. Charged with coordinating internal and external communication operations in the United States and 22 other countries, the vice president of public affairs enlisted experienced outside help:

EXHIBIT 3.1

CHECK LIST FOR SELECTING A FIRM

Competence and reputation

- Years in business
- Size—people and billings
- Full service—specialties
- Reach—local, regional, national, international
- Growth pattern/financial stability
- Types of accounts
- Experience with accounts similar to yours—any conflicts
- Samples of work
- Sample list of suppliers used

Clients

- Existing client list
- Past clients
- Average number of clients during past three years—retainer clients, project clients
- Oldest clients and length of service
- Average length of client–firm relationships
- Clients lost in last year

Staff

- List and qualifications of staff— full time, project clients, freelance/ consultants
- Names of several former employees
- Staff to be assigned to your account—qualifications and longevity with firm
- Percent of their time to be devoted to your account—other accounts they will handle
- Staff or personnel backup available
- Staff turnover in the past two years

Results and measurement

- Does firm understand your objectives/needs?
- How will progress be reported?
- How will results be measured?
- What will it cost—billing process, hourly rate, expenses billed, approval process?

Courtesy Harland W. Warner, APR, Fellow Warner Communication Counselors, Inc. Reprinted with permission of *Public Relations Review*.

By retaining their (Hill & Knowlton) services, we benefited from an existing network of media contacts, saving us some of the trouble of tracking down outlets we needed to contact with news of the joint venture. We also used their capabilities in resolving problems in translating, designing, and delivering documents in a manner appropriate to each of our markets.

If you don't have a structure in place, you should consider hiring the services of an outside firm that can provide you with the necessary expertise. . . . In a global setting, doing all this requires more effort, more forethought, and more skills than ever. There are simply more variables to contend with. And this puts ever greater demands on public affairs staff.[41]

Client–Firm Relationships

Sometimes counseling firms initiate contact with clients they think need help. More commonly, clients call counseling firms. For instance, an oil company may have a persistent problem with government regulation of offshore drilling, a long-planned enterprise in which millions of dollars have been invested. However, plans are held up because of opposition to exploration by environmental groups, investor concern that stock value will drop because of unfavorable reports in the business press, and public skepticism that the oil company will protect fragile ocean ecosystems. All of this is framed by memories of the Exxon *Valdez* oil spill off Alaska's Prince William Sound. The internal department convinces the chairman and CEO that it is time to seek the best outside help available to help design and manage a strategic plan to address these public relations problems. Unfortunately, it too often takes a *Valdez* oil spill, stock sell-off, or some other crisis to get top management's attention.

It is not uncommon for the client–firm relationship to begin with an emergency, as was the case when Arizona Economic Council officials called on Hill & Knowlton. After Arizona voters defeated a ballot initiative establishing a state holiday honoring Martin Luther King Jr., the National Football League announced that it would move the Super Bowl game from the Tempe, Arizona, stadium. In such emergencies, counsel provides advice and helps the client manage the crisis. Depending on the outcome, the firm may be retained on a long-term basis to prevent such crises in the future. In the Arizona situation, however, the Super Bowl game was moved to the Rose Bowl in Pasadena and Hill & Knowlton lost the Arizona Economic Council as a client.

Under more typical circumstances, a counseling firm begins its service after being invited to present a proposal. It begins by researching the client's problem situation and its relationships with the publics affected by or involved in the situation. Called a public relations audit, this initial exploration can take several days or even weeks. After doing the research, the counselor may report that there is no real problem or threat that requires outside assistance, or that the problems disclosed by the research are outside the counselor's area of expertise. More likely, however, the counsel arranges to make a presentation outlining the following:

1. Research findings and situation analysis of the problem or opportunity
2. Potential harm or gain to the organization
3. Projected difficulties and opportunities, given various courses of action or nonaction
4. Overall program goals, as well as objectives for various publics
5. Immediate action and communication responses, if needed to meet a crisis
6. Long-range plan for achieving the goals and objectives

7. Evaluation plans for monitoring the program and assessing impact
8. Staffing plans, budget, and timetable

Typically, competing firms make presentations (see Figure 3.6), and one is selected on the basis of its demonstrated capabilities and the presentation proposal. Once retained, the counselor usually functions in one of three ways:

1. Provides advice, leaving execution to the client's internal staff
2. Provides advice and works with the client's staff to execute the program
3. Provides advice and undertakes full execution of the program

Occasionally, client–firm relationships take a turn the client does not anticipate. To get the business (win the account), usually an "A-Team" of experienced professionals makes the presentation (new business pitch). The client is duly impressed by the talent and depth of experience they assume will be applied to their problems. In some instances, however, that is the last they see of many of these people. Instead, the account gets assigned to staff members who do not have the range of experience represented by the new business development team. Critics justifiably refer to this practice as a "bait-and-switch" tactic. The firm's senior executives show up just often enough to assure the client, but in fact the work has been delegated to junior staff. Firms employ such a strategy at the risk of losing clients.

Clients occasionally call for a review of the firm's work or even reopen the selection process by requesting proposals from competing firms. A review

FIGURE 3.6   COUNSELOR PRESENTATION

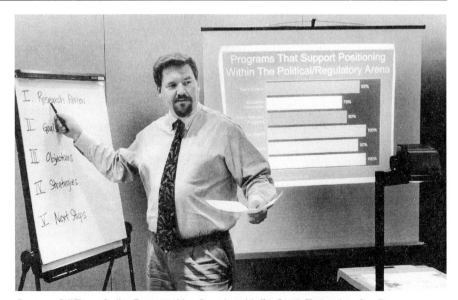

Courtesy Bill Trumpfheller, Executive Vice President, Nuffer, Smith, Tucker, Inc., San Diego.

may simply be a cover for having already decided to change firms. To soften the blow, the incumbent firm is given the "courtesy" of making the "short list" of finalists before another firm gets the account. In some cases, clients call for reviews and entertain proposals from competing firms simply to remind the incumbent firm that the client's business should not be taken for granted or given anything less than prime attention.

Some counselors suggest yet another reason why some clients conduct reviews and call for proposals: to get new ideas—free. The suspicion is that there is no real intention to replace the incumbent firm. The published request for proposals (RFP) or the invitation to selected firms represents an unethical search for new ideas without having to pay for the counsel. For that reason, firms try to discern how serious the client is about switching firms or bringing in outside counsel before investing in developing a presentation. A few firms will not do speculative pitches unless the client pays a fee that covers the cost of preparing the presentation. Critics of the RFP selection process say that quality is often sacrificed when price considerations lead to choosing the low bidder.

For the most part, client-firm relationships are amiable and long-lasting. Fleishman-Hillard, for example, has worked for client Anheuser-Busch (St. Louis) for more than 50 years; Rowland Worldwide for DuPont (Wilmington, DE) more than 35 years; and Ketchum Public Relations for Dow Chemical (Midland, MI) for more than 20 years. Trust and respect characterize many client-firm relationships that were built on a foundation of cooperation, collaboration, and collegiality developed while working together through both the worst and best of times.

Counselors' Advantages

Nine out of ten major corporations responding to one survey reported using external counsel at corporate headquarters, with half also hiring local counseling firms to supplement corporate-wide efforts and to handle regional problems and issues.[42] A Public Relations Society of America Counselors Academy survey found that almost three out of four corporations use outside counsel even though they have their own internal departments. Survey results from a wide range of organizations show increased use of outside counsel, even in government and nonprofit settings. The trend in the 1990s was to cut in-house staff and outsource work to external firms.[43] Clearly, external counsel provides valuable services not readily available internally.

Counselors rank *variety of talents and skills* as their greatest advantage over internal staffing. *Objectivity,* relatively untrammeled by the politics within an organization, ranks second. *Range of prior experience* is third; *geographical scope of their operations,* fourth; and the *ability to reinforce and upgrade a client's internal staff,* fifth.

Counseling firms with large staffs emphasize the *flexibility* of their personnel and operations as a prime advantage. In their offices, or no farther away than the telephone, are skilled researchers, artists, models, copy editors, magazine feature writers, media coaches and placement specialists, talk show experts, photographers, and legislative experts. A client can request a highly technical and specialized service, and an account executive can attend to the need immediately.

Flexibility is also tied to scope of operations and to range of experience. A firm based in New York, Washington, or Chicago can serve clients in Colorado, West Virginia, and California through its branches or affiliates. A global firm is as likely to have a network of branch offices or affiliated firms in London, Tokyo, and Melbourne as in Denver, Dallas, and Seattle. For example, Burson-Marsteller has more than 2,300 staff in 35 countries, with 19 offices in Europe. Among the first U.S. firms to open overseas offices, Burson-Marsteller opened its first office in Europe in 1961; in Asia, 1973; and in South America, 1978. Rowland Worldwide has 20 offices and more than 40 partner and affiliate firms; Edelman Public Relations Worldwide has 33 offices; and the largest network of independent firms, WORLDCOM Group, Inc., has 90 partner firms with 113 offices worldwide.

In the course of a year, counselors work on many different problems for several different clients. In effect, a public relations firm is a repository of living case histories. Each project adds to its fund of knowledge. Experience and versatility of staff make this synergy possible. The counselor approaches each situation bolstered by experience with similar situations and knowledge of the success or failure that attended previous encounters.

The counselor's *reputation* can be a major advantage. Externally, a counselor's reputation among the press and government officials can work to the advantage of clients. Internally, outside experts often can introduce ideas that internal staffers have struggled unsuccessfully to place on the agenda. Apparently paying a hefty fee increases top management's attention to public relations counsel. And from the client's point of view, knowing that the counselor's reputation and subsequent referrals are on the line also helps ensure performance.

Counselor's Handicaps

With rare exceptions, intervention by outside counsel—and this applies to almost all consultants—meets with *internal opposition* ranging from nonacceptance to outright rejection. This is, at least in theory, the counselor's most serious handicap. Antagonism toward and resistance to outsiders are natural human traits. The old guard resists change—the new idea, the new approach, the new look—and sees it as a threat to security and established ways of doing business.

The counselor more often than not makes suggestions in the form of recommendations. Those originally responsible can take offense and be alienated by these suggestions. Their realm is being invaded; their judgment is being criticized. The offended ask, "What does this outsider know about our organization, our way of doing things?"

Counselors, however, do not rank this problem at the top. They overwhelmingly cite *questions of cost* as the most frequent problem with clients. They list *threat to old guard and set ways* as the second most persistent handicap. *Resistance to outside advice* comes in third, and *unforeseen conflicts of personality or conviction* is fourth.

Other problems expressed frequently by counselors include a stubborn *lack of understanding of public relations by clients* and *unavailability of clients*—presumably the decision makers—at times when counselors want decisions. These suggest a problem of priorities on the part of clients.

Threatened insiders can create problems not related to the actual quality of service. Under the guise of scrutiny and concern, they raise questions about cost, return on investment, or qualifications. They point to the counselor's *superficial grasp of the organization's unique problems*: the local and historical angles on problems, the sacred cows, the things we never talk about. When those in the client organization raise such questions, it is an uphill battle for external counselors. Dealing with the internal staff and others in the client organization calls for special consulting skills.

Counseling Firm Costs

Clients retain the services of a counseling firm for specific projects or for an indefinite period of continuing service, reviewable and renewable at intervals. Fees for continuing services are established in one of three ways:

1. A monthly retainer covering a fixed number of hours and services
2. A minimum retainer plus monthly billing for actual staff time at hourly rates or on a per diem basis
3. Straight hourly charges, usually on a scale representing the range of experience and expertise

Fees for specific projects, on the other hand, are paid on an hourly fee basis or as a negotiated fixed fee covering the entire project. In recent years, the project fee basis for paying firms has changed the nature of business. Now instead of having a stable client list and steady cash flow from retainers and hourly fees, firms have to compete for contracts to do specific and limited projects. As one firm's principal put it, instead of having 30 clients, the firm has to have 300 clients because so much of the work is piecemeal.

Out-of-pocket expenses are generally billed at cost and are exclusive of the retainer fee. In some cases, the client deposits an advance with the firm to cover such expenses. Some firms, however, mark up actual costs of certain expenses by 15–20 percent to cover overhead costs. Ruder Finn (New York), for example, marks up advertising placements, photography, and printing by 20 percent but bills actual cost for entertainment, clipping services, and postage.

Fees vary widely. Large counseling firms have minimum retainer fees, usually in the range of $1,000 to $10,000, but up to $50,000 and more per month for major accounts. Wood products company Louisiana-Pacific (Portland) retained Fleishman-Hillard (St. Louis) for $60,000 per month, plus expenses. At the other end of the scale, a small client might pay as little as a $500-monthly retainer to write an occasional news release, or as little as $100 for a single news release.

Hourly fees range from a low of $25 an hour for assistant account executives or other junior support staff, to several hundred dollars for every hour worked by senior counselors and firm principals. Financial Relations Board

(Chicago) reportedly charges $60–$400 hourly for project staff. These rates typically reflect salary markups in the range of 2.5 to 3.5 times actual hourly staff costs. Figures differ from city to city, but four elements are reflected in counseling fees and charges:

1. Actual cost of staff time devoted to the project
2. Executive time and supervision
3. Overhead costs
4. Reasonable profit for doing the work, based on what the market will bear

The most common threat to client-firm relationships is conflict over the costs and hours billed. As a result, most firms use sophisticated accounting methods to record and track staff hours and project expenses. "Billable hours" often become a criterion for assessing employee productiveness. Some firms, formally or informally, expect each practitioner to bill a minimum number of hours each month, just as in most accounting and law firms. For example, it would not be unusual for an employee to "bill out" an average of more than 30 hours each week. In other words, the employee's time sheet—recorded in tenth- or quarter-hour units—documents 30 or more hours of work charged to specific client projects. (Exhibit 3.2 shows a typical form for recording hours.) Each client's monthly bill, then, reflects the total hours recorded on all staff time sheets designated to that account or project. The account executive monitors these time sheets and detailed expense records to keep costs in line with the client–firm agreement.

NEW APPROACHES

Increasingly, organizations are using a combination of internal departments and outside counsel to fulfill the public relations management function. Moreover, top management are increasingly recognizing how essential public relations is to organizational success. High-level practitioners are increasingly joining the executive decision-making group, or at least are being consulted on major decisions. Practitioners in firms are increasingly serving as counselors and strategic planners rather than acting merely as press agents and communication technicians. In short, public relations is changing and becoming an integral part of most organizations' management structure.

The president of one public relations firm predicts these changes will affect both internal departments and the firms serving them:

> Traditional, large, central PR departments will almost certainly become relics. Very tight, small and expert departments are likely to become the norm and outsourcing may be the word most commonly used. In many cases, the PR chief will use a broad array of consulting firms, rather than just one. He or she may conclude that it is far more effective to use a small, expert local company in a Third World country, rather than the local office of a U.S. multinational agency. The agencies, for their part, will need to find ways to demonstrate that they have significant comparative advantage relative to these small, local rivals.[44]

EXHIBIT 3.2

TIME SHEET

TIMESHEET

Name: _____ Employee #: _____ Date: _____

⏱	JOB# PFC	JOB	OPER. CODE	TOTAL HOURS	COMMENTS	⏱	JOB# PFC	JOB	OPER. CODE	TOTAL HOURS	COMMENTS
7:00						11:00					
7:06						11:06					
7:12						11:12					
7:18						11:18					
7:24						11:24					
7:30	684	342	100		Plan product	11:30					
7:36					launch event	11:36					
7:42						11:42					
7:48						11:48					
7:54						11:54				2.0	
8:00						12:00					
8:06						12:06					
8:12						12:12					
8:18						12:18					
8:24						12:24					
8:30						12:30	142	010	130		Follow-up on
8:36				.2		12:36					grand opening
8:42	684	342	110		meet w/client	12:42					pitch letter
8:48					re special	12:48					
8:54					event	12:54					
9:00						1:00					
9:06						1:06					
9:12						1:12					
9:18						1:18					
9:24						1:24					
9:30						1:30					
9:36						1:36					
9:42						1:42					
9:48						1:48				1.4	
9:54				1.3		1:54	201	010	110		Call re next
10:00	920	920			New business	2:00					year's program
10:06					hotel proposal	2:06				.3	
10:12						2:12	444	222	125		Brainstorm
10:18						2:18					special event
10:24						2:24					
10:30						2:30					
10:36						2:36				.5	
10:42						2:42	925	925			
10:48						2:48					
10:54						2:54					

Source: The New PR Client Service Manual, 3rd ed. (San Diego, CA: The Gable Group, 1997), p. 97a. Reprinted with permission.

Former AT&T public relations executive Edward M. Block, who oversaw what was at the time the largest public relations department (before the 1984 breakup of AT&T), agrees that the smaller departments will increasingly work with outside firms:

> Given the choice, I would never have built anything so large. . . . Rather than build huge staffs it (the firm) can be a cost-effective way to out-source noncritical functions. But the high priority, core responsibilities must remain in-house. A firm may even be a counselor, but not a substitute or surrogate for handling the vital pr roles.[45]

The trend to smaller public relations departments using outside firms is apparent in recent restructuring of major corporations: Hotel and gaming company ITT (New York) cut its corporate public relations staff from more than 180 in the mid-1980s to just two vice presidents in 1998. Likewise, Texaco (White Plains, NY), following the lead of competitor Mobil Oil (Fairfax, VA), cut 7 of the 39 staffers who had to "re-apply" for 32 positions in the downsized department. The new CBS Corporation (New York) retained only the senior vice president of corporate relations and terminated 5 staffers when it closed the Pittsburgh headquarters of the former Westinghouse Electric Corporation (which had acquired CBS in 1995). In the mid-1980s, CBS and Westinghouse had separate public relations departments with about 30 staffers in each. The large AT&T public relations staff, already reduced to just more than 800 after the 1984 breakup, was down to half that number in 1998.

Another change for firms and departments wanting to operate globally is the requirement to meet established quality standards. In Europe, for example, many client organizations require any vendor of services (including public relations firms) to be "ISO 9000 certified," meaning that the staff has been trained and operations have been tested to meet high standards of quality control established by Switzerland-based International Organization for Standardization. U.S.-based firms must also meet the international standards if they are to compete internationally. For example, Porter Novelli (New York) introduced ISO 9000 to other Omnicom Group–owned firms and agencies in order to more successfully compete in Europe. Burson-Marsteller and Fleishman-Hillard have also initiated the training and testing necessary for ISO 9000 certification in many of their offices, starting in Europe.

In response to growing concern about environment, the ISO developed a set of standards for assuring that manufacturing and production processes are environmentally sound. ISO 14000 certification is not a government mandate, however. Rather, it is a consumer-driven demand that retailers, suppliers, and manufacturers demonstrate commitment to protecting and improving the environment. According to an energy company executive in Mexico, "The shift in thinking here is that we are beginning to accept responsibility for our part in the environmental impact of a product through its entire life cycle."[46]

Although ISO 9000 and ISO 14000 are not yet routinely required in the United States, the trend is in that direction. Many companies advertise that their products are "green" and that their packaging is recyclable, suggesting a commitment to protecting the environment. Ford Motor Company (Detroit) awarded its "Q 1" quality designation to one of its marketing and public relations firms, a certification based on ISO 9000 standards. When Motorola (Shaumburg, IL) public relations department adopted the company-wide "Six Sigma" standard (3.4 defects per million steps in a process), it was leading the way in what is now a growing demand for integrating the function both within organizations and in the global practice.[47]

Global markets, strategic planning, and the convergence of communication and technology have attracted others to the public relations counseling field. Management and technology consulting firm Andersen Consulting (Chicago) posts open positions for "communications specialists." Job descriptions read much like position descriptions in traditional public relations firms. Some large law firms also have started offering "public relations counsel" to complement legal counsel and services in high-profile cases that attract media coverage.

Regardless of the source of counsel and services, public relations has an impact in an organization when people begin to tell each other that candor in communication is the best policy and that socially responsible actions are in the best interest of the organization. This means that public relations consciousness is gaining ground and there is growing confidence in the staff and outside counselors.

Exposing a clean organization to public gaze and operating in the mutual interests of itself and its publics does not mean that everything about the organization should be made public. In business there are competitors to consider. In the military there are security considerations. In health institutions there are ethical limitations on disclosure of patient information. In government agencies there are political and regulatory factors. Everywhere there are legal pros and cons. Common sense helps, but organizations must have specialized staff or counsel to perform the public relations function in an ethical and professional manner. That is a lesson from public relations' history, the topic of the next chapter.

NOTES

1. Quoted from introduction to David R. Drobis, "Stop Whining and Take a Seat! *The Public Relations Strategist* 2, no. 1 (Spring 1996): 37.
2. Lawrence G. Foster, "10 CEOs Send a Message to Public Relations," *The Public Relations Strategist* 1, no. 1 (Spring 1995): 8.
3. R. Wayne Pace, *Organizational Communication: Foundations for Human Resource Development* (Englewood Cliffs, NJ: Prentice-Hall, 1983), 16–17.
4. Henry H. Farquhar, "The Anomaly of Functional Authority at the Top," *Advanced Management* 7, no. 2 (April–June 1942): 51.
5. Bruce R. Barstow, "An Insider's Outside View of Public Relations," in *Precision Public Relations,* edited by Ray Eldon Hiebert (New York: Longman, 1988), 58–59. First published in *Public Relations Review* 10, no. 1 (Spring 1984): 10–17.
6. Gary F. Grates, "Why the Coveted Top Spot Is Losing Its Allure," *Communication World* 14, no. 3 (February 1997), 26.

7. Philip Lesly, "The Stature and Role of Public Relations," *Public Relations Journal* 37, no. 1 (January 1981): 15.

8. Martha M. Lauzen, "Public Relations Roles, Intraorganizational Power, and Encroachment," *Journal of Public Relations Research* 4, no. 2 (1992): 61–80.

9. Barstow, "An Insider's Outside View of Public Relations," 65.

10. James E. Grunig, ed., *Excellence in Public Relations and Communication Management.* Hillsdale, NJ: Lawrence Erlbaum Associates, 1992. The term "dominant coalition" is introduced on p. 24 and used throughout the book.

11. Adam Shell interview with Carol Sanger, Vice President of Corporate Communications, Federated Department Stores, "Talk from the Top: Communicating in Tumultuous Times," *Public Relations Tactics* 3, no. 4 (April 1996): 30–31.

12. *Jack O'Dwyer's Newsletter* 29, no. 42 (October 23, 1996), 7.

13. Jeff Cole, "Boeing Names New Managers, Alters Structure," *The Wall Street Journal,* 5 August 1997, p. B7.

14. Larissa A. Grunig, "Power in the Public Relations Department," *Public Relations Research Annual* 2 (1990): 115–55.

15. For a detailed analysis, see David M. Dozier, "The Innovation of Research in Public Relations Practice: Review of a Program of Studies," *Public Relations Research Annual* 2 (1990): 3–28.

16. David M. Dozier, with Larissa A. Grunig and James E. Grunig, *Manager's Guide to Excellence in Public Relations and Communication Management* (Mahwah, NJ: Lawrence Erlbaum Associates, 1995): 78–80.

17. Herbert A. Simon, *The New Science of Management Decision* (New York: Harper and Row, 1960): 5–6.

18. Robert L. Dilenschneider, "The Seven Deadly Sins," *PR Week* (November 14–20, 1988): 11. For a similar perspective with extensive case examples, see Dilenschneider's edited book, *Dartnell's Public Relations Handbook,* 4th ed. (Chicago: Dartnell Corporation, 1997).

19. Foster, "10 CEOs Send a Message," p. 11.

20. Ibid., p. 9.

21. Norman R. Nager and Richard H. Truitt, *Strategic Public Relations Counseling* (New York: Longman, 1987), 194.

22. Shell interview with Carol Sanger, "Talk from the Top," p. 31.

23. Roy T. Cottier, "Communication: A Management Strategy, Not a Professional Technique," *Vital Speeches* 53, no. 18 (July 1, 1987): 556–59. Speech to International Association of Business Communicators, Toronto. Cottier is former senior vice president of corporate relations at Northern Telecom Limited.

24. *Corporate Communications Benchmark 1997,* Section II. Report prepared by Edelman PR Worldwide, Opinion Research Corporation, and Integrated Marketing Communications Department, Northwestern University.

25. Clarence Randall, *The Folklore of Management* (Boston: Little, Brown, 1959), 24.

26. Thomas L. Harris, "IMC: A Concept for Today," *The Public Relations Strategist* 1, no. 3 (Fall 1995): 31.

27. Jim Arnold, "IMC: Much Ado About Little," *The Public Relations Strategist* 1, no. 3 (Fall 1995): 29.

28. Ibid.

29. Philip Lesly, "The Balkanizing of Public Relations," *The Public Relations Strategist* 2, no. 3 (Fall 1996): 43–44.

30. Ivy Lee, *Publicity: Some of the Things It Is and Is Not* (New York: Industries Publishing Company, 1925): 58–59.

31. See chapter 6 for more detailed discussion of legal considerations.

32. Ellen Joan Pollock, "Order in the Boardroom: Lawyers Rise to CEO," *The Wall Street Journal,* September 11, 1996, p. B1.
33. *Corporate Communications Benchmark 1997,* Section IV, p. 4.
34. Jean Cardwell, "Learning to Waltz with Human Resources," *The Public Relations Strategist* 2, no. 1 (Spring 1996), 44.
35. Ibid., 45.
36. Paul Sanchez, "Agents for Change," *Communication World* 14, no. 3 (February 1997), 53.
37. See current edition of *O'Dwyer's Directory of Public Relations Firms,* published by J. R. O'Dwyer Co., New York, for listings, addresses, executive names, number of employees, billings, and specialties. The 1997 edition lists more than 2,300 firms and departments of advertising agencies cross-listed with their 17,000-plus clients.
38. "Public Relations Consultancies—1998," *Marketing,* May 21, 1998, p. 33.
39. Letter to the editor, *O'Dwyer's PR Services Report* 11, no. 8 (August 1997), 61.
40. As quoted by Lee Levitt, "U.S. Firms Tap Foreign Shops for Client Work," *O'Dwyer's PR Services Report* 11, no. 6 (June 1997), 34.
41. Geoffrey L. Pickard, "Bridging the Gap in Joint Venture Communications: Global Public Affairs," *Vital Speeches* 53, no. 5 (December 15, 1986): 145–48.
42. *Corporate Communications Benchmark 1997,* Section II, C.
43. Thomas L. Harris & Co., Highland Park, IL, conducts an annual survey of clients using the largest public relations firms.
44. Frank Vogl, "Expectations of the Chief Corporate Public Relations Officer in 2001," speech presented to Arthur W. Page Society, Annual Spring Seminar, New York, March 28, 1996.
45. As reported in *john budd's plain talk* (a supplement to *pr reporter*), no. 14 (December 1, 1997), 3.
46. Robert W. Fisher, "The Future of Energy," *The Futurist* 31, no. 5 (September–October 1997), 46.
47. Charles A. Sengstock Jr., *Quality in the Communications Process* (Schaumburg, IL: Motorola University Press, 1997).

ADDITIONAL SOURCES

Dozier, David M., with Larissa A. Grunig and James E. Grunig. *Manager's Guide to Excellence in Public Relations and Communication Management.* Mahwah, NJ: Lawrence Erlbaum Associates, 1995. Chapters deal with power and change in organizations, building linkages to and working with top management, and global qualities of excellence.

Hammer, Michael, and James Champy. *Reengineering the Corporation: A Manifesto for Business Revolution.* New York: HarperCollins, 1993. The book that drove the reengineering craze that led to changes in processes, structures, and cultures in all types of organizations in the 1990s.

Maister, David H. *Managing the Professional Service Firm.* New York: Free Press, 1993. Widely read guide for maximizing service, satisfaction, and success (profitability) in firms.

O'Dwyer, Jack, ed. *O'Dwyer's Directory of Public Relations Executives* and *O'Dwyer's Directory of Public Relations Firms.* New York: J.R. O'Dwyer Co. Annual listings and descriptions of public relations executives, employers, and firms.

White, Jon, and Laura Mazur. *Strategic Communications Management: Making Public Relations Work.* Wokingham, England: Addison-Wesley Publishing Company, 1995. British perspective on many of the topics covered in this chapter.

Web Sites for selected public relations firms:

www.bm.com (Burson-Marsteller's award-winning web site links uses to information about the firm and a collection of public relations articles and sources.)

www.edelman.com (Address for Edelman Public Relations Worldwide—largest independent firm, with 35 offices and 1,300 staff.)

www.fleishman.com (Fleishman-Hillard International Communications)

www.mslpr.com (Manning Selvage & Lee Public Relations)

www.ogilvypr.com (Olgilvy Public Relations Worldwide)

www.pninternational.com (Porter Novelli International)

www.ruderfinn.com (Ruder·Finn)

www.worldcom.com (The WORLDCOM Group, Inc., link to network of 90 partner firms and 115 offices worldwide.)

HISTORICAL ORIGINS

Those who cannot remember the past are doomed to repeat it.
—*George Santayana*

OBJECTIVES

After studying chapter 4, you should be able to

▼ Use examples to illustrate how the development of public relations has occurred during attempts to mobilize public opinion in struggles for power and to promote change.

▼ Name major historical leaders in public relations and describe their respective contributions to the development of public relations and to current practice.

▼ Trace the evolution of public relations from its American beginnings to modern practice.

▼ Cite the origins of some of today's principles and techniques that guide public relations practice.

Studying how public relations evolved provides helpful insights into its functions, its strengths, and its weaknesses. Many practitioners do not have a sense of their calling's history and thus do not fully understand its place and purpose in society. Nor do they realize how U.S. history and the development of public relations are intertwined. Published histories typically oversimplify what is a complex and dramatic story by emphasizing novelty and a few colorful personalities. But understanding public relations' historical context is vital to the professionalization of today's practice.

The history of public relations cannot be told by simply saying that it grew out of press agentry. Nor can it be fully told in terms of people such as Ivy Lee or Arthur Page. Efforts to communicate with others and to deal with the force of public opinion go back to antiquity; only the tools, degree of specialization, breadth of knowledge, and intensity of effort are relatively new. This chapter highlights the evolution of the modern practice of public relations.[1]

ANCIENT GENESIS

Communicating to influence viewpoints or actions can be traced from the earliest civilizations. Archaeologists found a farm bulletin in Iraq that told farmers of 1800 B.C. how to sow their crops, how to irrigate, how to deal with field mice, and how to harvest their crops, an effort not unlike today's distribution of farm bulletins by the U.S. Department of Agriculture. Rudimentary elements of public relations also appear in descriptions of the king's spies in ancient India. Besides espionage, the spies' duties included keeping the king in touch with public opinion, championing the king in public, and spreading rumors favorable to the government.[2]

Greek theorists wrote about the importance of the public will, even though they did not specifically use the term "public opinion." Certain phrases and ideas in the political vocabulary of the Romans and in the writing of the medieval period relate to modern concepts of public opinion. The Romans coined the expression *vox populi, vox Dei*—"the voice of the people is the voice of God." Machiavelli wrote in his *Discoursi,* "Not without reason is the voice of the people compared to the voice of God," and he held that the people must be either "caressed or annihilated."

Public relations was used many centuries ago in England, where the kings maintained Lords Chancellor as "Keepers of the King's Conscience." There was an acknowledged need for a third party to facilitate communication and adjustment between the government and the people. So it was with the church, traders, and artisans. The word "propaganda" was born in the seventeenth century, when the Catholic Church set up its *Congregatio de Propaganda Fide*—"Congregation for Propagating the Faith."

AMERICAN BEGINNINGS: BORN IN ADVERSITY AND CHANGE

The American beginnings of public relations appear in the American Revolution's struggle for power between the patrician-led patriots and the commercial, propertied Tories. Later efforts to gain public support include the conflict between the trade and property interests led by Hamilton and the planter-and-farmer bloc led by Jefferson, the struggle between Jackson's agrarian pioneers and the financial forces of Nicholas Biddle, and the bloody Civil War.

Before the Revolution

Using publicity to raise funds, promote causes, boost commercial ventures, sell land, and build box-office personalities in the United States is older than the nation itself. The American talent for promotion can be traced back to the first settlements on the East Coast in the seventeenth century. Probably the first systematic effort on this continent to raise funds was that sponsored by Harvard College in 1641, when that infant institution sent a trio of preachers to England on a "begging mission." Once in England, they notified Harvard that they needed a fund-raising brochure, now a standard item in a fund drive. In response to this request came *New England's First Fruits*, written largely in Massachusetts but printed in London in 1643, the first of countless public relations pamphlets and brochures.[3]

Independence

The tools and techniques of public relations have long been an important part of political weaponry. Sustained campaigns to move and manipulate public opinion go back to the Revolutionary War and the work of Samuel Adams and his cohorts. These revolutionaries understood the importance of public support and knew intuitively how to arouse and channel it. They used pen, platform, pulpit, staged events, symbols, news tips, and political organization in an imaginative, unrelenting way. Adams worked tirelessly to arouse and then organize public opinion, proceeding always on the assumption that "the bulk of mankind are more led by their senses than by their reason." Early on, he discerned that public opinion results from the march of events and the way these events are seen by those active in public affairs. Adams would create events to meet a need if none were at hand to serve his purpose.[4]

Far more than most realize, today's patterns of public relations practice were shaped by innovations in mobilizing public opinion developed by Adams and his fellow revolutionaries. In fomenting revolt against England, these propagandists, operating largely from the shadows, developed and demonstrated the power of these techniques:

1. The necessity of an organization to implement actions made possible by a public relations campaign: the Sons of Liberty, organized in Boston in January 1766, and the Committees of Correspondence, also born in Boston in 1775.[5]
2. The use of symbols that are easily identifiable and emotion arousing: the Liberty Tree.
3. The use of slogans that compress complex issues into easy-to-quote, easy-to-remember stereotypes: "Taxation without representation is tyranny."
4. Staged events that catch public attention, provoke discussion, and thus crystallize unstructured public opinion: the Boston Tea Party.[6]
5. The importance of getting your side of a story to the public first, so that your interpretation of events becomes the accepted one: the Boston Massacre.[7]

6. The necessity for a sustained saturation campaign using these techniques through all available channels of communication to penetrate the public mind with a new idea or a new conviction.

The enormous difficulty of mobilizing public opinion to fight a revolution and to form a government is little appreciated today:

> They knew that there was a wide gap between their public professions and American reality. They knew that there was bitter opposition to Independence and that the mass of the people were [*sic*] mostly indifferent. They knew, too, that there were deep rivalries and serious differences among the colonies.[8]

In weak contrast to the revolutionists' effective communication, the Tories, supporters of King George and the British Empire, relied not so much on propaganda as on legal and military pressures, to no avail. It is little wonder that an exuberant Sam Adams would exult when he heard the firing at Lexington, "Oh, what a glorious morning is this!" He and his fellow propagandists had done their work well.[9] The emotion-laden revolutionary campaign set patterns for the nation's political battles that were to follow.[10]

The next public relations landmark in the new nation came with publication of 85 Federalist letters written to newspapers in 1787–1788 by Alexander Hamilton, James Madison, and John Jay. The letters urged ratification of the Constitution, in what one historian called the new nation's "first national political campaign":

> The political ordeal that produced the Constitution in 1787 and brought about its ratification in 1788 was unique in human history. Never before had the representatives of a whole nation discussed, planned, and implemented a new form of government in such a manner and in such a short time.[11]

Another historian, Broadus Mitchell, wrote:

> In parrying blows against and enlisting support for the constitution, the authors of the Federalist did the best job of public relations known to history. Objectors were not so much repulsed as refuted. Honest fears were removed. Ignorance was supplied with information and illustration. The manner was earnest rather than passionate, was persuasive by a candor that avoided the cocksure. He [Hamilton] addressed his readers's judgment in a spirit of moderation.[12]

Historian Allan Nevins credited Alexander Hamilton for "history's finest public relations job":

> Obtaining national acceptance of the Constitution was essentially a public relations exercise, and Hamilton, with his keen instinct for public relations, took thought not only to the product but to the ready acquiescence of thoughtful people; and he imparted his views to others. . . . Once the Constitution came before the country, the rapidity with which Hamilton moved was a striking exemplification of good public relations. He knew that if a vacuum develops in popular opinion, ignorant and foolish views will fill it. No time must be lost in providing accurate facts and sound ideas.[13]

Politics and Change

Twentieth-century developments in this field are directly tied to the power struggles evoked by political reform movements. These movements, reflecting strong tides of protest against entrenched power groups, have been the catalytic agents for much of the growth of public relations practice, because the jockeying of political and economic groups for dominance created the need to muster public support.

Public relations also grew in response to the need to gain public acceptance and utilization of swiftly advancing technology. For example, when the Bell Telephone System switched to all-number telephone dialing, it ran into a storm of public opposition on the West Coast from the Anti-Digit Dialing League, organized by Carl May against what he called the "cult of technology."[14] The U.S. Postal Service encountered similar resistance when it introduced zip codes.

The first clear beginnings of the public presidential campaign and of the presidential press secretary's function came in the era of Andrew Jackson. In the late 1820s and early 1830s, the common man won the ballot and the free public school was started. Literacy increased greatly and political interest was stimulated by a burgeoning, strident party press. As the people gained political power, it became necessary to campaign for their support. No longer was government the exclusive concern of the patrician few. With the rise of democracy in America came increasing rights for, and power of, the individual.[15] The ensuing power struggle produced an unsung pioneer in public relations, Amos Kendall.

As a key member of President Jackson's "Kitchen Cabinet," Kendall served Jackson as a pollster, counselor, ghostwriter, and publicist. The Kitchen Cabinet was unexcelled at creating events to mold opinion. On all vital issues that arose, Jackson consulted these key advisers, most of whom, like Kendall, were former newspapermen.

Jackson, unlettered in political or social philosophy, had difficulty getting his ideas across. Like many of today's executives, he needed a specialist to convey his ideas to Congress and the country. Jackson's political campaigns and his government policies clearly reveal the influence of Kendall's strategy, sense of public opinion, and skill as a communicator.[16]

Likewise, Bank of the United States president Nicholas Biddle and his associates were fully alert to the methods of influencing public opinion in their political battles with Jackson and Kendall. In fact, banks were the first businesses to use the press for this purpose; by loans to editors and placement of advertisements, they influenced many newspapers and silenced others. John C. Calhoun asserted as early as 1816 that the banks had "in great measure, control over the press." Biddle's publicist, Mathew St. Clair Clarke, saturated the nation's press with press releases, reports, and pamphlets pushing the bank's case. In March 1831, the bank's board authorized Biddle "to cause to be prepared and circulated such documents and papers as may communicate to the people information in regard to the nature and operations of the bank." But the pamphlets, the many articles planted in the press, and the lobbying efforts by Biddle and his associates did not prevail over the forces of Jackson and Kendall.[17]

The history of public relations is meaningful only when it is related to these power conflicts and recurring crises of change. It is not mere coincidence that in the past, business interests took public relations most seriously when their positions of power were challenged or threatened by the forces of labor, the farmer, the shopkeeper, government regulators, or a maturing generation. Nor is it a coincidence that labor's programs intensified when an adverse public reaction to labor was crystallizing in regulatory legislation or waning public support. Similarly, the most intense developments in public relations within government came in periods of crisis: World War I, the Great Depression and New Deal, World War II, the Korean War, Vietnam, the uneasy Cold War years with the Soviet Union, the invasion of Panama, the Persian Gulf War, and the continuing conflict with Iraq's Saddam Hussein.

THE MIDDLE YEARS

Many of the generating forces had their origins in the nineteenth century, although the modern concept of public relations was little known in young America. There were few inducements for its full-scale development and no means of mass communication on a national basis. Group relationships were relatively simple; people were relatively self-sufficient and independent, the majority then living on farms.

The roots of modern public relations can be traced to those times, however. As Alan Raucher wrote,

> Three major antecedents of twentieth-century publicity can be distinguished from their sometimes shady past. One of these was press agentry. Another was advertising. A third antecedent for publicity, rather unexpectedly, came from business critics and reformers. By the first decade of the century, those three elements, largely unnoticed by contemporaries, fused into a new compound.[18]

Press Agentry

To state that public relations has evolved from press agentry, although a gross oversimplification, contains a kernel of truth. Systematic efforts to attract or divert public attention are as old as efforts to persuade and propagandize. Much of what we define as public relations was labeled press agentry when it was being used to promote land settlement in our unsettled West or to build up political heroes.

Elements of press agentry are found in many public relations programs today, but not as strongly as critics assert. Press agentry, beginning with Phineas Taylor ("P. T.") Barnum and the theatrical press agents who followed, developed as an adjunct to show business. Box office enterprises are still the prime employers of press agents. Press agentry has reached its zenith in today's professional sports world promotions, such as the Super Bowl, Daytona 500, championship boxing matches, and NCAA basketball's Final Four.

Amos Kendall's time brought an effective demonstration of the buildup when Jackson's opponents created the myth of Davy Crockett in an effort to woo the frontier vote away from Old Hickory. Crockett's press agent was Mathew St. Clair Clarke. (The Davy Crockett legend was given an intensive, if short-lived, revival in the 1950s, when Walt Disney featured that "yaller flower of the forest" in movies, television programs, books, and records. Disney did not create the Crockett legend; he embellished it.)[19]

But the master of them all was P. T. Barnum, and he knew it. Barnum lived from 1810 until 1891, a period of great importance in the evolution of public relations, and his influence continues.

> Barnum's showmanship was evident not only in a canny instinct that enabled him to give the masses what they wanted, but also in his ability to dictate to them a desire for what he thought they should want. . . . Every man has his star. Barnum's star was an exclamation mark.[20]

Promoter Barnum even employed his own press agent, Richard F. "Tody" Hamilton.[21]

Railroad publicists played an important role in settling our nation and in creating the romantic aura that still surrounds the West. Beginning in the 1850s, railroads and land developers used publicity and advertising to lure people westward. Charles Russell Lowell, who directed the Burlington Railroad's publicity campaign launched in 1858, wrote, "We are beginning to find that he who buildeth a railroad west must also find a population and build up business." He had good advice for today's practitioner: "We must blow as loud a trumpet as the merits of our position warrants."[22] From then until the American frontier closed near the end of the century, press agents' publicity was a major force moving people to new lands and new lives.

Other promoters were quick to recognize the power of publicity and advertising. When the promoters of the World's Columbian Exposition in Chicago of 1893 found their grandiose plans ridiculed and misrepresented in the American and European press, they quickly set up a Department of Publicity and Promotion and hired a newspaperman, Moses P. Handy, "to utilize the printing press in every possible way."[23] Success crowned Handy's efforts.

Success begot imitators. Barnum led the way, and others followed in an ever-increasing number. During the two decades before 1900, press agentry spread from show business to closely related enterprises. But as press agents grew in number and their exploits became more outrageous—although successful, more often than not—it was natural that they would arouse the hostility and suspicion of editors and inevitable that the practice and its practitioners would become tainted. This stigma remains as part of the heritage of public relations.

Political Campaigning

Public relations strategists have played dominant roles in politics and political parties. Virginian John Beckley ranks among the first of a long line of political propagandists and organizers who have made the party system work. He was a devoted aide of Thomas Jefferson in building what was then known as the Republican party but today is the Democratic party. He was Jefferson's eyes and ears, his propagandist, "one of the leading party organizers of the 1790s."[24]

However, the development of modern political campaign methods and techniques, except insofar as these have been modified by television, satellite transmissions, and jet travel, is largely rooted in the last decades of the nineteenth century. Increasingly, "the activities of the public relations man [sic] have become a significant influence in processes crucial to democratic government."[25] In the 1880s and 1890s, techniques used by the political party managers followed from improved printing technology, an abundant supply of cheap paper, and increasing literacy, factors that were also increasing the number of newspapers.

The need seen by both parties to "educate" new immigrants spurred the evolution of the "literary bureaus" into press bureaus, now a standard fixture of political campaigns.[26] The hard-hitting Bryan-McKinley campaign of 1896 marked the first use of political campaigning methods. Both parties set up campaign headquarters in Chicago, from whence flowed a heavy stream of pamphlets, posters, press releases, and other campaign propaganda, not unlike contemporary American political campaigns. William Jennings Bryan, a Dem-ocrat with little money, used the campaign train, an innovation that lasted until the jet age and that is revived occasionally in an attempt to demonstrate a candidate's commitment to take the campaign to the people.

By 1900, political press bureau managers, both national and state, had assumed most of the functions that characterize the roles of political practitioners. Mass communication inevitably assumed its central role in American politics with the introduction of radio in the mid-1920s and air travel in the 1930s.[27]

Business Practices

The last two decades of the nineteenth century brought other discernible beginnings of today's practice. Frenzied and bold development of industry, railroads, and utilities in America's post–Civil War era set the stage for public relations in the twentieth century.

The post–Civil War period produced both mass production and mass media, resulting in the emergence of the advertising agent and increased use of press agents to promote business interests. Although advertising and publicity are distinct in today's business enterprise, they developed along parallel lines, with overlapping functions, blurred distinctions, and confusion in the public mind. Publicity evolved partly as a marketing support function but mainly for other purposes. Advertising, on the other hand, evolved to meet the marketing needs of business. For example, Swift & Company used advertising to promote packaged meats: "To break down consumer bias against eating meat that had been slaughtered weeks earlier and half a continent away, Swift turned to advertising."[28]

In the 25 breathtaking years from 1875 to 1900, America doubled its population and jammed its people into cities, went into mass production and enthroned the machine, spanned the nation with rail and wire communications, developed the mass media of press and magazines, and replaced the plantation owner with the head of industry and the versatile pioneer with the specialized factory hand. All this laid the foundation for a mighty industrial machine.

The rise of powerful monopolies, the concentration of wealth and power, and the roughshod tactics of the robber barons brought a wave of protest and reform in the early 1900s. Contemporary public relations emerged out of the melee of the opposing forces in this period of the nation's rapid growth. Goldman observes, "Shouldering aside agriculture, large-scale commerce and industry became dominant over the life of the nation. Big business was committed to the doctrine that the less the public knew of its operations, the more efficient and profitable—even the more socially useful—the operations would be."[29] In this era of "the public be damned," exploitation of people and of natural resources was bound to bring, ultimately, protest and reform once people became aroused.

The prevailing hard-bitten attitude of business people toward the public—be they employees, customers, or voters—was epitomized in the brutal methods used by Henry Clay Frick to crush a labor union in the Carnegie-Frick Steel Company's Homestead, Pennsylvania, plant in 1892. The employees' strike was ultimately broken and the union destroyed by the use of the Pennsylvania state militia. Cold-blooded power won this battle, but the employees eventually won the war. Much of public relations history is woven into the unending struggle between employer and employee.[30]

The Carnegie-Frick Steel strike marked the transition from craft control to managerial control. Historian Merle Curti observed, "Corporations gradually began to realize the importance of combating hostility and courting public favor. The expert in public relations was an inevitable phenomenon in view of the need for the services he could provide."[31]

Theodore N. Vail, who laid the public acceptance and public policy foundations of the nation's telephone system, recognized this as early as 1883, even though his buccaneering bosses did not. On December 20, 1883, Vail asked W. A. Leary of the Iowa Union Telephone and Telegraph Company these questions:

> What has been the tendency of the relationship between the public and the local Co's. for the past year, i.e., are the relations between the public and the Co's. improving?
>
> Where there has been any conflict between the local Exchange and the public, what has been the cause of the difficulties, and what has been the result?
>
> A full and detailed reply to me would be of great service.[32]

From 1897 on, the term "public relations" appeared with increasing frequency in railroad literature and in speeches of railroad tycoons. In the

American Association of Railroads' 1897 *Year Book of Railway Literature,* the stated objective was "to put annually in permanent form all papers or addresses on the public relations of railways, appearing or being delivered during the year, which seem to have enduring value."[33] The *Railway Age Gazette* pleaded for "better public relations" in a 1909 editorial entitled, "Wanted: A Diplomatic Corps."

The first corporate public relations department, in the contemporary meaning of this term, was established in 1889 by George Westinghouse for his new electric corporation. Westinghouse had organized his company in 1886 to promote his revolutionary alternating-current system of electricity. Thomas A. Edison had earlier established Edison General Electric Company, which used direct current. The now-famous "battle of the currents" ensued.

Edison, aided by the astute Samuel Insull, launched a scare campaign against the Westinghouse alternating-current system. As McDonald recorded:

> Edison General Electric attempted to prevent the development of alternating current by unscrupulous political action and by even less savory promotional tactics. . . . The promotional activity was a series of spectacular stunts aimed at dramatizing the deadliness of high voltage alternating current, the most sensational being the development and promotion of the electric chair as a means of executing criminals.[34]

When the state of New York adopted electrocution in 1888, Westinghouse realized that he had to get his story to the public. He hired a Pittsburgh journalist, Ernest H. Heinrichs, who served as his personal press representative until Westinghouse died in March 1914. Heinrichs later said that he was hired not because of the "battle of the currents," but because Westinghouse, like today's executive, did not have time to deal with the press. Heinrichs was the company's main channel through which news about the company passed to the press.[35] Then, as now, it took specialized skill to gain a hearing in the public forum and to deal with media demands. Moreover, then, as now, when Westinghouse's AC system won public acceptance in spite of the Edison-Insull propaganda scare campaign, it demonstrated "that performance and merit are the foundation stones of effective public relations."[36]

Other Activities

The fund-raising drive was born in the Civil War. Jay Cooke conceived and directed the first American fund-raising drive. Cooke sold war bonds for the Union by first selling patriotism and building a militant public opinion. Many of his techniques reappeared in the bond drives of World Wars I and II.

Also by the time of the Civil War, the U.S. Marine Corps was using advertising on a regular basis to attract recruits. In the Spanish-American War of 1898, the work of Cuban propagandists did much to arouse American sympathies for Cuba and to discredit Spain. The Cuban junta used press releases and mass meetings to raise funds and promote support for the Cuban cause from 1895 on.

Professional groups were paying attention to public opinion by the mid-1800s. In 1855, the American Medical Association (AMA) passed a resolution "urging the secretary of the Association to offer every facility possible to the reports of the public press to enable them to furnish full and accurate reports of the transactions." And in 1884, the AMA launched the first of its many programs to counter antivivisectionists' attacks, a problem that persists to this day as animal rights groups protest use of animals in research.

EVOLUTION TO MATURITY

Although the roots of today's practice lie far in the past, its definite beginnings date from the early 1900s, when the world entered the century that spanned from the horse and buggy to the space shuttle. The dividing lines blur a bit, but the growth can be traced through six main periods (see Figure 4.1) of development:

1. *Seedbed Era* (1900–1917) of muckraking journalism countered by defensive publicity and of far-reaching political reforms promoted by Theodore Roosevelt and Woodrow Wilson through the use of public relations skills.

FIGURE 4.1   TIME LINE OF DEFINING EVENTS AND PEOPLE IN PUBLIC RELATIONS

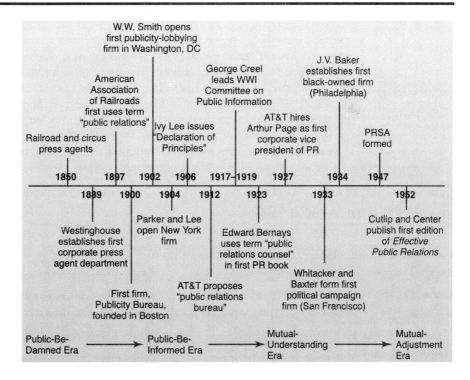

2. *World War I Period* (1917–1919) of dramatic demonstrations of the power of organized promotion to kindle a fervent patriotism: to sell war bonds, enlist soldiers, and raise millions of dollars for welfare.
3. *Booming Twenties Era* (1919–1929), when the principles and practices of publicity learned in the war were put to use promoting products, earning acceptance for changes wrought by the war-accelerated technology, winning political battles, and raising millions of dollars for charitable causes.
4. *Roosevelt Era and World War II* (1930–1945) of the Great Depression and World War II, with events profound and far-reaching in their impact, which advanced the practice of public relations. This period was dominated by Franklin D. Roosevelt and his counselor, Louis McHenry Howe.
5. *Postwar Era* (1945–1965) of adjustment as the nation moved from a war-oriented economy to a postindustrial, service-oriented economy and shouldered leadership of the free world. This era brought widespread acceptance of public relations as the number of practitioners passed the 100,000 mark. It also brought strong professional associations, the beginnings of public relations education, and the emergence of television as a powerful communications medium.
6. *Global Information Society* (1965–present), with its accelerating high technology, multiplying channels of communication, and the transition from a national economy to a world economy that features global interdependence and global competition. Stresses from these profound changes place ever heavier burdens on the function and its role in mediating conflicting interests to bring about mutual adjustment and accommodation.

These periods of development followed what Edward Bernays called the "public-be-damned" period of American enterprise, coming after the Civil War and lasting until about 1900. During public relations' seedbed era, Bernays suggested that the country had entered the "public-be-informed" period. He labeled the period following World War I as the time of "mutual understanding." Recent history documents antiwar protests, the consumer movement, environmental activism, civil rights, and other demonstrations of the increasing power of individuals and special interests. Mutual understanding has given way to the period of "mutual adjustment," representing a dramatic change from the public relations early in the twentieth century.

SEEDBED ERA: 1900–1917

Muckraking journalists—David Graham Phillips, Lincoln Steffens, Charles Edward Russell, Upton Sinclair, Ida Tarbell, and others—effectively exploited the newly developed national forums made possible by popular magazines, national wire services, and feature syndicates. Regier says, "Muckraking . . . was the inevitable result of decades of indifference to the illegalities and immoralities attendant upon the industrial development of America."[37] The reform and protest period extended roughly from 1900 to 1912. The muckrakers took their case to the people and got action. The agitation before

1900 had been primarily among farmers and laborers; now the urban middle classes took up the cry against government corruption and the abuses of big business.

The muckrakers thundered out their denunciations in boldface in the popular magazines and metropolitan newspapers, which now had huge circulations. By 1900, there were at least 50 well-known national magazines, several with circulations of 100,000 or more. The *Ladies Home Journal,* founded only 17 years before, was approaching a circulation of one million. The impact of the mass media was growing.[38] "It was muckraking that brought the diffuse malaise of the public into focus."[39]

The work was begun dramatically by Thomas W. Lawson's *Frenzied Finance,* appearing as a series in *McClure's* magazine in 1903. Ida Tarbell's *History of the Standard Oil Company,* described at the time as "a fearless unmasking of moral criminality masquerading under the robes of respectability and Christianity," and Upton Sinclair's novel, *The Jungle,* exposing the foul conditions in the meatpacking industry, both produced a violent public reaction. Public protest and reform brought regulatory legislation and a wave of trust-busting. Businesses were forced to take the defensive.

Long accustomed to a veil of secrecy, business leaders felt the urge to speak out in self-defense but did not know how. Their first instinct was to turn to their advertising planners and lawyers. In the first stages of the muckraking era, many great corporations sought to silence the attacks from the press by the judicious and calculated placement and withdrawal of advertising. U.S. Senator John F. Dryden, president of Prudential Insurance Company, by using the pressure of Prudential's advertising department, was able to squelch a critical article about him and get published instead a highly complimentary one in *Cosmopolitan* magazine.[40]

In the wake of New York State's Armstrong Committee's exposure of wrongdoing in the insurance industry, the New York Mutual Life Insurance Company commissioned N. W. Ayer to carry out an advertising campaign to restore public confidence in the insurance business.[41]

Early Firms

The Publicity Bureau. The nation's first publicity firm and forerunner of today's public relations firm was founded in Boston in mid-1900. George V. S. Michaelis, Herbert Small, and Thomas O. Marvin organized the Publicity Bureau "to do a general press agent business for as many clients as possible for as good pay as the traffic would bear." Michaelis, a Boston journalist once described by an associate as "a young man of many expedients," took the lead in organizing this new enterprise and was with it until 1909. One of the first people hired was James Drummond Ellsworth, who would later work with Theodore N. Vail in building the public relations program of American Telephone and Telegraph Company.[42]

Harvard University was the Publicity Bureau's first client. Michaelis, the firm's president, wrote to the president of Harvard boasting about the success of an early publicity effort: "We have met with very satisfactory success in publication of the articles, and I shall be glad to show you the clippings upon your return." And in a subsequent letter, he outlined what was surely the first fixed fee plus expenses arrangement:

> In the matter of payment, we understand that you are to pay the Bureau $200 a month for our professional services, and those of an artist where drawings seem to be required. That this sum is to include everything except the payment of mechanical work, such as printings and the making of cuts, and the postage necessary to send out the articles themselves to the various papers, which items are to be charged to the University.[43]

The reorganized Publicity Bureau came into national prominence in 1906, when it was employed by the nation's railroads to head off adverse regulatory legislation then being pushed in Congress by President Roosevelt. Ray Stannard Baker reported,

> The fountainhead of public information is the newspaper. The first concern, then, of the railroad organization was to reach the newspaper. For this purpose a firm of publicity agents, with headquarters in Boston, was chosen. . . . Immediately the firm expanded. It increased its Boston staff; it opened offices in New York, Chicago, Washington, St. Louis, Topeka, Kansas . . . and it employed agents in South Dakota, California, and elsewhere.[44]

According to Baker, the Publicity Bureau operated secretly, "careful not to advertise the fact that they are in any way connected with the railroads." This firm effectively used the tools of fact-finding, publicity, and personal contact to saturate the nation's press, particularly weeklies, with the railroads' propaganda. The campaign was to little avail, however, because the Hepburn Act, a moderately tough regulatory measure, was passed in 1906 after President Roosevelt used the nation's press and the platform to publicize a more persuasive case. Failure of their nationwide publicity effort caused railroad executives to reassess their public relations methods and, within a few years, to set up their own public relations departments. The Publicity Bureau faded into oblivion in 1911 when it last appeared in the American Newspaper Publishers Association antipublicity bulletin.[45]

Other industries turned to the specialist who could tell business's story in the public forum: the news reporter. Thus began the large-scale recruitment of journalists to serve as interpreters for corporations and other public institutions. Some reporters took the Publicity Bureau's lead and organized similar firms. With waves of the popular revolt beating against Capitol Hill, the opportunity for such a firm in Washington became apparent.

Smith & Walmer. The second firm was also the first to be based in Washington, DC. William Wolff Smith quit his job as correspondent for the *New York Sun* and the *Cincinnati Enquirer* in 1902 to open a "publicity business" with a partner named Walmer in the capital. (Walmer's role and tenure with the firm are not known.) A *New York Times* reporter later recalled that the Smith & Walmer firm solicited "press-agent employment from anybody who had business before Congress."[46]

From 1902 until 1914, Smith combined work as a freelance Washington correspondent for several newspapers, as an information source about Congress to affected trade associations, and as a publicist for those same trade groups. In 1916 he closed the firm and returned to law school, which he had quit in 1893 to take his first newspaper job, earning his law degrees in 1916. His "law practice," primarily devoted to lobbying the new regulatory agencies that resulted from the muckraking exposés, was the forerunner of the many law firms and public relations firms in Washington, DC, and state capitals engaged in lobbying. His law partner at the time later wrote of Smith:

> His practice was before the Departments and Congressional Committees more than in the courts. In this work he represented at various times a number of clients important in the commercial world, and, apparently to their satisfaction. He frequently appeared before Congressional Committees and Department Officers with success, and his briefs and other papers were ably prepared. He has a faculty of digging into a subject . . . which comes from his combined training as a newspaperman and a lawyer.[47]

Parker & Lee. Also during the seedbed era, former Buffalo reporter and veteran political publicist George F. Parker and young publicist Ivy Ledbetter Lee established the third firm in New York, Parker & Lee. They formed their partnership in 1904 after working together in the Democratic Party headquarters handling publicity for Judge Alton Parker's unsuccessful presidential race against Theodore Roosevelt. The firm lasted less than four years, but the junior partner—Lee—was to become one of the most influential pioneers in the emerging craft of public relations.

Hamilton Wright Organization, Inc. The fourth firm—The Hamilton Wright Organization, Inc.—was founded in 1908 when Hamilton Mercer Wright, a freelance journalist and publicist, opened a "publicity office" in San Francisco. Wright's first publicity work was for the California Promotion Committee, but he was also known for his promotion of Miami using pictoral publicity. His agency's first account was to promote the Philippine Islands on behalf of U.S. business interests, making his the first international firm. He moved to New York City in 1917, after spending 18 months doing freelance travel articles and sponsored publicity in Central and South America. World War I cut short his work promoting tourism in Central America for the United Fruit Company. His son and grandson, both carrying the same name, followed in the founder's footsteps by specializing in promotion of foreign countries in the United States. The Wrights closed the firm in 1969 after being subjected to hostile scrutiny in hearings held by Senator J. William Fulbright of the Senate Foreign Relations Committee in the mid-1960s. The hearings resulted in an amendment tightening enforcement of the Foreign Agents Registration Act of 1938. To the end, the Wrights maintained that they had never engaged in "political propaganda" for foreign clients, only tourism and trade publicity—"publicity on the industrial opportunities—publicity to attract attention to its natural resources."[48]

Pendleton Dudley and Associates. The fifth agency started during the first decade of this century lasted until 1988. Pendleton Dudley, who was to become an influential figure in public relations for half a century, took his friend Ivy Lee's advice and, in 1909, opened a publicity office in New York's Wall Street district. His first business client, AT&T, retained Dudley until his death at the age of 90 in 1966. For all those 57 years, Dudley remained the active head of his firm, which in 1946 had become Dudley-Anderson-Yutzy Public Relations when joined by Thomas D. Yutzy and George Anderson. In 1970, sisters Barbara Hunter and Jean Schoonover acquired the firm and changed the name to D-A-Y. The firm became a subsidiary of Ogilvy & Mather in 1983, and the separate identity and operation of D-A-Y was dropped in 1988.[49]

Thomas R. Shipp and Co. In 1914, Thomas R. Shipp organized the nation's sixth firm and the second located in Washington, DC. Shipp, like William Wolff Smith, was a native of Indiana and a former reporter. He spent six years learning publicity and politics from two experts, Theodore Roosevelt and Gifford Pinchot. In 1909 they gave Shipp administrative and publicity responsibilities for the newly formed National Conservation Association—"the center of a great propaganda for conservation"—which historians give credit for having established the terms "conservation" and "natural resources" in the public vocabulary.[50] Shipp opened his own "publicity company" as Smith was closing his to return to law school. When the United States entered World War I, Shipp headed the first American Red Cross fund drive. After the war, such corporations as General Motors, Standard Oil Company of New York, Swift & Company, and International Harvester retained Shipp as Washington public relations counsel. He died in 1952.

Early Pioneers

For the most part, big businesses hired former reporters to counter the muckrakers with whitewashing press agentry, demonstrating little grasp of the fundamental problems in the conflict. But there were exceptions. One was Georgia native Ivy Lee.

Ivy Ledbetter Lee. Lee, a Princeton graduate, a reporter covering the business world, saw the possibility of earning more money in the service of private organizations who were seeking a voice. After five years as a reporter, in 1903 Lee quit his low-paying job on the *World* to work in Seth Low's campaign for mayor of New York. This led to a job working with George F. Parker in the press bureau of the Democratic National Committee during the 1904 presidential campaign.

Parker had directed the publicity for Grover Cleveland's three campaigns for the presidency, but Cleveland was not wise enough to use him as a press secretary during his two terms as president.[51] In 1904, Parker was recalled to political battle to direct publicity for the Democratic National Committee in the futile campaign to unseat President Theodore Roosevelt. Lee was hired to assist him. Out of their campaign association came the decision to form the Parker and Lee partnership, which dissolved in 1908, when Ivy Lee became the Pennsylvania Railroad's first publicity agent. That year, Parker set up another partnership with C. A. Bridge, then city editor of the

New York Herald. The Parker–Bridge partnership folded in 1913, presumably because that year Parker was appointed to handle publicity for the Protestant Episcopal Church, a position he held until 1919. In 1920, Parker returned to politics when General Leonard Wood hired him to provide counsel for his campaign for the Republican party's presidential nomination.[52]

Lee, when hired to represent crusty George F. Baer and his associates in the anthracite coal strike in 1906, issued a "Declaration of Principles." Lee's statement of philosophy was to have a profound influence on the evolution of press agentry into publicity and of publicity into public relations. Eric Goldman observed that this declaration "marks the emergence of a second stage of public relations. The public was no longer to be ignored, in the traditional manner of business, nor fooled, in the continuing manner of the press agent."[53] It was to be informed. Lee's declaration, mailed to all city editors, reads as follows:

> This is not a secret press bureau. All our work is done in the open. We aim to supply news. This is not an advertising agency; if you think any of our matter ought properly to go to your business office, do not use it. Our matter is accurate. Further details on any subject treated will be supplied promptly, and any editor will be assisted most cheerfully in verifying directly any statement of fact. . . . In brief, our plan is, frankly and openly, on behalf of business concerns and public institutions, to supply to the press and public of the United States prompt and accurate information concerning subjects which it is of value and interest to the public to know about.[54]

Lee put this new approach to work in the anthracite coal strike. The work of reporters assigned to cover the strike was enormously simplified because channels of communication were comparatively open. Although reporters were not permitted at the strike conference, Lee did provide reports after each meeting. Lee was among the first to use the *handout* (now called *press release* or *new release*) system on a large scale. His success in generating favorable press coverage for the coal operators led to the retention of Parker and Lee by the Pennsylvania Railroad in the summer of 1906. Lee handled this account.[55]

During this period Lee used the term "publicity" to describe what is now called public relations; the concept and Lee's success grew steadily. In December 1914, at the suggestion of Arthur Brisbane, Lee was appointed as a personal adviser to John D. Rockefeller Jr. The Rockefellers were being savagely attacked for the strikebreaking activities of their Colorado Fuel and Iron Company. Lee served the Rockefellers until his death in 1934.

Ivy Lee did much to lay the groundwork for contemporary practice. Even though he did not use the term public relations until at least 1919, Lee contributed many of the techniques and principles that practitioners follow today. He was among the first to realize the fallacy of publicity unsupported by good works and to reason that performance determines the publicity a client gets. Lee propelled the growth of publicity departments and trained publicity advisers in many institutions. In his 31 years in public relations, Lee changed the scope of what he did from "pure agency" to serving as "a brain trust for the businesses we work with." One of the craft's most forceful representatives, he made public relations an occupation by his practice and preachments. However, Raucher warns, "Ivy Lee's reputation before World War I as the outstanding publicity specialist may easily obscure the general forces which created the new occupation. Lee built his career by exploiting problems of giant corporations in the early twentieth century."[56]

Lee's record, although substantial, is not free from criticism. When he died, he was under fire for his representation of the German Dye Trust, controlled by I. G. Farben. Lee advised the cartel after Adolf Hitler came to power in Germany and the Nazis had taken control. Although he never received pay directly from the Nazi government, Lee was paid an annual fee of $25,000 and expenses (a large sum at the time) by the Farben firm from the time he was retained in 1933 until his firm resigned the account shortly after his death in 1934.[57]

Rex F. Harlow. Others recognized the need for publicity services in other parts of the country. Rex F. Harlow began a lifetime career in 1912 in Oklahoma City when he was hired by an older brother to promote *Harlow's Weekly.* Harlow's career spanned the evolution of this young, uncertain calling to its maturity in the 1980s and helped shape today's practice. While teaching at Stanford University in 1939, he began teaching public relations courses and founded the American Council on Public Relations (ACPR). In 1945 he started the monthly *Public Relations Journal,* published until 1995 by the Public Relations Society of America, an organization formed in 1948 when Harlow's ACPR merged with the National Association of Public Relations Council.[58] (Harlow died April 16, 1993, at 100 years of age.)

Others of Influence

Theodore Roosevelt. The part played by Theodore Roosevelt in spurring the evolution has been little noted. The colorful president was a master in the art and power of publicity, and he used his knowledge and skill to gain his political ends. Observers claimed that Roosevelt ruled the country from the newspapers' front pages. One of his first acts upon assuming the presidency was to seek an understanding with the press. Veteran reporter David S. Barry later observed that Roosevelt "knew the value and potent influence of a news paragraph written as he wanted it written and disseminated through the proper influential channels." Roosevelt's successful and well-publicized antitrust suit against the Northern Securities Company turned the tide against the concentration of economic power. His conservation policies, effectively promoted by Gifford Pinchot in the government's first large-scale publicity program, saved much of America's resources from gross exploitation.

As one historian observed, "Roosevelt's colorful, outgoing personality and shrewd sense of publicity had his name constantly in the papers, and in ways to make him a national hero."[59] He saw the White House as a "bully pulpit."

With the growth of mass-circulation newspapers, Roosevelt's ability to dominate the front pages demonstrated a newly found power for those with causes to promote. He had a keen sense of news and knew how to stage a story so that it would get maximum attention. His skill forced those he fought to develop similar means. Roosevelt fully exploited the news media as a new and powerful tool of presidential leadership and remade the laws and the presidency in the process.

John D. Rockefeller. Business leader John D. Rockefeller never appeared to mind criticism, but philanthropist Rockefeller was cut to his Baptist quick by the accusation that his philanthropies were a means of buying public favor. When the "tainted money" issue flared yet again in 1905, he was hurt and angered. This led to his employment of Joseph Ignatius Constantine Clarke, a colorful Irish reporter, at a then-high salary of $5,000 a year. Clarke, attached to the legal department and given a staff of one stenographer, one office helper, and a person to paste clippings, worked hard to lift the veil of secrecy from Standard Oil and its founder, and with some success. Rockefeller became more open and courteous with reporters, and starting in October 1908, he published a series of autobiographical articles in *World's Work.* But as the legal and public attacks mounted, the company's executives quit giving Clarke information, and he resigned in frustration in 1913, the first in a long list of practitioners who have quit because of lack of administrative support.[60]

The period of 1900–1917 saw an intensive development of public relations skills by the railroads and the public utilities. These businesses, particularly the local transit companies, were the first to feel the heat of public anger and to be brought under public regulation. The Interstate Commerce Act set the pattern. In a five-year period, 1908–1913, more than 2,000 laws affecting railroads were enacted by state legislatures and by Congress.

Henry Ford. David Lewis, who chronicled Ford's public relations story, says, "The industrialist is revealed . . . as perhaps the most astute self-advertiser in the whole history of a land that has produced its full share of promoters and showmen." From 1908 on, Ford and his associates pioneered in the positive use of public relations in the automobile industry, seeking publicity, in sharp contrast to their publicity-shy business contemporaries of that era—which may explain why Ford prospered while many competitors fell by the wayside.[61]

Samuel Insull. Another businessman was equally innovative in the expanding utility field—Samuel Insull. In the late 1890s, Insull's Chicago Edison Company relied on sales techniques, free wiring, and rate cuts to increase the use of electricity. In 1901, Insull created an advertising department to ensure specialized treatment of his many messages to the public; in 1902 he built a demonstration "Electric Cottage"; in 1903 he started *The Electric City,* an external community publication, "to gain understanding and good will" in Chicago. Insull began using films in 1909, perhaps making him the first to use movies for public relations purposes. He initiated "bill stuffers" in 1912, and in later years used these for political messages. Most utilities do this today. He and his associates made countless public speeches, many of which were reprinted for wider distribution. Insull knew well that those identified with an institution are the prime determinants of its public reputation.[62]

Theodore N. Vail. The former American Telephone and Telegraph Company pioneered in public relations as well as in telephonic communications. Although public relations got short shrift between the time when Theodore N. Vail was forced out in 1887 until he was returned to power in 1902, the Bell company did organize a "literary bureau" in Boston around 1890 and was one of the first clients of the Publicity Bureau. After Vail returned as a director, the policies that became identified with AT&T began to take shape and they were brought to the fore when Vail became president in 1907. Vail hired *James Drummond Ellsworth* and began a publicity and advertising program.

The company tried to eliminate public criticism through efficient operation and consideration for the needs of subscribers. A systematic method of answering complaints was put into effect. Unlike other utilities, Bell did not fight public regulation but accepted it as a price for monopoly. Vail and Ellsworth, in collaboration with the N. W. Ayer advertising agency, began an institutional advertising campaign that continues to this day. AT&T showed the way in public relations advertising and public relations.[63] (See Exhibit 4.1.)

Growth in Other Areas

Equally important public relations developments were taking place outside the business community. For instance, the seedbed years brought innovative

EXHIBIT 4·1

*P*ROPOSAL FOR A PUBLIC RELATIONS BUREAU AT AT&T IN 1912 BY WALTER S. ALLEN

The establishment of a Public Relations Bureau in the American Telephone and Telegraph Company, in which all information concerning the relations of the telephone companies to the public should be concentrated and made available for use, would serve to coordinate much of the work now done independently by various departments of that company and the operating companies.

This bureau could bring together a large sum of material at present scattered, and a proper arrangement and collation of this would make it readily available and eliminate a considerable amount of duplication.

It would also be able to give its attention to the trend of public opinion and the drift of legislation, and by a study of these, bring to the attention of executive officers in a con-

densed form the broader lines of public sentiment in time to enable the telephone company to meet new phases of legislation and in many cases to forestall legislation by remedying conditions which have been the cause of trouble.

By employing a central organization to collect, analyze, and distribute material relating to these questions there will be a distinct saving in time of those actually engaged in work in the field and a broader and more efficient treatment of the problems.

All the available material can be brought together and everyone dealing with these questions be kept in touch with the trend of public opinion and action throughout the country. . . .

publicity programs to colleges and universities. At Yale in 1899, Anson Phelps Stokes converted the office of secretary into an effective alumni and public relations office. At Harvard in 1900, Charles W. Eliot, who in his inaugural address of 1869 had voiced the necessity of influencing "opinion toward advancement of learning," retained the Publicity Bureau. The University of Pennsylvania's public relations program dates from 1904, when it set up the University Bureau of Publicity. That same year, Willard G. Bleyer, pioneer journalism educator, organized a press bureau at the University of Wisconsin at the direction of public relations–minded President Charles R. Van Hise. But it was William Rainey Harper, the dynamic builder of the University of Chicago, who did more than any other educator to harness the power of publicity to the cause of higher education. His methods and his resulting success were observed and copied by many others.[64]

Churches, too, began to perceive the need for a public voice. One cleric wrote, "We will find that if we believe in the fruits of publicity we must believe also in the potential power of human nature to achieve goodness." Nonetheless, as in the case of business, it was the sharp attacks of critics that brought about the first programs. The Seventh Day Adventist Church, responding to public attacks on its opposition to Sunday laws, in 1912 established a publicity bureau with a former newspaper reporter in charge.[65] Trinity Episcopal Church of New York City, under biting public attack since 1894 for its exploitation of renters in its church-owned tenements, in 1909 became one of the early clients of Pendleton Dudley.

The whirlwind high-pressure campaign to raise money for charitable causes was first fabricated in 1905 in Washington, DC, by YMCA fund-raisers Charles Sumner Ward and Lyman L. Pierce. In their $350,000 drive for a new YMCA building, they were the first to use full-time publicists in a fund drive. The Y's successful techniques were soon used in the annual appeals of churches, colleges, civic centers, and health and welfare agencies.[66] The Ward–Pierce campaign format has endured the test of time and can be easily recognized in today's annual United Way drives.

Today's large-scale fund drives for health causes employ thousands of persons. The National Tuberculosis Association, founded in 1908, forerunner of the National Lung Association, was the first health group to use publicity to raise funds. That same year the American Red Cross hired its first publicity agent. The U.S. Marine Corps established a publicity bureau in Chicago in 1907 under Captain William C. Harllee, thus showing the way for present-day public relations programs in the nation's military.

Publicity's considerable extent in these early years of the new century was reflected in growing concern of journalists about the "perils of publicity." Don C. Seitz, business manager of the *New York World,* reported to the 1909 convention of the American Newspaper Publishers Association that the number of press agents was growing and that some were making $6,000 to $12,000 a year, very high pay in those years:

> Everybody was employing them; even the New York Orphan Asylum was paying a publicity man $75 a month. The advertising agencies—Albert Frank and Com-

pany, Lord & Thomas, N. W. Ayer & Son, J. Walter Thompson—had set up publicity departments which took fees for their services, fees diverted from the advertiser's newspaper advertising budget. Automobile manufacturers were sending a page of material each day to the *World,* and the cement, food, insurance, utilities, and other businesses were equally busy.[67]

WORLD WAR I PERIOD: 1917–1919

The contemporary practice of public relations first emerged as a defensive measure, but World War I gave it great offensive impetus. President Woodrow Wilson, who was keenly aware of the importance of public opinion, established The Committee on Public Information (CPI)—often referred to as the "Creel Committee." The CPI was to mobilize public opinion in support of the war effort and Wilson's peace aims in a country in which opinion was quite divided when war was declared. George Creel was made chairman.

George Creel. George Creel and his CPI demonstrated as never before the power of publicity to mobilize opinion. Creel had no campaign manual to guide him. He improvised as he went along. For example, he had no national radio or television to reach the nation quickly, so he created the Four Minutemen, a network of volunteers covering the nation's some 3,000 counties. These volunteers, alerted by telegrams from Washington, would fan out to speak to schools, churches, service clubs, and other gatherings. By the war's end nearly 800,000 of these four-minute messages had been delivered to some 400,000 persons. The CPI effort headed by Creel and Carl Byoir is chronicled in Creel's *How We Advertised America* and by Mock and Larson in *Words That Won the War.*[68]

Creel assembled as brilliant and talented a group of journalists, scholars, press agents, editors, artists, and other manipulators of the symbols of public opinion as America had ever seen united for a single purpose. The breathtaking scope of the huge agency and its activities was not to be equaled until the rise of the totalitarian dictatorships after the war. Creel, Byoir, and their associates were public relations counselors to the U.S. government, carrying first to the citizens of the country and then to those in distant lands the idea that gave motive power to the wartime undertaking of 1917–1918.[69]

The Liberty Loan drives were promoted by a separate campaign directed by Guy Emerson, later to pioneer in bank public relations, and John Price Jones, who later led the way in organized fund-raising. Their campaigns, based heavily on advertising techniques, taught many business people the values of public relations.

These successful demonstrations were to have a profound impact in the years ahead. Analyzing the influence of the Creel Committee, *The New York Times* commented in 1920,

> Essentially the species, if not a war product, is one which the war has mightily increased. Liberty Loans had to be advertised throughout the country. Publicity did

that. Five times, at short intervals, the newspapers of the nation stepped into line and "put across" to the man at the breakfast table, and in his office, in the factory, in the mine—into every phase of commerce and industry, in fact, the need of digging down deep into his pocket and "coming across." It worked. Beautifully and efficiently. Not only did he have a staff of press agents working immediately under him in a central office, but Creel decentralized the system so that every type of industry in the country had its special group of publicity workers. In this manner, more than in any other, were the heads and directors of movements of every type introduced to and made cognizant of the value of concentrating on publicity in so-called "drives."[70]

To illustrate the *Times*'s point, when America entered the war, the Red Cross had a membership of 486,194 in 372 chapters scattered across the nation and $200,000 in working funds. In September 1918, as the war neared its end, the Red Cross had 20 million members in 3,864 chapters and had raised more than $400 million in gifts and membership dues. Another example: On May 1, 1917, there were only some 350,000 holders of U.S. bonds; six months later, after two organized publicity and sales drives for Liberty Bonds, there were 10 million bondholders.

Equally impressive was Herbert Hoover's reliance on public relations to encourage food conservation by the nation's households, hotels, restaurants, and food dealers. The Food Administration, under the public relations direction of Ben Allen, former Associated Press correspondent, transmitted appeals about saving food to the public by every available means of communication. The nation's media donated nearly $20 million in advertising space, and an estimated 20 million people pledged their support by returning coupons inserted in publications or distributed at countless local meetings.

After the war there emerged an overly optimistic belief in the power of mass communication. A noted political scientist, Harold D. Lasswell, observed, "When all allowances have been made, and all extravagant estimates pared to the bone, the fact remains that propaganda is one of the most powerful instrumentalities in the modern world."[71] Unfortunately, many organizations still invest large sums in the outmoded all-powerful model of mass communication that emerged from the World War I experience.

Carl Byoir. The Creel Committee trained a host of practitioners who took their wartime experiences and fashioned a profitable calling. Among these were Carl Byoir and Edward L. Bernays. Byoir, who at age 28 had been associate chairman of the CPI, after a decade's tour into other endeavors founded in 1930 what would become one of the country's largest public relations firms until it was acquired by the Foote, Cone, & Belding advertising agency in 1978.[72] Bernays, who had a minor role in the CPI, beginning in the 1920s became one of the field's definers and tireless advocates.

BOOMING TWENTIES ERA: 1920–1929

Vigorously nourished by wartime developments, the public relations specialty quickly spread. It showed up in government, business, the churches, social work—now burgeoning in the war's aftermath—the labor movement, and social movements. The victory of the Anti-Saloon League in achieving national prohibition and the triumph of the women's suffrage movement, both in 1920, provided fresh evidence of the newly found power. And because the process of industrialization and urbanization had been pushed ahead several notches during the war, the growth and development of the practice, like much else in society, was accelerating.

Edward L. Bernays and Doris E. Fleischman. Among those vying with Ivy Lee for prominence and for business in the 1920s was Edward L. Bernays. Prior to World Way I, Bernays had worked as a press agent. While he worked for the Creel Committee during the war, his busy mind envisioned the possibility of making a life's work of what he called "engineering public consent."[73] Bernays is credited with coining the term "public relations counsel" in *Crystallizing Public Opinion,* the first book on public relations, in 1923. He broke more new ground the same year when he taught the first public relations course at New York University. Bernays continued in his roles as author, lecturer, advocate, and critic into the 1990s. *Life Magazine* included Bernays in its 1990 special issue, "The 100 Most Important Americans of the 20th Century." He died March 9, 1995, at age 103.

Bernays married Doris E. Fleischman in 1922. Together they ran their firm, Edward L. Bernays, Counsel on Public Relations, until formally retiring from active practice in 1962. She died in 1980. They counseled major corporations, government agencies, and U.S. presidents from Calvin Coolidge through Dwight Eisenhower, with Bernays taking the spotlight for most assignments. Although credited with being an equal partner with Bernays in the firm, with creating the first public relations newsletter and with collaborating with Bernays to develop the term public relations counsel, Fleischman struggled for professional equality because of her sex.[74] For example, in one of her two books she wrote,

> Many men resented having women tell them what to do in their business. They resented having men tell them, too, but advice from a woman was somewhat demeaning. I learned to withdraw from situations where the gender of public relations counsel was a factor or where suggestions had to be disassociated from gender. If ideas were considered first in terms of my sex, they might never get around to being judged on their own merits.[75]

Fleischman was an early feminist, who, after marrying Bernays, retained her birth name long before it was socially acceptable:

> During the next three decades, Fleischman continued to sign into hotels—and twice into maternity hospitals—as "Miss Doris E. Fleischman," and in 1925 she received the first U.S. passport granted to a married woman under her birth name. That was her name on the 1928 book she edited on careers for women and on the seven magazine articles and book chapters she published between 1930 and 1946.[76]

Bernays's book followed Walter Lippmann's 1922 *Public Opinion,* a book that reflected the growing interest in power and nature of public opinion. In all the years prior to 1917, only 18 books on public opinion and publicity were printed. At least 28 titles appeared between 1917 and 1925.

Scholarly interest also dates from this period. Social scientists began to explore the nature of public opinion and the role of mass communication in its formation. Although sophisticated opinion-measurement methods did not appear until the 1930s, the postwar work of social scientists contributed much to the development of market research, public opinion polls, and communication science.

Many other rapid-fire developments occurred during this postwar period. Several new counseling firms were established, including one founded by Harry A. Bruno, a British-born aviation enthusiast and wartime flier. After the airline he was working for went broke in 1923, he set up a firm in partnership with Richard Blythe. Most of Bruno's early clients were makers of airplane motors and instruments, seeking to promote aviation. He gained national prominence when he and Blythe handled the press relations for Charles A. Lindbergh's historic flight across the Atlantic in May 1927. Bruno's publicity and public relations projects did much to speed America's acceptance of the air age and commercial aviation.[77]

John W. Hill. Despite a booming economy and rapidly growing media, there were only six public relations firms listed in the Manhattan telephone directory in 1926. In 1927, John W. Hill, a Cleveland journalist, started a firm in that city. In 1933, he formed a partnership with Don Knowlton, and shortly thereafter moved to New York to found Hill & Knowlton, Inc. Knowlton remained to run the Cleveland office. The two firms, connected only by overlapping ownership, operated independently until 1964, when Knowlton retired and the Cleveland office was sold to a successor firm. Hill died in 1977. In 1980, JWT Group, the holding company that owned J. Walter Thompson Company advertising agency, acquired Hill & Knowlton for $28 million. The JWT Group of companies was acquired by the British conglomerate WPP Group, London, in 1989.

Long was viewed as an ethical and respected leader of public relations counseling. Hill's role in helping the major tobacco companies form the Tobacco Industry Research Committee (TIRC) threatens his legacy. On his recommendation, the presidents of the major tobacco companies agreed to fund the TIRC, with Hill fighting the tobacco wars on behalf of the cigarette industry until he retired from Hill & Knowlton in 1962. Throughout his professional life Hill saw himself as a man of integrity and principle, committing his views to paper:

> Should an existing client company adopt policies which the counsel believes are not in the public interest, he would advise against such policies—and, if he has integrity, be prepared to resign the account in case the client persisted.[78]

When asked directly about his role in the formation of the TIRC and in tobacco public relations, in 1966 Hill responded, "I decline to comment on this matter on the basis that this is an active, highly sensitive account" and did not cover Hill & Knowlton's tobacco account in his 1963 memoir, *The Making of a Public Relations Man.*[79] Long after Hill's death, however, there is little doubt about his role in creating a public relations front for the tobacco industry:

> Though John Hill had long since passed from such earthly battles, the fact remains that he was the guiding force in the formation of the Tobacco Industry Research Committee and later the Tobacco Institute. Thus, Hill must bear responsibility for that "brilliantly conceived and executed plan" that served the selfish interests of the tobacco industry at the expense of millions of Americans' good health.[80]

Two years before Hill set up shop in Cleveland, *Edward D. Howard II* had organized a public relations agency there that celebrates its 75th anniversary in 2000. Edward Howard and Company is not only Ohio's oldest public relations firm but is also the nation's longest surviving independently owned firm. It is now a member of the Pinnacle Worldwide network of independent public relations firms.

Another little-known pioneer was *Glenn G. Hayes* of Chicago, who established Hayes, Loeb and Company in 1921, an agency specializing in farm public relations. His partner, Sidney C. Loeb, landed Sears, Roebuck and Co. as the first big account when Sears needed a program to counteract a movement by thousands of local merchants to fight mail-order competition.

This period also saw increased use of public relations advertising as a tool. Illinois Central Railroad started a campaign in 1920 that sought "promotion of a better understanding and closer relationship with the patrons of our lines." In 1922, Metropolitan Life Insurance Company started a good-health campaign. In 1923, General Motors (GM) began to use advertising to sell itself as an institution.

Paul Garrett. GM, however, did not set up its own department until 1931, when GM president and management innovator Alfred P. Sloan Jr. brought in Paul Garrett, another influential pioneer. Garrett was the second corporate public relations practitioner to hold the office of vice president. He and Arthur W. Page at AT&T were among the first to use the new science of public opinion polling as the basis for planning and evaluating public relations programs. At GM Garrett built an innovative corporate program, which was widely copied by other corporations. He retired from GM in 1957 and was retained to counsel the then-new Xerox Corporation.[81]

Another development of the early 1920s was the wholesale adoption of the Creel Committee techniques. Beginning in 1919, for example, Samuel Insull and his cohorts in the utilities industry sparked a movement to persuade the American people of the blessings of privately owned utilities.[82] Despite the cloud that later crossed this program, it embodied some forward-looking concepts.

Quick-buck promoters also grasped the lessons taught by the success of wartime promotional campaigns. The disreputable Ku Klux Klan, born during Reconstruction, had been revived in Atlanta in 1915 as a "bottle club." By

1919, the club was floundering. Its promoter, William Joseph Simons, hired two publicists, Edward Y. Clarke and Bessie Tyler, who had formed the Southern Publicity Association as a firm to promote wartime fund drives. In just three years the Clarke-Tyler campaign multiplied the Klan's membership from a few thousand members in 1920 to about three million, earning great sums for themselves at the expense of a bitter legacy to the nation.[83]

Arthur W. Page. Among the pioneers shaping today's practice, Arthur W. Page stands at the summit. Page built three successful business careers, yet found time to contribute his talent to many public service endeavors. He was a writer and editor of *World's Work Magazine* and other periodicals of Doubleday, Page and Company from 1905 until 1927. Then he accepted Walter Gifford's offer to become vice president of American Telephone and Telegraph Co. to succeed James D. Ellsworth. At the outset Page made it clear that he would accept only on the conditions that he was not to serve as a publicity man, that he would have a voice in policy, and that the company's performance would be the determinant of its public reputation. Page's philosophy is summed up in this statement:

> All business in a democratic country begins with public permission and exists by public approval. If that be true, it follows that business should be cheerfully willing to tell the public what its policies are, what it is doing, and what it hopes to do. This seems practically a duty.[84]

Page retired from AT&T in 1947, after integrating public relations concepts and practices into the Bell System. From then until his death in 1960 at age 77, he served as a consultant to many large corporations and gave much of his time to the service of government, higher education, and other causes; but it was Page's work for AT&T that left his lasting imprint on public relations. His precepts and principles not only endure in the companies that used to be part of AT&T (broken up in 1984) but are being renewed and promoted by the Arthur W. Page Society. Founded in 1983, this society's membership includes primarily senior corporate public relations executives, leading counselors, and other leaders in public relations. According to the Page Society literature, Page practiced six principles of public relations:

1. *Tell the truth.* Let the public know what's happening and provide an accurate picture of the company's character, ideals, and practices.
2. *Prove it with action.* Public perception of an organization is determined 90 percent by doing and 10 percent by talking.
3. *Listen to the customer.* To serve the company well, understand what the public wants and needs. Keep top decision makers and other employees informed about public relations to company products, policies, and practices.
4. *Manage for tomorrow.* Anticipate public relations and eliminate practices that create difficulties. Generate goodwill.
5. *Conduct public relations as if the whole company depends on it.* Corporate relations is a management function. No corporate strategy should be im-

plemented without considering its impact on the public. The public relations professional is a policy maker capable of handling a wide range of corporate communications activities.

6. *Remain calm, patient, and good-humored.* Lay the groundwork for public relations miracles with consistent, calm, and reasoned attention to information and contacts. When a crisis arises, remember that cool heads communicate best.[85]

After World War I, and in part as a response to the dislocations caused by war, interest in and use of publicity techniques spilled over into the Community Chest movement and the new field of social work. As more and more money had to be raised to meet more and more needs of urban society, recognition of the importance of publicity and the need for trained publicists grew.

Advancement of social work publicity was spearheaded by Evart G. Routzahn and Mary Swain Routzahn of the Russell Sage Foundation. In the early 1920s, the Routzahns played key roles in the birth of the National Publicity Council for welfare agencies and of a Health Education Section in the American Public Health Association. What was first a committee on publicity methods in social work became, in 1922, the National Publicity Council for Welfare Services. From its inception until 1940, the council was used by the Routzahns to transport new ideas, new techniques, and missionary zeal to novices in health and welfare publicity work. This body, which attained 1,200 members, went through several reorganizations and name changes. In 1975 it became the National Communications Council for Human Services, and in 1977 it was merged into the Public Relations Society of America (PRSA).

Religious leaders also sensed the changing times. In 1918 the National Lutheran Council launched a strong national church publicity program. Later that same year, a Catholic organization, the Knights of Columbus, organized a publicity bureau with John B. Kennedy as its director. *The New York Times* noted at the time (quoting Kennedy), "They are quite frank in admitting that the 'biggest and most practical human lesson learned from the war is that nothing requiring organized effort can succeed without publicity and plenty of it.'" The YMCA and YWCA had long had publicity staffs, and they formed something of a nucleus for the spread of organized church publicity. Astute leaders everywhere were observing this "most practical human lesson from the war."

It was also during this period that a sense of identification and professionalism began to emerge in this new craft. The first national public relations organization was established in Chicago on June 15, 1915, as a part of the Associated Advertising Clubs of the World. Seven bankers founded the new organization and called it the Financial Advertising Association, reflecting that banking public relations in the era of World War I was seen as advertising, and stiff, high-collar advertising at that. In its early years, the association was mainly an "idea exchange" for its members, but it changed its name in 1947 to the Financial Public Relations Association, in 1966 to the Bank Public Relations and Marketing Association, and again in 1970 to the Bank Marketing Association, to express its purpose more accurately.

The next group to organize better exemplified the evolution of public relations. A handful of major universities and colleges had set up press bureaus prior to the war. More did so in the early 1920s, generally as an adjunct to a capital fundraising drive. Owing mainly to the determined efforts of T. T. Frankenberg, then publicity director for the Western College of Women in Oxford, Ohio, the Association of American College News Bureaus had been organized in April 1917. It lapsed into inactivity during the war, but came alive again in the 1920s.

Alice L. Beeman. At the 1925 convention, the organization took on new strength, reflecting the growth of the practice in higher education. Symbolic of its growth in ensuing years, the organization's name was changed in 1930 to the American College Publicity Association, in 1964 to the American College Public Relations Association, and in 1974—after a merger with the American Alumni Council—to the Council for the Advancement and Support of Education (CASE). This merger reflected a shift in emphasis in college public relations from publicity to development and fund-raising. CASE was launched under the leadership of its first president, Alice L. Beeman. She had previously been general director of the American Association of University Women, based in Washington, DC, and the AAUW Educational Foundation. In her new position as president of CASE, Beeman was the first woman to head a national public relations association.

ROOSEVELT ERA AND WORLD WAR II: 1930–1945

Propelled by wartime lessons and a changing America, the practice of public relations moved full speed ahead until the stock market crash in 1929. The ensuing Great Depression marks another milestone. That persistent economic catastrophe and Franklin D. Roosevelt's New Deal prompted development of the practice in many fields.

Louis McHenry Howe. FDR combined strong leadership with consummate skill to harness the forces of protest into an effective political coalition. He won his battles on front pages and over the radio, a new medium he used with matchless skill. Roosevelt's adroit moves in the public arena can be credited in large part to his public relations mentor, Louis McHenry Howe. The astute, tough-minded Howe served FDR faithfully and effectively from 1912 until Howe's death in 1936. He gave his life to being Roosevelt's right-hand man and did much to advance him to the White House.[86]

FDR's success in winning public support spurred the efforts of the conservative forces, particularly the business community, to counter his appeals. But such a cataclysmic event as the Depression was bound to produce a sharp readjustment of values, and a new trend set in, marked by wider acknowledgment of an institution's or industry's social responsibility. Increasingly leaders in many settings realized that mutually beneficial public relationships could be built only by coupling responsible performance with persuasive publicity.

Events flowing from the Depression and the New Deal brought home to every group the need to build informed public support. New Dealers soon found that this was essential to pave the way for their radical reforms, and government public relations had its greatest expansion under Franklin Roosevelt. School administrators were made to realize the dangers of an uninformed public as hard-pressed taxpayers chopped off the frills in education. The Depression brought a tremendous expansion in social welfare needs and agencies, whose administrators also came to realize the need for better public understanding. Military leaders, looking apprehensively at the buildup of the Nazi and Fascist war machines, began to promote support for more adequate armed forces. Colleges and universities, caught in the web of financial woes, turned more and more to public relations to raise funds.

Business leaders turned increasingly to public relations specialists for help in fighting against Roosevelt's biting criticisms and his legislative reforms. There was a marked trend away from occasional and defensive efforts and toward more positive and continuous programs, administered by newly established departments. A growing labor movement, too, found that it had problems and needed guidance. Growth was stimulated all along the line by the social and economic upheavals of the Depression.

This period also brought the tool that promised more precise, more scientific measurement and assessment of public opinion. The Roper and Gallup polls, begun in the mid-1930s, won wide respect in the presidential election of 1936. Perceptive practitioners began using this new tool to advise management and to formulate programs. The public opinion poll, with the application of new sampling methods, has steadily improved in reliability and in utility. George Gallup, who did much to make polling a key tool of public relations, politics, marketing, and scholarship, died in 1984.

Joseph Varney Baker. In 1934, the first minority-owned firm opened in Philadelphia. Joseph Varney Baker left his position as city editor of the *Philadelphia Tribune* to provide counsel to the Pennsylvania Railroad Company. Baker was the first Black to serve as president of a PRSA chapter and the first to be accredited by PRSA. His firm's list of clients included Chrysler, Gillette, Procter & Gamble, NBC, RCA, and Scott Paper Company. One authority on minorities in public relations concluded that during the 40 years that Baker's firm existed, it "was hired to communicate only with the black consumer market, and the practice has continued to this day."[87]

Clem Whitaker and Leone Baxter. This era also produced the forerunner of a major segment of today's practice: the political-campaign specialist. In 1933, husband and wife Clem Whitaker and Leone Baxter formed the first agency specializing in political campaigns, headquartered in San Francisco. California, with its heavy reliance on the initiative and referendum and its weak political party organizations, provided fertile ground for the growth of political firms. From 1935 through 1958, the firm managed 80 major campaigns and won all but six. This agency brought a new approach to politics, including the media blitz in the final days of the campaign. Today it has countless imitators.

World War II produced more violent changes in the environment, accelerating the development of public relations. Once more the government led the way, with a breathtaking demonstration of the power of an organized informational campaign. This time the instrument was the Office of War Information.

When war broke out after the Japanese bombing of Pearl Harbor on December 7, 1941, the government's information machine, which had been built largely in the New Deal years, was in some disarray. Three major information agencies overlapped and jousted for dominance: the Office of Facts and Figures, headed by Archibald MacLeish, the poet; the Office of Government Reports, headed by Lowell Mellett, former Washington correspondent; and the Division of Information in the Office of Emergency Management, headed by Robert Horton. President Roosevelt was reluctant to create a central information agency, even with the chaos, fearing that Congress and the press would interpret it as a "propaganda instrument to propel America into war." FDR knew well how the Creel Committee had become a whipping boy when its slogans of World War I turned to bitter irony in the 1920s. It was in that period that propaganda had become a sullied, useless word.

After Pearl Harbor, however, the urgency of the situation prompted Roosevelt to issue Executive Order 9182 in June 1942 creating the Office of War Information (OWI) and appointing Elmer Davis as its director.[88] George Creel, who had brilliantly directed the CPI in World War I, was never consulted by FDR. Davis, veteran news reporter and radio commentator, never effectively brought the warring forces in the OWI under control, nor did he play the role Creel did in counseling the president, but he and the OWI set the pace for extensive expansion of the practice in the armed forces, in industry, and in allied fields. OWI developed more techniques and trained many more practitioners than did the Creel Committee.

In the opinion of two public relations scholars, the OWI's greatest contributions derived from its work as the predecessor of the United States Information Agency. OWI was the agency that pointed out the danger in not countering distorted ideas of the United States throughout the world.[89] Others learned this lesson during these tumultuous years.

Public relations in the armed forces today constitutes a major segment of the practice. Prior to the outbreak of World War II, however, it had been given scant support by authoritarian military leaders. In 1935, General Douglas MacArthur, then chief of staff, appointed a young major, Alexander Surles, to head up a public relations branch with the "dual job of getting before the public the War Department's anxiety over things to come in Europe and to help newsmen pry stories out of the War Department."[90] In January 1941, Surles was asked to draft a plan for "a man-sized bureau of public relations."

With the advent of war, this staff quickly grew from three to 3,000 officers and civilians. Concurrently, the Navy Department moved to expand and strengthen its public relations. The Army Air Corps, under the imaginative leadership of General H. H. "Hap" Arnold, a former information officer, quickly recruited a host of skilled public relations and advertising specialists. Their task was to sell air power in an age of trench-minded generals. Even though the armed forces went into the war ill-equipped for public relations, they acquitted themselves well. The work was largely a matter of publicity, censorship, and assistance to war correspondents. In the process they trained countless numbers of practitioners for this work after the war and built a solid foundation for practice in the postwar boom.

World War II brought paid advertising to the fore as a major tool of public relations, now in its many forms: public relations advertising, public service advertising, issue or advocacy advertising, and institutional advertising. Two forces spurred this development. In World War I many makers of goods quit advertising because the products for the civilian market were in short supply and thus needed no advertising. When many of these manufacturers returned to the civilian market after the war, they found that many people had forgotten brand names. Advertising executives pounded this lesson home in the 1920s. The second force at work was the advertising industry's concern with its tarnished reputation. In the wake of the 1929 market crash and the ensuing Depression, advertising was singled out as one of the villains. New Dealers sought legislation to eliminate fraud in advertising and to require government grade labeling. At the same time, several antiadvertising books became best sellers.

These forces gave birth in 1942 to the War Advertising Council, which worked with industry and the government to make advertising a major tool in getting citizens to produce for the war, to ration scarce resources, to buy war bonds, and to serve in the armed forces. In advocating the council, James Webb Young called for advertising's power to be used in open propaganda in international relations, to create understanding and reduce friction. Likewise, he advocated its application to the arts, music, and literature and promoted it as a servant of "all the forces of righteousness."[91] Young reflected what Bernays called "a movement toward public responsibility in private business," a movement required if business were to work its way back to credibility. As a result of this wartime development, advertising is used widely as a major public relations tool.

POSTWAR BOOM: 1945–1965

World War II brought new opportunities; new demonstrations of the utility of public relations in motivating war production, military morale, and civilian support; and new techniques and channels of communication. The war also schooled about 75,000 persons in the practice. The tensions and problems of the uneasy years of conversion from a wartime to a peacetime economy and the transition from an industrial to a postindustrial, service-oriented society accentuated and extended these developments. For example, in the late 1940s, industry was wracked by a series of bitter, prolonged strikes as organized labor fought to redress grievances built up in the no-strike war period and to keep wartime gains in pay. These struggles and increased public criticism of big business placed heavy demands on the function in business and industry.[92]

Similarly, the postwar baby boom and the GI-fed enrollment bulge brought new and heavy demands on the nation's schools and colleges, forcing administrators to accept the need for public relations counsel. School districts had to promote one bond issue after another to build additional schools, and the nation's institutions of higher education had to scramble for funds for more teachers and buildings to meet the exploding demand for higher education and research.

Expanding world trade and political conflict extended the practice around the world, with American practitioners leading the way. Advances in telecommunication and transportation brought the peoples of the world into the closest contact in the history of civilization. The same ecological factors that compelled the development of public relations in the United States were now operating on a global scale, only faster. For example, the Cold War between the world's superpowers, the United States and the Soviet Union, necessitated conversion of the OWI to what today is the U.S. Information Agency (USIA) and the maintenance of large public relations staffs in the armed forces.

Today's USIA grew from several information and cultural exchange bodies born in World War II and the early postwar years. The Office of International Information and Educational Exchanges was created by the Fulbright Act in 1946. Heightening Cold War tensions prompted passage of the U.S. Information and Educational Exchange Act of 1948, known as the Smith-Mundt Act. Dissatisfaction with the resulting split authority resulted in creation of the U.S. Information Agency on August 1, 1953, under President Eisenhower's Reorganization Plan No. 8. This made USIA independent of the State Department, which at the time had authority over cultural and educational exchanges.

The advent of television as a powerful national forum and its consequent widespread impact on a more educated society likewise brought new public relations opportunities and problems to institutions and their executives. Television's role in politics, for example, spawned the political campaign specialist, now a major role in the nation's political system. Eventually television prompted many leaders in business, government, the military, and so forth to undergo media training to become adept at talking in sound bites, controlling the agenda in interviews, and fielding questions with answers based on a message strategy.

These and kindred developments during the postwar decades of rapid expansion brought increased stability and maturity to the field. This era saw the number of practitioners pass the 100,000 mark. This era also saw the foundations for a profession being put in place by strong professional associations and the beginning of public relations education in the nation's colleges. Both these developments were fed by rapid growth in books and journals, which were published to build a common body of knowledge for the field. The following developments highlighted the 1945–1965 boom period:

1. Steady growth in the number of programs in industries, institutions, social agencies, government bureaus, and trade associations. Already-established programs tended to mature and to move beyond publicity.
2. Stabilization in the number of independent counseling firms, especially in the communication hubs of New York, Washington, Chicago, and Los Angeles.

3. A tremendous spurt in the number of books, articles, and journals devoted to the practice and its philosophy, problems, and techniques. The literature is voluminous, although somewhat repetitive.
4. Organization of new associations for practitioners and redirection or consolidation of those already established. Many of these are now mature.
5. Growth in the number of college courses and students and in the breadth and depth of the courses. Increased support for collegiate preparation from practitioners and great acceptance of young graduates in the job market.
6. Internationalization of the practice and its standards, reflected in the formation of the International Public Relations Association in 1955.

Another force pushing the practice toward professionalism came from campuses. In this period, public relations education, which had its origins in publicity courses in the 1920s, developed slowly, because the function was suspect in the minds of many academicians. A 1946 survey identified 30 major institutions offering public relations courses.[93] Ten years later a PRSA survey found that 92 were offering courses designed to prepare students for this work, with 14 schools offering a major.[94] By 1964, as this era ended, 14 institutions offered a bachelor's degree in public relations, 29 had undergraduate sequences, and all told, 280 were offering instruction in various courses.[95]

Public relations education gained some cohesion with the formation of the Council on Public Relations Education at the 1956 convention of the Association for Education in Journalism meeting at Northwestern University. Approval came only after a spirited floor fight in which many traditional journalism teachers opposed the move. The council's purpose was "to promote fuller exchange of information and ideas among teachers" and to enlist the support of practitioners. That educators' group is now a large and recognized division in the expanded Association for Education in Journalism and Mass Communication. Later that same year, PRSA created the Foundation for Public Relations Research and Education. This foundation—no longer affiliated with PRSA—is now known as the Institute for Public Relations Research and Education and is based at the University of Florida, Gainesville. In 1990, PRSA established another foundation with a mission similar to that of its original foundation—to advance research and education and to advance the field toward professionalism.

Additional impetus for the growth of professionalism came with establishment of one strong general organization and emergence of a number serving specialized fields of practice. PRSA was born August 4, 1947, when representatives of the West Coast American Council on Public Relations and the East Coast National Association of Public Relations Counsel met in Chicago. Members of the Washington-based American Public Relations Association voted not to come in at that time but ultimately capitulated in 1961. Dr. Rex F. Harlow, who had organized the council, was the moving force in bringing this merger about. In 1945, while president of the council, Harlow had started the *Public Relations Journal,* which became the monthly magazine of PRSA after the merger.[96] In this and other ways, Rex Harlow played a major role in the professionalization of public relations.

GLOBAL INFORMATION AGE: 1965–PRESENT

Since the mid-1960s, public relations has increased in importance and complexity. Far-reaching trends early in this period made government affairs a main public relations task and brought "issues management" and management by objectives to the function's lexicon. In 1950, only 17 percent of workers held information jobs; by the early 1980s, more than 60 percent were similarly employed. In 1960, the United States had about 25 percent of the world market share in manufacturing, but by the 1980s, this had slipped to less than 17 percent. These trends presaged the end of the industrial era in the United States.[97]

But the driving force in contemporary practice has been the onrush of the global information age. Although this new age had its roots in the 1950s, it really took off in the mid-1960s. Naisbitt sets the beginnings of the information society in 1956 and 1957. In 1956, for the first time in American history, white-collar workers outnumbered workers in industrial production. A year later, 1957, brought the Soviet satellite, Sputnik, and with it the era of global satellite communications. By the 1980s, the output of information was accelerating by some 40 percent annually. That means, says Naisbitt, "data will double every twenty months. The on-line information selection business is now a multi-billion-dollar enterprise."[98]

Computer technology is to the information age what the mechanized assembly line was to the industrial age. Public relations and new media scholar John Pavlik says that the computer has evolved from simply a calculator to a "sophisticated mutlimedia global communications tool."[99]

> If the trend in the falling price of computing power continues, twenty years from now most homes will have a device in their living room with the power of today's supercomputers—but at a cost of just $500. For the creators of multimedia software, interactive television and other new media content, the implications are that all software—programming—can be vastly different than today. Rather than endless reruns of *Gilligan's Island,* the interactive TV future might offer viewers the opportunity to trek across the North Pole or converse with William Shakespeare. The limits will be only those of our own imaginations.[100]

The implications for public relations communication are no less revolutionary.

As then-president and chief executive officer of Dow Chemical Company Frank Popoff told the 1989 graduating class at Alma College (Michigan),

> Twenty years ago people talked in terms of air travel shrinking space and time, making it possible to move among nations and continents in hours instead of days. Today, with the advent of telecommunications, business people in Japan, Europe and Midland, Michigan, can meet simultaneously without leaving their offices. . . . Once people talked about industrialization, about nations developing the ma-

chinery and the skills to manufacture and distribute products on a large scale at affordable cost. Now we talk about globalization, about the world as a global community where nations and people can share one economy, one environment, one technology and, at least in commerce, one language.[101]

NOTES

1. The authoritative references on public relations history are by Scott M. Cutlip, *Public Relations History: From the 17th to the 20th Century* (Hillsdale, NJ: Lawrence Erlbaum Associates, 1995), and *The Unseen Power: Public Relations— A History* (Hillsdale, NJ: Lawrence Erlbaum Associates, 1994). In two volumes totaling 1,100 pages, Cutlip details the people and events that affected U.S. history and the development of public relations.
2. A. L. Basham, *The Wonder That Was India* (London: Sidgwick and Jackson, 1954), 122.
3. Samuel Eliot Morison, *The Founding of Harvard College* (Cambridge: Harvard University Press, 1935), 303. Also see Hugh T. Lefler, "Promotional Literature of the Southern Colonies," *Journal of Southern History* 33 (1967): 3–25.
4. Philip Davidson, *Propaganda and the American Revolution, 1763–1783* (Chapel Hill: University of North Carolina Press, 1941), 3.
5. Cass Canfield, *Sam Adams' Revolution (1765–1776)* (New York: Harper and Row, 1976).
6. Benjamin Woods Labaree, *The Boston Tea Party* (New York: Oxford University Press, 1966).
7. For the account that imprinted the patriots' version on history, see James Bowdoin, Dr. Joseph Warren, and Samuel Pemberton, "Short Narrative of the Horrid Massacre in Boston," in *Tracts of the American Revolution, 1763–1776*, edited by Merrill Jensen (New York: Bobbs Merrill, 1967).
8. Merrill Jensen, "The Sovereign States," in *Sovereign States in an Age of Uncertainty*, ed. Ronald Hoffman and Peter J. Albert (Charlottesville: University of Virginia Press, 1981).
9. For the Tory side of the propaganda battle, see Carol Berkin, *Jonathan Sewall, Odyssey of an American Loyalist* (New York: Columbia University Press, 1974).
10. William Baldwin Jr., "Bicentenary of a Classic Campaign," *Public Relations Quarterly* 10 (Spring 1965).
11. Robert A. Rutland, *The Ordeal of the Constitution: The Antifederalists and the Ratification Struggle of 1787–88* (Boston: Northeastern University Press, 1983), 3.
12. Broadus Mitchell, *Alexander Hamilton: Youth to Maturity, 1755–1788* (New York: Macmillan, 1957), 422–23.
13. Allan Nevins, *The Constitution Makers and the Public, 1785–1790* (New York: Foundation for Public Relations Research and Education, 1962), 10. Also in *Public Relations Review* 4, no. 3 (Fall 1978), 5–16.
14. John Brooks, *Telephone: The First Hundred Years* (New York: Harper and Row, 1976), 270–71.
15. T. Swann Harding, "Genesis of One 'Government Propaganda Mill,' " *Public Opinion Quarterly* 11 (Summer 1947): 227–35. (A history of public relations in the U.S. Department of Agriculture.)
16. For one example of Kendall's work, see Lynn Marshall, "The Authorship of Jackson's Bank Veto Message," *Mississippi Valley Historical Review*, vol. L (December 1963). For an additional view of Kendall, see *Autobiography of Amos*

Kendall (Micro-Offset Books, 1949, reprinted). For an estimate of Kendall's influence, see Arthur M. Schlesinger Jr., *The Age of Jackson* (Boston: Little, Brown, 1945).

17. For accounts of this epic public relations battle, see James L. Crouthamel, "Did the Second Bank of the United States Bribe the Press?" *Journalism Quarterly* 36 (Winter 1959); and Bray Hammond, *Banks and Politics in America* (Princeton: Princeton University Press, 1957).

18. Alan Raucher, *Public Relations and Business, 1900–1929* (Baltimore: Johns Hopkins University Press, 1968).

19. For accounts of Davy Crockett's buildup, see James A. Shackford, *David Crockett, the Man and Legend* (Chapel Hill: University of North Carolina Press, 1956); Marshall Fishwick, *American Heroes: Myths and Realities* (Washington, DC, 1954), 70–71; and Vernon Parrington, *Main Currents in American Thought* (New York: Harcourt Brace Jovanovich, 1930), vol. 2, 173–78.

20. Irving Wallace, *The Fabulous Showman: Life and Times of P. T. Barnum* (New York: Alfred A. Knopf, 1959).

21. Dexter W. Fellows and Andrew A. Freeman, *This Way to the Big Show* (New York: Viking, 1936; Halcyon House, 1938), 193; and Phineas Taylor Barnum, *The Life of P. T. Barnum Written by Himself* (New York: Redfield, 1855), 154–74.

22. Richard C. Overton, *Burlington West* (Cambridge, MA: Harvard University Press, 1941), 158–159.

23. Rossiter Johnson, ed., *A History of the World's Columbian Exposition,* vol. 2 (New York: D. Appleton, 1897), 1–31.

24. Noble E. Cunningham Jr., "John Beckley: An Early American Party Manager," *William and Mary Quarterly* 13 (January 1956): 40–52.

25. Stanley Kelley Jr., *Professional Public Relations and Political Power* (Baltimore: Johns Hopkins University Press, 1956). (One of the first books to point out the growing role of public relations in politics gives examples from the late 1940s and early 1950s.)

26. Luther B. Little, "The Printing Press in Politics," *Munsey's Magazine,* 23 (September 1900): 740–44.

27. For a full account, see Stanley L. Jones, *The Presidential Election of 1896* (Madison: University of Wisconsin Press, 1964).

28. Ray Ginger, *The Age of Excess* (New York: Macmillan, 1965), 25.

29. Eric F. Goldman, *Two-Way Street* (Boston: Bellman Publishing Co., 1948). A sketchy potboiler.

30. For a concise account, see Leon Wolff, *Lockout* (New York: Harper and Row, 1965).

31. Merle Curti, *The Growth of American Thought,* 3rd ed. (New York: Harper and Row, 1964), 634.

32. Copied from original in AT&T Archives.

33. Cutlip, *Public Relations History,* 208.

34. Forrest McDonald, *Insull* (Chicago: University of Chicago Press, 1962), 44–45. (Biography of the utility magnate who blazed many public relations trails before he crashed in ruin.)

35. "America's First Press Agent a Well-Known Pittsburgher," clipping in Westinghouse Company files, circa 1906.

36. Cutlip, *Public Relations History,* 203.

37. C. C. Regier, *The Era of the Muckrakers* (Chapel Hill: University of North Carolina Press, 1932). (Regier neglects the role of metropolitan newspapers in this muckraking.) For a generous sampling of newspaper articles, see Arthur Wein-

berg and Lila Weinberg, eds., *The Muckrakers* (New York: Simon and Schuster, 1961). For a more recent discussion of the most prolific, if lesser known, muckraker, see Robert Miraldi, "Charles Edward Russell: 'Chief of the Muckrakers,' " *Journalism & Mass Communication Monographs* 150 (April 1995).

38. Parrington, *Main Currents in American Thought,* vol. 3, pp. 404–5. For details on the rise of the mass media, see Edwin Emery, *The Press and America* (Englewood Cliffs, NJ: Prentice-Hall, 1972); Theodore Peterson, *Magazines in the Twentieth Century* (Urbana: University of Illinois Press, 1964); and Stephen Fox, *The Mirror Makers* (New York: Morrow, 1984).

39. Richard Hofstadter, *The Age of Reform* (New York: Alfred A. Knopf, 1955), 185.

40. Robert D. Reynolds Jr., "The 1906 Campaign to Sway Muckraking Periodicals," *Journalism Quarterly* 56 (Autumn 1979): 513.

41. Ralph H. Hower, *The History of an Advertising Agency: N. W. Ayer & Son at Work,* 1896–1939 (Cambridge: Harvard University Press, 1939), 117. See also p. 95 of the 1949 revised edition.

42. For details, see Scott M. Cutlip, "The Nation's First Public Relations Agency," in *The Unseen Power,* 10–26. See also "The Nation's First Public Relations Firm," Journalism Quarterly 43 (Summer 1966). (It was in fact a publicity agency, not a public relations firm.)

43. Cutlip, *The Unseen Power,* 11.

44. Ray Stannard Baker, "Railroads on Trial," *McClure's Magazine* 26 (March 1906): 535–44. The story is also told in Weinberg and Weinberg's, *The Muckrakers.*

45. Cutlip, *The Unseen Power,* 16.

46. "Department Press Agents," Hearing before Committee on Rules, House of Representatives, May 21, 1912, 62d Congress, 2d session (Washington, DC: Government Printing Office, 1912), 16. Also see William Kittle, "The Making of Public Opinion," *Arena* 41 (1909): 443–44.

47. As quoted in Cutlip, *The Unseen Power,* 30.

48. Ibid., 75.

49. Ibid., 92–103.

50. Ibid., 32–33.

51. Gordon A. Moon II, "George F. Parker: A 'Near Miss' as First White House Press Chief," *Journalism Quarterly* 41 (Spring 1964): 183–90.

52. Correspondence in Box 141, *General Leonard Wood Papers,* Library of Congress, suggests that the Parker and Bridge firm continued into the 1920s with Parker and Roy Mason as partners.

53. Goldman, *Two-Way Street.*

54. Quoted in Sherman Morse, "An Awakening on Wall Street," *American Magazine* 62 (September 1906): 460.

55. *Ivy L. Lee Papers,* Princeton University Library. Lee's correspondence of 1907 includes a letter from the president of Pennsylvania Railroad to a colleague in Southern Pacific, saying that he had concluded that the time had come to take measures to "place our case before the public."

56. Raucher, *Public Relations and Business.* For the definitive biography, see Ray Eldon Hiebert, *Courtier to the Crowd: The Story of Ivy L. Lee and the Development of Public Relations* (Ames: Iowa State University Press, 1966).

57. For testimony on this case, see *Investigation of Nazi and Other Propaganda: Public Hearings before a Subcommittee of the Committee on Un-American Activities, Hearing Number 73-NY-7* (Washington, DC: Government Printing Office 1934); and *Trials of War Criminals before the Nurenberg Military Tribunal,* volumes 7 and 8, Case Six, U.S. v. Krauch, "The I. G. Farben Case" (Washington, DC: Government

Printing Office, 1963). See also *Activities of Nondiplomatic Representatives of Foreign Principals in the United States, Hearings before Committee on Foreign Relations, U.S. Senate,* parts 1–13 (Washington, DC: Government Printing Office, 1963).

58. Rex F. Harlow, "Years of Challenge," an unpublished autobiography, 1982. Harlow's writings are cited elsewhere in this chapter and in chapter 1. His American Council on Public Relations is discussed in more detail in chapter 5.

59. George Juergens, *News from the White House: The Presidential-Press Relationship in the Progressive Era* (Chicago: University of Chicago Press, 1981), 70.

60. See full story in Joseph I. C. Clarke, *My Life and Memories* (New York: Dodd, Mead, 1955); and "A New Press Agent," *Editor and Publisher* 4 (May 12, 1906).

61. For the story of Ford's public relations, see David L. Lewis, *The Public Image of Henry Ford: An American Hero and His Company* (Detroit: Wayne State University Press, 1976).

62. Samuel Insull, *Central Station Electric Service* (Chicago: privately printed, 1915), 356.

63. See Noel L. Griese. "James D. Ellsworth, 1863–1940," *Public Relations Review* 4 (Summer 1978): 22–31.

64. For more on the development of public relations in higher education, see Scott M. Cutlip, "Advertising Higher Education: The Early Years of College Public Relations," *College and University Journal* 9 (November 1970), part I, and 10 (January 1971), part II.

65. Howard Weeks, "The Development of Public Relations as an Organized Activity in a Protestant Denomination" (Master's thesis, American University, 1963).

66. For a full account of public relations' role in fund-raising, see Scott M. Cutlip, *Fund Raising in the United States: Its Role in America's Philanthropy* (New Brunswick, NJ: Rutgers University Press, 1965), and Kathleen S. Kelly, *Effective Fund-Raising Management* (Mahwah, NJ: Lawrence Erlbaum Associates, 1997), Part II, "Historical Context of Fund Raising."

67. Edwin Emery, *History of American Newspaper Publishers Association* (Minneapolis: University of Minnesota Press, 1950), 125–30.

68. George Creel, *How We Advertised America* (New York: Harper & Brothers, 1920), and James O. Mock and Cedric Larson, *Words That Won the War* (Princeton: Princeton University Press, 1939).

69. Mock and Larson, *Words That Won the War,* 4.

70. *New York Times,* February 1, 1920, p. 9, col. 1.

71. Harold D. Lasswell, *Propaganda Techniques in the World War* (New York: Alfred A. Knopf, 1927), 220.

72. See Cutlip, *The Unseen Power,* 531–88, for detailed descriptions of the growth and tumultuous times of the Carl Byoir & Associates.

73. For a detailed chronicle of his own career, see Edward L. Bernays, *Biography of an Idea: Memoirs of Public Relations Counsel Edward L. Bernays* (New York: Simon and Schuster, 1965).

74. Pamel J. Creedon, "Public Relations History Misses 'Her Story,' " *Journalism Educator* 44, no. 3 (Autumn 1989): 26–30.

75. Doris Fleischman Bernays, *A Wife Is Many Women* (New York: Crown, 1955), 171. As quoted by Creedon in "Public Relations History," p. 28.

76. Susan Henry, "Dissonant Notes of a Retiring Feminist: Doris E. Fleischman's Later Years," *Journal of Public Relations Research* 10, no. 1 (1998), 1. (In 1955, she identified herself as "Doris Fleischman "Bernays" on the title page of her book, *A Wife Is Many Women*—as Henry's description of Fleischman's later life also so vividly portrays.)

77. Cutlip, *The Unseen Power,* 278–307.

78. Hill Papers (December 3, 1958, memo), as quoted in Cutlip, *The Unseen Power,* 518.

79. Cutlip, *The Unseen Power,* 487–88.

80. Ibid., 501.

81. Ibid., 527.

82. For this unsavory page in history, see *Utility Corporations: Efforts by Associations and Agencies of Electric and Gas Utilities to Influence Public Opinion,* Summary Report Prepared by Federal Trade Commission, 70th Congress 1st session, Senate Document 92, Part 71-A (Washington, DC: Government Printing Office, 1934). A popular summary is Ernest Gruening, *The Public Pays* (New York: Vanguard, 1931). For a kinder view, see McDonald, *Insull.*

83. John M. Shotwell, "Crystallizing Public Hatred: The Ku Klux Klan in the Early 1920s" (Master's thesis, University of Wisconsin-Madison, 1974).

84. George Griswold Jr., "How AT&T Public Relations Policies Developed," *Public Relations Quarterly* 12 (Fall 1967): 13. (A special issue devoted to AT&T's public relations.) Also see Noel L. Griese, "He Walked in the Shadows: Public Relations Counsel Arthur W. Page," *Public Relations Quarterly* 21 (Fall 1976).

85. *Membership Directory 1998* (New York: Arthur W. Page Society, 1998).

86. For a balanced view of Howe's contributions to FDR's career and his public relations ideas, see Alfred B. Rollins Jr., *Roosevelt and Howe* (New York: Alfred A. Knopf, 1962).

87. Marilyn Kern-Foxworth, "Minority Entrepreneurs Challenge the Barriers," *Public Relations Journal* 45, no. 8 (August 1989): 19.

88. Allan M. Winkler, *The Politics of Propaganda: The Office of War Information 1942–45* (New Haven: Yale University Press, 1978), 4.

89. For a quick study of the OWI, see Robert L. Bishop and LaMar S. Mackay, "Mysterious Silence, Lyrical Scream: Government Information in World War II," *Journalism Monographs* 19 (May 1971), based on their Ph.D. dissertations written at the University of Wisconsin.

90. Information based on Colonel Sidney A. Knutson's thesis, "History of Public Relations Program of U.S. Army" (University of Wisconsin, 1953). Also see Gordon W. Keiser, *The U.S. Marine Corps and Defense Unifications 1944–47* (Washington: National Defense University Press, 1982).

91. Thomas S. Repplier, "Advertising and 'The Forces of Righteousness,' " in *The Promise of Advertising,* edited by Charles H. Sandage (Homewood, IL: Richard D. Irwin, 1961), 59.

92. "Business Is Still in Trouble," *Fortune* 39 (May 1949) reflects business' postwar public relations problems. For a biting critique of some business efforts to deal with critics, see William H. Whyte, *Is Anybody Listening?* (New York: Simon and Schuster, 1952).

93. Alfred McClung Lee, "Trends in Public Relations Training," *Public Opinion Quarterly* 11 (Spring 1947): 83–91.

94. Public Relations Society of America, "Public Relations Education in American Colleges and Universities," August 1956. (Study directed by Hale Nelson, chairman of PRSA Education Committee.)

95. Ray E. Hiebert, "Public Relations Education in American Colleges and Universities 1964." (Report prepared for the Public Relations Society of America, 1964.)

96. Rex Harlow, "A Timeline of Public Relations," *Public Relations Review* 6 (Fall 1980): 5.

97. For implications of transition from a postindustrial to an information society, see Robert B. Reich, *The Next American Frontier* (New York: Times Books, 1983); and Rosabeth Moss Kanter, *The Change Masters* (New York: Simon and Schuster, 1983).

98. John Naisbitt, *Megatrends: Ten New Directions Transforming Our Lives* (New York: Warner Books, 1982); and John Naisbitt and Patricia Aburdene, *Megatrends 2000: Ten New Directions for the 1990s* (New York: William Morrow and Co., 1990) are still useful analyses of the implications of accelerating change.

99. John V. Pavlik, *New Media and the Information Superhighway* (Needham Heights, MA: Allyn & Bacon, 1996), 39.

100. Ibid., 40.

101. Frank Popoff, "The Incredible Shrinking World," *The Point Is . . .*, no. 127 (May 18, 1989): Dow Chemical Company, Midland, MI.

ADDITIONAL SOURCES

Creedon, Pamela J., ed. *Women in Mass Communication: Challenging Gender Values.* Newbury Park, CA: Sage Publications, 1989.

Cutlip, Scott M. *The Unseen Power: Public Relations—A History.* Hillsdale, NJ: Lawrence Erlbaum Associates, 1994.

Cutlip, Scott M. *Public Relations History: From the 17th to the 20th Century.* Hillsdale, NJ: Lawrence Erlbaum Associates, 1995.

Foxworth, Marilyn Fern. "African-American Achievements in Public Relations." *Public Relations Journal* 47, no. 2 (February 1991): 18–19.

Henry, Susan. "Anonymous in Her Own Name: Public Relations Pioneer Doris E. Fleischman." *Journalism History* 23, no. 2 (Summer 1997): 51–62.

Henry, Susan. "Dissonant Notes of a Retiring Feminist: Doris E. Fleischman's Later Years." *Journal of Public Relations Research* 10, no. 1 (1998): 1–33.

Hon, Linda Childers. "To Redeem the Soul of America: Public Relations and the Civil Rights Movement." *Journal of Public Relations Research* 9, no. 3 (1997): 163–212.

Olasky, Marvin N. *Corporate Public Relations: A New Historical Perspective.* Hillsdale, NJ: Lawrence Erlbaum Associates, 1987; and "The Development of Corporate Public Relations, 1850–1930." *Journalism Monograph* 102 (April 1987), by the same author. Critic recasts historical role of public relations as an attempt by corporations to limit competition.

Paisley, William J. "Public Communication Campaigns: The American Experience." In *Public Communication Campaigns,* 2d ed., edited by Ronald E. Rice and Charles K. Atkin, 15–38. Newbury Park, CA: Sage Publications, 1989.

Pearson, Ron. "Perspectives on Public Relations History." *Public Relations Review* 16, no. 3 (Fall 1990): 27–38.

Pratt, Cornelius B. "The 40-Year Tobacco Wars: Giving Public Relations a Black Eye?" *Public Relations Quarterly* 42, no. 4 (Winter 1997–98): 5–10.

"Public Relations in American History" (special issue). *Public Relations Review* 4 (Fall 1978). Lectures by historians Allan Nevins, Ray Allen Billington, Frank E. Vandiver, George F. G. Stanley, Eric F. Goldman, and Joe B. Frantz.

Raucher, Alan R. "Public Relations in Business: A Business of Public Relations." *Public Relations Review* 16, no. 3 (Fall 1990): 19–26.

ETHICS AND PROFESSIONALISM

5

If I have done my job well for the right purpose, my life has substance and meaning. If I have done my job poorly or for the wrong purpose, I have squandered my life, however much I have prospered.

—*John Kultgen*[1]

O B J E C T I V E S

After studying chapter 5, you should be able to

▼ Identify the major justification and motivations behind concern for professional ethics in public relations practice.

▼ List and briefly discuss the five positives of socially responsible public relations, as well as the three major negatives attributed to public relations when it is not practiced in the public interest.

▼ Outline the major arguments for and against licensing and accreditation of practitioners.

▼ List and describe the major professional organizations serving the field.

▼ Outline and apply some of the major articles from the Public Relations Society of America Code of Professional Standards.

Any discussion of the professional status of public relations necessarily begins with ethics. In fact, adherence to a code of professional ethics separates professions from other skilled occupations. Ethical issues take on added importance because professionals with special expertise have unprecedented power in decisions that affect every aspect of society. In the global village, where information and influence reach most parts of the world with amazing speed and ease, professional power and impact do not stop at national or cultural boundaries. Ethics and professionalism are global concerns, with social responsibility no longer simply a local issue.

This chapter explores the ethical and professional foundations of public relations practice. It also chronicles aspects of an occupation adopting the philosophy and trappings of a calling and an *emerging profession.*

ETHICAL FOUNDATIONS

You do not have to be a cynic to question the ethical foundations of some established professions. Evening news reports tell of physicians prescribing unnecessary tests and medications sold by laboratories and pharmacies that they themselves own, committing Medicare or insurance fraud, and performing costly (and sometimes risky) but unnecessary surgery. Critics point to some lawyers making top dollar as hired guns for special interests by filing lawsuits to harass and intimidate, to frustrate judicial process, or to obscure facts in legalese. Others have been convicted for absconding with clients' estates. Investigative journalists and prosecutors expose television ministers living in luxury and lust while preying on those most susceptible to fund-raising appeals and least able to support bogus but high-sounding missionaries.

Absence of rigorous policing of such pretenders and charlatans erodes public confidence. Ideally, professional societies or associations engage in self-policing to deter malfeasance, to enforce the collective morality, and to ensure that professionals will engage in what one writer calls "right conduct."[2] Spike Lee said the same thing in his movie title *Do the Right Thing.* Surely, the primary goal is to protect the client of professional services. At the same time, however, self-policing in the professions protects the professional franchise and maintains public trust and support for professional privilege.

Professional Ethics

Right conduct suggests that actions are consistent with moral values generally accepted as norms in a society or culture. In professions, the application of moral values in practice is referred to as "applied ethics."[3] Established professions translate widely shared ideas of right conduct into formal codes of ethics and professional conduct. These statements of applied ethics guide professional practice and provide the basis for enforcement and sanctions.

Thus, professional conduct is based on what are generally considered virtuous motives, monitored and assessed against established codes of conduct, and enforced through concrete interpretation for those who deviate from accepted standards of performance. The principle behind professional ethics is that one's actions are designed to create the greatest good for both the client and community as a whole rather than to enhance the position and power of the practitioner.

Why this concern for ethics and enforcement of codes of conduct? The answers are at the same time both simple and complex. The simple answer is to protect those who entrust their well-being to the professional. The more complex answer also includes concerns about protecting the profession itself: professional privilege, status, and collegiality.

The Imperative of Trust

Clients' relationships with professionals differ from their relationships with other providers of skills and services. For example, if you go to a hospital emergency room, it is unlikely that you will know the doctors and nurses who take care of you. Yet you will most likely have some degree of confidence that they are qualified and capable and, furthermore, that they will perform with your best interests in mind. Even if you are alert and able, it is unlikely that you will delay their performance while you check their transcripts to make sure they took the appropriate courses and passed all their exams, or ask them to justify their fee schedule or itemize anticipated costs. Contrast your relationship with these doctors and nurses with the one you establish with the mechanic or repair shop when your car needs major or emergency service.

The difference centers on the nature of fiduciary relationships. When you seek the services of a professional, you put yourself—not just your things—at risk. Your well-being is subject to the judgment and actions of the professional. Except in extreme circumstances, you maintain ultimate control, but you typically must reveal aspects of your person and behavior that normally remain private. In other words, you *trust* the professional with information and access that often are withheld from even your closest friends and family. Often, you actually *entrust* yourself and your possessions to the professional. That is, you enter a *fiduciary relationship,* meaning the professional holds you, and possibly your possessions, in trust and is obliged to act in your best interest. This obligation differentiates the professional from other knowledgeable and skilled artisans.[4]

Professional Privilege

Professionals traditionally hold privileged positions in society because of the value and trust inherent in fiduciary relationships. Additionally, professionals do work that is seen as especially valuable, in part because of the preparation and practice needed to develop the required knowledge and skills. Because money alone does not justly reward such work, society extends privileges to its practitioners. So not only must professionals invest a great deal of time to acquire and maintain their own knowledge and skills, but they must also commit themselves to uphold the profession by honoring its obligations and values.

When professionals violate fiduciary relationships or otherwise exploit clients, or when they perform substandard practice, they threaten not only their client's welfare but that of their entire profession. Professional privilege rests on the foundation of public trust and confidence in both the professional's expertise and right conduct.

To protect both clients and their own privileged positions in society, professions establish codes of ethics and standards of practice. These codes often have the weight of law and the power of state sanctions. The argument for codes and rigorous enforcement rests on the belief that professional work involves special and valuable knowledge and skill essential to the public good and is so esoteric and complex that only those deemed qualified may engage in practice.[5]

Professional privilege rests, therefore, on the implicit agreement among the profession, the public, and the state. Here is "the deal":

> Protect my members from the unfettered competition of a free market, and you can trust them to put your interest before their own. I will select them carefully and train and organize them to provide competent and ethical service.[6]

Simply put, professional privilege extends beyond an individual practitioner's relationship with client and colleagues; it also includes obligations derived from an implicit contract with the larger society.

Social Responsibility

Professions, then, must also fulfill expectations and moral obligations at the level of society. Commitment to serve society applies to both individual practitioners and the profession collectively. It means that right conduct takes into account the welfare of the larger society as the professional helps clients solve problems. It also means that associations of professionals exercise collective power as moral agents and watchdogs for the betterment of society. To fulfill their social responsibilities, professionals are expected to do more than provide knowledge and skilled services; they are "held responsible for improving the institutions administering those services."[7]

Because public relations has impact well beyond the boundaries of client organizations, individual practitioners must be concerned with both the intended and the unintended consequences of the function. Collectively through their professional associations they must take responsibility for prescribing standards of competence, defining standards of conduct, establishing educational and accreditation requirements, encouraging research to expand the body of knowledge that guides the practice, and representing the profession in matters affecting the profession's charter and social mission.[8]

Ultimately, public relations is judged on its impact on society. Public relations' social utility is enhanced when (1) it promotes the free, ethical competition of ideas, individuals, and institutions in the marketplace of public opinion; (2) it reveals the sources and goals underlying attempts to influence; and (3) it enforces high standards of conduct. Social utility is diminished when (1) it suppresses or otherwise limits competition of ideas, (2) it hides or ascribes to others the true sources of public relations efforts, and (3) it leaves unchallenged incompetent or unethical practice.

Positives

The major positives of socially responsible public relations include:

1. Public relations improves professional practice by codifying and enforcing ethical conduct and standards of performance.
2. Public relations improves the conduct of organizations by stressing the need for public approval.
3. Public relations serves the public interest by making all points of view articulate in the public forum.
4. Public relations serves our segmented, scattered society by using communication and mediation to replace misinformation with information, discord with rapport.
5. Public relations fulfills its social responsibility to promote human welfare by helping social systems adapt to changing needs and environments.

Much good can be credited to ethical public relations practice, and opportunities for serving the public interest abound. Public relations' benefits are apparent in the billions of dollars raised to construct buildings, endow professorships, and provide scholarships in universities; in campaigns to eradicate disease and substance abuse, reduce poverty, improve nutrition, and house the homeless; in the lessening of ethnic, racial, and religious discrimination and conflict; in responsive economic enterprises providing profit for investors, jobs for employees, and goods and services for consumers; and in greater understanding of global problems and relations. The potential good inherent in ethical, effective public relations is limitless. So is the potential for social dysfunction.

Negatives

Three major negatives can be attributed to the practice:

1. Public relations gains advantages for and promotes special interests, sometimes at the cost of the public well-being.
2. Public relations clutters already choked channels of communication with the debris of pseudoevents and phony phrases that confuse rather than clarify.
3. Public relations corrodes our channels of communication with cynicism and credibility gaps.

Too often the thrust of public relations is to obfuscate and obscure rather than to clarify complex public issues. Robert Heilbroner recognized public relations as a social force and charged it with a major part "in the general debasement of communications from which we suffer." He said,

> No one can quarrel with the essential function that public relations fills as a purveyor of genuine ideas and information. No one denies that many public relations men, working for corporations as well as for colleges or causes, honestly commu-

nicate things which are worth communication. Nor can anyone absolve public relations for loading the communications channels with noise. We read the news and suspect that behind it lies the "news release." We encounter the reputation and ascribe it to publicity. Worst of all, we no longer credit good behavior with good motives, but cheapen it to the level of "good public relations."[9]

Practitioners also stand accused, with some validity, of loading our communication channels with noise and clogging them with the clutter of manufactured stories. Expressing these concerns, historian Daniel Boorstin argued that "pseudoevents" blur, rather than clarify, public issues. In his book, *The Image,* Boorstin wrote,

> The disproportion between what an informed citizen needs to know and what he can know is even greater. The disproportion grows with the increase of the officials' power of concealment and contrivance. The news gatherers' need to select, invent, and plan correspondingly increases. Thus inevitably our whole system of public information produces always more "packaged" news, more pseudoevents.[10]

Although Boorstin primarily blamed journalists for this, practitioners produce the majority of pseudoevents covered by the media. Surely few would deny that events planned to promote a cause in the public interest do have a legitimate place in public relations. It is the phony events to promote dubious causes that come under fire. Precious news space and time given to a celebrity's honorary degree, a ribbon-cutting ceremony, or an orchestrated photo opportunity preempts explaining the complexities of the plight of the homeless, the national debt, the breakup of the Soviet Union, or international trade relations. Ethical public relations contributes to clarification of public issues, not to their displacement, distortion, or obfuscation.

This social aspect of right conduct reminds us that both individual practitioners and the profession as a whole are entrusted with the welfare of larger society as a condition on how they serve clients. This aspect of ethics is referred to as the profession's "social responsibility." When choosing such work and life, one also takes on the social responsibility of the profession, as well as its knowledge, skills, trust, and privileges.

In summary, to qualify as a profession, practitioners—both individually and collectively—must operate as moral agents in society. Ethical professional practice requires placing public service and social responsibility over personal gains and private special interests.

OTHER PROFESSIONAL FOUNDATIONS

Concern for the ethical behavior in public relations addresses the emerging profession's effort to qualify morally. Other moves toward professional status derive from the caliber of training required of aspiring professionals and the conduct of basic research to guide the practice. These represent efforts to qualify through knowledge and expertise. In addition, practitioners and their organizations increasingly take on the institutional, procedural, and membership rules of other professions, in short, to qualify *functionally*.

Keep in mind, however, that the concept of a profession is not the product of logic. Rather, as legal historian Willard J. Hurst pointed out in an early issue of *Public Relations Journal,* "practice and experience in making society function have led to the definition of some occupations as professional, and have from time to time determined which ways of earning a living should fit the professional category."[11] Many callings—nursing, financial planning, and real estate, to name but a few—are striving for professional status. Few have earned it. Much of the effort is self-serving; some of it is public-spirited.

Attempts to achieve professional status might be considered selfish by some, but the results of increased professionalism benefits society as a whole. Professionalization institutionalizes the best practices and establishes standards of quality that serve the public interest. Professionalization has, by and large, brought us better health care; safer highways and bridges; better houses; faster cars and airplanes; and higher standards in business, banking, and accounting. We would add to this list more competent public relations counsel.

To assess the progress of contemporary practice and the calling toward achieving the status of a profession, we need criteria. In addition to the ethical foundation and moral imperative outlined in the previous section, other indicators of professional status include the following:

1. Specialized educational preparation to acquire unique knowledge and skills, based on a body of theory developed through research
2. Recognition by the community of a unique and essential service
3. Autonomy in practice and acceptance of personal responsibility by practitioners
4. Codes of ethics and standards of performance enforced by a self-governing association of colleagues

In summary, for public relations to achieve professional status, there must be specialized educational programs, a body of knowledge, community recognition, individual accountability, and commitment to abide by established codes that protect the public interest and spell out social responsibility.

PROFESSIONAL EDUCATION

As a leading public relations practitioner told students at Ball State University, "Public relations will never reach the status of a profession as long as people can get into the field and prosper without having completed a fairly rigorous course of study in the field."[12] True enough, established professions require extended periods of training to learn the knowledge and skills needed to practice; generally the more rigorous the training and the more esoteric the knowledge, the higher the professional status.

Because preparation is standardized and demanding, those entering professions go through similar initiations to the values and expectations of practice. Their common socialization experience not only standardizes the practice but also encourages commitment to lifelong careers and strong bonds with colleagues. Because of the commitment, time, and effort invested in acquiring the knowledge and skill base, professionals value achievement in the intellectual aspects of their fields.[13]

Degree Programs

University-level instruction in public relations dates from 1920. Concurrent with the beginning of the publicity boom of that era, Joseph F. Wright introduced a publicity course at the University of Illinois, frankly admitting that the course was created to bring prestige to his new calling. Two years later, in 1922, Frank R. Elliott introduced a publicity course at Indiana University. Both Wright and Elliott organized the first institutional publicity programs for their universities. Teaching the publicity courses on a part-time basis gave these pioneers the faculty status they needed to earn support among colleagues who looked askance at "propagandists."[14]

Edward L. Bernays, who had just written *Crystallizing Public Opinion,* offered the first public relations course in 1923. Bernays taught the one-semester-credit course for two years in the journalism department of New York University's School of Commerce, Accounts, and Finance. By 1946, 30 colleges offered 47 courses.[15] In 1956 the Public Relations Society of America (PRSA) made the first comprehensive survey of public relations education and found that the number of colleges offering courses had tripled in a decade.[16] Another survey financed by PRSA in 1970 identified 303 institutions offering one or more courses and increasing scholarly research activity.[17] The 1981 Commission on Public Relations Education estimated that 10,000 students were taking public relations courses at some 300 institutions.[18] In 1987 a similar commission found more than 160 colleges and universities offering public relations sequences or degree programs associated with journalism schools and departments but made no estimate of how many programs reside in communication and speech departments.[19] PRSA's 1991 guide, *Where to Study Public Relations,* lists 212 colleges and universities in the United States, Canada, Puerto Rico, and Australia.[20] In addition, there are respected programs in Austria, England, and Germany.

Wherever it is housed, public relations education has attracted the attention of practitioners, as well as large numbers of students. The most recent commission recommended that undergraduate public relations programs contain no more than 25 percent course work in the major, with the rest devoted to liberal arts, sciences, and other general education courses. The commission also recommended that only half the course work in the major be specifically identified as public relations content. Without identifying specific courses, the commission listed five core content areas of study:

1. *Principles, practices, and theory of public relations:* Introduces theories, managerial tasks, and ethical responsibilities. This is a concepts and principles course, not a skills or production course.

2. *Public relations techniques:* Writing, message dissemination, and media networks. Stresses writing, designing, editing, and distributing written materials used in public relations practice. Includes print, broadcast, and audiovisual media.
3. *Public relations research for planning and evaluation:* Introduces the use of research to identify problems and publics, to determine action and communication strategies, and to assess program results. Includes both fact-finding and evaluative research methods used in public relations decision making.
4. *Public relations strategy and implementation:* Employs case-method and campaign-planning approaches to give students experiences in program planning, managerial analysis, and program administration. Applies decision theory and management theories to public relations strategic planning.
5. *Supervised public relations experience:* Provides hands-on experience in an internship, practicum, or cooperative education setting. Typically takes the form of a carefully structured, supervised professional assignment in a public relations department or firm.[21]

The commission also suggested specialized advanced study in a specialized area of public relations practice, such as publicity and media relations, community relations, financial and investor relations, employee relations, or international relations. Additional recommended course work includes communication theory and process; history and structure of mass communication; and communication production: writing and editing, graphics and typography, photography, electronic media, and public speaking.

The recommended graduate curriculum includes either a thesis research project or comprehensive examinations and the following core courses:

1. *Communication Theory:* Examines principal theories, processes, and models, including concepts and systems.
2. *Communication Research:* Includes data analysis and logic related to research design and procedures.
3. *Research Design and Critical Analysis:* Examines contemporary research methodology and original research designs emphasizing hypothesis testing.
4. *Communication in Society:* Explores role and impact of communication (particularly mass media). Considers historical, legal, and economic issues.
5. *Advanced Public Relations Case Studies:* Examines representative public relations organizations, their problems, and their procedures.
6. *Public Relations Management:* Analyzes public relations as a primary management responsibility, emphasizing resolution of conflicts between private and public sectors of society.[22]

Europe's first postgraduate degree in public relations was offered by the School of Management at the University of Stirling, Scotland, UK. Established in 1988, the Master of Science in Public Relations includes a curriculum similar to what is offered in U.S. universities, emphasizing theory and practice, management, ethics, research and evaluation, and media training.

Continuing Education

Professions require continuing education to keep practitioners current in theory and skills. PRSA and International Association of Business Communicators (IABC) now encourage members to earn continuing education units (CEUs) for participating in some professional development seminars and workshops. For example, IABC program literature explains:

> CEUs allow you to build a permanent record of achievement which may be used as evidence of increased performance capabilities and job advancement. The CEU officially is defined as 10 contact hours of participation in an organized continuing education experience under responsible sponsorship, capable direction and qualified instruction.

As of 1993, all accredited (APR) members of PRSA must earn points from continuing education, professional development, and public service to maintain their accredited status. The requirement to maintain current expertise and skills and to perform public service moves the field even closer to the more established professions. Continuing education also demonstrates commitment to the lifetime of learning needed to provide clients current and competent service, part of any profession's implicit contract with society.

RESEARCH AND THE BODY OF KNOWLEDGE

Ideally, professional higher education introduces aspiring practitioners to the body of theory and skills upon which the profession is based. Continuing education then keeps practitioners up to date on research developments that expand the body of knowledge. Not everyone, however, accepts the concept of a body of knowledge and the value of basic research. Few practitioners subscribe to or read the field's research journals. Even some board members of foundations and institutes ostensibly established to encourage basic research talk about scholarly research with disdain and try to divert resources to producing "news you can use."

One sure sign of advancement toward professional status is the increasing demand for research and critical examination of the conventional wisdom guiding the practice. Public relations problems in business and industry, for example, are every bit as tough and complicated as the problems faced by engineering, finance, production, or distribution. Practitioners must approach them as methodically and as thoroughly prepared as engineers, economists, and other managers approach their own. Such a scientific approach requires understanding based on a body of knowledge developed through extensive research. Hence, the oft said, "Nothing is more practical than a good theory."

Body of Knowledge Project

The PRSA research committee headed by then–US West Communications public relations executive George Fowler began in 1986 what became known as the PRSA Body of Knowledge Project. This group took on the tasks of identifying relevant theory and research publications, abstracting the books and articles included in the inventory, and publishing updated bibliographies and abstracts.[23]

The literature serving the field reflects the gap between the immediate information needs of practitioners and the theory-building research conducted by scholars. For example, the content of PRSA's *Public Relations Tactics* and IABC's *Communication World* primarily reflect practitioners' interest in day-to-day problems and techniques related to designing and implementing programs and what one practitioner called "news you can use." The independent *Public Relations Quarterly* features commentaries and scholarly analyses, book reviews, and regular columnists of interest to practitioners. PRSA's slick *Public Relations Strategist* quarterly addresses issues and trends of interest to public relations professionals and—according to the magazine's promotional literature—their peers, meaning "the chief executive officer, marketing managers, and financial and human resources executives." On the other hand, the scholarly journals—*Public Relations Review* and *Journal of Public Relations Research*—report research on the social context of public relations, professionalism, and theory development related to the practice. The literature mirrors classic concerns of other emerging professions: preoccupation and introspection during the search for collective identity, justification, and recognition.[24]

Support for Research

Because professions draw upon a specialized body of knowledge developed through research, practitioners are obligated to support the advancement of professional knowledge. To that end, PRSA established the Foundation for Public Relations Research and Education in 1956 to advance professionalism in public relations by funding research, disseminating scholarly writings, and promoting professional education. The foundation initiated a fellowship program enabling university faculty to work in counseling firms or corporations and awarded scholarships to public relations graduate students. The foundation began sponsoring a series of annual lectures in 1961. Perhaps its most important contributions, however, were in subsidizing much-needed books, publishing *Public Relations Review* (the field's first scholarly journal), and funding a series of public relations bibliographies.

During the 1980s, however, the foundation drifted from its original mission and began to exert its independence from PRSA. Directors funded failed attempts to introduce public relations education in business schools and pushed to broaden the appeal of *Public Relations Review* beyond the scholarly research audience. In 1988, culminating a long-running debate over the role of the scholarly journal, the foundation cut off financial support and transferred ownership to the founding editor. In the foundation's announcement of ownership change, it promised a new publication providing "information and ideas based primarily on the day-to-day experience of experts," but none appeared. Completing the change and separation from PRSA in 1989, the foundation changed its name to the Institute for Public Relations Research and Education. It also broadened its mission to "improve the effectiveness of organizational management by advancing the knowledge and practice of public relations and public affairs."

The institute, now based at the University of Florida, continues to fund public relations research projects, publish important books for the field, recognize outstanding scholarship, and award undergraduate and graduate scholarships. Its annual Pathfinder Award recognizes outstanding research contributions to the body of knowledge. The annual master's thesis award and graduate research grants encourage advanced public relations studies. The Institute's annual Ketchum Public Relations–funded "SMART" (Scientific Measurement And Research Techniques) grant supports a graduate student's research and includes a paid eight-week internship in Ketchum's New York office.

During the late 1980s and 1990s, however, the IABC Research Foundation became the major funding agency for public relations research. Estimated to total more than $400,000, its Excellence in Public Relations and Communication Management project explored the function's contributions to the bottom line and identified factors contributing to organizational success. Professor James Grunig at the University of Maryland led a team of researchers from the United States and the United Kingdom that produced comprehensive reviews of theory and research and also collected data from more than 200 organizations in the United States, Canada, and the United Kingdom.[25]

The Literature

The University of Wisconsin Press published the first comprehensive bibliography of public relations books and periodical literature in 1957. This first bibliography of the field was compiled by Scott M. Cutlip and was funded by a grant from the then Foundation for Public Relations Research and Education. The second edition, published in 1965, carried nearly 6,000 entries of books and articles relevant to the practice. The third edition in 1974 added 4,000 titles to the growing body of literature. The fourth issue of *Public Relations Review* in 1975 began that journal's series of updated bibliographies.[26] The first such bibliography produced in conjunction with the PRSA Body of Knowledge Project appeared in the spring 1988 issue of *Public Relations Review*.[27] Dramatic increases in the number of scholarly books and journals relevant to public relations practice indicate a growing knowledge base for study and practice and make annual attempts to catalog all new entries more difficult.

Publication in 1975 of public relations' first scholarly journal, *Public Relations Review,* marked an important milestone for the field. The Foundation recognized that there was an increasing number of scholars engaged in theory-building research. The same foundation funded a second scholarly journal in 1984—*Public Relations Research and Education.* Although only three semiannual issues were published, it provided the impetus for three subsequent volumes of *Public Relations Research Annual* (1989–1991). Reflecting the continuing growth of scholarly research, in 1992 the annual became the quarterly *Journal of Public Relations Research. Public Relations Review* and *Journal of Public Relations Research* are the primary publications sharing scholarly research, theoretical discourse, and criticism of the field.

PRSA's monthly *Public Relations Journal*—started in 1944 by one of the organization's founders, Rex F. Harlow—ceased publication in 1995. Like its successor, the tabloid-format *Public Relations Strategist,* it emphasized professionalism, discussed techniques used in practice, presented case histories, and provided a forum for debate on practice and ethics. *Public Relations Quarterly,* started in 1954 as the publication of the then-named American Public Relations Association (APRA), is similar in purpose and content, although its articles are somewhat longer and less how-to oriented. Since 1961, when APRA merged with PRSA, *Public Relations Quarterly* has been privately published. The International Public Relations Association began a quarterly journal, *International Public Relations Review,* in 1977. Edited in the organization's Geneva office, this journal includes thoughtful commentaries, status reports on public relations around the globe, and an international perspective on the practice.

Three national weekly newsletters—the major ones in a growing field—report current news, opinions, and how-to information: *Public Relations News,* started in 1944; *pr reporter,* started in 1958; and *Jack O'Dwyer's Newsletter,* started in 1967. In addition, publications such as *PR Week* (weekly) and *O'Dwyer's PR Services Report* (monthly), as well as numerous regional and specialized newsletters, publish news, features, and how-to articles of interest to practitioners. (See Exhibit 5.1, pg. 156.)

Of course, volumes of analyses and research reports do not get published and widely disseminated. Most research conducted by public relations departments and firms is considered proprietary and is therefore not shared beyond the sponsoring organization. Often such research addresses specific issues and publics at a particular time and does not draw on or contribute to the body of theory. If publications do result from such case studies and descriptive surveys, they tend to take the form of "how-public-relations-saved-the-day" reports. As a result, much of what passes as research in the literature consists of selectively published narratives that do not test or build theory and therefore add little to the body of knowledge and literature of the field.

LICENSING AND ACCREDITATION

Pioneer counselor Edward L. Bernays was among the first to advocate licensing. In 1953 he argued, "In the entire history of professions, licensing standards and criteria and finally codes of ethics in public conduct have been necessary . . . to exclude those who are not properly qualified."[28] The indefatigable Bernays was still thumping the same drum more than 50 years later: "We must get the two words, public relations, defined by law with licensing and registration of practitioners, as is the case with lawyers, medical doctors and other professionals. Today the term 'public relations' is in the public

EXHIBIT 5.1

PUBLICATIONS

Scholarly Journals

Journal of Public Relations Research, Lawrence Erlbaum Associates, Inc., 10 Industrial Avenue, Mahwah, NJ 07430 (Ed.: Elizabeth L. Toth, School of Public Communications, Syracuse University, 215 University Place, Syracuse, NY 13244)

Public Relations Review, JAI Press Inc., 55 Old Post Road No. 2, P.O. Box 1678, Greenwich, CN 06836 (Ed.: Ray E. Hiebert, College of Journalism, University of Maryland, College Park, MD 20742)

Professional Periodicals

Communications World, International Association of Business Communicators, One Hallidie Plaza, Suite 600, San Francisco, CA 94102 (nine issues annually)

International Public Relations Review, International Public Relations Association, CP 2100, CH-1211, Geneva 2, Switzerland (quarterly)

O'Dwyer's PR Services Report, J. R. O'Dwyer Company, Inc., 271 Madison Avenue, New York, NY 10016 (monthly)

Public Relations Strategist, Public Relations Society of America, 33 Irving Place, New York, NY 10003 (quarterly)

Public Relations Quarterly, 44 West Market Street, Rhinebeck, NY 12572

PR Week, PR Publications Ltd., 220 Fifth Avenue, New York, NY 10001

Newsletters

Jack O'Dwyer's Newsletter, 271 Madison Avenue, New York, NY 10016

PR News, Phillips Publishing, Inc., 7811 Montrose Road, Potomac, MD 20854

PR Reporter, PR Publishing Company, Inc., P.O. Box 600, Exeter, NH 03833

---

domain and anyone—many without training, education, or ethical behavior—is welcome to use it to describe what he or she professes to do."[29] Yet practitioners in the United States remain divided on the feasibility and desirability of licensing.

Legal Considerations

The issue of occupational licensure—the permission granted by the state to engage in a specific occupation—raises three basic constitutional issues: (1) the right of freedom of expression, (2) the right of the states to regulate occupations, and (3) the right of individuals to pursue occupations without unjustified state interference. Licensure must be justified on the grounds that it is crucial to the well-being and preservation of society.

Two serious constitutional issues are raised in the matter of licensing. One is the problem of demonstrating a compelling state interest; the other is safeguarding the practitioner's freedom of expression. The right of the states to regulate occupations is based on the Tenth Amendment, which reserves for states (or people) all powers not specifically delegated to federal government. Of course the First Amendment protects freedom of speech.

In recent years, the courts have raised the lower limits of what is defined as "compelling state interest." The two broad reasons generally given for public relations licensure—protection of society and professionalization of practition-ers—must be considered carefully in the light of "compelling state interest."

The first of these reasons, that public relations can harm society by "cor-rupting the public channels of communications," is the stronger of the two, yet it is weak in the eyes of the courts. Although public relations has the po-tential for abuse, its actions may be no more dangerous to society as a whole than would be those exercised directly by the organization for whom the practitioner might act. And although public relations may be controversial, the courts have argued in cases such as *Adams* v. *Tanner,* 244 U.S. 590 (1917), and *Baker* v. *Daly,* 15 F. Supp.2d 881, that controversy is not sufficient cause to regulate. The argument that licensing would protect society is directly re-futed in law. The courts have consistently found that even abusive communi-cation merits protection under the First Amendment.

The second of these reasons, that licensure would professionalize the practice, also gets short shrift in the law. It may be a powerful professional ar-gument, but it has no legal basis. In no case have the courts suggested that be-cause licensing would be beneficial, it would be justifiable. Licensing cannot be imposed simply for the benefit of those in an occupational group, either to raise standards or to fence out competition.

Nor can the question of infringement of freedom of expression be easily dismissed. If the state did license practitioners, the exact degree of infringe-ment of the practitioner's right of expression would most likely be minimal. What is at issue here is the right to the title "certified public relations coun-selor." The Supreme Court stated in *Time* v. *Hill,* 385 U.S. 374, that constitu-tional guarantees of free speech and press are not so much for the benefit of those concerned "as for the benefit of the citizens generally." In developing a measure of fitness that involves the competence to communicate, the state would be recognizing different competencies in individuals. Yet the right to freedom of expression is accorded to all, as contrasted with the privilege of practicing medicine, which is not guaranteed in the Constitution.

Advocates counter that licensing would be voluntary, thereby avoiding conflicts with the constitutionally protected rights. Likewise, organizations cannot be forced to hire only licensed practitioners. Instead, state licensing would limit only the use of the title "licensed public relations practitioner" or a similar title using the "licensed" label, not the right of free expression. Ad-vocates also point out that employers and clients would soon learn the value of hiring licensed professionals. They also argue that states could work out reciprocity agreements whereby licenses issued by one state would be hon-ored by other states, assuming similar examinations and criteria are estab-lished.[30]

A bill "to provide for the issuance of licenses for public relations coun-selors" was introduced in the Massachusetts legislature in late 1991 to com-memorate the late Edward Bernays's 100th birthday. If it had been passed, the bill would have established a licensing board; spelled out "good character, education and examination" as requirements for licensure; prohibited those without licenses from using titles that include "public relations," "communica-tion," or "corporate communication"; and authorized use of current accreditation exams for the purposes of licensing. The 1992 legislative hearings made it clear that the bill was more symbolic and honorific of Bernays than reflective of a consensus in the public relations community. On the whole, it appears that licensure will not soon provide a means of elevating and standardizing the preparation, ethics, and competence of practitioners.

Accreditation

In the absence of state licensing, PRSA, IABC, and several state and specialized associations have programs to certify practitioners. Such accreditation programs typically require a written examination and an oral defense before a panel of qualified peers. Beginning in 1991, PRSA began an accreditation maintenance program, requiring accredited members to remain active in continuing education and public service. To retain their "Accredited Public Relations" designation (or APR, printed after their names), accredited members must earn 10 points every three years through education, professional development, and public service activities. PRSA lifted the maintenance requirement in 1996 for all members who earned their APR prior to 1991. IABC's accreditation program—Accredited Business Communicator—requires a portfolio presentation in addition to written and oral examinations. According to IABC literature, "'ABC' after your name is a mark of professional achievement and commitment" that indicates that a practitioner has moved "from craft levels to communication management levels."

Approximately one of every five eligible PRSA members—those in practice five or more years—are accredited, or 4,000. An even smaller number of IABC members (about 600)—less than 5 percent of the membership—have passed that organization's accreditation exam.

For almost two decades, advocates of accreditation have proposed consolidation of the many accreditation programs under a single certification program. One suggestion was to form a "public relations council" as a single accrediting body and to bring the combined weight of the many associations and societies to bear on practitioners who violate codes of ethics and professional behavior. Such a council would set and maintain high professional and commercial standards and arbitrate complaints about the conduct of individual practitioners, departments, and firms.

Unfortunately, proposals for a single accreditation program usually died because of lack of interest and territorial jealousies among the professional organizations. For example, when the North American Public Relations Council proposed "universal accreditation" (UA) in 1998, the Agricultural Relations Council, Florida Public Relations Association, Maine Public Relations Council, Society for Healthcare Strategy & Market Development, Southern Public Relations Federation, and Texas Public Relations Association joined PRSA to create a new standardized accreditation process. IABC opted to keep its accreditation program separate. IABC's Accreditation Council chair said UA "is not in the best interest of our members worldwide" because

> (1) IABC's program has an evaluative segment (portfolio) as part of the process; UA does not; (2) IABC's program is entirely peer-created and peer-reviewed; UA

is not; (3) IABC's program is global; the UA program currently only covers only North America.

In summary, a single, well-publicized, and strongly enforced accreditation program is needed to move public relations toward professional status. Current practice continues to be guided by weak voluntary codes, splintered efforts by different associations and societies, and no state licensing. This situation weakens claims of professionalism and high ethical standards.

PROFESSIONAL ORGANIZATIONS

The growth of professional associations reflects the serious efforts being made by many practitioners to surround the function with status and to advance its competence. One directory lists 215 such groups in 72 countries with combined membership of more than 150,000.[31] Although these associations include only a small portion of all those working in the public relations field, they exert considerable influence through their publications, conferences, seminars, awards programs, and advocacy for the practice.

 ### Public Relations Society of America (PRSA)

The largest professional organization is the Public Relations Society of America, with more than 20,000 members in 113 chapters. Headquartered in New York City, PRSA traces its origins to three older associations established to bring together practitioners of this growing vocation.

PRSA was formed February 4, 1948, by the merger of the National Association of Public Relations Counsel (NAPRC) and the American Council on Public Relations (ACPR). The NAPRC was first organized in 1936 as the National Association of Accredited Publicity Directors. Composed largely of New York City practitioners without any official accreditation process, it used the words *national* and *accredited* in a very loose sense. It changed its name in 1944 to reflect the shift of emphasis to public relations. The ACPR was started in San Francisco in 1939 as an association for West Coast practitioners.

The goal of forward-looking practitioners and educators for a strong national association, serving all fields of practice, was finally realized July 1, 1961, when the American Public Relations Association (APRA) merged into PRSA. Headquartered in Washington, DC, and dominated by trade-association practitioners, APRA had been organized in 1944 after a seven-year effort by Washington practitioners. At the time of the merger in 1961, PRSA had 3,359 members and the APRA 826; 100 practitioners held membership in both organizations.

APRA made two contributions to the advancement of public relations: its Silver Anvil Awards to recognize successful programs and its *Quarterly Review of Public Relations,* later renamed in turn *PR Quarterly* and *Public Relations Quarterly.* PRSA continued the Silver Anvil Awards program but dropped APRA's quarterly publication in favor of the now-discontinued monthly *Public Relations Journal,* which ACPR had begun in 1944.

PRSA fosters the exchange of ideas through its publications and meetings, promotes a sense of professionalism, provides opportunities for continuing education, and encourages ethical behavior and high standards of practice. Its strength and scope were greatly enhanced in 1977 when the National Communication Council for Human Services, the organization of practitioners serving the health and welfare fields, voted to consolidate its membership and services with those of PRSA.

The counselors in the PRSA organized a "counselors' section" in 1960 as a means of dealing more effectively with the problems of special concern to public relations firms. This section studied counseling fees, issued a booklet defining the role of the counselor, and in 1963 gained PRSA's approval of a voluntary plan of self-accreditation, based on character, experience, and examination. This section is now the Counselors Academy and requires PRSA accreditation (APR) for membership. PRSA members who were engaged in association work followed suit in 1963 when they won approval for a "business and professional association section," now known as the Association Section. A government section—now Public Affairs and Government Section—was formed in 1970, and other interest groups have since organized. There are now 16 sections: Association, Corporate, Counselors Academy, Educational and Cultural Organizations, Educators, Employee Communications, Environment, Financial Communications, Food and Beverage, Health Academy, International, Multicultural Communications, Professional Services, Public Affairs and Government, Technology, and Travel and Tourism.

Following the split with the Foundation (now the Institute) for Public Relations Research and Education in 1989, PRSA established another foundation to support research, to fund scholarships, and to publish materials. Its major projects have been establishing the Body of Knowledge Project and establishing a series of awards and scholarships to encourage research and professionalism in public relations.

 ## International Association of Business Communicators (IABC)

Progress toward increased professionalism and higher standards in public relations has been greatly advanced by the emergence of the IABC as a strong organization. Founded in 1970 when the Association of Industrial Editors and the International Council of Industrial Editors merged, IABC grew from 3,500 members to almost 13,000 members today. In 1974 the association became an international organization when the Corporate Communicators of Canada merged with IABC. U.S. membership totals approximately 9,500, Canadian membership 2,500, and there are 1,000 in other countries. The association has 120 chapters in 14 countries, including Australia, Belgium, Canada, Hong Kong, Malaysia, Mexico, Netherlands, New Zealand, Philippines, Slovenia, South Africa, United Kingdom, United States, and Southern Africa. IABC also has affiliations with European Association of Public Relations Officers (CERP PRO) and the British Association of Communicators in Business (BACB). The IABC headquarters is in San Francisco.

To advance the competence and ethics of this field, IABC created a professional development guide for practitioners to help them identify the skills and knowledge necessary for attaining career goals and an ethics review committee to enforce a code of ethics. The code of ethics emphasizes that the principles of professional communication—it is legal, ethical, and in good taste—apply worldwide. Its Gold Quill and EXCEL awards programs set standards for and recognize excellence in communication program design and implementation. Its *Communication World* magazine, published nine times a year, serves as a news source on emerging issues and a reference on communication trends, theory, and practice. IABC's belief that communication should be a management function is supported with a program to reach key educators. IABC also formed a foundation in 1982 to support education and research. Its primary activities during the 1990s included publishing reports from the Excellence in Public Relations and Communication Management and Velvet Ghetto projects, recognizing leadership in the field, and continuing to commission research.

Canadian Public Relations Society (CPRS)

Founded in 1948, the same year as PRSA, CPRS has almost 2,000 members in 15 chapters. One-third of the members are accredited. CPRS publishes a quarterly newsletter, *Communiqué,* and holds an annual conference. Headquartered in Ottawa, Ontario, CPRS closely parallels PRSA in philosophy and programming.

Institute of Public Relations (United Kingdom) (IPR)

Also founded in 1948, IPR has 12 regional groups and a total of 3,500 members. It has long been a leader in establishing and enforcing codes of professional and ethical conduct and in encouraging academic preparation and professional development within the profession. IPR publishes *Public Relations* eight times a year and sponsors the Communication Advertising and Marketing Education Foundation.

Public Relations Consultants Association (United Kingdom) (PRCA)

The Public Relations Consultants Association, an association of "consultancies"—called "firms" in the United States—was formed in 1969 to promote professional standards in consultancy practice, to act as a clearinghouse for clients seeking counseling in public relations, and to represent members' interests. Only its 160 member consultancies may use the title "registered public relations consultants." In addition to publishing consultancy costs and other research, the association works closely with IPR in promoting the profession and in establishing standards of practice. For example, in 1998 PRCA introduced mandatory standards for member firms. The association's charter, definitions, guidelines, codes, and arbitration and disciplinary procedures formed the basis for those adopted by the European Community nations.

PRCA guidelines for member consultancies suggest that all staff members pledge compliance with the association's charter requirements. Furthermore, the guidelines call for a clause of charter compliance in all employment contracts. As longtime professional leader Tim Traverse-Healy told the authors in London, the guidelines indicate the way "responsible practitioners here are beginning to think and act."

International Public Relations Association (IPRA)

French Stamp

When IPRA was formed in London in 1955, it had only 15 members in five countries. Membership now totals 1,000 in 77 countries, with headquarters in Geneva, Switzerland. IPRA is formally recognized by the United Nations, and its members serve as consultants to the UN Economic and Social Council. In 1965 it adopted the Code of Athens, based on the UN Declaration of Human Rights. To commemorate IPRA's 25th anniversary in 1980, the French Post Office Authority issued the first and only stamp dedicated to public relations.

IPRA promotes professional recognition, high standards, and ethics among practitioners working in international aspects of public relations. In addition, it supports professional development and recognition in parts of the world where public relations is just developing and helps establish new national associations. IPRA meets twice each year, annually recognizes "outstanding contribution to better world understanding," publishes *International Public Relations Review* quarterly, and issues "Gold Papers" on major issues of interest to the global public relations community.

Specialized, Regional, and Local Associations

The growing memberships of several specialized national organizations attest to the field's growing sense of common interests, developing esprit de corps, and professionalism. For example, hospital practitioners formed a society affiliated with the American Hospital Association in 1964. Now almost 4,300 members belong to the Society for Healthcare Strategy and Market Development, formed in 1996 with the merger of two AHA-affiliated groups—American Society for Health Care Marketing and Public Relations, and the Society for Healthcare Planning and Marketing. Members receive *Spectrum,* a bimonthly newsletter, and *Hospitals & Healthcare Networks,* a twice-monthly magazine.

Also typical of these specialized groups is the National Association of Government Communicators (NAGC). Organized in January 1976, it combined the memberships of the Government Information Organization and the Federal Editors Association. Most NAGC members work in the Washington, DC, area, but there are regional NAGC chapters in Frankfort, Kentucky; Minneapolis; Philadelphia; Denver; Susquehanna Valley, Pennsylvania; Austin, Texas; Hampton Roads, Virginia; and Chicago. Goals are to gain recognition for government communicators in the policy-making process and to advance professionalism among members through workshops, seminars, and annual meetings. It also works with the Civil Service Commission to update and write meaningful job standards. Another of NAGC's goals is to get Congress to repeal laws that restrict and hobble the public relations function in government.

Also growing is the network of Black Public Relations Society chapters in Atlanta, Chicago, Los Angeles, New York, Philadelphia, and Washington, DC. The first chapters were formed in 1973, and the most recent was formed in New York in 1991. Chapters provide mentoring and networking opportunities and encourage African American students to enter public relations careers. A similar organization for Hispanic practitioners, the Hispanic Public Relations Association, was founded in 1984 in Los Angeles.

Other specialized associations include the following:

Religious Public Relations Council	Founded 1929
National School Public Relations Association	1935
Agricultural Relations Council	1953
Baptist Public Relations Association	1954
National Society of Fund Raising Executives	1960
National Investor Relations Institute	1969
Council for Advancement and Support of Education (CASE)	1975
Issue Management Council	1982

Florida Public Relations Association, founded in 1938, is one of several state associations. Others include Maine Public Relations Council, Public Relations Association of Mississippi, and Texas Public Relations Association. Similar to the state groups, most major cities have public relations clubs, publicity clubs, and other associations not affiliated with PRSA, IABC, or other national and international organizations.

In addition, a number of "exclusive" groups have developed over the years, with varying degrees of impact in shaping the practice. These include the Wise Men, begun in 1938 by John W. Hill, Pendleton Dudley, and T. J. Ross; Public Relations Seminar, started in 1951 as an outgrowth of the National Conference of Business Public Relations Executives; and Pride and Alarm, founded in 1957 by New York–based practitioners who style themselves "junior Wise Men." Such groups function informally and hold their meetings in private. Exclusivity for the in-group is their hallmark.

The newest by-invitation-only group is the Arthur W. Page Society, formed in 1983 when the giant AT&T public relations unit anticipated being splintered among AT&T and seven newly formed regional telephone companies as a result of divestiture. The group's literature spells out the vision statement:

> The Arthur W. Page Society is committed to the belief that public relations as a function of executive management is central to the success of the corporation. The membership of the Society will embrace those individuals who epitomize the highest standards of public relations practice, as exemplified by the Page Principles. (See Exhibit 5.2, pg. 164.)

Outside the United States, there are more than 100 national and regional associations in some 70 countries, and the total is increasing as public rela-

EXHIBIT 5.2

ARTHUR W. PAGE PRINCIPLES

The Arthur W. Page Principles

TELL THE TRUTH

Let the public know what's happening and provide an accurate picture of the company's character, ideals and practices.

PROVE IT WITH ACTION

Public perception of an organization is determined ninety percent by doing and ten percent by talking.

LISTEN TO THE CUSTOMER

To serve the company well, understand what the public wants and needs. Keep top decision makers and other employees informed about public reaction to company products, policies and practices.

MANAGE FOR TOMORROW

Anticipate public reaction and eliminate practices that create difficulties. Generate goodwill.

CONDUCT PUBLIC RELATIONS AS IF THE WHOLE COMPANY DEPENDS ON IT

Corporate relations is a management function. No corporate strategy should be implemented without considering its impact on the public. The public relations professional is a policymaker capable of handling a wide range of corporate communications activities.

REMAIN CALM, PATIENT AND GOOD HUMORED

Lay the groundwork for public relations miracles with consistent, calm and reasoned attention to information and contacts. When a crisis arises, remember that cool heads communicate best.

Courtesy Arthur W. Page Society.

tions gains recognition in the global community. Examples include the Public Relations Institute of Australia (established in 1960); Brazil's Federal Council of Public Relations Professionals (1969); the French Public Relations Federation (1971, membership composed of six separate associations of individuals and consultancies); the German Society of Public Relations (1958), the Public Relations Society of India (1958), and the Nigerian Institute of Public Relations (1963).

Student Organizations

Development of the Public Relations Student Society of America (PRSSA) under the auspices of PRSA has strengthened education and recruitment into the field. PRSA's interest in organizing student chapters first surfaced in 1950, but it was not until April 1967 that now-retired Professor Walter Seifert of Ohio State University proposed such an organization to the PRSA assembly. The proposal won quick approval, and the first chapter was chartered in 1968. In 1998 there were PRSSA chapters on 203 campuses with almost 6,000 members. PRSSA's purpose is "to cultivate a favorable and mutually advantageous relationship between students and professional public relations practitioners." To ease graduating PRSSA students' transition into the field, PRSA established a preassociate membership with reduced fees and special programs.

IABC also sponsors student chapters on 45 U.S. campuses, three in Canada, and one in Hong Kong, with a total membership of 600. Students also hold membership in professional chapters. Territorial disputes between PRSA and IABC emerged when one university's student public relations club tried to affiliate with both PRSSA and IABC. PRSSA's rule forbidding dual affiliation illustrates the absence of common purpose and shared goals among the many professional associations and societies governing public relations.

CODES OF ETHICS

In addition to a self-governing organization, a basic requirement for professions is adherence to a set of professional norms, usually referred to as codes of ethics. As acceptance of professionalism and a sense of cohesiveness have developed, there has been increasing concern for standards of professional responsibility. Many practitioners are making an earnest effort to qualify morally. Others see codes of ethics as so much window dressing and high-sounding puffery.

Attempts to advance the ethics in this field are reflected in the number of codes of professional standards for public relations practice. In the United States, the principal code is that of the Public Relations Society of America. PRSA's first Code of Professional Standards was adopted in 1954 and revised in 1959, 1963, 1977, 1983, and 1988 (see Exhibit 5.3, pg. 166).

The 1963 revisions strengthened ethical guidelines for financial practice. Following several years of investigation, the Securities and Exchange Com-

EXHIBIT 5.3

PUBLIC RELATIONS SOCIETY OF AMERICA CODE OF PROFESSIONAL STANDARDS FOR THE PRACTICE OF PUBLIC RELATIONS

(This Code was adopted by the PRSA Assembly in 1988. It replaces a Code of Ethics in force since 1950 and revised in 1954, 1959, 1963, 1977, 1983, and 1988.)

Declaration of Principles

Members of the Public Relations Society of America base their professional principles on the fundamental value and dignity of the individual, holding that the free exercise of human rights, especially freedom of speech, freedom of assembly, and freedom of the press, is essential to the practice of public relations. In serving the interests of clients and employers, we dedicate ourselves to the goals of better communication, understanding, and cooperation among the diverse individuals, groups, and institutions of society, and of equal opportunity of employment in the public relations profession.

We pledge:

To conduct ourselves professionally, with truth, accuracy, fairness, and responsibility to the public;

To improve our individual competence and advance the knowledge and proficiency of the profession through continuing research and education;

And to adhere to the articles of the Code of Professional Standards for the Practice of Public Relations as adopted by the governing Assembly of the Society.

Code of Professional Standards for the Practice of Public Relations

These articles have been adopted by the Public Relations Society of America to promote and maintain high standards of public service and ethical conduct among its members.

1. A member shall conduct his or her professional life in accord with the *public interest.*
2. A member shall exemplify high standards of *honesty and integrity* while carrying out dual obligations to a client or employer and to the democratic process.
3. A member shall *deal fairly* with the public, with past or present clients or employers, and with fellow practitioners, giving due respect to the ideal of free inquiry and to the opinions of others.
4. A member shall adhere to the highest

mission issued a biting indictment of the malpractice of a handful of practitioners. Revision of the code in 1977 responded to the threat of antitrust litigation against the PRSA by the Federal Trade Commission (FTC). The commission's Bureau of Competition had decided that code provisions barring contingency fees and banning one member from encroaching upon another member's clients were in violation of free competition. Two provisions of the code were in contention:

A member shall not propose to a prospective client or employer that the amount of his fee or other compensation be contingent on or measured by the achievement of specified results; nor shall he enter into any fee agreement to the same effect.

standard of *accuracy and truth,* avoiding extravagant claims or unfair comparisons and giving credit for ideas and words borrowed from others.

5. A member shall not knowingly disseminate *false or misleading information* and shall act promptly to correct erroneous communications for which he or she is responsible.

6. A member shall not engage in any practice which has the purpose of *corrupting* the integrity of channels of communications or the processes of government.

7. A member shall be prepared to *identify publicly* the name of the client or employer on whose behalf any public communication is made.

8. A member shall not use any individual or organization professing to serve or represent an announced cause, or professing to be independent or unbiased, but actually serving another or *undisclosed interest.*

9. A member shall not guarantee the achievement of specified results beyond the member's direct control.

10. A member shall *not represent conflicting or competing interests* without the express consent of those concerned, given after a full disclosure of the facts.

11. A member shall not place himself or herself in a position where the member's *personal interest is or may be in conflict* with an obligation to an employer or client, or others, without full disclosure of such interests to all involved.

12. A member shall *not accept fees, commissions, gifts or any other consideration* from anyone except clients or employers for whom services are performed without their express consent, given after full disclosure of the facts.

13. A member shall scrupulously safeguard the *confidences and privacy rights* of present, former, and prospective clients or employers.

14. A member shall not intentionally *damage the professional reputation* or practice of another practitioner.

15. If a member has evidence that another member has been guilty of unethical, illegal, or unfair practices, including those in violation of this Code, the member is obligated to present the information promptly to the proper authorities of the Society for action in accordance with the procedure set forth in Article XII of the Bylaws.

16. A member called as a witness in a proceeding for enforcement of this Code is obligated to appear, unless excused for sufficient reason by the judicial panel.

17. A member shall as soon as possible sever relations with any organization or individual if such relationship requires conduct contrary to the article of this Code.

A member shall not encroach upon the professional employment of another member. Where there are two engagements, both must be assured that there is no conflict between them.

The latter provision had long been a source of debate inside and outside PRSA because it did not apply to the many practitioners who did not belong to PRSA. Thus, it appeared to protect only counselors who were PRSA members, making fair game of those who were not. In fact, the provision was never meaningfully enforced.

Although PRSA membership did not agree with the FTC's charges, the two provisions in question were deleted from the code April 29, 1977. Nevertheless, PRSA leaders made it clear that the society does not condone pirating accounts or contingency fees. The Federal Trade Commission on October 27, 1977, accepted from PRSA an agreement containing a consent order that prohibits the society from "promulgating rules that affect fee arrangements or business solicitations." Thus, the FTC approved the society's amended code.

Whereas the revised code also removed "sexist concepts and language," it retained another hotly debated provision:

> A member shall adhere to truth and accuracy and to generally accepted standards of good taste.

The phrase "generally accepted standards" remained a bone of contention among thoughtful practitioners. Its elasticity allowed more than one unethical practice to go unpunished until the 1988 revision of the code, after a case was brought before the grievance board.

The case involved a practitioner's disclosure of a potential client's plans to a competitor. Two articles were reworded to cover "potential" as well as past and present clients. The 1988 revision did not change the major provisions of the code. Rather, the Code of Professional Standards for the Practice of Public Relations was expanded to 17 articles and reworded to make them more understandable. In addition, revisions aligned PRSA's code with that proposed by the 13-member organizations of the North American Public Relations Council.

PRSA members agree to conduct their professional lives in accordance with the code. Compliance is enforced in confidential proceedings, following complaints of code violations by a PRSA member, by a nonmember, or through media exposure. A nine-member national Board of Ethics and Professional Standards acts somewhat as a grand jury, investigating complaints and deciding whether or not to file charges. Disciplinary cases are referred to either six-member judicial panels in each of PRSA's nine national districts or directly to PRSA's board of directors. Exhibit 5.4 outlines the rather cumbersome process.

Enforcement by PRSA's Board of Ethics and Professional Standards has been uneven over the years. The first penalty for violation was meted out in 1962, when a member was censured for attempting to take away the account of another member. Two members were censured in 1963, and another was suspended in 1964 in the wake of the Fulbright Committee's investigation of counselors representing foreign governments. Since those early cases, however, fewer than one out of five cases gets referred to judicial panels or the board of directors. Most cases are dismissed because of lack of evidence, settled to the satisfaction of all parties, or dropped because the charged member died or simply resigned. One of the quirks in the code is that it applies only to members.

A headline-grabbing case occurred in 1986 when PRSA President Anthony Franco resigned from PRSA after media reports that the Securities and Exchange Commission (SEC) had charged him with insider trading in a client's stock. According to the SEC's complaint filed in U.S. District Court in

EXHIBIT 5.4

PRSA CODE ENFORCEMENT PROCESS

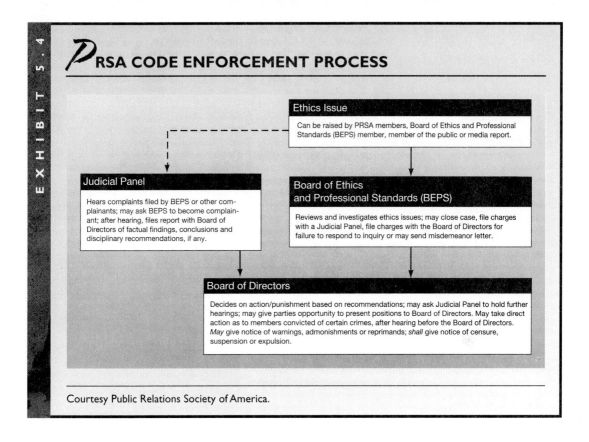

Ethics Issue

Can be raised by PRSA members, Board of Ethics and Professional Standards (BEPS) member, member of the public or media report.

Judicial Panel

Hears complaints filed by BEPS or other complainants; may ask BEPS to become complainant; after hearing, files report with Board of Directors of factual findings, conclusions and disciplinary recommendations, if any.

Board of Ethics and Professional Standards (BEPS)

Reviews and investigates ethics issues; may close case, file charges with a Judicial Panel, file charges with the Board of Directors for failure to respond to inquiry or may send misdemeanor letter.

Board of Directors

Decides on action/punishment based on recommendations; may ask Judicial Panel to hold further hearings; may give parties opportunity to present positions to Board of Directors. May take direct action as to members convicted of certain crimes, after hearing before the Board of Directors. *May* give notice of warnings, admonishments or reprimands; *shall* give notice of censure, suspension or expulsion.

Courtesy Public Relations Society of America.

Washington, DC, the American Stock Exchange noticed an unusually large purchase of a small Michigan company's stock. A purchase of 3,000 shares at $41 per share had occurred the day before public announcement that a private investment group would buy the company for $50 per share. The stock exchange traced the purchase to Franco, who had helped the company—his client—prepare an announcement of the impending sale. The SEC complaint alleges that Franco had denied the purchase but later telephoned his broker to rescind the trade.[32]

Almost a year after the incident, without admitting or denying the allegations in the SEC complaint, Franco signed a consent decree accepting terms of a Final Judgment of Permanent Injunction in which he and his agents are "restrained and enjoined from, directly or indirectly" any practices designed to defraud, mislead or deceive, in connection with the purchase or sale of such security.[33]

The Franco case prompted an amendment in the bylaws to allow continuation of an investigation for up to 90 days after a member resigns from PRSA. The PRSA president or a designated officer is to announce the results of judicial proceedings, including "any disciplinary action which would have been taken had the member not resigned."[34] This closes the loophole that prevented prosecution after a member resigned.

EXHIBIT 5.5

INTERNATIONAL ASSOCIATION OF BUSINESS COMMUNICATORS CODE OF ETHICS

Preface

Because hundreds of thousands of business communicators worldwide engage in activities that affect the lives of millions of people, and because this power carries with it significant social responsibilities, the International Association of Business Communicators developed the Code of Ethics for Professional Communicators. The Code is based on three different yet interrelated principles of professional communication that apply throughout the world.

These principles assume that just societies are governed by a profound respect for human rights and the rule of law; that ethics, the criteria for determining what is right and wrong, can be agreed upon by members of an organization; and, that understanding matters of taste requires sensitivity to cultural norms.

These principles are essential:

- Professional communication is legal.
- Professional communication is ethical.
- Professional communication is in good taste.

Recognizing these principles, members of IABC will

- engage in communication that is not only legal but also ethical and sensitive to cultural values and beliefs;
- engage in truthful, accurate and fair communication that facilitates respect and mutual understanding; and,
- adhere to the following articles of the IABC Code of Ethics for Professional Communicators.

Because conditions in the world are constantly changing, members of IABC will work to improve their individual competence and to increase the body of knowledge in the field with research and education.

Articles

1. Professional communicators uphold the credibility and dignity of their profession by practicing honest, candid and timely communication, and by fostering the free flow of essential information in accord with the public interest.
2. Professional communicators disseminate accurate information and promptly correct any erroneous communication for which they may be responsible.
3. Professional communicators understand and support the principles of free speech, freedom of assembly, and access to an open marketplace of ideas; and act accordingly.

IABC takes a different approach to its code of ethics for communicators (last revised in 1995). Rather than playing an enforcement role, IABC's Ethics Committee encourages professional development activities related to ethics and offers counsel to individual members on how to deal ethically with specific situations. Widespread dissemination of the code in several languages promotes compliance. If a governmental agency or judicial body finds a member guilty of a serious offense, however, the IABC executive board is authorized to employ procedures spelled out in the bylaws to terminate membership. (See Exhibit 5.5.)

Most people recognize that the adoption of a code of ethics does not au-

4. Professional communicators are sensitive to cultural values and beliefs and engage in fair and balanced communication activities that foster and encourage mutual understanding.
5. Professional communicators refrain from taking part in any undertaking which the communicator considers to be unethical.
6. Professional communicators obey laws and public policies governing their professional activities and are sensitive to the spirit of all laws and regulations and, should any law or public policy be violated, for whatever reason, act promptly to correct the situation.
7. Professional communicators give credit for unique expressions borrowed from others and identify the sources and purposes of all information disseminated to the public.
8. Professional communicators protect confidential information and, at the same time, comply with all legal requirements for the disclosure of information affecting the welfare of others.
9. Professional communicators do not use confidential information gained as a result of professional activities for personal benefit and do not represent conflicting or competing interests without written consent of those involved.

10. Professional communicators do not accept undisclosed gifts or payments for professional services from anyone other than a client or employer.
11. Professional communicators do not guarantee results that are beyond the power of the practitioner to deliver.
12. Professional communicators are honest not only with others but also, and most importantly, with themselves as individuals; for a professional communicator seeks the truth and speaks that truth first to the self.

Enforcement and Communication of the IABC Code for Professional Communicators

IABC fosters compliance with its Code by engaging in global communication campaigns rather than through negative sanctions. However, in keeping with the sixth article of the IABC Code, members of IABC who are found guilty by an appropriate governmental agency or judicial body of violating laws and public policies governing their professional activities may have their membership terminated by the IABC executive board following procedures set forth in the association's by-laws.

IABC encourages the widest possible communication about its Code.

Courtesy International Association of Business Communicators.

tomatically bring morality to a calling. But having a code usually reflects a sincere desire among a vast majority of leaders and members to raise standards of ethical practice and to provide criteria to guide and judge individual behavior. But a code without commitment, training, and enforcement means little in practice. Demonstrating their commitment to ethical practice, some public relations firms—Epley Associates, Inc.; Ketchum Public Relations; and Manning, Selvage & Lee—require new employees to sign an agreement that obligates them to practice according to the PRSA code, even if they are not themselves members of PRSA. (See Exhibit 5.6, pg. 172, for examples of ethics in practice.)

EXHIBIT 5.6

PUBLIC RELATIONS ETHICS IN PRACTICE

Situation 1: Your firm is one of several under consideration by a manufacturer planning to introduce a new service. The company anticipates severe opposition from certain groups and politicians. You are given confidential information as to the service and the company's plans so you can develop a proposal. The company awards the contract to a competing firm. Can you disclose the information to the manufacturer's opposition?

Answer: You are obligated by the PRSA code Article 13 to safeguard the confidences and privacy rights of present, former, and prospective clients or employers.

Situation 2: Your firm publishes a newsletter directed to brokerage houses. A corporate executive—one of your clients—asks you to help make the company better known among stockbrokers. You publish a highly optimistic forecast of the company's business prospects, leaving out some information about problems. You also fail to indicate your firm's relationship with the company. Were you under any obligation to disclose this relationship? Should you print a correction that includes all the information you have about the company?

Answer: According to Article 5 of the code, you must immediately print a correction in your newsletter, giving all the facts and clarifying your relationship with the company. Not only is your incomplete and optimistic report in violation of federal security regulations but you are also in violation of several articles of the code: Articles 1, 3, 4, 5, 7, and 8. Your publication clearly was not in the public interest, did not deal fairly with the public, and did not adhere to the highest standards of accuracy and truth. The code forbids disseminating false or misleading information and representing an undisclosed interest while professing to be independent or unbiased. The code also requires that you be prepared to identify clients or employers on whose behalf communication is made.

Situation 3: Your employer directs you to set up a supposedly independent citizens' organization to demonstrate support for a new real estate development that requires planning commission approval. The new organization will be financed secretly by your company and a group of contractors who will participate in building the homes. Is there anything wrong with establishing this organization?

Answer: You may not set up an organization that purports to serve an independent

A distinguished Canadian counselor once pointed out that "Unfortunately, these codes have little real value unless they are accepted in turn by the employers of practitioners and applied to the conduct of the business itself."[35] Longtime leader and crusader for higher ethics in public relations Frank Wylie admonished, "We shouldn't allow ourselves to accept the lowest common denominator of behavior—the negative and retrogressive 'it won't really hurt anyone' philosophy. We must aspire to a better level of ethics, and we must persevere to achieve that goal."[36] Public relations ethics scholar Donald Wright likewise does not let individual practitioners off the hook: "Although there always will be some peer-imposed discipline based on codes of ethics, the bottom-line of ethical decision making in our field will continue to rest in the laps of individual practitioners."[37]

cause but actually carries out a private or unannounced interest of a PRSA member, client, or employer (Article 8).

Situation 4: A pharmaceutical company hires your firm to set up a press conference for an independent British scientist who has tested one of your client's new products and written a favorable research article. You are also to arrange speaking engagements for the visiting scientist. After your successful press conference, which gains wide media coverage, you learn that the scientist is actually an employee of the pharmaceutical company's research subsidiary. What actions should you take?

Answer: You must sever relations with this client as soon as possible (Article 17) and cancel all speaking engagements you arranged for the scientist (Article 5). To continue the relationship and program would violate Articles 1, 2, 3, 4, 6, and 8: to act in the public interest, exemplify high standards of honesty and integrity, deal fairly with the public, adhere to the highest standards of accuracy and truth, not corrupt the integrity of communication channels, and not use an individual purported to be independent to serve an undisclosed interest.

Situation 5: Your employer asks you to give a series of talks in communities served by your company. You are to discuss the new plant being built and its operations. You visit the plant before giving the speech prepared by your immediate supervisor. During the tour you learn that several claims in the speech are not true. Can you give the speech as originally written?

Answer: Knowingly presenting false or misleading information to the public is a clear violation of Articles 1, 2, and 5. If your employer insists that you give the speech as written, then your only choice is to resign (Article 17).

Situation 6: A client asks you to help arrange a public offering of stock. You decline because you have no experience in corporate finance or financial relations. Instead, you refer the client to your friend, a fellow PRSA member, who specializes in financial relations. The practitioner sends you a check for $500 in appreciation of the referral. Can you accept the money?

Answer: You may keep the payment from your appreciative friend only if your client knows about the payment and approves (Articles 11 and 12).

Adapted from article written by the late Donald B. McCammond, APR, while he served as chairman of PRSA's Board of Ethics and Professional Standards. "Ethics: The Right Choice," *Public Relations Journal* 43, no. 2 (February 1987): 8–10. Used with permission of *Public Relations Journal*.

TOWARD NEW HORIZONS

Even after the considerable progress recorded since the mid-1900s, public relations still stands short of public acceptance as a true profession. The field lacks standardized educational requirements, mandatory certification or licensing, full-fledged devotion to serving the public interest, public acceptance of its social utility, and effective self-regulation. There is a growing consensus on a fairly standardized curriculum in the nation's schools and departments of journalism and communication but still no educational requirements for entry to the practice.

And although accreditation—even universal accreditation—is encouraged by many professional associations and societies, proposals to certify or license practitioners are either rejected without serious consideration or posed as symbolic gestures. And whereas codes of ethics and standards of practice are held up as evidence of professional status, enforcement poses little threat or is easily subverted when the subject of enforcement simply drops his or her membership.

As a result, the field continues to be plagued with press agents parading as counselors and with practitioners who are more interested in manipulating the opinions of others than in understanding them. There is still ample evidence that the function is not fully and widely understood, even among its practitioners. In sum, the field still takes in many who cannot qualify morally through a commitment to ethical practice or functionally through knowledge and expertness gained in specialized education. Fortunately, the ranks of those who can are growing.

The future looks promising, but there are still those who say that public relations is an art, not a profession. They apparently chose not to notice that the difference lies in the fiduciary relationship that is built into professional practice but not into art.[38] Likewise, they chose to ignore the growing body of knowledge and related specialized skills required to practice the mature public relations. On the other hand, preoccupation with professional status may detract from the real value of professionalism: the ideal of providing competent and ethical service to those in need. One without the other falls short of the ideal: Ethics without competence is meaningless; competence without ethics is directionless. European scholar Hans-Martin Sass makes the point clearly:

> Ethics and expertise belong together; only together do they constitute true professionalism and provide a morally acceptable foundation for professional fiduciary services. The client . . . expects not general expertise . . . or general commitment to virtues or moral or religious principles from the expert; rather, he or she expects experienced expertise in making good technical and good moral judgments in concrete cases.[39]

Whether public relations qualifies as a profession is a less important question than the extent to which its practitioners do good and do no harm. If practitioners as a group are to measure up, they will have to practice positive public relations. They will have to take ethical stands and be a force in the institutionalization of ethics within their organizations. Yet researcher Kathy Fitzpatrick found that fewer than 7 percent of ethics officers have public relations backgrounds, and only about 12 percent of all organizations' ethics committees include public relations officers.[40]

In the final analysis, professional status will not be achieved by singing hymns of faith and self-congratulations. Simply put, behavior speaks louder than words. As a respected practitioner, the late T. J. Ross said many years ago in an interview with *Fortune* magazine, "Unless you are willing to resign an account or a job over a matter of principle, it is no use to call yourself a member of the world's newest profession . . . for you are already a member of the world's oldest."[41]

Almost a century ago a handful of pioneers staked a claim on what we call public relations. Moves to professionalize the practice and to accept the nobility of serving the public interest continue to strengthen educational programs, build the body of knowledge, toughen admission requirements, and raise the standards of ethics and acceptable behavior. These moves will ensure that public relations continues to progress professionally and will provide opportunities to achieve professional status to those with the necessary moral commitment, knowledge, and skills. Practitioners committed to high standards of ethics and professionalism will distinguish public relations practice from other skilled occupations and make it a calling in the service of the public interest.

NOTES

1. John Kultgen, *Ethics and Professionalism* (Philadelphia: University of Pennsylvania Press, 1988), 371.
2. R. M. Veatch, "The Danger of Virtue," *Journal of Medicine and Philosophy* 13 (1988): 445–46.
3. Baruch Brody, *Ethics and Its Applications* (New York: Harcourt Brace Jovanovich, 1983).
4. Robert Sokolowski, "The Fiduciary Relationship and the Nature of Professions," in *Ethics, Trust, and the Professions: Philosophical and Cultural Aspects,* edited by Edmund D. Pellegrino, Robert M. Veatch, and John P. Langan (Washington, DC: Georgetown University Press, 1991), 23–43.
5. For more detailed discussion of the bases for professional privilege, see Eliot Freidson, "Nourishing Professionalism," in Pellegrino, Veatch, and Langan, eds., *Ethics, Trust, and the Professions,* 193–220.
6. Ibid., 196.
7. Kultgen, *Ethics and Professionalism,* 248.
8. Ibid., 183–84.
9. Robert Heilbroner, "Public Relations: The Invisible Sell," in Reo M. Christenson and Robert 0. McWilliams, *Voice of the People,* 2d ed. (New York: McGraw-Hill, 1967), 485.
10. Daniel Boorstin, *The Image* (New York: Atheneum, 1962), 17.
11. Willard J. Hurst, "The Professions of American Life," *Public Relations Journal* 13, no. 8 (August 1957).
12. David Ferguson, "A Practitioner Looks at Public Relations Education," 1987 Vern C. Schranz Distinguished Lecture in Public Relations (Ball State University, Muncie, IN).
13. Freidson, "Nourishing Professionalism," 195–97.
14. Scott M. Cutlip, "History of Public Relations Education in the United States," *Journalism Quarterly* 38 (Summer 1961).
15. Alfred McClung Lee, "Trends in Public Relations Training," *Public Opinion Quarterly* 11 (Spring 1947).
16. Hale Nelson, "Training for Public Relations," *Public Relations Journal* 12, no. 9 (September 1956).
17. Ray Eldon Hiebert, *Trends in Public Relations Education, 1964–1970* (New York: Foundation for Public Relations Research and Education, 1970). Also see "PR in Classroom," *Public Relations Journal* 26 (September 1970).

18. Kenneth O. Smith, "Report of the 1981 Commission on Public Relations Education," *Public Relations Review* 8 (Summer, 1982): 66–68.

19. William P. Ehling and Betsy Plank, *Design for Undergraduate Public Relations Education* (Chicago: Commission on Undergraduate Public Relations Education, 1987).

20. Public Relations Society of America, *Where to Study Public Relations* (New York: Public Relations Society of America, 1991).

21. Ibid., 23–27.

22. Smith, "Report of the 1981 Commission," 68.

23. See James K. VanLeuven, "Public Relations Body of Knowledge: A Task Force Report," *Public Relations Review* 13, no. 4 (Winter 1987): 11–18, for a description of the project. See "Public Relations Body of Knowledge Task Force Report," *Public Relations Review* 14, no. 1 (Spring 1988): 3–40, for the first listing of selected sources. *Public Relations Review* continues to publish annual bibliographies of selected books and articles in periodicals.

24. Glen M. Broom, Mark S. Cox, Elizabeth A. Krueger, and Carol M. Liebler, "The Gap between Professional and Research Agendas in Public Relations Journals," *Public Relations Research Annual* 1 (1989): 141–54.

25. The research team included Professor David M. Dozier, San Diego State University; Professor William P. Ehling, Syracuse University; Professor Larissa A. Grunig, University of Maryland; and public relations consultants Fred C. Repper, Ingram, TX, and Jon White, Bedford, UK. Books reporting the project results include James E. Grunig, ed., *Excellence in Public Relations and Communication Management: Contributions to Effective Organizations* (Hillsdale, NJ: Lawrence Erlbaum Associates, Publishers, 1992), and David M. Dozier, *Manager's Guide to Excellence in Public Relations and Communication Management* (Mahwah, NJ: Lawrence Erlbaum Associates, 1995)

26. Scott M. Cutlip, *A Public Relations Bibliography* (Madison: University of Wisconsin Press, 1957, 1965); Robert L. Bishop, *Public Relations: A Comprehensive Bibliography* (Ann Arbor: University of Michigan Press, 1974); and Bishop's two updates published in *Public Relations Review* 1, no. 4 (Winter Supplement 1975–1976), 3, no. 2 (Summer 1977). Albert Walker has compiled the annual bibliographies for *Public Relations Review* since 1978.

27. PRSA Task Force, "Public Relations Body of Knowledge," *Public Relations Review* 14, no. 1 (Spring 1988): 3–39.

28. Edward L. Bernays, "Should Public Relations Counsel Be Licensed?" *Printers Ink,* December 25, 1953.

29. Edward L. Bernays, "The Case for Licensing PR Practitioners," *Public Relations Quarterly* 28 (Spring 1983): 32.

30. Raymond P. Ewing, "Master Plan," *Public Relations Journal* 43, no. 7 (July 1987), review of Edward L. Bernays's book, *The Later Years: Public Relations Insights 1956–1986* (Rhinebeck, NY: H and M Publishers, 1986). See Paul S. Forbes's letter to the editor response, "Pro test," in *Public Relations Journal* 43, no. 9 (September 1987): 6–7.

31. John M. Reed, ed., *Reed's Worldwide Directory of Public Relations Organizations,* 2d ed. (Washington, DC: Pigafetta Press, 1991).

32. *SEC* v. *Anthony M. Franco,* United State District Court, District of Columbia, Civil Action 86 Civ. 2382, Litigation Release No. 11206 (August 26, 1986).

33. Final Judgment of Permanent Injunction as to Anthony M. Franco, *SEC* v. *Anthony M. Franco,* USDC, District of Columbia, Civil Action 86 Civ. 2382.

34. See Section 7 of Article XII of PRSA bylaws.

35. Leonard Knott, *Plain Talk about Public Relations* (Toronto: McClelland and Stewart, 1961), 3. Written by one who pioneered and shaped the practice in Canada.
36. Frank Wylie, "Professional Ethics and Other Misconceptions." Address before the Publicity Club of Chicago, April 20, 1977.
37. Donald K. Wright, "Ethics Research in Public Relations: An Overview," *Public Relations Review* 15, no. 2 (Summer 1989): 4.
38. Sokolowski, "The Fiduciary Relationship," 31.
39. Hans-Martin Sass, "Professional Organizations and Professional Ethics: A European View," in *Ethics, Trust, and the Professions,* edited by Pellegrino, Veatch, and Langan, 270–71.
40. Kathy Fitzpatrick, "The Role of Public Relations in the Institutionalization of Ethics," *Public Relations Review* 22, no. 3: 256.
41. Quote from J. Handly Wright's 1979 Gold Anvil Award acceptance speech, Public Relations Society of America National Conference, 1979. Wright is retired vice president of the Association of American Railroads.

ADDITIONAL SOURCES

Baker, Lee. *The Credibility Factor: Putting Ethics to Work in Public Relations.* Homewood, IL: Business One Irwin, 1993.

Black, Jay, ed. *Journal of Mass Media Ethics* 4, no. 1 (1989). This issue is devoted to articles on ethics in public relations.

Cutlip, Scott M. "The Tobacco Wars: A Matter of Public Relations Ethics." *Journal of Corporate Public Relations* 3 (1992-1993): 26–31.

Donaldson, Thomas. *Ethics in the Global Market.* London: Oxford University Press, 1989. Author outlines rights both multinational and domestic corporations are bound to respect as part of their moral mission.

McElreath, Mark P. *Managing Systematic and Ethical Public Relations Campaigns.* Madison, WI: Brown & Benchmark Publishers, 1996. Presents in-depth discussion of ethical decision making in public relations for individuals, groups, organizations, publics, society, and culture.

Sallot, Lynne M., Glen T. Cameron, and Ruth Ann Weaver Lariscy. "Professional Standards in Public Relations: A Survey of Educators." *Public Relations Review* 23, no. 3 (Fall 1997): 197–216.

Seib, Philip, and Kathy Fitzpatrick. *Public Relations Ethics.* Fort Worth, TX: Harcourt Brace College Publishers, 1995. Examines principles of professional ethics, arguing that individual practitioners' ethical behavior affects the professional status of the entire field.

VanLeuven, Jim, ed. "Special Issue: Education in Public Relations." *Public Relations Review* 15, no. 1 (Spring 1989).

Wright, Donald K., ed. "Special Issue: Ethics in Public Relations." *Public Relations Review* 15, no. 2 (Summer 1989).

LEGAL CONSIDERATIONS

It is the purpose of the First Amendment to preserve an uninhibited marketplace of ideas in which truth will ultimately prevail.
—*Justice Byron White*

OBJECTIVES

After studying chapter 6, you should be able to

▼ Outline the major principles underlying First Amendment protection of free speech, commercial speech, political expression, and political participation for organizations.

▼ Define and explain libel, slander, privacy, copyright, and trademarks as they relate to public relations practice.

▼ Describe practitioners' rights, responsibilities, and limits on lobbying and serving as representatives for foreign interests.

▼ Describe the legal restrictions on communication between labor and management during union elections and collective bargaining, as outlined in the Taft-Hartley Act of 1947.

▼ Outline the Securities and Exchange Commission's disclosure requirements that apply to publicly owned companies.

This chapter was written in collaboration with Professor Kathy R. Fitzpatrick, APR, Southern Methodist University. Professor Fitzpatrick holds a juris doctor degree and is a member of the state bar of Texas. She formerly worked in corporate public relations for two Fortune 100 companies and now has a consulting practice specializing in strategic communications, law, and ethics.

Public relations operates in an increasingly complex legal climate. Increased concern about sexual harassment; age, gender, and race discrimination; privacy; and labor abuse put these issues on the public agenda and led to new laws and regulations in the workplace. Growing concern about product quality, safety, nutrition and health, and environmental protection led to greater media scrutiny and accountability in the marketplace. Enhanced technology, increased access to the Internet, and instantaneous on-line journalism and commentary have made organizations easy targets of uncontrolled communication in unregulated cyberspace. What all this means for public relations professionals is that today's practitioner must be more knowledgeable about the law and how legal issues affect public relations practices and organizational reputation.

The Institute for Crisis Management reported that business crisis news stories jumped 19 percent in 1997, continuing a three-year trend that indicated growing public concern about business crises in the United States and abroad.[1] At the same time, a shift in crisis causes from industrial and environmental accidents to management, financial, and technology problems has been reported.[2] As public relations counselor Robert Dilenschneider says, "Crises aren't what they used to be."[3]

Legal scholars studying how organizations respond to crises involving legal issues found that legal strategy dominates organizational decision making. In one study, almost two-thirds of official spokespersons used a legal strategy rather than a public relations strategy as the basis for their public responses to charges. Typically, the spokespersons denied being guilty of charges, acted indignant, or said "no comment" or as little as possible. In contrast, those few using a public relations strategy either stated their organization's policy or position on the issue or announced what investigations were underway. Only one admitted that a problem existed.[4]

The researchers suggest that ignoring public relations consequences is "shortsighted and potentially costly" and recommend a collaborative approach to crisis management.[5] In other words, a company's need to set the record straight with a public that has been exposed to negative accusations should not be ignored. In many cases, if a reputation is destroyed by negative publicity, a later victory at the courthouse may not matter at all.[6]

The increased recognition of the tremendous impact of public opinion on organizations involved in legal controversies spawned the development of a specialty practice area in public relations called "litigation public relations." Those practicing litigation public relations help organizations address important interests that extend beyond legal concerns. For example, a company might be concerned about the effect of litigation on its shareholders and the price of its stock, on its employees and the company's effort to recruit, on its customers and the sale of its products, and on its relationships with industry partners such as distributors and suppliers and others. In short, because the damage caused outside the courtroom can be greater than that incurred in resolving the legal issues, it is in a company's best interest to seek both legal and public relations counsel.

Public relations professionals must be mindful of how laws and regulations affect communication activities. In litigation public relations, for instance, a company may not engage in communication campaigns that could prejudice the outcome of the legal proceedings, that is, interfere with due process. In other areas of public relations work, communication may also be restricted. Those who are unfamiliar with the laws that affect public relations practices place both themselves and their organizations at risk of increased legal liability, as one study found:

> The finding that most practitioners are only somewhat or not at all familiar with important legal issues, combined with the finding that most of their work is either not reviewed or subject to limited review by legal counsel, suggests that many public relations practitioners may be placing both themselves and their clients at risk of legal liability.[7]

Whether practitioners are knowledgeable or not, legal considerations often define, limit, and regulate modern public relations practice. That is not likely to change any time soon. As a result, most large communication businesses—public relations firms, advertising agencies, and news media—have specialized lawyers on staff or law firms on retainer.

This chapter outlines major areas of law relevant to public relations, but space does not permit exhaustive discussion of legal requirements imposed on practitioners. Practitioners should consult their attorneys or corporate counsel on specific questions about legal matters. This chapter first outlines the increasing impact of First Amendment decisions on public relations law and then discusses areas of regulation.

Although they do define the terms "commercial speech," "advertising," and "advertisement," commonly used legal dictionaries and encyclopedias do not list "public relations." Consequently, it has no "legal meaning."[8] Yet self-government is based on the philosophy of open, robust debate in a free marketplace of ideas. As the late Supreme Court Justice William O. Douglas wrote,

> When ideas compete in the market for acceptance, full and free discussion exposes the false and they gain few adherents. Full and free discussion keeps a society from becoming stagnant and unprepared for the stresses and strains that work to tear all civilization apart.[9]

The First Amendment to the Constitution protects freedom of expression from government control. The First Amendment says that Congress shall make no law "abridging the freedom of speech, or of the press; or the right of the people peaceably to assemble, and to petition the Government for a redress of grievances."

Although adopted in 1791, the First Amendment was not interpreted by the Supreme Court until the twentieth century. In decisions over the last eight decades, the Supreme Court has ruled that First Amendment restrictions on government interference with freedom of expression apply to both the federal government and state governments.[10] The Court has also ruled that the First Amendment applies to most media, including newspapers, books, magazines, broadcasting, and film.[11] Thus, publishers and broadcasters have a constitutionally protected right of expression just as do individuals. The Supreme Court has also ruled that charitable appeals for funds, on the street or door to door, are protected under the First Amendment because they involve the "communication of information, the dissemination and propagation of views and ideas, and the advocacy of causes."[12]

Not all content comes under First Amendment protection, however. "Fighting words" which provoke another to violence and certain symbolic actions that interfere with government, such as burning a draft card, have been ruled to be outside First Amendment protections.[13] Until recently, commercial advertising and most corporate expression was not protected from government regulation or suppression by the First Amendment. Moreover, no Supreme Court First Amendment decision ever specifically referred to public relations.[14]

Expression that does come under the First Amendment is not protected absolutely. Persons or corporations whose expressions defame, invade the privacy, or disturb the peace of others may have to pay damages. Generally a person will be held accountable for speech that damages another only after he or she expresses it, but in rare circumstances the government can block the dissemination of expression by issuing a prior restraint. Prior restraints on expression, however, are presumptively unconstitutional.[15]

The U.S. Supreme Court ruled in 1992 that so-called hate speech cannot be banned simply because its content is offensive to some. In the case before the Court, the city of St. Paul, Minnesota, had prosecuted a youth under a law intended to punish those who burn crosses, display swastikas, or otherwise express racial or religious bigotry and hate. Justice Antonin Scalia wrote that governments may not punish those who "communicate messages of racial, gender or religious intolerance" simply because those targeted may be offended or emotionally distraught. The Court was unanimous in overturning the St. Paul "hate speech" law, thus broadening First Amendment protection and limiting use of the "Fighting Words Doctrine" to suppress potentially offensive expressions of bigotry.[16] Similarly, university regulations against hate speech on campuses have been declared unconstitutional because they were used "broadly and indiscriminately" to limit speech "simply because it was found to be offensive."[17]

Furthermore, governments cannot pass overly broad laws that infringe upon First Amendment rights by allowing law enforcement officers too much power to limit demonstrations or the circulation of fliers at reasonable hours and places.[18] The Court has ruled that it is a violation of the First Amendment for a city to prohibit charitable groups from soliciting contributions if more than 25 percent of the funds raised are used for administrative expenses and overhead.[19]

The Supreme Court has been most concerned about protecting political expression. For example, in *The New York Times* v. *Sullivan* the Court said that the United States has

> a profound national commitment to the principle that debate on public issues should be uninhibited, robust, and wide-open, and that it may well include vehement, caustic, and sometimes unpleasantly sharp attacks on government and public officials.[20]

The Court's decisions foster a "marketplace of ideas" free of most government regulation. By contrast, the Constitution permits considerable regulation of communication about the commercial marketplace of goods and services. A conflict for communicators arises when businesses and organizations are not allowed to communicate public messages that would be protected by the First Amendment if originated by a newspaper or private individual. In recent years, however, the Court has extended limited First Amendment protections to commercial advertising and corporate speech.

Commercial Speech

The Supreme Court summarily ruled in 1942 that the First Amendment does not protect "purely commercial advertising."[21] The Court reconsidered its almost casual dismissal of commercial advertising in 1976. In *Virginia State Board of Pharmacy* v. *Virginia Citizens Consumer Council,* the Supreme Court ruled that the First Amendment bars a state from prohibiting pharmacists from advertising the prices of prescription drugs. In his opinion for the court, Justice Harry Blackmun came close to equating the traditionally protected marketplace of ideas with the more regulated commercial marketplace:

Advertising, however tasteless and excessive it sometimes may seem, is nonetheless dissemination of information as to who is producing and selling what product, for what reason and at what price. So long as we preserve a predominantly free enterprise economy the allocation of our resources in large measure will be made through numerous private economic decisions. It is a matter of public interest that those decisions, in the aggregate, be intelligent and well informed. To this end the free flow of commercial information is indispensable.[22]

Since *Virginia Pharmacy,* the Court has struck down other statutes prohibiting commercial expression. Because of Supreme Court decisions, states may not bar attorneys from advertising the prices of "routine" legal services, home owners from advertising their houses by placing "For Sale" signs in their yards, and drugstores from advertising contraceptives.[23]

When deciding commercial speech cases, the Court employs a four-part test established in 1980 in *Central Hudson Gas & Electric Corp.* v. *Public Service Commission of New York.*[24] Initially the Court looks to see if the expression is protected by the First Amendment. To be protected, the expression must concern a lawful activity and not mislead. The Court also asks if the asserted governmental interest is substantial enough to justify regulation. If the expression is protected and the government interest is substantial, the Court then asks whether the regulation directly advances the governmental interest and whether the regulation is more extensive than necessary to serve that interest.[25]

The Court has not accorded the same degree of protection to commercial advertising that it insists upon for other protected content. Because of "commonsense" differences between commercial speech and political expression, the Court says advertising can be more heavily regulated by government and trade and professional associations. For example, in 1986 the Court ruled in *Posadas de Puerto Rico Associates* v. *Tourism Company of Puerto Rico* that it was constitutionally permissible for the government to forbid gambling casino advertising directed to local residents while promoting casino gambling directed to nonresidents. Although the 5:4 decision seemingly violates the four-part test from *Central Hudson,* the Court justified its position, saying, "In our view, the greater power to completely ban casino gambling necessarily includes the lesser power to ban advertising of casino gambling."[26]

The Court also abandons the presumption against the constitutionality of prior restraints when applying the First Amendment to commercial advertising. In addition, the tolerance normally shown for caustic, misleading, and even false charges in the political arena does not extend to commercial advertising. Regulatory bodies, the Court has said, are still free to require the inclusion of "additional information, warnings and disclaimers, as are necessary" to ensure that advertisements are not deceptive, such as in cigarette advertising.[27]

An advertising law scholar points out that deception in advertising is something of a paradox. On one hand the law allows "puffery" because it does not work, meaning that reasonable people are not misled by such "legalized lying." On the other hand, why would advertisers use puffery if they truly thought it did not work? However, concern about repressing advertising content that may be useful to some consumers and a cautious attitude about possible violation of First Amendment guarantees of free speech limit prosecution of what many might consider deceptive advertising.[28]

Thus, either by design or through neglect, a company's First Amendment protection for advertising its products and services, although extended, hardly represents a sturdy bulwark against government controls. Beginning in 1990, for example, the Federal Trade Commission reversed its 1980s hands-off posture regarding questionable advertising practices. For example, the FTC has issued guidelines for advertisers' claims of environmental benefits of their products, claims about health and nutrition, claims of fuel economy, and claims that something is free even if there is a charge for postage and handling. The FTC also issues rules—sometimes mandated by statute—to prevent unfair and deceptive advertising. In 1995, for example, the FTC ordered telemarketers to "promptly and clearly" disclose their identities and that they are trying to sell something. The FTC can halt advertising, order changes in advertisements, and even require corrective advertising designed to correct misstatements and false claims made in previous advertisements.[29]

Other federal agencies with regulatory power over advertising include the Federal Communication Commission, the Federal Drug Administration, the Securities and Exchange Commission, the U.S. Postal Service, and the Bureau of Alcohol, Tobacco, and Firearms. Although none have as much control over advertising as does the FTC, they generally monitor advertising content to protect the public against misleading, fraudulent, and even "obscene and indecent" ads. For example, in 1995, it was the Federal Drug Administration, not the FTC, that ordered tobacco companies to restrict advertising to children, claiming that cigarettes are subject to FDA authority because they are an addictive drug.[30]

Corporate Political Expression

Corporate political expression is also more restricted than political expression by individuals and the media. Traditionally newspapers and other news media have been the only corporations with the same right of free expression as an individual. Although all corporations enjoy the rights of due process like any private individual, courts and legislatures have prohibited unregulated corporate and union participation in the political arena. This is apparently out of fear that large organizations would use their immense resources to dominate what is supposed to be a free marketplace of ideas. There has also been concern that stockholders, union members, and utility rate payers are unfairly coerced if their investments, dues, and utility bills are used to support political causes in which they may not believe. As a result of these concerns, the Labor Management Relations Act of 1947 (known as the Taft-Hartley Act and passed over President Harry S. Truman's veto) prohibits corporations and unions from making either contributions to, or expenditures on behalf of, political candidates for federal office.[31]

Elections

The prohibition on corporate and union contributions and expenditures was incorporated into the Federal Election Campaign Act of 1971 and its amendments.[32] The Federal Election Campaign Act also placed limits on the amount that individuals could contribute to candidates and spend independently on behalf of a candidate. An *expenditure* is independent if it is not made in cooperation or consultation with the candidate. An expenditure made as part of and in coordination with a candidate's campaign is a *contribution*.

In 1976, the Supreme Court struck down the spending limits on individuals in *Buckley* v. *Valeo*. The Court ruled that individual expenditure limits violate the First Amendment because they put a substantial restraint "on the quantity and diversity of political speech."[33] But the Court did uphold the constitutionality of limits on contributions individuals could make to a candidate. Under the act, individuals cannot contribute more than $1,000 to any one candidate and a total of $25,000 in any one year to all candidates. Violating the limits is taken seriously, as the former chairman and principal of then Robinson Lerer Sawyer Miller Inc., later Robinson Lake Lerer & Montgomery (RLLM) learned. James Lake of New York pleaded guilty to making illegal campaign contributions to a candidate for Congress in 1993 by asking RLLM associates to make campaign contributions that he would reimburse. A federal judge ordered Lake to write an essay on the Federal campaign finance law and fined him $150,000.[34]

Unlike limits on expenditures, the Court said, limits on contributions impose only a "marginal restriction upon the contributor's ability to engage in free communication."[35] Contributions are only a symbolic expression of support, the Court said, whereas expenditures by individuals are direct expression that cannot be limited without violation of the First Amendment. The Court also upheld the provisions of the Federal Election Campaign Act requiring political committees and candidates to report their contributions and expenditures to the Federal Election Commission, the regulatory body created by the act. These reports of who contributes, spends, and receives money are open to the public so that voters can learn which interests support which candidates.

The Supreme Court did not rule in *Buckley* on the constitutionality of prohibiting corporate contributions and expenditures in elections. It did note, however, that large contributions undermine "the integrity of our system of representative democracy" to the extent they are given "to secure political quid pro quo from current and potential office holders." The Court added that avoiding the "appearance of corruption" is of almost equal concern.[36] The Supreme Court also upheld a section of Michigan's Campaign Finance Act that prohibits corporations from spending corporate funds to support or oppose candidates running for state offices. The Court agreed that Michigan's restriction on campaign expenditures by the Michigan Chamber of Commerce was justified in order to "avoid corruption or the appearance of corruption."[37]

Interpreting the statutory prohibitions on corporate contributions and expenditures, the Federal Election Commission has ruled it is illegal for a corporation to grant a loan to a candidate without charging a normal rate of interest and requiring repayment at a normal due date. It is also illegal to allow the use of corporate facilities to produce election materials without reimbursement at the usual commercial rates. Leave time used to aid a candidate, however, is not a contribution, even if paid, as long as the company granting leave does not direct an employee to aid a candidate.[38]

Whereas corporations and unions may not make contributions or expenditures in an election, they are permitted a narrow range of partisan and nonpartisan communications. Partisan messages by corporations can include extremely opinionated, even vitriolic, communication about candidates or elections. Delivery of such messages, however, must be restricted to a corporation's executive and administrative personnel, its shareholders, and their families. Unions may also distribute partisan communications to members and their families. Permitted, but closely regulated, nonpartisan activities include using posters and newsletters to urge employees to register and vote, distributing registration materials, and buying newspaper ads urging citizens to vote.[39]

Corporations and unions can also help their employees and members make contributions and expenditures by setting up and administering separate segregated funds, or *political action committees*. A PAC, as these committees are called, can contribute up to $5,000 to as many candidates as its members wish. PACs are limited to contributing $15,000 each year to national political parties and $5,000 to other political committees but are not limited on "independent expenditures" for advertising and other campaign activities.[40]

Political action committees play a powerful role in American elections, raising concern that their influence leads to "the best Congress money can buy." Without forming PACs, however, corporations and unions themselves are allowed very little communication in elections. They are allowed more in referenda and other political issue campaigns where the chance of corruption is thought to be less.

Referenda and Political Issues

Massachusetts once had a statute prohibiting corporations from trying to influence a ballot question that did not relate directly to their businesses. In 1978, the Supreme Court struck down that law in *First National Bank of Boston* v. *Bellotti*. First National Bank and four other companies wanted to buy advertising to oppose a referendum on establishing a state personal income tax. Bellotti, the attorney general of Massachusetts, threatened action against the companies if they bought advertising opposing the proposal.

In striking down the statute, the Supreme Court appeared to establish a First Amendment right for corporations. Justice Louis F. Powell Jr., writing for the Court, said that the inherent worth of speech that informs the public "does not depend upon the identity of its source, whether corporation, association, union, or individual."[41] Justice Powell dismissed the argument that corporations are too powerful to be allowed participation in the marketplace of ideas. There is no evidence, he said, "that the relative voice of corporations has been overwhelming or even significant in influencing referenda in Massachusetts, or that there has been any threat to the confidence of the citizenry in government."[42] The Court also rejected the attorney general's argument that corporate advertising in a referendum amounted to a forced contribution by shareholders to support causes in which they did not necessarily believe.

But the Court stopped short of creating a First Amendment right of expression for corporations similar to that of individuals or media companies. As in the Court's earlier commercial advertising cases, Justice Powell placed the First Amendment protection on the content of the speech rather than on the speaker. Powell said the proper question is not whether corporations have First Amendment rights but whether the Massachusetts statute abridges free expression.[43] The Court struck down the statute because it prohibited political expression that "was at the heart of the First Amendment's protection." An advertisement expressing a view on a tax referendum "is the type of speech indispensable to decision making in a democracy, and this is no less true because the speech comes from a corporation rather than an individual."[44]

The *Bellotti* decision opens the door for corporations to participate in government affairs. There are many referenda on taxes, rent control, beverage container deposits, and other issues on which corporations and public interest groups wish to state their views. But companies can also comment on political issues other than referenda. In 1980, the Supreme Court struck down a New York Public Service Commission ruling that barred utilities from including messages about public issues along with a customer's monthly bill. The Consolidated Edison Company had included a bill insert advocating the development of nuclear power. The Court said the public service commission's prohibition "strikes at the heart of the freedom to speak."[45] In a companion case the Court held that an electric utility could not be barred from promoting the use of electricity.[46]

The Court has also ruled that contributions cannot be limited where they will be used to support ballot issues. In *Citizens against Rent Control* v. *City of Berkeley,* the Court struck down an ordinance limiting contributions to an organization opposing a rent control referendum proposal to $250. In its decision the Court blurred the constitutional distinction between contributions and expenditures established in *Buckley* v. *Valeo.* In *Buckley,* the Court said that limits on contributions in an election are only a "marginal restriction" on expression because contributions are symbolic speech. But in *Citizens against Rent Control,* the Court said limits on contributions in a referendum are "beyond question a very significant form of political expression."[47]

Logically, the *Buckley* and *Bellotti* decisions would allow corporations to advertise their views in candidate elections. If independent election expenditures by individuals are pure speech, as the Court ruled in *Buckley,* so too, it could be argued, are independent expenditures by corporations. If the source of speech does not determine whether it is protected, as the Court ruled in *Bellotti,* then, arguably, corporate election advertisements could enjoy as much protection as corporate advertisements in referenda and political issues. Before courts agree, however, they will have to be persuaded that the potential for corporate and union corruption of democratic processes is not greater in elections than in political issues where there are no candidates. In the meantime, companies may spend and contribute freely to advertise their positions on referenda and political issues, subject to media acceptance of their ads.

LOBBYING: THE RIGHT TO PETITION

Many practitioners represent clients or employers as lobbyists before federal and state legislatures. In fact, lobbying has been one of the fastest growing specialties in public relations practice. Lobbyists attempt to influence legislation and regulations, primarily by providing information. Those who represent foreign governments or businesses typically must register as "foreign agents."

Lobbying

Lobbyists were first required to disclose their activities under Title III, the Federal Regulation of Lobbying Act of 1946.[48] That law required any persons whose principal purpose is to influence legislation to register with Congress and file quarterly financial statements detailing their lobbying expenses and sources of income. The Supreme Court narrowed the law, in decisions in 1953 and 1954, so that it applied only to people and organizations whose main purpose is to influence legislation through "direct communication with members of Congress on pending or proposed federal legislation."[49] Not everybody agreed, however, that the 1946 law and its amendments worked as intended, leading to it being repealed in 1995 and replaced by a new lobbying act.

To more effectively regulate lobbying and protect public confidence in government, Congress enacted and President Clinton signed the Lobbying Disclosure Act of 1995, with new definitions, new disclosure requirements, and restrictions (S 1060—PL 104-65).[50] The new law defines "lobbyist," "lobbying firm," and "lobbying contact" as follows:

A lobbyist [is] someone who was employed or retained by a client, made more than one contact on behalf of that client, and spent at least 20 percent of his or her time during a six-month period providing that service to the client.

A lobbying firm was defined as an entity that had at least one person who was hired to represent someone other than his or her employer. The term also applied to self-employed individuals who represented other people or entities.

A lobbying contact was defined as a communication, either oral or written, on behalf of a client to a covered executive or legislative branch official regarding legislation, rules, regulations, grants, loans, permits, programs or the nomination of anyone subject to Senate confirmation.[51]

Lobbying includes direct pressure on members of Congress through an "artificially stimulated letter writing campaign."[52] But lobbying does not include general public relations campaigns that attempt to "saturate thinking of the community" about public issues.[53] Nor does it include testimony before a committee of Congress, or magazines and newspapers which, in the ordinary course of business, publish news items and editorials urging the passage or defeat of legislation.[54] Lobbying does not include contacts with a member of the executive branch who then contacts a member of Congress.

Lobbyists and lobbying firms must register with the Secretary of the Senate and the Clerk of the House within 45 days of either being hired or making a contact defined as lobbying, whichever happened first. They must register if they receive or expect to receive more than $5,000 in a six-month period. So must in-house lobbyists who expect to spend more than $20,000 on lobbying activities during a six-month period. Both lobbyists and lobbying firms must report names, addresses, places of business, and phone numbers of their own business, their clients, and anyone else who contributes more than $10,000 in a six-month period to lobbying activities conducted by the registrant. In addition to registering, all registrants must file reports twice a year, providing "good faith estimates" of the amounts paid by clients or spent on lobbying.[55]

The new law allows nonprofit charitable, educational, and other tax-exempt organizations to simply file a copy of their IRS Form 990, which reports lobbying expenditures, rather than requiring them to file a separate report. Nonprofit organizations that do engage in lobbying are prohibited from receiving federal grants, awards, contracts, and loans. For example, the law precludes the most powerful lobbying organization in Washington, DC—the American Association of Retired Persons (AARP)—from receiving such government largess because it lobbies the federal government on Social Security, Medicare, taxes, and other issues important to its members. The act exempts public officials, the working press, and those who provide testimony before congressional committees. It also excludes those whose total work for a client consists of less than 20 percent activities qualifying as lobbying. In the final analysis, some experts "inside the Beltway" predict that the new law will lead to an increase in lobbying efforts not covered by the definition of lobbying, "as their access to legislators will be more closely monitored and regulated."[56] One estimate is that the new law will increase the number of those required to register as lobbyists by up to 10 times the number registered when the law passed (from about 6,000 to as many as 60,000).[57]

Grassroots Lobbying

Successful lobbyists typically use "grassroots lobbying" and other campaign techniques, such as issue or advocacy advertising, to mobilize public support outside the nation's capital and state capitals. The goals, of course, are to sway public opinion, to activate constituents, and thereby to increase pressure on legislators and government agencies. In effect, grassroots lobbying combines the strengths of direct lobbying with the power of political movements. As the late Speaker of the House Thomas P. "Tip" O'Neill (D–MA) said, "All politics is local."

Grassroots lobbying is part of an organization's First Amendment right to express itself on public issues. But if a powerful corporation uses a public relations campaign to do damage to another, it may run afoul of antitrust laws. In *Eastern Railroad Presidents Conference* v. *Noerr,* the U.S. Supreme Court ruled that antitrust laws, which prohibit anticompetitive restraints of trade, do not bar corporations from joining with public relations counsel in a "no-holds-barred" public relations campaign to affect legislation. In *Noerr*, the Court said railroads could try through public opinion to kill legislation favored by truckers. However, the Court said there may be situations where a publicity campaign, "ostensibly directed toward influencing governmental action, is a mere sham to cover . . . an attempt to interfere directly with the business relationships of a competitor."[58] In such a case, the antitrust laws might apply.

Foreign Agents

Counselors serving foreign governments must register under the Foreign Agents Registration Act of 1938 (FARA), whether they are lobbyists or not.[59] Congress passed the Foreign Agents Registration Act to limit Nazi and Fascist propaganda in the United States and to identify foreign agents working here. The legislation resulted from the activities of two early public relations firms: "These firms were Carl Byoir & Associates, which took the German railroads account to promote tourism in Germany, and Ivy Lee & T. J. Ross and Associates, which represented the interests of I. G. Farben."[60]

In his report to the House of Representatives, Congressman Emanuel Celler summarized legislators' motivations for passing the law:

> We believe that the spotlight of pitiless publicity will serve as a deterrent to the spread of pernicious propaganda. We feel that our people are entitled to know the sources of any such efforts, and the person or persons or agencies carrying on such work in the United States.[61]

Under the amended Foreign Agents Registration Act, all persons who are working as agents of foreign governments, companies, or political parties must register within 10 days with the U.S. Attorney General. They also must report under oath every six months the names of the foreign interests for whom they work, the activities they carry out, and where they get and how they spend their money. The law defines "agent" as anyone in the United States who works as a public relations counsel, publicity agent, information service employee, or political consultant for a foreign principal. However, diplomatic officers, officials of foreign governments, journalists for American publications, and those engaged in charitable or religious activities are exempted from registration.[62]

Three examples illustrate the types of activities covered by the act and the amounts of money that can be involved: The government of India retained The Washington Group at $25,000 a month to represent its economic and political interests in Washington, DC. Similarly, Turkey awarded a $540,000-one-year contract to the Abernathy MacGregor Group, New York, to help build support for full membership in the European Union, to help win approval for an oil pipeline, and to counter Committee to Protect Journalists' (New York) charges that Turkey persecutes and imprisons journalists who write stories unfavorable to the government. The Netherlands Foreign Investment Agency selected Ruder Finn, New York, to promote U.S. business investments in Holland, budgeting an estimated $1.5 million. Each firm had to register as a foreign agent under FARA.

In addition, foreign agents must label lobbying materials and "political propaganda" as being distributed by a registered foreign agent. They also must provide copies to the attorney general. Political propaganda includes communication intended to influence public opinion about foreign policy; promote racial, religious, or social tensions; or advocate the forceful overthrow of other Western Hemisphere countries.[63]

ACCESS TO THE MEDIA

Public relations plays an important role in the marketplace of ideas, even on a global scale. Its practitioners are responsible for making certain that the ideas, information, or causes of their employers and clients get public hearings. The job requires access to the media, but U.S. law allows media to refuse any story or advertisement they do not wish to run.

Print Media

Constitutional protection of freedom of the press has thus far blocked creation of a legal right of access to the print media for any particular cause, idea, or spokesperson. Some First Amendment scholars argue that the right of expression is rather thin if it can be exercised only by the managers of mass communication. It may have been appropriate, so the argument goes, in the eighteenth century to grant publishers absolute control of their publications under the First Amendment. At that time virtually anyone could start a newspaper. Contrast that situation with today, when most major cities are served by only one metropolitan newspaper. In a time of monopoly newspapers, protecting the right to publish does not guarantee that the marketplace of ideas will be robust.[64]

So far, only one lowly court has recognized a right of access to the print media, and that was a long time ago—1919. In *Uhlman* v. *Sherman,* a lower court in Ohio held that public dependence on the community's only newspaper imposed an obligation on the publisher to open his advertising columns to the public on an equal basis.[65] However, courts since then have consistently held that a publisher can refuse any editorial or advertising copy, provided the publisher does not break a contract or violate the antitrust laws.[66] In the *Home Placement Service* v. *Providence Journal* decisions, the courts ruled that the newspapers involved violated antitrust laws by denying a would-be competitor the opportunity to buy advertising space.[67]

The U.S. Supreme Court has firmly refused to recognize a right of access to the print media. In 1974, the Court struck down a Florida statute requiring a newspaper to give a candidate for public office space to reply to criticism in the publication. Pat Tornillo, a teacher who had led a strike in Miami, brought suit against the *Miami Herald* when the paper refused to give him space to reply to an editorial calling him a "czar" and a lawbreaker while he campaigned for the state legislature.

The Supreme Court ruled the Florida access statute an unconstitutional abridgment of freedom of the press. In a unanimous opinion written by Chief Justice Burger, the Court rejected the argument that the public needs a right of access to the print media. "A responsible press," the Chief Justice wrote, "is an undoubtedly desirable goal, but press responsibility is not mandated by the Constitution, and like many other virtues, cannot be legislated."[68]

Broadcast Media

Until the mid-1980s, there was stronger legal support for access to broadcast media than to print. Broadcasting has been subject to more government regulation since its inception. The government has issued licenses for use of the limited broadcast band since early in the century. The Federal Communications Act of 1934, which established the current regulatory framework for broadcasting, requires that stations licensed by the government operate in the "public convenience, interest or necessity." Under this affirmative obligation, broadcast license holders have been required to provide public access to airtime on radio and television stations. Broadcasters, unlike publishers, were obliged under the Fairness Doctrine and the Equal Time Rule to treat a wide variety of issues with balance.

The Fairness Doctrine, first enunciated by the Federal Communications Commission in 1949, was incorporated into Section 315 of the Federal Communications Act 10 years later. Section 315 required broadcasters to afford reasonable opportunity for the discussion of conflicting views on issues of public importance. To fulfill their fairness obligations, broadcasters were required to seek out controversial issues and then treat all sides fairly.

Those obligations began to diminish during the "deregulation" era of the 1980s, however. First, the Supreme Court in 1984 declared unconstitutional the Federal law barring the public radio and television stations from broadcasting editorials (*FCC* v. *League of Women Voters,* 468 U.S. 364). That case opened the door to a series of challenges and eventual changes in FCC requirements, including the elimination of the Fairness Doctrine.

In deciding in favor of the League of Women Voters, the high court overturned for the first time federal content restrictions on broadcasters' First Amendment rights. Although not a direct test of the Fairness Doctrine, Justice William J. Brennan's footnote to the majority ruling questioned the scarcity rationale that had so long justified restrictions on broadcast content:

> The prevailing rationale for broadcast regulation based on spectrum scarcity has come under increasing criticism in recent years. Critics, including the incumbent Chairman of the FCC, charge that with the advent of cable and satellite television technology, communities now have access to such a wide variety of stations that the scarcity doctrine is obsolete. We are not prepared, however, to reconsider our long-standing approach without some signal from Congress or the FCC that technological developments have advanced so far that revision of the system of broadcast regulations may be required.[69]

When the FCC abolished the Fairness Doctrine in 1987, FCC Chairman Dennis Patrick concluded "that the Fairness Doctrine chills free speech," and that doing away with it will "extend to the electronic press the same First

Amendment guarantees that the print media have enjoyed since our country's inception."[70]

The case began before the FCC had abolished the Fairness Doctrine. The FCC had ruled that a Syracuse, New York, television station had violated the Fairness Doctrine when it refused to provide airtime to a group opposed to the construction of a nuclear power plant. The station had carried commercials in favor of the plant. The station appealed the FCC's ruling. The federal court sent the case back to the FCC, ordering it to take into account the First Amendment. The FCC responded by abolishing the Fairness Doctrine. Backed by pro–Fairness Doctrine groups, the opposition group challenged the FCC's right to abolish the Fairness Doctrine. The Court of Appeals ruled that the FCC acted within the law. By simply refusing to review the case rather than ruling it unconstitutional, however, the Supreme Court left open the possibility that Congress could some day restore the Fairness Doctrine.[71] When some in Congress pushed to reinstate the Fairness Doctrine in 1989, President Bush announced that he would veto such legislation. When the Supreme Court declined to review a case in 1990, the Fairness Doctrine was put to rest, at least for the time being.

Although the controversial Fairness Doctrine is no longer in effect, Section 315 of the Communications Act still requires broadcasters to provide equal access to the airways for political candidates during election campaigns. Under the Equal Time Rule, or "equal opportunity provision," if a broadcaster permits any candidate for public office to appear on the station, the broadcaster must give all other bona fide candidates for the same office in the same election equal opportunity to appear. The requirement for nonfederal elections differs from the requirement for federal elections.

For example, a broadcast station may choose to sell advertising time only to major party candidates running for local office in the primary race, because minor party candidates are not running against the major party candidates. In the general election, however, all candidates for the same office must be given the opportunity to buy equal amounts of advertising time at the same rates. Section 312(a)(7) of the Communications Act requires stations to provide "reasonable access" to all candidates for federal office.[72]

After studying broadcasters' sales practices during election campaigns, the FCC determined that not all candidates were being offered the lowest rates. This practice was in violation of the lowest unit charge provision of Section 315(b). The FCC rewrote the rules in 1991 to require all broadcasters to offer all candidates the lowest cost airtime sold to any other advertiser in all the classes of available airtime. News coverage of candidates and debates among major candidates—considered bona fide news—are exempt from the Equal Time Rule.[73]

The Equal Time Rule also requires broadcasters to carry advertisements from political candidates *without censorship,* even when some might consider the content offensive. In the 1992 campaign, for example, some pro-life candidates included pictures of dead fetuses in their campaign ads. Some candidates used character assassination tactics, but stations were required to run the ads. The Supreme Court ruled, however, that because under Section 15 they cannot censor or otherwise limit what politicians say in their ads, after carrying the advertisements broadcasters have immunity from libel and slander suits.[74]

The rule applies even when an on-air employee of a station runs for office. In other words, if an on-air reporter or disk jockey runs for public office, the station must give other candidates for the same office equal broadcast time at no charge. For example, when a Sacramento television reporter wanted to run for city council in his community, the station said he would have to take unpaid leave to avoid other candidates getting equal airtime. When the reporter appealed, the FCC and courts sided with the station.[75] So even though legislators and broadcasters periodically call for its repeal, as was the case with the Fairness Doctrine, the Equal Time Rule remains in effect with no indication that it will be weakened any time soon.

ACCESS TO GOVERNMENT INFORMATION AND MEETINGS

To encourage open government and an informed electorate, the federal government and all 50 states have open records and meeting laws. The federal Freedom of Information Act (FOIA), enacted in 1966 and strengthened in 1976 by the Government in the Sunshine Act, has significantly increased public access to government records and proceedings.[76]

The Freedom of Information Act was amended in 1974, requiring agencies to publish lists of records and fee schedules for making requested copies. In 1986 Congress reduced the fees that agencies were charging news organizations and educational institutions and raised the fees that they charged commercial businesses. Businesses requesting information now must not only pay the costs of copying documents but also must cover the time spent searching for and reviewing documents. Instead of citizens and journalists being the major benefactors of the act, lawyers are the most frequent users. Historians and other academicians also are frequent users.[77]

The act gives anyone access to all records of all federal agencies unless those records fall within one of nine exemptions. Agencies do not have to release information that would jeopardize national security, reveal business trade secrets, invade an individual's privacy, or interfere with a law enforcement investigation. Nor are regulatory agencies required to release reports dealing with banking and other financial institutions, or oil and gas exploration data and maps. Internal agency memoranda and information specified by federal statutes are also exempted from disclosure. Interpretation of these exemptions continues to be controversial and a way for agencies to withhold information.

In addition, the courts have etched away at the power granted to those outside government under the Freedom of Information Act. For example, in 1980 the Supreme Court ruled that reporters could not have former Secretary of State Henry Kissinger's diary of official telephone calls because he took the diary home with him. Unless the government compelled him to return it, the diary was beyond the reach granted under the act.[78] Many of the Central Intelligence Agency's records were excluded in a case decided by the Supreme Court in 1985.[79] Then in 1989 the high court restricted access to FBI records, ruling out public access to criminal histories on the basis that such information "can reasonably be expected to invade that citizen's privacy."[80]

The Government in the Sunshine Act requires about 50 federal agencies' central policy-making and governing boards to announce and open meetings to the public. The limitations on this requirement, however, roughly parallel the exemptions allowed under the Freedom of Information Act. When an agency does hold a closed meeting, it must record the proceedings or document what happened in detailed minutes. After the meeting, the agency must report what happened and the results of any votes taken, including how each of those present voted. The act excludes most informal gatherings and unofficial meetings.[81] And none of the rights granted under the open meetings act apply to private businesses, except under the provisions of the Securities Exchange Act to be discussed in subsequent sections.

Even with the sometimes controversial exemptions and limitations, the Freedom of Information Act and Government in the Sunshine Act and their counterparts at lower levels of government have opened the files and meetings of government to public scrutiny. Public relations practitioners in government must make sure that officials are aware of their obligations under these two acts and must respond appropriately to press requests for access to information and meetings. In fact, public affairs officers in government often confront the conflict between government agencies' desire to work in relative secrecy and journalists' demand for full disclosure. Claims of national security and individual privacy have often been covers for concealing official abuses of position and other misconduct in government. In 1995, however, the Clinton administration issued new guidelines for classifying national security and foreign policy documents, providing greater access and making it more difficult for government officials to classify materials exempt from FOIA access.[82]

LIBEL AND PRIVACY

Practitioners responsible for writing news releases, speeches, corporate reports, newsletters, house organs, and other communications are constantly watchful for pictures and statements that might defame or invade privacy. Libel and privacy civil law has become increasingly important, as lawyers and aggressive clients have been encouraged by juries voting large damage awards. Both practitioners and their employers or clients can be held liable for tort violations (see Exhibit 6.1 for definitions of some legal terms). For example, if a public relations agency issues a news release that attributes libelous statements to a company spokesperson, the public relations writer could be held accountable on the same basis as the spokesperson and the organization he or she represents. Anyone who "republishes" a defamatory statement can be named as a defendant in a defamation lawsuit.

Libel and Slander

Defamation occurs as *libel* (published written defamation) and *slander* (spoken defamation). It includes statements or communications that diminish re-

EXHIBIT 6.1

DEFINITIONS OF KEY LEGAL TERMS

Administrative law includes rules and decisions of the numerous governmental agencies charged with writing and enforcing regulations. Such law is designed to adjudicate disputes arising in regulated areas and activities such as communication (Federal Communication Commission), advertising and trade (Federal Trade Commission), public trading of stocks (Securities and Exchange Commission), and communication between labor and management (National Labor Relations Board). Thousands of government bodies have the power to write administrative law—writing rules and adjudicating among conflicting interests.

Common law is the oldest type of law because it derives from the accumulation of rulings (legal precedents) over the long history of court cases. U.S. common law is based on English common law that goes back at least 1,000 years. There is no federal common law, however, because each state has its own judicial traditions that are subject to change as conditions and values change.

Constitutional law represents the basic legal charters of the federal and state governments, spelling out basic legal principles, rights, and authorities. This type of law also spells out how each level of government is to relate to others and defines the areas of responsibility for each. The federal constitution, however, is the final arbiter of constitutional law, because no law in conflict with the U.S. Constitution can be enforced.

Criminal law spells out what is collectively considered an offense against society and the penalties for committing acts that violate what the people have said is wrong. The government must prove that the party charged with having committed an antisocial act is "guilty beyond a reasonable doubt." As the O. J. Simpson trials demonstrated, however, the burden of proof in *civil law* rests on the "preponderance of the evidence," a lower standard than that in criminal cases. In civil cases, one party is charging another with having been harmed, even though it is not at a level covered by criminal law. The courts provide a neutral venue for resolving the conflict without government participation.

Statutory law is the body of statutes and ordinances written and passed by legislative bodies. This type of law includes everything from acts of Congress to ordinances passed by city councils. Unlike common and constitutional law, statutory law is recorded by subject and collected by subject matter, making it accessible through published codes. For example, "United States Code" is recorded and indexed by subject or related subjects.

A *tort* is anything considered legally wrong that one party does to another, such as libel, invasion of privacy, or trespass. The party doing the wrong becomes the "defendant" being sued for monetary damages by the "plaintiff" under civil law. The plaintiff can be awarded "damages" in the form of compensation for loss or injury ("general damages"), reimbursement for actual monetary losses ("special damages"), and payment designed to punish the defendant ("punitive damages").

Sources: Definitions adapted from Kent R. Middleton, Bill F. Chamberlin, and Matthew D. Bunker, *The Law of Mass Communication*, 4th ed. (New York: Longman Publishers USA, 1997), and Wayne Overbeck, *Major Principles of Media Law*, 1997–1998 ed. (Fort Worth: Harcourt Brace College Publishers, 1998).

spect, goodwill, confidence, or esteem; or produce other adverse feelings about a person or institution. Related laws are designed to protect the reputations of persons and institutions. Four conditions—sometimes five—must be met before a statement is held legally libelous. The statement must do the following:

1. Hurt someone's reputation—be *defamatory.*
2. *Identify* the victim by name or by some other way obvious to others.
3. Be *communicated*—published or broadcast—to an audience other than the victim.
4. Contain an element of *fault*—proof of a falsehood being disseminated with either malice (if a public figure) or negligence (if a private individual).
5. Or in the absence of the fourth condition, proof of *damages or injury.*[83]

Newsletters covering public relations periodically report cases of practitioners suing in state courts under libel laws because of statements made after they were fired from public relations firms or other organizations. Similarly, practitioners responding to press inquiries about terminated executives must be aware of their own state's libel laws, because statements may be seen as damaging someone's reputation or future employment opportunities. Common law defenses, however, are well established, including the following:

1. *Truth* is the oldest and strongest defense. The burden of proving falsity is on the one bringing suit. The plaintiff must prove not only that the statement is false but also that it was made with malice or negligence.
2. *Privilege* protects otherwise libelous statements that are fair and accurate accounts of what occurs in government proceedings and documents.
3. *Fair comment* includes opinions about the performance of those in the public limelight—actors, politicians, sports stars, musicians, and other celebrities.[84]

Any individual has the right to sue for libel, as do corporations. In some states, nonprofit organizations and other small groups can sue for libel. Governments cannot sue for libel, but public officials may sue as individuals when they think their reputations have been subjected to defamatory statements that cause injury or actual damages. Suing may not be the wisest course, however.

Corporations and executives considering suits against critics who they believe have defamed them must consider the public relations ramifications of their suits in the court of public opinion as well as their chances of winning in a court of law. Moreover, practitioners must remind thin-skinned executives about the constitutional protection for caustic and even false comments in the public arena. Educational institutions, manufacturers, art galleries, advertising agencies, public relations firms, and others who offer their work to the public are subject to "fair comment."

Privacy

Citizens express increasing concern about protecting their private lives as computers make it increasingly easy to identify specific individuals and asso-

ciate them with records of past and current behavior. For example, if you donate to a favorite cause, your name and other vital information may be sold
or traded to organizations pushing similar causes. Soon after your first check
is cashed, similar organizations begin soliciting you for donations. Telephone
calls during dinner hours and an avalanche of mail solicitations make it clear
that the first organization shared information about you with others. Your response may be feeling that your right to privacy has been violated and you
just want to be let alone.

Such concern is reflected in statutes and court cases that place limits on
what information can be collected about citizens and who has access to the
information. Several states have passed laws severely limiting the use of electronic surveillance devices, the results of medical and substance abuse tests,
and personal data. Public relations practitioners have increasing responsibilities to safeguard the privacy of employees.

Legal scholar William L. Prosser divided the law of privacy into four different torts, each of which is "an interference with the right of the plaintiff
. . . 'to be let alone.' " The four categories include

1. *Intrusion* upon the plaintiff's seclusion or solitude, or into his or her private affairs
2. *Public disclosure* of embarrassing private facts about the plaintiff
3. Publicity that places the plaintiff in a *false light* in the public eye
4. *Appropriation,* for the defendant's advantage, of the plaintiff's name or
   likeness[85]

Each of the four categories affects public relations. For example, *intrusion*
is the tort of invading a person's solitude or seclusion, usually through illegal
entry, unlawful search, or electronic eavesdropping. Secretly taping conversations, whether in person or over the phone, may lead to privacy claims. "The
law has long held that it is illegal to peep, snoop, or eavesdrop on people in
private places," including using a telephoto lens, hiding a microphone, or tres-
passing outside a window.[86]

Public disclosure of private facts is similar to libel in that it violates the
personality and may cause mental anguish. But the private facts tort differs
from defamation in that the communications in a disclosure case are true but
embarrassing, and reputation is not necessarily damaged. Courts have found
the private facts tort when intimate medical information, identity of sex crime
victims, or name of a juvenile offender is revealed, as well as when photographs show someone in an embarrassing pose. Practitioners working at
public institutions, particularly where medical information is stored, should
be familiar with statutory limitations on the release of client or patient information. Most such organizations have written guidelines for releasing information. As a general rule, a public relations practitioner should get written
permission before releasing personal information. Parents must give permission for the release of private information about minors.

A person is placed in a *false light* when he or she is made to appear other
than he or she is. Like libel, this tort involves false statements or portrayals,

but unlike libel, a person's reputation need not be harmed. False light results when personal humiliation and mental anguish are demonstrated. For example, the false light tort has been found when captions accompanying photographs mislead or misrepresent. The "general rule," according to one authority, is:

> A photograph is reasonably safe if the caption is not misleading . . . However, if the caption creates a false impression about the people in the picture, or if it is used for commercial (i.e., noneditorial) purposes, the risk of a lawsuit for invasion of privacy is much greater.[87]

Appropriation occurs when someone uses the name or picture of another for advertising or trade purposes without consent. Appropriation occurs, for example, when an advertiser uses a celebrity's picture without permission. Practitioners should get a signed release from anyone whose name or picture is being used in commercial promotions or other publications. Employees may provide an implied consent when they willingly offer information and photos for in-house news publications. But employees have claimed appropriation where employers used employees' pictures in publications outside the corporate "family."

A legal spin-off of the appropriation tort is violation of a person's right of publicity. This is the right to exploit one's own talents. For example, in 1992 the Supreme Court refused to review a 1989 award of $400,000 to singer Bette Midler. Midler had sued Young & Rubicam for using a singer who intentionally sounded like Midler in advertisements produced for Ford's Mercury Sable.[88] Courts also have held that companies violate a person's right of publicity when they record an entertainer's entire act or sell memorabilia capitalizing on his or her personality without permission. Courts in some states have held that the right of publicity can be passed to one's heirs, making it an inheritable property right rather than a personal right. Such a case in California involved sales of souvenirs using the likeness of Bela Lugosi, star of the original Dracula film.[89] In Elvis Presley cases in Tennessee, however, a series of court decisions ended with the court concluding that Presley's right of publicity did not survive his death, and in fact passed to the public domain.[90] Of course this decision is moot for those who claim to have seen Elvis shopping last week at their local K-Mart or Kroger store.

In summary, organizations cannot use a living person's name or likeness for advertising or commercial purposes without consent, and in some states the same applies to deceased celebrities' names and likenesses. Practitioners must get consent before using someone's name, voice, photograph, or other portrayal. It is an oversimplified statement, but people generally have a legal right to their privacy.

COPYRIGHT AND TRADEMARKS

Public relations communicators frequently use the words and pictures of others in brochures, news releases, pamphlets, reports, and speeches. Sometimes public relations officers use excerpts of others' work; sometimes they hire outside contractors to write copy or take pictures. Publishing and selling the creative work of others and protecting property rights in one's own work is the province of copyright and trademark law.

Copyright

The copyright statute was revised in 1976 to take into account developments in photocopiers, videotapes, motion pictures, broadcasting, cable television, and other technologies since the original act was adopted in 1909. It has been amended many times since then. For example, in 1988 Congress enacted the National Film Preservations Act to regulate movie colorization and passed the Visual Artists Rights Act in 1990 to give sculptors, painters, and other visual artists control over whether or not their names can be used on works that have been altered with or without their permission.

Copyright law provides that the copyright owner "shall have exclusive right" to reproduce, distribute, and use original works of expression fixed in a tangible medium. A copyright exists automatically the moment a work is created. Contrary to popular belief, neither registration nor publication is required for a copyright to be valid. You can copyright written, musical, dramatic, pictorial, graphic, and sculptural works. You cannot copyright ideas, methods of operation, concepts, or utilitarian objects such as lamps or typefaces. For example, you can copyright the photograph of a famous landmark building on your campus, but your copyright does not prevent others from photographing the same building. The copyright protects only your photographic image—the composition and placement of elements—from being used without your consent.[91]

A public relations practitioner writing stories and taking pictures during the regular course of employment creates "works made for hire" that belong exclusively to the employer. However, contracts must be written to define an employer's rights in works created by employees during off-hours or by outside contractors and freelancers. A freelancer who sells a work without a contract usually gives up only rights to first publication.

Claiming formal copyright requires attaching a copyright notice to the work and registering with the Copyright Office of the Library of Congress in Washington, DC. Within three months of publication, the owner must file a four-page form, include two copies of the material to be copyrighted, and pay a fee based on the number of pages in the document. Although registration is not necessary for the copyright to be valid, it is helpful in case a copyright owner brings suit for infringement.

The copyright notice on the work consists of the following: (1) the word "Copyright," the abbreviation "Copr.," or the copyright symbol ©; (2) the year of first publication; and (3) the name of the copyright owner—for example, "Copyright 1999 by (your name here)." Copyright for an individual lasts for the life of the author plus 50 years. For a work made for hire, copyright lasts for 75 years from the date of publication or 100 years from the date of creation, whichever is shorter.

Limited or "fair use" of copyrighted works is not an infringement. Critics, scholars, news reporters, and public relations professionals can quote briefly from copyrighted works while evaluating or commenting upon them. But use of a substantial portion of another's work may be an infringement, particularly if that use lessens the potential market for the copyright owner. For example, copying and distributing chapters of this book violates the publisher's copyright protection of the material. Distributing photocopies of magazine articles to several corporate departments to save subscription costs also infringes upon a publisher's copyright.

Determining whether use of copyrighted material qualifies as fair use under the statute involves the following criteria:

1. The purpose and character of the use, including whether such use is of a commercial nature or is for nonprofit educational purposes
2. The nature of the copyrighted work
3. The amount and substantiality of the portion used in relation to the work as a whole
4. The effect of the use upon the potential market for or value of the copyrighted work[92]

For example, in 1991 a federal court ruled that the widespread practice of copying and selling packets of course readings does not qualify as fair use. As a result, Kinko's Graphics Corp. and other campus copying services must now get permission to copy and agree to pay royalties (if required) on previously published materials such as journal articles and book chapters.[93] In another case, the court found that it was not fair use for a large group of Texaco scientists to make single copies of journal articles even though the corporation had legal subscriptions to the journals.[94]

Practitioners and broadcast news monitoring service executives testified in 1992 before a Senate Judiciary Committee subcommittee in favor of a bill that would extend the fair use exception to the broadcast equivalent of print clipping services. Some broadcast monitoring services record news and public affairs programming about or of interest to their client organizations. Broadcasters have charged that these recordings constitute infringement of copyrighted material. Not surprisingly, public relations professionals and monitoring service executives argue that such use falls under the fair use exemption.

In the 1993 case *Georgia Television Company* v. *Television News Clips of Atlanta,* the court rejected a video clipping service's claim of a First Amendment right to provide video clippings to clients. The court held that the service violated the Copyright Act.[95] After Congress failed to pass legislation exempting such clipping services from copyright restrictions, the services entered lengthy negotiations with the major networks and local stations. The major networks have authorized video clipping services to use broadcast programming for modest licensing fees. Still underway, however, are attempts to develop an industry-wide agreement to cover similar use of local broadcasts by clipping services.[96] So far, broadcast monitoring services do not have to pay royalties to broadcast stations.

Trademarks

The Lanham Act of 1946 and its amendments protect *trademarks*—words, names, and symbols used by companies to identify and distinguish their goods or services from those of another. A trademark can be a product brand name such as Kleenex. A *trade name,* on the other hand, identifies the commercial name of the producer. Kimberly Clark Corporation, a trade name, manufactures Kleenex tissues, a trademark.

Trademark rights are created through adoption and use of the mark on goods in trade. Trademark rights are protected under common law, but registration of a trademark with the U.S. Patent and Trademark Office creates presumptions of ownership that are important should infringement be claimed. Application for trademark registration can be filed before or after the mark is used in commerce, but usually after a commercial research firm has confirmed that no other party has registered the name, phrase, or logo intended as a trademark. Applications include (1) a written application form, (2) a drawing of the trademark, (3) the filing fee ($245), and (4) three examples of how the trademark is being used. The ® symbol or the phrase "Registered in U.S. Patent and Trademark Office" indicates a registered trademark. Often the "TM" subscript is used when the registration is pending. The registration lasts for 10 years, with 10-year renewals for as long as the mark is used in commerce.

Organizations with valuable trademarks have legal staffs to police their use. Infringement can lead to public relations problems. The Coca-Cola Company, for example, made network news when it brought suit against a popular pizza parlor in California for misrepresenting the soft drink.[97] In another case, Pizzeria Uno Corporation sued a restaurant owner for infringement when two "Taco Uno" restaurants opened their doors.[98]

Owners of trademarks frequently run advertisements reminding journalists and public relations practitioners to use trademarks as adjectives, not as nouns or verbs, and to use capital letters when referring to their product. You may use a *Xerox* photocopier, or simply a photocopying machine; you do not "Xerox" a document. These policing efforts are designed to avoid losing exclusive use of a trademark by allowing it to fall into common usage as a generic word.

Some words and phrases cannot be trademarked. One example of this involved two of America's largest brewing companies. When Genesee Brewing Company sued the Stroh Brewing Company for infringing on its right to use the term "Honey Brown" to describe one of its popular specialty beers, the Court found that because the words "honey brown" were generic as applied to Stroh's product, Genessee could not recover for trademark infringement.[99] Reminding that generic marks are never entitled to trademark protection, the Court cited an earlier case involving the retailer Ambercrombie & Fitch: "No matter how much money and effort the user of a generic term has poured into promoting the sale of its merchandise and what success it has achieved in securing public identification, it cannot deprive competing manufacturers of the product of the right to call an article by its name."[100]

Public relations specialists in corporations and unions must be mindful that the Labor Management Relations Act of 1947 (Taft-Hartley Act) not only regulates communications during political elections but also prohibits management from interfering with labor's right to organize and to bargain collectively once a union is established. The Taft-Hartley Act prohibits both unions and management from engaging in unfair labor practices.

Representation Elections

The National Labor Relations Act of 1935 (known as the Wagner Act) required strict neutrality in communications to employees that involve organization of employees or collective bargaining. But in 1941 the Supreme Court ruled that an employer could not be barred "from expressing its view on labor policies." The employer, the Court said, is free "to take any side it may choose" on a controversial labor issue as long as the employer does not restrain or coerce his employees.[101] The Court views management's course of conduct as coercive rather than any individual statement.

The Supreme Court's holding was codified in the Taft-Hartley Act of 1947. Section 8(c) says that no management view, argument, or opinion will be an unfair labor practice as long as the expression contains "no threat of reprisal or force or promise of benefit."[102] The purpose of Section 8(c), according to the legislative conference committee, was "to protect the right of free speech when what the employer says or writes is not of a threatening nature or does not promise a prohibited favorable discrimination."[103]

Management does not engage in an unfair labor practice if it communicates to employees through speeches, talks, and letters to tell workers about the strike history of the union, the likely dues and assessments, and the merits of working for a company without a union. But management cannot threaten to fire or punish employees because of union activities, make promises to influence votes, spy on union meetings, or call employees separately to discuss the union. Management also cannot urge employees individually to vote against the union.

Collective Bargaining

Section 8(d) of the Taft-Hartley Act requires companies and unions "to meet at reasonable times and confer in good faith with respect to wages, hours, and other terms and conditions of employment." This means that both parties are supposed to enter negotiations with open minds and with a willingness to reach an agreement. If management is unwilling to meet or is unreasonably firm in its offers, labor may file an unfair labor practice charge with the National Labor Relations Board (NLRB).

The U.S. Court of Appeals for the Second Circuit upheld an NLRB ruling that General Electric engaged in an unfair labor practice when it combined "'take-it-or-leave-it' bargaining methods with a widely publicized stance of unbending firmness" in its negotiations with the International Union of Electrical, Radio and Machine Workers (IUE).[104] For several years, General Electric had followed a firm policy vis-à-vis its unions, backing up a hard-line policy with an intensive program of employee communication. Union critics labeled the program as "Boulwarism" because it was formulated largely by Lemuel R. Boulware. Looking at the "totality of conduct," the NLRB hearing examiner said General Electric flooded employees with

> a constant stream of communications plugging the merits of its bargaining position. In some instances it advanced arguments not only more full but different from those presented to the union negotiators at the bargaining table, a circumstance found herein to constitute the clearest evidence of bargaining bad faith.[105]

Furthermore, the company stressed to employees the finality of the company's offer, the futility of further negotiations, the "selfish" and "irresponsible" motives of the union leadership, and the jeopardy of employees' jobs.[106]

Unfair labor practices by unions include mass picketing that physically prevents nonstriking employees from entering a plant, acts of violence on a picket line, threats to employees that they will lose their jobs unless they support the union, and refusal to bargain in good faith.

FINANCIAL PUBLIC RELATIONS

Financial public relations, one of the highest-paid specialties in public relations practice, requires both an understanding of corporate finance and legal knowledge. Public Relations Society of America defines this part of public relations as follows:

> The dissemination of information that affects the understanding of stockholders and investors generally concerning the financial position and prospects of a company, and includes among its objectives the improvement of relations between corporations and their stockholders.[107]

Under the Securities and Exchange Commission's "integrated disclosure system," corporations in which members of the public own shares must continuously provide information about the health of the company. "Investor relations" specialists issue press releases, draft speeches, conduct annual meetings, and write quarterly and annual reports to achieve the "adequate and accurate information" required under federal law.

Investor relations practice is regulated by several statutes passed after the stock market crash of 1929. For example, the 1933 Securities Act restricts corporate communication before and during the period that new securities offerings are being registered with the Securities and Exchange Commission.[108] The Securities and Exchange Commission of 1934, which regulates trading of securities after their initial distribution, requires periodic reporting about a company.[109] The Investment Company Act of 1940 and the Investment Advisers Act of 1940 regulate investment companies and advisers.[110] In addition, practitioners in financial public relations are subject to the disclosure rules of the stock exchange that lists their company's stock.

Disclosure

Disclosure takes two forms: that which is mandated by statute and that which is required to avoid fraud. The Securities Act of 1933 and the Securities and Exchange Act of 1934 mandate disclosure. The 1933 act requires filings with the Securities and Exchange Commission when securities are offered to the public.

The Securities Act of 1933 requires that companies provide "material information" about new security offerings so that investors can make purchasing decisions based on facts. Information is considered "material" if the information is likely to have a significant effect on securities prices, or if it is likely to be considered important by a reasonable investor when making decisions to buy, hold, or sell shares. The act also requires a company to register its stock with the Securities and Exchange Commission and provide detailed information about its financial history and prospects.

Section 5 of the 1933 act prohibits a company from offering to sell or to buy a security before the security is registered with the SEC. During the pre-filing period and 20-day waiting period after securities are filed, a company can distribute a "red herring" prospectus that describes the stock but clearly indicates it is not an offering for sale. Not until a securities offering is registered can brokers and dealers issue written offers to sell the stock. During the registration period, companies do continue the usual flow of advertising, informational press releases, quarterly and annual reports, and proxy statements. Two cases illustrate this disclosure requirement.

In a case held to violate Section 5 of the 1933 act, two New York underwriters issued a press release before a registration statement was filed with the SEC. The press release touted more than 100,000 acres of prime Florida land "in the area of the Gold Coast" of Florida on which industrialist Arthur Vining Davis's Arvida Corporation would undertake a "comprehensive program of orderly . . . development." Within a short time the press release resulted in newspaper stories nationwide and stimulated investments totaling more than $500,000.

The SEC ruled that the references in the press release to the 100,000 acres on the Gold Coast began the selling process illegally before the securities were registered. Arvida's final prospectus, issued after registration, revealed that development might be more difficult than the press release had indicated. It turned out that much of the land was not conveniently located and that some of the money raised through the stock offering might have to be used to retire debt rather than to develop new properties.[111]

The SEC, in July 1984, published a report of an investigation of Howard Bronson & Co., a New York public relations firm, in which the agency and Thomas F. Pate, a vice president in the firm, were rebuked for dissemination of "false and misleading statements of material facts made in connection with the offer and sale of unregistered securities of a foreign issuer whose common stock was traded over-the-counter." Pate, who supplied a report to some 50 broker-dealers recommending the stock of International Technologies Corporation, failed to disclose that this was done for a "consideration of $3,000 per month," according to the SEC release dated July 12, 1984. This investigative report was issued under provisions of Section 21(a) of the 1934 Securities Exchange Act. The SEC release concluded,

> Although the Commission does not consider public relations firms to be guarantors of the information they gather for distribution, such firms should not view themselves as mere publicists or communicators of information with no attendant responsibility whatsoever for the contents of such information. Indeed, these firms must be aware of their obligation not to disseminate information concerning their clients which they know or should have reason to know is materially false or misleading.[112]

Congress overrode President Clinton's veto of the Private Securities Litigation Reform Act of 1995, thereby making several reforms to the Securities Act of 1933 and the Securities Exchange Act of 1934.[113] Major changes include restricting abusive litigation practices such as routine filing of class action lawsuits against public companies following sharp drops in stock prices and abuse of the discovery process by plaintiffs' attorneys to extort settlements from publicly traded companies that might settle simply to avoid costly litigation.

Additionally, the act created a new "Safe Harbor for Forward-Looking Statements" to encourage dissemination of information without fear of litigation. Companies may be protected from liability for predictions about earnings and performance as long as such forecasts are tempered by "meaningful" cautionary statements telling investors why the projections might fail to come true.[114] The law covers such statements as projections of revenues, income, earnings, expenditures, and dividends; plans and objectives of future operations; and management discussion and analysis of financial conditions or results of operations.

A quick review of *PR Newswire* shows that many companies' news releases now include "forward looking statements," which are duly noted as falling within the provisions of the new act, as well as the required "meaningful cautionary statements" listing the factors that could cause actual results to differ materially from those projected.

Securities Trading

The Securities Exchange Act of 1934 mandates disclosure to insure that investors have accurate information during the trading of securities. Section 13 of the act requires companies registered with the SEC to file quarterly, annual, and other reports with the SEC. Section 14 regulates the solicitation of proxies.

The annual report has long been regarded the most effective medium for disseminating corporate financial information to the investment community.

There are two kinds of annual reports: the usually glossy publication sent to shareholders and the four-part report filed on Form 10-K with the SEC. For many years the content of these two reports was often quite different. The SEC demanded extensive disclosure of market information, financial data, five-year summaries of sales and assets on Form 10-K, whereas the annual report to shareholders often contained much less. The 10-K was always available to the public, but investors seldom requested it. However, since 1982, annual reports to shareholders must contain most of the financial information and discussion required in Form 10-K.

Notable for the financial public relations practitioner is the required Management Discussion and Analysis (MD&A) in which the SEC asks management to describe in detail company liquidity, capital resources, results of operations, and future prospects. Practitioners often write drafts of the MD&A after canvassing officers and directors for suggestions.

Besides writing annual reports, the public relations professional is likely to have an important role in issuing proxy materials and organizing the company's annual meetings. Proxies are the statements companies must provide under Section 14 of the 1934 act to tell shareholders when and where the annual meeting will be held and what business will be conducted. Stockholders who cannot attend the meeting can vote their shares by proxy—giving specific directions in writing about how their votes are to be cast. The practitioner may have a hand in writing management policy proposals, publishing them in the proxy statements and organizing and conducting the annual meeting at which proposals will be voted upon. In proxy fights, in which a group of shareholders tries to sway votes to oppose management, the public relations practitioner may help choose issues, plan appeals to stockholders, and buy editorial advertising to promote management's positions.

Practitioners also participate in the updating of information—"continuous disclosure"—required by the securities laws and the rules of the stock exchanges. Under Section 12 of the 1934 act, companies must file quarterly reports on SEC Form 10-Q within 45 days of the end of the first three quarters and "current reports" on Form 8-K within 15 days of any material change in the company. Changes that must be reported on Form 8-K include shifts in the control of the company, acquisition or disposition of assets, bankruptcy or receivership, changes in the company's certifying accountants and financial statements, and resignations of directors.

In addition, the antifraud provisions of the securities laws—Section 10b of the 1934 Act and Rule 10b-5 in the Code of Federal Regulations—require corporate officers with access to nonpublic information—"insiders"—to make "immediate disclosure" of material changes if the insiders plan to trade the company's stock. Furthermore, stock exchange rules also require immediate disclosure of material changes in a company.

Simply issuing a press release may not be sufficient to fulfill the disclosure requirements. The American Stock Exchange disclosure policies, for example, require a company, "at a minimum" to release announcements of material information simultaneously to the national business and financial news wire services, the national news wire services, *The New York Times, The Wall*

Street Journal, Moody's Investors Service, and Standard & Poor's Corporation. Appropriate disclosure procedure depends on the size of a company and the dispersion of its stockholders, but the basic principle remains the same—public statements must be truthful.

SEC Chairman Arthur Levitt Jr. apparently believes that public statements also should be understandable. He announced that beginning October 1, 1998, critical parts of mutual fund prospectuses and other documents put out by publicly traded companies for stock and bond offerings must be written in plain English. The cover page and the section summarizing risk factors "must use everyday, concrete words, no legal jargon or highly technical business terms and should use lists of 'bullet' points for complex material whenever possible."[115]

Fraud

Section 10(b) of the 1934 Exchange Act and Rule 10b-5 prohibit fraud in securities trading. Rule 10b-5 makes it unlawful, in connection with the purchase or sale of any security, (a) to employ any device, scheme, or artifice to defraud; (b) to make any untrue statement of a material fact or to omit to state a material fact; and (c) to engage in any act or practice that operates as a fraud or deceit.

In order for there to be fraud in the buying and selling of securities, it is usually necessary to show that insiders are using nonpublic information to help them trade securities profitably or that insiders are "tipping" friends and clients with information that gives them an unfair advantage over the average investor. "Insiders" barred from tipping or trading on information not available to the public include corporate executives, public relations personnel, and outside accountants, lawyers, outside public relations counsel, and other professionals with access to corporate plans.

The SEC charged a public relations firm with insider trading for the first time in early 1986. (Recall that the second case of Anthony Franco discussed in chapter 5 occurred later in 1986.) In the first case, the SEC said that Ronald Henegen of R. F. Henegen Inc., a financial public relations firm, passed insider information about one of the firm's clients to a stockbroker. Based on the advance knowledge that Puritan Fashions Corporation (now part of C.K. Holdings, Inc.) would not achieve its sales and profit projections, the stockbroker advised another stockbroker and clients to sell Puritan stock amounting to some $2 million. In a third case, the SEC charged a senior vice president of Ruder Finn (New York) and a former senior account executive of tipping a relative and his friend to make a $250,000 profit on stock in a company about to be acquired by RF client Sandoz. The two public relations executives settled without admitting guilt by promising not to violate SEC laws in the future and by paying back the profits and a fine. "RF was not accused of any wrongdoing and pointed out it has a strict policy against the misuse of insider trading."[116] These cases illustrate that public relations practitioners "must not only know the law, they must take steps to ensure it will be followed."[117]

In the 1968 *Texas Gulf Sulphur* case, the Second Circuit Court of Appeals ruled that insiders and the company violated Rule 10b-5 by responding to rumors with a press release that misleadingly downplayed the importance of mineral samples taken at a Canadian mine. After some promising samples were found, but before a press release was issued, corporate insiders bought TGS stock. At least one officer tipped outsiders, who also bought stock.[118]

In *Schlanger* v. *Four-Phase Systems, Inc.,* the courts held that the company had issued a misleading statement denying knowledge of any corporate development that would account for market activity in its stock. At that very time, however, the company was actively engaged in merger discussions.[119] In a similar case, the SEC decided that *Carnation Company* issued "materially misleading" statements when it said there were no corporate developments that would account for unusual market activity in its stock. Carnation issued the statement while it was engaged in preliminary acquisition talks with Nestlé, S.A., which ultimately led to Nestlé's acquisition of Carnation.[120]

In its report of the Carnation Company ruling, the SEC encouraged public companies to respond promptly to market rumors concerning material corporate developments. Referring to the *Texas Gulf Sulphur* and *Four-Phase Systems* cases, the SEC concluded,

> Whenever an issuer makes a public statement or responds to an inquiry from a stock exchange official concerning rumors, unusual market activity, possible corporate developments or any other matter, the statement must be materially accurate and complete. If the issuer is aware of nonpublic information concerning acquisition discussions that are occurring at the time the statement is made, the issuer has an obligation to disclose sufficient information concerning the discussions to prevent the statements from being materially misleading.[121]

Because public relations firms may be held legally liable for issuing false or misleading statements, many insert clauses in client contracts to protect themselves should information provided by a client lead to charges of fraud. A typical clause reads as follows:

> You agree to indemnify and hold harmless from and against any and all losses, claims, damages, expenses, or liabilities which [name of public relations firm] may incur based upon information, representations, reports, or data furnished by you to the extent such material is furnished or prepared by or approved by you for use by [name of public relations firm].

During the mid- to late 1980s national news headlines featured a litany of SEC prosecutions of securities fraud and insider-trading cases. In May 1986, the SEC and federal prosecutors charged Dennis Levine with profiting $12.6 million through insider trading. In November 1986, Ivan F. Boesky agreed to pay a $100 million penalty to settle SEC charges of insider trading. In December 1987, Boesky was sentenced to three years in prison. In September 1988, the SEC charged Drexel Burnham Lambert and the now-infamous Michael Milken with insider trading, stock manipulation, fraud, and other federal securities laws violations. In December of the same year, the Drexel firm pleaded guilty to six felonies, settled the SEC charges, and paid a $600 million fine. The firm filed for bankruptcy court protection in February 1990. In April of that year, Milken pleaded guilty to six felonies and paid a $600 million fine. He began a 10-year prison sentence in November of 1990. These are only the major players in a series of scandals that reached from New York to Beverly Hills, contributing to the collapse of the junk-bond market, and some say the stock market crash of 1987.[122] It is little wonder that the SEC remains vigilant in the areas of financial public relations, stock manipulation, and insider trading.

OTHER LEGAL ISSUES

Legal issues also guide the business practices of public relations professionals. Contract law in particular calls for frequent specialized legal counsel. For example, since an advertising agency successfully sued when more than half the employees left with most of the agency's business in 1954, employment contracts routinely contain "noncompete" clauses. The principle established was that employees cannot use their employer's time and facilities to develop their own separate business. For example, Manning, Selvage & Lee sued three former executives in the Atlanta office—Glen Jackson, Boling Spalding, and Joseph Ledlie—who quit to start their own firm, Jackson Spalding Ledlie. The two firms settled out of court.[123]

In the majority of cases, however, the courts have not upheld noncompete clauses in employment contracts, favoring employees over their former employers seeking damages. Most contractual noncompete agreements apparently fail to meet one or more of three tests: (1) they must be reasonable, being no broader than necessary to protect the legitimate business interests of the employer without placing undue restriction on an employee's ability to earn a living; (2) they must be supported by some consideration, such as the offer of employment, raise, promotion, or continuing employment; and (3) they must protect only the employer's legitimate business interests, such as unique products and services, trade secrets, and goodwill. Attempts to eliminate competition or other purposes not related to the three tests have led courts to not uphold noncompete clauses.[124]

In other areas, the tobacco lawsuits have raised concerns that public relations firms increasingly will be targeted by plaintiffs seeking damages in cases involving charges of fraud or conspiracy (which, by definition, requires more than one defendant). For example, a public relations firm was named as a defendant in the Texas case *Feagin v. Brown & Williamson Tobacco Corp. et al.*, in which conspiracy was the sole cause of action.[125] The plaintiff claimed that the tobacco manufacturer, a research organization, and a public relations firm conspired to negate the effects of scientific studies linking smoking with health hazards, including cancer. These cases illustrate both the need to inquire about the truthfulness of information disseminated and the importance of understanding the potential legal implications of public relations work.

The threat of malpractice suits has even spawned a modest interest among public relations professionals in malpractice insurance policies. These examples suggest that to work in public relations, one must know enough about legal matters to be sensitive to potential problems and to recognize when to seek legal counsel.

A single chapter can introduce only a small array of issues that cut across many areas of practice. It is rare, however, that public relations problems are settled in a court of law. More often they are resolved in the court of public opinion.

NOTES

1. "ICM Crisis Report: News Coverage of Business Crisis Events during 1997," *The ICM Crisis Report* 6, no. 1 (February 1998).
2. Ibid.
3. Robert L. Dilenschneider, "Work Place Crises Aren't What They Used to Be," *Communication World* 14, no. 9 (October–November 1997), 24–27.
4. Kathy R. Fitzpatrick and Maureen Shubow Rubin, "Public Relations vs. Legal Strategies in Organizational Crisis Decisions," *Public Relations Review* 21, no. 1 (Spring 1995), 30–31.
5. Ibid., 31.
6. See Kathy R. Fitzpatrick, "The Court of Public Opinion," *Texas Lawyer,* September 30, 1996, 30.
7. Kathy R. Fitzpatrick, "Public Relations and the Law: A Survey of Practitioners," *Public Relations Review* 22, no. 1 (Spring 1996): 6–7.
8. Catherine A. Pratt, "First Amendment Protection for Public Relations Expression: The Applicability and Limitations of the Commercial and Corporate Speech Models," *Public Relations Research Annual,* 2 (1990): 207.
9. *Dennis* v. *United States,* 341 U.S. 494, 584 (1951).
10. *Near* v. *Minnesota,* 283 U.S. 697 (1931). This famous case actually only *limited* the *kind* of government interference.
11. For example, *Red Lion Broadcasting Co.* v. *Federal Communications Commission,* 395 U.S. 367 (1969) (broadcasting): *Burstyn* v. *Wilson,* 343 U.S. 495 (1952) (film).
12. *Village of Schaumburg* v. *Citizens for a Better Environment,* 444 U.S. 620, 632 (1980). The Independent Sector played a major role in this case.
13. For example, see *Chaplinsky* v. *New Hampshire,* 315 U.S. 568 (1942) (fighting words): *Miller* v. *California,* 413 U.S. 15 (1973) (obscenity).
14. Pratt, "First Amendment Protection for Public Relations Expression," 207.
15. *Nebraska Press Association* v. *Stuart,* 427 U.S. 539, 96 S.Ct. 2791 (1976).
16. *R.A.V.* v. *St. Paul,* 505 U.S. 377 (1992), 112 S.Ct. 2538 (1992).
17. *Doe* v. *University of Michigan,* 721 F. Supp. 852 (E.D. MI, 1989).
18. For example, *Skokie* v. *National Socialist Party of America,* 69 Ill. 2d 605, 373 N.E. 2d 21 (1978).
19. *Village of Schaumburg* v. *Citizens for a Better Environment,* 444 U.S. 620 (1980). In 1984 the Court also ruled that state-imposed limits on the amount of money charities may spend on fund raising violate the charities' constitutional right of free speech (*Maryland* v. *Munson,* 467 U.S. 947 [1984]). The vote was five to four.
20. *New York Times* v. *Sullivan,* 376 U.S. 255, 270 (1964).
21. *Valentine* v. *Chrestensen,* 316 U.S. 52, 54 (1942).

22. *Virginia State Board of Pharmacy v. Virginia Citizens Consumer Council*, 425 U.S. 748, 765 (1976).
23. *Bates v. State Bar of Arizona*, 433 U.S. 350 (1977) (legal advertising): *Linmark Associates, Inc. v. Township of Willingboro*, 431 U.S. 85 (1977) (signs): and *Carey v. Population Services International*, 431 U.S. 678 (1977) (ads for contraceptives).
24. *Central Hudson Gas & Electric Corp. v. Public Service Commission of New York* 447 U.S. 557 (1980).
25. *Central Hudson Gas & Electric Corp. v. Public Service Commission of New York*, 447 U.S. 557, 563–64 (1980).
26. *Posado de Puerto Rico Associates v. Tourism Company of Puerto Rico*, 478 U.S. 328 (1986).
27. *Virginia State Board of Pharmacy v. Virginia Citizens Consumer Council*, 425 U.S. 748, 771–72, n. 24 (1976).
28. Ivan L. Preston, *The Great American Blow-Up: Puffery in Advertising and Selling*, rev. ed. (Madison: University of Wisconsin Press, 1996).
29. Kent R. Middleton, Bill F. Chamberlin, and Matthew D. Bunker, *The Law of Public Communication*, 4th ed. (New York: Longman, 1997): 326–35.
30. Ibid., 330.
31. 29 U.S.C. sec. 141 *et seg.* (1988).
32. 2 U.S.C. sec. 441b. (1988).
33. *Buckley v. Valeo*, 424 U.S. 1, 19 (1976).
34. Reported by *O'Dwyer's Newsletter* 31, No. 5 (February 4, 1998), p. 5. This newsletter reported the charges against Lake and his departure from RLLM in the October 25, 1995, issue (Vol. 28, No. 42).
35. *Buckley v. Valeo* at 20–21.
36. Ibid. at 26.
37. *Austin v. Michigan Chamber of Commerce*, 494 U.S. 652 (1990).
38. See 2 U.S.C. sec. 441b (1988). See also 11 C.F.R. secs. 100.7 and 114.9 (1992).
39. 2 U.S.C. sec. 441b, 11 C.F.R. sec. 114, and Federal Election Commission Advisory Opinion 1980–20.
40. Middleton, Chamberlin, and Bunker, *The Law of Public Communication*, 268–69.
41. *First National Bank of Boston v. Bellotti*, 435 U.S. 765, 777 (1978).
42. Ibid. at 789–90.
43. Ibid. at 776.
44. Ibid. at 777.
45. *Consolidated Edison Co. of New York, Inc., v. Public Service Commission of New York*, 447 U.S. 530, 535 (1980).
46. *Central Hudson Gas & Electric Corp. v. Public Service Commission of New York*, 447 U.S. 557 (1980). In December 1983, the California Public Utilities Commission ordered Pacific Gas & Electric to include a fund-raising appeal from a watchdog group, TURN, in its bills four times a year.
47. *Citizens against Rent Control v. City of Berkeley*, 102 S.Ct. 434, 438 (1981).
48. 2 U.S.C. sec. 261 *et seq.* (1988).
49. *United States v. Harris*, 347 U.S. 612, 620 (1954). See also *United States v. Rumely*, 345 U.S. 41 (1953).
50. The Senate passed S 1060, 98-0, July 25, 1995. The House passed HR 2564, 421-0, then cleared S 1060, Nov. 29, 1995. President Clinton signed S 1060 into law (PL 104–65), Dec. 19, 1995.
51. "Lawmakers Enact Lobbying Reforms," *Congressional Quarterly 1995 Almanac: 104th Congress* (Washington, DC: Congressional Quarterly, 1996), sec. 1, 40.
52. *Harris*, 345 U.S. at 620.

53. *Rumely,* 345 U.S. at 47.

54. 2 U.S.C. sec. 267 (1988).

55. "Lobbying Reforms," *Congressional Quarterly 1995 Almanac,* sec. 1, 40.

56. Vance Hickin, "Grassroots Lobbying inside the Beltway: Public Relations and Advocacy in the Political Arena" (Senior research paper, San Diego State University, December 1995).

57. Adam Clymer, "Congress Passes Bill to Disclose Lobbyists' Roles," *New York Times,* November 30, 1995, sec. A, p. 1.

58. *Eastern Railroad Presidents Conference* v. *Noerr,* 365 U.S. 127, 144 (1961).

59. 22 U.S.C. sec. 611 *et seq.* (1988). See original act at 52 U.S. Statutes at Large, pp. 631–33, or PL 583, 8 June 1938.

60. Scott M. Cutlip, *The Unseen Power: Public Relations—A History* (Hillsdale, NJ: Lawrence Erlbaum Associates, 1994): 73–74.

61. 83 *Cong. Rec.,* 7, 8022 (1938).

62. 22 U.S.C. sec. 611(c)(1)(iii), (1988).

63. Ibid., secs. 611 and 614.

64. See Jerome Barron, *Freedom of the Press for Whom?* (Bloomington: Indiana University Press, 1973). See also Benno C. Schmidt Jr., *Freedom of the Press* v. *Public Access* (New York: Praeger, 1976).

65. *Uhlman* v. *Sherman,* 22 Ohio N.P.N.S. 225, 31 Ohio Dec. 54 (1919).

66. *Shuck* v. *Carroll Daily Herald,* 215 Iowa 1276, 247 N.W. 813 (1933); *Chicago Joint Board, Amalgamated Clothing Workers of America* v. *Chicago Tribune Co.,* 435 F. 2d 470 (7th Cir. 1970).

67. *Home Placement Service* v. *Providence Journal Co.,* 682 F.2d 274 (1st Cir. 1982), *cert. denied,* 103 S.Ct. 1279 (1983).

68. *Miami Herald Publishing Co.* v. *Tornillo,* 418 U.S. 241, 256 (1974).

69. Wayne Overbeck, *Major Principles of Media Law,* 1997–1998 ed. (Fort Worth: Harcourt Brace College Publishers, 1998): 397.

70. Ibid., 341.

71. *Syracuse Peace Council* v. *Federal Communications Commission,* 867 F.2d 654 (D.C. Cir. 1989).

72. Section 312(a)(7) was upheld in *Columbia Broadcasting System, Inc.* v. *Federal Communications Commission,* 453 U.S. 367 (1981).

73. Middleton, Chamberlin, and Bunker, *The Law of Public Communication,* 541–44.

74. *Farmers Educational and Cooperative Union of America* v. *WDAY, Inc.,* 360 U.S. 525 (1959).

75. *Branch* v. *Federal Communications Commission,* 824 F.2d 37 (D.C. Cir. 1987). In 1988 the U.S. Supreme Court refused to review the decision of the U.S. Court of Appeals.

76. Freedom of Information Act, 5 U.S.C. sec. 552 (1966), and Government in Sunshine Act, 5 U.S.C. sec. 552b (1976).

77. Overbeck, *Major Principles of Media Law,* 303–23.

78. *Kissinger* v. *Reporters Committee for Freedom of the Press,* 445 U.S. 136 (1980).

79. *Central Intelligence Agency* v. *Sims,* 471 U.S. 159 (1985).

80. *U.S. Department of Justice* v. *Reporters Committee for Freedom of the Press,* 489 U.S. 749 (1989). This decision was extended in *John Doe Agency* v. *John Doe Corp.* 493 U.S. 146 (1989) to include many other government documents obtained by the FBI during investigations.

81. *Federal Communications Commission* v. *ITT World Communications,* 466 U.S. 463 (1984). For a summary of the Government in the Sunshine Act and similar

access laws at state and local levels, see Overbeck, *Major Principles of Media Law,* 323–32.

82. Middleton, Chamberlin, and Bunker, *The Law of Public Communication,* 487.
83. Overbeck, *Major Principles of Media Law,* 101–2.
84. Ibid., 102–3.
85. William L. Prosser, 48 *Calif. L. Rev.* 383 (1960).
86. Middleton, Chamberlin, and Bunker, *The Law of Public Communication,* 177.
87. Overbeck, *Major Principles of Media Law,* 178.
88. *Midler* v. *Ford Motor Company,* 849 F.2d 460 (9th Cir. 1988).
89. *Lugosi* v. *Universal Pictures,* 25 Cal. 3d 813, 603 P.2d 425, 160 Cal. Rptr. 323 (1979).
90. *Memphis Development Foundation* v. *Factors,* 616 F.2d 956 (6th Cir. 1980) and *Factors* v. *Pro Arts, Inc.,* 652 F.2d 278 (2nd Cir. 1981).
91. Middleton, Chamberlin, and Bunker, *The Law of Public Communication,* 220.
92. Ibid., 238.
93. *Basic Books* v. *Kinko's Graphics Corp.,* 758 F. Supp. 1522 (S.D.N.Y. 1991).
94. *American Geophysical Union* v. *Texaco,* 85 Civ. 3446, 802 F. Supp. 1 (S.D.N.Y. 1992).
95. *Georgia Television Company* v. *Television News Clips of Atlanta,* 983 F.2d 238 (1993).
96. Middleton, Chamberlin, and Bunker, *The Law of Public Communication,* 210.
97. *Coca-Cola Co.* v. *Overland, Inc.,* 692 F.2d 1250 (9th Cir. 1982).
98. *Pizzeria Uno Corporation* v. *Temple,* 747 F.2d 1522 (1984).
99. *Genesee Brewing Company, Inc.* v. *Stroh Brewing Company,* 124 F.3d 137 (1997).
100. *Ambercrombie & Fitch Co.* v. *Hunting World, Inc.,* 537 F.2d 4 (2d Cir. 1976).
101. *National Labor Relations Board* v. *Virginia Electric & Power Co.,* 314 U.S. 469, 477 (1941).
102. 29 U.S.C. sec. 158(c) (1988).
103. National Labor Relations Board, 1, *Legislative History of the Labor Management Act,* 549 (1948).
104. *National Labor Relations Board* v. *General Electric Co.,* 418 F.2d 736, 762 (2d. Cir. 1969).
105. National Labor Relations Board, "General Electric Company and International Union of Electrical, Radio, and Machine Workers, AFL-CIO, Case No. 2-CA-7851," April 2, 1963.
106. *Intermediate Report,* appended to *General Electric Co. and International Union of Electrical, Radio, and Machine Workers,* AFL-CIO, 150 N.L.R.B. 192, 277 (1964).
107. "Code of Professional Standards for the Practice of Public Relations: An Official Interpretation of the Code as It Applies to Financial Public Relations," *The Blue Book of Public Relations Practitioners: 1997–98 Registry Issue* (New York: Public Relations Society of America, 1997), 27.
108. 15 U.S.C. sec. 77a *et seq.* (1988).
109. 15 U.S.C. sec. 78a *et seq.* (1988).
110. 15 U.S.C. sec. 80a-1 *et seq.* (1988) and 15 U.S.C. sec. 80b-1 *et seq.* (1988).
111. *Securities and Exchange Commission* v. *Arvida Corp.,* 169 F. Supp. 211, 213–14 (S.D.N.Y. 1958).
112. Securities and Exchange Commission Release of July 12, 1984, "In the Matter of *Howard Bronson & Co. and Thomas F. Pate,*" 10. See also Scott M. Cutlip, "Attendant Responsibility: Public Relations and the SEC," *Public Relations Journal* 41, no. 1 (January 1985): 26–31.

113. Private Securities Litigation Reform Act of 1995, Pub. L. No. 104-67, 109 Stat. 737 (1995).

114. See Mary S. Diemer, "Reforms Change Landscape of Securities Litigation," *Litigation News* 21, no. 3 (March 1996): 1, 4.

115. "Fund Prospectus in Plain English?" (Associated Press), *San Diego Union-Tribune,* February 8, 1998, sec. I, p. 3.

116. "Two RF Employees Charged by SEC," *Jack O'Dwyer's Newsletter* 30, no. 13 (March 26, 1997), p. 7.

117. Frank Walsh, "Public Relations Firm Charged with Insider Trading," *Public Relations Journal* 42, no. 5 (May 1986): 10.

118. *Securities and Exchange Commission* v. *Texas Gulf Sulphur Co.,* 401 F. 2d 833, 860–2 (2d. Cir. 1968) (*en banc*) *cert. denied,* 394 U.S. 976 (1969).

119. *Schlanger* v. *Four-Phase Systems, Inc.,* 582 F. Supp. 128 (S.D.N.Y. 1984).

120. Securities and Exchange Commission Release No. 22214 of July 8, 1985, "In the Matter of *Carnation Company.*"

121. Ibid., 7.

122. James B. Stewart, "Scenes from a Scandal: The Secret World of Michael Milken and Ivan Boesky," *The Wall Street Journal* (Marketplace Section), October 2, 1991, pp. B1 and B8. The article was adapted from James B. Stewart, *Den of Thieves* (New York: Simon & Schuster, 1991).

123. "MS&L, JSL of Atlanta Settle Lawsuit," *Jack O'Dwyer's Newsletter* 30, no. 13 (March 26, 1997): 7.

124. "Are Non-Compete Clauses Enforceable?" *Public Relations Tactics* 4, no. 12 (December 1997): 10.

125. See Gordon Hunter, "Dallas Tobacco Case Hinges Solely on Unusual Conspiracy Theory," *Texas Lawyer,* August 19, 1996, 7.

ADDITIONAL SOURCES

Fitzpatrick, Kathy R. "Public Relations and the Law: A Survey of Practitioners." *Public Relations Review,* 22, no. 1 (Spring 1996), 1–8.

Fitzpatrick, Kathy R., and Maureen Shubow Rubin. "Public Relations vs. Legal Strategies in Organizational Crisis Decisions." *Public Relations Review,* 21, no. 1 (Spring 1995), 21–33.

Ingelhart, Louis Edward. *Press and Speech Freedoms in America 1619–1995.* Westport, CT: Greenwood Publishing, 1997. Provides anecdotes to illustrate the history of press freedom and free speech in America, drawing from 2,400 cases and quotations.

Moore, Roy L., Ronald Farrar, and Erik Collins. *Advertising and Public Relations Law.* Mahwah, NJ: Lawrence Erlbaum Associates, 1997.

Ivan L. Preston. *The Great American Blow-Up: Puffery in Advertising and Selling,* rev. ed. Madison: University of Wisconsin Press, 1996.

Roschwalb, Susanne A., and Richard A Stach. *Litigation Public Relations: Courting Public Opinion.* Littleton, CO: Fred B. Rothman, 1995. Judges, lawyers, and public relations specialists present cases to illustrate public relations involvement—strategy, publicity, media relations, etc.—during legal processes.

Smith, Craig R. *All Speech Is Created Equal.* Long Beach, CA: Freedom of Expression Foundation, 1990. A conservative perspective on extending First Amendment protection to commercial speech and on resisting attempts to resurrect the FCC's Fairness Doctrine. Author uses summaries of many of the cases cited in this chapter to argue his points.

Walton, Wesley S., and Charles P. Brissman. *Corporate Communications Handbook: A Guide for Managing Unstructured Disclosure in Today's Corporate Environment.* New York: Clark Boardman Co., 1989. The authors—both lawyers—present case studies, case law, and SEC guidelines to illustrate legally required disclosure.

THEORETICAL UNDERPINNINGS: ADJUSTMENT AND ADAPTATION

7

Our organizations are living systems, existing in a turbulent environment that constantly tests their abilities to survive . . . the forces of
fierce global competition, dizzying technological advances, vacillating
economies, and highly sophisticated and demanding customers.[1]

—*Carol Kinsey Goman*

OBJECTIVES

After studying chapter 7, you should be able to

▼ Describe some of the major social, economic, and technological trends and changes that make organizations and
their public increasingly interdependent.

▼ Define a *system* and explain how systems theory is useful
for explaining how adjustment and adaptation are essential
to public relations.

▼ Explain the differences between open and closed systems,
using notions of *reactive* and *proactive* public relations.

▼ Define major concepts from systems theory, including
homeostasis, static and dynamic states, morphogenesis,
negative and positive feedback, and cybernetics.

▼ Diagram, label, and explain the open systems model of
public relations.

This chapter presents a theoretical model for public relations. Such a framework is necessary for understanding, organizing, and integrating the many activities and purposes of public relations. In addition, the professionalization of the field requires a body of knowledge grounded in theory.

As defined in chapter 1, *public relations* deals with the relationships that organizations build and maintain with publics. These relationships are subjected to political, social, economic, and technological change pressures in an ever-changing environment. Careful assessment of these forces is essential if organizations are to steer a safe, steady course through uncharted territory in the increasingly global community. Why is Sears a strong organization entering the 21st century and Wards struggling to survive and Woolworth's 400 five-and-dime stores now gone from the scene? To paraphrase Darwin, it is not the powerful organizations that will survive in the new millennium, it is those able to adjust and adapt to a changing world.

THE ECOLOGICAL APPROACH

This was the first public relations book to suggest using a social systems perspective when in 1952 it introduced the concept of *ecology* to public relations. Borrowed from the life sciences, the term helped students and practitioners understand that public relations deals with the *interdependence* of organizations and others in their environments. Viewed in this perspective, public relations' essential role is to help organizations adjust and adapt to changes in their environments.

Organizations depend upon their environments for many things: charters to operate, personnel, funds to operate and grow, freedom to pursue missions, and too many others to list. To prosper and endure, all organizations must (1) accept the public responsibility imposed by an increasingly interdependent society, (2) communicate, despite multiplying barriers, with publics that are often distant and diverse, and (3) achieve integration into the communities that they were created to serve. The first point represents the source of *public relations thinking in management.* The second point explains the growth of public relations as a *specialized staff function.* The third point states the *goal* of both management and the specialized practice.

In short, the job of public relations is to help organizations adjust and adapt to their environments. Public relations counselors monitor public opinion, social change, political movements, cultural shifts, technological developments, and even the natural environment. They then interpret these environmental factors and work with management to develop strategic plans of organizational change and responsiveness.

Years ago Alvin Toffler foresaw a more dynamic environment emerging from what he called the "technology-driven Information Age." He said the changes would include "new family styles; changed ways of working, loving, and living; a new economy; new political conflicts; and beyond all this an altered consciousness as well."[2] The revolution in information and communication is not so much about technology as in the social consequences of the new communication systems, according to communication scholar Frederick Williams: "Never before in history have so many people had so much information at their fingertips."[3]

Public relations specialists must anticipate and monitor such changes in an organization's environment and help interpret them to management. The successful public relations counselor constantly surveys the environment, always trying to extend vision farther beyond the horizon and trying to increase both the size and the resolution of the picture of present and future realities. In essence, such attempts to see clearly and to anticipate are designed to give the organization time to plan, an opportunity to be *proactive* rather than simply *reactive* to environmental changes.

Specific changes and forces at play must be identified, studied, and understood for particular situations and organizational settings. At the same time, however, some overriding basic changes drive other change pressures and produce consequences for all organizations.

SOME BASIC TRENDS AND CHANGES

Committing words to paper on trends and basic changes is risky business when the world is changing with unparalleled speed. By the time you read this section, no doubt scientific and technological advances, economic and political reforms, and even changes in social attitudes and individual freedoms may make parts of the list obsolete. Surely the specifics will have to be rewritten almost weekly before being factored into organizational decision making. With that acknowledgment of the limitations, following are brief discussions of seven areas of great change that have far-reaching impact on most organizations and their publics.[4]

Protecting the Environment

Environmental issues dominate public debate and public policy and will do so well into the 21st century. Faith Popcorn calls this movement the "Save Our Society" trend and says it is "the issue for the soon-to take-over generation."[5] Concerns about the environment have prompted changes in which products are purchased, how they are packaged, how much of the raw material is recycled, and how and where they are discarded. "Green," "biodegradable," and "recyclable" are valued attributes in the increasingly environmentally sensitive marketplace.

Destruction of the protective ozone layer in the atmosphere calls for international concern and action. Burning fossil fuel deposits billions of tons of carbon in the air each year, causing an increasing concentration of carbon dioxide. Global warming threatens to turn large portions of Africa, Asia, and Latin America into arid wasteland. The greenhouse effect could also change coastlines, flood cities, and change agriculture by changing rainfall patterns and commerce by raising sea levels. Stopping destruction of rain forests will require international action and cooperation to avert an environmental disaster. Other concerns include air and water quality, acid rain, trash in landfills, disposal of toxic materials, and human encroachment on remaining wilderness areas.

Public opinion surveys show that damaging the environment is seen as the most serious business crime. Likewise, surveys of leaders in business and government, as well as in public relations, consistently show protection of the environment as their major concern. Concern for protecting the environment also has fueled a "green" movement even among investors, sometimes previously viewed as interested only in the financial bottom line. They are using their dollars to make the same point an environmental activist made on CBS-TV news: "Clean up your (environmental) act, not just your image."

A majority of large corporations now have formal environmental policies and management committees to help make their organizations and products more environmentally friendly. Organizations also set goals related to reducing waste disposal, recycling, and cutting air pollution, some would say because of pressure from environmental groups and the threat of governmental regulations. Some futurists see signs of progress:

> By 2010 or so we should expect manufacturers to have adopted "green" methods, and a significant portion of energy will be derived from renewable sources and biomass. Improvements in fossil-fuel efficiency will reduce greenhouse-gas emissions by one-half by 2016. . . . By 2017, high-speed-rail systems will connect major cities of the developed world.[6]

Examples of how the environmental movement affects organizations are numerous. In fact, almost any activity that has potential impact on the environment requires an increasingly rigorous environmental impact review and public hearings. For example, the U.S. Fish and Wildlife Service declared almost 12 million acres of forest as "critical habitat" for the now-famous and threatened spotted owl. Of the acres set aside, 3 million acres are private forest, including 200,000 acres owned by Weyerhaeuser. As a result, the company says that it will have to spend $700,000 to locate the owls on its properties and that each owl or pair that it finds on the Olympic Peninsula "locks up enough forestland to provide homes for 20,000 American families."[7]

The U.S. Navy introduced new sandblasting methods, switched to non-toxic types of paints for ships, and enforced strict new guidelines for refuse disposal at sea in response to environmental concerns. McDonald's started selling its burgers and other fast-food items in biodegradable packages in response to the green movement. In short, no organization can escape the growing concern and increasingly militant activism related to protecting the environment. One futurist consultant recycled a term long used by soil conservationists to describe this responsibility—*stewardship,* or "the task of caring for and preserving the earth and all its resources, to return them in as good or better shape to each succeeding generation."[8]

Maybe most promising is consumer demand for products that are manufactured using environmentally sensitive processes. The number of manufacturers seeking ISO 14000 certification by the International Organization for Standardization in Geneva, Switzerland, provides dramatic evidence of the growing concern for the environment. Some retailers and wholesalers around the world require that manufacturers and suppliers be certified, indicating that their products meet internationally accepted criteria covering the environmental impact of products throughout their life cycle.[9]

Health Care Reform

Health care costs are a major cost of doing business for many organizations. Medical expenses prevent many people from seeking treatment and can bankrupt others. Company-sponsored health insurance coverage has become an employment benefit available to fewer and fewer. Many unemployed and underemployed simply go without coverage, and without health care, they increase health risks for themselves and others.

National health insurance, health care reform, and managed care became national issues in the 1990s, often dominating national debate and elections. More and more people began to question the morality of the inequalities in health care for the haves and the have-nots. Policy makers shaved millions of dollars from current budgets by not funding prenatal care and proper nutrition for children, simply postponing the social costs that threaten to bankrupt state and federal governments in the future. In the meantime, advances in medical science and technology continue to push the envelope on extending life and increasing health care costs. In response, Oregon led the way by rationing health care based on expert judgments about which procedures are most cost-effective uses of the state's limited health care budget.

Amid questions about the morality of not making all medical science and technology available to everyone, political pressure continues to grow for national reform of the health care industry as more and more hospitals fail, while others switch from being nonprofit community hospitals after being purchased by large health care corporations. Some futurists call for major changes in how hospitals operate and how health care is paid for:

> Much as fast-food chains have succeeded by offering a limited menu by stressing efficiency and consistent quality, a chain of focused factor outlets could succeed by specializing in a single type of operation (such as open-heart work or joint replacement) or by providing the complete spectrum of supplies and services needed to deal with one common condition (e.g., diabetes or asthma). But this could only happen if consumers have the freedom to select their own health-service providers and pay the bills themselves.[10]

At the same time that many urge reform in the health care system, the ever-expanding genetic engineering and pharmaceutical industries introduce new gene therapies and drugs to cure or prevent diseases. Optimists predict that in a few years the focus will switch from concerns about disease to wanting to live longer, stronger, and smarter.

AIDS

Not all experts share the same optimism about finding a way to prevent infection by HIV, the virus that causes AIDS: "We're not going to end infectious disease any more than detectives and our other law enforcement brethren are going to stop violent crime."[11] The health care system will crumble, according to some, under the weight of the worldwide acquired immune deficiency syndrome, or AIDS, epidemic. For example, up to 900,000 in the United States are infected with the AIDS virus. In some African cities, as many as 40 percent of the population already carry the HIV that ultimately causes AIDS in most of those infected. Harvard University researchers estimate that as many as 120 million people worldwide will be infected by the virus by the year 2000, and 25 million will have AIDS. The Harvard experts predict that the greatest number of cases will be in Southeast Asia and Africa, with Latin America and the Caribbean also suffering major epidemics.[12]

AIDS education and safe-sex campaigns have become commonplace in many organizations. "Universal precautions" and safety training programs in health care settings have changed the practice of medicine, nursing, and dentistry, as well as emergency services such as police and fire fighting. Prison guards, blood-bank staff, medical laboratory technicians, waste-disposal crews, and even housekeeping personnel see themselves at risk. Few organizations can avoid the impact of the AIDS crisis or the impact of people's perceptions of being at risk.

Globalization of Business and Economies

In *Megatrends 2000*, authors John Naisbitt and Patricia Aburdene preface their view of the new millennium by describing what they accurately saw as a global economic boom in the 1990s. To illustrate the impact of new economic forces in the global community, they raise the question, "Who is more important and known, Jan Carlzon, head of SAS, and Pehr Gyllenhammar, head of Volvo, or the top political figures whose names are not even known outside Sweden?"[13] Their point is that the international landscape shaped by political and military alliances formed during 20th-century wars are giving way to economic alliances. Acquiring territory—the old goal of international conflicts—is being replaced by the goal of building economic advantage in international trade.

This scenario includes free trade and common currency among nations. Linking 15 European Union countries in 1992 was simply the most visible indicator of the move toward free trade worldwide. In 2002, for example, 11 of the EU countries will begin using the same currency—Euro coins and paper notes—in place of their sometimes centuries-old francs, schillings, marks, and lira (go to **www.europa.eu.int/info-en/htm**). At the same time, economic alliances are breaking down regional trade barriers in North America, South America, Latin America, the South Pacific, Southeast Asia, the Persian Gulf, and West Africa. It is conceivable that talk of trade imbalances and trade deficits between countries soon will be no more meaningful than talk of trade imbalances between New York and Chicago, Los Angeles and San Francisco, Kyoto and Tokyo, or Munich and Stuttgart. For example, Japanese automobile companies manufactured automobiles in Tennessee, Ohio, and Illinois. Sony manufactured television sets in southern California. At the same time, Coca-Cola and Pepsi bottled their American soda pops around the globe. In other words, even past barriers often were more political than real.

Speeding the demise of the last vestiges of protective barriers are millions of miles of fiber-optic cables linking computers, fax machines, telephones, and local communication networks worldwide. The global marketplace thrives on this rapidly developing global telecommunication system. Being "out of the loop" takes on new and real meaning when we are talking about world trade and the global economy. Few organizations can truly isolate themselves from these global economic forces. In fact, most will have to link their activities and products just to stay in business. That means that government policy and business practice must take into account the new realities of the global market.

For example, U.S. policy makers have not been able to agree on what computer code encryption products can be exported or on what role government will play in regulating computer security software. As a result, major software producers in Germany, Ireland, Canada, Israel, and the United Kingdom ship encryption products across borders without the obstacles limiting U.S. entry to this global market.

> Our policy, ironically, encourages the growth of foreign producers at the same time it retards growth here. . . . The global market is rendering our policy obsolete. And I fear that will soon make our products obsolete as well. The lack of agreement is caused by the unwillingness to compromise.[14]

Global Communication in the Information Age

Few could have imagined that Marshall McLuhan's 1950 forecast of a "global village" would include Saddam Hussein and Bill Clinton tuned to the same Atlanta-based Cable News Network program in order to monitor missile strikes in the Persian Gulf. Likewise, few could have predicted the collective mourning experienced by a worldwide audience attending Princess Diana's funeral via international television. Founders of the modern Olympics could not have imagined that the games would become the world's largest media event, transforming the global village into the largest audience in history, even sharing the horror when a bomb distracted attention from the Atlanta games.

An array of fixed-position satellites provides two-way communication anywhere in the world. Pocket-sized transmitter-receivers that were once science fiction within the reader's lifetime are now commonplace in international commerce, government, and even social exchange. Even though English is the language of international business, computers are extending the reach of the new information age by translating documents, transcribing voice communication, and empowering those formerly excluded from international discourse. And the messages, whatever their intended content, tell distant peoples about each other and events of common interest. Simply put, the window on the world is opening wider and wider to more and more people.

Communication satellites and fiber-optic networks deliver electronic mail, television and radio coverage, newspaper and magazine content, and "secure" commercial transactions and government communications. No doubt some of the information is about the latest developments in artificial intelligence, virtual reality, robotics, and other technology spawned by computers and the information age. What organization can suceed in the new millennium while disregarding these developments?

In summary, new communication technology is changing the world in unexpected and powerful ways. Central to these changes are new kinds of communities—"metanational" entities—bringing together every imaginable group of persons. These "telecommunities" are

> Powerful, incorporeal communities built on shared interest; they are not wedded to geography or contained by national boarders. The growth of these placeless communities will have a major impact on society economically, politically, and culturally, and they will challenge traditional sovereignty in many virtually unstoppable ways.[15]

Realignment of the Family and Work

No longer do most American families look like the families portrayed in old movies: Dad drives off to work in the family car; mom gets the kids (one girl and one boy) ready for school; the kids hold hands and walk a short distance to their neighborhood school; mom goes about her daily chores, paying particular attention to getting the ring around the collar out of dad's shirts; after school, the boy delivers newspapers while the girl helps mom prepare dinner; dad returns from work in time to loosen his tie and to rest with the evening paper before dinner; and finally, the family spends the evening together reading, playing board games, or doing school homework. It is safe to say that you probably do not know a family like this now.

Variations on family structure are too numerous to describe, but a few examples will help make the point: families headed by single parents, mixed families that include children from previous marriages and stepparents, extended families in which grandparents are parenting their grandchildren, and even bicoastal families in which one parent works back East and the other works out West. Experts point out that almost one-fourth of all children live with only one parent (usually the mother) and that one-third of those families live in poverty. What organization can ignore the impact of family life on its most important public, its employees? What organization can ignore the impact of these same forces on customers, clients, neighbors, and others in the community?

Potomac Electric Power could not: It now offers employees free child care placement services. Nor could Lockheed Martin: This company provides employees a toll-free 24-hour hotline so they can talk to counselors about stress, child care options, or elder-care services for aging parents. Also responding to the changing needs of families, cable television company Discovery Communications instituted flextime options such as taking work home and altering days and hours in the office. These companies will not be alone as an aging population will increase the number of workers who exercise their rights under the federal family leave law for unpaid leave to care for elderly parents. Likewise, renewed interest in "balancing the new work-family equation" and child care puts added pressure on employers to be "family friendly."[16]

Not only families benefit when employees' satisfaction with their work and appreciation of management support increase. Aetna, the insurance company, saved an estimated $2 million within five years after instituting a family-friendly maternity leave program that allowed employees to work part-time after leave. About 90 percent of all women returned to the company after their leave, or double the rate before the new leave program. First Tennessee Bank found that employee satisfaction translated into reduced employee turnover, greater customer satisfaction and retention, and revenue growth well above the industry average. Likewise, Sears has hard data linking employee satisfaction with greater customer retention, according to Executive Vice President Tony Rucci: "If we improve employee satisfaction by five points we can predict a two-point improvement in customer satisfaction. And a quarter after that, revenue will grow by 1.67 percent."[17]

Civil Rights and the Empowerment of Individuals

Amnesty International makes a point of keeping the spotlight on countries that violate individual rights and freedom. Global communication networks make the spotlight bright indeed. Under the glare of global attention, even South Africa's apartheid gave way to a new public policy recognizing the rights of all citizens. Nike also found itself in that spotlight when accused of using unfair labor practices in its Asian plants. And following the well-established pattern, increased literacy and education continue to spur greater individual rights and freedom worldwide.

In no small way, the demise of Soviet-style socialism around the world will ultimately enhance individual opportunities to participate in the emerging global economy. Even with their obvious potential for abusing individuals, the new democratic economies will benefit more individuals than did centrally controlled production and distribution. Unlike economies run by governments, those driven by individual enterprise (entrepreneurs) and individual consumers will empower individuals. Even formerly die-hard socialists now call for "market-driven socialism" and "free-market socialism." Regardless of the new labels designed to gloss over fundamental change, however, new forms of entrepreneurial spirit and capitalism are replacing socialism because of relentless pressure by individuals who want to participate in the global economy and new communication technology that makes their participation possible and often free of government control.

TRACKING THE TRENDS

This discussion of major trends and changes is far from complete, but it indicates how major forces affect organizations. It simply is not possible to build an omnibus list that would cover all situations. Instead, the role of public relations is to track and analyze the specific trends and forces at play in particular situations.

For example, how will the growing animal rights movement affect an organization's ability to accomplish its mission? The *Los Angeles Times Magazine* reported that the Maryland-based animal rights group People for the Ethical Treatment of Animals (PETA) "has grown from humble origins to an 800-pound gorilla . . . the largest organization of its kind in the country, claiming more than 350,000 members."[18] Cosmetics manufacturers, medical research laboratories, meat packers, and even federal government agencies have had to factor the views of this new activist force into their decision making.

The animal rights movement forced Avon, Estée Lauder, Benetton, and Tonka Toy Company, among others, to stop testing products on rabbits, guinea pigs, and other animals. It forced the National Institutes of Health to close a research clinic that used animals in research and the Pentagon to halt wound tests on animals. A slaughterhouse in Texas was ordered shut after PETA pressure. PETA is also winning the battle for public opinion, as an overwhelming majority support animal rights and think it should be illegal to kill animals for fur or use animals in cosmetics research.

Consider the issue of education reform: As more and more Americans enter the job market without basic writing, math, and problem-solving skills, American industry slips further behind in the competitive global marketplace. At the same time, parents must cope with ever-increasing costs for post-secondary education. RJR Nabisco Corporation in 1992 began matching employees' annual contributions to a tax-deferred educational savings plan. RJR Nabisco contributes up to $4,000 toward the costs of college, everything from a two-year college to an Ivy League university. Many other companies have "adopted" schools to help promote improvement in the educational system. Others have started their own basic education programs in an attempt to equip employees with basic job skills. Few organizations escape problems brought on by the education crisis, the changing family, new technology, or global competition.

A SYSTEMS PERSPECTIVE

This discussion of changes and their impact on organizations suggests a systems perspective for public relations. The systems perspective applies because mutually dependent relationships are established and maintained between organizations and their publics.

The concepts of adjustment and adaptation, as well as our definition of public relations, employ concepts and propositions from *systems theory*. For

EXHIBIT 7.1

TRACKING TRENDS AND ISSUES

Picture yourself as the captain of the Starship Enterprise.

You want to be sure that you have a radar system that can accurately anticipate fast-moving meteors and the location of nearby planets to avoid impending disasters.

While moving through space at warp speeds, you don't want to wait until these obstacles are in sight to adjust your course and keep the ship out of danger.

The same is true about an organization—your organization—facing a meteor shower of issues in today's rapidly changing environment.

As issues affecting your organization arise, it is best to have a radar system in place that will help management *anticipate* trends and issues likely to affect your organization and its publics, rather than waiting until it's too late to do anything except react defensively.

If you are in public relations, you must start being more systematic in the tracking and management of issues. If you don't, someone else in your organization will. It's a prerequisite for organizational survival.

Even the Starship Enterprise would find it difficult to navigate through the turbulent issues environment most organizations face today.

Quote from Kerry Tucker, President, Nuffer, Smith, Tucker, Inc., San Diego, CA. Used with permission.

---

example, a university is part of a system composed of alumni, donors, neighbors, employers, high school counselors and teachers, and other universities in the area, to name but a few of the many publics. Even the simplest definition of a system—a set of interdependent parts—illustrates this perspective. However, an elaborated definition better serves our analysis:

> **A system is a set of interacting units that endures through time within an established boundary by responding and adjusting to change pressures from the environment to achieve and maintain goal states.**

In the case of public relations, the set of interacting units includes the organization and the publics with which it has or will have relations. They are somehow mutually affected or involved. Unlike physical and biological systems, however, social systems are not especially dependent on the physical closeness of component parts. Rather, specification of organization–public interactions defines systems. In other words, an organization–publics system consists of an organization and the people involved with and affected by the organization. Whereas the organizational component in the system is relatively easy to define, publics are abstractions defined by the public relations manager applying the systems approach. In fact, different publics, and therefore a different system boundary, must be defined for each situation or problem.

This principle of systems theory can be illustrated by comparing a university's publics when the goal is recruiting students as opposed to when the goal is raising money for a new business school computing center. The student recruitment campaign might include college-bound high school students, their parents, high school counselors, students currently enrolled at the university, and alumni. Because the university tends to attract students from a particular region or segments of the population, program planners would have to identify the geographic and sociographic territory to be covered in the recruitment effort. In effect, each of these decisions defines the components and boundary of the system for the student recruitment program.

The capital campaign for the new computing center at the same university, on the other hand, calls for a different definition of the organization–publics system. Program planners would determine what groups or entities are most interested in such a facility or most likely to benefit from its presence on campus. Surely the local business community would include potential donors. In cities far from the campus, corporate foundations that have historically funded innovative educational programs would be included as prospective contributors. More specifically, computer hardware and software companies that hire computer scientists would be identified as a third public for this campaign. Not all alumni are likely contributors, but those who have succeeded in professions calling for computing skills could be selected from the alumni list to make up a fourth public.

In both situations, definitions of the publics include those with whom the organization must establish and maintain enduring and mutually beneficial relationships. Most relationships, however, extend well beyond the period of such specific campaigns. Therefore, even though relationships must be defined specifically for each situation and program goal, they also must be viewed in the larger context of the university's overall public relations program.

Public relations efforts, then, are part of an organization's *purposive* and, therefore, *managed* behavior to achieve goals. For example, a fire that destroys a museum certainly has an impact on the museum's relationships with donors and others. Such an unplanned event, however, clearly is not part of the public relations program. On the other hand, the fund-raising campaign, groundbreaking ceremony, and grand opening gala are public relations responses to the situation created by the fire. These events are intended to establish or maintain relationships necessary for rebuilding the museum.

In some cases, goals can be achieved by simply maintaining existing relationships in the face of changing conditions. More likely, however, organizations must continually adjust their relationships with publics in response to an ever-changing social milieu. Because organization–publics systems exist in changing environments, they must be capable of adapting their goals and relationships to accommodate change pressures from their complex and dynamic settings. A classic case of adjustment and adaptation is the redirection of March of Dimes fund-raising and research to birth defects after the polio vaccine eliminated the disease for which the organization–publics system was originally created.

Environmental Change Pressures

Systems theorists typically define the environment as anything that generates change pressures—information, energy, and matter inputs—on a system. Environmental inputs to organization–publics systems take many forms. For example, news reports about abuses by top executives at United Way—lavish lifestyles, high salaries, consulting fees paid to associates, limousine and luxury hotel expenses, and even Concorde flights to Europe—certainly affected the charity's relationships with donors and local United Way chapters. And the impact was not limited to United Way, as all charities braced for a donor backlash, greater public scrutiny, and even government investigations of high salaries and generous benefits packages of nonprofit organizations executives. Soon after the United Way case made headlines in the nation's news media, the biweekly *Chronicle of Philanthropy* reported that more than one-fourth of the nation's largest 117 charities paid top executives $200,000 or more annually. Years later, the issue of charity executives' pay made headline news: "Officials at AIDS Charities under Fire over $100,000-Plus Salaries."[19]

Changes in educational levels and values of those entering the local workforce affect relationships between a local manufacturing company and labor unions, community groups, local government, and other employers in the area. Shifts in university students' majors—from history to business, for example—put stress on the rather rigidly structured faculty and resources at a university. Changes in the university in turn affect relationships with its various publics: prospective students, current students, faculty, alumni, trustees, donors, legislators, and prospective employers of graduating students. Relationships with other institutions of higher education will change as the universities compete for history majors and refer business students to each other's campuses.

Even "an insignificant leak" of radioactive water in a power utility's nuclear-generating reactor puts stress on a utility's relationships with regulators, antinuclear citizen groups, and the financial community. Or recall the media coverage of protest groups picketing tuna-canning companies because their fishing practices killed dolphins. Almost immediately sales slumped, government scrutiny increased, children and parents alike erroneously accused the companies of killing "Flipper" for profit, and protest stickers were attached to the product on grocery store shelves. Socially conscious investors sold tuna stock as prices plummeted.

These examples illustrate that change pressures on organization–publics systems come from many types of environmental sources. In turn, organization–publics relationships change in response to these environmental pressures. If they do not change, old relationships become dysfunctional because the organization acts and reacts in ways inappropriate to the new circumstances. If they are unmanaged and nonpurposive in their responses to environmental changes, systems tend to degenerate to maximum disorder, what systems theorists call "entropy." In social systems this means that coordinated behavior to attain mutually beneficial goals is no longer possible. In effect, systems break up. Public relations is charged with keeping organizational relationships in tune with the mutual interests and goals of organizations and their publics.

Subsystems and Suprasystems

To this point, a system has been defined as including the organization and its publics. Similarly, the organization is itself composed of a set of interacting units. From this perspective, the organization can also be viewed as a system. Because organizations exist in dynamic social settings, they must modify internal processes and restructure themselves in response to changing environments. In the absence of such adjustment and adaptation, organizations—just like any other social system—become out of step with the world around them. As counselors to line management, the public relations staff is charged with keeping the organization sensitive to environmental changes, anticipating as well as reacting to change pressures.

Likewise, the organization–publics system can be part of a larger set of interacting units, thus viewed as a component of a higher-order social system. For example, a local United Way–publics system is but one component of the community's charitable social service system. It is also only one subsystem in the national system of affiliates, which in turn is but one component of the nation's charitable social service system. Eventually, of course, one could project this series of ever-larger systems to the highest level on earth, the world. Many public relations specialists work at the level of the private enterprise system, health care system, educational system, or international development system, to name but a few examples of regional, national, and international systems.

The systems perspective, then, suggests that the level and definition of the system must be appropriate to the concern or the problem situation. A component—a subsystem—in one system may be itself analyzed as a system in another context. Likewise, a system defined as such for one purpose may be but a component or subsystem in a higher-order suprasystem when the reason for the analysis changes.

For example, when reorganizing the local United Way's internal structure and programming, the organization is viewed as the system and the publics are viewed as parts of the environment. When the United Way scandal made the headlines, however, for some purposes each of the 2,100 local United Way organizations and their publics became local systems within an even larger environmental context. Likewise, the national United Way of America, made up of national headquarters and all 2,100 local units, can be viewed as but one component in the national or international charity system. And the charities taken as a group are but one component in the larger set of tax-exempt, nonprofit organizations some have referred to as the "third sector" of the economy.

The United Way scandal illustrates the latter level of systems analysis, as news of national United Way President William Aramony's high salary and extravagant lifestyle produced change pressures on all tax-exempt charitable, religious, and educational groups and foundations. Individual donors called for more accountability and greater scrutiny of what charities do, as did the National Committee for Responsive Philanthropy. A congressional subcommittee called for more Internal Revenue Service staff members to monitor the more than one million tax-exempt organizations. (The one million total does not include almost 350,000 churches and other national groups such as 4-H, Boy Scouts, Girl Scouts, and Boys and Girls Clubs!) Television evangelists, national foundations, universities, and even local charities all felt the heat of media attention and increased public scrutiny.

Systems theorist James G. Miller uses the concept of higher-order systems to define a system's environment:

> The immediate environment is the suprasystem minus the system itself. The entire environment includes this plus the suprasystem and systems at all higher levels which contain it. In order to survive, the system must interact with and adjust to its environment, the other parts of the suprasystem. These processes alter both the system and its environment. It is not surprising that characteristically living systems adapt to their environment and, in return, mold it. The result is that, after some period of interaction, each in some sense becomes a mirror of the other.[20]

Organizations as Systems

Miller says "living systems" engage in exchanges with their environments, producing changes in both the systems and their environments. Such imagery of exchange processes, structural change, and adaptation captures the essence of the public relations function in organizations. Specifically, public relations is part of what organization theorists call the *adaptive* subsystem, as distinct from the *production, supportive-disposal, maintenance,* and *managerial* subsystems.[21] The latter—the managerial subsystem—is defined as "direction, adjudication, and control" of the other subsystems.

Adaptive subsystems vary in their sensitivity to their environments, just as do the public relations functions within organizations. Some organizations actively monitor their social environments and make adjustments based on what is learned. An example is a church that begins offering single-parent counseling and social events in response to the growing number of households headed by divorced and single parents. On the other hand, given public concerns about health care costs and excessive corporate profits, how sensitive was the pharmaceutical company that charged 100 times more for a drug when it was used to treat human cancer than when the same drug was sold as an antiparasitic agent in farm animals?

The amount of resources, time, and effort an organization devotes to monitoring its environment is determined by

1. The degree of conflict or competition with the external environment, typically related to the extent of involvement with and dependence on government
2. The degree of dependence on internal support and unity
3. The degree to which internal operations and external environment are believed to be rationalized, that is, characterized by predictable uniformities and therefore subject to planned influence, and affecting all of these
4. The size and structure of the organization, its heterogeneity of membership and diversity of goals, its centralization of authority[22]

Organizational adjustment and adaptation to new conditions depend in part on how open organizations are to their environments. Differences in how sensitive organizations are to their environments provide a useful basis for further systems analysis of the public relations function.

All systems—mechanical, organic, and social—can be classified in terms of the nature and amount of interchange with their environments. The continuum ranges from closed systems on one extreme to open systems on the other. *Closed systems* have impermeable boundaries, so they cannot exchange matter, energy, or information with their environments. *Open systems,* on the other hand, exchange inputs and outputs through boundaries that are permeable. Of course, social systems cannot be completely closed or totally open, so they are either *relatively open* or *relatively closed.* The distinction is important.

The extent to which systems are closed is an indication of their insensitivity to their environments. Closed systems do not take in new matter, energy, or information. In short, closed systems do not adapt to external change and eventually disintegrate. On the other hand, open systems are responsive to environmental changes. Survival and growth of open systems depend on interchange with its environment. The most successful organizations are "especially adroit at continually responding to change of any sort in their environments."[23]

Open systems adjust and adapt to counteract or accommodate environmental variations. Inputs from the environment can be reactions to a system's own outputs or the result of changes independent of system outputs. In either case, inputs have an impact on system goal states, those conditions the system holds as "ideal" or "desired." Inputs can cause deviations from these system goal states. When that happens, feedback within a system causes adjustments in both system *structure* (what the system *is*) and *processes* (what the system *does*). The adjustments are intended to reduce, maintain, or increase the deviations. The output of adjustments can be directed internally or externally, or both. Internal outputs change or maintain goal states. External outputs change or maintain environmental conditions. Which type of output should public relations stress? That depends, for "there is no property of an organization that is good in any absolute sense; all are relative to some given environment, or to some given set of threats and disturbances, or to some given set of problems."[24] And does it mean that an open system will adjust effectively? Not necessarily, for "there is maladjustment as well as adjustment; the function concept only poses the question of adequacy but does not settle it beforehand."[25] (Figure 7.1 represents the cyclical nature of an open system's interchange with its environment, assessment and reassessment, and adjustment and adaptation essential to the system maintenance and change.)

The ultimate goal of systems, of course, is survival. But because they exist in changing environments, open systems must continually adjust to maintain states of equilibrium or balance. The conditions necessary for survival are represented as the "goal states" in the model. Paradoxically, open systems must continually change to remain the same, an enduring set of interacting units. To differentiate the *dynamic* states of relatively open systems from the *static* states of relatively closed systems, systems theorists refer to the changeable goal states as *homeostasis.* This term is used "to avoid the static connota-

FIGURE 7.1   OPEN SYSTEMS MODEL

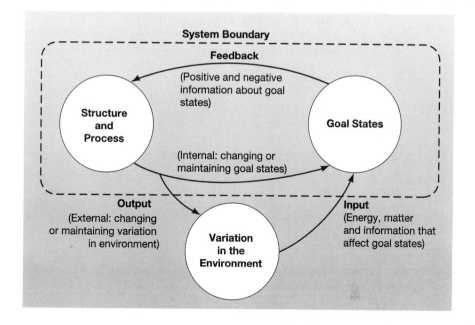

tions of equilibrium and to bring out the dynamic, processual, potential-maintaining properties of basically unstable . . . systems."[26] The person credited with coining the term homeostasis said it "does not imply something set and immobile, as stagnation," but rather "a condition which may vary."[27]

Homeostasis, then, refers to goal states that, although *relatively stable,* are subject to change as a result of system inputs. For example, your academic department attempts to maintain a certain student population, but that goal may change if the state reduces the university's budget. The student census goal could be increased if new resources were added, such as a newly endowed lectureship made possible by wealthy alumni. Yet another term is needed, however, to describe other changes characteristic of open systems that adjust and adapt to environmental inputs.

Whereas homeostasis represents the maintenance of dynamic system goal states, *morphogenesis* refers to changes in the structure and process element in the open systems model in Figure 7.1. For example, press and public criticism of how the state fair is being managed prompts the board of directors to appoint a new administrator and to reorganize the business office. In addition, the board revises procedures for awarding contracts. Notice that the structure and processes may change even if the goal states do not, and vice versa. What changes and to what extent depends on the nature of the feedback in the system. According to Littlejohn,

> Feedback can be classified as positive or negative, depending on the way the system responds to it. Negative feedback is an error message indicating deviation;

the system adjusts by reducing or counteracting the deviation. Negative feedback is the most important type of feedback in homeostasis because negative feedback maintains a steady state.

A system can also respond by amplifying or maintaining deviation. When this happens, the feedback is said to be positive. This kind of interaction is important to morphogenesis, or system growth (e.g., learning). . . . The response to negative feedback is "cut back, slow down, discontinue." Response to positive feedback is "increase, maintain, keep going."[28]

Systems, then, can adjust and adapt their goals, structures, or processes, depending on the kind and amount of feedback. Open systems not only generate different types of feedback as a result of system inputs, but they exhibit more flexibility in adjusting to inputs. Choices among alternative adaptive strategies are made on the basis of which ones are most effective in helping the system maintain or achieve system goals in the context of environmental change pressures. As one systems theorist put it, "All systems are adaptive, and the real question is what they are adaptive to and to what extent."[29]

CYBERNETICS IN OPEN SYSTEMS

Study of this input-output self-regulation process in systems is referred to as *cybernetics.* Buckley's general cybernetic model (Figure 7.2) portrays what tends to occur or would occur ("were it not for complicating factors") in goal-seeking systems. The model contains five elements: (1) goals established in a control center; (2) outputs related to the goals, which have impact on the state of the system and its environment; (3) feedback to the control center on the effects of the output; (4) a comparison of the new system state with the goal state; and (5) control center determination of the need for corrective output.[30]

FIGURE 7.2   CYBERNETIC CONTROL MODEL

From Walter Buckley, *Sociology and Modern Systems Theory* ©1973, p. 173. Reprinted with permission from Prentice-Hall Inc., Englewood Cliffs, NJ.

Cybernetic control systems used for navigation on space shuttles, airplanes, and ships are good examples. Early in the 20th century, sailors called the first such navigational system "iron mike." This relatively simple cybernetic system contained a course-setting device, a course indicator to signal discrepancies from the set course, and a mechanism for activating the rudder to make course corrections. Compare that with the sophisticated cybernetic control system on the most advanced and largest sailing ship, the 617-foot *Club Med 1:*

> A hard gust of wind generates pressure on the sails. The extent of that increase in pressure is measured, and the computer instructs the sheets, which are attached to the clews of the sails, to slacken off—spilling the incremental wind and thereby easing the tension. Simultaneously, the computer instructs the windward seawater ballast to ingest more water, while the leeward ballast chamber rushes to empty its supply of water. It is most terribly important to do all of this before the ship lists over more than two degrees, that being, on *Club Med 1,* the limit of official toleration. If the ship were to heel more than two degrees, passengers might notice that they were under sail, and that isn't really the idea, on the world's largest sailboat. So that everything described above happens within approximately three seconds.[31]

Even a thermostat–furnace system can be described as a cybernetic system. Just as does *Club Med 1,* this system responds (corrective actions) to deviations from the goal state (the temperature set in the thermostat). Its responses, however, include either production or cessation of heat only: turning the furnace on or off. Similarly, relatively simple organisms have limited options for dealing with variations in their environments. For example, the cuttlefish (Figure 7.3)—a squidlike marine mollusk—indiscriminately squirts an inky fluid when it encounters something in its surroundings.

Organizations, much like the *Club Med 1,* have so many sophisticated options available for dealing with environmental change that they make turning on the heat and squirting ink seem primitive. Or do they? Some public relations programs are routinized to the point that, regardless of the problem and without regard to environmental conditions, the response is to get out a press release "telling our story." In other words, the response is both predetermined and applied indiscriminately from situation to situation. Maybe the cuttlefish's strategy for squirting ink at problems is not unique to that species!

Simple mechanical cybernetic systems and living organisms typically do not change structurally except when pushed to the limit of system tolerance. For example, even though the cuttlefish makes cosmetic changes to blend in with its environment, structural change is not an option when it confronts threats in its surroundings. Social systems and complex cybernetic systems such as those used in "smart buildings," on the other hand, have the capacity to use cybernetic self-regulation to make relatively major structural changes. Such changes help the system to adapt to new environmental conditions or to modify outputs to change or neutralize the sources of change pressure. This interchange between systems and their environments is characteristic of open

FIGURE 7.3   CUTTLEFISH

Photograph courtesy Gerhard Saueracker, Perth, Western Australia.

systems and makes morphogenesis—purposive changes in structure and process—possible. In short, open systems have the capacity to adjust and adapt to constantly changing environments.

Another quality of open systems becomes apparent when social systems are compared with mechanical systems and many living organisms. Simple, relatively closed systems *react* to outside events only if the input—change pressure—is sufficient to penetrate the system boundary. Complex, relatively open systems monitor—and in some cases actively probe—their environments to detect and predict changing conditions. In other words, sophisticated open systems *anticipate* changes in their environments and initiate corrective actions designed to counteract or neutralize the changes before they become major problems.

Public relations exhibits a similar range of closed versus open approaches. When public relations practitioners get together, they often use the terms "reactive" and "proactive" to describe programs. Reactive programs employ relatively closed systems approaches to program planning and management. Like the cuttlefish squirting ink, a reactive public relations program activates only when disturbed. For example, *Forbes* magazine suggested that Weyerhaeuser's management philosophy "minimizes outside pressures for performance on management." The magazine went on to say, "The company is structured in ways that once made sense but no longer do." According to *Forbes*, the longtime chairman's (the founder's great-grandson) "reaction to criticism was to shrug it off," hiring from the outside "was nearly taboo," and "change moves at a glacial pace in this company." Completing the picture of a relatively closed systems approach, the magazine reported that company representatives "declined to talk with *Forbes* for this story, citing among other things a negative story that ran 13 years ago. Like an elephant, Weyerhaeuser never forgets. Like an elephant, it is also hard to turn around."[32]

Similarly, apparently Amarillo city officials and the Texas beef industry were operating in the reactive mode of relatively closed systems when they dealt with Oprah Winfrey, the nation's top-rated talk show host. Oprah taped her show in Amarillo while defending herself in court against charges that she had defamed beef during a program about mad cow disease. Texas cattlemen and the Texas Beef Group sued. Chamber of Commerce leaders decided not to welcome Oprah and forbade Chamber employees to attend tapings of the program. Oprah won in the court of law and in the court of public opinion, increasing her position as one of the most popular talk show hosts on television. City officials missed an opportunity to put the city in a good light when they refused to cooperate with Oprah's staff and did not provide information about Amarillo and its attractions. Typical of such closed systems' responses, the mayor was quoted afterward as saying, "I didn't realize the depth and breadth of Oprah's popularity."[33]

Proactive programs, in contrast, use their early-warning "radar" to gather information, to make adjustments, and to generate internal and external output to prevent or avoid problems. Digital Research's announcement that it would no longer merely issue a steady stream of press releases is an example of an organization changing from a closed systems approach to public relations to a more open systems model. Instead of indiscriminately squirting ink like a cuttlefish, the computer software company adopted a proactive open systems approach. To that end Digital Research not only retained a public relations firm but also added the firm's head to its board of directors. The first step in the new approach was a series of strategic planning sessions—a proactive response.

Similarly, even a power utility, long thought of as the corporate equivalent of an elephant, can behave as a proactive open system. For example, while other utilities were fighting acid rain regulations and legislation, Minneapolis-based Northern States Power Company had already factored pollution control and reduction into operations. "Their policy is to exceed every environmental requirement that's placed on them," according to a Minnesota pollution-control agency program chief. Northern States, for example, to comply with new emission regulations started buying low-sulfur Western coal years before it needed to. By doing so it locked in prices and transportation costs well beyond the year 2000. Meanwhile, other Midwest utilities continued to burn the cheaper, high-sulfur Midwestern and Eastern coals. As a result, these coal-burning utilities now pay premium prices for the cleaner-burning Western coal. Northern States also installed scrubbers to clean sulfur from smoke and gases emerging from its furnaces in the early 1970s and has improved their efficiency since then. Utilities that waited until the 1980s and 1990s paid more than five times as much for scrubbers. The company's president and chief executive took the long view: "You have to be environmentally responsible to have a hope for success or longevity."[34]

EXHIBIT 7.2

ADJUSTMENT AND ADAPTATION—"MA BELL" STYLE

Before government and media attention to Microsoft's alleged domination of the software industry, maybe no organizational change received as much attention as did the court-ordered divestiture of the Bell System. On January 1, 1984, the then-107-year-old American Telephone and Telegraph split into eight separate companies: AT&T and seven regional companies. The old AT&T had been the world's largest company, secure in its position as a virtual monopoly and employer of almost a million "telephone people." It began with the famous words of Alexander Graham Bell, "Mr. Watson, come here. I want to see you." Its transformation stands as an extreme example of system adjustment and adaptation to a changed environment.

Even during the long court fight against divestiture, AT&T was planning a new structure to respond to the new legal, social, economic, and technological environments. AT&T's chair-

man had decided that the fight would have gone on for years with little hope of avoiding the inevitable breakup. When it happened, advertisements announced, "We've been working to make the biggest change in our lives a small change in yours."

The response should have been anticipated: Theodore N. Vail, twice chairman of AT&T—1878 to 1887 and 1907 to 1920—pioneered in making the corporation responsive to its social setting. He did not fight public regulation and hired James D. Ellsworth to begin a public relations program that responded to public interests. Arthur W. Page succeeded Ellsworth. Page's philosophy of public relations and corporate social responsibility endures (see chapter 4).

By the early 1990s, AT&T and the seven regional companies had broadened their missions and product lines well beyond what was once thought of as "the telephone com-

OPEN SYSTEMS MODEL OF PUBLIC RELATIONS

Output of a steady stream of press releases and other traditional reactive public relations responses is suggestive of closed systems thinking. This all-too-common approach to the function is apparently based on two assumptions: (1) that the purpose of public relations is limited to effecting changes in the environment, and more mistakenly, (2) that organizations have the power to change their environments, thereby eliminating the need to change themselves. Does this kind of thinking remind you of the cuttlefish and thermostat–furnace system? On the other hand, an open systems approach casts public relations in the role of bringing about changes in both environments and organizations as a result of environmental inputs.

Bell and Bell refer to the first approach to public relations as functionary and the second as *functional*. In their view, the *functionary* role is similar to a closed systems approach:

> Public relations functionaries attempt to preserve and promote a favorable image of the organization in the community on the hypothesis that if the organization is "liked" the public will continue to absorb the organization's outputs. Such func-

pany." They manufactured computers and other communication equipment, expanded their publishing businesses, diversified their communication services, and became leaders in the generation and transmission of information. Cable television companies, other manufacturers, publishers, and the other telephone companies faced not one, but eight competitors. By the late 1990s, mergers had reduced the number of regional "integrated telcos" to five, and AT&T had once again divested, spinning off its Bell Laboratories to form a new company—Lucent Technologies—and spinning off former cash register manufacturer NCR as a computer company. AT&T also began building high-speed fiber-optic voice and data transmission networks, and even reentered the local telephone service business in 1999 by linking its operations with Time Warner's millions of cable television lines.

In short, AT&T transformed itself into a powerful player in a new digital, wireless, and multimedia environment. It is no longer "The Telephone Company" or "Ma Bell." The old AT&T adjusted and adapted.

It was not an easy transition, however. Longtime AT&T consultant Chester Burger recalls that in the early 1980s there were 1,700 full-time public relations specialists on AT&T's payroll with a total budget of about $170 million. Much of the public relations effort was to defend the company's historic monopoly in providing telephone service and the equipment that could be connected to the system. Burger concludes, however, that (1) public relations strategy can't overcome broad social factors, (2) it is easy to convince yourself that corporate self-interest coincides with the public interest, and (3) technology is changing the world.[*]

Simply put, AT&T either had to change or it would have followed other corporate dinosaurs into extinction.

---

[*] Chester Burger, APR, Fellow PRSA, "Last Word: When Public Relations Fails," *The Strategist* 3, no. 3 (Fall 1997): 56.

tionaries are only concerned with supplying information about the organization to the environment and not with supplying information to the organization about the environment. Because functionaries do not supply feedback information, they do not function in decision-making or even in advisory roles in relation to environmental concerns. Therefore, *they have little to say about* what *is said; they are mainly concerned with* how *things are said.*[35]

In this approach to public relations, the emphasis is on maintaining the status quo within the organization while effecting change in the organization's publics. The goal of building and maintaining relations between the organization and its publics is to bring the publics into line with the organization's plans.

In contrast, a functional view of public relations calls for an open systems approach, changing both the organization and the environment. Relations between the organization and its publics are maintained or changed on the basis of reciprocal output–feedback adjustment. In the functional approach:

[Public relations] has the potential to act in an advisory capacity and to have impact on decision-making. This potential in turn leads to some control over its own

FIGURE 7.4   REACTIVE PUBLIC RELATIONS

Courtesy Doug Marlette, *The Charlotte Observer.*

domain in times of crisis and, as a sensing device, public relations can be effective in preventing many potential crisis situations. Management properly remains the "large wheel" but the small wheel that is public relations may occasionally be capable of influencing the larger one. If observations of external and internal environments indicate that a policy or practice is detrimental to the best interests of the organization (and, increasingly, society) management can be encouraged to adjust.[36]

The functionary approach casts public relations practitioners in the technician role discussed in chapter 2. In this limited role, they monitor the environment (if at all) to make communication output more effective, not to make changes within the organization. In organizations in which public relations operates in the functional mode, on the other hand, practitioners become part of top management, "the dominant coalition."

Practitioners with the knowledge, training, and experience to practice a two-way model of public relations are more likely to be included in the organization's dominant coalition. They also are more likely to have power in that coalition rather than to serve it in an advisory role. When public relations managers have power in the dominant coalition, they can influence organizational ideology and the choice of publics in the environment for which strategic public relations programs are planned. At that point, public relations practitioners can fulfill a communication counseling and management role—and truly practice the profession defined for them in public relations textbooks but seldom fulfilled in the real world.[37]

In effect, public relations practiced in the closed systems (functionary) model attempts to maintain the status quo within organizations while directing change efforts at the environment. When public relations is part of organizations' strategic attempts to adjust and adapt to their dynamic environments, the practice reflects the open systems (functional) model.

The open systems approach radically changes the practice from how it is widely practiced. Whereas the more common functionary version attempts to exercise control over environmental forces, the open systems model suggests adjustment and adaptation as the more realistic and appropriate responses. Most definitions of organizational environment suggest that it includes factors outside organizational boundaries and often outside organizations' control. An organization's *specific environment* includes those "constituencies that can positively or negatively influence the organization's effectiveness. It is unique to each organization and it changes with conditions."[38]

The open systems model uses "two-way symmetric" approaches, meaning that communication is two-way and that information exchange causes changes on both sides of organization–public relationships. The difference between one-way and two-way communication led the Grunigs to propose yet another way to describe closed and open systems public relations: craft public relations versus professional public relations.

> Practitioners of craft public relations seem to believe that their job consists solely of the application of communication techniques and as an end in itself. To them, the purpose of public relations simply is to get publicity or information into the media or other channels of communication. Practitioners of professional public relations, in contrast, rely on a body of knowledge as well as technique and see public relations as having a strategic purpose for an organization: to manage conflict and build relationships with strategic publics that limit the autonomy of the organization.[39]

Both approaches emphasize the primary role of communication in social systems. As Buckley put it, "the interrelations characterizing higher levels (of systems) come to depend more and more on the transmission of *information*—a principle fundamental to modern complex system analysis."[40]

Applying the open systems approach to public relations first and foremost calls for purposeful sensing of the environment to anticipate and detect changes that affect organizational relationships with publics. Following an open systems approach, public relations must be selectively sensitive to specifically defined publics that are mutually affected or involved by organizational policies, procedures, and actions. The open systems model of public relations calls for research skills to monitor publics and other environmental forces, as well as forces within organizations.

Open systems public relations also has the capacity to initiate corrective actions within organizations and direct programs to affect knowledge, predisposition, and behavior of both internal and external publics. The outcomes sought are maintenance or achievement of goals that reflect the mutual interests of organizations and their publics. Those found in conflict with mutual interests are changed or eliminated, *before* they become issues or problems. Proactive corrective action may be the major and most useful aspect of the open systems model of public relations. Steps taken in advance reduce both the amount of effort required and the trauma associated with crisis-oriented reactive public relations.

Thus, organizations employing open systems public relations maintain their relationships by adjusting and adapting themselves and their publics to ever-changing social, political, and economic environments. (Figure 7.5 illustrates the open systems model applied to public relations.)

As early as 1923, in one of the earliest public relations books, *Crystallizing Public Opinion,* Edward L. Bernays wrote about the role of the "public relations counsel" in a democratic society. Expressing a model of public relations similar to our open systems approach, he said that the public relations counsel recognizes changes in the organization's social setting and advises clients or employers how the organization should change itself and respond so as to establish a "common meeting ground." Not many years later, Harwood Childs said that the function of public relations is to "reconcile or adjust in the public interest" those aspects of organizations that have social significance. This concept of public relations, based on the open systems theoretical model, serves as the basis for the many activities under the banner of public relations and spells out its essential role in organizations and society.

FIGURE 7.5   OPEN SYSTEMS MODEL OF PUBLIC RELATIONS

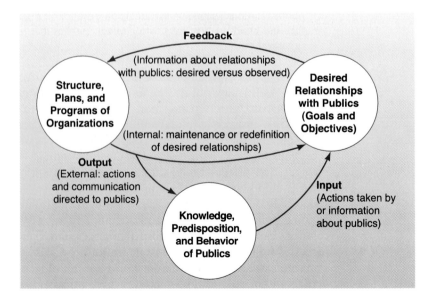

In the final analysis, public relations practitioners are applied social and behavioral scientists working as part of a strategic plan. According to employee communication expert Paul Sanchez at Watson Wyatt Communication Consulting Practice, a public relations plan "also tilts the balance toward proactive communication, thus avoiding wasted time on purely reactive communication that does not support strategic goals."[41]

Working on behalf of their organizations and in the public interest, public relations professionals are *agents* and *managers of change,* both inside and outside their organizations. They plan and facilitate organizational and social adjustment and adaptation using primarily communication, the topic of the next chapter.

NOTES

1. Carol Kinsey Goman, "Energizing a Restructured Work Force," *Communication World* 14, no. 3 (February 1997), 55–57.
2. Alvin Toffler, *The Third Wave* (New York: Bantam Books, 1980), paperback, 9. See also Toffler's *Future Shock.*
3. Frederick Williams, *The New Communications,* 3d ed. (Belmont, CA: Wadsworth Publishing Company, 1992), 340.
4. Some of this information is adapted from William E. Halal, Michael D. Kull, and Ann Leffmann, "Emerging Technologies: What's Ahead for 2001–2030," *The Futurist* 31, no. 6 (November–December 1997): 20–25.
5. Faith Popcorn, *The Popcorn Report* (New York: Doubleday Currency, 1991), 86. Futurist and marketing forecaster outlines 10 basic trends and shows how they will change consumer demand, lifestyles, and organizations.
6. Halal, Kull, and Leffmann, "Emerging Technologies," p. 23.
7. "Special Report: Whooooo Cares?" *Weyerhaeuser Today* (Weyerhaeuser Company, August 1991): 1–4.
8. Edith Weiner, "Business in the 21st Century," *The Futurist* 26, no. 2 (March–April 1992): 13–17. The concept of stewardship is credited to Aldo Leopold, who joined the U.S. Forest Service in the Southwest in 1909, moved to Wisconsin in 1933 to manage the Forest Products Laboratory, took on various conservation leadership posts in Wisconsin, and was a professor at the University of Wisconsin-Madison until his death in 1948.
9. Robert W. Fisher, "The Future of Energy," *The Futurist* 31, no. 5 (September–October 1997): 43–46.
10. Lane Jennings, "Paying for Tomorrow's Health Care," *The Futurist* 32, no. 3 (April 1998): 6. Author highlights conclusions from two books calling for health care reform.
11. C. J. Peters, Chief of Special Pathogens, Centers for Disease Control, as quoted by Dan Johnson, "Virus Hunters Pursue Our Invisible Enemies," *The Futurist* 32, no. 1 (January–February 1998): 8.
12. Data from Scripps Howard News Service, Lou Kilzer, "Many Too Optimistic about War on AIDS," *San Diego Union-Tribune,* May 3, 1998, p. A25, and Associated Press report, "New Study Predicts 25 Million Will Have AIDS by Year 2000," *San Diego Union-Tribune,* June 4, 1992. The full report, *AIDS in the World 1992,* was published by Harvard University in late 1992.
13. John Naisbitt and Patricia Aburdene, *Megatrends 2000: Ten New Directions for the*

1990s (New York: William Morrow and Company, 1990), 22. A useful summary of the trends highlighted by television news and magazine cover stories.

14. Remarks by U.S. Secretary of Commerce William M. Daley, U.S. Department of Commerce, Washington, DC, April 15, 1998. The quotations were from the complete text at the Office of the Secretary's web site **(www.osec.doc.gov/ops/econ.htm).**

15. George Bugliarello, "Telecommunities: The Next Civilization," *The Futurist* 31, no. 5 (September–October 1997): 23.

16. James A. Levine and Todd L. Pittinsky, *Working Fathers: New Strategies for Balancing Work and Family* (Reading, MA: Addison-Wesley Publishing Company, 1997). Authors suggest that "paying serious attention to both working mothers and working fathers . . . can transform today's work-family challenge into win-win solutions for America's business and America's families" (p. 9).

17. Michelle Neely Martinez, "The Proof is in the Profits," *Working Mother* 20, no. 5 (May 1997), pp. 27–30.

18. Howard Rosenberg, "Fighting Tooth and Claw: Ingrid Newkirk's Combative Style and Headline-Grabbing Stunts Have Shaken Up the Animal-Rights Movement," *Los Angeles Times Magazine,* March 22, 1992, p. 18.

19. Jonathan D. Salant, Associated Press story published in the *San Diego Union-Tribune,* May 7, 1998, p. A–11.

20. James G. Miller, *Living Systems* (New York: McGraw-Hill Book Company, 1978), 29–30.

21. For complete explications of these subsystems, see Chris Argyris, *Integrating the Individual and the Organization* (New York: John Wiley and Sons, 1964), and Daniel Katz and Robert L. Kahn, *The Social Psychology of Organizations* (New York: John Wiley and Sons, 1966), 39–47.

22. Harold L. Wilensky, *Organizational Intelligence: Knowledge and Policy in Government and Industry* (New York: Basic Books, 1967), 10.

23. Thomas J. Peters and Robert H. Waterman Jr., *In Search of Excellence* (New York: Harper and Row, 1982), 12.

24. R. Ashby, "Principles of the Self-organizing System," in *Principles of Self-organization,* edited by H. Von Foerster and G. W. Zopf (New York: Pergamon Press, 1962), 266.

25. Siegfried F. Nadel, *Foundations of Social Anthropology* (London: Cohen and West, 1951), 375.

26. Walter Buckley, *Sociology and Modern Systems Theory* (Englewood Cliffs, NJ: Prentice-Hall, 1967), 14.

27. Walter B. Cannon, *The Wisdom of the Body* (New York: W. W Norton and Company, 1939), 24.

28. Stephen W. Littlejohn, *Theories of Human Communication,* 4th ed. (Belmont, CA: Wadsworth Publishing Company, 1992), 47. Chapter 3 presents a good summary of systems concepts and their application to communication. The most complete reference on systems theory is Miller's previously cited 1,100-page *Living Systems.* More readable and probably most cited is Ludwig von Bertalanffy, *General Systems Theory: Foundations, Development, Applications,* rev. ed. (New York: George Braziller, 1968).

29. Lotfi A. Zadeh, as quoted by George J. Klir, *Facets of Systems Science* (New York: Plenum Press, 1991), 143.

30. Buckley, *Sociology and Modern Systems Theory,* 172–76. Cybernetic theory of self-regulating systems was first detailed in Norbert Wiener's *Cybernetics* (Cambridge, MA: MIT Press, 1948) and revised in a 1961 second edition (New York: John Wiley and Sons).

31. William F. Buckley Jr., "Haut Boat," *Forbes FYI* (March 16, 1992), 88 and 90.
32. John H. Taylor, "Rip Van Weyerhaeuser," *Forbes* 148, no. 10 (October 28, 1992): 38–40. The story goes on to report changes in top management, structure, and incentive programs to make the company more responsive and profitable.
33. Billy Layne Smith, "When Oprah's Cattle Battle Came to Amarillo," *Public Relations Tactics* 5, no. 4 (April 1998): 1, 9, and 27.
34. Steve Weiner, "Profit without Pollution," *Forbes* 139, no. 11 (May 18, 1987): 46.
35. Sue H. Bell and Eugene C. Bell, "Public Relations: Functional or Functionary?" *Public Relations Review* 2, no. 2 (Summer 1976): 51–52.
36. Ibid., 53.
37. James E. Grunig and Larissa Schneider Grunig, "Toward a Theory of the Public Relations Behavior of Organizations: Review of a Program of Research," *Public Relations Research Annual* 1 (1989): 60.
38. Stephen P. Robbins, *Organization Theory: Structure, Design, and Applications,* 3d ed. (Englewood Cliffs, NJ: Prentice-Hall, 1990), 207.
39. James E. Grunig and Larissa A. Grunig, chapter 11, "Models of Public Relations and Communication," in *Excellence in Public Relations and Communication Management,* edited by James E. Grunig (Hillsdale, NJ: Lawrence Erlbaum Associates, 1992), 312.
40. Buckley, *Sociology and Modern Systems Theory,* 47.
41. Paul Sanchez, "Agents for Change," *Communication World* 14, no. 3 (February 1997): 53.

ADDITIONAL SOURCES

Cadwallader, Mervyn L. "The Cybernetic Analysis of Change in Complex Social Organizations." In *Communication and Culture: Readings In the Codes of Human Interaction,* pp. 396–401. Edited by Alfred G. Smith. New York: Holt, Rinehart and Winston, 1966.
Cancel, Amanda E., Glen T. Cameron, Lynne M. Sallot, and Michael A. Mitrook. "It Depends: A Contingency Theory of Accommodation in Public Relations." *Journal of Public Relations Research* 9, no. 1 (1997), 31–63. Presents the theory that variables affect the degree of accommodation in public relations practice, in contrast to Grunig's normative two-way symmetrical model.
Churchman, C. West. *The Systems Approach.* New York: Dell Publishing Co., 1979. Applies systems approach to management and decision making.
Hage, Jerald. *Theories of Organizations: Form, Process, and Transformation.* New York: John Wiley and Sons (Wiley-Interscience), 1980. Seminal work on organizations as adaptive systems.
Heath, Robert L., and Douglas D. Abel. "Proactive Response to Citizen Risk Concerns: Increasing Citizens' Knowledge of Emergency Response Practices." *Journal of Public Relations Research* 8, no. 3 (1996): 151–71.
Klir, George J. *Facets of Systems Science.* New York: Plenum Press, 1991. Volume 7 of the International Series on Systems Science and Engineering, International Federation for Systems Research. Contains 11 chapters that synthesize and update systems theory in science and 35 reprinted articles representing significant authors and publications of the field.
Knoke, William. *Bold New World: The Essential Road Map to the Twenty-First Century.* New York: Kodansha America, 1996). Investment banker's optimistic views about how social, political, and technological changes will change as-

sumptions about place, time, space, organizations, relationships, government, and work.

Kotter, John P. *Leading Change.* Boston, MA: Harvard Business School Press, 1996. Outlines eight-step process for organizational change, as well as the obstacles communicators and managers must overcome in change efforts.

Kuhn, Alfred J. *Organizational Cybernetics and Business Policy: System Design for Performance Control.* University Park: Pennsylvania State University Press, 1986. Presents a seven-phase model for applying systems theory to the design and management of complex business organizations. Uses General Motors as a case study.

Monge, Peter R. "Systems Theory and Research in the Study of Organizational Communication: The Correspondence Problem." *Human Communication Research* 8 (Spring 1982): 245–61.

Rapoport, Anatol. *General Systems Theory: Essential Concepts and Applications.* Tunbridge Wells, UK: Abacus, 1985.

Weiner, Edith, and Arnold Brown. *Insider's Guide to the Future: A Preview of What Life Will Be Like over the Next 20 Years.* Greenwich, CT: Boardroom Books, 1997. Introduces concept of "emotile" society, suggesting that concerns about personal well-being (emotion) combined with impatience and acceptance of impermanence (mobility) will shape future society.

COMMUNICATION AND PUBLIC OPINION

No human capability has been more fundamental to the development of civilization than the ability to collect, share, and apply knowledge. Civilization has been possible only through the process of human communication.[1]

—*Frederick Williams*

OBJECTIVES

After studying chapter 8, you should be able to

▼ Outline the tasks of public relations communications in the crowded message environment.

▼ Define communication as a two-way process taking place within intrapersonal, interpersonal, and social contexts.

▼ Diagram the communication model and label and briefly discuss the elements.

▼ List and briefly discuss the effects of public relations communication.

▼ Identify and discuss the five dimensions of public opinion.

▼ Define an attitude and an opinion and distinguish between them.

▼ Diagram and explain the model of individual orientation and the model of coorientation.

▼ Define the four states of coorientational consensus.

The force of public opinion has steadily gained strength around the world as mass communication has become a global phenomenon. Governments and institutions formerly somewhat isolated from the glare of media attention and public scrutiny now see their actions or nonactions reported via international news media. For example, international pressure was marshaled against Saddam Hussein because of media portrayals of his troops' invasion of Kuwait and atrocities there, never mind that some of the so-called atrocities turned out to be unsubstantiated fabrications! Or recall the video showing the lineup of tobacco company executives taking the oath before testifying to a Congressional committee that they had no knowledge that nicotine is addictive. Soon thereafter, copies of internal documents—including handwritten notes and memoranda—from these same tobacco companies' files were being displayed and read in every news medium and the Internet. Exposure of the long-secret scientific and marketing research reports speeded settlements in several state legal proceedings and energized the national antismoking movement to phase out tobacco advertising and distribution to children.

Television and Internet pictures of oil-coated birds and sea otters and dead fish on even the most remote beaches stir emotions and activate protests against those seen as responsible. Few successfully hide from the peering eye of the world's media: not the despotic dictator, not the crooked savings and loan executive, not the military officer charged with sexual harassment, not the government official living a life of luxury within a nation of starving children, not the university president using public funds to purchase and maintain a yacht, not the corporate executive drawing millions of dollars in salary and benefits while investors and employees witness the demise of their company.

Nor can the world's audiences ignore the constant stream of messages about the people, events, and places in the global village. Television satellite signals and the Internet carry pictures of starving children, death, and relief camps in Ethiopia, Somalia, Zambia, and war-torn Kosovo, causing an outpouring of sympathy and aid from around the world. News and pictures of famine from closed-off North Korea sear our minds with images of widespread famine. Media have expanded the "world outside" and increased the number of "pictures in our heads," to borrow from Walter Lippmann in *Public Opinion*.[2] The media themselves have multiplied to the point that competition for audience attention has never been greater, prompting even greater pursuit of distant, novel, interesting, and sensational news and information.

THE BATTLE FOR ATTENTION

Each year U.S. book publishers issue more than 50,000 new titles. During the same period, a typical U.S. child sees 20,000 television commercials. There are at least 12,000 magazines, approximately 10,000 radio stations, almost 12,000 daily and weekly newspapers, more than 1,200 television stations, and new media technologies too numerous to count in the United States. Each attempts to attract an audience. Estimating how many messages each of us is exposed to each day by all these media has become something of a guessing game. Suffice it to say that each of us is exposed to or seeks out hundreds, even thousands, of messages each day.

You chose to read this section of *Effective Public Relations,* but more likely during the rest of the day you were exposed to or will be exposed to many more messages, many of which you did not or will not seek out. You will probably screen out many because you have little or no interest in the content. You will skip some because you do not have time to pay attention. You will miss others simply because you are preoccupied with something else and "tune out." In short, your attention is the object of fierce competition. The contenders are many. To defend against the onslaught of attention seekers, you may become choosy, even resistant. Few messages get through. Even fewer have an impact. No wonder one communication scholar referred to "the obstinate audience."[3]

Public relations communications compete in this crowded message environment. The first task is to get the *attention* of target publics. The second is to stimulate *interest* in message content. The third is to build a *desire* and *intention* to act on the message. And the fourth is to direct the *action* of those who behave consistent with the message. Unfortunately, the communication process is not as simple as many apparently believe.

DISSEMINATION VERSUS COMMUNICATION

The myth of communication suggests that sending a message is the same as communicating a message. In essence, dissemination is confused with communication. This confusion is apparent in public relations when practitioners offer media placements (clippings and broadcast logs) as evidence that communication has occurred. These practitioners probably subscribe to the communication model introduced by information scientists Shannon and Weaver, based on their work for Bell Telephone Laboratories in the late 1940s.[4]

Shannon and Weaver's model consists of an information source, message or signal, channel, and receiver or destination. Not surprisingly, because of their telephone perspective, the communication process produces relatively few and simple problems. *Technical* problems arise when the signal or chan-

FIGURE 8.1   COMMUNICATION PROCESS MODEL

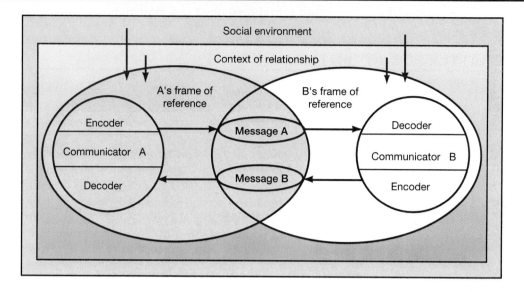

nel limits or distorts the message being transmitted from the source to the sender. *Semantic* problems occur when the receiver's perception of the message and meaning are not the same as those intended by the sender. *Influence* problems indicate that the sender's message did not produce the desired result on the part of the receiver. As Weaver wrote,

> The questions to be studied in a communication system have to do with the amount of information, the capacity of the communication channel, the coding process that may be used to change a message into a signal and the effects of noise.[5]

But as public relations practitioners will tell you, communication with target publics is much more complicated than this set of questions suggests. As the late Wilbur Schramm pointed out, communication is complicated by people:

> Communication (*human* communication, at least) is *something people do.* It has no life of its own. There is no magic about it except what people in the communication relationship put into it. There is no meaning in a message except what the people put into it. When one studies communication, therefore, one studies people—relating to each other and to their groups, organizations, and societies, influencing each other, being influenced, informing and being informed, teaching and being taught, entertaining and being entertained—by means of certain signs which exist separately from either of them. To understand the human communication process one must understand how people relate to each other.[6]

This is no simple task. In fact, Schramm's concept of communication requires a two-way-process model in which sender and receiver operate within the contexts of their respective frames of reference, their relationship, and the social situation.

As Figure 8.1 illustrates, communication is a reciprocal process of exchanging signals to inform, instruct, or persuade, based on shared meanings and conditioned by the communicators' relationship and the social context.

The process of *informing* involves four steps: (1) attracting attention to the communication, (2) achieving acceptance of the message, (3) having it interpreted as intended, and (4) getting the message stored for later use. The more demanding process of *instruction* adds a fifth step: stimulating active learning and practice. The process of *persuasion* goes beyond active learning to the sixth step of accepting change: yielding to the wishes or point of view of the sender. Clearly, barriers to achieving the outcomes of informing, instruction, and persuasion increase with the addition of the fifth and sixth steps in the processes.[7]

ELEMENTS OF THE COMMUNICATION MODEL

Early communication researchers studied the individual elements in the communication process model to determine the effect of each on the effectiveness of the process. Most studies dealt with persuasion as the desired outcome, but more recent studies have expanded the range of effects studied.

The Sender

Characteristics of message sources affect receivers' initial acceptance of the message but have little effect on long-term message impact. Hovland and his colleagues called this long-term source impact the "sleeper effect."[8] For example, according to the theory of source credibility and attractiveness, safe-sex messages promoting prevention of HIV infection among college students are more readily accepted as believable when presented by highly credible sources, such as a recognized medical authority, than when presented by peers. In a few weeks, however, recipients of the message will retain about the same amount of information whether they got it from a credible source or from a fellow college student.

More recent research suggests both short-term and long-term source impact. Source credibility amplifies the value of information, according to one scholar. The theory suggests that the perceived status, reliability, and expertness of the source add weight to messages. Multiplying the three source characteristics by each other yields the weight factor of the source in the communication process.[9]

Researchers have concluded that although source characteristics affect the communication process, their impact varies from situation to situation, from topic to topic, and from time to time. At a minimum, however, source characteristics affect receivers' initial receptivity to messages.

The Message

Message characteristics surely have an impact in the communication process, but many communication scholars agree that "meaning is in people, not words." This observation leads naturally to the conclusion that different people receiving the same message may interpret it differently, attribute different meanings to it, and react to it in different ways. All the same, message characteristics can have powerful effects, even if they do not conform to simple and direct cause-and-effect explanations. As suggested by the notion of the obstinate audience, message effects are mediated by receivers, thereby frustrating the search for rules that apply in all communication situations.

Early persuasion research on message characteristics produced few such rules, but did provide guidance still used in public relations today. For instance, if you wish to persuade, should the message contain only one side of the issue, or should it address both sides of an argument? Research findings generally support the following recommendations:

1. If receivers oppose your position, present arguments on both sides of the issue.
2. If receivers already agree with your position, your message will have greater impact—probably reinforcement—if you present only arguments consistent with the receivers' views.
3. If receivers are well educated, include both sides of the argument.
4. If you use messages containing both sides of the argument, do not leave out relevant arguments on the opposing side, or receivers who notice the omission will grow suspicious of your presentation.[10]
5. If receivers are likely to be exposed later to persuasive messages countering your position, use two-sided messages to "inoculate" the audience to build resistance to the later messages.[11]

Recent message research suggests that gaining compliance is a complicated process, however. If the message source has little power or control to exercise over the receiver, then persuasion becomes the primary strategy. If, on the other hand, the sender has power or control, then instruction or direction becomes the relevant strategy. Researchers list four major approaches to gaining compliance through communication:

1. *Sanction strategies* use rewards and punishments controlled by the sender, the receiver, or the result of the situation.
2. *Altruism strategies* call upon the receiver to comply so as to help or come to the aid of the sender or some third party represented by the sender.
3. *Argument strategies* employ (a) *direct requests,* in which the sender does not give the receiver the rationale or motivation for the request; (b) *explanations,* in which the sender gives the receiver one or more reasons for complying; and (c) *hints,* in which the sender sets up the situation or suggests circumstances from which the receiver draws the desired conclusion and compliance.
4. *Circumvention strategies* misrepresent the situation, give false rationales, or promise rewards and punishments not within the sender's power to deliver.[12]

Research on the impact of message characteristics supports the general conclusion from the previous section: Message impact is mediated or conditioned by receivers. For example, the classic study of order of presentation—"primacy" versus "recency"—demonstrated that the first part of the message has the greatest effect on receivers with low initial interest. The last part of the message has the greatest effect on those with high initial interest.[13]

Another line of message research initiated by Hovland and his associates at Yale deals with the use of fear to achieve compliance. After conducting an experiment using messages about dental hygiene, Janis and Feshback concluded that low-fear messages produce more compliance than do high-fear messages. High-fear messages apparently produce defensive reactions in the receiver that led to distortion, denial, or rejection of the message.[14] Some recent research on fear appeals, however, suggests a much more complicated relationship in which several factors influence the relationship between fear messages and subsequent compliance.

For example, high-fear messages about the dangers of smoking and of venereal disease, when combined with believable recommendations, produce high scores on intended compliance. Three factors affect the impact of fear messages: (1) the seriousness or harmfulness of the subject, (2) the likelihood or probability of the feared event, and (3) the efficacy of the recommended course of action. Apparently receivers evaluate fear-producing messages on these three characteristics before making a decision to adopt recommended courses of action. Researchers refer to this decision process as "protection motivation."[15]

In the final analysis, however, many characteristics of the source, receiver, and communication situation mediate the impact of messages on receivers. One writer concluded,

> When main-effect findings demonstrated relationships between the selected variable and some measure of attitude/behavior change, additional variables such as source characteristics, power, and receiver variables were investigated.[16]

The Medium or Channel

New technologies for delivering messages challenge conventional wisdom. For example, widespread adoption of fax machines during the 1980s revolutionized business communication. The same can be said about all phone communication with the introduction of answering machines, cordless and cellular phones, and voice mail. In many organizations, e-mail has changed communication within organizations and even across national boundaries.

For example, almost six out of ten Unisys employees access the company's electronic newsletter at their own workstation terminals. Rather than having to wait for the next issue of a printed newsletter or until announcements get posted on bulletin boards, employees sign on to the company's mainframe computer to get news that can be updated at any time. Employees ranked the Unisys News Network as their preferred information source, ranking it over their bosses, printed newsletters, and even the ever-popular grapevine. Because of the success of the electronic newsletter, Unisys dropped its printed newsletter. No one complained.[17]

Surprisingly, Unisys employees selected the electronic newsletter over interpersonal communication with their bosses. Communication scholars and practitioners historically have considered face-to-face interpersonal communication the most direct, powerful, and preferred method for exchanging information. In contrast with mass communication, interpersonal communication involves as few as two communicators (typically in close proximity), uses many senses, and provides immediate feedback. This description of the interpersonal communication situation, however, does not take into account the possibility that mass media messages may be directed to only a few (or only one!) in the audience. Likewise, physical proximity can be less important than the nature of the relationship between communicators, what one scholar calls the "intimacy-transcends-distance phenomenon." What begins as impersonal communication when people initially exchange messages can become interpersonal communication as the communicators develop a relationship.[18]

Extending time and distance, however, often requires using message delivery systems other than in-person presentations. In much of contemporary society, face-to-face contacts give way to mediated transmissions. Spoken words give way to written communication. Individually addressed letters give way to printed messages. Printed publications give way to broadcast words and pictures. Broadcast messages give way to networks of computers carrying digital signals translated into all manner of information. Choosing the right *medium* (singular) or *media* (plural) requires an understanding of media and media effects.

Interest in media selection intensified after Marshall McLuhan's famous assertion that "the medium is the message."[19] Untangling media effects from those of other elements of the process, however, remains an unfinished task. Attempts to demonstrate "all-powerful" media effects—sometimes referred to as the "hypodermic model"—have largely failed to do so. For example, concern about powerful media effects on children usually motivates both criticism and research.[20] First the 1929–1932 Payne Fund studies of how movies influenced children led to production codes and reinforced the prevailing "legacy of fear." Next, publication of *Seduction of the Innocent* in 1954 led to the "great comic book scare." The book's author concluded that comic books lead children to delinquency, cruelty, violence, and undesirable sexual behavior, but not all children. Not all these conclusions were supported by the evidence, but that did not keep the author from concluding that comic books are "definitely and completely harmful."[21]

Soon after this, comic books gave way to television as the object of concern and study. Between 1959 and 1960, Stanford University researchers studied almost 6,000 students, almost 2,000 parents, and hundreds of teachers and others in 11 communities, comparing television communities with those without television, urban communities with suburban communities, and industrial communities with agricultural communities. The researchers wanted to learn how television affects children. They learned that most children are not sitting targets for television. Instead it was children who used television for entertainment, information, and social purposes. Not surprisingly, the researchers found that many factors in the communication process and context mediate the effects of television on children.[22]

One media effects theory suggests that print and television have different effects because of characteristics of the media themselves. "High-involvement" print media tend to produce effects that follow a "see-learn-feel-do" sequence. Television, as a "low-involvement" medium, produces gradual shifts in perceptions, often through repetition. Latent effects on perceptions are activated later when the situation demands a decision or other response, such as when making a purchase. In other words, television's effects on subsequent behavior may not appear for some time. Additionally, attitude changes may follow the behavior. The explanation is that the left hemisphere of the brain processes high-involvement print media messages, whereas the right hemisphere processes low-involvement media messages.[23]

Notice that explanations of low-involvement and high-involvement media effects rely on differences in receivers' brain activities. Research using recent advances in brain wave measurement technology, however, does not support this explanation. Researchers tested the media involvement model, asking, "Do television viewing subjects show a larger amount of beta (conversely, a smaller amount of alpha) in the right brain hemisphere than in the left?" They found that neither hemisphere dominates during television viewing, concluding that television viewing produces brain wave patterns much like those produced by other activities. In other words, according to the researchers, "television viewing appears to be nothing special."[24]

The Receivers

Communication models—and public relations programs—often consider the audience passive recipients at the end of a message transmission process. This tradition continues even though research evidence and constant references to "two-way" suggest a different model and role for the audience.

In early mass communication studies, however, mass society audiences were viewed as vulnerable to messages and media manipulated by those in control. Concerned critics saw people as alienated and isolated from the kind of strong social and psychological forces found in traditional societies, as a consequence of industrialization, urbanization, and modernization. It was this notion of vulnerable audiences that motivated both early research on media effects and the growing concern of critics.[25]

The evidence gathered on audience effects, however, suggests a different type of receiver. Apparently children are not as uniformly vulnerable to film, comic books, and television as media critics feared. Moreover, the Yale persuasion experiments demonstrated that receivers are not uniformly influenced by messages designed to change attitudes. For example, receivers who value group membership are relatively unaffected by messages espousing positions counter to those of the group. Those who are persistently aggressive toward others tend to be resistant to persuasive messages. On the other hand, receivers with low self-esteem and feelings of social inadequacy are influenced more by persuasive messages than are people with high self-esteem and feelings of indifference toward others.[26]

In short, the notion of a monolithic and passive mass audience does not describe reality. Rather, the more accurate description suggests selected active receivers processing messages designed for the few, not the masses:

> Since audiences are known to be evasive at best and recalcitrant at worst, every effort is made to communicate artfully and well. While communication is conceptualized as a one-way flow, efforts are directed at targeting messages for different audience segments and promoting audience involvement wherever possible.[27]

Context of the Relationship

Communication occurs within the context of the communicators' relationship. The range of such relationships includes close and intimate relationships such as in friendships and marriage, as well as formal, competitive, and conflictual interpersonal relationships in a variety of settings. The point, of course, is that the relationship itself affects much about the communication process.

For example, one theory of friendships suggests that four dialectical factors influence the nature and amount of communication between friends. The first is *independence versus dependency*. Communication between friends occurs under contradictory pressures: to let each other make their own decisions while at the same time providing support and help. The second is *affection versus instrumentality*. Friends communicate within the context of giving affection as an end in itself, versus using the friendship to achieve some other end. The third dialectic is *judgment versus acceptance*. For example, friends are supposed to accept each other without conditions, but what kind of friend are you if you do not provide "constructive criticism" to help your friend? (Good luck on that one!) The fourth dialectic influencing communication between friends is *expressiveness versus protectiveness*. The conflict here is between spontaneity and honesty versus strategy and caution. Overriding all of these cross pressures is the notion that friendship is a private relationship played out within a set of public expectations. No wonder communication is a complicated process, even between friends.[28]

Conflict provides a similarly complicated context for communication. Conflict occurs when two or more people have the power to inflict sanctions on each other while trying to achieve mutually exclusive objectives. The combatants may have different values and may define the conflict situation differently. Each has the means or resources to engage the other. Conflict ends when the combatants sense victory or defeat or that the probable outcome does not justify the cost of continuing.[29]

All relational communication reflects four basic dimensions: (1) emotional arousal, composure, and formality; (2) intimacy and similarity; (3) immediacy or liking; and (4) dominance–submission.[30] For example, your supervisor announces changes in scheduled work hours for student assistants without consulting with the students (the first dimension) by posting the new schedule on the office bulletin board (the second dimension). The notice also expresses the supervisor's hope that the new schedule does not inconvenience any of the assistants (the third dimension) but indicates that the supervisor has the power to establish work schedules (the fourth dimension).

Not surprisingly, nonverbal behaviors play important roles in relational communication. *Proximity* communicates intimacy, attraction, trust, caring, dominance, persuasiveness, and aggressiveness. *Smiling* communicates emotional arousal, composure, formality, intimacy, and liking. *Touching* suggests intimacy. *Eye contact* intensifies the other nonverbal behaviors.[31] Of course, these interpretations of nonverbal behaviors do not take cultural differences into account. For example, in some cultures, such as Arab and Latin American cultures, close proximity does not necessarily indicate dominance or aggressiveness. Likewise, in Navajo and some Asian cultures eye contact can be interpreted as a sign of disrespect or challenge. In some cultures, touching in public is practically forbidden.

Whether verbal or nonverbal, communication in relationships helps the parties make predictions about others in the relationship. Communication reduces uncertainty about the probable outcomes of future exchanges and provides a basis for the continuing relationship. Understanding the communication process, however, requires not only an understanding of the relationship between the communicators but also the larger social context within which communication occurs.

The Social Environment

Communication affects and is affected by the social setting. Thus, communication occurs as a structured process within evolving systems of related components and activities. Social systems include families, groups, organizations, and all kinds of collectivities that are at the same time both producers and products of communication.

For example, when people think they can achieve something through joint action that they cannot accomplish individually, they form groups. Communication in groups depends on the nature of the group (primary versus secondary, formal versus informal, task-oriented versus experiential), characteristics of group members, group size, group structure, group cohesiveness, and group purpose.[32] Apart from understanding the determinants and consequences of group communication, researchers and practitioners alike are concerned with group effectiveness in making decisions.

Successful group decision making requires accomplishing four tasks: (1) developing an adequate and accurate assessment of the problem, (2) developing a shared and complete understanding of the goal and the criteria for success, (3) agreeing on the positive outcomes of decisions, and (4) agreeing on the negative outcomes of decisions. Decision-making effectiveness, therefore, depends on the extent to which members' communication helps achieve these group functions.[33]

Organizations impose additional layers of complexity and constraints on communication. But nobody said this was going to be easy. Recall that the forces at play in the larger society (outlined in chapter 7) affect how all communicators—individuals, groups, and organizations—approach their publics, shape the content of their messages, define communication goals, and condition audience responses. Recall also the central point of the last chapter: All elements of a system are interdependent and mutually influenced by forces in their environment. In short, communication—when it occurs—results from a complex reciprocal process in which communicators try to inform, instruct, or persuade within the contexts of their relationships and the larger social setting.

EFFECTS OF THE PROCESS

Communication effects have long been the object of concern and study. The range of effects run the gamut from early concerns about "all-powerful" media to "no effects." Hypothesized unlimited effects of movies on helpless children motivated the Payne Fund studies of the 1920s. Maybe critics simply feared too much. After ambitious public persuasion and political campaigns in the 1940s and 1950s produced disappointing results, many concluded that mass communication has almost no impact. Maybe the campaign planners simply asked too much of mass communication. More recent evidence supports theories in which mass communication effects occur under specified conditions. Apparently, the answer depends on what question you ask.

Creating Perceptions of the World around Us

Early theorists cast mass communication in the role of telling us about events, things, people, and places we could not experience directly ourselves. Walter Lippmann said it best when he wrote about "the world outside and the pictures in our heads." He described a "triangular relationship" between the scene of action (interpreted to include people, places, actions, and the entire range of possible phenomena), perceptions of that scene, and responses based on the perceptions. The last side of the triangle is complete when the responses have impact on the original scene of action. Mass media fit in the model between the scene of action and audience perceptions (see Figure 8.2).[34]

Lippmann pointed out that most of us cannot or do not have direct access to much of the world; it is "out of reach, out of sight, out of mind." The mass media help us create a "trustworthy picture" of the world that is beyond our reach and direct experience. His notions of media impact on public perceptions not only set the stage for studying mass communication effects but arguably established the conceptual basis for much of what later became public relations.

Setting the Agenda

The "agenda-setting" theory of mass communication effects builds on Lippmann's notion of media impact by distinguishing between *what we think about* and *what we think*. The difference is that the former includes what we know about (cognition) whereas the latter refers to our opinions and feelings (predisposition). Agenda setting suggests that mass media can have substan-

FIGURE 8.2   MASS MEDIA IN PUBLIC OPINION FORMATION

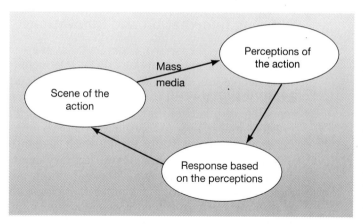

Source: Based on "triangular relationship" in Walter Lippmann, *Public Opinion* (New York: Harcourt, Brace and Company, 1927), pp. 16–17.

tial and important impact on the cognitive level without affecting predisposition.[35] But it should be clear that even if media are limited to this one effect, setting the agenda is not a trivial consequence.

For example, early explorations of agenda setting by the press during presidential elections found that relative media emphasis on issues has a cumulative effect on the electorate. The same issues, with the same relative emphasis as that given by the media, make up the voters' agenda. In other words, the issues considered least to most important by voters reflect patterns of media coverage rather than a particular political agenda. Furthermore, the relative number of people concerned about issues parallels the relative media emphasis of those issues. Media and public agendas were most similar during the early stages of the campaign and for those issues least likely to be within peoples' direct experience.[36]

Imagine the potential consequences of media agenda setting. First of all, media coverage can elevate the public standing of issues, people, organizations, institutions, and so forth. Second, changes in the amount of media attention can lead to changes in public priorities. Third, the more concerned people are about something, the more they tend to learn about it, the stronger their opinions of it, and the more they tend to take action on it. (Notice, however, that the agenda-setting theory does not predict what information they will seek, which way their opinions will change, or what types of actions they will take.) Fourth, media coverage can affect the agenda priorities of some specific and important publics, such as legislators, regulators, and other policy makers.

In summary, mass communication can affect public opinion by raising the salience of issues and positions taken by people and groups in the news.[37] Furthermore, like Lippmann's theory of media effects, the agenda-setting theory contributes to the conceptual foundation for public relations mass communication.

Diffusing Information and Innovations

Beyond setting the issue agenda, research in a variety of settings shows that mass communication facilitates social interaction and change. For example, some people use mass media to get information from sources unlike themselves. The sources may come from different social, economic, and educational backgrounds but are accessible through the media. The media, then, provide information from sources that would otherwise not be available through interpersonal networks in which "like talks to like." Once people get information from the media, however, they enter conversations armed with useful new information. What we learn from the mass media often determines what we talk about with others, providing the common ground needed to begin conversation: "Did you see in this morning's paper that . . . ?" or "Wasn't Jay Leno funny last night when he said . . . ?" In effect, mass media provide information to those who seek it and supply information needed for subsequent interpersonal communication.[38]

Originally communication scholars referred to the mass media–interpersonal sequence of communication as the "two-step flow" model. This model of communication effects suggests that ideas flow from the media to opinion leaders, who in turn inform others through interpersonal conversations. Most now agree, however, that communication is a multistep-flow process in which media are more effective than interpersonal conversations in spreading information. Interpersonal communication is more effective than mass media, however, in forming or changing predisposition toward an issue of innovation. On a wide range of issues and innovations, people are more likely to turn to their interpersonal networks of near-peers for subjective evaluations than to mass media sources.[39] Of course, mass media can extend the reach of peers, and thus the care with which spokespersons are chosen.

Characteristics of the innovation or new idea as well as characteristics of the adopters influence the adoption process. Ideas or innovations are more readily adopted if they are (1) more advantageous than the current situation, (2) compatible with previous experience and other aspects of the situation, (3) simple, (4) easily tried, and (5) observable with readily apparent outcomes. "Innovators" are the first to adopt new ideas, followed by "early adopters," "early majority," "late majority," and "laggards." Characteristics of the individuals in each of the categories vary with the nature of change being adopted and the context.[40]

Diffusion and adoption processes illustrate the impact that mass communication has on interpersonal communication and networks. More important, they show how mass and interpersonal communication interact in social systems and in social change.

Defining Social Support

The *spiral of silence* theory suggests a phenomenon referred to as "the silent majority." Individuals who think their opinion conflicts with the opinions of most other people tend to remain silent on an issue. Carried to an extreme, even if a majority actually agree but do not individually recognize social support, their silence and inactivity can lead to the erroneous conclusion that not many people support a particular view. On the other hand, individuals who think that many others share their view, or that the number of people who agree is growing rapidly, are more likely to express their views. Under these conditions, a vocal minority that sees itself on the winning side can appear to represent a widely shared perspective.[41] In either case, as Lippmann pointed out more than 50 years before the spiral of silence theory appeared, people "respond as powerfully to fictions as they do to realities, and . . . in many cases they help to create the very fictions to which they respond."[42]

In essence, public opinion arises as individuals collectively discern about support for their views through personal interaction and by attending to the mass media. Individuals observe and assess their social environments, assessing the distributions of opinions, estimating the strength and chances of success for each, and determining the social sanctions and costs associated with each. The spiral begins when individuals choose to remain silent or to express their views. It continues as others observe the presence or absence of support for their own views. It gains apparent legitimacy when increasing numbers of individuals translate their observations into public silence or expression. It is reinforced when the media cover the views being displayed most forcefully and most frequently and do not make an effort to determine the actual distribution of views.

Media coverage can reflect, enforce, or challenge the spiral of silence effect on public opinion. But understanding the dynamics of individuals' collective observations of their social environments and public opinion translates rather directly into public relations practice. Examples include public information campaigns designed to break the spirals of silence associated with smoking, drinking and driving, substance abuse, domestic violence, sexual harassment, and safe sex, to list only a few. In each instance, and for many other public issues, mass communication played a key role in redefining socially accepted expression and behavior.

As illustrated in Figure 8.3, mass media messages can provide individuals pictures of their social environment, of whether there is social approval or disapproval of their views or actions. This "sociocultural model" of communication effects suggests that "messages presented via the mass media may provide the appearance of consensus regarding orientation and action with respect to a given object or goal of persuasion."[43]

PUBLICS AND THEIR OPINIONS

Nineteenth-century writer and first editor of *Atlantic Monthly* James Russell Lowell said, "The pressure of public opinion is like the atmosphere. You can't see it, but all the same it is sixteen pounds to the square inch." Lowell's words have even more relevance now. Public opinion has never been more powerful, more fragmented, more volatile, and more exploited and manipulated.

FIGURE 8.3   SOCIOCULTURAL MODEL OF PERSUASION

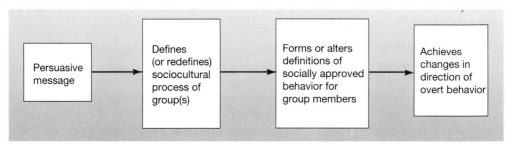

Source: Melvin L. DeFleur and Sandra J. Ball-Rokeach, *Theories of Mass Communication,* 4th ed. (New York: Longman, 1982), p. 225.

For example, media coverage and public opinion of the president's character played a major role in the 1996 presidential campaign between Republican challenger Bob Dole and incumbent Bill Clinton. Public satisfaction with pocketbook issues (the economy), however, won out over Republican charges of ethical transgressions in the Clinton White House and frequent references to the long-running investigation of the Arkansas Whitewater scandal. Researchers studying the campaign coverage found ample evidence of a powerful media effect:

> News media coverage, *alone,* explained a substantial portion of the variance in the public's preference for either Clinton or Dole in 1996 . . . suggestive of a powerful relationship between news media coverage and public opinion in presidential elections.[44]

They concluded, however, that "positive evaluations of Clinton generated from favorable conditions in economic and world affairs may have made the public less susceptible to persuasion from positive or negative media coverage of Dole."[45] Public opinion polls reflected the President's advantage throughout the campaign and guided the campaign away from engaging the character issues.

Public opinion polls have long guided politics, government programs, entertainment programming, and even corporate decision making. In short, much as Lowell suggested, public opinion is an always-present, dynamic force. It is part of public relations' mission to help organizations recognize, understand, and deal with this powerful influence in their environments.

It is not an easy task, however. As the former vice president of AT&T says:

> Public opinion is not necessarily logical; it is amorphous, ambivalent, contradictory, volatile. Consequently, those of us who would hope to influence public opinion can only expect that our efforts, over time, may nudge the consensus toward some reasonable perception of the issues.[46]

His experience led him to conclude that publics have "an astounding ability to ignore very material facts when those facts don't interest them, and increasing the supply of information does not necessarily increase public knowledge."[47]

Nevertheless, public opinion is a powerful force in modern society. Organizations of all types must deal with *real* and *perceived* public opinion as they establish and maintain relationships with their many internal and external publics. But organizations are the actors; public opinion is simply the "energizer" of their actions.

> (Public opinion) is not a decorporalized general will; neither is it a statistical construct made up of individual data points. It is an expression of social energy that integrates individual actors into social groupings in ways that affect the polity. This understanding takes the concept of public opinion out of metaphysics and . . . avoids reducing it to a set of discrete individualized observations that cannot account for its composite sociopolitical significance.[48]

Definition of Public Opinion

The common notion of public opinion holds that it is simply the aggregation of individual views on some issue. This "individual agreement" approach to defining public opinion, however, misses the point that it is *public.* Individual cognition may or may not represent the *consensus,* or "thinking together," that more fully represents the kinds of opinions that form and are formed by public discussion among those sharing a "sense of commonness."

Thus, public opinion represents more than the collected views held by a particular category of individuals at one point in time. Public opinion is not adequately defined as simply a *state* of individual cognition. Instead, it reflects a dynamic *process* in which ideas are "expressed, adjusted, and compromised en route to collective determination of a course of action."[49]

> It occurs within groups of communicating people, who together determine what the issue is, why it is a cause for public concern, and what can be done about it. While the process unquestionably involves private cognition, individuals' thoughts about a social issue are largely dependent for both form and content on public discussion. This is why communication is so often metaphorically equated with externalized cognition: Communication requires "thinking together."[50]

In practice, however, both researchers and public relations practitioners take "snapshots" of public opinion, essentially freezing the process at one point in time so as to describe it at one time and compare it with at other times. Their surveys too often measure only direction and intensity, ignoring other important dimensions.

Direction of opinion indicates the evaluative quality, telling us the "positive-negative-neutral," "for-against-undecided," or "pro-con-it-depends" quality of predisposition. In its simplest form, direction is a yes-no answer to a survey question. Media frequently report public opinion survey results as simply the percentages for or against some issue, proposition, or candidate. For example, stories reporting poll results, popularity, margin, and other indicators of the direction of public opinion about the candidates—"Horse race content"—dominated coverage of the 1996 presidential campaign, comprising 38 percent of all stories.[51] (Character stories were second at 18 percent.) Direction clearly represents the most basic and most frequently used measure of public opinion.

Intensity measures show how strongly people feel about their opinions, whatever the direction. For example, throughout Kenneth Starr's investigations of Whitewater and the Clinton White House, pollsters asked registered voters to indicate "on a scale of 1 to 10" how strongly they felt about a wide range of issues and actors related to the special counsel's "search for the truth." Likewise, surveys often ask respondents to mark "strongly disagree / disagree / neutral / agree / strongly agree" to indicate both direction and intensity of feelings. Intensity measures provide an initial estimate of the relative strength of predisposition. Intensity and direction are often reported to indicate not only how people feel about issues such as abortion, school vouchers, and clear-cutting forests, or people such as President Clinton, Kenneth Starr, and Yasser Arafat, but also how deeply they hold the feelings.

Stability refers to how long respondents have held or will hold the same direction and intensity of feelings. Measures of stability require observations taken at two or more points in time. Think of this dimension as something like the charts that track stock prices or temperature patterns over time. During the long-running bull market, when Alan Greenspan made off-the-cuff comments about interest rates, stock prices immediately reflected his remarks. Presidential candidates experience a "bump" in support after the national conventions. In effect, the stability measure provides evidence of how reactive public opinion is to events or other information.

Informational support refers to how much knowledge people hold about the object of opinion. For example, partisan voters often have strong opinions of their respective candidates, yet do not hold much information to back up their predisposition. In political campaigns, voters who have little information about candidates or issues tend to focus on who they see as being involved or associated with a candidate or issue and how they think the candidate or issue affects them personally. Better-informed voters, in contrast, "are more likely to ignore consideration of the specific groups involved in favor of a more general interpretation of the issue," concentrating more on democratic values and the abstract rights of individuals.[52]

> People gradually learn, through exposure to public discussion on the issue, to base their opinions on certain pertinent aspects of the issue, and at the same time they learn not to pay attention to other features of the issue deemed to be irrelevant. Exposure to information therefore narrows one's focus on an issue to a small number of relevant interpretations when there is general agreement among opinion leaders about how to think about the issue.[53]

Other researchers studying a mayoral election found that those more informed about issues hold stronger opinions about the issues, but the direction of the opinions are not easily predicted. Furthermore, those with more knowledge and strong opinions are more likely to vote and to contact local officials.[54]

Absence of "information mass" behind an opinion on relatively nonpartisan issues may indicate that the direction and intensity are susceptible to change. For example, if Monsanto finds that public opinion against field testing of genetically engineered plants is not well informed, the company could mount a public information campaign designed to educate community members about the risks and benefits involved, taking care to frame the messages in the context of who is affected and involved (including the consensus views of community leaders), as well as how the field tests will affect those in the community—potential risks (if any) and benefits.

Social support measures provide evidence of the extent to which people think their opinions are shared by others in their social milieu. The persuasion model in Figure 8.3 indicates the power of perceptions of social approval or disapproval. Pollsters probing this dimension of public opinion ask respondents to report their impressions of what significant others think about an issue, or to estimate the distribution of public opinion on the issue under study. In effect, measures of social support show how people define the nature of the consensus on issues.

The social context of opinion may be simply the tendency to think that other people are more influenced by media or events than ourselves. Researchers have found "third-person effects" under various conditions—people tend to underestimate impact on themselves and overestimate impact on others. Such effects could have consequences in how public policy is determined (protecting those perceived to be vulnerable others), how political campaigns are conducted (influencing easily persuaded voters), and how juries decide libel cases and award damages (estimating the harm done to reputations). "So the third-person effect may have a number of behavioral implications, even though it is basically a perceptual phenomenon."[55]

Think of both informational and social support as giving predisposition weight or inertia. If, for example, people with a strong opinion on an issue hold a lot of information—pro and con—about that issue and see their particular position as being widely shared, then the direction and expression of the opinion are not likely to change. Much as the direction of a bowling ball is little affected by the air movement created by air conditioner and furnace fans, opinions with much informational and social support have great mass and are not susceptible to easy or quick change. On the other hand, even strongly held opinions can change if they are not backed by information and perceived social support. They can change direction as frequently and rapidly as a Ping-Pong ball in an El Niño–driven storm!

In other words, describing and understanding public opinion requires greater measurement sensitivity and depth than the simple yes-no questions often used in telephone polling. Public opinion reflects a dynamic process of interpersonal and media communication on issues among groups and collectivities of people who have the capacity to act in similar ways. "Thinking together" often leads to "acting together," the real reason for understanding public opinion.

The Publics

First of all, practitioners of public relations must discard notions about "the general public." The mosaic of the many different ethnic, racial, religious, geographic, political, occupational, social, and special-interest groupings that would be included make the general public concept of little, if any, value in public relations. Rather, effective programs communicate and build relationships with specifically defined "target publics." Without such specific definitions and detailed information about intended audiences of messages, how do program planners measure public opinion, establish program objectives, develop meaningful message and action strategies, select media to deliver messages selectively and effectively, and determine whether the program worked?

Chapter 11 outlines specific contemporary approaches to defining publics, but the basic concept traces back to the early 1900s. Philosopher and educator John Dewey defined a public as an active social unit consisting of all those affected who recognize a common problem for which they can seek common solutions. He wrote that publics are formed by "recognition of evil consequence brought about a common interest." Without communication, however, it "will remain shadowy and formless, seeking spasmodically for itself, but seizing and holding its shadow rather than its substance."[56]

Grunig expands on Dewey's concept by outlining three factors that move *latent* publics to become communicating *active* publics:

1. *Problem recognition* represents the extent to which people are aware that something is missing or amiss in a situation, thereby knowing that they need information.
2. *Constraint recognition* represents the extent to which people see themselves limited by external factors, versus seeing that they can do something about the situation. If people think they can make a difference or have an effect on the problem situation, they will seek information to make plans for action.
3. *Level of involvement* represents the extent to which people see themselves being involved and affected by a situation. In other words, the more they see themselves connected to a situation, the more likely they will communicate about it.[57]

After testing his "situational theory" of publics on a variety of environmental issues, Grunig concludes that environmental publics defined according to their communication behavioral similarities are not the same as those identified by demographic attributes or attitudes.[58] He consistently finds four types of publics:

1. *All-issue publics* are active on all issues.
2. *Apathetic publics* are inattentive and inactive on all issues.
3. *Single-issue publics* are active on one or a limited number of related issues. (Such publics include the pro-life and animal rights groups.)

4. *Hot-issue publics* are active after media expose almost everyone and the issue becomes the topic of widespread social conversation. (Character during the 1996 presidential campaign and global warming created publics after attracting extensive media attention.)[59]

As suggested by Grunig's situational theory of publics, cross-situational definitions do not apply readily in specific situations. For example, useful definitions of publics go beyond demographics or "psychographics" to include relevant indicators of common recognition of mutual interests and situational variables that tie certain individuals, but not others, to specific situations or issues. In other words, publics result from specific issues or situations, not shared cross-situational traits. Dewey said that when

> a church, a trade union, a business corporation, or an educational institution conducts itself so as to affect large numbers outside of itself, those who are affected form a public which endeavors to act through suitable structures, and thus to organize itself for oversight and regulation.[60]

Dewey's concept of a public logically extends to include structures, rules, sanctions, and punishments imposed by those affected when "it is deemed necessary to have those consequences systematically cared for."[61]

Specific issues and situations determine each public's composition, size, and range of responses. For example, an organization's philanthropic donation to support construction of a controversial abstract sculpture in a park can activate many individuals to respond in a variety of ways. Some, if not most, of those who see themselves affected by the organization's charity probably have no direct contact with the organization making the donation and do not live near the park. On the other hand, if the same organization proposes a complex restructuring of its long-term debt, then probably only a few top executives who fear being presented early retirements, financial analysts, and institutional investors may respond to the proposed changes. From the perspective of the publics that come into existence in the two situations, a wider range of publics and a greater number of people are moved to react in a variety of ways by the charitable contribution than by the restructuring proposal. It is conceivable, however, that the long-term "evil consequences" of financial restructuring will have a much greater impact on the community than will the existence of an avant-garde piece of public art.

INDIVIDUAL ORIENTATIONS AND COORIENTATION

The different publics and reactions stimulated by the two situations in the previous scenarios suggest both individual and shared orientations. Individual orientations, however, do not become public opinion until they are shared—or perceived to be shared—by others. The realization, rightly or wrongly, that an individual's views of a situation are similar to those held by others evokes a sense of identification among individuals and the perception of a common interest. In other words, individual orientations include perceptions of issues or objects in one's environment, as well as perceptions of significant others' views of those same issues or objects. When two or more individuals' orientations include the same issues or objects and each other, they are in a state of "coorientation."

Orientation

Individuals hold opinions of varying degrees of relevance and intensity. Individuals assign value to objects in their environment on the basis of both their previous history with the objects and their assessment of the objects in the current context. (See Figure 8.4.) The former value is *salience,* or the feelings about an object derived from an individual's experiences and reinforcements from previous situations. Salience refers to what the individual brings to a situation as a result of history. The second source of value is *pertinence,* which refers to the relative value of an object on the basis of object-by-object comparisons on the basis of some attribute or attributes. Pertinence value can vary depending on which attribute is used to make the comparison or what other objects are used in the comparison.[62] In other words, salience indicates how individuals feel about an object, independent of the situation, whereas pertinence depends on how the individual defines the situation. To describe and understand an individual's opinion about some object, then, you have to measure both salience and pertinence. The distinction helps clarify the relationship between attitudes and opinions.

An *attitude* is the cross-situational predisposition or preference with respect to an object. Attitudes predispose individuals to respond in certain ways

FIGURE 8.4   MODEL OF INDIVIDUAL ORIENTATION

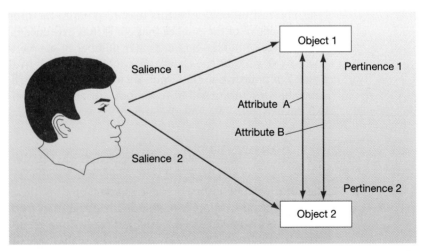

Source: Adapted from Richard F. Carter, "Communication and Affective Relations," *Journalism Quarterly* 42, no. 2 (Spring 1965), p. 204.

toward objects from one situation to another, based on a lifetime of accumulating and evaluating information and experiences. Crespi substitutes "attitudinal system" when referring to what others call "attitude." He defines attitude systems as comprising of four components:

1. Evaluative frames of reference (values and interests).
2. Cognition (knowledge and beliefs).
3. Affection (feelings). Because many use the term *attitude* as referring only or primarily to the affective mode, whereas others use attitude more generally, an added benefit of adopting this nomenclature is that it avoids confusing the affective response mode with the entire system.
4. Conation (behavioral intentions).[63]

On the other hand, an opinion is the judgment expressed about an object in a particular situation or given a specific set of circumstances. Opinions tend to reflect an individual's related attitudes but also take into account aspects of the current situation.

Scholars have generally distinguished between attitudes and opinions in two ways:

> First, opinions are generally considered to be verbal, or otherwise overt responses to a specific stimulus (an issue), while attitudes are more basic global tendencies to respond favorably or unfavorably to a general class of stimuli. While opinions are largely situational, attitudes are more enduring with a person across situations. Second, opinions are considered to be more cognitive and somewhat less affective in their makeup. . . . An attitude is an immediate, intuitive orientation while an opinion is a thought-out, reasoned choice between alternatives for action in a social matrix.[64]

The notion that opinions are expressed makes them important to the formation and study of public opinion. On the other hand, unexpressed intrapersonal predisposition does not affect *public* opinion formation. Not until attitudes get expressed through opinions in discussion or other public communication do they have an impact on the processes of forming and changing public opinion. That opinions are public expressions establishes public opinion as a social phenomenon.

Coorientation

The social or interpersonal concept of public opinion requires two or more individuals oriented to and communicating about an object of mutual interest. In other words, they are "cooriented" to something in common and to each other.

The coorientational model in Figure 8.5 illustrates the *intrapersonal* and *interpersonal* elements of communication relationships.[65] First, the intrapersonal construct of *congruency* describes the extent to which your own views match your estimate of another's views on the same issue. Some refer to this variable as "perceived agreement." On the basis of this estimate, you formu-

FIGURE 8.5   MODEL OF COORIENTATION

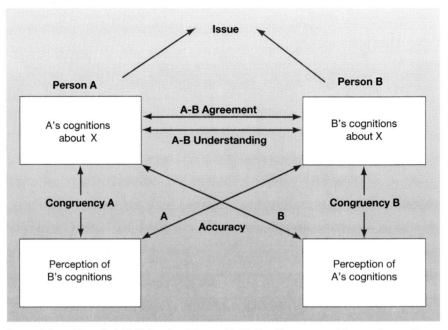

Source: Adapted from Jack M. McLeod and Steven H. Chaffee, "Interpersonal Approaches to Communication Research," in *Interpersonal Perception and Communication,* ed. Steven H. Chaffee and Jack M. McLeod, special edition of *American Behavioral Scientist,* 16, no. 4 (March–April 1973), pp. 483–88.

late strategies for dealing with the other person or for spontaneously responding in interactions.

The extent to which you accurately estimate another's views determines the appropriateness of your actions. Each of us recalls instances in which we misjudged another person's position on some issue of mutual interest, and responded to them inappropriately until we learned what the person really thought about the issue. *Accuracy,* then, represents the extent to which your estimate matches the other person's actual views. Because it requires a comparison of observations taken from two different people, accuracy represents an interpersonal construct.

The other interpersonal constructs include *agreement* and *understanding.* Agreement represents the extent to which two or more persons share *similar evaluations* of an issue of mutual interest. Understanding measures the *similarities in the definitions* of two or more persons. In terms used in the individual orientation paradigm, agreement compares saliences, whereas understanding compares pertinences.

Coorientational Consensus

By including many individuals simultaneously oriented to issues of mutual concern and interest, the interpersonal coorientational model is extended to large social groupings. A coorientational concept of public opinion in communities and society provides an alternative to the usual psychological approaches to describing states of consensus.

First, the coorientational approach does not use the traditional "individual agreement" approach to describing public opinion, that is, an aggregation of individual orientations to some issue or topic. Instead, the coorientational approach casts public opinion as the product of both individual perceptions on an issue and their perceptions of what significant others think about the same issue.

Social scientists long ago recognized the need to take into account *perceptions of agreement* in addition to *actual agreement.* Scheff, for one, argued that perceptions of agreement can be independent of actual agreement and that perceptions of agreement more likely affect public behavior than does actual agreement. In fact, it is often the case that those involved in issues of public debate do not know the state of actual agreement, operating instead on their perceptions of agreement.[66]

Conceiving public opinion—or consensus—in this way makes it a complex social phenomenon that can be described using coorientational concepts. For example, the state of *monolithic consensus* represents high levels of actual agreement accurately recognized as such by those involved. *Dissensus* exists when high levels of actual disagreement are accurately perceived as such. (See Table 8.1.)

Public opinion based on inaccurate perceptions of agreement is more troublesome in relationships. Unlike actual agreement or disagreement, however, inaccurate perceptions are at least subject to change as a result of effective communication. For example, after extended interaction, two or more persons may simply agree to disagree. At least they each know where the other stands on the issue. The same cannot be said about situations based on inaccurate perceptions of each other's views.

False consensus exists when there is actual disagreement but the majority of those involved think they agree. *Pluralistic ignorance* represents the state of public opinion in which a majority perceive little agreement, but in fact

TABLE 8.1	TYPES OF COORIENTATIONAL CONSENSUS		
		Perceives That Majority Also Agrees on Issue	Perceives That Majority Does not Agree on Issue
	Majority actually agrees on issue	Monolithic Consensus	Pluralistic Ignorance
	Majority does not agree on issue	False Consensus	Dissensus

Source: Adapted from Thomas J. Scheff, "Toward a Sociological Model of Consensus," *American Sociological Review,* 32, no. 1 (February 1967), p. 39.

there is widespread agreement. When those involved do not accurately recognize the state of actual agreement, they act on the basis of their inaccurate perceptions. In the cases of false consensus and pluralistic ignorance, their responses and public expressions (that is, public opinion) are not consistent with the actual distribution of individual orientations on issues of common interest. Accurate perceptions of others' views, however, are surely the most likely outcome of public communication and the greatest motivation for maintaining communication in society and in relationships.

What may appear as logical in the context of this discussion, however, apparently is not widely recognized by those who commission or practice public relations. Instead of trying to increase the accuracy of cross perceptions in social relationships, most communication efforts attempt to influence levels of agreement, or to "engineer consent." But actual agreement can exist independent of perceptions of agreement, leading to Scheff's more useful definition of coorientational public opinion:

> Complete consensus on an issue exists in a group [read "public"] when there is an infinite series of reciprocating understandings between the members of the group [read "public"] concerning the issue. I know that you know that I know, and so on.[67] (Words in brackets added.)

In the context of public relations, the coorientational approach to consensus and relationships is also useful for describing the nature of organization–public relationships.

Coorientational Relationships

The coorientational approach helps identify three public relations problems that call for rather straightforward communication strategies:

1. An organization and a public hold different definitions of an issue. They simply are not talking about the same thing when they engage in communication about "the issue." They are talking about different issues.
2. The organization's perceptions of a public's views of an issue (evaluations "and" or "or" definitions) do not match the public's actual views. Organizational management makes decisions about a public based on inaccurate estimates of the public's views. Not surprisingly, the relationship suffers when members of that public are subjected to the organization's actions and communications.
3. Members of a public hold inaccurate perceptions of an organization's positions on an issue of mutual concern. Public responses to the organization's management, its products, its actions and procedures, and so forth are based on inaccurate estimates of management policy and values.

Note that in all cases, the nature of the organization–public relationship is threatened by differing definitions and inaccurate perceptions, not by disagreement over the issue itself. None of the situations calls for communication designed to change the level of agreement–disagreement on the issue.

Communication that helps create shared definitions and increase accuracy improves the relationship and makes each side's dealings with the other more appropriate. (See Figure 8.6.)

For example, even though the Army Corps of Engineers communicated the advantages of a proposed flood-control project to the various publics who would be affected, they apparently did not do the same for the project's disadvantages. Convinced that the various publics supported the project, the Corps scheduled what was to be the final public hearing for project approval. Project planners were surprised by the suspicions, concerns, objections, and uncertainties expressed at the hearing. The project was delayed for the additional meetings and negotiations needed to improve accuracy in both the Corps's and publics' perceptions of the project and each other's views.[68] Had the Corps initially used the coorientational approach to assess public opinion of the project, they might have identified their relationship problems and taken steps to avoid the costly delays.

As this example illustrates, the coorientational approach serves three major purposes in public relations planning. First, coorientational measures provide the information needed to identify and describe problems in organiza-

FIGURE 8.6   **COORIENTATIONAL MODEL OF ORGANIZATION–PUBLIC RELATIONSHIPS**

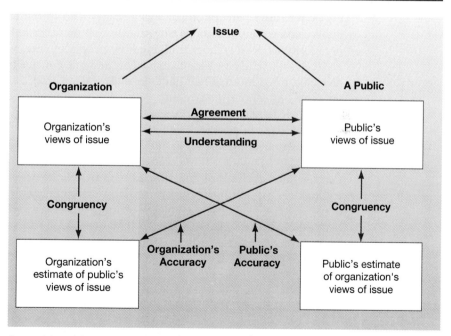

Source: Adapted from Jack M. McLeod and Steven H. Chaffee, "Interpersonal Approaches to Communication Research," in Interpersonal Perception and Communication, eds. Steven H. Chaffee and Jack M. McLeod, special edition of American Behavioral Scientist, 16, no. 4 (March–April 1973), pp. 483–88.

tion–public relationships. Rather than defining problems in ways that limit strategies to those designed to increase agreement by changing public perceptions, this approach calls for an assessment of all parties' views in order to understand relationships.

Second, coorientational measures provide useful guidance for planning appropriate messages and responses to correct organization–public relationship problems. Coorientational assessments of relationships can lead to atypical, yet efficient, solutions. For example, imagine that the analysis shows that management has an inaccurate perception of a public's views on an issue and as a result is proposing what will be an inappropriate action or response. Simply reporting the public's actual views on the issue to management may be the only corrective action needed.

Third, repeated use of coorientational measures indicates how the relationship changes as a result of the communication and other corrective actions. In other words, agreement, understanding, congruency, and accuracy serve as outcome criteria for assessing the impact of public relations efforts on organization–public relationships.[69]

In conclusion, public relations establishes and maintains relationships between organizations and their publics by—but not limited to—facilitating two-way communication. The communication, however, may have less impact on the extent to which parties agree or disagree than on the accuracy of their cross-perceptions of each other's views. In the final analysis, Lippmann's "pictures in our heads" of the "world outside" include our estimates of what others think. These perceptions of social reality lead to the formation of active publics and condition actions toward others, both other individuals and other organizations. Researchers studying how people interact with their computers, television, and new media arrived at the same conclusion: "What *seems* to be true is often more influential than what really is true. . . . *Perceptions* are far more influential than reality defined more objectively."[70] As Lippmann said, "That is why until we know what others think they know, we cannot truly understand their acts."[71]

Communication, then, not only moves information from one party in a relationship to another but also defines the relationships and social environment within which we all function: as citizens, employees, managers, and policy makers. Not surprisingly, the media of communication—the topic of the next chapter—play essential roles in shaping both issues and their social contexts. Mass media make possible the thinking together that shapes and represents the states of consensus in complex organizations, in communities, and in the larger global society.

NOTES

1. Frederick Williams, *The New Communications,* 3d ed. (Belmont, CA: Wadsworth Publishing Company, 1992), 9.
2. Walter Lippmann, *Public Opinion* (New York: Harcourt, Brace and Company), 1922, 3 and 4.

3. Paul F. Lazarsfeld, Bernard Berelson, and Hazel Gaudet, The People's Choice: How the Voter Makes Up His Mind in a Presidential Campaign, 3d ed. (New York: Columbia University Press, 1968), 151.

4. Warren Weaver, "The Mathematics of Communication," in *Communication and Culture: Reading in the Codes of Human Interaction,* edited by Alfred G. Smith (New York: Holt, Rinehart and Winston, 1966), 17. Reprinted from *Scientific American,* 181 (1949): 11–15. Original theory published in Claude E. Shannon and Warren Weaver, *The Mathematical Theory of Communication* (Urbana: University of Illinois Press, 1949).

5. Ibid., 17.

6. Wilbur Schramm, "The Nature of Communication Between Humans," in *The Process and Effects of Mass Communication,* rev. ed., edited by Wilbur Schramm and Donald F. Roberts (Urbana: University of Illinois Press, 1971), 17.

7. Ibid., 38–47.

8. Carl I. Hovland, Irving L. Janis, and Harold H. Kelley, *Communication and Persuasion* (New Haven: Yale University Press, 1953). The World War II "Yale studies" provided the foundation for persuasion theory still used for designing both persuasion effects research and public communication campaigns.

9. Norman H. Anderson, "Integration Theory and Attitude Change," *Psychological Review* 78, no. 3 (May 1971): 171–206.

10. Adapted from Carl I. Hovland, Arthur A. Lumsdaine, and Fred D. Sheffield, "The Effect of Presenting 'One Side' versus 'Both Sides' in Changing Opinions on a Controversial Subject," in *Experiments on Mass Communication* (Princeton: Princeton University Press, 1949), 201–27. Also in Schramm and Roberts, *The Process and Effects of Mass Communication,* 467–84.

11. Arthur A. Lumsdaine and Irving L. Janis, "Resistance to 'Counterpropaganda' Produced by One-Sided and Two-Sided 'Propaganda' Presentations," *Public Opinion Quarterly* 17, no. 3 (1953): 311–18. See also William J. McGuire, "Persuasion, Resistance, and Attitude Change," in *Handbook of Communication,* edited by Ithiel de Sola Pool and others (Skokie, IL: Rand McNally, 1973), 216–52.

12. Adapted from Richard L. Wiseman and William Schenck-Hamlin, "A Multidimensional Scaling Validation of an Inductively Derived Set of Compliance-Gaining Strategies," *Communication Monographs* 48, no. 4 (December 1981): 257–58.

13. Carl I. Hovland, ed., *The Order of Presentation in Persuasion* (New Haven: Yale University Press, 1957). Reports series of experiments from the Yale studies of message effects in persuasion. The order of presentation, however, turned out to be a relatively minor factor in the communication process, inspiring little research over the years.

14. Reported in Hovland, Janis, and Kelley, *Communication and Persuasion.*

15. Ronald W. Rogers, "A Protection Motivation Theory of Fear Appeals and Attitude Change," *Journal of Psychology* 91 (September 1975): 93–114. See also Rogers and C. R. Mewborn, "Fear Appeals and Attitude Change: Effects of a Threat's Noxiousness, Probability of Occurrence, and the Efficacy of Coping Responses," *Journal of Personality and Social Psychology* 34, no. 1 (July 1976): 54–61.

16. Michael Burgoon, "Messages and Persuasive Effects," in *Message Effects in Communication Science: Sage Annual Reviews of Communication Research* 17, edited by James J. Bradac (Newbury Park, CA: Sage Publications, 1989), 157.

17. From letter to the editor, "Success Story for On-Line News," by Katharine Marshall, director, Internal Communications, Unisys, Blue Bell, PA, in *Communication World* 9, no. 6 (May–June 1992): 5.

18. See Gerald R. Miller, "Interpersonal Communication," chapter 5 in *Human Com-*

munication: Theory and Research, edited by Gordon L. Dahnke and Glen W. Clatterbuck (Belmont, CA: Wadsworth Publishing Company, 1990), 91–122, for a review of interpersonal communication.

19. Marshall McLuhan, *Understanding Media: The Extensions of Man* (New York: McGraw-Hill, 1965), 7.

20. Shearon A. Lowery and Melvin L. DeFleur, *Milestones in Mass Communication Research: Media Effects,* 2d ed. (New York: Longman, 1988). Summarizes 13 major studies that attempted to document media effects.

21. Frederic Wertham, *Seduction of the Innocent* (New York: Rinehart, 1954). See Lowery and DeFleur, *Milestones in Mass Communication Research,* 213–43, for a summary of Wertham's all-out condemnation of comic books.

22. Wilbur Schramm, Jack Lyle, and Edwin B. Parker, *Television in the Lives of Our Children* (Stanford, CA: Stanford University Press, 1961). See Lowery and DeFleur, *Milestones in Mass Communication Research,* 245–70, for a summary.

23. Herbert E. Krugman, "The Impact of Television Advertising: Learning without Involvement," in *The Process and Effects of Mass Communication,* edited by Schramm and Roberts, 485–94. (First published in *Public Opinion Quarterly* 24 (1965): 349–56.) See also Krugman, "Memory without Recall, Exposure without Perception," *Journal of Advertising Research* 17, no. 4 (1977): 7–12.

24. William Miller, "A View from the Inside: Brainwaves and Television Viewing," *Journalism Quarterly* 62, no. 3 (Autumn 1985): 508–14.

25. Summary of "Developing Frameworks for Studying Mass Communication," chapter 1 in Lowery and DeFleur, *Milestones in Mass Communication Research,* 1–29.

26. Lowery and DeFleur, *Milestones in Mass Communication Research,* 151–61.

27. Brenda Dervin, "Audience as Listener and Learner, Teacher and Confidante: The Sense-Making Approach," in *Public Communication Campaigns,* 2d ed., edited by Ronald E. Rice and Charles K. Atkin (Newbury Park, CA: Sage Publications, 1989), 69.

28. William K. Rawlins, "A Dialectical Analysis of the Tensions, Functions, and Strategic Challenges of Communication in Young Adult Friendships," in *Communication Yearbook* 12, edited by James A. Anderson (Newbury Park, CA: Sage Publications, 1989), 157–89.

29. Michael E. Roloff, "Communication and Conflict," in *Handbook of Communication Science,* edited by Charles R. Berger and Steven H. Chaffee (Newbury Park, CA: Sage Publications, 1987), 484–536. See also Charles Watkins, "An Analytical Model of Conflict," *Speech Monographs* 41, no. 1 (1974): 1–5.

30. Stephen W. Littlejohn, *Theories of Human Communication,* 5th ed. (Belmont, CA: Wadsworth Publishing Company, 1996), 252. Good survey of communication theory. See also Judee K. Burgoon and Jerold L. Hale, "The Fundamental Topoi of Relational Communication," *Communication Monographs* 51 (1984): 193–214.

31. Littlejohn, *Theories of Human Communication,* 252.

32. Marvin E. Shaw and Dennis S. Gouran, "Group Dynamics and Communication," in *Human Communication: Theory and Research,* edited by Gordon L. Dahnke and Glen W. Clatterbuck (Belmont, CA: Wadsworth Publishing Company, 1990), 123–55.

33. Randy Y. Hirokawa, "Group Communication and Decision Making Performance: A Continued Test of the Functional Perspective," *Human Communication Research* 14, no. 4 (Summer 1988): 487–515.

34. Walter Lippmann, "The World Outside and the Pictures in Our Heads," chapter 1, *Public Opinion* (New York: Harcourt, Brace and Company, 1922). Reprinted in *The Process and Effects of Mass Communication,* rev. ed., edited by Schramm and Roberts, 265–86.

35. Maxwell E. McCombs and Donald L. Shaw, "The Agenda-Setting Function of Mass Media," *Public Opinion Quarterly* 36, no. 2 (Summer 1972): 176–87. First of many reports of media agenda-setting effects on a variety of issues in a variety of settings.

36. Maxwell McCombs, Edna Einsiedel, and David Weaver, *Contemporary Public Opinion: Issues and the News* (Hillsdale, NJ: Lawrence Erlbaum Associates, 1991), 12–17.

37. Ibid., 17–21.

38. Steven H. Chaffee, "The Interpersonal Context of Mass Communication," in *Current Perspectives in Mass Communication Research,* vol. 1, edited by F. Gerald Kline and Phillip J. Tichenor (Beverly Hills, CA: Sage Publications, 1972), 95–120.

39. Everett M. Rogers, "Communication and Social Change," in *Human Communication,* edited by Dahnke and Clatterbuck, 259–71.

40. Ibid.

41. Elisabeth Noelle-Neumann, "The Theory of Public Opinion: The Concept of Spiral of Silence," in *Communication Yearbook* 14, edited by James A. Anderson (Newbury Park, CA: Sage Publications, 1991), 256–87. Noelle-Neumann first published her theory in "The Spiral of Silence: A Theory of Public Opinion," *Journal of Communication* 24, no. 2 (Spring 1974): 43–51, and later in book form, *The Spiral of Silence: Public Opinion—Our Social Skin* (Chicago: University of Chicago Press, 1984).

42. Lippmann, *Public Opinion,* 14.

43. Melvin L. DeFleur and Sandra J. Ball-Rokeach, *Theories of Mass Communication,* 4th ed. (New York: Longman, 1982), 226.

44. David Domke, David P. Fan, Michael Fibison, Dhavan V. Shah, Steven S. Smith, and Mark D. Watts, "News Media, Candidates and Issues, and Public Opinion in the 1996 Presidential Campaign," *Journalism & Mass Communication Quarterly* 74, no. 4 (Winter 1997): 733.

45. Ibid., 734.

46. Edward M. Block, "How Public Opinion Is Formed," *Public Relations Review* 3, no. 3 (Fall 1977): 15.

47. Ibid., 10.

48. Irving Crespi, *The Public Opinion Process: How the People Speak* (Mahwah, NJ: Lawrence Erlbaum Associates, 1997): 10.

49. Vincent Price and Donald F. Roberts, "Public Opinion Processes," in *Handbook of Communication Science,* edited by Berger and Chaffee, 784.

50. Ibid., 782–83.

51. Domke et al., "Public Opinion in the 1996 Presidential Campaign," 728.

52. Dennis Chong, "Creating Common Frames of Reference on Political Issues," chapter 8 in *Political Persuasion and Attitude Change,* edited by Diana C. Mutz, Paul M. Sniderman, and Richard A Brody (Ann Arbor: University of Michigan Press, 1996): 199.

53. Ibid., 200.

54. Dan Drew and David Weaver, "Media Attention, Media Exposure, and Media Effects," *Journalism Quarterly* 67, no. 4 (Winter 1990): 740–48.

55. Vincent Price, Li-Ning Huang, and David Tewksbury, "Third-Person Effects of News Coverage: Orientations toward Media," *Journalism & Mass Communication Quarterly* 74, no. 3 (Autumn 1997): 525.

56. John Dewey, *The Public and Its Problems* (New York: Henry Holt and Company, 1927), 15–17.

57. James E. Grunig and Fred C. Repper, "Strategic Management, Publics, and Is-

sues," in *Excellence in Public Relations and Communication Management,* edited by James E. Grunig (Hillsdale, NJ: Lawrence Erlbaum Associates, 1992), 135–37.

58. See also James E. Grunig, "Communication Behaviors and Attitudes of Environmental Publics: Two Studies," *Journalism Monographs* 81 (March 1983): 40–41.
59. Grunig and Repper, "Strategic Management, Publics, and Issues," 139.
60. Dewey, *The Public and Its Problems,* 28–29.
61. Ibid., 16.
62. Concepts and paradigm of individual orientation adapted from Richard F. Carter, "Communication and Affective Relations," *Journalism Quarterly* 42, no. 2 (Spring 1965): 203–12.
63. Crespi, *The Public Opinion Process,* 19.
64. Price and Roberts, "Public Opinion Processes," 787.
65. Model and coorientational concepts from Jack M. McLeod and Steven H. Chaffee, "Interpersonal Approaches to Communication Research," in *Interpersonal Perception and Communication,* edited by Steven H. Chaffee and Jack M. McLeod, special edition of *American Behavioral Scientist* 16, no. 4 (March–April 1973): 483–88.
66. Thomas J. Scheff, "Toward a Sociological Model of Consensus," *American Sociological Review* 32, no. 1 (February 1967): 32–46.
67. Ibid., 37.
68. Keith R. Stamm and John E. Bowes, "Communicating During an Environmental Decision," *Journal of Environmental Education* 3, no. 3 (Spring 1972): 49–56.
69. Glen M. Broom, "Coorientational Measurement of Public Issues," *Public Relations Review* 3, no. 4 (Winter 1977): 110–19. See also Glen M. Broom and David M. Dozier, *Using Research in Public Relations* (Englewood Cliffs, NJ: Prentice-Hall, 1990): 36–39.
70. Byron Reeves and Clifford Nass, *The Media Equation* (Cambridge, UK: Cambridge University Press, 1996): 253.
71. Lippmann, *Public Opinion,* 13.

ADDITIONAL SOURCES

Ettorre, Barbara. "The Care and Feeding of a Corporate Reputation," *Management Review* 85 (June 1996): 39–46.

Ewen, Stuart. *PR! A Social History of Spin* (New York: Basic Books, Division of HarperCollins, 1997). Almost 500 pages outlining a critical view of how public relations evolved from the work and thoughts of Edward Bernays and Walter Lippmann.

Gaziano, Cecilie. "Forecast 2000: Widening Knowledge Gaps," *Journalism and Mass Communication Quarterly* 74, no. 2 (Summer 1997): 237–64. Updates research on predictors and consequences of knowledge inequities in society.

Glasser, Theodore L., and Charles T. Salmon, eds. *Public Opinion and the Communication of Consent.* New York: Guilford Press, 1995. Assembles 17 chapters written by 30 leading scholars of the nature, contexts, processes, and impact of public opinion.

Jeffres, Leo W. *Mass Media Effects,* 2nd. ed. Prospect Heights, IL: Waveland Press, 1997. Summarizes and updates literature on media effects previously published as two books.

Knapp, Mark L., and Anita L. Vangelisti. *Interpersonal Communication and Human Relationships.* Boston: Allyn and Bacon, 1992. Summary of literature and theory related to dialogue, interaction rituals, relationships, and other aspects of relational communication.

O'Keefe, Garrett, Dennis P. Rosenbaum, Paul J. Lavrakas, Kathaleen Reid, and Renee A. Botta. *Taking a Bite Out of Crime: The Impact of the National Citizens' Crime Prevention Campaign.* Thousand Oaks, CA: Sage Publications, 1996. Tracks impact of campaign from its beginning in 1979, presenting findings of effectiveness of print, radio, and television media campaign.

Perloff, Richard M. *Political Communication: Politics, Press, and Public in America.* Mahwah, NJ: Lawrence Erlbaum Associates, 1997. Provides social-scientific perspective on media and government, press–presidential relations, and communication theory applied to 1996 presidential campaign and the Clinton health reform effort.

Mutz, Diana C., and Joe Soss. "Reading Public Opinion: The Influence of News Coverage on Perceptions of Public Sentiment," *Public Opinion Quarterly* 61 (1997): 431–51.

Rogers, Everett M., James W. Dearing, and Soonbum Chang. "AIDS in the 1980s: The Agenda-Setting Process for a Public Issue," *Journalism Monographs* 126 (April 1991). Traces agenda-setting process for a single issue over time, in contrast to the usual cross-sectional approach used in many agenda-setting studies.

Wanta, Wayne. *The Public and the National Agenda: How People Learn about Important Issues* (Mahwah, NJ: Lawrence Erlbaum Associates, 1997). Examines agenda-setting effects by examining demographic, psychological, and behavioral influences. Provides exhaustive list of agenda-setting references.

MEDIA AND MEDIA RELATIONS

9

Every newspaper when it reaches the reader is the result of a whole series of selections as to what items shall be printed, in what position they
shall be printed, how much space each shall occupy, what emphasis each
shall have. There are no objective standards here. There are conventions.[1]

—Walter Lippmann

OBJECTIVES

After studying chapter 9, you should be able to

▼ Outline some of the major changes resulting from the use
of new communication technology.

▼ Define employee communication as a part of the public relations function, using the basic elements of the definition
of public relations.

▼ List the major goals of employee communications.

▼ Discuss the major controlled media used in employee
communication.

▼ Discuss the major media used for communicating with external publics.

▼ Define the relationship between practitioners and journalists as being mutually dependent and mutually beneficial,
but sometimes as adversaries.

▼ Outline basic guidelines for building good media relations
and working with the press.

Practitioners of public relations use printed words, spoken words, images, and combinations of all these communication forms. They use both *controlled media* and *uncontrolled media* to communicate with their organizations' many publics. Controlled media include those in which practitioners have the say over what is said, how it is said, when it is said, and—to some extent—to whom it is said. Uncontrolled media are those over which practitioners have no direct role in decision making about media content. Instead, media gatekeepers decide what is reported, how it is reported, when it is reported, and to whom it is reported.

Technology is changing our notions about media, especially the concept of mass media. As one scholar concluded, "The net effect of all these technologies will be to make channels, and the kinds of content they carry, differentially available to the public."[2] Notions about mass, undifferentiated passive audiences are also being outdated as interactive media replace conventional one-way channels. Technology that was originally developed to increase output has often resulted in more individualized communications.

For example, computerized word processing and high-speed printers began by generating large numbers of letters that *appeared* to be addressed to individuals. Now more sophisticated software programs linked to databases produce letters that address individuals by name and refer to specific information needs. Individually targeted direct mail has changed the media mix in many advertising budgets and is increasingly being used to reach individuals with important public relations messages. Some meeting and convention planners are incorporating interactive audience response systems such as IRIS to get immediate feedback on the topics being discussed. Movie producers are experimenting with audience participation in determining story lines and outcomes with interactive systems to replace passive movie viewing. Faxes and call-in polls have made even magazines and television two-way media. Fiber-optic systems hold promise for creating veritable information freeways that can change communication, commerce, and social relationships at all levels. In short, media are undergoing rapid change and "demassification."

What follows is a snapshot of the major media as they are now used and some of the developments that hold promise for the future. The first part of this chapter summarizes some of the new media developments that are changing communication at an unprecedented rate. In fact, no textbook can keep up with the almost daily changes in the media landscape. The second part of the chapter examines the media used primarily for—but not limited to—communicating with internal publics. The third section reviews media typically used for reaching large and dispersed, primarily external, publics. The chapter concludes with a discussion of media relations, one of public relations' primary assignments.

NEW MEDIA, NEW CHALLENGES

The Internet represents the most ubiquitous leading edge of what is a major communication revolution. The digital world has changed communication within organizations and between organizations and their various publics. To paraphrase the words of a song, if you work in public relations in some organizations, it's the information superhighway or no way. New media expert John Pavlik summarized the impact of technology:

> Journalists, public relations practitioners, and advertisers all use new technology to do their work more effectively. They use new technologies to increase their work efficiency and speed, as well as to reduce cost. Moreover, new technologies can enable communication professionals to do things in new and creative ways or even do entirely new things.[3]

Advancing technology has changed the way communication is produced, distributed, displayed, and stored. And although many recognize that new reality and are experimenting with new media technology, few, if any, know the whys, hows, and so-whats of their application in daily practice. The Institute for Public Relations Research and Education assembled public relations and communication leaders in late 1997 and asked them to identify some of the technology-driven changes and their real or potential impact on how organizations communicate.[4] Following are some of their conclusions and those of others, as well as other information to help illustrate the impact of new media technology:

1. **Intranets and Internets make two-way communication possible as never before.** The interconnected networks of communication technology "represents a paradigmatic shift in corporation communication." For example, corporate leaders say that e-mail has become a fundamental means of communicating within their organizations as well as to their external stakeholders. They also say that this new communication method has improved their two-way communication with publics.

   Researchers and practitioners alike are beginning to learn how the new media work. One researcher studying interpersonal relationships found that e-mail, newsgroups, and on-line chat rooms can create friendships with similarities to the long tradition of pen pals.[5] In fact, Stanford researchers concluded that media experiences are similar to interpersonal experiences:

People's responses show that media are more than just tools. Media are treated politely, they can invade our body space, they can have personalities that match our own, they can be a teammate, and they can elicit gender stereotypes. Media can evoke emotional responses, demand attention, threaten us, influence memories, and change ideas of what is natural. Media are full participants in our social and natural world.[6]

What Reeves and Nass called "the media equation" may explain what admissions officials at the University of Georgia learned about "operating a cutting-edge World Wide Web site" that applicants could access to check on the status of the applications. Officials shut down the new interactive system, concluding that, "Learning about one's rejection through a computer . . . would be 'too cold.' "[7]

In *Being Digital,* Nicholas Negroponte wrote about "pulling versus pushing," suggesting that big media companies, such as publishers and broadcast networks, are based on the complex distribution of "atoms." "Moving bits, by contrast, is far simpler and, in principle, precludes the need for these giant corporations. Almost."[8] Instead of distributors deciding which atoms of content to package and "push" to people, digital technology linked by the vast network of computer networks makes it possible for people to search, select, and "pull" bits to themselves. This change causes major rethinking about how media work, and the roles of those who previously had some power over the selection and filtering of information available to others. In short, technology that makes almost any information readily available to anyone with access to the World Wide Web changes how public relations people will communicate in both their internal and external relationships.

2. **The new media landscape is changing rapidly and will continue to do so for several years to come.** Although public relations officers will have to manage and exercise some control over an organization's web site and other strategic communications, it is neither likely nor efficient for them to develop and maintain web sites or to attempt to control or screen communication. The balance of power is shifting rapidly to the millions of users sitting at networked computers engaging in what some have called new media's "many-to-many" capabilities, in place of the old "one-on-one" model of communication.

The federal government and attorneys general in 20 states filed antitrust suits against Bill Gates's Microsoft in 1998 for trying to gain monopolistic control over access to the Internet. The legal maneuvering will no doubt go on for years, even as new players come and go in the emerging and competitive new media marketplace. Antitrust suits were not necessary in the case of the short-lived New Century network, created in 1997 by nine old media giants—Advance Publications, Cox Enterprises, Gannett, Hearst, Knight-Ridder, *New York Times, Times Mirror, Tribune,* and *Washington Post*—to beat back competition from new media. *Business Week* reported

While the wired world moved at warp speed, New Century spent 18 months hiring a permanent CEO and two years creating an electronic doorway to 140 newspapers. By the time it became wired . . . not only was Microsoft ahead with its Sidewalk.com online city guides, but New Century's own partners also had launched competing ventures.[9]

New Century's board of directors essentially wrote off the $25 million investment and closed shop—one of many casualties of what promises to be an era of change for the turbulent new media environment.

3. **Technology makes it possible to distribute and capture more data and information than ever before possible.** With change comes opportunity, but there is also the possibility of change occurring too rapidly for the system to manage. For example, with a search of the World Wide Web now requiring sorting through 320 million pages not protected by passwords or other blocks to browsers and search engines, even the most sophisticated search engines access and index only one-third of those pages. And it is going to get worse. Steve Lawrence of NEC Research Institute reports in the journal *Science* that the growth of Internet pages will grow 1,000 percent by 2003, totaling 3.5 billion pages. Even today, however, a search on a keyword or name can produce a listing of millions of pages, "leaving people drowning in data, while still thirsting for information," according to Associated Press reporter Paul Recer.[10]

Public relations specialists are surely contributing to the ocean of data, as mass communication student Joerg Hoewner at Germany's Ruhr University discovered. He did content analyses of 106 public relations firms' web sites, with 77 of the firms based in the United States. In an average of 21 pages, fewer than half of the firms offered profiles of the CEO and key staff members, only 45 percent listed clients, 29 percent stated their corporate philosophy, 24 percent provided pricing information, and only 9 percent reported clips or case studies of past successes for clients.[11]

Anyone connected to an Intranet or the Internet is subject to the glut of information. Junk mail is now a phenomenon of the digital age, as newsgroups and listservs distribute messages to literally thousands of destination computers with no more effort than sending a message to a coworker or friend. Blast faxes indiscriminately activate fax machines all around the globe, prompting many to screen incoming calls to prevent this new form of junk mail.

Trying to trace in detail changes in new media produces information with the shelf life of lettuce. The overriding conclusion is that the rapidly changing technologies and the blurring of media distinctions as they converge in the digital world promise to send shock waves of change in how media are used to communicate both internally and externally—the topics of the sections that follow.

MEDIA FOR INTERNAL PUBLICS

An organization's most important relationships are those with employees at all levels. The terms *internal publics* and *employee publics* refer to both the supervisors and those being supervised. These publics represent an organization's greatest resource, its people. According to Alvie Smith, former director of corporate communications at General Motors, two factors are changing employee communication and enhancing management's respect for this part of the public relations task:

1. The value of understanding, teamwork, and commitment by employees in achieving bottom-line results. These positive aspects of worker behavior are strongly influenced by effective, way-of-life interactive communications throughout the organization.
2. The need to build a strong manager-communication network, one that makes every supervisor at every level accountable for communicating effectively with his or her employees. This needs to be more than just job-related information and should included key business and public issues affecting the total organization.[12]

In Smith's view, organizations miss out on a sizable share of their human resource potential because they do not put a high priority on effective two-way communication as the foundation for management–employee relations and overall job performance. He calls the consequence of result "slothing on the job":

> The ugly truth is that employee disloyalty and lack of commitment to organizational goals may be costing American businesses more than $50 billion a year. This is probably a conservative figure when you include the cost of absenteeism, labor grievances, production interruptions, poor quality, repair and warranty expenses for fixing poor quality and—highly important—owner disloyalty, loss of repeat customer sales and credibility. Perhaps most costly of all is inaction by employees who withhold their best efforts and ideas; who cruise along with just passable performance.[13]

The coordination and mediation necessary for dealing with employees today puts the public relations staff, with its communication savvy and skills, square in the middle of managing internal relationships. Apple Computer, for example, sees employee communication "as a key factor in maintaining a wide-open progressive work environment as well as the most important channel in keeping a far-flung, empowered and decentralized organization aligned and coordinated."[14] Delta Air Lines chairman and CEO Ronald W. Allen, who rose through the ranks by running departments such as personnel and training, sees his primary job as cultivating a motivated and loyal work force.[15]

Day-to-day working relationships involve a great deal of contact, but effective employee communication develops in a climate of trust. Ideally, working relationships are characterized by at least seven conditions:

1. Confidence and trust between employer and employees
2. Candid information flowing freely up, down, and sideways
3. Satisfying status and participation for each person

4. Continuity of work without strife
5. Healthful surroundings
6. Success for the enterprise
7. Optimism about the future

The chief executive must establish that climate and underwrite it as formal policy. Even with such support from the top, however, many barriers stand in the way of free-flowing, two-way communication in organizations.

Opinion Research Corporation has tracked employee opinions of organizational internal communication since 1950. Large majorities consistently give their organizations favorable scores on *credibility,* but less than half say their organizations do a good job of letting them know what is going on, or *downward communication.* Similarly, less than half give high marks to their organization's willingness to listen to their views, or *upward communication.* A similar survey conducted by the consulting firm Towers, Perrin, Forster and Crosby found the grapevine second only to immediate supervisors as employees' major source of organizational information. Nine out of ten surveyed ranked their immediate supervisor as the "preferred source" and ranked the grapevine as the least preferred source. (See Figure 9.1, pg. 290.)

A Watson Wyatt Company survey of corporate readers of its employee communication newsletter identified "help employees understand business direction–mission" as the number one objective of employee communication programs. Employee publications, bulletin boards, group meetings, personnel handbooks, and memos are the most frequently used media for management communication directed to employees. Face-to-face communication with an "open-door policy" is the primary medium for encouraging upward communication and building good working relationships with employees.

Balancing the needs for employee satisfaction with the success of the enterprise is but one aspect of the continuous adjustment and reconciliation in the employer–employee relationship. As a part of the larger public relations function, however, the goals of employee communication are to establish and maintain mutually beneficial relationships between an organization and the employees on whom its success or failure depends.

PRINTED WORDS

Even with the new communication technology, printed publications remain the primary media for internal communication in most organizations. Imagine the competition for attention these publications must overcome when they reach the homes of employees and their families. The usual goals of such publications include the following:

1. Keeping employees informed of the organization's lines of business, direction, and goals
2. Providing employees the information they need to perform their assignments proficiently

FIGURE 9.1   MANAGERS: THE MISSING LINK

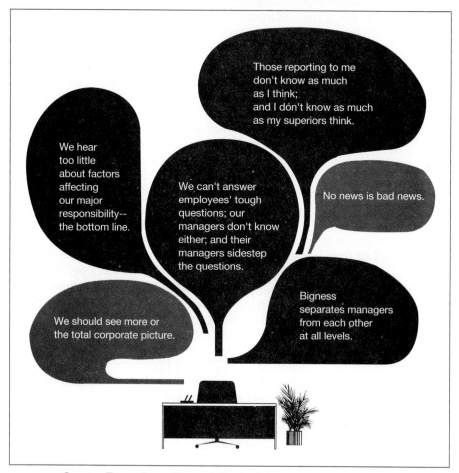

Courtesy Towers, Perrin, Forster & Crosby, Atlanta.

3. Encouraging employees to maintain and enhance the organization's standards for and commitment to quality improvement, increased efficiency, improved service, and greater social responsibility
4. Recognizing employees' achievements and successes

Each publication, each issue, each printed word is part of a coordinated employee communication program designed to achieve these and specific goals set in response to particular organizational settings and situations. Because of their impact, permanence, and reference value, printed words remain the workhorses of employee communication.

Organizational Publications

Estimates of the number of organizational publications in the United States range from 100,000 up to more than a million, if you count all the newsletters. Probably two-thirds are internal, or employee, publications. Their impact, formerly considered indirect—even intangible—is now viewed as direct and measurable.

An organizational publication can take the form of a simple newsletter, a tabloid newspaper, or a "magapaper" that combines the format of a newspaper with the style of a magazine. Many are high-quality, four-color publications. A few carry advertising to help pay the costs of production. In Great Britain some industrial firms sell their organizational magazines rather than give them away. They take the position that employees tend to place more value on the publications if they have monetary worth. Two out of every three British coal miners, for example, buy the *Coal News* tabloid newspaper published by the National Coal Board.

All organizational publications have these characteristics in common: They satisfy the organizational need to go on record with its positions and to communicate information essential for achieving organizational objectives; they permit the organization to deliver messages to specific target publics; and they let the organization communicate in its own words, in its own way, without interruption or alteration. In short, they give the organization a means of controlled communications.

The organizational publication is versatile. It can be edited to serve the narrow interests of its sponsor. It can be edited to shed light on issues important to employees and other publics. Most often it combines editorial content that both espouses the sponsor's point of view and addresses concerns of targeted publics. (Without the latter, of course, it would die for lack of readers outside the inner circle of top management.)

Organization publications are directed to many publics, but the most common use is in employee communication. Practitioners responding to surveys usually rate employees as a primary audience for organizational publications. The major advantage of publications is their ability to deliver specific and detailed information to narrowly defined target publics. As a result, many organizations have several employee publications, each designed to meet the information needs of particular employee groups. For example, because about half of Callaway Vineyards' employees speak Spanish, it prints its employee publication in both English and Spanish. Ciba-Geigy Canada Ltd. publishes its employee publications in both English and French. The front cover and pages to the center staple are in one language; flip the publication and the back cover becomes the cover for the half published in the other language.

Many organizations attempt to make their publications two-way: inviting questions and conducting surveys, then reporting the results. (See Figure 9.2, pg. 292.) This requires the full cooperation of top management because of the time required to respond to questions and the expense of conducting surveys. Two-way communication also demands a climate of trust. Employees are of-

FIGURE 9.2   EMPLOYEE "SPEAK OUT" FORM

FOLD DOWN ALONG THIS LINE ▲

Use this form
to get answers
to your
    Questions
    Suggestions
    Complaints
    Comments

Please use separate form for
each subject.

SPEAK OUT!

Only one person should sign this form–the answer will
be mailed to you at your home.
As space permits, letters of general interest will be
published.
Your name will be kept confidential by the editor.

Postage
Will Be Paid
By
Addressee

No
Postage Stamp
Necessary
If Mailed in the
United States

BUSINESS REPLY MAIL
FIRST CLASS PERMIT NO. 1

EDITOR WILL DETACH AND KEEP THIS PORTION

Check Here ☐ if you do not want your letter published

Check Here ☐ if, instead of a mailed reply, you prefer to discuss this matter with a qualified person.

Name _____
(Please Print)

Home Address _____

City _____ **State** _____ **Zip Code** _____

Department _____

(Note: This information is only to assist the editor. Remember: If you don't include your name, you cannot receive an
answer unless it is chosen for publication. This part of the form will be held in confidence by the editor and destroyed
after your letter is answered.)

ten reluctant to submit questions or to write for publication. Nonetheless, internal publications provide an excellent mechanism for feedback and responsive communication.

Newsletters are the most common form of periodical publication. Because of readily available and inexpensive desktop publishing technology, newsletters are relatively easy, fast, and inexpensive to produce. As a result, most organizations rely on newsletters to communicate news in a timely and targeted fashion. According to Paul Swift, managing editor of the *Newsletter on Newsletters:*

> Newsletters are a medium that is here to stay . . . and grow. . . . There is more value being put on targeting communication with the corporate world and between associations and their members, as opposed to mass media. They [newsletters] are good for getting a specific message to a targeted audience in a specific context. Narrowcasting—what newsletters are, as opposed to broadcasting—is growing coincidentally with the desktop revolution.[16]

Supplemental publications—pamphlets, brochures, manuals, and books—have three major uses:

1. Indoctrination. Publications welcome new employees, mem- bers, students, or visitors. Indoctrination literature helps the newcomer get off on the right foot. It spells out the rules of the organization and the benefits of playing by the rules. It seeks to instill team spirit by communicating that the newcomer has joined a winning team. ("Collateral materials" and product manuals for the consumer or product owner usually originate in the marketing function.)
2. Reference. Many publications deal with group insurance plans, pension plans, suggestion systems, hospitalization programs, profit sharing, housekeeping and safety, recreation programs and facilities, training and educational programs, and organizational policies and procedures. These handbooks give employees or members specific information and guidance.
3. Institutional. Institutional publications typically spell out the organization's philosophy, values, and guiding principles. Messages relate to quality, competitiveness, environmental issues, the free enterprise system, social responsibility, multicultural diversity, and the organization's role in the community. Other reports are tied to dedications, celebration, awards, history, organizational success, founders, and organizational heroes. An example of this type of publication is Dow Chemical Canada's *Dow's Secret Weapons,* a book summarizing Dow's day-to-day operational philosophies. The content consists mainly of quotations from internal presentations and publications by Dow executives and directors, along with well-known authors on corporate management.

There are no most effective formats or methods for distributing handbooks. Dow sent *Dow's Secret Weapons* to selected executives and waited for others to request copies. It became a valued reference for hundreds of managers as the public relations staff filled orders. Sometimes books are written by authors commissioned to produce organizational books distributed in the commercial book market, in addition to serving internal institutional purposes. For example, *Schweppes, The First 200 Years* chronicles the history of the originator of carbonated mineral water and the soft drink industry.

Organizational books are found in libraries, reception lobbies, wall racks, and employee lounges. They are usually mailed to leaders in the community, business and industry, education, government, and the financial community. Employees and members get their copies either at work or in the mail at home. Dealers' copies are delivered by sales representatives. Books published by government agencies are available from the Superintendent of Documents. Associations sometimes issue such books as part of convention or meeting packets, or they mail copies to members.

Books and lengthy booklets tracing the history of organizations or biographies of founders are usually subsidized by sponsors and published by commercial publishers. Sponsors distribute copies to libraries and selected influentials. Although high in initial cost, sponsored books can pay long-term dividends if they are accurate, well written, and distributed to appropriate libraries and individuals. Once catalogued into libraries, such histories become source material for writers, students, and others doing research on organizations and their founders.

Basic questions must be considered: (1) Does the type of book under consideration fit the needs it is designed to fill? (2) Will the nature and purpose of the book attract a capable outside writer? (3) Is the book to be sold commercially or given away? (4) Should it have a prestige hard cover or be a paperback? (5) What are possible tie-ins to promote it? (6) Does it further the organization's basic public relations objectives?

Letters

Even in the age of fax, e-mail, and cell phones, *letters* remain the backbone of internal and external organizational communication. With the aid of word processing software, individualized letters are being used increasingly to establish direct, speedy communication with employees and other specific publics. Letters supplement the slower, less frequently published employee magazine. They offer an opportunity for the chief executive to communicate with employees and their families in a conversational, personalized, and newsy manner. Among their advantages are economy, a direct and individualized approach, an impressive appearance, impact, and speed. Letters support line communication by ensuring the accuracy of information, pointing out what is important and newsworthy in the organization's affairs and adding importance to line communication. This support is increasingly important in large, diversified organizations.

Letters go from organization officials to community opinion leaders, to members of selected professions such as medicine or education, to legislators, suppliers, retailers, or media executives and reporters. Computers and high-speed printers have the obvious advantage of individualized addresses and salutations, in addition to specific references in the body of the letter.

Even more important than periodic letters is an organization's daily correspondence. The normal flow of letters and memos constitutes an important and influential means of communication. The importance of effective letters that evoke pleased reactions, not irritation or confusion, is obvious. Yet many organizations continue in the rut of cold, stilted, hackneyed letters that do more to confuse and obscure than to clarify.

Inserts and Enclosures

Anyone who has received bills from utilities or oil companies knows about *inserts* and *enclosures*. A common form is the "payroll stuffer" that goes into paycheck envelopes. Typical uses range from news vignettes to offers of merchandise and services. The insert is an important public relations medium for appealing to natural constituencies for support and for important notices and news. Examples include calls for employees or stockholders to write legislators in support of an organization's stand on a public policy issue or notification of changes in benefits or procedures.

One obvious advantage of the insert is that the message goes to a favorably predisposed audience. Readership and receptivity can be high. Another advantage is economy. A small, lightweight printed insert need not add to the postage or change the classification of the mail.

Reprinted Speeches, Position Papers, and "Backgrounders"

Expressing an organization's position in reprints is a common method of communicating with select publics about controversial issues and public policy. The simple explanation is that as more organizations find their traditional policies and methods under investigation or challenge, they respond formally in speeches or by providing testimony in congressional hearings. Reprinting their responses in their entirety provides full disclosure of what was said and offers a rebuttal to the sometimes selective reporting by news media.

The major uses are to inform and reassure important individuals concerned about issues of mutual interest. Thus, these materials are sent to employees, legislators and other government officials, financial analysts, leaders of pressure groups, the media, and community opinion leaders. The downside of this medium is that it sometimes serves primarily to massage the egos of executives by espousing narrow interests and speaking in glittering generalities or trying to win business for the organization by touting its products or services. Typically, readers see through these transparent uses.

A similar method of extending the reach of limited circulation materials is reprinting articles from publications. With permission from the original publications, favorable publicity, analyses of important issues, and other coverage of interest to an organization's publics can be reprinted and distributed. This adds control to what would otherwise be uncontrolled media coverage.

Bulletin Boards

The use of *bulletin boards* is widespread and here to stay. If there were no other reason, laws requiring the posting of an ever-increasing number of notices would preserve this medium. The nature of the medium is changing, however, as large numbers of employees in many organizations work at computer terminals that have the capability of "electronic bulletin boards" and messages. Employees often begin their workdays by checking their e-mail for notices and messages on their terminals.

Bulletin boards offer a good place to corroborate information with brief messages publicly. They provide quick access for spiking rumors and for making desirable information stick. The dynamic board gets regular attention; it needs to be updated often. Seeing the same notice again and again becomes an annoyance and soon leads to inattention. In somewhat the same category are the *posters and placards* on walls or columns in work areas. The themes of such posters are usually safety, health, housekeeping, productivity, and security.

To work with all these publications, practitioners must know desktop publishing and be skilled in writing, editing, photography, layout, and design. For most, the PC has replaced the paper page as the primary medium for producing printed words in the information age.

The important thing to remember is that publications supplement but do not replace the face-to-face communication needed in successful work relationships. A handbook for the new employee is no substitute for the personal handshake, for a thorough orientation program and tour, or for regular and frequent communications from immediate supervisors.

Publications and the printed word are being redefined as communication technology makes new media available. T. Michael Forney predicted in 1982 that the information age would change public relations in ways similar to what Gutenberg's press did to calligraphers: "Within the next decade, the computer will be as commonplace in the home and office as the telephone is today." He was right. He also correctly predicted that organizational publications would be replaced by something that will take full advantage of new, enhanced communication linkages, including the following:

1. Instant contact, rather than the present cumbersome, time-consuming production process from typewriter to printer to mailroom to desk
2. Message flexibility, which allows information to be tailored automatically to different levels and types of employees
3. Instant file and retrieval, which provides ready access to past information at the touch of a key
4. Interactivity, offering users the opportunity to get the information they want, in the form and detail they want, and to ask for further clarification if they so desire[17]

Paradoxically, the newspaper *USA Today* dropped paper entirely for its internal newsletters. It circulates four electronic letters, one for each of the paper's sections—News, Money, Sports, and Life—by video display terminal. According to public relations manager Steve H. Anderson, "It's the easiest and most efficient way to get company news out to the employees."[18]

New means of verbal communication also are changing and enhancing traditional face-to-face communication, but the oldest form of all still deserves first attention.

The Grapevine

The grapevine is neither a formal nor a controlled medium, but word of mouth is often the quickest means for communicating some information. The grapevine is a potent line of communication. It carries information much more exciting than simple facts or truth. And e-mail makes the grapevine work with the speed of electrons on copper wire or the speed of light over the fiber-optic network!

Sometimes the grapevine is actually harmful, or threatens to be. Rumors of downsizing and layoff, of a hostile takeover by a competitor, of friction among officials, of sexual harassment charges, or of bad blood between factions can hurt. The word travels far beyond the local group, becoming more and more distorted as it spreads. Hints of trouble tend to breed trouble wherever there happens to be a chip on somebody's shoulder.

The public relations staff usually stays tuned in to the grapevine. When the gossiping and rumoring are harmless, they do nothing. When real trouble brews, they squelch the gossip by releasing the full facts on the topic. Once in a while a counterrumor or an exposé of the facts among the natural leaders of an organization is effected to offset a harmful rumor.

In either case, too often the grapevine is the source of information for employees, even though it is not their preferred source. The lesson for the public relations practitioner is that the grapevine will fill the information gaps left by an inadequate communication program. The informal, uncontrolled channels will take over where the formal, controlled channels stop.

Meetings

Meetings bring people together, providing both opportunities to speak and opportunities to listen, a two-way communication. Work-group meetings, quality control circles, and participative management sessions are examples of small, task-oriented meetings. Such face-to-face get-togethers are expensive in time away from routine tasks but economical in the long run because of both the ideas they produce and the team-building effects.

Just as with other communication strategies, a meeting requires specific objectives, careful planning and staging, and skillful direction. Exchange of viewpoints can be open but controlled so that the meeting does not drag or get diverted from its purpose. Effectiveness depends on the moderator's ability to lead and articulate. For some meetings, specially trained group process facilitators serve this vital role while participants delve into important content issues. One school of thought is that important meetings involving people of different levels trying to resolve conflicts or make critical decisions should be guided by a process facilitator so that power, content, and process are not vested in one person, the boss. This approach may be useful only for special meetings or for training purposes, because part of any manager's role is to bring together the work group for problem-solving meetings and discussions.

For large gatherings, particularly those bringing together the entire employee force or important external publics, the public relations staff is called upon to plan the meeting. Annual meetings, for example, require a great deal of preparation time for top executives and a commitment of time from shareholders expecting a return on their time investment. Checklists for preparing such large meetings are extensive, so much so that many organizations contract with specialized firms to provide meeting management services.

Traditional meetings requiring face-to-face meetings in a single room are all but obsolete, according to one communication expert:

> New technologies such as PCs and digital audio-visual tools have created a whole new class of "electronic meeting." Conference calls, computer-interfaced meeting technologies, satellite connections, electronic bulletin boards and facsimile networks have forever blurred the meaning of meetings.[19]

To accomplish group decisions, many organizations now use the latest telecommunication and computer technologies to bring ideas and people together. One approach is to give members gathered around a table their own individual key pads connected to a single computer. Forcing communication through the computer screen enhances the exchange by giving timid group members and subordinates the same access as obnoxious talkers and opinionated bosses.

Some major global corporations have created state-of-the-art electronic meeting systems capable of connecting people around the world instantaneously to work together on a single problem. For example, IBM installed twenty "TeamFocus electronic meeting rooms" with personal computers and multimedia capabilities on a global network. Whether installed in a single room or designed as a multimedia global network, these new electronic "group decision support systems" are replacing traditional meetings.

Speeches and Speakers' Bureaus

There are few organizations of any size without some officials who can get on their feet and talk informatively and interestingly to select groups. *The Executive Speechmaker* lists these advantages for speeches:

1. Provides the most direct and persuasive means of communication because it involves face-to-face contact with a live audience.
2. Helps "personalize" an organization, particularly at a time when many people see large organizations as being excessively impersonal.
3. Often allows opportunity for give-and-take between speaker and audience, a two-way dialogue that can be informative for both parties.
4. Helps demonstrate the organization's openness and its desire to be a constructive participant in industry and community activities.

5. Brings prestige to both the speaker and the organization.
6. Gets the organization's views on public record.
7. Provides authoritative source material for other communications.[20]

Not all speeches accomplish these objectives effectively. Sometimes the blame can be attributed to public relations practitioners, because they are frequently called on to research a speech, prepare an outline, develop visuals, and sometimes write the entire speech. In addition to preparing materials for speakers, practitioners coach executives preparing for public appearances.

A *speakers' bureau* provides speakers on request. The subject matter usually represents a compromise between a desire simply to express organizational views on important issues and the need to provide requesting groups with informative programs. As such, a speakers' bureau is a valuable medium for any organization with something important to say to key groups of influentials and community groups.

There are four points worth remembering in providing speakers:

1. Carefully select and coach the lineup of speakers.
2. Select topics that serve the needs of potential audiences and carry the organization's story or positions on important issues of public debate.
3. Provide speakers visual aids: flip charts, slides, overhead transparencies, or videotapes.
4. Promote and publicize the availability of the speakers to appropriate groups.

IMAGES AND WORDS

The oft-predicted demise of printed and spoken words as major employee communication techniques has not happened. New technology simply expanded the reach and possibilities for communication and speeded up the process of distribution.

Teleconferencing

Technological advances in satellite communication have also expanded the range of possibilities for meetings and speeches. For example, key speakers unable to take time to travel to participate in person can be beamed to the meeting via satellite teleconferencing. Or simultaneous sessions in several cities can be linked electronically with speakers shown on large-screen television equipment. The savings in travel time and costs, meeting facilities, and boarding of participants can more than offset the costs of using this new technology.

The primary reason for using teleconferencing is to reach people at many locations all at the same time with the same message. AT&T chairman Bob Allen's teleconference to discuss the company's special early retirement program reached some 100,000 managers at 250 U.S. locations. The chancellor of the California State University system used teleconferencing to keep administrators, faculty, staff, and students informed during the budget crises brought on by the faltering California economy of the early 1990s. (See Figure 9.3 for illustration of how the system works.)

Ford Motor Company's 275 manufacturing and sales offices all receive one-way video feeds from the Dearborn, Michigan, headquarters. Twenty-five North American locations have two-way video transmission capabilities. The major U.S. facilities of General Motors (GM) are linked via satellite telecon-

FIGURE 9.3   SATELLITE TELECONFERENCING

Courtesy VideoStar Connections, Inc., Atlanta.

ferencing to facilitate the exchange of design, research, and production information among employees. Federal Express has one of the largest corporate employee satellite television systems:

> A system with more than 1,000 downlinks in the United States, Canada, Great Britain and Europe and 400-plus broadcasts a year. Its program places heavy emphasis on job-related information, including daily business updates, discussion of recurring-problem areas and ideas for improving performance at all levels.[21]

Not all satellite teleconferencing is limited to internal communication. During the Tylenol poisoning crisis, Johnson & Johnson used teleconferencing to hold national press conferences in 30 cities to answer reporters' questions and to keep the media updated on developments. International Association of Business Communicators (IABC) conducted a teleconference for 1,200 members in 22 cities. The National Safety Council held a meeting of almost 2,000 participants in 45 cities across the United States on "Back Injury, Prevention and Rehabilitation." Part of the program consisted of a question-and-answer period in which participants engaged in two-way communication with the speakers.

Closed Circuit Television (CCTV)

GM's newest assembly plants have built-in CCTV capabilities. There are 60 "team centers," each seating 32 employees. The system makes it possible to telecast live or by videotape and film to almost 2,000 employees at the same time. "Built to accommodate the strong emphasis on employees as business teams, each of these centers can also be split into rooms accommodating sixteen people, approximately the size of average work teams," according to the former director of corporate communications at GM, Alvie Smith. He is also cautious about the use of CCTV:

> It is critical that the financial, personnel and equipment requirements be evaluated thoroughly—also factor in the availability of up-to-date videotape materials from within the organization and outside. And remember that if you decide to take employees off their jobs to watch CCTV shows, that's lost production and therefore expensive. So the programs have to be substantive to be worth the cost—not just a case of amateur TV producers having fun.[22]

Georgia-Pacific executives have grown accustomed to "going on camera" to keep thousands of employees in its many sites informed of developments in the forest products industry. The corporation's video production department produces about 70 training, sales, marketing, safety, and news programs each year. The broadcast-quality videotape productions eliminate the need to fly in hundreds of sales representatives to a central location or to various plants for product training and sales meetings.

The growing use of teleconferencing and television means that public relations practitioners have to understand these media that combine the spoken word with the visual image. Whereas the transmission technologies are relatively recent developments, these skills have long been part of the practice.

Video, Film, and Slide Presentations

Sponsored videos and films are those conceived within and commissioned by an organization for sales, training, or public relations purposes. The intent is not to reap direct, immediate monetary return at the box office, but rather to develop favorable ideas, motivations, attitudes, or behaviors in viewing audiences. The most widely seen company film celebrated its 40th year of distribution in 1998: Aero Mayflower Transit Company's *The Mayflower Story.*

An example of the potential impact and audience for film is the Allstate Insurance Company short subject, *Ridin' the Edge.* Allstate campaigned vigorously to make air bags standard safety equipment on new cars, whereas some auto manufacturers resisted. A crash scene in the Hollywood movie *Moving Violation* called for a stunt driver to crash into a concrete wall at almost 33 miles per hour. Allstate provided air bag–equipped cars from their test fleet and technical advice in exchange for the right to use the scene footage in *Ridin' the Edge.* The film short was shown more than 125,000 times during the first four years and seen by more than 46 million people. Follow-up research on opinions toward air bags indicated that 27 percent more viewers approved of air bags than nonviewers. Only 2 percent of viewers disapproved of air bags, compared with 9 percent for nonviewers.[23]

The film was shown on commercial, public, and cable television; as a short in theaters; and to all types of groups and classes. Many police academies, driver education instructors, and insurance class teachers still use the film. Allstate public relations staff members think the short sponsored film helped keep air bags on the public agenda in spite of strong resistance by automobile manufacturers.

Motion pictures and video offer the following communication strengths:

1. They combine the impact of sight, sound, drama and movement, color, and music.
2. They present ideas involving motion that cannot be described effectively by print or audio means.
3. They attract sustained and exclusive attention to a message for the length of the showing.
4. They make explicit the time factor in any operation or series of events
5. They provide a believable record of events.
6. They show processes that cannot ordinarily be seen by the naked eye.
7. They bring the past and the distant to the viewer.
8. They enlarge, reduce, or simplify objects, as well as illustrate abstractions through the use of photography, cartoons, and graphics.
9. Above all, they let the viewers see with their own eyes: seeing is believing.

Many of the strengths and principles of video and film apply to slide presentations. If motion is not critical to the message, a less expensive slide presentation often can be as effective.

Displays and Exhibits

In almost every factory or hospital there is a reception room, showroom, cafeteria, or lounge. Every college has the equivalent of an Old Main, student union, or reception or visitor's center. Every branch of the military has its sites to perpetuate its memories, receive guests, and show its progress, as illustrated in Figure 9.4. These places are natural areas for displays and exhibits. For anyone who has ever taken a plant tour or visited a major fair, the content of such exhibits needs no explanation. Displays must be conceived as part of the total public relations program designed to reach target publics.

Another important use of displays and exhibits is the trade show or convention. Almost every major city has a convention center to host conventions and trade shows of all types. Exhibits at these gatherings often have marketing and sales objectives but also include the following public relations uses:

1. Create or maintain a specific perception of the organization
2. Maintain contact with important audiences
3. Show the depth and breadth of the organization's operations
4. Generate inquiries for more information
5. Get feedback for evaluating strategies
6. Recruit personnel

Displays and exhibits are also distributed much like films and videotapes for use at special events and local gatherings. The U.S. Department of Agriculture and Cooperative Extension Service based at state land-grant universities have long provided displays and exhibits for local meetings and fairs.

FIGURE 9.4   "FAT MAN" AND "LITTLE BOY" EXHIBIT, BRADBURY SCIENCE MUSEUM, LOS ALAMOS NATIONAL LABORATORY, NEW MEXICO

Many government agencies and corporations publish catalogues from which users order for local showings.

Permanent installations at theme parks, zoos, museums, airports, and other public attractions have become major public relations tools. Corporate displays now serve as both entertainment and information attractions at the major Walt Disney centers in Florida and California, as well as Sea Worlds in Florida, Ohio, and California. For years the University of Illinois College of Agriculture has provided educational exhibits for Chicago's Lincoln Park Farm-in-the-Zoo as a way to reach urban residents with information about agriculture.

Exhibitors know that the objective is to entice the footsore visitor to stop at the display, to retain attention long enough for the visitor to study the presentation, and to impart information or stimulate immediate or future action. Usually displays and exhibits are constructed by specialized firms, but the purpose, concept, and message are typically the products of public relations programming and creativity.

This section has not covered all the controlled media available to practitioners. The intent here was to introduce a few of the major media over which the practitioner has a high degree of control. Controlled media are the primary media for communicating with internal publics. Moreover, they are the preferred means for reaching external publics when resources and time are available and when audience size and dispersion make the use of controlled media possible. Because external publics are often large and dispersed, sometimes making controlled media impractical, uncontrolled media and other mass media are the topics in the sections that follow.

MEDIA FOR EXTERNAL PUBLICS

The economical, effective method of communicating with large and widely dispersed publics is through the mass media: newspapers, magazines, trade publications, AM and FM radio, television, cable, WebTV, books, and so on. To handle this part of the job, practitioners must understand the role of information, the various media and their mechanics, and the values of those who control access to them. Practitioners also need to understand that media are constrained by their mechanical requirements, their values, their rules, and—for many—the necessity of delivering an audience to advertisers. Today's communicators are confronted with a paradox: Multiplying channels of communication permit a sharper focus of messages but greatly escalate competition for audience attention.

Mass media reach into nearly every home and workplace, showering citizens with far more messages than they can absorb. General and specialized media appear to represent an easily used means of disseminating ideas and information to publics, but this can be delusive. Just because these media have audiences and convey messages does not necessarily mean that those messages are received, accepted, or acted upon. For example, print messages have no direct impact on the millions of illiterate Americans. Moreover, there are other nonreaders, either because of lack of interest or because they read and speak a language other than the one used in the publication.

For another thing, the public media have a relatively fixed capacity; newspapers and magazines have a limited number of columns for editorial matter, and there are only 24 hours in a broadcast day. Hence, these media cannot possibly accommodate all the messages fed into them. Receivers also have limited time and attention to give to the millions of messages. In a world stuffed with messages, only a tiny fraction gets past the door and into the home. Even fewer get attention.

Nonetheless, power in America is largely exercised through control of the means and content of mass communications. Mass media constitute the key components in the nation's public-information system, a system in which public relations practitioners play an important role. Competition for access to media is spirited and becoming more so with each passing day. Practitioners must adjust their work to rapidly changing media, owing to a combination of the impact of computers, innovations in signal transmission, and new ways to send and retrieve information and images. As one political public relations specialist advises,

> My advice is to watch *USA Today* and its imitators, pay attention to cable TV, and listen to the audio channels on transcontinental flights (where futurism/millennialism is in vogue). And remember, radio call-ins defeated the congressional pay raise.[24]

Newspapers

Although the number of daily and weekly newspapers declined in the 1980s, the newspaper remains the workhorse of the public information system. When people think of publicity, they almost instinctively think of the newspaper. American newspapers—daily, weekend, Sunday, weekly, semiweekly, ethnic, labor, religious, scholastic, and foreign language—are read by most literate people. Publicity in newspapers, day in and day out, forms the foundation of most information programs. Reading the newspaper is as much a part of the influential citizen's daily habits as are eating and sleeping. As a result, the influence of the world's great newspapers is great. Journalism scholar and educator John C. Merrill refers to these as "internationally elite newspapers":

> Such papers—mainly dailies—are read by the world's intellectuals, political and opinion leaders, and cosmopolitan, concerned citizens of various countries. They are directed at a fairly homogeneous audience globally and have a greater interest in international relations and the arts and humanities than the general run of mass-appeal papers. They are well-informed, articulate papers that thoughtful people the world over take seriously.[25]

U.S. papers on Merrill's list of elite dailies include *The New York Times, Los Angeles Times, Washington Post,* and *Christian Science Monitor.* His European list includes *Le Monde* of France, *Neue Zürcher Zeitung* of Switzerland, *El País* of Spain, *Daily Telegraph* of England, and *Svenska Dagbladet* of Sweden. Asia's elite dailies include Japan's *Asahi Shimbun* and *Mainichi Shimbun* and India's *Times of India* and *Statesman*. According to Merrill, "The elite papers recognize that they will not reach many people, but they seek to have an impact that no other medium does on the serious, intellectual, opinion-leading segment of the world community."[26]

Newspapers are a moving force in society. The late Justice Felix Frankfurter once said, "To an extent far beyond the public's own realization, public opinion is shaped by the kind, the volume, and the quality of the news columns." Newspaper scholars have suggested that the power of the press comes from its dissemination of information and its impact on public interest in important issues (the agenda-setting function discussed in chapter 8). Nor should editorial endorsement be totally discounted. Newspapers are a primary means of reaching community publics in these days of specialized media and fragmented audiences. Although no longer the primary news medium for the majority, newspapers are still a powerful force in shaping the public agenda and influencing the outcome of debate. And for individuals seeking political content, surveys in many parts of the country reveal that they tend to turn to newspapers.[27]

From the early part of the 20th century until World War II, when newspapers were the prime source of news and entertainment, the number of *daily newspapers* has declined. (See Exhibit 9.1 for one reporter's opinion on the state of the newspaper today.) The number began to stabilize at mid-century

EXHIBIT 9.1

*W*HAT'S HAPPENED TO THE PRESS?

Obviously, the place of the daily paper in American life has changed. In my early days, we were the first purveyors of the news, but radio and television changed all that, and when the old man checks the next morning's newspaper for the latest locker room gossip on the baseball game he watched on television the night before, it merely says "Late Game" and doesn't even give him the score. What is more ominous for the future, the children are no longer picking up the newspaper habit by reading the comic strips, but find the latest TV murders much more exciting than "Little Orphan Annie" or even "Peanuts."

. . . I don't agree with those who think the newspaper is in decline, and I don't notice much red ink on their balance sheets.

In fact, I think we are witnessing the greatest expansion of information since the invention of movable type. On the three hundredth anniversary of America's first newspaper (Benjamin Harris's *Publick Occurences Both Foreign and Domestick,* published in Boston on September 25, 1690), there were 1,625 U.S. dailies with a circulation of over 62 million, and it was said that many of them were hauling in an average of 20 percent in profit before taxes—a record matched by few industries.

James Reston, *Deadline: A Memoir* (New York: Random House, 1991), 470–71. Used with permission of the author.

and remained about the same through the mid-1970s. There were 1,772 daily papers in 1950, for example, and only 16 fewer, 1,756, in 1975. By 1997, however, the number had dropped to only 1,509 dailies because of mergers and discontinued editions during the 1980s and early 1990s.[28]

Although the number of dailies declined during the 1980s and early 1990s, the average circulation for surviving papers increased and newspaper reading remained fairly stable despite increased media competition. Daily newspaper readership figures compiled by Simmons Market Research Bureau show that approximately 59 percent of all adults say they read a daily newspaper; 69 percent read them on Sundays. Adults spend an average of 28 minutes with their daily newspaper. Only 48 percent of 18- to 24-year-olds read a newspaper daily, but 59 percent read one on Sundays.[29]

A study of newspaper readers in Brazil identified five types. *Instrumental readers* use newspapers to get information they think will be useful for daily living. Reading is purely an information-seeking activity to understand what is happening and why it is happening. *Opinion makers* use newspapers to get advice and guidance for forming and validating opinion. Newspapers help them make up their minds on issues and provide insight on what others are thinking. *Pleasure readers* use newspaper reading as an enjoyable habit. They see newspapers as a source of enjoyment and reading as an end in itself, not as a means for accomplishing some other purpose. *Ego boosters* use newspapers as a source of information for impressing others. They read to enhance their self-image and status with others. *Scanners* use newspapers for many and varied reasons, but there is no single motivation or pattern strong enough to suggest they belong in one of the other four types.[30]

The number of weekly and semiweekly newspapers is declining, but circulation remains strong. In 1980 there were 7,954 weeklies with a circulation of 42.3 million. By 1997 the number had dropped to 7,214 weeklies, but circulation was more than 70 million.[31] These newspapers still offer an effective, direct, and intimate means of reaching the people of suburbs, small towns, and rural areas, who are often the source of grassroots opinion. Readers of weekly newspapers are loyal and read their papers thoroughly. A weekly newspaper arguably exerts a far greater impact on readers' opinions than does the typical daily. And these opinions often count beyond their numbers.

Most weeklies emphasize news of local government, schools, public affairs, and personal news. Public relations practitioners, walled in by skyscrapers and stuck in traffic jams or crowded mass transit, should not forget the people of small-town and suburban America or the newspapers that help shape their opinions. In fact, many executives (with public relations assistance) write op-eds for the opinion-editorial page. These pieces, by design, focus on one subject—usually local and controversial—and openly express the organization's position on the issue. Key to placing op-ed pieces is timeliness. For example, if a bill being debated in Congress is not getting much media attention, an op-ed piece on how the bill will affect the local community or your company may catch the editorial page editor's eye.[32]

The Sunday paper generally gets a longer, more intensive and leisurely reading. It tends to emphasize feature material—stories without a time element—often more like a magazine than like a daily paper. Special features and pictures without a time peg are supplied early in the week. And because news can be relatively scarce on Sundays and Mondays, newspapers often are more receptive to material on these publication days. Practitioners should not overlook the national Sunday supplement magazines and local weekend magazines developed by large-city newspapers for reaching large audiences. For example, more than 300 newspapers include *Parade* every Sunday, reaching some 70 million readers.

Newspaper space allocated to news has decreased in recent years, at least relative to the increased glut of newsworthy information pouring into newsrooms, including that from practitioners. Typically newspapers devote about 50 percent of their space to editorial matter; some as little as 25 percent. The rest is advertising (about 46 percent) and unpaid public service (4 percent). Local news makes up the largest proportion of editorial content: about 75 percent of all news published.

The strengths of newspapers are many. No other medium offers comparable audience size and breadth day in and day out, or the range and depth of content. Most newspapers are produced in local communities and are indigenous to those communities. They have a firsthand intimacy with their local publics. The local YMCA can reach its community public through its local newspaper. The state health department can reach its publics through the state's daily and weekly newspapers. A commercial concern with regional distribution can reach its publics by a regional selection of newspapers. Similarly, a national organization can reach most national audiences with newspapers.

American newspapers—from the mass-circulation giants down to small weeklies with circulations of less than 2,000—vary a great deal in content, character, and audience, yet all have a fairly standardized definition of news. The number, locale, and variety of newspapers enable practitioners to pinpoint the geography of publicity, as well as audiences, with precision. This capability has been enhanced by the development of city, state, regional, and national paid publicity wires.

There are other advantages. A person buys a newspaper as something that is wanted, not as something that is required. Newspapers constitute a medium of sustained interest and information. Readers are generally the interested, influential people. Because they reach most of their readers daily, major newspapers are the most acceptable medium for a cumulative publicity buildup and thus are especially valuable in promotional campaigns. Newspapers are read at the reader's leisure and convenience, in sharp contrast with the broadcast media, where a program missed is difficult to retrieve or gone forever. And finally, the perceived credibility of newspapers is hard to match.

Newspapers also have limitations. An important one is that typical readers read only one-fifth to one-fourth of the editorial content of their daily newspaper. Only 56 percent of readers say they read or scan all their daily newspaper's pages. Thus, it is a mistake to assume that publicity printed is publicity read. As important as newspapers are, they cannot carry the information task alone. The press must be used in coordination with other channels of communication.

New media and online services have changed the nature and structure of both newspaper organizations and how they process news and information. Most major U.S. and Canadian newspapers have launched online services, including Web sites and partnerships with consumer online companies. Visit the "Hotlinks" and "The Digital Edge" pages at **www.naa.org** for the latest information on newspaper new media activity. (See Exhibit 9.2, pg. 310, for how the *Los Angeles Times* operates in the new digital media world.)

Another limitation is imposed by the newspaper journalists' fetish for speed and the resulting haste with which newspapers are put together. This pressure leads to many inaccuracies and fragmented, superficial coverage, a fact of life with which practitioners must cope. In contacts with the daily newspaper, practitioners quickly learn the importance of dealing with specialized reporters. If it is a sports-related story, work directly with the sports department. If it is a straight news story of local interest, deal with either the city editor or the reporter on the specific assignment. Newspapers have specialists covering the environment, health, science, international relations, business, and others areas too numerous to mention here. (Caution: No two newspaper organizations are exactly alike, so the same titles may mean different things at different newspapers.)

Wire Services and News Syndicates

For high-reader-interest stories and spot news of state, regional, national, or international significance, the wire services offer the most economical and effective outlet. Publicity with a local angle can be directed to individual newspapers where that interest exists. For timely stories not limited to a locale, placing them on the wires increases the likelihood of immediate and widespread coverage. It also increases the acceptability of the practitioner's copy. A well-written wire story can reach newspaper readers, radio listeners, and TV viewers across the nation. Transmitting millions of words and pictures daily, the wire services are influential beyond calculation. Access to these networks is through the nearest bureau or stringer correspondent.

Each of the two major wire services in the United States operates with national trunk wires, regional wires, and state wires. In addition to their newspaper networks, both serve broadcast stations with wire copy and audio feeds. Associated Press, founded in 1848, has its headquarters in New York City, with bureaus and clients around the world. The privately owned and scaled-down United Press International (UPI) is headquartered in Washington, DC. It was formed in 1958 by the merger of United Press (founded in 1907 by newspaper magnate E. W. Scripps) and William Randolph Hearst's International News Service. UPI also provides worldwide service, although annual losses, reorganization in bankruptcy court, and restructuring have taken their toll.

Associated Press—better known as AP—is a cooperative owned by its member newspapers. Subscribers include almost 1,600 daily and weekly news-

EXHIBIT 9.2

YOUR FATHER'S NEWSPAPER AND A WHOLE LOT MORE

Carol Perruso
President, LATimes.com
Los Angeles Times

Although an ink-on-paper product delivered every 24 hours is still the predominant distribution form for daily newspapers, journalists and publishers have begun to realize that the traditional news cycle and format don't always meet the needs of their readers.

Some of a newspaper's most valuable content—enterprise reporting, information graphics and analysis—has a shelf life considerably longer than 24 hours. For example, a series on HMOs or a map showing earthquake faults or a personal investment column often finds its greatest usefulness at a later date—when the reader is choosing a new health care plan, buying a house, or deciding on an IRA.

Calls and letters from readers requesting recipes, reviews, and travel stories tell editors and reporters that there also are aftermarkets for their work.

In the mid-1990s, prompted by the need for new revenue streams and the fear of losing readers, newspapers began experimenting with alternative delivery of news. These in-

cluded fax newspapers, audiotext, and on-line services. They also got more aggressive about marketing their archived content, including same-day delivery of archives to the major commercial vendors such as Lexis-Nexis, fax-on-demand services, and research services provided by *Los Angeles Times* staff members. Graphics were turned into posters, columns into booklets, and major news stories became instant books.

At the *Los Angeles Times* we have tried them all, starting in 1991 with Moscow Fax, delivered to top Russian officials before the break-up of the Soviet Union. Then came the pay-per-call telephone services that delivered stock quotes, sports scores, and horoscopes.

Next was TimesLine, an advertiser-supported phone information service launched in 1993 that provided stocks and sports news and more. The newsroom started using TimesLine to give readers recorded excerpts of records or CDs reviewed in the Calendar section. Or when a major political figure died, TimesLine played excerpts from his or her speeches, which proved a popular feature. Election results were provided in near-real time, as fast or faster than broadcast media.

About the same time we launched the subscription- and advertiser-supported Financial Fax and Mortgage Rate Fax, weekday compilations of news and financial information.

An "instant" book, produced within three weeks of the 1994 Northridge, California, earthquake became the paper's all-time top-selling book. In addition to books, a dozen or more booklets and posters have been pro-

papers and 5,900 radio and television stations. In addition, AP markets its news services to nonmedia clients. Beginning in early 1993, AP began transmitting publicity photos for a fee, putting it in direct competition with the publicity wire services.

Newspapers also subscribe to news services from *The New York Times,* duced, compilations columns or other "news-you-can-use" content. These include personal finance, recipes, retirement, and other subjects.

For a few years, reprints of recipes, travel stories, and series were sold through an automated fax-on-demand service. The same services continue to be available through Times on Demand, the paper's call-in reprint service. It offers the public access, at prices much less than commercial online databases, to the paper's electronic archive of stories.

In 1995, the New Business Development Department launched a custom publishing business, to work with paying clients to create marketing publications, which used previously published newspaper content. We produced guides for visitor bureaus, magazines for Metrolink riders, and reprints of stories about corporate clients.

Several of these endeavors produced sufficient revenue (and profit) to remain in business: Mortgage Rate Fax, Financial Fax, corporate reprints, Times on Demand, books. Most lucrative has been the sale of electronic archives to commercial on-line services. The other products were relatively short-lived as we learned what worked and what didn't in the business of finding new purposes for editorial content.

Eventually, however, most new business development resources and investment were moved to on-line. First came TimesLink, on the Prodigy service, followed in 1996 with a World Wide Web site, **www.latimes.com.**

The fit and the timing are right. The medium allows journalists new ways of telling stories, including audio, video, and interactivity. And it gives them unlimited editorial space for sidebars, and other content. It also allows the newspaper to compete with television on breaking stories.

In the 1998 winter Olympics in Nagano, time differences meant that events occurring after 4:00 P.M. Japan time would not make the next day's paper. Reporters filed separate stories for LATimes.com, allowing the paper to compete with broadcast. When Frank Sinatra died shortly before midnight on May 14, 1998, most of the paper's press run was complete. The web site had the story and a prepared obituary within two hours, and a short time later, the web site's coverage also included audio excerpts of his music as well as an obituary and lifetime photo collections.

For advertisers, the medium allows measurable, direct response advertising as well as brand advertising. And for the highly profitable classified ads, on-line is the perfect medium, allowing searching in ways not possible in print.

The *Los Angeles Times* experience with alternative means of delivering its content and developing auxiliary revenue streams is a fairly common one among major newspapers. Many experimented with fax, audiotext, and reprint services and still operate them. Most papers now have active and growing web sites. Where it all will lead, none of us know. The Internet and the new avenues of communication it offers keep changing the newspaper on a daily basis, almost as rapidly as the news itself.

The mission of the *Los Angeles Times* is the same: gathering and editing the news, and providing an advertising marketplace. But the package it is wrapped in may come on the wings of electrons as often as it does in the hands of newspaper carriers.

Washington Post, Los Angeles Times, Knight-Ridder, and newspaper syndicates such as King Features Syndicate, National Newspaper Syndicate, News America Syndicate, United Features Syndicate, and Newspaper Enterprises Syndicate.

Internationally, Reuters (United Kingdom), Agence France-Presse

(France), New China News Agency (People's Republic of China), and Kyoto (Japan) are a few of the major news services providing news and features for not only newspapers but also radio, television, magazines, and private subscribers. These are large organizations with reporters, editors, and other staff in most major capitals and market centers. Reuters, for example, has a staff of almost 300 in its New York office, just one of its many offices.

Standing beside AP and UPI equipment in most of the nation's major newsrooms are high-speed teleprinters provided by commercial PR wires. Practitioners use these distribution services to speed time-critical press releases simultaneously into newsrooms. Increasingly time-sensitive press relations brought on the dramatic growth of domestic and international publicity wire networks.

PR Newswire (PRN) introduced electronic distribution of news releases in New York City in 1954. Other local PR wires copied the concept. The idea quickly evolved into national systems in the United States, Canada, and England, followed by worldwide news-release distribution systems. Although they differ greatly in size, all these wires operate in essentially the same way: charging clients to transmit releases to the media, with fees based on the extent and type of distribution ordered. For example, PRN offers more than 60 distribution options in the United States, ranging from local coverage to national distribution. Media receive these news services at no charge.

Because they offer fast, simultaneous transmission to all the media on a network, practitioners use these wires to flash news ranging from major corporate developments and earnings reports, sporting events, and obituaries to invitations to press conferences. They are especially useful in times of emergency. For example, a baby food manufacturer had an urgent need to distribute a product recall to many media outlets quickly and simultaneously when glass shards were found in one shipment of food products.

PRN serves about 1,500 media, covering every major area of the country. Operating from its headquarters in New York City, PRN transmits news releases and photos internationally through its Canada News-Wire and PR Newswire International Services. International distribution services include coverage in individual countries, as well as regional distribution packages such as European Financial Capitals, European General Pack, and Pacific Rim Pack. PRN reports that each year more than 15,000 news sources use these services to send 100,000 messages to newsrooms, trade publications, and selected offices.

Another large portion of newspaper content is supplied by the feature, photo, and specialized news syndicates. As in the case of the wire services, placement of a feature or a picture with a syndicate ensures wide, economical distribution and increases the acceptability of material. Most syndicates distribute columns and comics. For example, Universal Press Syndicate distributes both text features and comic strips, including Scott Adams's "Dilbert," Gary Larson's "The Far Side," Ted Martin's "Pavlov," and Jim Unger's "Herman." Syndicates charge fees based on each client newspaper's circulation.

The world's largest feature news service, Newspaper Enterprise Association (NEA), provides news features, Washington columns, op-ed features, editorials, pictures, sports, family page and food features, astrology columns, and crossword puzzles. It serves 750 daily newspapers in the United States and Canada. In addition, nearly 400 weekly papers use features distributed through the Suburban Features division of NEA. A carefully targeted story carried by the right syndicate can get nationwide coverage. Material can be channeled to the press through such syndicates as NEA, King Features Service, and United Feature Syndicate, to name but a few. Others deal in specialized news, such as Auto News Syndicate, Religious News Service, and Fashion 'n' Figure. A complete list of feature and specialized syndicate outlets for publicity is published annually in the Editor and Publisher International Yearbook.

As in the case of paid publicity wires, there are also feature services that supply newspapers and periodicals with client-sponsored material without charge. Clients pay the bill. Typical is the Derus Media Service, Chicago, which mails out a clipsheet, *Editorial PACE,* to dailies and weeklies. It also distributes individual releases. Another such service is North American Precis Syndicate, Inc. (NAPS), with offices in New York, Washington, Chicago, and Los Angeles. NAPS distributes news, features, and reprints to the nation's dailies and weeklies.

Magazines

More than 12,000 (some estimate more than 20,000) magazines and specialized publications published in the United States offer effective specialized channels of communication to narrowly defined audiences. Variations in the content and audience appeal of magazines are almost limitless, and ever changing. Some 300 new magazines are started each year, but only one in 10 is successful. Many never make it to the first issue. Others fail after the first year or two, disappointing enthusiastic publishers who had visions of attracting both subscribers and advertisers.

One author refers to magazines as "the first national mass medium," referring to Benjamin Franklin's *General Magazine,* published in February 1741. Technically, however, Andrew Bradford's *American Magazine* was the first American magazine, because it appeared in print three days before Franklin's magazine. Historians, however, give Franklin credit for originating the concept of a magazine.[33]

Magazines' broad array and variety—from the circulation giants such as *Modern Maturity, Reader's Digest, TV Guide, National Geographic, Better Homes and Gardens, Family Circle, Time, Newsweek, U.S. News and World Report, Cosmopolitan,* and *Good Housekeeping;* more narrowly targeted magazines such as *Ms., Rolling Stone, Sports Illustrated, PC World, Wired,* and *Architectural Digest;* and trade and business journals such as *Women's Wear Daily, Business Week, Fortune,* and *Forbes;* to such recreational magazines as *World Tennis, Video Review, Popular Photography, Snowboarding,* and *Ski Magazine*—provide effective communication media to reach large audiences who share common interests. Thus, magazines often enable communicators to target a specific message to a specific audience more economically than with other media.

The changing magazine market—from general to specialized publications—reflects the nation's changing interests and lifestyles. There is a magazine or periodical catering to almost every known interest, vocation, and hobby. Advances in offset printing and computerized production have stimulated circulation and advertising revenues by giving advertisers options for buying targeted portions of the total circulation. Regional advertising in such national magazines as *Time* or *Newsweek,* for example, allows advertisers to sell to a market within a market, even local markets. *Farm Journal,* the first national magazine to publish regional editions (1952), now produces up to 9,000 different versions of each issue. Specialized editions are tailored to match the information needs of selected groups of farmers, based on "the most complete database on farmers in the U.S.," according to the publisher.[34]

Several thousand business and professional publications serve the specialized needs of professional groups, trade associations, or business and industry. These publications generally use prepared news releases if the content serves their readers' economic or professional needs. Each of these publications caters to a carefully defined audience, usually representing the membership lists of the organization publishing the magazine. Examples include PRSA's *The Strategist,* IABC's *Communication World,* and the American Medical Association's *American Medical News.* In addition to collecting subscription fees built into membership fees, many of these publications carry advertising of products and services specific to readers' occupations or professional practices.

A guide to the audiences and content of magazines is provided by two indispensable tools of the practitioner: *Writer's Guide* and *Writer's Market.* Audit Bureau of Circulation (ABC) publishes verified circulation figures of member magazines. Advertisers use these figures for making decisions about where to place advertisements. Public relations practitioners use these sources to estimate audience size and characteristics for magazine coverage.

The following facts illustrate the advantages of using magazines. Opinion leaders read many magazines. Magazines provide more durable information than newspapers. Magazine readers have the opportunity to read, reread, discuss, and debate the information gleaned from this source. The trend is away from fiction and entertainment features toward more investigative and interpretative reporting of controversial issues. Readers with special interests turn to magazines for in-depth treatment of topics, such as when older citizens report that magazines are second only to health care specialists as a source for health information. The vitality and force of magazines in shaping opinions, creating fashions, designing houses, setting standards for professions or businesses, and enlisting political support have been demonstrated many times over since those first two American magazines appeared in 1741.

Publicity placement in a magazine should be preceded by a careful analysis of the publication's readers, its editorial formula, its advertising content, and the market it serves. The smart practitioner studies the magazine's topics, style, policies, trends, format, and so forth and then applies this knowledge by slanting news and features to the particular publication. Publicists generally do not submit unsolicited material, however. Rather, they work on a tip or query basis when they have something that would have reader appeal. They submit story outlines or feature suggestions. If one is accepted, they work with the magazine's staff or freelance writers to develop the story. The practitioner's jobs are to sell ideas to editors and then to cooperate with writers and photographers, who build the ideas into articles.

Magazine publicity placement is almost essential for organizations seeking to influence national or specialized audiences. Yet many practitioners fail in their efforts to get such publicity because they do not understand the long lead time of national magazines, the length of time it takes to put a story idea into final, publishable form, and the stiff competition for space; and also because they do not make adequate circulation studies so that material is targeted for the particular audience. The competition comes from editors and staff writers on the magazines, frequent contributors, and freelance writers who write regularly for national magazines.

An approach often used but sometimes overlooked is that of dealing with freelancers. Freelance writers who sell to national magazines are interested in an account of an institution, a person, or an event that possesses at least one of these three qualities: (1) national importance or significance; (2) elements of struggle, conflict, contest, or drama; or (3) anecdotal enrichment and entertainment value. It is common practice to give a freelancer a good story to develop. The freelancer gets a check; the practitioner gets a publicity placement in a magazine. The Society of Magazine Writers in New York City operates a Dial-a-Writer Service for those seeking writers for special projects.

Radio

Once thought to be fading because of television and cable, radio today serves a useful and pervasive role in our public information system. Radio offers a wide range of publicity possibilities. It is a mobile medium suited to a mobile people. (Newspaper people like to point out that their medium is also "mobile," and no batteries are required.) It reaches the bedroom and breakfast table in the morning and rides to and from work in the car, lulls us to sleep at night, and goes along to the beach, to the woods, and on fishing trips, a flexibility no other medium can match. For example, in the aftermath of Hurricane Andrew, radio became the primary medium for communicating to the citizens of Florida's South Bay. No other medium reached the many citizens who had lost their homes, telephone and power lines, and transportation.[35]

There are close to 500 million radio sets, and radio listening has increased to more than three hours a day. The typical household has at least five radios. Almost 80 percent of all U.S. citizens listen to radio daily. As one radio specialist says, "It's the first source of news. It's there when you wake up. It's there when you go to sleep."[36]

There are more than 10,000 radio stations in the United States, of which 1,260 are public stations. About 5,000 are AM, and 5,000 are FM. There has been a marked shift in radio programming and listening patterns from AM to FM. In the early 1970s, AM stations attracted three-fourths of the audience. By the early 1990s, more than three-fourths of the total radio listening audience tuned to FM stations. The AM dial is so crowded that nearly half the

AM stations—"daytimers"—have to shut down 15 minutes after sunset to avoid interfering with others. FM also gained listeners because of its high-quality stereo sound, which coincided with the development of noise-free recordings.

Radio news releases are usually fed to stations over telephone lines, sometimes to networks such as the Texas Radio Network and USA Radio Network. Audio news services, such as North American Network (based in Washington, DC) and News/Broadcast Network (Milwaukee and New York City), use telephone distribution to target stations by region and format. News/Broadcast Network, for example, reaches 2,200 stations through its daily feeds on the Associated Press and Mutual Broadcasting wires. To increase airings on local stations, audio news services often localize national stories by including local interviews or sound bites.[37]

Even though it is a mass medium, radio possesses the qualities of a direct, personal touch, because it uses the spoken word, for the most part, to convey its message. Broadcast pioneer Arthur Godfrey put his finger on this intimate quality in describing the turning point in his career:

> Lying in that hospital listening to the radio, I realized for the first time how really intimate the medium is and how ridiculously ineffective most of the speakers were. . . . They were not *talking,* they were *reading,* and therefore convincing no one. . . . I decided I'd do things differently. . . . When I face a mike I have a mental image of only one person listening to me and I talk to that one person.

The practitioner should realize radio is a person-to-person medium that flourishes on conversation. Call-in talk shows now play a major role in setting the public agenda and in providing a forum for public debate. Writing in *New York Magazine,* Joe Klein said that radio talk-show hosts killed a proposed congressional pay raise:

> A gaggle of radio talk show hosts . . . rallied their listeners against the pay raise. They (along with consumer activist Ralph Nader) mounted the most effective lobbying campaign of the past decade—an effort that raised the daunting specter of radio populism on the rampage and talk hosts as the political organizers of the '90s.[38]

Talk shows certainly played a role in the Bush–Clinton and Clinton–Dole presidential campaigns, with candidates and their spokespersons appearing on the nationally syndicated *Larry King Show* to make major announcements. Rush Limbaugh has a national radio audience, whereas Boston's Jerry Williams, another conservative, has political impact on listeners throughout New England. Almost every major city has its own radio all-talk shows capitalizing on local conflict, sensational topics, and legitimate public debate of important issues. Increased emphasis on the discussion type of program opens up many possibilities for practitioners. Talk shows and telephone interviews focusing on controversial issues have become increasingly popular and have an almost insatiable appetite for guests with a message—however controversial it may be.

Listener surveys show newscasts and talk programs at the top or near the top of programs preferred by most listeners. By providing news scripts or recorded interviews for radio newscasts, practitioners can get a wide hearing for stories within the audience limits of a given station or set of stations. Radio newsrooms want news prepared for radio, not copies of newspaper releases. They want news written for bulletin presentation. Radio news editors want all difficult names and words spelled out phonetically for the announcer. The lead story on a typical newscast is 100 words or fewer. News is written for the ear, not for the eye. Radio news must be informal, conversational, brief, to the point, and—above all—accurate. Once spoken, errors cannot be recalled and corrected; besides, one never gets exactly the same audience twice in radio. Radio journalists expect and deserve equal treatment with print journalists in releasing news and covering special events.

Many organizations provide stations with dial-access recorded newscasts, which are updated as news develops. Copy for these newscasts is prepared in the public relations office, then recorded on automatic playback systems. Stations are given an unlisted telephone number for these recorded newscasts. The AFL-CIO operates an automated telephone bulletin service to serve radio stations, as do many state highway patrol offices, weather reporting services, and stock and commodity brokers.

Public service time is seldom prime listening time, but it is not without value. Since the Federal Communications Commission relaxed its public service requirements for broadcasters, many stations have reduced the number of public service and other nonrevenue programs they broadcast. Yet most stations provide some free time to nonprofit agencies as part of the station's community relations program. In nonprime time the competition for air time is less intense than during the more desirable—and salable—drive time and other high-listenership hours. That is not to say, however, that an effective program cannot attract and hold listeners.

An effective way is to provide radio and TV *public service announcements* (PSAs) 10 seconds, 30 seconds, or 60 seconds in length. A PSA is any announcement for which no charge is made that promotes programs and services of government and voluntary agencies. Stations set their own standards, but most use well-prepared PSAs. And they can be effective. For example, a PSA prepared by the Aluminum Association to urge recycling of cans was used by 244 TV stations more than 15,000 times, adding up to nearly 164 broadcast hours. The "Recycle and Save" PSA increased the number of logged toll-free calls from 433 a month to 9,500 calls within nine months.

Television

The communications phenomenon of the 20th century, television, has great force and scope as a publicity medium. No other medium matches television's ability to provide a window on the world. What other medium could transmit live coverage of the Mars Explorer vehicle making its first tentative steps on that faraway planet? How could anyone ignore the human tragedies in Bosnia shown so vividly on the evening news? Many recall the soot-smudged faces of those fleeing the bombed federal building in Oklahoma City. And long-lens cameras gave us live pictures of Princess Diana's funeral procession and her sons solemnly following their mother's casket on the way to Westminister Abbey.

A medium that permits the use of the printed word, spoken word, pictures in motion, color, music, animation, and sound effects—all blended into one message—possesses immeasurable potency. It offers a vast range of possibilities for telling a story, from a terse, 60-second video on a TV newscast to a half-hour or 1-hour documentary film to a miniseries extended over several evenings. And with satellite transmission now commonplace, the powerful, pervasive impact of television is worldwide. Yet many practitioners do not fully capitalize on TV's power. Television took the lead from newspapers in 1963 as the primary source of news, a fact many practitioners, many of whom once worked in print media, fail to recognize.

More than 1,500 TV stations broadcast almost around the clock to nearly every household. The number of cable channels now give viewers more options than they can carefully consider. The average time spent with television now approaches the length of a typical workday. Children spend more time watching TV than with their teachers in classrooms. They grow up using the remote-control clicker to explore a seemingly endless array of program services such as Disney, Discovery, Black Entertainment TV, TNT, HBO, CNN, and C-SPAN, to name but a few. As former FCC chairman Newton Minow says,

> Choice has skyrocketed. The VCR means you can watch a program when you want to see it, not just when the broadcaster puts it on the schedule. If you are a sports fan, a news junkie, a stock market follower, a rock music devotee, a person who speaks Spanish, a nostalgic old-movie buff, a congressional-hearing observer, a weather watcher—you now have your own choice. The FCC objective in the early '60s to expand choice has been fulfilled—beyond all expectations.[39]

This is our most intimate mass medium, yet it can attract half the population to watch Michael Jackson perform during Super Bowl halftime. It can entice advertisers to pay almost one and a half million dollars to run a 30-second ad during the Super Bowl, or more than $150,000 for the same 30 seconds during the regular program schedule.

Television has become a dominant force in the rearing of our young, the prime source of news and entertainment for most Americans, and a powerful soapbox from which citizens' protests can be communicated to the nation and the world. This medium has greatly altered national election campaigns and has diminished the role of the political parties. Researchers in Germany, for example, found that TV newscasts not only caused changes in awareness of problems but also had consequences on voting intentions.[40] National and international wire services and global TV news networks have created a truly global forum. Events made large by TV shape public opinion worldwide. What other explanation is there for the carefully scripted and choreographed TV appearances of both George Bush and Saddam Hussein during the Kuwait–Persian Gulf crisis?

Television greatly heightens citizen awareness of the conduct of public institutions and emphasizes the impersonal, interdependent nature of the environment. It also creates a sense of frustration for citizens, who are witness to much that they cannot control, be it the police beating Rodney King in Los Angeles, Coast Guard cutters intercepting boats overloaded with Haitian refugees, bloated stomachs of starving children in Somalia, pro-life protesters blockading the entrance to a health care clinic, the wretched life of homeless families, or developers scraping hillsides bare to build more look-alike houses. TV brings these and many more pictures of the world into our homes.

TV's influence is potent and pervasive because Americans spend more than seven hours per day watching TV. But viewing habits and patterns are changing: The three major commercial networks now attract only about 60 percent of the viewing audience, compared with more than 90 percent in the early 1960s. The VCR has freed the viewer from being tied to program schedules. New transmission technology is expanding the channel-carrying capacity of cable networks, giving cable subscribers the choice of hundreds of program services and channels. As Newton Minow concludes, "The most important educational institution in America is television. More people learn more each day, each year, each lifetime from television than from any other source."[41]

Heavy reliance on TV news as a primary source of news disturbs thoughtful observers who know that the limits of time and dominance of dramatic pictures inevitably oversimplify and thus distort the news. For example, evening network shows, watched by more than 50 million people each night, must tell the story of the world in 4,000 words or fewer, the equivalent of four columns in a standard-sized newspaper. Fifty-eight seconds is a major story. Before retiring from the *MacNeil-Lehrer News Hour* on PBS (now the *News Hour*), Robert MacNeil bluntly admitted,

> In most of the stories television cares to cover there is always the "right bit," the most violent, the most bloody, the most pathetic, the most tragic, the most wonderful, the most awful moment. Getting the effective "bit" is what television news is all about.[42]

The compression involved in a TV news program, coupled with today's news values and technology, brings a compound of fiction and fact in terse fragments to viewers around the world. Adam Clayton Powell III says major TV networks have entered agreements with video news services around the world or formed alliances to get news once covered by their own foreign bureaus, "capturing images on videotape and distributing them within seconds to dozens or even hundreds of newsrooms around the country and around the world for immediate use."[43]

Even when doing news documentaries, television blurs the line between entertainment and objective journalism:

> The documentary's claims to offer unprejudiced rendering of objective reality were strained by a number of factors associated with the story-telling conventions of popular television, including considerations of plot, character, pursuit of an af-

fective response from audiences, and conscious competition with entertaining programming. . . . Editing and camera techniques also suggested the malleable nature of the medium. Indeed, these techniques helped to generate debate over what is commonly referred to in the industry as "actuality," that is, material captured by photographic or audio equipment which "documents" the analysis of the producer.[44]

Success or failure of entertainment programs is determined by their ratings and the consequent amount of advertising the programs can attract, not by their quality. These same criteria are applied all too often to television news programs. But according to one critic, shallowness and the emphasis on entertainment value are not necessarily givens of the medium itself:

> By its very nature, we are told, television emphasizes the visual over the ideational. Action events, national leaders, and political candidates have visual appeal; issues and policy analysis do not. Hence there is bound to be more surface than substance in the news. . . . Rather than being a criticism, this "blaming the nature of the media" is a disguised defense. It gets everybody off the hook and treats television, or whatever medium, like a disembodied technological force all its own. However, it is not television as such that chooses to cling to surface events but the people who run it. With the right script and right intentions, visual media can offer engrossingly informative and penetrating presentations on vital subjects.[45]

Selling story ideas to TV producers is a common approach for using television. Producers are the ones who decide if an author's new book is reviewed or the author is interviewed or if a personality appears on shows such as NBC's *Today* and *Leno* or on syndicated shows such as *Oprah, Regis and Kathie Lee,* and *Rosie O'Donnell.* The most common technique, however, is providing video for news or documentary programs in the form of a video news release, or VNR.

TV Guide blew the whistle on the growing use of VNRs in newscasts without viewers being informed that the video was provided by an outside source. The magazine referred to the video press releases as "fake news," suggesting that VNRs blur the line between news and commercials.[46] Others have expressed concern that VNRs can be aired without first having passed journalistic standards for verifying accuracy, can be shown without identifying the source, can be used to manipulate media content in favor of the VNR source, and can violate generally accepted ethical principles in public relations and journalism.[47]

Responding to such concerns, a special committee of the Public Relations Service Council established a "Code of Good Practice for Video New Releases" (see Exhibit 9.3) and a logo to be used by those agreeing to abide by the code.

Practitioners are learning how to produce VNRs more acceptable to news directors. Bob Kimmel of News/Broadcast Network (a New York City VNR producer) lists techniques to avoid to increase the chances that stations will use a VNR:

EXHIBIT 9.3

CODE OF GOOD PRACTICE FOR VIDEO NEWS RELEASES

1. The objective of a VNR is to present information, pictures, and sound that TV journalists can use and rely on for quality, accuracy and perspective.
2. Information contained in a VNR, to the extent possible, must be accurate and verifiable. Intentionally false or misleading information must be avoided.
3. A VNR must be clearly identified on the video's opening slate and any advisory material and scripts that precede or accompany tape distribution.

4. The sponsoring company, organization or individual must also be clearly identified on the video slate.
5. The name and phone number of a responsible party must be provided on the video for journalists to contact.
6. Persons interviewed in the VNR must be accurately identified by name, title, and affiliation on the video.

Used with permission of Public Relations Service Council.

1. Don't mix natural sound with voice-over narration.
2. Don't overuse stills as a substitute for action video.
3. Don't place titles of "supers" on the video news segment itself. Provide the information separately so stations can insert titles in their regular fonts and styles.
4. Don't use fancy special effects and repetitive dissolves not ordinarily used in news packages.
5. Don't commercialize the VNR with blatant product or service presentations.
6. Don't put your own reporter on the screen.
7. Don't produce a VNR unless you have a news story or a timely feature of general interest.[48]

"At one time, VNRs were assailed by TV journalists because they too closely resembled advertisements. VNRs are under attack today, video experts say, because they deliver what they promise: news!"[49]

When there is not enough time to distribute a VNR on tape, satellite transmission makes it possible to instantaneously distribute public relations messages. Satellite media tours (SMTs), used so frequently in presidential campaigns, make it possible for candidates to appear on local television news and public affairs programs across the nation. The "tour," however, happens by satellite transmission technology without requiring the subject to move from the source station studio. The SMT no doubt will replace the time-consuming and expensive city hopping formerly part of political campaigns, crisis communication programs, and other breaking news stories calling for top management appearances on the global television medium.

Cable Television

The growth of cable television with its 500-channel-capacity has profoundly altered the nation's communication and viewing patterns. Cable was born in 1948, when the first community-antenna television (CATV) system was built in a small Pennsylvania community that suffered from poor television reception. The number of systems increased steadily until the early 1970s but increased rapidly in 1975 when Time, Inc. put Home Box Office on the air and the FCC lifted restrictions on programming and advertising. It was Cable News Network's (CNN) live coverage of the 1986 Challenger disaster and the round-the-clock coverage of the 1991 Gulf War, however, that made cable news a major player in the global information system. For example, CNN had 125 staffers covering the Persian Gulf region when the war with Iraq began. ABC, CBS, and NBC each had between 60 and 80. CNN coverage was so much more complete that several network affiliates carried CNN reports rather than their own network feeds.[50]

As new technology expands the channel-carrying capacity of old and new systems alike, cable TV may become only part of the packages of services carried. For example, International Cablecasting Technologies of Los Angeles and Digital Cable Radio in Hatboro, Pennsylvania, offer compact disk–quality music delivered by cable. Cable companies offer interactive cable television services such as shopping and banking, information databases, and emergency alert connections to police and fire departments. Fiber-optic networks link home television sets with central computers to give users access to their bank accounts, advertisements and other product information services, and news databases and libraries. Viewers are connected directly to a central computer by way of WebTV and home terminals to call up or send information. In fact, as futurists predicted, the line between television, telephone, and home computers is blurring as both information and entertainment services are delivered to homes over cable systems.

Then again, there may be no wire or cable at all. Multipoint distribution systems (MDS) use microwave transmitters to distribute programs to subscribers. Satellite-delivered pay television was introduced in Australia in 1993. Widespread use of direct-broadcast satellite systems will occur when technology and economics converge to make it possible to replace the large home satellite dishes with small antennas mounted in attics or on windows. A small Texas town became the first wireless telephone community in 1993, changing its switch-and-wire system to digital wireless technology. The system reportedly gives the same quality, privacy, and data transmission capabilities as the old wire technology while lowering costs.[51]

In the meantime, telephone companies around the world are entering the video-transmission business. Using new asymmetric digital subscriber line (ADSL) technology, Bell Atlantic experimented with video-on-demand services in suburban Washington, DC, over its existing copper wire network. In the Tampa, Florida, area, GTE Corporation built a fiber network to carry video from city hall, performing arts theaters, and sports venues to local television stations and other carriers. Telcom Australia installed a fiber-to-home network. The company already delivers CNN International and VIP Australian tourist information service to hotels and some businesses in major cities over its fiber-optic network.[52]

WORKING WITH THE MEDIA

Knowing about the media—knowing how to work with each medium, produce content for each, meet the deadlines of each, adhere to specific style requirements, and appeal to each medium's audience—is a major part of many practitioners' jobs. Practitioners responsible for dealing with the media and media gatekeepers must build and maintain relationships of mutual respect and trust. The relationship, although mutually beneficial, remains an adversarial relationship at its core, because journalists and practitioners are not in the same business and often do not have the same communication goals.

The Person in the Middle

To be effective in the go-between and mediating roles, practitioners must have the confidence of both their organization and the media. This is not an easy job. CEOs and other line managers are naturally suspicious of the media, just as journalists are by nature questioning and somewhat untrusting of those they put in the spotlight. Practitioners and others in organizations complain, "Why does the press always sensationalize things?" "Journalists never get things right." "I didn't say that!" "They take things out of context . . . or twist things to fit their story." Journalists counter with, "That organization never tells the truth!" "We don't get to talk with the person who has the real story and real news." "What we get is PR crap." "You get the feeling they're trying to hide something."

The adversarial—even hostile—feelings that exist between practitioners and journalists often spill over into public debate. Herbert Schmertz, Mobil Corporation vice president of public affairs during the 1980s, criticized journalists and media performance by providing what he called "constructive, responsible criticism."[53] Mobil periodically uses its advocacy advertising to criticize the media (see Figure 9.5, pg. 324), to which Schmertz credits substantial progress in improving print coverage of his corporation and business in general. He saved his harshest criticism for television news and

> the questionable values that afflict TV journalism—the slavery to ratings . . . the pandering to the lowest common denominator . . . the emotional presentation to entice a larger audience . . . the subversion of news values to entertainment values . . . the ruthless compression of facts to fit preordained timetables.[54]

Schmertz was not alone in his criticism. Unhappy with television coverage of the B-2 bomber and the plane's price tag, veterans' organizations and the defense industry counterattacked:

> By its very nature, television news suffers from a variety of limitations and con-

4. The myth of the open airwaves

There is a simple, yet overwhelming, difference between the print media and television journalism. Newspapers and magazines offer regular access to their pages to those who wish to rebut what has been printed. The major television networks do not.

Access to television is supposed to be governed largely by the Federal Communications Commission's Fairness Doctrine. That doctrine owes its existence to the theory that the airwaves are a scarce resource and must therefore be allocated among potential users. The doctrine requires owners of broadcast licenses "...to encourage and implement the broadcast of all sides of controversial public issues..." and to play "...a conscious and positive role in bringing about the balanced presentation of the opposing viewpoints." In theory, the Fairness Doctrine doesn't preclude anything. In reality, the networks have turned it into a doctrine of unfairness.

Under a mandate to present all sides of a public issue, the networks confine debate through controls imposed by their own news departments. Through their news staffs, the networks exercise total control over the agenda of issues, and who may speak to the public. Unfortunately, the result of this network control, with no system or forum for rebuttal, has resulted in a narrow and selective discussion of major public issues—and the systematic exclusion or distortion of many viewpoints.

Mobil has often been denied the opportunity to rebut inaccurate television news broadcasts. Frequently, the broadcasts appeared at times when critical energy legislation was under debate in Congress—legislation regarding oil company divestiture, natural gas deregulation, oil decontrol, and the "windfall profit" tax. At such times, the networks' systematic exclusion of ideas and information impaired the public's ability to rationally decide fundamental policy issues.

Other companies have experienced similar frustrations in their attempts to gain adequate airtime to rebut erroneous television newscasts. Kaiser Aluminum & Chemical Corporation had to threaten a slander suit and had to ask the FCC to order ABC to give it time to respond to charges made on a 1980 *20/20* segment, before ABC finally gave the company the opportunity for an unedited reply. It took more than a year, however, before the rebuttal was aired on prime-time TV.

In response to a 1979 CBS *60 Minutes* broadcast, Illinois Power Company produced its own tape to point out the network's distortions. Called "60 Minutes/Our Reply," the power company's rebuttal exposed the bias of the broadcast by including CBS film footage not included in the original segment. The program has been widely shown to various groups across the country, but it has not been aired on television.

The networks not only block rebuttals, they refuse to air advertisements on "controversial" issues, and have rejected Mobil advocacy commercials since 1974—despite evidence that public support for issue advertising is strong. (Network policies would preclude the very message you are currently reading.) A 1980 survey by the Opinion Research Corporation found that 85 percent of the American public think corporations should be allowed to present their views on controversial matters in television commercials. And most independent stations and network affiliates have opened their doors to advocacy advertising, without creating the chaos the networks profess to fear.

As the Supreme Court affirmed in its 1978 *Bellotti* decision: "The press does not have a monopoly on either the First Amendment or the ability to enlighten."

Mobil®

Courtesy Mobil Corporation.

straints. The process by which television editors, producers, and reporters compile, summarize, and synthesize complicated issues often leads to misrepresentations or outright distortions of the news. . . .

Network television shies away from complicated events, focusing instead on simplicity. Entertainment. Images . . .

Absent an image, television journalists do not seem capable of presenting the news. Even with an image, broadcast journalism is less serious, and oftentimes less responsible, than print journalism.[55]

General Motors counterattacked when in late 1992 NBC News reported a staged accident and fire involving GM's full-sized pickups manufactured from 1973 through 1987. The report aired on *Dateline NBC* under the title "Waiting to Explode." Exhibit 9.4, pgs. 326–327, summarizes one case in which the media admitted fault and apologized to viewers and to GM.

The acrimony is not one-sided. When Meg Greenfield was *Washington Post* editorial page editor, she issued a memo barring practitioners from editorial offices: "We don't want any of that damned crowd around here." Subsequently, *Post* executive editor Ben Bradlee extended the ban on talking to public relations sources to reporters, a directive quickly ignored because of reporters' dependence on public relations sources.[56] A scholarly look at public relations "information subsidies" of news media led the study's author to conclude,

In journalistic folklore there is a distrust, or mistrust, of public relations practitioners as biased "flacks" engaged in puffery and manipulations of information, and indeed public relations practitioners themselves are indoctrinated to expect that attitude of distrust from journalists.[57]

In fact, practitioners and journalists operate in a mutually dependent and mutually beneficial relationship, sometimes as adversaries, sometimes as colleagues cooperating in respective self-interest. Not as frequently, but occasionally, the news media are manipulated by the practitioner, who may have more resources, as well as control access to news sources. With at least equal frequency, news media frustrate practitioners in their attempts to get information to publics. In short, there is a dynamic tension in the relationship between practitioners and journalists that is "firmly embedded in journalistic culture."[58] All too often neither practitioners' employers nor journalists understand practitioners' mediator role in establishing and maintaining media relations.

Guidelines for Good Media Relations

The underlying conflict of interests necessarily makes the practitioner–journalist relationship adversarial. The practitioner advancing a particular cause or organization stands in stark contrast to the journalist's drive to dig up news through good reporting and journalistic initiative. Given the experience of at least a century, the adversarial relationship appears to serve the public interest and the needs of the public information system.

EXHIBIT 9.4

GENERAL MOTORS VERSUS NBC NEWS

Alvie L. Smith, APR
Director of Corporate
Communications (retired)
General Motors Corporation

The Situation

In November 1992, a 16-minute segment entitled "Waiting to Explode" on the television news magazine *Dateline NBC* focused on what it called the unsafe design of GM full-sized pickups built from 1973 through 1987. The show included a 1-minute segment of "unscientific" demonstration crashes conducted by the Institute for Safety Analysis (ISA) in which one truck catches fire after being struck in the side by a car.

Seventeen million viewers saw apparent visual support for interviews with safety experts who claimed that the trucks were vulnerable to fires and explosions because of fuel tank design and placement.

The television segment also included interviews with the parents of a 17-year-old who was killed when his pickup was broadsided by a car driven by a drunk driver. GM officially complained to NBC that the show was "grossly, unfair, misleading and irresponsible."

In February 1993, the jury found GM "negligent" and awarded the parents $105.2 million. GM appealed, claiming that the 70-miles-per-hour impact into the cab, not the fire, killed the truck driver.

Although NBC and ISA claimed that the test vehicles had been destroyed after the demonstration crashes, GM investigators found them and got court approval to study the vehicles to recreate the demonstrations and results.

GM's Response

In a February 8, 1993, press conference in Detroit, GM's chief counsel presented a well-researched refutation of the *Dateline NBC* segment. GM locations throughout the world

The sound approach for organizations and practitioners is to view media relations as an investment. Accuracy and fairness in press coverage does not result from reporters' work alone. Ultimately, however, the relationship between practitioners and journalists has an impact on the quality of new coverage about organizations.[59] Those relationships can best be achieved when practitioners follow a few basic rules: (1) shoot squarely, (2) give service, (3) do not beg or carp, (4) do not ask for kills, and (5) do not flood the media.

1. **Shoot squarely.** It is not just politically correct to counsel that "honesty is the best policy" in dealing with the press; it is good business and good common sense. Jerry Dalton Jr., past PRSA president and manager of corporate communications at Vought Aircraft Company, says the practi-

and North American dealers received the press conference via satellite. Hundreds of videotapes of the press conference were distributed. While displaying the crash truck fuel tank and slow-motion sequences of the crash, GM's counsel pointed out major deceptions in the report and test crash:

1. NBC did not tell viewers that incendiary rocket devices were taped under the trucks and timed to go off on impact to ignite any spilled gasoline.
2. The fuel tank had been "topped off" before the test and fitted with a nonstandard cap that allowed gasoline to escape as the incendiary device was fired.
3. There was no puncture of the gas tank, as had been claimed in the NBC report.
4. Impact speeds in the demonstration crashes were significantly higher than those NBC reported: one at 39 miles per hour, not 30, and the other at least 47, not 40.

GM filed a lawsuit against NBC and ISA for defaming its reputation. This was the first such action in GM's history.

NBC's Response

NBC carried highlights of GM's charges in its February 8 newscast, but NBC News President Michael Gartner defended the segment. On February 10, however, *Dateline NBC* coanchors Jane Pauley and Stone Phillips read a lengthy retraction negotiated by NBC and GM that day. NBC did not contest any of GM's accusations. "NBC deeply regrets using the one-minute crash segment," Phillips said. "We apologize to our viewers and to GM."

Results

GM accepted NBC's apology and dropped the lawsuit, with the provision that NBC pay GM's research expenses, about $2 million. Quick acceptance of NBC's apology and dropping legal action took the matter out of the media spotlight. In March 1993, Gartner resigned from *NBC News* and three other executives were fired. A group of independent lawyers hired by NBC had scathing criticism for the show's producers. NBC announced it would reorganize its procedures to ensure future accuracy and fairness. *Detroit Free Press* columnist Steven Brill wrote: "NBC's candid apology was a pivotal event in the annals of journalism—a refreshing reversal of the usual arrogance and stonewalling and hiding behind a justifiably permissive law."

tioner's most important asset in dealing with the media is credibility: "It must be earned, usually over a period of time. It means simply that a reporter can trust [the practitioner] totally, and vice versa. It means never lying. If you can't, for some legitimate reason, speak the truth, then say nothing."[60] Journalists point out that good and bad news tend to even out over time, so if practitioners are honest with bad news, then they are more likely to be trusted with good news.

Another fundamental principle is that a practitioner cannot favor one news outlet at the expense of others. The safest rule is that spot news should go out as fast as possible, letting the media determine the cycle in which it breaks. News and feature material should be alternated evenly among the competitors. As a corollary, practitioners must protect journalistic initiative. If a reporter gets a tip and asks for information, it belongs to the journalist. The same information should not be given to other outlets unless they come after it. This is a policy with which no reporter can justly quarrel, because each of them would demand the same protection for their scoops.

2. **Give service.** The quickest, surest way to gain the cooperation of journalists is to provide them with newsworthy, interesting, and timely stories and pictures that they want when they want them and in a form they can readily use. Journalists work with fixed and sometimes tight deadlines. Practitioners who hope to place stories in the news media must know and adhere to media lead times (see Exhibit 9.5).

Journalists also count on and cooperate with the practitioner who willingly responds to a midnight call for a photo and biographical sketch of an executive who just died. News, a highly perishable commodity, occurs around the clock, as do news deadlines in the global village. Therefore, some practitioners are on call around the clock. As Dalton points out,

> "News doesn't wait—for anyone or anything. In many instances, it's now or never to respond on behalf of your organization. The well-written, properly-reviewed, thoroughly-coordinated reply or statement will never see the light of day unless it gets to the media in time for their deadlines."[61]

3. **Do not beg or carp.** Nothing irritates journalists and their editors and news directors more than the practitioner who begs to have stories used or complains about story treatment. Journalists have finely developed senses of journalistic objectivity and news value. If information is not sufficiently newsworthy on its own merits to attract their interest, no amount of begging and carping can change the quality of that information. And do not ask journalists to send tear sheets. Hire your own clipping service or monitor the media yourself.

Nothing, however, is more offensive to a journalist than a practitioner who tries to pressure the editorial side to use a story, change a story treatment, or kill a story by holding hostage the organization's advertising business. That kind of pressure does not work when up against journalistic integrity and will surely lead to resentment or to an immediate public response. For example, a threat to "pull our advertising" can lead to a banner headline or the lead story on the evening news, pitting the media against a corporate bully. The rule of thumb is that advertising belongs in the advertising department, and news—good and bad—is for journalists to report in news columns or newscasts.

4. **Do not ask for kills.** Practitioners have no right to ask the press to suppress or kill a story. It seldom works, is unprofessional, and brings only ill will. To journalists, this is a crude insult and an abuse of the First Amendment. It is asking journalists to betray their public trust. The best way to keep unfavorable stories out of the press is to prevent situations that produce such stories.

There are occasions when it is perfectly legitimate to request a delay

EXHIBIT 9.5

MEDIA LEAD TIMES

*By Roxanne Ruben
and Judy Lynes
The Phelps Group
Los Angeles*

"Lead time" means the amount of time needed by a medium to receive press materials and then turn a story around for publication or airing. Lead times also determine when you should (or shouldn't) send information to a medium.

So, the next time you're pitching a story or sending a news release, show editors you have publicity savvy by knowing their lead times. You'll not only score points, you'll also avoid missing a potentially "hot" media opportunity. The importance of meeting deadlines with the media can't be stressed enough. Once you've missed a deadline, there's no turning back—you can't recreate a story and use it a second time with the media.

Most lead times vary considerably among print, radio and television and are fairly consistent for each type of medium. For example, trade and consumer magazines generally have different lead times. But if a story qualifies as "breaking news," then lead times don't always apply. Faxes and overnight delivery services have made deadlines for lead times easier to meet if you are caught off guard. The bottom line, however, is that you should be aware of standard lead times.

When in doubt call a reporter and ask what the lead time is. In the meantime, here are a few guidelines:

Print	Lead Time
Newspapers (some sections—food, travel, calendar listings—have longer lead times)	One to two weeks (dailies) Three weeks (weeklies)
Trade Magazines (monthly)	Six weeks to two months
Consumer Magazines (monthly)	Five to six months
Metro Magazines (monthly)	Three to four months
Weekly Magazines	One to two months
Newspaper Sunday Magazines	Three to four months
Television	
Public Service Announcements (PSAs)	Six to eight weeks
National Morning Shows	Two weeks to one month
Local Talk Shows	Two to three weeks
Local News	Two days
Radio	
Public Service Announcements	Six to eight weeks
Promotions	Two weeks to two months
Talk Shows	Four days to one month
News	Two days

Courtesy The Phelps Group, Los Angeles. (Photo by Mike Caroff.)

in publication or to explain to the press any part of the story that might be damaging to the public interest. As the Pentagon learned during the 1991 Gulf War, however, the press does not take such requests lightly. Imposing tight restrictions on journalists in press pools and requiring security reviews of all dispatches in the name of national security brought charges of censorship and reminders of California U.S. Senator Hiram Johnson's 1917 claim, "The first casualty when war comes is truth."[62]

However, if the press reports an inaccurate or misleading story, ask for a correction. Many news media, in the interest of their own public relations, have adopted policies of publishing or broadcasting corrections. At the same time, however, practitioners should also ask that the erroneous information be corrected in the computerized database, what used to be called the "morgue" or library. Some organizations provide updated background information about the organization, its finances, its products or services, or executives to media so it will be in the file when stories break. For example, the Pharmaceutical Manufacturers' Association sends a file of information to news outlets with this note: "If your files on the prescription drug industry don't include the information in this folder, your files may be incomplete." Many organizations send annual fact books to the media (see Figure 9.6).

5. **Do not flood the media.** Study and experience teach the boundaries of newsworthiness, and common sense dictates respect for them. If a financial editor receives information appropriate for the sports or real estate editor, the financial editor loses respect for the practitioner who engages in blanketing the media with releases. The best advice includes the following: (1) stick to what journalists will consider news, (2) keep media mailing lists current, and (3) send to only one—the most appropriate—journalist at each news medium.

To document how much his reporters and editors have to cull each day, Paul Steiger, *The Wall Street Journal's* New York managing editor, asked the 17 domestic bureau managers to save all news materials they received on 1 day. They sent him press releases, public relations wire stories, faxes, and letters, but not electronic news releases still in computer memory. The stack of boxes and bins in Steiger's office was more than 2 feet high and 10 feet long.[63] An avalanche of material similar to that at *The Wall Street Journal* occurs in newsrooms around the globe. Journalists strike a bargain with their audiences to supply important and interesting information. These gatekeepers require that practitioners do likewise.

Guidelines for Working with the Press

Former CBS news reporter and experienced counselor Chester Burger says that the press "is often unfair, unreasonable, and simply wrong. But even if it isn't our friend, it is the best friend the nation has, and we should be thankful for it."[64] Based on notions of a free and independent press, as well as principles of sound public relations practice, seasoned practitioners offer the following guidelines for working with the press:

FIGURE 9.6   UCLA MEDIA GUIDE

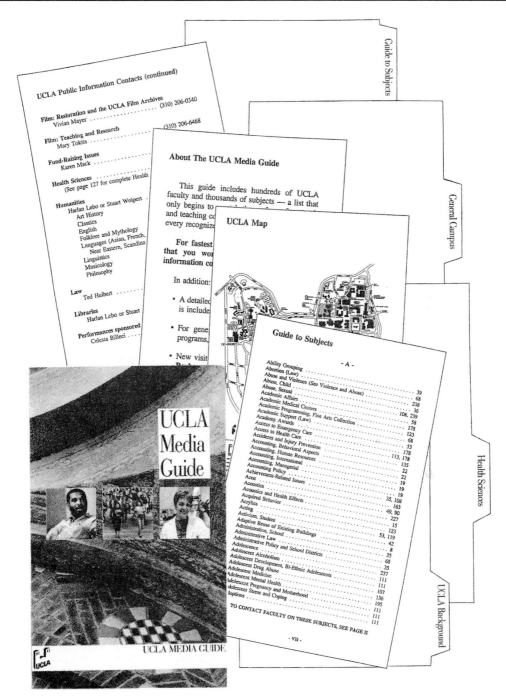

Courtesy UCLA Public Information Office.

1. Talk from the viewpoint of the public's interest, not the organization's. The soft-drink bottler who launches a campaign to collect and recycle bottles can frankly admit that it does not want to irritate the public by having its product litter the landscape.

2. Make the news easy to read and use. Use a short, punchy headline to attract attention and give potential users an indication of the topic. Do not use jargon, unfamiliar acronyms, or technical terms. Personal pronouns, names, and quotations make your copy easier to read and more interesting. Put the name, address, and phone number of the news source and contact at the top of releases.

3. If you do not want some statement quoted, do not make it. Spokespersons should avoid talking "off the record," because such statements may well wind up published without the source. Some news organizations forbid reporters to accept such information. Moreover, it is certainly too late to qualify something as off the record after you make a statement to a reporter.

4. State the most important fact at the beginning. A manager's logical presentation may first list the facts that led to a decision, but news reporters want the decision. The first-level response to a reporter's question is a short summary of your position or newsworthy announcement. The second-level response includes a concrete example or evidence to back up your first statement. If the reporter persists, return to the first-level summary statement.

5. Do not argue with a reporter or lose your cool. Understand that journalists seek an interesting story and will go to great lengths to get the story. To paraphrase an old public relations maxim, do not argue with people who buy printers ink by the barrel or with people who own the transmitter or cable system; these people have the final say.

6. If a question contains offensive language or simply words you do not like, do not repeat them even to deny them. Along the line of having final say, reporters also can select quotes, portions of quotes, or even single words for the final story. Reporters often use the gambit of putting words into subject's mouths, such as, "Do you mean . . . ?" or "Is what you are really saying . . . ?" For example, ABC-TV's Sam Donaldson is well known for his ability to goad subjects into saying headline-making statements using this technique.

7. If the reporter asks a direct question, give an equally direct answer. Feeling pressure to say something more than what is called for by a question is a common error. If the appropriate answer is "yes" or "no," give the correct response and say no more. Some reporters will remain silent after getting an answer in hopes that the subject will volunteer more information. Assume that the camera is on at all times; otherwise the unguarded comment will be the sound bite on the evening news! Media adviser Roger Ailes's rule of thumb is that the tougher the question, the shorter the answer should be.

8. If spokespersons do not know the answer to a question, they should simply say, "I don't know, but I'll get the answer for you." This is a commit-

ment to follow through by providing the information as quickly as possible. Better yet, prepare for the interview by anticipating what questions will be asked, by developing succinct answers, and by rehearsing with someone playing the role of the reporter.

9. Tell the truth, even if it hurts. Do not think for a moment that bad news will go away or that the media will miss it. Treat it as you would any other story: Prepare as if it were good news and take it to the media. Not only does that mean that you will keep some control over the story and how it is covered, but it means that you are not on the defensive, making yourself vulnerable to charges of trying to hide the facts or of having been exposed by the media. This may be the most difficult position to sell to those in top management, who often see the practitioner's job as keeping bad news out of the media.

10. Do not call a press conference unless you have what reporters consider news. When is a news conference justified? Seldom. In fact, call a news conference only when there is no other means to get an important breaking story to the media in a timely fashion. Examples include important controversial matters such as labor–management disputes and settlements, important political announcements, and major policy changes affecting large numbers of people. The determining factor is the need to give reporters an opportunity to ask questions and pursue the story rather than simply issuing a statement or making an announcement. Complex matters that require backgrounding and detailed explanation, such as a technological breakthrough, may justify a press conference. Simple, straightforward, or noncontroversial announcements rarely justify the expense and effort of media coverage. And finally, if you do call a press conference, follow the suggestions outlined in steps 1 through 9.[65]

These suggestions can help practitioners build and maintain good relations with those in the news media. Because of the crucial gatekeeper role played by reporters and editors in both print and broadcast media, practitioners have little choice but to earn and keep the respect of journalists in the news media. At the same time, although the public has a right to *public information*, there are limits. Some information is confidential, and some information cannot be disclosed because of individual privacy. Knowing how to keep control of the agenda when dealing with the press is part of the media training required for all those acting as spokespersons.

In the final analysis, however, the practitioner–journalist relationship is an adversarial relationship. After being accused of doing something immoral by teaching people how to deal with the press, Roger Ailes told a journalism seminar:

> We always advise our clients to tell the truth. But the thing that disturbs me most is that you are here in journalism school learning how to ask the questions, yet you would deny a person the right to learn how to answer those questions.[66]

Part of the motivation for giving managers media training is that the top executives in many organizations are public figures without training or experience in dealing with this aspect of their public life. Some have suggested that the CEOs are obliged to deal with the media and face the public when their organizations make important decisions or are involved in crises that have impact beyond the organization. This obligation applies to leaders in corporations, nonprofit agencies, health and health care organizations, educational institutions, government, and all other organizations concerned about their relationships with publics.

Because a free press plays a central role in our free society, this is the era of the media-savvy top executive. Media training designed to help executives deal directly with the press is a responsibility of the public relations department and an essential investment in maintaining good media relations.

NOTES

1. Walter Lippmann, *Public Opinion* (New York: Harcourt, Brace and Company, 1922), 354.
2. James G. Webster, "Audience Behavior in the Media Environment," *Journal of Communication* 36, no. 3 (Summer 1986): 83.
3. John V. Pavlik, *New Media and the Information Superhighway* (Boston: Allyn & Bacon, 1996): 6.
4. Donald K. Wright (Principal Investigator), *Corporate Communications Policy Concerning the Internet: A Survey of the Nation's Senior-Level Corporate Public Relations Officers* (Gainesville, FL: The Institute for Public Relations Research and Education, 1998).
5. Bianco P. Floyd, "Profile," *The Chronicle of Higher Education,* April 10, 1998, p. A38.
6. Byron Reeves and Clifford Nass, *The Media Equation: How People Treat Computers, Television, and New Media Like Real People and Places* (Cambridge, UK: Cambridge University Press, 1996): 251.
7. Lisa Guernsey, "U. of Georgia Decides That Rejecting Applicants on Line (*sic*) Is "Too Cold," *The Chronicle of Higher Education,* April 10, 1998, p. A36.
8. Nicholas Negroponte, *Being Digital* (New York: Vintage Books, 1995): 83–85.
9. I. Jeanne Dugan, "New-Media Meltdown," *Business Week,* March 23, 1998, p. 11.
10. Paul Recer, "Web pages number 320 million; search engines overwhelmed," *The San Diego Union-Tribune,* April 3, 1998.
11. "Web Site Story," *Public Relations Tactics* 3, no. 8 (August 1996): 3.
12. Alvie L. Smith in letter to authors, March 28, 1993.
13. Alvie L. Smith, "Getting Managers Off Their Butts and into the Communication Game," *Communication World* 9, no. 1 (January 1992): 35.
14. Christopher Eschar, "Innovative New Strategies Enhance Employee Relations," *PRSSA Forum* 23, no. 3 (Spring 1991): 4.
15. Linda Grant, "The Ascent of Delta," *Los Angeles Times Magazine,* June 16, 1991, pp. 17–19, 32–33.
16. *pr reporter* 35, no. 50 (December 21, 1992): 1 and 3.
17. T. Michael Forney, "The New Communication Technology," *Public Relations Journal* 38, no. 3 (March 1982): 22.
18. Gene Goltz, "Making Harmony with House Organs," *Presstime* 13, no. 2 (February 1991): 33.

19. Michael Finley, "The New Meaning of Meetings," *Communication World* 8, no. 4 (March 1991): 25.

20. *The Executive Speechmaker: A Systems Approach* (New York: Foundation for Public Relations Research and Education, 1980).

21. Alvie L. Smith, *Innovative Employee Communication: New Approaches to Improving Trust, Teamwork and Performance* (Englewood Cliffs, NJ: Prentice-Hall, 1991), 147. This must-read for those interested in employee communication details the Federal Express case and many other examples by former GM director of corporate communications.

22. Ibid., 145.

23. Don Costa, "Winning with a Short-Subject Film," *Public Relations Journal* 38, no. 9 (September 1982): 24–26.

24. Frank Mankiewicz, "From Lippmann to Letterman: The 10 Most Powerful Voices," in "The Opinion Makers," special issue of *Gannett Center Journal* 3, no. 2 (Spring 1989): 96.

25. John C. Merrill, "Global Elite: A Newspaper Community of Reason," in "World Media," special issue of *Gannett Center Journal* 4, no. 4 (Fall 1990): 93.

26. Ibid., 101.

27. Stacey Frank Kanihan and Steven H. Chaffee, "Situational Influence of Political Involvement on Information Seeking: A Field Experiment." Paper presented to the Annual Convention of the Association for Education in Journalism and Mass Communication, Anaheim, CA, August 1996, p. 28.

28. Facts About Newspapers 1998, published by Newspaper Association of America, Vienna, VA (www.naa.org).

29. Ibid.

30. A. Carlos Ruotolo, "A Typology of Newspaper Readers," *Journalism Quarterly* 65, no. 1 (Spring 1988): 126–30.

31. Facts About Newspapers 1998.

32. Mary Jane Genova, "Op-ed Articles Express Client's Point of View," *Public Relations Journal* 47, no. 9 (September 1991): 35.

33. Shirley Biagi, *Media/Impact: An Introduction to Mass Media,* 2d ed. (Belmont, CA: Wadsworth Publishing Company, 1992): 82–83.

34. *pr reporter* 34, no. 8 (February 25, 1991): 4

35. According to Professor Joseph V. Trahan in a presentation to the New Mexico Public Relations Society of America Professional Development Seminar, Albuquerque, January 29, 1993. Trahan, also a major in the U.S. Army Reserves, coordinated on-site press relations for federal agencies responding to the Hurricane Andrew crisis.

36. Keith Elliot Greenberg, "Radio News Releases Make the Hit Parade," *Public Relations Journal* 48, no. 7 (July 1992): 6.

37. Ibid.

38. Charles Price, "ATTACK of the Radio Talk-Show Hosts," *California Journal* 20, no. 9 (September 1989): 366.

39. Newton N. Minow, "How Vast the Wasteland Now?" Address given at the Gannett Foundation Media Center (Now Freedom Forum Center for Media Studies), Columbia University, New York City, May 9, 1991 (the 30th anniversary of Minow's "Vast Wasteland" speech to the National Association of Broadcasters).

40. Hans-Bernd Brosius and Hans Mathias Kepplinger, "Beyond Agenda-Setting: The Influence of Partisanship and Television Reporting on the Electorate's Voting Intentions," *Journalism Quarterly* 69, no. 4 (Winter 1992): 893–901.

41. Minow, "How Vast the Wasteland Now?"
42. Robert MacNeil, *The Right Place at the Right Time* (Boston: Little, Brown, 1982), 129.
43. Adam Clayton Powell III, "The Global TV News Hour," in "World Media" issue of *Gannett Center Journal* 4, no. 4 (Fall 1990): 119.
44. Michael Curtain, "Packaging Reality: The Influence of Fictional Forms on the Early Development of Television Documentary," *Journalism Monographs* 137 (February 1993): 19.
45. Michael Parenti, *Inventing Reality: The Politics of the Mass Media* (New York: St. Martin's Press, 1986), 9–10.
46. David Lieberman, "Fake News," *TV Guide 40,* no. 8 (February 22, 1992), 10–14, 16, and 26.
47. K. Tim Wulfemeyer and Lowell Frazier, "The Ethics of Video News Releases: A Qualitative Analysis," *Journal of Mass Media Ethics* 7, no. 3 (1992): 151–68.
48. "Ten Tips on How to Get Your VNR Aired," *Communication World* 9, no. 9 (September 1992): 10.
49. Adam Shell, "VNRs: In the News," *Public Relations Journal* 48, no. 12 (December 1992): 21.
50. Patrick Mott, "New King of the Hill," *The Quill* 79, no. 2 (March 1991): 14–16.
51. "Wireless City," *The Futurist* 27, no. 2 (March–April 1993): 5.
52. Information about cable trends and developments, such as those reported here, are extensively reported in the weekly trade journal *Cable World,* Cable World Associates, 1905 Sherman Street, Suite 1000, Denver, CO 80203. Other sources include *Broadcasting* (weekly trade journal), 1735 DeSales Street, N.W., Washington, DC 20036, and *Journal of Broadcasting* (quarterly research journal), Ohio State University, Columbus, OH 43210.
53. "Inquiry: Press Can't Have the Right to Lie," *USA Today,* November 4, 1983, p. 11A.
54. Herbert Schmertz, "The Press and Morality." Remarks to Guild Hall Discussion Series, East Hampton, NY, July 12, 1983.
55. Stephen Aubin, "The B-2 and Network News: A Case Study in Media Distortion." Report published by the Aerospace Education Foundation (an affiliate of the Air Force Association), Arlington, VA, January 1991, p. 1.
56. "Flack Attack: The Post Spurns P.R. 'Wolves,' " *Time,* May 10, 1982, p. 101; and Carl Cannon, "The Great Flack Flap," *Washington Journalism Review* 4 (September 1982): 35.
57. Judy VanSlyke Turk, "Information Subsidies and Media Content: A Study of Public Relations Influence on the News," *Journalism Monographs* 100 (December 1986): 26–27.
58. Michael Ryan and David L. Martinson, "Journalists and Public Relations Practitioners: Why the Antagonism?" *Journalism Quarterly* 65, no. 1 (Spring 1988): 139.
59. Mark S. Cox, "Media Relations and the Content of Business News" (Master of Science in Mass Communication thesis, San Diego State University, May 1983).
60. H. J. Dalton Jr., personal letter and enclosure—"50 Basic Thoughts on Good News Media Relations" (presentation to Veterans Administration public affairs training seminar).
61. Ibid.
62. Paul McMasters, "Journalists Aren't Winning Their Gulf War," *The Quill* 79, no. 2 (March 1991): 8. See also Richard Zoglin, "The Press: It Was a Public Relations Rout Too," *Time,* March 11, 1991, pp. 56–57.

63. "News Is Stacked Up at *Wall St. Journal,*" *Jack O'Dwyer's Newsletter,* August 26, 1992, p. 4.
64. Chester Burger, "Phony Communication Is Worse Than None at All." Arthur W. Page Society Hall of Fame induction speech, Amelia Island, FL, September 23, 1992.
65. Adapted from Roger Ailes (with Jon Kraushar), *You Are the Message: Secrets of the Master Communicators* (Homewood, IL: Dow Jones-Irwin, 1988); Chester Burger, "How to Meet the Press," *Harvard Business Review,* July–August 1975; Christel K. Beard and H. J. Dalton Jr., "The Power of Positive Press," *Sales and Marketing Management,* January 1991: 37–43; and Dalton, "50 Basic Thoughts on Good News Media Relations."
66. Ailes, *You Are the Message,* 165.

ADDITIONAL SOURCES

Grunig, James E. "Symmetrical Systems of Internal Communication." In *Excellence in Public Relations and Communication Management,* edited by James E. Grunig, 531–75. Hillsdale, NJ: Lawrence Erlbaum Associates, 1992. Grunig concludes that internal communication does increase employee job satisfaction if the system is designed as a symmetrical, information-sharing system.

Hickson, Mark III, and Don W. Stacks. *Organizational Communication in the Personal Context.* Needham Heights, MA: Allyn & Bacon, 1998. Outlines role of communication in organization, tracing the function from the employee's perspective "from interview to retirement."

Howard, Carole, and Wilma Mathews. *On Deadline: Managing Media Relations,* 2nd ed. Prospect Heights, IL: Waveland Press, 1994. Summarizes how to deal with reporters, prepare spokespersons, and other aspects of making media relations effective.

Hudson, Howard Penn. *Publishing Newsletters,* 3rd ed. Rhinebeck, NY: H&M Publishers, 1997. Remains the classic reference on how to produce effective newsletters, from the publisher of the *Newsletter on Newsletters.*

Johnson, Melissa A. "Public Relations and Technology: Practitioner Perspectives." *Journal of Public Relations Reseach* 9, no. 3 (1997): 213–36. Reports study of how new communication technologies affect public relations roles and work.

Shaw, Donald L. "The Rise and Fall of American Mass Media: Roles of Technology and Leadership." Roy W. Howard Public Lecture in Journalism and Mass Communication Research 2 (April 4, 1991), School of Journalism, Indiana University, Bloomington. Traces the evolution of major media, concluding that media never regain the dominant position once it is lost. Rather, media innovate to find ways to better serve a loyal audience and develop new users.

Shoemaker, Pamela J., and Stephen D. Reese. *Mediating the Message: Theories of Influences on Mass Media Content.* New York: Longman, 1991. Reviews research on the various influences on media content, including the impact of media professionals, media routines, organizational factors, outside sources, and ideological perspectives.

Weaver, David H., and G. Cleveland Wilhoit. *The American Journalist: A Portrait of U.S. News People and Their Work.* 2d ed. Bloomington: Indiana University Press, 1991.

Willis, Jim. *Journalism: State of the Art.* New York: Praeger Publishers, 1990. Synthesizes scholarly research on journalists, their work settings, their ethics, their relationships with news sources, and their decision-making processes. Written for those who would probably not chose to read the original scholarly reports.

www.nua.ie/surveys/ Internet newsletter published by one of Europe's leading Internet consultancies and developers—Nua. Reports current news, statistics, and international developments.

STEP ONE: DEFINING PUBLIC RELATIONS PROBLEMS

The old "flying by the seat of the pants" approach to solving public relations problems is over.

—*Edward J. Robinson*

OBJECTIVES

After studying chapter 10, you should be able to

▼ Outline the four-step problem-solving process as it applies to public relations.

▼ Define research, identify its major purpose as reducing uncertainty in decision making, and discuss why it is essential in public relations program management.

▼ Describe the attributes of a useful problem statement.

▼ Differentiate between informal ("exploratory") and formal methods of research, giving examples of both.

Dr. Edward Robinson wrote the obituary for the "seat-of-the-pants" approach to doing public relations in 1969. He saw the public relations practitioner as "an applied social and behavioral scientist" using "research to help in the problem solving process." He may have been a bit premature in his assessment, however, when he wrote this in the first public relations research book. Intuitive, individualistic approaches to problem solving often still guide the practice in many settings, even though, as Robinson wrote, research is "the most powerful tool available to the applied practitioner."[1]

The open systems approach discussed in chapter 7 combines rational problem solving and proactive strategic planning. From its origins as the art of reacting to outside threats, public relations has evolved to an applied science. No longer do hunches, gut feelings, and personal experiences, alone or in combination, serve as an adequate basis for public relations programs. And rarely do top managers or clients accept a practitioner's recommendations or simple assertions that a program was successful on faith alone.

MANAGEMENT PROCESS

In its most advanced form, public relations is a scientifically managed part of an organization's problem-solving and change processes. Practitioners of this type of public relations use theory and the best available evidence in a four-step problem-solving process:

1. Defining the problem (or opportunity). This first step involves probing and monitoring knowledge, opinions, attitudes, and behaviors of those concerned with and affected by the acts and policies of an organization. In essence, this is an organization's intelligence function. It provides the foundation for all the other steps in the problem-solving process by determining "What's happening now?"

2. Planning and programming. Information gathered in the first step is used to make decisions about program publics, objectives, action and communication strategies, tactics, and goals. This involves factoring the findings from the first step into the policies and programs of the organization. This second step in the process answers, "Based on what we have learned about the situation, what should we change or do, and say?"

3. Taking action and communicating. The third step involves implementing the program of action and communication designed to achieve the specific objectives for each of the publics to accomplish the program goal. The questions in this step are, "Who should do and say it, and when, where, and how?"

4. Evaluating the program. The final step in the process involves assessing the preparation, implementation, and results of the program. Adjustments are made while the program is being implemented, based on evaluation feedback on how it is or is not working. Programs are continued or stopped after learning, "How are we doing, or how did we do?"

Each step is as important as the others, but the process begins with gathering intelligence to diagnose the problem. Information and understanding developed in the first step motivate and guide subsequent steps in the process. In practice, of course, diagnosis, planning, implementation, and evaluation cannot be so neatly compartmentalized, because the process is continuous and cyclical and is applied in a dynamic setting. Figure 10.1 illustrates the continuous, overlapping, and cyclical nature of public relations problem solving.

How an oil company's public relations staff managed a problem situation some years ago illustrates the four-step process. The company decided to close one of its sales divisions as part of a reorganization to increase efficiency. This meant that 600 employees would have to move or find new jobs, the community where the division was located would suffer economic loss, customers of the sales division would be concerned about getting equally good service under the new setup, and investors would be curious about the meaning of the move.

The first task was to marshal all the facts through research so that the move could be explained and justified in terms of those concerned. The next step was to plan the announcement. Timing was important. The news had to be broken swiftly, before rumors started, released simultaneously to all those affected, and communicated in such a way as to explain satisfactorily the necessity and wisdom of the change.

Materials included a procedure memorandum to guide the staff, a presentation script for meetings, letters to several different groups of employees, letters to all dealers, a news release, a statement on banking arrangements for community banks, a general office letter, and plans for meetings. The news

FIGURE 10.1   FOUR-STEP PUBLIC RELATIONS PROCESS

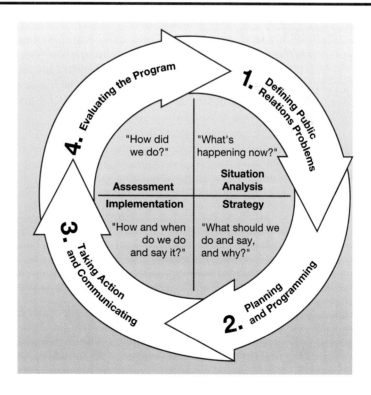

was released in a coordinated program of meetings, letters, and media coverage. Finally, evaluation focused on the department's original assessment of the problem situation, the techniques used, and the reactions of those affected, with an eye to improving procedures. The lessons learned were put to good use a few years later when the company closed a plant in another location, demonstrating how systematic research and evaluation improves the practice over time.

Obviously, this is an oversimplified presentation of what actually happened. The process includes many smaller steps within each of the four major steps represented in the model. These will be outlined in greater detail in this and the next three chapters. In this chapter we will concentrate on the research and fact-finding methods necessary for beginning the strategic planning process.

ROLE OF RESEARCH IN STRATEGIC PLANNING

Monitoring the social environment is not only the first step in the process; it is the most difficult one. One is reminded of the fable of the elephant and the six blind men of Indostan: Each encounters only a single part of the beast and describes the elephant based on that limited information. For example, the one who grabs the trunk concludes, "The Elephant is very like a snake!" The one who feels the knee says, "'Tis clear enough the Elephant is very like a tree!" This process continues, with each experiencing only a portion of the elephant. In the end, each was partly right and mostly wrong about the nature of the beast but argued "loud and long" based on his respective encounter with the elephant.[2] Without researching a problem situation, practitioners run the risk of acting like the six blind men from Indostan.

Surveys of practitioners routinely show that research training tops the list of needed professional continuing education. Surveys also show that practitioners often say that they do not do more research because they lack funds and have too little time. A better explanation of why so little research is used in public relations, however, is a combination of (1) not understanding how to do and use research and (2) many employers' and clients' views that research is not necessary. While in college, few practitioners studied research methods or anticipated that research would be part of their professional work. Once they began professional practice, they felt little pressure from employers and clients, who often did not demand or fund research. As one corporate public relations executive responded in a Ketchum Public Relations survey, "The problem is not with research methodology, but with the inability—or perhaps laziness—of PR professionals who prefer to fly by the seats of their pants."[3]

For years, executives and practitioners alike bought the popular myth that public relations deals with intangibles that cannot be measured. With each passing day it becomes increasingly difficult to sell that position to results-oriented management (many with MBA degrees) accustomed to making decisions based on evidence and objective analysis. A practitioner in a nonprofit organization attributes "the decline of PR . . . to the lack of monitoring and substantive evaluation of results. That's why PR is seen by CEO's as 'fluff.' "[4]

Without research, practitioners are limited to asserting that they know the situation and can recommend a solution. With research and analysis, they can present and advocate proposals supported by evidence and theory. In this context, research is the systematic gathering of information to describe and understand situations and to check out assumptions about publics and public relations consequences. It is the scientific alternative to tenacity, authority, and intuition. Its main purpose is to reduce uncertainty in decision making. Even though it cannot answer all the questions or sway all decisions, methodical, systematic research is the foundation of effective public relations.

RESEARCH ATTITUDE

Computers and management information specialists have greatly increased organizations' abilities to gather, process, transfer, and interpret information. The increase in MBA-prepared, information-conscious middle and upper managers intensifies the pressure on public relations for accountability. In short, a research orientation is necessary for those practicing public relations in the information age. An early researcher who helped build the automotive industry, C. F. Kettering, once described this attitude toward research in these words:

> Research is a high-hat word that scares a lot of people. It need not. It is rather simple. Essentially, it is nothing but a state of mind—a friendly, welcoming attitude toward change. Going out to look for change, instead of waiting for it to come. Research . . . is an effort to do things better and not be caught asleep at the switch. The research state of mind can apply to anything. Personal affairs or any kind of business, big or little. It is the problem-solving mind as contrasted with the let-well-enough-alone mind. It is the composer mind, instead of the fiddler mind; it is the "tomorrow" mind instead of the "yesterday" mind.[5]

Research is no longer a specialized activity delegated to "chi-square types" tucked away in the bowels of an organization. As Rossi and Freeman put it, "It is also a political and management activity, an input into the complex mosaic from which policy decisions and allocations emerge for the planning, design, implementation, and continuation of programs."[6]

Modern managers are a fact-minded lot; they want figures. In many organizations, these executives tend to be isolated from problems by cadres of specialists and subordinates. When the public relations aspect of organizational problems must be brought home to them, the research-based approach is most effective. As other parts of organizations such as marketing, finance, and personnel have adapted a research-based approach, so must public relations. In fact, research findings suggest a strong linkage between doing research and earning one of the few seats at the management strategy table. Studies of practitioners show that participation in management increases when practitioners do research.[7]

LISTENING AS SYSTEMATIC RESEARCH

Effective public relations starts with listening, which requires openness and systematic effort. Too often, what purports to be communication is simply opposing ideas passing each other in different one-way channels, for example, in a management-versus-labor bargaining situation with each side merely wanting to score points, not listening to the other's views. As Wilbur Schramm explained, "Feedback is a powerful tool. When it does not exist or is delayed or feeble . . . then the situation engenders doubt and concern in the communicator, and frustration and sometimes hostility in the audience."[8] Also using his words, "Feedback tells the communicator how his message is being received."[9]

Listening is not an easy task. Channels from the worker out in the plant or from the alumnus in Seattle must be created and kept open. Failure to listen often leads to purposeless "communications" on issues that do not exist to publics that are not there. Unless you know the orientation, predisposition, and language of your audience—learned through empathetic listening—you are not likely to communicate effectively. Research is simply one method of structuring systematic listening into the communication process. (See Exhibit 10.1.)

An able listener of another time, Abraham Lincoln, knew the importance of listening. Twice a week, Lincoln set aside a time for conversations with ordinary folk: housewives, farmers, merchants, and pension seekers. He listened patiently to what they had to say, no matter how humble their circumstances or how trivial their business. A military aide once protested to the president that he was wasting valuable time on these unimportant people. Lincoln rebuked him, saying, "I tell you, Major . . . that I call these receptions my public opinion bath . . . the effect, as a whole is renovating and invigorating."[10] Today the White House has sophisticated and elaborate methods for monitoring constituent opinion: daily analyses of media and mail content, sophisticated telephone voice mail tabulations of calls, as well as regular polling of public opinion.

Prudence dictates the systematic listening to an organization's publics through scientific research. Yet many organizations fail to utilize this public relations tool fully. In some, two-way communication is seen as organized back talk and a potential threat, rather than an essential tool of modern management. More likely, systematic listening to obtain reliable feedback is limited because it takes effort and skill. The amount of information input, however, determines the extent to which an organization operates as an open rather than a closed system in dealing with problems.

DEFINING PUBLIC RELATIONS PROBLEMS

In closed systems, of course, problems are allowed to define themselves, often as crises. The public relations effort then necessarily reverts into "fire fighting" rather than "fire prevention." Examples include spending millions of dollars to counter proposals made by dissident stockholders; paying millions of

EXHIBIT 10.1

WALTER BARLOW ON RESEARCH AS LISTENING

At the end of a meeting with the CEO of a large corporation some years ago, he asked me, "Son, tell me, just what kind of 'racket' are you in?"

I replied, "Well, if you will let me ask a few questions, I think I can demonstrate what I do, but I warn you, the questions might cause you to throw me out of this office."

"Go ahead," he said.

"Well, how much of your business day would you say is spent in communication of some sort—having a conversation like this, attending meetings and conferences, reading reports, calling on the phone, and all the rest?"

He thought for a moment and replied, "You have pretty much described how I spend all of my time. I'm either communicating in some way, preparing for it, or seriously thinking about it."

That warmed me up a bit, because I felt safe to proceed. "Well, you have just told me that your time, valued at about $800,000 in salary last year, is spent in the *process* of communication. Now, tell me, in this communicating, do you do all the talking?"

He smiled right away, "Of course not!"

"Would you say that you spend, say, 40 percent of your communicating time in listening, or taking in information in some way?"

"That would probably be about right. I know I talk a lot, but I do listen too."

"Suppose I had asked the top fifty executives in your company the same question, do you think I would have gotten agreement on at least 40 percent?"

Again, he replied immediately, "I damned well hope you would."

"Now, we have established something else, and that is that you allocate around $320,000 of your base salary to the process of listening, and if I multiplied that 40 percent times the salaries of the fifty others, we would have a figure in the millions."

He was now totally absorbed in the interchange. "Yes, I see. I had never thought of it that way."

Here I had a chance to move in with the clincher: "Well, I happen to know that your advertising budget is in the neighborhood of $35 million, and if we added in all the other corporate 'talking,' we would certainly come up with a figure over $100 million." I had his total attention now.

"And just how much does your corporation spend in listening? Is it any wonder that from time to time you must feel that nobody really understands you?"

I did not get an answer to the question, because the point had been made: whatever listening was going on had to be a tiny fraction of the talking, a situation he would never have brooked in his personal corporate life.

"Well, corporations like yours can't listen like you're doing now. The only way we have found yet to do that is through scientifically planned research. It can reflect back to you how people are reacting to the corporate talking you do in so many ways.

"And that is the racket I am in: helping corporations close the loop and listen to their constituencies."

Courtesy Walter G. Barlow, President, Research Strategies Corporation, Princeton, NJ.

dollars for advertising time and space to apologize for past actions and to announce corrective measures; and suffering costly construction delays because active citizen groups resorted to legal action to stop proposed, yet unexplained, projects.

Such situations have long histories, and sometimes neither side recalls what caused the blowup. Heading off such blowups is part of the task. The earlier a complaint is caught, the easier it is to handle. Continuous fact-finding uncovers many problems while they are still small enough to permit corrective action and communication before becoming major public issues. The same attentive listening catches rumors before they become widespread and part of the public's perceptions of the organization.

Problem definition begins with someone making a value judgment that something is either wrong, could soon be, or could be better. Implicit is the notion that organizational goals provide the criteria for making such judgments. Goal states serve as the basis for deciding if and when a real or potential problem exists. Once a judgment is made, however, the process becomes an objective, systematic research task designed to describe in detail the dimensions of the problem, the factors contributing to or alleviating the problem, and the publics involved in or affected by the situation. In short, research is used to determine "What's happening now?"

Problem Statement

A useful problem statement summarizes what was learned about the problem situation: (1) It is written in the present tense, describing the current situation. (2) It describes the situation in specific and measurable terms, detailing most of or all of the following:

What is the source of concern?
Where is this a problem?
When is it a problem?
Who is involved or affected?
How are they involved or affected?
Why is this a concern to the organization and its publics?

(3) A problem statement does not imply solution or place blame. If it did, program strategies would be predetermined and limited, much like the cuttlefish's limited options for responding to its environment. The classic example of a problem statement that has an implied solution is the overused, "What we have here is a communication problem." Communication is part of the solution, not the problem!

The real problem could be that only 5 percent of new graduates join the alumni association during the first year following graduation, compared with 21 percent of all graduates, resulting in lost contact and reduced support for the university. Or in the case of a fund-raising effort for a new youth center, the problem could be stated as, the building fund is $200,000 short of the amount needed to complete and equip the new gymnasium by the planned June 1 opening. If you had worked for one of the major oil companies several years ago, you might have been concerned about the "divestiture problem": A plurality (47 percent) of Americans agree with proposals to break up each of the major oil companies into four separate and competing operating companies, thus encouraging some in Congress to vote in favor of divestiture legislation.

Notice that each of these problem statements contains concrete measures of the problem situation based on objective research and documentation. Notice also that solutions are not implied, meaning that no particular strategy is suggested in any of the problem statements. In other words, communication may be part of the solution, but it is not stated as part of the problem. Finally, notice that the three examples describe the current situation—"What's happening now?"—not the future.

Situation Analysis

A problem statement represents a concise description of the situation, often written in a sentence or short paragraph. In contrast, a situation analysis is the unabridged collection of all that is known about the situation, its history, forces operating on it, and those involved or affected internally and externally. A situation analysis contains all the background information needed to expand upon and to illustrate in detail the meaning of a problem statement. In the process of analyzing the situation, one is able to clearly and specifically define and refine the problem statement. Typically, the definition process begins with a tentative problem statement, followed by investigation of the situation, which leads to refining the problem definition, and so on. The situation analysis results in what some practitioners call their "fact book," often in the form of information assembled in three-ring binders or files.

The section on *internal factors* deals with organizational policies, procedures, and actions related to the problem situation. Rather than direct all the attention to the publics and other external factors, a situation analysis begins with a thorough and searching review of perceptions and actions of key actors in the organization, structures and processes of organizational units relevant to the problem and the history of the organization's involvement.

The internal situation analysis also includes a "communication audit"—a systematic documentation of an organization's communications for the purpose of understanding how it communicates with its publics. One practitioner describes the communication audit as follows:

> A complete analysis of an organization's communications—internal and/or external designed to "take a picture" of communication needs, policies, practices, and capabilities, and to uncover necessary data to allow top management to make informed, economical decisions about future objectives of the organization's communication.[11]

Consistent with the open systems model, practitioners do an audit to learn in detail how, what, and to whom they communicate. An audit provides decision makers a clear picture of what is currently done and a basis for deciding what changes need to be made.

Another essential part of the internal portion of a situation analysis is a constantly updated organizational almanac. This file not only serves as an essential organizational background reference when working on specific problems but also provides ideas and information for speeches, pamphlets, special reports, exhibits, and media requests. Most organizations do not have librarians or historians, so public relations departments often handle queries that cannot be answered by others. Journalists expect and need quick answers. Ready access to complete and accurate information on an organization, its history, performance, and managers can give the public relations department a start on crises or rumors in the making.

After developing an understanding of the organizational side of the problem situation, an analysis focuses on the *external factors,* both positive and negative. The starting point may be a systematic review of the history of the problem situation outside the organization. A situation analysis also calls for detailed study of who is currently involved or affected and how. Much of what is done under the banner of public relations research includes gathering information about *stakeholders:* what they know, how they feel, and what they do that is related to the problem.

"Stakeholder analysis" is the process of identifying who is involved and who is affected in a situation. Stakeholders are *people*—in the imagery of system theory—who are part of the same system as an organization. They are in interdependent relationships with an organization, meaning that what they know, feel, and do has impact on the organization and vice versa. In the interest of building and maintaining mutually beneficial relationships, organizations undertake periodic stakeholder analyses to monitor how organizational policies, procedures, decisions, actions, and goals affect others. The different stakeholder groups can be ranked or rated according to the extent to which each is interdependent with an organization in a particular problem situation. Notice that not all those identified as stakeholders necessarily become publics for a program designed to address a particular problem (more on defining publics in the next chapter).[12]

How could you set objectives for each of the publics if you do not know what they currently know, what their opinions are, and how they behave? How could you develop action and communication strategies without a detailed understanding of and empathy for the target publics? At least four additional questions must be answered through research:

1. How much do people use information in the problem situation? Communication is effective only if receivers see a need for information. The situation analysis research must determine to what extent different people actually feel a need for and use information related to a given problem situation.
2. What kinds of information do people use? Whereas "why" questions make up 20 to 35 percent of the questions people typically ask in situations, these are the ones least likely to be answered successfully in communication programs. Programs that respond to audience needs rather than the interests of the source are based on knowledge of what information different people want.

3. How do people use information? Information is rarely an end in itself, because people use information in many different ways. Receivers see information as useful if they think that it relates to a specific action, topic, or plan they consider important. Rarely are they helped simply because they received general information.
4. What predicts information use? Demographics or other cross-situational characteristics often do not predict how people use information. Rather, where receivers are in the decision-making process relevant to a problem, or how they see themselves in the situation, determines whether or not they will use the information. In other words, you must know how different individuals see themselves involved in or affected by the situation.[13]

The importance of situation-specific understanding of stakeholders is also evident in VanLeuven's theory of message and media selection: "(1) the user selects media and messages for his or her own rational-appearing and personally relevant purposes; (2) the user will attach his or her own personal meanings to a selected message; (3) the user's behavior reflects anticipated future communication satisfaction as well as a history of prior motivation, intentionality, and reinforcement."[14]

Researching the stakeholders before planning program strategies tests the accuracy of assumptions about who they are, what they know, how they feel about the situation, how they are involved or affected, what information they see as important, how they use it, and even how they get information. With that information in hand—and only then—can program planners write objectives for each public and develop strategies to achieve them.

Systematic definition and study of the stakeholders is needed also to determine an order of priority. Rarely does a practitioner have the staff or money to mount programs directed to all stakeholders. Priorities must be assigned based on which of them are most central to the particular problem at hand, not in response to internal or external pressures not related to the problem situation.

Increased understanding of the stakeholders helps determine their information needs and uses: message content. Researching their communication patterns and media preferences helps practitioners select the most effective and efficient media strategy for delivering those messages.

Only after the situation has been completely analyzed can practitioners set realistic program goals. Lacking complete and accurate information, practitioners can be guilty of overpromises and underdelivery. Without a complete understanding of the problem situation, practitioners run the risk of developing programs that do not address the major causes of the problem. No amount of public relations communication can change bad performance into good performance or socially irresponsible action into responsible behavior. Neither can it compensate for lack of integrity or persuade publics that an unfair or self-serving policy is fair and unselfish. Overenthusiastic selling of the function often results from incomplete comprehension of the problem situation and leads to the appearance of program failure.

Researching the situation gives practitioners and their employers and clients the timely, complete, and accurate information they need to understand the problem and to serve as a basis for decision making. (Exhibit 10.2 lists topics covered in a situation analysis.) Research is simply an attempt to reduce uncertainty, or as one executive put it, "to help really see what's there to be seen."

Detailed analyses of the internal and external factors in the problem situation provide practitioners with the information they need to assess organiza-

---

EXHIBIT 10.2

CONTENT OF SITUATION ANALYSIS

I. Internal Factors

1. Statements of the organization's mission, charter, bylaws, history, and structure
2. Lists, biographies, and photos of key officers, board members, managers, and so forth
3. Descriptions and histories of programs, products, services, and so forth
4. Statistics about resources, budget, staffing, sales, profits, stockholders, and so forth
5. Policy statements and procedures related to the problem situation
6. Position statements (quotations) by key executives regarding the problem situation
7. Description of how the organization currently handles the problem situation
8. Descriptions and lists of the organization's internal stakeholders
9. Lists of organizational media (two-way) for communicating with internal groups

II. External Factors

1. Clippings from newspaper, magazine, trade publication, and newsletter coverage of the organization and the problem situation
2. Reports, transcripts, and tapes of radio, television, and cable coverage
3. Content analyses of media coverage and Internet sources
4. Lists of media, journalists, columnists, talk-show hosts, freelance writers, and producers who report news and features about the organization and issues related to the problem situation
5. Lists of and background information on individuals and groups who share the organization's concerns, interests, and positions on the problem situation (including their controlled internal and external media outlets)
6. Lists of and background information on individuals and groups who oppose the organization's concerns, interests, and positions on the problem situation (including their controlled internal and external media outlets)
7. Results of surveys and public opinion polls related to the organization and the problem situation
8. Schedules of special events, observances, and other important dates related to the organization and the problem situation
9. Lists of government agencies, legislators, and other officials with regulatory and legislative power affecting the organization and the problem situation
10. Copies of relevant regulations, legislation, pending bills, referenda, government publications, and hearing reports
11. Copies of published research on topics related to the problem situation
12. Lists of important reference books, records, and directories, as well as their locations in the organization

---

tional strengths (S) and weaknesses (W) and to identify the opportunities (O) and threats (T) in the external environment. In practice, practitioners refer to this approach to summarizing the situation analysis as "SWOT" or "TOWS" analysis. Several strategic implications logically flow from this analytic framework:

1. SO strategies build on organizational strengths to take advantage of opportunities in the external environment.
2. ST strategies also build on organizational strengths to counter threats in the external environment.
3. WO strategies attempt to minimize organizational weaknesses to take advantage of external opportunities.
4. WT strategies attempt to minimize both organizational weaknesses and environmental threats.[15]

Another analytic technique for summarizing the findings of a situation analysis is "force-field analysis." Before researching the situation, practitioners and others on the management team brainstorm the negative forces contributing to or causing the problem, as well as the positive forces alleviating or solving the problem. The research on the internal and external forces helps determine the extent to which each contributes positively or negatively to the problem situation. Just as with SWOT analysis, the results of a force-field analysis lead to strategic decisions designed to minimize or neutralize the impact of negative forces and to maximize or enhance the contributions from positive forces.[16]

RESEARCH PROCESS

The central roles of research in modern public relations, addressed further in chapter 13, are demonstrated here. Sometimes practitioners do the research themselves. Other times practitioners hire research specialists or research firms to design the research, gather the information, or analyze the data. In either approach, practitioners must know the research process and concepts. Simply put, you cannot satisfactorily explain to someone else something you do not understand yourself. Ann H. Barkelew, senior vice president and general manager of Fleishman-Hillard's Minneapolis office, says, "You cannot practice public relations today—successfully or effectively—without research."[17]

Scientists have developed a generally accepted approach to research. The process begins with a clear statement of the problem under investigation. Some choose to phrase the problem in the form of a question. Others pose hypothetical relationships between observable phenomena for testing and theory building. The next step is to develop the research design, the plan for making the observations related to the research problem. Is a survey needed? An experiment? Or will the observations be taken from published census reports? This is followed by the specific methods for gathering, analyzing, and interpreting data.[18]

Whereas two research projects are seldom the same in the specifics of how they are implemented, they share a common goal of increasing our understanding of situations and society. The approach and methods chosen for a particular project will depend on the problem being addressed, the skills and preferences of the researcher, the available resources, and the constraints imposed by others or as a result of the situation.

INFORMAL OR "EXPLORATORY" METHODS

Informal methods still dominate public relations research even though highly developed social science methods are available. Informal methods can be useful, however, if practitioners recognize their weaknesses and purposes. The major problem—samples of unknown representativeness—results from how samples are selected. The issue is the extent to which the results from samples represent anybody other than the few from whom information was gathered. For example, the results may represent only the opinions of a vocal minority rather than the majority.

If viewed as good methods for *detecting* and *exploring* problem situations and for pretesting research and program strategies, then informal methods serve valuable purposes. If the results are used as the basis for program planning and evaluation as if the findings were representative of target publics, then these methods are misused. "Exploratory" best represents the probing nature of informal methods.

The following sections describe some of the informal methods used in public relations.

Personal Contacts

In 1893 Lord Bryce said, "The best way in which the tendencies at work in any community can be best discovered and estimated is by moving freely about among all sorts and conditions of men." Politicians have been doing this for a long time. Skill in sizing up people's awareness, opinions, and attitudes has long been and always will be a prime qualification of public relations professionals.

For example, when management requested an employee communication campaign against drug abuse, a corporate practitioner, posing as a patient, checked into a drug treatment center and spent three days acquiring firsthand knowledge about drugs, their use, and their potential effects on employees. Others have worked in wheelchairs to gain perspective on what it is like to go for coffee breaks, use the bathroom, or complete other tasks in facilities not designed for easy access. Trade shows, community and professional meetings, or other occasions that attract stakeholders provide opportunities for practitioners to listen carefully and gain understanding.

Feedback from periodic personal visits can be encouraged, extended, and amplified in many ways. For example, when the late Los Angeles Mayor Thomas Bradley first took office, he opened his door to local citizens one day a month. They were given a chance to talk to the mayor about poor sewer facilities, increases in school vandalism, or whatever was on their minds. The mayor of Utica, New York, went a step further. To encourage people to drop in and air their complaints, he took his door off its hinges and put up a sign over his couch that read, "The Town's Living Room." The president of Delta Airlines maintains an open-door policy for employees.

A more structured use of personal contacts is exemplified by the annual shareholder meetings held each year by publicly owned corporations. For example, managers in one company visited shareholders in their homes after business hours. Each year management personnel in various locations personally talked with shareholders about the company's business. In another aggressive approach to getting feedback, a state highway department used a travel trailer as a mobile information center to collect citizens' views on proposed highway projects. The trailer provided an atmosphere for candid one-on-one discussions with highway personnel and gave people who are reluctant to speak in public meetings an opportunity to air their views.

Key Informants

Practitioners commonly talk with key informants, a variation on personal contacts. This approach involves selecting and interviewing knowledgeable leaders and experts. The interview typically takes the form of an open-ended discussion in which selected individuals are encouraged to talk about the problem or issue in their own terms. Because in-depth interviews with key informants take so long to complete and require such careful content analysis, the technique is limited to a relatively small number of respondents.

Many practitioners regularly consult influential people such as authors, editors, reporters, ministers, labor leaders, professors, civic leaders, bankers, and special interest group leaders. Some have consulted bartenders and taxi drivers. The basis for selecting key informants is their perceived knowledge of an issue and their ability to represent others' views. The major limitation, of course, is that because they were selected purposely because they are seen to have special knowledge and leadership roles, by definition they do not reflect current views of followers. In-depth interviews with key informants often yield early warning signals on important issues.

Focus Groups and Community Forums

It is only a short step from personal contacts and key informants to asking groups for ideas and feedback. The range of groups runs from open town meetings, such as those used by the Clinton Administration, to the highly structured and videotaped focus group, a technique commonly used in both public relations and consumer marketing research. An effective moderator who is an able interviewer and facilitator of the group process is key to the success of this approach.

Practitioners use focus groups and community forums to explore how people will react to proposals and to gather information useful for developing questionnaires to be used in more formal research methods. Unexpected insights are gained from the sometimes spirited dialogue among participants.

Researchers call such information "serendipitous findings," but unanticipated reactions may be the best reason for using these informal research methods. It is better to learn such things before going to the field with a full-blown survey or program test.

For example, the United Soybean Board (USB) developed a fruitful variation of the community forum when it held a series of town hall meetings for soybean producers. An influential producer was asked to invite neighbors to hear presentations and to comment on how the organization was spending producers' funds contributed through a mandatory checkoff on soybean sales. Producers hosted a total of 375 meetings in 28 states, providing USB useful feedback on its program and producers' interests. Similarly, the Chicago Welfare Council staged a "listen-in" for community leaders to get guidance and reactions for program planning. Government agencies have long used this exploratory strategy to solicit information and participation. The Forest Service, the Army Corps of Engineers, and the Environmental Protection Agency regularly conduct public meetings and hearings to get information and reactions to various project and program proposals. One of the lessons learned from their experiences is that community input must be sought early and often to keep agencies responsive to citizen interests.

Focus groups represent a more structured approach. Typically, focus groups include six to 12 carefully selected representatives from a target public. They are asked to discuss a specific issue or program proposal in depth. Sessions are videotaped and the recordings carefully analyzed to catch the smallest detail in participants' comments. For example, one organization conducted focus-group research to learn what middle school teachers want in curriculum materials provided by outside sources. One authority says the major strengths of focus groups is the open, spontaneous, and detailed discussions they generate, even among people who did not know each other before the session began.[19] They can be planned, conducted, and analyzed in a matter of days, providing insights and understanding that can be factored into program planning.

Even when members of a group are carefully selected, as with information gained from personal contacts, the results cannot be used to make inferences to a larger population or public. Because the group is small, selection is usually not truly random, and the group-discussion context introduces an artificial setting, the results are not representative—in a scientific sense—of a public or the publics from which the participants were selected. As with other informal methods, focus groups are typically small groups of unknown representativeness.

Moderators also can have an effect on what and how the group discusses. Those viewing the session filter what is said through their own subjective perceptions and interpretations. It is simply not appropriate to suggest that findings from this approach can be used in place of data gathered from scientifically selected samples. The major functions are to identify and explore issues for further study in formal surveys and to pretest program strategies before full-blown field testing.

Advisory Committees and Boards

A standing committee, panel, or board can sometimes be more useful than a single group session, particularly for long-running programs and issues. In some instances such a group can serve as a continuous feedback mechanism for detecting possible changes in public opinion on issues even before they would show up in polls and surveys. There is a price, however, for using advisory committees and boards. Their advice must be given earnest consideration, or this method will backfire. Members quickly sense when they are being used for cosmetic purposes or being showcased to demonstrate concern for community input. Appoint such a committee or board only when the major motivation is to solicit input and guidance on a regular basis, and be prepared to act on the input.

Nonprofit organizations use this approach to tap the professional public relations community for both expertise and services. Almost every chapter of the United Way, the Arthritis Foundation, Easter Seals, and similar organizations has a public relations advisory committee. Committee service is one way public relations practitioners fulfill their public service obligation as professionals.

Other organizations, for-profit and nonprofit alike, use advisory committees and boards. For example, your city's children's hospital, chamber of commerce, and police department probably use this method of gathering information. The insurance industry created advisory committees and complaint bureaus to facilitate policyholder feedback in response to the consumer movement. An accounting firm set up a public review board to provide an outside perspective on operations. A board of education set up a 24-member community advisory committee to give the board a better sense of community attitudes and needs. The New York Stock Exchange created an advisory committee of 15 senior corporate officers to facilitate communication with the corporations listed on the exchange. The American Frozen Food Institute formed an advisory board on frozen goods made up of food editors and home economics instructors.

Advisory committees and boards provide valuable information and guidance, but they cannot substitute for formal approaches to determining the distribution of opinions and reactions among target publics. They provide effective forums for increasing interaction, participation, and in-depth probing of issues. In other words, they are exploratory techniques used to supplement more formal methods.

Ombudsman

The term *ombudsman* originated when the Swedish government established the first such position in 1713. Growing dissatisfaction with ever-longer lines of communication to increasingly isolated managers and bureaucrats has brought about widespread adoption of this informal information-gathering method in government agencies. In countless corporations the ombudsman concept has proved useful in providing feedback and ideas for solving problems while they are still manageable.

Two kinds of ombudsmen are used. One, true to the roots of the original, investigates and solves problems. The second, who at best parries problems, often is there to protect the bureaucracy and to create the illusion of a responsive organization. The former has independent authority to take action on complaints; the latter facilitates communication and seeks authority from others to implement remedies.[20]

The ombudsman's role and scope of its authority vary widely. Dow Chemical Company once established an "ombudswoman" to help promote the advancement of women in the company. At Bronx Community College the ombudsman, appointed by the president, acts as a conduit for student complaints but has no authority to make full-scale investigations. At the University of Nebraska–Lincoln, on the other hand, the ombudsman sees the job as "reporting to nobody and responsible to everyone." The U.S. Navy Family Ombudsman program, started in 1809, says the role is one of cutting governmental red tape and acting as liaison between interested parties and the Navy offices. The ombudsman "investigates organizational problems and makes recommendations for remedial action to improve the quality of administration and redress individual grievances." A large New York hospital employs, as do many hospitals, a "patient representative" to serve as an advocate of patients "to help them and their families find satisfactory solutions to problems." ARCO has an ombudsman to mediate problems dealers cannot get resolved through usual channels: "In a sense, I'm the court of last resort, so this office manages to resolve nearly all disputes."

In each of these settings, the ombudsman provides an effective means for facilitating greater management awareness of public reactions and views. If sincerely used and competently staffed, the ombudsman position can be an important means of obtaining organizational feedback, as well as for helping people get solutions for their problems and answers to their questions. But because this method relies on people who seek out the opportunity to make their feelings and complaints known—a self-selected sample—it also is an exploratory, informal approach to gathering information. Although it *can help identify and detect problems,* information gathered by an ombudsman may not accurately describe the frequency or distribution of problems or concerns among the larger group, particularly those of less assertive members.

Call-In Telephone Lines

Toll-free 800 numbers are commonly used to obtain instant feedback and to monitor the concerns and interests of various publics. Johnson & Johnson tracked telephone calls during the consumer panic associated with the seven deaths caused by cyanide-laced Extra-Strength Tylenol capsules. Similarly, Procter & Gamble (P&G) monitored more than 100,000 calls on its 800 number when a rumor was circulating that P&G promoted Satanism. The calls not only gave the companies opportunities to respond to concerned consumers but also provided constantly updated information on public concerns and reactions.

Companies also recognize the public relations value of giving consumers and customers access to the corporation and of answering questions directly.

By doing so, consumer and customer hot lines provide companies feedback on their products, service, facilities, and employees. For example, General Electric's customer-service Answer Center gets more than 6,000 calls a day. Whirlpool Corporation, among the first in the 1960s to provide a customer call-in service in response to growing customer dissatisfaction, found that about 70 percent of its "Cool Line" service calls were from customers who wanted information on repairs.

Some organizations use this method to field questions from employees; some hospitals use it to provide information and take complaints from patients and their families; other health care centers use toll-free numbers both to provide help and to determine the extent of health problems; and many government agencies use them to help citizens find their way through the bureaucratic maze. For example, the Internal Revenue Service Form 1040 publication lists toll-free 800 numbers for every state, the District of Columbia, and Puerto Rico. Taxpayers can ask IRS representatives how to complete tax forms or other tax questions. By dialing 1-800-TAX-FORM, taxpayers may order IRS forms. Both services help the IRS track taxpayer interests and needs.

To be effective, a call-in service must be used with sincerity. For example, the U.S. Bureau of Mines, acting in the wake of several major mine disasters, announced with great fanfare that it was installing hot-line telephones at the entrance of every coal mine so that miners could alert the bureau if they found unsafe conditions. The bureau promised "instant action" on the reports. A few months later a reporter for *The Wall Street Journal* found that the bureau had not monitored the recorded calls for almost two months. The newspaper reported that bureau employees "had forgotten about the machine."

Nonprofit organizations also use analyses of telephone calls to track stakeholder concerns. For example, the American Red Cross analyzed more than 1,700 calls about AIDS to determine information needs and which messages to target to different publics. In addition, program planners learned that many people did not understand some of the words used in AIDS educational messages. Based on their analyses of the telephone calls, program planners learned not only what questions needed to be answered but also what words to use and avoid when answering.[21]

A pejorative description of radio talk shows, however, serves as a reminder of the danger in putting too much stock in analyses of telephone calls: SLOP, which stands for a self-selected listener opinion poll. Surely analyses of telephone calls can provide early evidence for detecting potential problems and public opinions. The caution, however, is that detecting problems and opinions cannot substitute for describing the frequency of problems or the distribution of opinions in an organizations' publics.

Mail Analysis

Another economical way of collecting information is periodic analysis of incoming mail. Stakeholders' correspondence reveals areas of favor and disfavor and information needs. Letter writers, however, tend to be critical rather than commendatory. Letters may serve as early warnings of ill will or problem relationships, but they do not reflect a cross section of public opinion or even the views of a particular public.

President John F. Kennedy borrowed a leaf from Franklin D. Roosevelt's book on keeping in touch with constituents. Kennedy directed that every 50th letter coming to the White House be brought to him. Periodic mail samples helped both these leaders bridge the moat surrounding the White House. Other chief executives in organizations of all kinds use daily or weekly reports on the mail to read the pulse of citizens' concerns and opinions. Many organizations file brief summaries of letters to track public concerns.

At its peak, Ford Motor Company's "We Listen Better" campaign brought in 18,000 letters a week from Ford owners. Letters were answered personally, not with form letters, which required a large investment in money and human resources. Comments, suggestions, and criticisms were carefully coded and keyed into a computer file. Printouts of the running tallies provided Ford executives useful information, even though the data came from a self-selected sample.

The exploratory nature of mail analysis nevertheless provided information useful for detecting concerns and problems before they became widespread. Those who feel so strongly about something that they take time to write letters may not be representatives of entire publics, but they may be the first of many to follow. In this role, those who write letters join those who call 800 numbers as early-warning signals of situations that need attention and may indicate a need for formal research.

On-Line Sources

New communication technology creates opportunities for friend and foe to talk about each other, as well as about organizations, causes, and events. Prudent public relations practitioners now also monitor what is being said about their organizations on-line. Rumors on the Internet have the potential to influence labor negotiations, attract regulatory attention, drive stock prices up or down, and increase or decrease sales. Among those accessing messages on the Internet, an organization's reputation can be damaged, its brand franchise can suffer, and its hard-earned goodwill can be diminished.

Jackson and Stoakes referred to the Internet's "dark side, where the spread of false and misleading information can cause serious injury to an unprepared target." They recommend that public relations practitioners monitor the Internet to prevent a "cybercrisis" because "rumors that originate on the Internet often make their way into print and broadcast media before a company even knows they exist."[22] Two search programs are particularly useful for scanning what is being said on the World Wide Web: DejaNews **(www.deganew.com)** searches all Usenet newsgroups for messages dated 1995 and after. Alta Vista **(www.altavista.com)** conducts searches based on phrases, links, URLs, and domains.

Again, such searches are informal methods for detecting what is being said on the Internet; they cannot produce profiles of public opinion. And that may be the most important point: monitoring on-line sources can help practitioners tap into the rapidly expanding channels of interactive communication and to intervene in the virtual conversation.

Field Reports

Many organizations have district agents, field representatives, or recruiters who live in and travel the territories served. These agents should be trained to listen and observe and be given an easy, regular means of reporting their observations. In this way they can serve as the eyes and ears of an organization.

Studies of organizational intelligence and communication demonstrate, however, that such representatives tend to gild the lily and to report what they think will set well with their bosses. This is particularly true if field staff know that their reports will pass through a gauntlet of superiors, the same people who hold power over their futures in the organization.

For example, to assess the impact of a company's "progress week," management asked sales representatives to evaluate the program. Forty percent ventured no opinion. About half of those who did respond said the week's promotion had produced more favorable opinions of the company. A formal survey later found that only about one in 10 of the target population was inclined to be more favorable in their opinion of the company. After comparing the field reports with the survey results, it was clear that only 12 of the 42 grassroots observers accurately assessed the results of the promotion. The comparison serves as a reminder that all subjective reports such as field reports must be used with caution. Like the other informal methods, field reports serve best as an early warning to detect situations that may call for more thorough investigation.

FORMAL METHODS

The purpose of both informal and formal methods is to gather accurate and useful information. Formal methods are designed to gather data from scientifically representative samples. Formal methods help answer questions about situations that simply cannot be answered adequately using informal approaches.

The danger is that practitioner-researchers can become more concerned about the methods used than the purpose of the study. As one writer put it, "In science as in love, concentration on technique is quite likely to lead to impotence." Those who get bogged down in research techniques at the expense of usefulness often spend time and resources to produce volumes of data that sit unused on shelves.

Formal methods are useful, however, only if the research question and objectives are clearly determined *before* the research design is selected (see Exhibit 10.3, pg. 360). Done correctly, each approach can yield information that describes phenomena and situations within established ranges of accuracy and tolerance for error. These approaches also make it possible to use inferential statistics, the process of using data from representative samples to

EXHIBIT 10.3

CHECKLIST FOR STARTING A RESEARCH PROJECT

1. How will the results obtained from the research be used? This may seem like an obvious question, but it is often easy, particularly in time of crisis, to jump into a research project without a plan for using the results.

2. What is the specific population (public) being studied, and how should the sample be chosen? In some studies, determining the population in question can constitute one of the more difficult aspects. Wise sample selection can minimize project costs and maximize the accuracy of results.

3. What type of research technique is most appropriate in this instance? Do not automatically assume that a survey is best. Perhaps a focus group or secondary research will yield better results.

4. If a survey is to be used, what sort of field methodology will be most efficient? There are three primary choices here: mail, telephone, and in-person interviews. The practitioner should be familiar with the pros and cons of each.

5. Are closed-ended questions, open-ended questions, or a combination of the two recommended? The response to the first question above will have a major effect on the types of questions used.

6. What is the experience level of the research firm being considered, and what are the backgrounds of its personnel? It is especially important to inquire into the firm's experience with the particular type of research being contemplated. Do not be afraid to ask for references.

7. How will the data be analyzed and the results reported? This is very important! Many practitioners have assumed that they were purchasing complete reports, only to be handed stacks of computer runs as the final product.

8. How soon will the results be provided? The luxury of proper planning, when available, can prevent a research project from becoming an unnecessarily costly undertaking.

9. How much will it cost? Professional research is expensive. It is wise to obtain written proposals from three firms. At the same time, many problems can be prevented by insisting that the proposals address each of these nine questions.

Courtesy David L. Smith. Adapted and reprinted with permission from June 1980 issue of *Public Relations Journal.* Copyright 1980.

estimate characteristics of populations. In other words, systematic formal methods make it possible for practitioners to make accurate statements about publics based on evidence drawn from scientifically representative samples.

Successful public relations managers know about formal research methods and statistics. Public relations education at many universities now includes a research methods course as part of the curriculum. Continuing education programs for practitioners typically include offerings on how to use research in program planning, management, and evaluation. The following sections introduce some of the methods and issues in conducting formal research.

Secondary Analysis and On-Line Databases

Doing research does not always call for gathering data yourself. Secondary analysis reuses data gathered by someone else, often for other purposes.[23]

Numerous governmental and commercial organizations conduct national, regional, and local surveys. Some of these surveys track issues and trends. For example, the U.S. Bureau of the Census has a long history of developing standardized definitions, sampling techniques, sophisticated methods, and publications of findings. Within government, specialized departments have large research staffs tracking major developments and trends in agriculture, labor, business, the economy, and education, to name but a few of the areas under constant study.

Since the 1930s, major commercial polling firms such as those formed by A. C. Nielsen, George Gallup, Elmo Roper, and Louis Harris have made their names synonymous with measures of public opinion. Almost every major city has similar research firms tracking local public opinion trends and conducting marketing research. Major newspapers, television stations, and other news organizations regularly conduct and report surveys. The results of these surveys often can be segmented on the basis of geography, demographics, and other attributes relevant to public relations problem situations.

Sometimes overlooked are the survey research centers maintained by almost all major universities. Research conducted with public funds is often published and available for the asking. Most public agencies can provide listings of data sets and publications. For much less than the cost of conducting a survey, additional analyses of available data often can be done to help answer questions not asked in the original analysis.

Special-interest publications and scholarly journals regularly publish research data. A great deal of research is conducted to answer questions previously answered by competent researchers and reviewed by knowledgeable editorial boards. On-line searches now make it easy and cost effective to search research literature for studies done on specific topics. It makes little sense to design and conduct research until after exploring the possibility that someone else has already done the work and published the results.

The most frequently used research approach to information gathering in public relations, however, is researching on-line databases. Some of the most-used databases include Lexis-Nexis, Dun and Bradstreet, Dow Jones News/Retrieval, NewsNet, Data Times, Wise Wire, News Sites, and Burrelle's Broadcast Database (all are brand names). Practitioners use these services to access and search through news and technical publications, business information services, market research, financial reports, government records, and broadcast transcripts. For example, the New York public relations firm Chacma, Inc., conducted database searches for economic and political facts on foreign governments and clients dating back 10 to 12 years. On-line feeds of international news wires allowed the firm to track developments abroad, with summary printouts available each morning.[24]

Some on-line database companies customize services to meet the specific needs of subscribers. For example, to track the over-the-counter cold remedy field, the manager of information services at Ketchum Public Relations in New York subscribed to Dow Jones's customized service to get relevant information faxed to her office as soon as it goes on line. NewsNet and Lexis-Nexis will set up special files for subscribers, making it easy for customers to access information without the usual cost of a conventional search of the entire database.[25]

Content Analysis

Content analysis is the application of systematic procedures for objectively determining what is being reported in the media.[26] Press clippings and broadcast monitor reports, all available from commercial services, have long been used as the bases for content analyses. They indicate only what is being printed or broadcast, *not* what is read or heard. And they do not measure whether or not the audiences learned or believed message content. For example, a content analysis of newspaper clippings provides a useful measure of what messages are being placed in the media, but it does not indicate readership or impact.

Analyzing the editorials and letters to the editor may yield little more than the views of the editor and publisher. The range of letters sent is seldom represented by those chosen for publication.[27] And the editorial page does not represent public opinion, as is made abundantly clear when candidates receiving newspaper endorsements do not win elections. As agenda-setting researchers caution, media are better at telling us what to think about than they are at telling us what to think.[28]

As John Naisbitt demonstrated in his popular books on trends, however, content analysis can provide valuable insights into what is likely to be on the public agenda in the future. Recognizing the role of the media in reporting and influencing trends, in 1968 Naisbitt began publishing a quarterly newsletter, *Trend Report,* based on content analyses of 206 metropolitan newspapers. Now the national and regional newsletters report content analyses of more than 6,000 newspapers. Based in Washington, DC, but no longer owned by Naisbitt, these newsletters give corporate and government subscribers an early-warning system for forecasting social and economic conditions, often long before they are apparent to most observers.

Increasingly, public relations firms are helping their clients anticipate issues by either subscribing to issues-tracking services or by doing their own media content analyses. It is important to note, however, that these media content analyses employ a more systematic, formal method than the usual informal approaches used for monitoring the media. The key differences are the representativeness of the content selected for analysis and the objectivity used in measuring and coding the content.

Surveys

Mailed questionnaires and in-person interviews are the two major approaches used in survey research. The adequacy of both depends on the sampling procedures used, what questions are asked, and how the questions are asked.

Advantages of *mailed questionnaires* include considerable savings of time and money, convenience for respondents because they determine when to answer the questions, greater assurance of anonymity, standardized wording, no interviewer bias, access to respondents not readily reached in person by interviewers, and opportunity for respondents to take time to gather information needed to complete the questionnaire.

The biggest disadvantages of many surveys are that researchers have no control over who responds and that low response rates are typical. Whereas the original mailing list may have been a randomly selected and representative sample, unless all respond there is no assurance of an unbiased sample. Even a 90 percent response rate could be inadequate if those not responding represent a significant and uniform segment of the population being studied. Remember that elections are often won by fractions of a percent. There is no basis for the conventional wisdom that a 50 percent return is adequate. The unanswered question remains, which half of the sample did or did not respond?

Other disadvantages include lack of control over the conditions under which the questionnaire is completed, no assurance that the intended respondent completed the questionnaire, lack of flexibility in how questions are asked if the respondent does not understand what is being asked, and difficulties in getting and maintaining current mailing lists.

A variation of the mailed questionnaire takes the form of a page included in publications or distributed with other materials. Whereas the cost of a separate mailing is saved, all the advantages and disadvantages of the mailed questionnaire apply and in some cases are magnified.

In-person interviews give researchers increased control over the sample, but the increased cost of that control becomes the major disadvantage. Telephone interviews offer a fast and cost-effective way to complete interview studies while providing more anonymity to respondents. More than 95 percent of households have telephones, but not all are listed in directories. Computer-assisted random digit dialing (RDD) has helped solve the sampling problem caused by incomplete directory listings. But even with the most sophisticated software, sampling phone numbers produces only about two working phone numbers for every three numbers dialed. The reasons for the relatively low—and dropping—rate of working phone numbers among those dialed are modems, faxes, and second and third lines. New area codes make frequent changes in the dialing software necessary. So although the numbers selected for calls may be representative, answering machines and refusal rates have made it more difficult to obtain representative samples and have driven up costs.[29]

For example, the research firm Survey Sampling, Inc., estimates that researchers must call five phone numbers to complete one interview in Chicago and three calls to complete one interview in Cincinnati. Moreover, although 36 percent of adults have refused to participate in a research study, they said inconvenience was the major reason for refusing. Notably, more people than ever are participating in surveys. Forty-two percent of all adults have participated in some type of survey. Even 84 percent of those who had refused to cooperate in one survey said that they had participated in another survey.[30]

In-person doorstep interviews may be the most flexible and thorough method, but the costs are proportionately greater. In both telephone and doorstep approaches the interviewers themselves can influence the information gathered, so interviewer training is an essential element of this approach.

Advantages of interview studies include high response rates, greater flexibility in dealing with the respondents, more control over conditions under which the questions are asked, increased control over the order and completeness of questioning, and opportunity to observe and record reactions not covered by the questionnaire. In addition to the relatively greater cost and potential influence of interviewers, disadvantages include the inconvenience imposed on respondents, less anonymity for respondents, increased difficulty in contacting those selected in the sample, and respondents' negative reactions resulting from misuse of survey approaches by salespersons and other solicitors posing as researchers.

Usually single surveys are conducted on *cross-section samples* of a population or public. If the study is designed to learn how people change over time or to track a process, however, a panel study may be the better approach. In panel studies the same respondents are interviewed several times during the study, are asked to complete a series of questionnaires on a fixed schedule, or are required to maintain a diary during the study period. Two problems common to this approach are that respondents drop out during the study ("panel mortality") and that respondents become more attentive to the issues being studied because of the repeated observations ("sensitization").

In summary, formal research methods follow the rules of science, use representative samples, and employ other systematic procedures for making the observations, taking the measurements, and analyzing the data. Like other skills based on specialized knowledge, doing formal research requires study and practice. Done correctly, however, formal research helps practitioners describe reality accurately. Research findings, combined with experience and judgment, provide the foundation for defining public relations problems and for designing programs to address those problems. In other words, research builds the information foundation necessary for effective public relations practice and management.

This chapter highlights only some of the approaches for gathering the qualitative and quantitative information needed to understand and define public relations problem situations. Whereas research is often viewed as a necessary step for evaluating program impact, it is equally necessary in the initial step of the problem-solving process—defining the problem situation. Not only does research provide the information necessary for understanding the problem, but this "benchmark" description serves as the basis for monitoring and evaluating program effectiveness. How do you plan the program if you do not know what you are dealing with? How do you determine how the program is working if you do not know where you started?

Practitioners know that research initiates, monitors, and concludes the problem-solving process. It is the essential ingredient that makes public relations a management function as well as a managed function.

NOTES

1. Edward J. Robinson, *Public Relations Research and Survey Research: Achieving Organizational Goals in a Communication Context* (New York: Appleton-Century-Crofts, 1969). The first book devoted to using social science survey research methods in public relations.

2. From the fable, "The Blind Men and the Elephant," by John Godfrey Saxe (1816–1887), quoted by Henry Mintzberg, "Strategy Formation: Schools of Thought," in *Perspectives on Strategic Management,* edited by James W. Fredrickson (New York: Harper Business Division of Harper & Row, 1990): 105–6.

3. Quoted in Walter K. Lindenmann, "Research, Evaluation, and Measurement: A National Perspective," *Public Relations Review* 16, no. 2 (Summer 1990): 14.

4. Ibid.

5. C. F. Kettering, "More Music Please, Composers," *Saturday Evening Post* 211, no. 32 (1938).

6. Peter H. Rossi and Howard E. Freeman, *Evaluation: A Systematic Approach,* 4th ed. (Newbury Park, CA: Sage Publications, 1989), 27.

7. David M. Dozier, "The Innovation of Research in Public Relations Practice: Review of a Program of Studies," *Public Relations Research Annual* 2 (1990): 3–28. See also Jon White and David M. Dozier, "Public Relations and Management Decision Making," in *Excellence in Public Relations and Communication Management,* edited by James E. Grunig (Hillsdale, NJ: Lawrence Erlbaum Associates, 1992), 91–108.

8. Wilbur Schramm, *Men, Messages, and Media: A Look at Human Communication* (New York: Harper and Row, 1973), 51.

9. Wilbur Schramm, "The Nature of Communication between Humans," in *The Process and Effects of Mass Communication,* rev. ed., edited by Wilbur Schramm and Donald F. Roberts (Urbana: University of Illinois Press, 1971), 26.

10. Carl Sandburg, *Abraham Lincoln: The War Years* II (New York: Harcourt, Brace and World, 1939): 236–37.

11. Joseph A. Kopec, "The Communication Audit," *Public Relations Journal* 38, no. 5 (May 1982): 24.

12. For more on the distinction between "stakeholders" and "publics," see James E. Grunig and Fred C. Repper, "Strategic Management, Publics, and Issues," in *Excellence in Public Relations,* 127–46.

13. Adapted from Brenda Dervin, "Audience as Listener and Learner, Teacher and Confidante: The Sense Making Approach," in *Public Communication Campaigns,* 2d ed., edited by Ronald E. Rice and Charles K. Atkin (Newbury Park, CA: Sage Publications, 1989), 67–86.

14. Jim VanLeuven, "Expectancy Theory in Media and Message Selection," *Communication Research* 8, no. 4 (October 1981): 431.

15. Heinz Weihrich, "The TOWS Matrix: A Tool for Situational Analysis," in *Strategic Planning: Models and Analytical Techniques,* edited by Robert G. Dyson (Chichester, UK: John Wiley and Sons, 1990), 17–36.

16. Kerry Tucker and Doris Derelian, *Public Relations Writing: A Planned Approach for Creating Results* (Englewood Cliffs, NJ: Prentice-Hall, 1989), 41–46.

17. Glen M. Broom and David M. Dozier, *Using Research in Public Relations: Applications to Program Management* (Englewood Cliffs, NJ: Prentice-Hall, 1990), 20.

18. For more detailed discussion of research methods, see Broom and Dozier, *Using Research in Public Relations.*

19. Larissa A. Grunig, "Using Focus Group Research in Public Relations," *Public Relations Review* 16, no. 2 (Summer 1990): 36–37.

20. For an account of the origins and uses of the ombudsman concept, see Donald C. Rowat, ed., *The Ombudsman: Citizen's Defender,* 2d ed. (London: George Allen and Unwin, 1968).

21. Meryl Davids, "Panic Prevention," *Public Relations Journal* 43, no. 3 (March 1987): 21.

22. Amy Jackson and Unity Stoakes, "Internet Vigilance: Monitoring Public Opinion Online," *Public Relations Tactics,* November 1997, p. 12.

23. David W. Stewart and Michael A. Kamins, *Secondary Research: Information Sources and Methods,* 2d ed. (Newbury Park, CA: Sage Publications, 1993). Discusses how to locate information from various sources, including government agencies, on-line information search services, and CD-ROM delivery systems.

24. *O'Dwyer's FARA Report* 1, no. 2 (March 1991): 5. (Monthly newsletter reporting developments under the Foreign Agents Registration Act.)

25. John Masterton, "Discovering Databases: On-Line Services Put Research at Practitioner's Fingertips," *Public Relations Journal* 48, no. 11 (November 1992): 12–19, 27.

26. For more detailed descriptions of content analysis procedures, see Robert P. Weber, *Basic Content Analysis* (Beverly Hills, CA: Sage Publications, 1985); and Guido H. Stempel III, "Content Analysis," in *Research Methods in Mass Communication,* edited by Guido H. Stempel III and Bruce H. Westley (Englewood Cliffs, NJ: Prentice-Hall, 1981), 119–31.

27. David L. Grey and Trevor R. Brown, "Letters to the Editor: Hazy Reflections of Public Opinion," *Journalism Quarterly* 47 (Autumn 1970): 450–56, 471.

28. For a good summary of two decades of agenda-setting research, see the special issue of *Journalism Quarterly* 69, no. 4 (Winter 1992); and Maxwell McCombs, Edna Einseidel, and David Weaver, "The Agenda-Setting Role of Mass Communication," chapter 2 of *Contemporary Public Opinion: Issues and the News* (Hillsdale, NJ: Lawrence Erlbaum Associates, 1991), 11–21.

29. Terrence Coen, "Improve Phoneroom Efficiency," *The Frame,* November 1997, p. 1. (Quarterly newsletter published by Survey Sampling, Inc., Fairfield, CT.)

30. Pat Lewis, "Cooperation Rates, the Ups and the Downs," *The Frame* 14, no. 1 (1991): 2.

ADDITIONAL SOURCES

Broom, Glen M., and David M. Dozier. *Using Research in Public Relations: Applications to Program Management.* Englewood Cliffs, NJ: Prentice-Hall, 1990.

Fink, Arlene. *How to Analyze Survey Data* (The Survey Kit, Vol. 8) and *How to Report on Surveys* (The Survey Kit, Vol. 9). Thousand Oaks, CA: Sage Publications, 1995.

Fowler, Floyd J. Jr. *Survey Research Methods,* 2d ed. Newbury Park, CA: Sage Publications, 1993. Covers essentials of survey research and adapts it to personal computers for data entry and analysis.

Greenbaum, Thomas L. *The Handbook for Focus Group Research,* 2nd ed. Thousand Oaks, CA: Sage Publications, 1997. Author summarizes 20 years of experience in focus group research.

Hyman, Herbert H. *Secondary Analysis of Sample Surveys: Principles, Procedures, and Potentialities.* New York: John Wiley and Sons, 1972. Considered the classic reference on doing secondary analyses.

Lavrakas, Paul J. *Telephone Survey Methods,* 2d ed. Newbury Park, CA: Sage Publications, 1993. Outlines the use of new technology for conducting telephone research, sampling techniques, supervising interviewers, and securing cooperation of respondents.

Miller, Delbert C. *Handbook of Research Design and Social Measurement,* 5th ed. Newbury Park, CA: Sage Publications, 1991. This may be the most complete manual on social science research methods. Most valuable are the guides to doing research and presentations of selected scales and indices.

Williams, Frederick. *Reasoning with Statistics,* 4th ed. New York: Holt, Rinehart and Winston, 1991. Uses communication examples to introduce statistics.

STEP TWO: PLANNING AND PROGRAMMING

Strategy is a driving force in any business or organization. It's the intellectual force that helps organize, prioritize and energize what they do. No strategy; no energy. No strategy; no direction. No strategy; no momentum. No strategy; no impact.

—*Jim Lukaszewski*[1]

OBJECTIVES

After studying chapter 11, you should be able to

▼ Define *strategic thinking* and *strategy,* and explain how they apply to *strategic public relations management.*

▼ Describe the application of management by objectives (MBO) to public relations planning and management.

▼ Outline the major steps in the planning and programming process.

▼ List and describe the major approaches to defining publics.

▼ Discuss the characteristics of useful program objectives and write examples.

▼ Describe and give examples of the three major categories of disasters and crises that practitioners must anticipate and plan for.

Once the public relations problem or opportunity has been defined through research and analysis, practitioners must devise a strategy for coping with the problem or for capitalizing on the opportunity. This is planning and programming—making the basic strategic decisions about what will be done in what order in response to or in anticipation of a problem or opportunity. The effectiveness of the tactics used in the next step of the process—taking action and communicating (chapter 12)—depends on the sound planning done in this, the second step. Yet many practitioners do not take the time necessary to give planning more than a glancing blow; they do "pseudoplanning."[2] Like the cuttlefish squirting ink, inadequate planning leads to routine responses whose origins and motivations are lost in history. Such reaction-based programs may or may not be appropriate in the present context.

STRATEGIC THINKING

Strategic thinking involves predicting or establishing a desired future goal state, determining what forces will help and hinder movement toward the goal, and formulating a plan for achieving the desired state. But as President Dwight D. Eisenhower is quoted as having said when he commanded U.S. forces during World War II in Europe: "The plan is nothing. Planning is everything!" When planning a program, an organization is, in effect, making tomorrow's decisions today. Skimping on the strategic planning step in the process results in programs that may reinforce controversy rather than resolve it, waste money on audiences that are not there, or cause misunderstanding and confusion instead of understanding and clarification.

Many difficult public relations problems were born of yesterday's spur-of-the-moment decisions. For example, the American Heart Association's short-lived "seal-of-approval" program for food products was canceled under heavy pressure from the U.S. Department of Agriculture and other interested parties. Surely the PGA Tour regretted its announcement that disabled tour pro Casey Martin could not use a golf cart. The IRS regretted and retracted its announcement that fans who caught Mark MacGwire's record-setting home run balls would have to pay a large "gift tax." Another example is the public relations disaster that resulted when Nestlé marketed in developing nations an infant-formula substitute for breastfeeding. The company apparently did not take into account that the formula would be mixed with water unsafe for babies. Exxon's handling of the tanker *Valdez* oil spill cleanup in Prince William Sound on the Alaskan coast provides yet another case study of inadequate planning and programming for such a disaster. One writer described Exxon's response in an article titled "Exxon *Valdez*: How to Spend Billions and Still Get a Black Eye."[3]

In all these cases, program planners apparently made strategic decisions based on inadequate situation analyses or without fully considering possible unintended consequences of their program tactics. In effect, programs represent strategic interventions for which both planners and their organizations are held responsible.

Public Relations as Part of Strategic Thinking

A definition of strategy captures the essence of strategic thinking and management expectations:

> Strategy can be defined as the determination of the basic long-term goals and objectives of an enterprise, and the adoption of courses of action and the allocation of resources necessary for carrying out these goals.[4]

Corporate-level strategy provides the overall goal and direction within which an organization's divisions operate. Business-level strategy establishes the goals and directions for each division, each operating unit, or, in diversified organizations, each business. In a *planning mode,* strategy takes the form of a systematic plan and guidelines for achieving corporate- and business-level strategies. In an evolutionary mode, strategies develop over time, representing a pattern of decisions that respond to opportunities and threats in the environment. Whereas the planning mode has been the preferred model, the *evolutionary mode* is increasingly accepted as the more appropriate approach for dealing with rapidly changing organizations and environments.[5] As such, plans that spell out the goals and strategy—including the public relations components—become dynamic documents that reflect the open systems approach discussed in chapter 7.

Reliance on research findings as the basis for strategic planning to achieve effective public relations varies widely. Walter Lindenmann, senior vice president and director of research at Ketchum Public Relations in New York, surveyed practitioners to learn how many use research as the basis for program planning. Seventy-five percent of all those surveyed reported that they "occasionally" or "frequently" do research specifically for the purpose of planning. Counselors were most likely to use research, 89 percent, whereas practitioners in nonprofit settings were least likely, 68 percent.[6]

Another study concludes that practitioners' use of strategic thinking and program evaluation are correlated with the number of social science, statistics, and computer courses taken by practitioners. Seat-of-the-pants approaches are not correlated with taking social science or statistics courses and are negatively correlated with course work in using computers. Furthermore, the more practitioners engage in various types of research, the more likely they are to approach their work as managers and to be involved in management decision making.[7] As one practitioner put it, "If you don't have information to take to the table, then you don't get invited to the table [management meetings]."

Management Expectations

In many organizations, top management limits public relations participation in management decision making. "Many public relations people fantasize their roles in strategic planning, but few are really involved in any meaningful fashion," according to a principal of a major public relations firm.[8] Responding to management expectations requires practitioners to think outside the boundaries of public relations by analyzing and understanding the needs and concerns of operating units. In short, line managers expect public relations efforts to help achieve organizational goals, or in the words of some managers, "affect the bottom line."

Longtime AT&T public relations executive Ed Block outlined a CEO's expectations of the chief public relations officer:

> In this role, I need someone with an exquisite public relations "gut" combined with a comprehensive knowledge of the business and its external and internal environment. I want someone who is in touch with the "soul" of the business, someone who shares my vision and understands my sensibilities. I don't need a "handler" or a gate keeper. I need someone whose counsel, over time, will influence my thinking in broad terms, not someone who hectors me on every piddling issue that crosses my desk. I also want someone whose counsel is sought out by others in top management because it is timely and thoughtful and helpful—not because it comes from someone who has special access to me.[9]

In the information age of instant computer communication and on-line databases, the days of playing hunches and simply replaying the past as the primary bases for planning are history. Others in the organization may make strategic decisions based on financial, legal, or technical considerations and data. It is the responsibility of the public relations practitioner to anticipate the impact of those decisions on various stakeholder groups. In the words of another telephone company executive, "We lead an issues management group that functions as an early warning sentinel for the corporation." He credits the environmental scanning and "up-front counseling" for public relations' company-wide acceptance in the strategic planning process. "Or to put it another way," he concludes, "we help plan the parade, not just carry the shovels afterward!"[10] AT&T's CEO and chairman, Robert E. Allen, made the same point, "I need PR people at my side not in my wake."[11]

Prudent long-range planning, anticipating conceivable developments, is more likely to result in the following:

1. An integrated program in which the total effort results in definite accomplishments toward specific goals.
2. Increased management participation and support.
3. A program emphasis that is positive rather than defensive.
4. Careful deliberation on choice of themes, timing, and tactics.

Even though the values of planning are evident and widely acknowledged, there is too little emphasis on this step in public relations. The following appear to be the main obstacles:

1. Failure of employers and clients to include the practitioner in deliberations that lead to policies and programs; a failure often born of lack of confidence in the public relations officer or counselor.
2. Absence of clearly agreed-upon objectives for implementing the public relations program.

3. Inadequate time because of the pressures of meeting daily problems.
4. Frustrations and delays that practitioners encounter in getting internal clearance and in coordinating with other departments.

Despite the problems, in the final analysis management expects public relations to help manage threats from the environment, to enhance the organization's competitive edge (usually in the form of marketing support), and—most important—to protect an organization's most important assets, its good name and reputation. "Buildings depreciate, patents expire, but, properly managed, a company's name and reputation grow in value every year."[12]

Often the health of the bottom line depends on the health of an organization's reputation. An organization's market share, its ability to attract and retain valuable employees, its attractiveness to prospective donors and members, its autonomy and freedom to carry out its missions, and even its stock price are affected by its reputation among various stakeholders. Management expects the public relations unit to manage the organization's reputation and good standing with the same strategic thinking that goes into managing other assets.

Counselor Davis Young says there is no quick and easy way to build an organization's reputation:

> If you want people to regard your organization highly, that must be a priority to which you allocate both time and money, one for which you plan and budget as you would for any aspect of your business. . . . *It may take years to build a reputation but only a monment to destroy one.* . . . A reputation is a priceless asset to be protected and managed at all times.[13]

STRATEGIC MANAGEMENT

Strategic management represents the open systems approach to public relations rather than the closed systems, reactive approach. One counselor defines strategic management as "a process that enables any organization—company, association, nonprofit or government agency—to identify its long-term opportunities and threats, mobilize its assets to address them and carry out a successful implementation strategy."[14]

Strategic planning in public relations involves making decisions about program goals and objectives, identifying key publics, setting policies or rules to guide selection of strategies, and determining strategies. There must be a close linkage between the overall program goal, the objectives established for each of the publics, and the strategies selected. The key point is that strategies are selected to achieve a particular outcome (as stated in a goal or objective). On the other hand, if you don't care where you end up, any route will get you there.

Public relations practitioners work with other managers to develop strategic program plans. Although each program calls for specifically tailored and unique elements, the overall approach is similar from plan to plan. The planning and programming process typically includes the following steps:

1. Defining roles and missions. Determining the nature and scope of the work to be performed.
2. Determining key results areas. Determining where to invest time, energy, and talent.
3. Identifying and specifying indicators of effectiveness. Determining measurable factors on which objectives may be set.
4. Selecting and setting objectives. Determining results to be achieved.
5. Preparing action plans. Determining how to achieve specific objectives.
   A. *Programming*. Establishing a sequence of actions to follow in reaching objectives.
   B. *Scheduling*. Establishing time requirements for objectives and action steps.
   C. *Budgeting*. Determining and assigning the resources required to reach objectives.
   D. *Fixing accountability*. Determining who will see to the accomplishment of objectives and action steps.
   E. *Reviewing and reconciling*. Testing and revising a tentative plan, as needed, prior to commitment to action.
6. Establishing controls. Ensuring the effective accomplishment of objectives.
7. Communicating. Determining the organizational communications necessary for achieving understanding and commitment in the previous six steps.
8. Implementing. Securing agreement among all key people on who and what needs to be committed to the effort, what approach will work best, who needs to be involved, and what immediate action steps need to be taken immediately.[15]

Mission Statements

The four-step public relations process outlined in chapters 10 through 13 is based on the assumption that the organization has clearly defined its overall mission and goals and that public relations is part of the plan to achieve them.

Most organizations have a written statement of goals and objectives, long range and immediate. The purpose is to state succinctly why an organization exists, such as Merck Pharmaceutical's, "We are in the business of preserving and improving human life." Mission statements typically make public commitments of citizenship obligations and social responsibility. They often give the organization's attitude in dealing with its employees, members, clients, neighbors, and donors. They may state the organization's posture on government regulation or environmental issues, explain how it measures its own progress, and so on. In short, they are idealistic and inspirational statements designed to give those in the organization a sense of purpose and direction. (See Exhibit 11.1, pgs. 376–377, for examples.)

Mission statements without management commitment and support, however, become simply cosmetic additions to brochures, reports, and speeches.

The challenge is to instill a sense of mission, values, and behavior standards throughout an organization. Each organization has to define its own unique mission, matching its strategy and values, and creating its own culture.[16]

Whether these documents are kept private for competitive or security reasons or are open statements of mission, standards of conduct, or specific purposes, public relations staff are privy to them. In organizations where no such statements have been set down, there is an urgent need for the top public relations officer to propose one.

Mission statements of organizational goals, obligations, values, and social responsibility serve two important purposes in public relations: First, they commit the whole organization to accountability, and that means visibility or communication of some sort. Second, the attitudes expressed provide a framework in which public relations can devise its goals and objectives, build its budgets, direct its talents, devise its programs, and assess its impact.

The mission statement for the public relations function builds upon the organization's mission statement. Typically the mission of public relations is to help the organization achieve its mission by doing the following:

1. Collecting and analyzing information on the changing knowledge, opinions, and behaviors of key publics and stakeholder groups.
2. Serving as the central source of information about an organization and as the official channel of communication between an organization and its publics.
3. Communicating significant information, opinions, and interpretations to keep an organization's publics and other stakeholders aware of organizational policies and actions.
4. Coordinating activities that affect an organization's relationships with its publics and other stakeholder groups.

To the extent that these activities and an organization's mission are connected to measurable goals and objectives, then public relations is part of management. To attain organizational maturity, the function must be mainstream in every sense, not a sideshow, and have management agreement of a clear-cut charter, or mission.

Management by Objectives

As executives have become sophisticated in the ways of public relations, they have become more demanding. Most organizations operate on the basis of management by objectives (MBO) or, as others term it, management by objectives and results (MOR). Simply put, MBO systematically applies effective management techniques to running an organization. It specifies the outcomes (consequences, results, impact) to be achieved, thereby establishing the criteria for selecting strategies, monitoring performance and progress, and evaluating program effectiveness.

As now applied, MBO operates at two levels of outcomes: goals and objectives. Goals are summative statements that spell out the overall outcomes of a program. Such a program may involve many different parts of an organi-

MISSION STATEMENTS

Weyerhaeuser Company (Tacoma, Washington)

Our Vision. The Best Forest Products Company in the World.

Our Strategies. We shall achieve our vision by: Making Total Quality the Weyerhaeuser way of doing business. Relentless pursuit of full customer satisfaction. Empowering Weyerhaeuser people. Leading the industry in forest management and manufacturing excellence. Producing superior returns for our shareholders.

Our Values. Customers: We listen to our customers and improve our products and services to meet their present and future needs. **People:** Our success depends upon high-performing people working together in a safe and healthy workplace where diversity, development and teamwork are valued and recognized. **Accountability:** We expect superior performance and are accountable for our actions and results. Our leaders set clear goals and expectations, are supportive, and provide

and seek frequent feedback. **Citizenship:** We support the communities where we do business, hold ourselves to the highest standards of ethical conduct and environmental responsibility, and communicate openly with Weyerhaeuser people and the public. **Financial Responsibility:** We are prudent and effective in the use of the resources entrusted to us.

New York Stock Exchange

Mission Statement. Support the capital-raising and asset-management process by providing the highest quality and most cost-effective, self-regulated marketplace for the trading of financial instruments; promote confidence in and understanding of that process; and serve as a forum for discussion of relevant national and international policy issues.

Johnson & Johnson

Our Credo. We believe our first responsibility is to the doctors, nurses and patients, to

zation as well as many different strategies. Goals state what the coordinated effort is intended to accomplish and by when it will be accomplished. Goals establish what will be accomplished if the objectives set for each of the publics are achieved.

Objectives represent the specific knowledge, opinion, and behavioral outcomes to be achieved for each well-defined target public, what some call "key results." The outcome criteria take the form of measurable program effects to be achieved by specified dates. In practice, objectives do the following:

1. Give focus and direction for developing program strategies and tactics.
2. Provide guidance and motivation to those implementing the program.
3. Spell out the criteria for monitoring progress and for assessing impact.

An organization's overall goals provide the outcome criteria for unit and individual goals, including those for the public relations department. Just as an organization has a written MBO plan, so should public relations have a long-range MBO plan on paper. A separate document should give guidance mothers and fathers and all others who use our products and services. In meeting their needs everything we do must be of high quality. We must constantly strive to reduce our costs in order to maintain reasonable prices. Customers' orders must be serviced promptly and accurately. Our suppliers and distributors must have an opportunity to make a fair profit.

We are responsible to our employees, the men and women who work with us throughout the world. Everyone must be considered as an individual. We must respect their dignity and recognize their merit. They must have a sense of security in their jobs. Compensation must be fair and adequate, and working conditions clean, orderly and safe. We must be mindful of ways to help our employees fulfill their family responsibilities. Employees must feel free to make suggestions and complaints. There must be equal opportunity for employment, development and advancement for those qualified. We must provide competent management, and their actions must be just and ethical.

We are responsible to the communities in which we live and work and to the world community as well. We must be good citizens—support good works and charities and bear our fair share of taxes. We must encourage civic improvements and better health and education. We must maintain in good order the property we are privileged to use, protecting the environment and natural resources.

Our final responsibility is to our stockholders. Business must make a sound profit. We must experiment with new ideas. Research must be carried on, innovative programs developed and mistakes paid for. New equipment must be purchased, new facilities provided and new products launched. Reserves must be created to provide for adverse times. When we operate according to these principles, the stockholders should realize a fair return.

Used with permission. Courtesy Weyerhaeuser Company, New York Stock Exchange, and Johnson & Johnson.

within the department. Just as managers or general officers are periodically subject to performance review by a superior officer, so is the public relations manager. If line departments and other staff functions hold annual conferences to reenergize the staff, so should public relations. Most important, however, public relations must operate within and as part of an organization's overall MBO plan, must be held accountable in the same way as other functions, and must show how public relations contributes to the achievement of the organization's mission and goals.

Strategy and Tactics

The terms *strategy* and *tactics* are often confused. Borrowed from the military, strategy involves the crucial decisions of a war or campaign, such as whether to rely on missiles or aerial bombardment. Strategy represents the overall game plan. Tactics are decisions made during the course of battle. Tactics represent on-the-spot decisions necessitated because of developments as the strategic plan is implemented. In effect, tactics are the decisions or actions taken to make the strategy fit the reality and contingencies of the field of battle.

In public relations practice, however, strategy typically refers to the overall concept, approach, or general plan for the program designed to achieve a goal. Tactics refer to the operational level: the actual events, media, and methods used to implement the strategy. For example, the Wisconsin Milk Marketing Board's (WMMB) successful program to pass a referendum illustrates the difference between strategies and tactics.

WMMB wanted to win dairy producers' support for increasing, from five to 10 cents per hundredweight of milk produced, the amount directed to state and regional promotions of dairy products. Congress mandated that dairy farmers nationwide contribute 15 cents for each hundredweight of milk they sell to do research and to promote the sale of dairy products. Of the mandatory checkoff, five cents goes to the National Dairy Promotion and Research Board and five cents goes to state or regional organizations. Dairy farmers then choose which organization gets the other five cents, often called the "middle nickel." WMMB wanted Wisconsin producers to direct the discretionary five cents to the state organization.

Program strategies included reinforcing the producers' belief in the need to build markets for Wisconsin dairy products; demonstrating WMMB's successes in marketing, research, and education; and enlisting influential third-party endorsements to reach targeted groups of producers. Tactics included check stuffers, newsletters, informational meetings, an 800 telephone number information service, the annual report, and exhibit booths at Farm Progress Days and the World Dairy Expo. Ninety-three percent of the producers who cast ballots in the referendum voted in favor of directing the middle nickel to WMMB.

Reasons for Planning

Preparing a plan does not guarantee success, but it greatly enhances its chances. Strategic planning, however, is not universally accepted as part of public relations practice. The excuses practitioners give for not planning are similar to those offered by other managers:

1. "We don't have time." Practitioners who feel that they are already overloaded with work offer this excuse. Of course, they are missing the point that those with a plan typically make better use of their time, thus making time spent planning a wise investment.
2. "Why plan when things are changing so fast?" Plans get modified in light of changing circumstances; they are not cast in concrete. Having a plan, however, provides the baseline from which modifications can be made with full awareness that changes in strategy and direction are occurring. In fact, the more turbulent the environment, the greater the need to chart the changing course to the desired result, to have a plan.
3. "We get paid for results, not for planning." Public relations practitioners tend to be oriented more to activities than to strategic planning. A dollar spent on research and planning is often viewed as a dollar not available for implementing program activities. This orientation generally leads to count-

ing activities rather than results that count. In fact, practitioners are paid for results that happen according to a plan.

4. "We're doing O.K. without a plan." Short-term success can change to failure if conditions change. For example, it is easy to see how an injury to a football team's star quarterback can change an entire football season. Such was the case in a business setting when the founder and CEO of a new and successful computer company died in an automobile accident the very day the company's stock went public. The stock offer was withdrawn until new management was in place. A few weeks later the company stock was again offered but commanded a substantially lower price. Soon thereafter Eagle Computer went out of business. Part of planning involves building in strategies for handling contingencies such as industrial accidents and other operational crises; top management decisions that attract media and public scrutiny; changes in management and other key personnel; and charges by government agencies, consumer groups, unions, or whistle-blowers.[17]

Planning is for the purpose of making something happen or preventing it from happening, for the purpose of exploiting a situation or remedying one. Public relations practice is engaged more often in trying to create a viewpoint or a happening than trying to prevent one and trying to take advantage of an opportunity more often than trying to remedy an undesired situation. There remain, however, many situations and occasions when remedial public relations measures are required because preventive measures were not taken.

Public relations calls for long-term planning and programming in many areas, such as public policy and social problems, but crises often give birth to public relations planning. Preventive public relations is tied most often to long-term planning. Remedial public relations actions tend to be of short duration and have minimal time for planning. The immediate need quite often is to pick up the pieces of a negative situation or to exploit a positive one. The latter works best if done within the framework of a long-term plan that includes strategies for such contingencies.

WRITING THE PROGRAM

Writing the program is a challenge. When the program meshes with organizational goals, the employer knows that the public relations practitioner understands what management is trying to do and is part of the management team. Counselor Jim Lukaszewski paraphrases the CEO's position: "Please spare me from another amateur corporate strategist—the person who doesn't have a clue about how the company operates, my goals or our critical strategic needs; but who yaps at me every day and calls it strategy."[18]

The task of writing an overall program or a proposal would rarely fall on a new member of a staff. It is important, however, that all members understand how proposals and presentations evolve. By seeing how all the parts come together, all members are better able to perform their own segment or specialty when programs are implemented. Plans and programs are generally infused with enthusiasm. That helps get approval by employers and clients. But overenthusiasm carries with it the serious danger of overpromising: "This employee communication program has everything necessary to eliminate the turnover problem." Those are dangerous words. Suppose the program falls short, reducing employee turnover by "only" 50 percent? Ordinarily such a reduction might be considered an acceptable performance, but evaluated against the unrealistic earlier statement, it might be considered not up to the level promised.

Program Plan

A public relations plan starts with the organization's mission statement. It proceeds from the specific role assigned to it in the form of a public relations mission. It engages in whatever fact-finding is indicated, as discussed in chapter 10. An orderly investigative process involves the following four aspects of a situation analysis:

1. A searching look backward. There is no organization, no problem, no opportunity without a history. Learning that history is the first step. In a newly created entity, who founded it? For what purpose? Is it time for an anniversary event, an institutional museum, a biography of the founder? Can public relations help? Background information is also essential if public relations is brought into a going entity to deal with a pressing problem. What is the background of the problem? What has happened that has caused public relations to be involved in a new or different way? Public relations problems, too, have a history.

2. A wide look around. Where there has been no continuing monitoring of public opinion toward the organization, that is the next step. How do employees feel about the conditions of their employment, their leadership? How do the neighbors feel about the presence and conduct of the organization? Is there a breakdown in understanding between the organization and any of its constituent publics? Is there a resentment simmering somewhere? In a crunch, on whom could the organization depend? In that crunch, what groups would delight in the troubles or embarrassment of the organization?

3. A deep look inside. Every organization has a character and a personality. Both tend to be reflections of those who control the organization by their ownership, management, votes, membership, or tenure or in some other way. Character can be discovered by examining the policies set down and by determining if day-to-day actions square with the words. Personality is evident in the style of administration: centralized authority or generous delegation, openness and candor or secretiveness and suspicion. It is portrayed by contemporary or traditional decor and equipment, open or closed doors on executive offices, symbols of stature, approachability of officials, and whether communication is formalized, as by memo, or casual, as by phone. The practitioner needs to know what makes the organization tick and whether it ticks with convictions, values, and standards that the practitioner can share and honestly promote.

4. A long, long look ahead. Is the mission of the organization realistically attainable? Can public relations planning and programming fit in? Can they make a practical contribution? Will this organization be around in ten years? Will it be larger and more solidly entrenched, or will it be engaged in a slow retreat toward oblivion? What are the pros and cons? What are the forces that will affect the organization's chances for success or failure? Are the game and the outcome worth getting involved?

Implementing these steps has been greatly enhanced by advances in technology and resources. On-line databases, for example, as well as increasingly sophisticated issue-tracking techniques and services enable practitioners to meet executives' demands for data as a basis for planning. These data are used to build the foundation of the program: the problem statement and situation analysis (discussed in chapter 10) and the program goal. The final plan (or proposal) typically includes the ten components outlined in Exhibit 11.2, pg. 382.

Role of Working Theory

A program plan represents someone's working theory of what has to be done to achieve a desired outcome. In the words and form of a theoretical statement, "If we implement these actions and communications, then we will achieve these outcomes with our publics, which should lead to accomplishing the program goal." Theory also determines the selection of tactics. Someone's working theory guides how a special event is designed, how a newsletter or press release is worded, and how a community function is conducted. The theory that guides how each tactic is executed represents the practitioner's idea of what will cause a desired result. So when people say a program is "all theory," they are right!

The role of theory is obvious, but not always made explicit, at every step of the planning process. Otherwise how would decisions be made? For example, theory clearly guides the process when writing program objectives and determining the strategies to achieve them. Assume that the goal of an employee communication program is to reduce the number of employees seriously injured or killed while driving to and from work and while driving on the job. The situation analysis background research shows that traffic accidents are the leading cause of workplace fatalities and cost U.S. employers almost $55 billion annually. The federal Department of Transportation estimates that 2,000 people die each year in work-related crashes, or 40 percent of all workplace deaths. Investigation within the organization shows that a surprisingly large percentage of employees do not wear seat belts while driving or when a passenger. Program planners decide to develop a program to increase seat belt use among employees. (Clearly, their theory is that increased seat belt use will lead to a reduction in serious injuries and deaths.)

The situation analysis research also shows, however, that delivery drivers are the ones most frequently injured or killed in accidents and that the accidents occur during work hours. Program planners decide that to have the greatest impact on solving the problem and achieving the program goal, the program should target delivery drivers and car parking-lot attendants. Plan-

EXHIBIT 11.2

PUBLIC RELATIONS STRATEGIC PLANNING PROCESS

Four-Step Process	Strategic Planning Steps and Program Outline
A. Defining the Problem (chapter 10)	**1.** The Problem, Concern, or Opportunity "What's happening now?" **2.** Situation Analysis (Internal and External) "What positive and negative forces are operating? "Who is involved and/or affected?" "How are they involved and/or affected?"
B. Planning and Programming (chapter 11)	**3.** Program Goal "What is the desired situation?" **4.** Target Publics "Who—internal and external—must the program respond to, reach, and affect?" **5.** Objectives "What must be achieved with each public to accomplish the program goal?"
C. Taking Action and Communicating (chapter 12)	**6.** Action Strategies "What changes must be made to achieve the outcomes stated in the objectives?" **7.** Communication Strategies "What message content must be communicated to achieve the outcomes stated in the objectives?" "What media best deliver that content to the target publics?" **8.** Program Implementation Plans "Who will be responsible for implementing each of the action and communication tactics?" "What is the sequence of events and the schedule?" "How much will the program cost?"
D. Evaluating the Program (chapter 13)	**9.** Evaluation Plans "How will the outcomes specified in the program goal and objectives be measured?" **10.** Feedback and Program Adjustment "How will the results of the evaluations be reported to program managers and used to make program changes?"

ners then outline what each of the two publics must learn from the program, what opinions each must hold after the program, and what each must do to reach the goal of increased seat belt use: another complex theoretical model of what the program must achieve. Their working theory follows the "learn-feel-do" causal sequence that guides most public communication programs:

Information Gain → Opinion Change → Behavioral Change

The working theory is made explicit when stated in the form of objectives for the two target publics. After the objectives are written, planners then turn to developing strategies and tactics to cause the sequence of outcomes specified by the objectives. If during implementation or after the program, the expected (theorized) outcomes are not being achieved, then program planners must decide whether their theory was flawed or whether the program implementation was flawed.

It is indeed the wise practitioner who keeps track of the conditions under which theorized cause-and-effect relationships appear to work and when those assumptions about the linkages between program activities and program effects do not occur. For example, did the third-party endorsements used in the Wisconsin Milk Marketing Board referendum campaign actually make a difference in the number of votes cast in favor of the middle nickel checkoff? If so, maybe the strategy can be generalized to other programs. If not, are dairy producers unique and more resistant to such endorsements?

In summary, working theory drives every program decision, whether the assumptions about the causal relationships behind the decisions are made explicit or not. Practitioners are continually devising and testing their working theories. Those who can bridge the gap between theory and practice are the ones most likely to achieve management positions in the 21st century.[19]

Defining Target Publics

First of all, practitioners define publics; they are abstractions imposed by program planners. Planners must reify publics so as to develop the objectives, strategies, and tactics necessary for implementing a program. Reification is treating an abstraction as if it exists as a concrete or material entity. The "general public" is the grandest and least useful reification of all; there simply is no such thing. Given unlimited resources, practitioners could avoid the need to reify by targeting individuals. Useful and practical definitions of publics, however, necessarily represent some degree of reification.

The usual demographic and cross-situational approaches to defining publics typically provide minimal useful guidance for developing program strategy. Simply listing general categories of potential stakeholder groups gives those planning and implementing a program little information about how people in each of the categories uniquely contribute to or are affected by the problem situation and organization.

Stakeholder categories such as employees, stockholders, alumni, consumers, community groups, government, and so forth, each may contain what public relations scholar James Grunig calls "nonpublics, latent publics, aware publics, and active publics."[20] *Nonpublics* are people who do not face a problem or situation in which they are mutually involved with or affected by either an organization or other people. Their level of involvement is so low that they have no impact on the organization and the organization has no recognizable impact on them. *Latent publics* include people who are simply unaware of their connections to others and an organization with respect to some issue or other problem situation. *Aware publics* are those people who recognize that they are somehow affected by or involved in a problem situation shared by others but have not communicated about it with others. When they begin to communicate and organize to do something about the situation, they become *active publics*.

Useful definitions describe program publics on the basis of how people are involved in or affected by the problem situation or issue, who they are, where they live, what relevant organizations they belong to, what they do that is relevant to the situation, and so forth. The definitions derive from the particular situation for which a public relations intervention is being planned.

For example, suppose that a university has the goal of increasing the number of incoming freshmen for the next academic year. The target publics for the program might include staff members in the admissions and academic advising offices (internal publics); high school students and others who have written or called academic departments requesting information about particular majors; high school seniors with grade points of at least 3.0 in high schools within 100 miles of the university and their parents; and high school guidance counselors in those same schools. When a local newspaper accuses two starting football players at the same university of receiving bogus academic credit for summer work experience, however, the public relations office will define different target publics for the university's response. It is obvious that different people, with different kinds of connections to the university, are involved in and affected by the potential crisis in the university's football program.

Following are approaches used alone and in combination to define target publics from among the various stakeholder groups:

1. Geographics—natural or political boundaries—indicate where to find people but give little useful insight about important differences within the boundaries. This approach is useful for selecting media and allocating program resources according to population density. ZIP codes, telephone area codes, city limits, county lines, and so forth, are examples of the geographic approach to defining publics.
2. Demographics—gender, income, age, marital status, education—are the most frequently used individual characteristics but provide little understanding of why or how people are involved or affected. Demographics and geographics help practitioners make the first cut, but without additional information about how people are involved or affected by an issue, problem, or situation, they usually give little guidance to developing strategy and tactics.
3. Psychographics—psychological and lifestyle characteristics (cross-situational)—widely used under the name "VALS," segment adults on the basis of "psychological maturity." Knowing about lifestyle and values is useful but typically only when combined with other attributes that tie the segments to something related to a particular situation.
4. Covert power—behind-the-scenes political or economic power—describes

people at the top of a power pyramid who operate across situations. They exert power over others on a wide range of issues but often not in ways easily observed. Identifying these people requires a combination of careful observation over time, interviews with others in the problem situation, analyses of documents that record or track the exercise of covert power, or any combination of the three.

5. Position uses the positions held by individuals, not attributes of the individuals themselves, to identify target publics. People are identified as important in a particular situation because of the roles they play in positions of influence in particular situations. The positions they hold make them important players in the efforts to achieve program goals and objectives.

6. Reputation identifies "knowledgeables" or "influentials" based on others' perceptions of these individuals. These publics are referred to as "opinion leaders" or "influencers," but they are defined as such by people in the situation of interest and are not to be confused by the cross-situational covert power group or defined as opinion leaders by the observer using some cross-situational definition.

7. Membership uses appearance on an organizational roster, list, or affiliation as the attribute relevant to a particular situation. For example, membership in a professional association or special-interest group signals a person's involvement in a situation, not the individual attributes of the member. Usually members receive controlled media from the organization with whom they affiliate.

8. Role in the decision process calls for observing the decision-making process to learn who plays what roles in influencing decisions in a particular situation. This approach helps identify the most active among the active publics, those who really make decisions, take action, and communicate. Again, knowing their individual attributes can be less important than knowing how they behave in the process that leads to decisions related to the issue or problem of interest.

The key to defining publics is to identify how people are involved and affected in the situation for which the program intervention is being developed. Program planners can develop specific and responsive program objectives and strategies if they know what different people know about an issue or situation, how they feel about it, and what they do that is either contributing to it or reacting to it. This understanding of what they know, how they feel, and what they do, combined with who and where they are, provides the basis for writing useful program objectives for each target public.

Writing Program Objectives

Objectives spell out the key results that must be achieved with each public to reach the program goal. In practice, objectives

1. Give focus and direction to those developing program strategy and tactics.
2. Provide guidance and motivation to those charged with implementing the program.

3. Spell out the outcome criteria to be used for monitoring and evaluating the program.

All too often, however, public relations program objectives either describe the tactic, or means, rather than the consequences, or ends, to be achieved. For example, "To issue 12 monthly issues of . . ." and "To inform people about . . ." both describe activities, not results. Objectives should outline the intended impact of the 12 issues and of the effort to inform.

Objectives also make concrete the working theory behind the program, usually in the "learn-feel-do" causal sequence. Program objectives for each public specify the desired outcomes and in what sequence, by what dates, and in what magnitude they are needed to achieve the program goal. (See Exhibit 11.3.) The more specific the objectives, the more precise is everything that fol-

EXHIBIT 11.3

$\mathcal{S}$AMPLE PROGRAM GOAL AND OBJECTIVES

Program Goal

To reduce the number of delivery drivers seriously injured or killed while driving on the job from a five-year average of five per year to no more than two in the next fiscal year.

Objectives for Delivery Drivers

1. To increase, within 6 weeks after starting the program, the percentage of drivers from 8 percent to at least 90 percent who are aware that in a typical year four company delivery drivers are seriously injured and one is killed while driving on the job.

2. To increase, within 2 months after starting the program, the percentage of drivers from 5 percent to at least 80 percent who know that 55 percent of all fatalities and 65 percent of all injuries from vehicle crashes could be prevented if seat belts were used properly.

3. To increase, within 2 months after starting the program, drivers' awareness to at least 85 percent that 95 percent of all city employees, police, and emergency vehicle drivers use shoulder restraints and seat belts

any time they drive on the same city streets.

4. To reduce, within 3 months after starting the program, the number of drivers from 67 percent to less than 25 percent who feel that using seat belts while driving adds to delivery time and extends the time needed to complete routes.

5. To decrease, by the end of the third month after the program begins, the number of drivers from 70 percent to less than 35 percent who "agree" or "strongly agree" with the statement that their own safe driving prevents serious driving accidents to the point that seat belts are not necessary.

6. To increase the percentage of drivers who use seat belts from the current 51 percent to at least 70 percent within 3 months after the program begins, to at least 80 percent within 5 months, and to at least 90 percent by the end of the first year.

7. After the 90 percent level of use is achieved, to maintain that level of seat belt use among all permanent and all temporary replacement drivers.

lows. Following are examples of useful program objectives for the three levels of outcomes:

1. Knowledge outcome: By July 1, to increase the number of local homeowners from 13 percent to 27 percent who know that wildland fires destroyed 2,500 homes during the past three fire seasons.
2. Predisposition outcome: To increase neighboring property owners' confidence in our ability to conduct field tests safely from a mean confidence rating of 2.7 to 3.5 by January 15.
3. Behavioral outcome: To increase the percentage of employees who use seat belts when driving on the job from the current 51 percent to at least 70 percent within 30 days after the program begins.

These examples illustrate the elements and form of useful program objectives:

1. Begin with "to" followed by a verb describing the direction to the intended outcome. There are three possibilities: "to increase," "to decrease," and "to maintain."
2. Specify the outcome to be achieved. Again, there are three possible categories of what is to be maintained or changed: what people are aware of, know, or understand (knowledge outcomes); how people feel (predisposition outcomes); and what people do (behavioral outcomes). Each objective should spell out a single, specific outcome.
3. State the magnitude of change or level to be maintained in measurable terms. To provide useful and verifiable outcome criteria, objectives must be stated in quantifiable terms. Surely the levels must be realistic and consistent with the resources available to those implementing the program. Experience and judgment, plus evidence from the situation analysis research, provide the bases for setting the levels of outcomes to be achieved. Without benchmark data, judgment dominates when setting the outcome levels.
4. Set the target date for when the outcome is to be achieved. Dates stated in the objectives follow the working theory of the sequence of what has to happen. Typically, outcomes must be achieved in order, with one necessary before another. Each successive outcome is a logical consequence of the previous outcomes. Dates also provide guidance for those developing strategy and tactics, even down to deciding when to schedule communications and events.

Objectives should be in writing, with copies available to each person working on the program. Objectives become the primary basis for developing and implementing program strategy and tactics. Objectives should be discussed frequently, because they provide the guidance for planning, managing, and evaluating program elements and the overall program. As the topic of staff discussions, objectives keep the program on track. As conditions change, program planners change the objectives to reflect the different program environment.

Without objectives, programs drift according to the whims and desires of clients and employers and the intuitions and preferences of practitioners. People in power choose program strategy and tactics because they like them, not because they are logically related to intended outcomes. Practitioners select strategy and tactics because of habit, comfort based on previous experience, or because they worked last time. In effect, objectives provide a road map, derived from the working theory, to the desired goal.

PLANNING FOR PROGRAM IMPLEMENTATION

Plans, if they are to be carried out effectively, must be monitored at each step of the way. Preparation and follow-up support are necessary to ensure a return on the investment made in planning and programming. Anticipation and follow-through on plans are just as important in the practice of public relations as in sports.

Writing Planning Scenarios

Writing planning scenarios is the art of forecasting and describing the range of possible future states. Scenarios provide either longitudinal or cross-sectional summative statements about the future for the purpose of planning. Forecasters working in the Rand Corporation in the 1950s were the first to refer to "scenario writing" when describing their more qualitative approach to forecasting the future. The process differs from more traditional quantitative forecasting in that planners develop a number of plausible predictions of the future rather than relying on a single projection as the bases for charting strategy.[21]

The origins of scenario writing are more qualitative than quantitative. In fact, the pioneer of the technique said that the most important parts of the process are "simply to think about the problem" and to engage in "systematic conjecture."[22] The goal is to help clients anticipate more than one possible future state and plan for events that may have no history upon which to build.

Futurists generally agree that the range of useful scenarios is two to four, but that the idea number is three. And although the labels may vary, they represent high-, low-, and middle-ground future states, with the middle-ground scenario often viewed as the one most likely to occur. Some experienced planners, however, argue that to avoid the appearance of assigning probabilities, scenarios should be titled according to some major theme or major attribute. Still others suggest "optimistic, surprise-free, and pessimistic" labels, again without suggesting probabilities. These planners point out that futurists cannot predict an uncertain future with certainty, so they cannot attach probabilities to scenarios.[23] Catastrophic events, political revolutions, and other dramatic and unanticipated changes in the social, political, economic, and technological environments demonstrate that scenarios represent possibilities. In contrast, the vision of hindsight reported in case studies gives the appearance of predictability; but note that case studies describe the past, not the future.

The danger of labeling one scenario as "most likely" or "probable" is that program planners tend to develop strategy for only that one possible future state, thereby defeating the purpose of having developed scenarios. After all, the purpose of writing scenarios is to construct descriptions of possible future states so that contingency planning can help prepare for the range of possibilities. The greater the future uncertainty, the greater the need for planning scenarios. Predictions based on historical data, traditional forecasting models, and trend analyses may not meet the needs of public relations planners who must be prepared for the unexpected. This is not to say that one would be wise to abandon traditional quantitative methods, however.

Anticipating Disasters and Crises

Whereas public relations practitioners typically cannot predict a specific disaster or crisis, they can anticipate that the unexpected will occur. It is the "unexpected" nature of events that creates a crisis situation: "An organizational crisis is a low-probability, high-impact event that threatens the viability of the organization and is characterized by ambiguity of cause, effect, and means of resolution, as well as by a belief that decisions must be made swiftly."[24]

First, though, practitioners must determine the types of crises, because the response depends in part on the type and duration of possible scenarios. A scholar of crisis management categorized eight types of crises caused by either management failures or environmental forces: *natural, technological, confrontation, malevolence, skewed management values, deception, management misconduct,* and *business and economic.*[25] Somewhat in jest, some use the "banana index" to describe crises: *green*—new and emerging issues and problem situations; *yellow*—current and ripe; and *brown*—old and moldy. A serious attempt to define crises also uses time as the critical variable:

1. Immediate crises—the most dreaded type—happen so suddenly and unexpectedly that there is little or no time for research and planning. Examples include a plane crash, product tampering, death of a key officer, fire, earthquake, bomb scare, and workplace shooting by a disgruntled former employee. These call for working out in advance a consensus among top management for a general plan on how to react to such crises to avoid confusion, conflict, and delay.
2. Emerging crises allow more time for research and planning, but they may erupt suddenly after brewing for long periods. Examples include employee dissatisfaction and low morale, sexual harassment in the workplace, substance abuse on the job, overcharges on government contracts, and the GM pickup fuel tank. The challenge is to convince top management to take corrective action before the crisis reaches the critical stage.
3. Sustained crises are those that persist for months or even years despite the best efforts of management. Rumors or speculation get reported in the media or circulated by word of mouth, outside the control of public relations. No amount of denial or countering seems to stop the rumor or purge the news database, meaning that reporters working on a new story will see the old story and may repeat the misinformation. Examples include persistent rumors of eminent downsizing, suggestions that Procter & Gamble's logo contains Satanic symbolism (this paragraph is an example of how

such rumors get repeated to new audiences!), and the charges of promiscuity that have plagued President Bill Clinton throughout his two terms.[26]

Practitioners who prepare for the worst are anticipating and responding to the needs of top management. For example, in the insurance industry, a string of catastrophic losses—earthquakes, fires, floods, hurricanes, and tornadoes—and the politicization of insurance issues helped establish the role of public relations in planning and management. In an industry in which disasters and crises are part of the business, senior managers regard public relations as essential to maintaining the industry's public franchise.[27]

Most organizations know how to deal with operational crises internally. It is the "unplanned visibility" following such crises, however, that can turn them into events that threaten reputation, credibility, and market position.[28] Some crisis management experts attribute the seemingly heightened interest in crisis management to what *Time* magazine called the "magazining of TV news" and fierce competition for "high-impact, hot-button stories":

> And everyone in magazineland seems to agree on what the good stories are: consumer rip-offs, miscarriages of justice, teary tales of people victimized by bad doctors or trampled on by insensitive government agencies. Like the one-hour dramas they have replaced on the prime-time schedule, the magazines serve up morality tales of black hats vs. white hats, with the reporter as avenging U.S. marshal. Instead of a six-gun, his or her weapons are a hidden camera (for the inevitable undercover exposé) and a hand-held mike, thrust at reluctant witnesses before they slam the car door. It's "Gotcha!" journalism.[29]

Common mistakes in handling crises include the following:

1. Hesitation—which leads to public perception of confusion, callousness, incompetence, or lack of preparation.
2. Obfuscation—which leads to the perception of dishonesty and insensitivity.
3. Retaliation—which increases tension and intensifies emotion rather than reducing them.
4. Prevarication or equivocation—which creates the biggest problem, because nothing substitutes for truth.
5. Pontification—which creates vulnerability by taking a high-handed approach without really dealing with the issue at hand.
6. Confrontation—which provides others visibility by keeping the issue alive, giving them a platform, and giving them more to respond to.
7. Litigation—which guarantees even greater visibility and may eliminate more reasonable solutions.[30]

The key to anticipating and avoiding crises is assessing what can go wrong, what can affect people or the environment, and what will create visibility. Guidelines for preparing for public relations crises include the following:

1. Identify things that can go wrong and become highly visible; assess vulnerabilities throughout the organization.

2. Assign priorities based on which vulnerabilities are most urgent and most likely.
3. Draft questions, answers, and resolutions for each potential crisis scenario.
4. Focus on the two most important tasks—what to do and what to say—during the first critical hours following a crisis.
5. Develop a strategy to contain and counteract, not react and respond.[31]

The value of having such a plan was demonstrated by a fire on the then-new $200-million luxury liner Crystal Harmony. The Los Angeles–based ship's captain called by radio phone to report that a fire in the ship's auxiliary engine room had disabled the ship. There were no deaths or injuries among the 920 guests and 540 crew members, but the ship was dead in the water. Public relations director Darlene Papalini turned to the company's 61-page "Crisis Communication Manual." It covered five types of emergency scenarios: (1) trade: labor strike or delayed sailing; (2) business page: "bad press," unfavorable financial news, or sale of a company; (3) shipboard: natural catastrophes, such as a hurricane or accidents such as a ship running aground; (4) media: a bomb threat, fire, or threat of sinking; and (5) international: terrorist or other attack. Each executive member of the crisis management team has a copy of the manual at home as well as a copy at the office.

The crisis was successfully handled with passengers, media, port agents, employees, vendors, and suppliers in part because such a crisis had been anticipated as a possible scenario and plans had been put on paper. According to Papalini, "We certainly do not want to go through such a thing again, but we were most pleased that people understood the plan and followed it; it worked."[32]

Successful handling of this and other crises requires an ability to anticipate possible emergencies and vulnerabilities, skills in planning strategy for responding to possible emergency scenarios, recognition of the early stages of crises, and the capacity to respond immediately as part of a systematic crisis management planning process. (See Exhibit 11.4, pg. 392.)

Establishing an Information Center

Many organizations have discovered the dangers of rumors and the need to provide authentic information. When a crisis arises, it suddenly becomes apparent that some seemingly unimportant facets of an operation have been overlooked and must be given hurried attention. Inevitably one such area of weakness is the availability of information. A knee-jerk response usually results in a jerry-built rumor center that operates through the crisis period, then fades away without serious thought until the next crisis comes.

There are three major points to remember in planning for an information center. First, the center must be recognized for what it is: a place where information moves from the institution directly to an organization's publics. It is not a press operation. To saddle an organization's press office with an added responsibility of answering questions from other publics reduces the effectiveness of both functions. Press and public information centers must be closely coordinated, but where the organization can afford it, they must be separate entities, each directed toward its own specific function.

EXHIBIT 11.4

*C*HECKLIST FOR CRISIS COMMUNICATION

Do the Following:

✓ Get out your prepared crisis plan, call together the crisis management steering committee, call in experts to help analyze and explain the crisis, and open the lines of communication.

✓ Notify top management and refer them to the crisis plan. Give them the task of making impact projections in preparation for inquiries from employees, government agencies, and the media.

✓ Channel all inquiries to the designated spokesperson, who was selected and trained in advance as part of the crisis planning preparation. Notify receptionists, operators, secretaries, and others to direct all inquiries to the designated spokesperson without giving their own versions or opinions.

✓ Set up a news center for media and begin providing information as quickly as it becomes available. Provide information background packets, telephones, computers and printers, fax machines, and a place for television interviews away from the crisis scene.

✓ Be open and tell the full story. If you do not, someone else will and you will lose control as journalists turn to other sources and outside experts to fill in gaps in the story.

✓ Demonstrate the organization's concern for what is happening and for the people who are involved and affected. At the same time, explain what the organization is doing or planning to do to solve the problem.

✓ Have someone on call 24 hours a day and stay with the story as long as the media are interested.

✓ Reconvene the crisis management team afterward to summarize what happened, to review and evaluate how the plan worked, and to recommend improvements in the crisis plan.

On the Other Hand:

✓ Do not speculate publicly about what you do not know to be fact. And do not respond to reporters' questions designed to solicit speculation.

✓ Do not minimize the problem or try to underplay a serious situation. The press will find out the truth soon enough.

✓ Do not let the story dribble out bit by bit. Each new disclosure becomes a potential headline or lead story.

✓ Do not release information about people if it will violate their privacy or if it blames anyone for anything.

✓ Do not say "no comment" or make off-the-record comments. If you cannot say something on the record, then explain why and tell reporters when they can expect the information. If information is simply not available, say so and assure reporters that you will get it to them as soon as you can.

✓ Do not play favorites among the media or the reporters. Respect reporters' work by not undercutting their scoops and enterprise.

✓ Do not try to capitalize on media attention and interest by trying to promote the organization, cause, products, or services. Do not do what will be perceived as a self-serving pitch while in the crisis spotlight.

Adapted from Claudia Reinhardt, "Workshop: How to Handle a Crisis," *Public Relations Journal* 43, no. 11 (November 1987): 43–44. Used with permission of *Public Relations Journal.*

Second, the center should be in two parts. Rumor centers are almost exclusively telephone operations. Of course, there must be an answering service or information center. So one group deals directly with the publics, taking questions and providing answers. If that group does not have the information, they promise to have it within a certain period of time. The second group, however, is a coordinating agency: the point of contact between the information center and the institution's staff and agencies. The coordinating agency goes to the institution's staff for information and checks material with the highest level of the administration for accuracy, coordinates it with the press office, and relays it to the center for use. Hence, all information flows through the coordinating agency, where it can be accounted for and logged. In addition to raw information—the factual material used to answer direct and simple questions—the coordinating agency should have qualified people available to speak on policy or to conduct philosophical discussions of current issues. As the sole source of material for the information center, this agency controls the center and what is being said to the various publics. Although not an official spokesperson, it does provide for a "one-voice" response to the institution's problems.

Third, and perhaps the most important, any such center must have credibility established long before any crisis; it must be the accepted source of accurate information. This cannot be accomplished during the period of crisis alone. The flow of credible information must be established during routine times. The function must become an accepted part of the institution on a full-time, continuing basis, identical in crisis or routine situations. It must also, over an extended period, encourage both internal and external publics to use it with faith and confidence. This amounts to more than establishing a reputation for truth; it involves education.

Internally, all agencies of the institution must be made aware that such a system exists and must be encouraged to use it to make information for which they are responsible available. At the same time, employees at every level in the organization must be advised to direct all calls to the information center. One crisis management specialist warns,

> The most damaging information or story points will come from individuals who work with us or who have worked for us; from documents or studies that should never have been written or done; from hand-written notes in the margins of otherwise innocuous documents; or from dumb, colorful statements or phrases a spokesperson just couldn't resist saying.[33]

Such an information or fact center, operating normally over a long period of time, sets the pattern within an institution for quickly and efficiently moving information. If the institution is tuned to such an operation in routine times, the transition is far less shattering in troubled times. When all the pieces of the crisis management plan work, some crises are avoided or preempted, and others are managed in such ways as to minimize damage. Pearson and Clair outline a broader definition of success, however:

> Effective crisis management involves minimizing potential risk before a trigger-

Old

New

ing event. In response to a triggering event, effective crisis management involves improvising and interacting by key stakeholders so that individual and collective sense making, shared meaning, and roles are reconstructed. Following a triggering event, effective crisis management entails individual and organizational readjustment of basic assumptions, as well as behavioral and emotional responses aimed at recovery and readjustment.[34]

The difficulties of dealing with one type of crisis—a pernicious rumor—are illustrated by giant Procter & Gamble's handling of a wild rumor that it was in "league with Satan" and giving part of the corporation's money to the "church of Satan." Evidence for such claims was Procter & Gamble's logo, which had evolved over more than a century, showing the man in the moon and stars. To deal with this rumor, the company went to the press, the pulpit, and the courts to stop the wild charges emanating from religious fanatics. But in April 1985, Procter & Gamble gave up the fight and announced that it would remove the logo from its products. In 1991, Procter & Gamble modernized its logo for the first time since 1930 but did not use it on products or in advertising for several years thereafter.

Budgeting

There is as much art and artistry in public relations budgeting as there is science. Available literature on the subject is sparse. Few practitioners study accounting and finance as part of their professional education. Canadian practitioners rated budgeting as their weakest skill, with 60 percent reporting that they had never received financial training.[35] Other surveys of practitioners reveal that they typically use their computers for word processing and desktop publishing but not to manage financial data. Yet about 40 percent of them manage budgets of $1 million or more.[36]

No doubt practitioners in other countries suffer from the same deficiency in their professional preparation. At professional seminars the most frequently mentioned guideline seems to be, "Always ask for more than you need." Of course the deliberate, habitual padding of budget requests is not peculiar to public relations. It has become part of the system but cannot be recommended as responsible management.

In established departments, budgets generally relate to one of four control factors. One is the total income or funds available to the enterprise, the second is the "competitive necessity," the third is the overall task or goal set for the organization, and the fourth is the profit or surplus over expenses.

When *total income* or *funds available* is the basis, as in marketing or fund-raising activities, public relations is generally allocated a percentage. The percentage relates to the organization's total operating budget, to gross sales, to funds raised, or to funds allocated from taxes. When *competitive necessity* is the criterion, the amount spent by a similar charity or a competing organization is matched or exceeded. This method is very risky. The *task* or *goal* basis usually provides for public relations to have a share of the funding set aside to achieve the desired end result. For example, to achieve a fund-raising goal, a museum might increase the percentage of the operating budget allocated to "development" activities. The final approach—based on how much money is "left over"—usually sets a fluctuating figure that can go up or down, depending on "the point at which we break even," or in a nonprofit operation, "the point at which we cover all expenses." Not only is it difficult to plan and staff under this option, but it also reinforces the impression that public relations is something you do if you have money to spend after covering the essentials.

Budgeting is rarely a one-person job. Each specialist is called on to estimate and itemize variable costs that will be incurred to implement the public relations plan during the next budget year. Variable costs are those associated with projects and activities, such as printing, rent for special events facilities, speakers' fees, photographers, advertising, travel, and entertainment. The department head, or someone designated, adds the estimated variable costs to the unit's fixed costs, including such expenses as salaries and benefits, overhead for office space, phone, service, equipment leases, supplies, subscriptions, and service contracts. The next executive up the line evaluates the budgets from the departments for which he or she is responsible, negotiates and adjusts the budget requests to fit the total available or needed, and finally either approves or forwards the budgets to the next level for approval. (See Figure 11.1.)

Three guidelines may be helpful:

1. Know the cost of what you propose to buy. If you plan to do a special mailing, find out the exact costs for photography and artwork, printing and folding, mailing lists, labeling and sorting, delivery, postage, and everything else needed to complete the job. Do not guess, because you will have to live within the budget that gets approved and deliver what was promised.
2. Communicate the budget in terms of what it costs to achieve specific results. The actual details of actual variable and fixed costs used to develop the budget may not be of interest to management or to a client. Managers who must approve the budget typically want to know how much it will cost to achieve goals and objectives. They look to you to manage the process in a cost-effective fashion.
3. Use the power of your computer to manage the program. Develop a master spreadsheet, as well as spreadsheets for individual projects. By tracking each project and linking each to the master spreadsheet, you can estimate cash-flow requirements in advance and monitor expenditures against cost estimates.

Too often, budgets are put aside after they are approved and are not used as management tools. Used in conjunction with other elements of program planning, however, budgets provide guidance for scheduling staff resources, contracting for services, tracking project costs, and establishing accountability. Individual staff members, as well as the entire unit, should refer to the budget when assessing performance against expectations.

Budgets often play an important part in shaping and maintaining the relationship between the public relations staff and their clients and top management. In the final analysis, practitioners must have realistic budgets, must use them to direct staff efforts, must review them frequently with clients and top management, and must be able to link costs to performance and outcomes.

FIGURE 11.1 **PUBLIC RELATIONS BUDGETING AND PLANNING PROCESS**

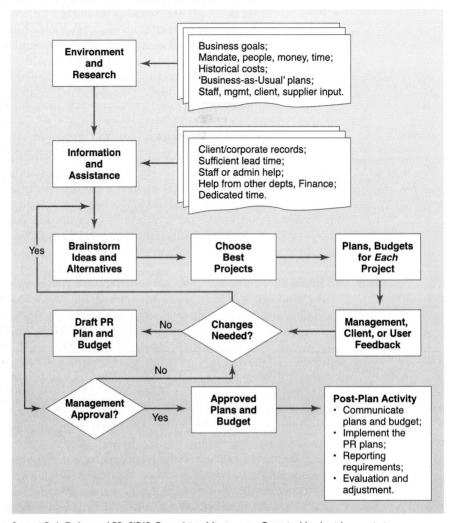

Source: Bob Delaney, APR, SIRIS Consulting, Mississauga, Ontario. Used with permission.

Pretesting Program Elements

Once the strategic plan is formulated, it should be tried on a pilot basis. Marketers have been doing this for decades. Only recently has pretesting a plan of action and communication become somewhat routine in public relations.

Many qualitative and quantitative tools are available: interviews with opinion leaders, focus groups, controlled laboratory tests, and field tests in pilot communities. Careful pretests of strategy, tactics, and program materials provide estimates of how they will work, provide comparisons of alternatives to determine which works best, and detect possible backlash effects of unanticipated, unfavorable results.

Backlash effects can be avoided by conducting a response analysis. This means using a sample audience to observe immediate reaction to specific communication content. As an example, the Occupational Safety and Health Administration (OSHA) would have been spared much embarrassment had it pretested its 16-page booklet "Safety with Beef Cattle." A pretest would have eliminated such nonsense warnings as, "Be careful not to step into the manure pits," "If your ladder is broken, do not climb it," and "Beams that are too low can hurt you."

Message pretesting also can help increase the understandability of the information for its intended audience. The symbolism chosen for a public relations document may represent perfect clarity to its creator but be both uninteresting and unintelligible to the reader. Or the symbol may be inappropriate, as when Caterpillar Tractor Company sent 10,000 calendars to its Saudi Arabia dealer, Zahid Tractor. When government inspectors opened the shipment they found that the calendar contained a picture of a village in Iceland showing a church with two crosses. Workers blotted out the crosses with heavy black markers because Christian symbols are forbidden in the devoutly Islamic nation. The blotches created 10,000 reminders of the need to pretest even the smallest detail in program communications and activities.

A few years ago an experimental program of health education was undertaken in an isolated Peruvian community high in the Andes. As part of the program, a film on the transmission of typhus by lice, featuring graphic close-up shots, was prepared and shown to the villagers. It became apparent that the message was not getting through. A survey of the people who had seen the film revealed that although they had many lice in their homes, they had never been bothered by the "giant" kind shown on the screen. To get results, appeals and symbols must be appropriate and understood.

A cautionary note on pretesting must be inserted. The stream of public opinion rushes along swiftly. An idea that worked well in a pretest might prove a fiasco upon widespread use because of a time lag. Seasons change and with them so change people's concerns, recreational pursuits, and so forth. Overpowering events can quickly alter the public opinion climate overnight with an unexpected news event; for example, the United Way of American national headquarters scandal dramatically changed the climate for fund-raising campaigns run by local United Way organizations. When using pretest results as a guide to communication programs, practitioners need to be as certain as possible that program conditions are similar to those that existed during the pretest and that pretest subjects are representative of the program target publics.

Selling the Plan

Research, analysis, precedents, and experience must be converted into program forms acceptable to those who are not public relations executives and to clients. Some are not sensitively attuned to public opinion. Some are cost oriented, or publicly gun-shy, or both. Some do not commit comfortably to speculative expenditures with no guarantee of return. Some are nervous about issuing information to news media. Goals and objectives not tied directly to sales or profits are ephemeral to many. The more specific the institutional goals, the more specific and effective the public relations plan can be.

Selling the program proposal puts the practitioner's persuasive and technical communication skills to the test. It calls for effective writing, persuasive speaking, skillful use of presentation audiovisual materials, and careful reading of those around the conference table. But effective selling begins with an effective program proposal.

After a program has been approved at the policy level, it becomes necessary to familiarize colleagues with what is to follow. Otherwise, these important collaborators may wind up uninformed, like an outside counselor who is not allowed to participate in the planning. Then, they would not be able to do their part. They would not be in a position to solicit support from the people under their supervision.

Some generally accepted tenets related to introducing others to the program merit noting. Explain the basic problems in terms of the harm that can be done if they are left unattended. Then, explain the immediate remedial measures in relation to long-term plans. Use similar case examples, precedents, and survey results to substantiate the plan. Eliminate personal opinion except as it applies to special knowledge of related cases. Relate the program to the climate in which the organization operates and that it hopes to enjoy in the future. Stress that the activities will have a desirable ultimate effect on public opinion. Keep explanations short and to the point. Be decisive and have conviction in the plan, qualities highly respected by administrators.

Staff orientation and indoctrination are best handled through informal sessions in which people can air their views and talk things out. Quite often, meetings are arranged in which the practitioner presents the program and then throws the meeting open to discussion. When this is done, a summary should be supplied afterward to all participants in the discussion. It can take the form of meeting minutes, a program timetable, a roster of projects, or a report explaining the plans. It is important for future relationships that the programming agreed upon be a matter of record. Getting it down on paper tends to make the planning and programming steps real and tangible for those charged with implementing the program.

NOTES

1. Jim Lukaszewski, "Let's Get Serious about Strategy," *strategy* I (Supplement to *pr reporter* newsletter), March 2, 1998, p. 1.

2. David M. Dozier and Larissa A. Grunig, "The Organization of the Public Relations Function," in *Excellence in Public Relations and Communication Management,* edited by James E. Grunig (Hillsdale, NJ: Lawrence Erlbaum Associates, 1992), 412–13.

3. William J. Small, "Exxon *Valdez*: How to Spend Billions and Still Get a Black Eye," *Public Relations Review* 17, no. 1 (Spring 1991): 9–25.

4. Stephen P. Robbins, *Organization Theory: Structure, Design, and Applications,* 3d ed. (Englewood Cliffs, NJ: Prentice-Hall, 1990), 121.

5. Ibid., 121–23.

6. Walter K. Lindenmann, "Research, Evaluation, and Measurement: A National Perspective," *Public Relations Review* 16, no. 2 (Summer 1990): 8.

7. David M. Dozier, "The Innovation of Research in Public Relations Practice: Review of a Program of Studies," *Public Relations Annual* 2 (1990): 15–21.

8. Robert W. Kinkead and Dena Winokur, "How Public Relations Professionals Help CEOs Make the Right Moves," *Public Relations Journal* 48, no. 10 (October 1992): 19.

9. Ed Block, "Expectations of PR: A Colloquy," *Arthur W. Page Society Newsletter* 7, no. 2 (June 1991): 4.

10. David M. Bicofsky of New York Telephone Company, quoted in Kinkead and Winokur, "How Public Relations Professionals Help CEOs," 23.

11. Quoted in Dena Winokur and Robert W. Kinkead, "How Public Relations Fits into Corporate Strategy," *Public Relations Journal* 49, no. 5 (May 1993): 23.

12. Kinkead and Winokur, "How Public Relations Professionals Help CEOs," 21.

13. Davis Young, *Building Your Company's Good Name* (New York: American Management Association, 1996): 12.

14. Paul S. Forbes, "Applying Strategic Management to Public Relations," *Public Relations Journal* 48, no. 3 (March 1992): 32.

15. Adapted from George L. Morrisey, *Management by Objectives and Results for Business and Industry,* 2d ed. (Reading, MA: Addison-Wesley Publishing, 1982), 107, 216–20.

16. Andrew Campbell, "The Power of Mission: Aligning Strategy and Culture," *Planning Review* 20, no. 5 (September–October 1992): 10–12, 63.

17. Adapted from Patrick J. Below, George L. Morrisey, and Betty L. Acomb, *The Executive Guide to Strategic Planning* (San Francisco: Jossey-Bass Publishers, 1987), 17–19; and Robert B. Irvine, "The Crisis Outlook for '92 and Beyond," *Public Relations Journal* 48, no. 10 (October 1992): 8, 34.

18. Lukaszewski, "Let's Get Serious about Strategy," pp. 2–3.

19. Winokur and Kinkead, "How Public Relations Fits into Corporate Strategy," 23.

20. James E. Grunig and Fred C. Repper, "Strategic Management, Publics and Issues," in *Excellence in Public Relations and Communication Management,* edited by James Grunig (Hillsdale, NJ: Lawrence Erlbaum Associates, 1992), 127.

21. Steven P. Schnaars, "How to Develop and Use Scenarios," in *Strategic Planning: Models and Analytical Techniques,* edited by Robert G. Dyson (Chichester, UK: John Wiley and Sons, 1990), 153–67.

22. Herman Kahn, *The Japanese Challenge* (New York: Thomas Y. Crowell, 1979), 5, as quoted in Schnaars, "How to Develop and Use Scenarios," 160.

23. Schnaars, "How to Develop and Use Scenarios," 158–65.

24. Christine M. Pearson and Judith A. Clair, "Reframing Crisis Management," *Academy of Management Review* 23, no. 2 (January 1998): 60.

25. Otto Lerbinger, *The Crisis Manager: Facing Risk and Responsibility* (Hillsdale, NJ: Lawrence Erlbaum Associates, 1997), Part II.

26. Adapted from Claudia Reinhardt, "Workshop: How to Handle a Crisis," *Public Relations Journal* 43, no. 11 (November 1987): 43–44.

27. Robert J. Gore, "In a High-Profile, Crisis-Laden Business, Insurance CEOs Rely on Public Relations," *Public Relations Journal* 49, no. 5 (May 1993): 21.

28. James E. Lukaszewski, "How to Handle a Public Relations Crisis," *World Executive's Digest* 12, no. 6 (June 1991): 68.

29. Richard Zoglin, "The Magazining of TV News," *Time* (July 12, 1993): 50–51.

30. Adapted from Lukaszewski, "How to Handle a Public Relations Crisis," 68–69.

31. Ibid.

32. Norman Sklarewitz, "Cruise Company Handles Crisis by the Book," *Public Relations Journal* 47, no. 5 (May 1991): 34–36.

33. Lukaszewski, "A Primer on the News Magazine Shows," *Executive Action* (January/February/March 1997). Quote from The Lukaszewski Group Inc. newsletter. Used with permission.

34. Pearson and Clair, "Reframing Crisis Management," p. 66.

35. Bob Delaney and Michael Lewis, "Planning and Budgeting for Public Relations Professionals." Paper presented to the 1990 Annual Conference of the Canadian Public Relations Society, June 1990.

36. *Profile 1997* (San Francisco: International Association of Business Communicators, 1997): V–6.

ADDITIONAL SOURCES

Dozier, David M., with Larissa A. Grunig and James E. Grunig. *Manager's Guide to Excellence in Public Relations and Communication Management.* Mahwah, NJ: Lawrence Erlbaum Associates, 1995.

Fearn-Banks, Kathleen. *Crisis Communications: A Casebook Approach.* Mahwah, NJ: Lawrence Erlbaum Associates, 1996. Presents case studies of how problems can turn into crises, then catastrophes, if not managed effectively.

Kendall, Robert. *Public Relations Campaign Strategies.* New York: HarperCollins, 1992. How-to approach to applying four-step public relations process and campaign principles to public relations.

Lerbinger, Otto. *The Crisis Manager: Facing Risk and Responsibility.* Mahwah, NJ: Lawrence Erlbaum Associates, 1997. Builds case for central role of communication in the management of crises.

Lukaszewski, James E. "Establishing Individual and Corporate Crisis Communication Standards: The Principles and Protocols." *Public Relations Quarterly* 42, no. 3 (Fall 1997): 7–14. Summarizes lessons learned by crisis communication management expert.

McElreath, Mark P. *Managing Systematic and Ethical Public Relations Campaigns,* 2nd ed. Dubuque, IA: Brown & Benchmark Publishers, 1996. Outlines "how-to" steps of researching, planning, implementing, and evaluation of public relations campaigns.

Nager, Norman R., and T. Harrell Allen. *Public Relations Management by Objectives.* Lanham, MD: University Press of America, 1984. (Originally published by Longman.) Still the most comprehensive effort to date to apply MBO to public relations.

Rayfield, Robert E., Lalit Acharya, J. David Pincus, and Donn E. Silvis. *Public Relations Writing: Strategies and Skills.* Dubuque, IA: William C. Brown Publishers, 1991. Approaches public relations writing as the application of communication and other social science theory.

Rice, Ronald E., and Charles K. Atkin, eds. *Public Information Campaigns,* 2d ed. Newbury Park, CA: Sage Publications, 1989. Useful reference for students and practitioners with interests in government and politics, and public health.

Tucker, Kerry, Doris Derelian, and Donna Rouner. *Public Relations Writing: An Is-*

sue-Driven Behavioral Approach, 3d ed. Englewood Cliffs, NJ: Prentice-Hall, 1997. Applies theory to developing public relations strategy and tactics.

U.S. Department of Health and Human Services, Office of Cancer Communications. *Making Health Communication Programs Work: A Planner's Guide.* National Institutes of Health Publication No. 89-1493 (1989). Discusses principles and processes for developing health communication programs. Includes examples and specific step-by-step guidelines applicable in other contexts.

STEP THREE: TAKING ACTION AND COMMUNICATING

Words are merely words, and they can be purely cosmetic if they aren't backed by convictions, actions and policies.[1]

—*Harold Burson*

OBJECTIVES

After studying chapter 12, you should be able to

▼ Differentiate between the *action* and *communication* components of program strategy.

▼ Define action strategy to include primarily *internal* adjustment and adaptation.

▼ Discuss major issues related to: (a) framing the message, (b) semantics, (c) symbols, and (d) barriers to communication.

▼ List and briefly describe the six criteria traditionally applied by gatekeepers to determine news value of messages.

▼ Outline the five major reasons why information campaigns fail and the three major ways to increase their chances of success.

▼ Outline the five stages of acceptance in the diffusion of new ideas.

The third step of the management process moves the public relations program into implementation. This stage applies to the fact-finding and strategic planning of the first two steps. Once a problem has been defined and a solution worked out, the next steps are *action* and *communication*.

ACTION AND COMMUNICATION

Public relations has matured into the role of helping organizations decide not only what to say but what to do, according to Harold Burson. In its infancy and into the 1960s, public relations simply crafted and distributed the message handed down from management. Indicating their view of the role of the function, management asked, "How do I say it?" In response to the social changes of the 1960s, organizations and their CEOs were increasingly held accountable on such issues as public and employee safety, equal opportunity, and the environment. In addition to how to say something, management asked public relations, "What shall I say?" Beginning in the 1980s, however, public relations entered a third stage; in addition to asking communication questions, management now asked, "What do I do?"[2]

Burson attributes this new role to unavoidable and increasingly detailed public scrutiny of what organizations do and say. Public response is also quick because of almost instantaneous worldwide communication. Modern communication technology closes the loop between message and behavior to the point that they are almost one and the same: What an organization does can be reported as quickly as what the organization says. As a result, all organizations need public relations more than ever, first to help determine what to do, and then to work out what to say and how to say it.[3]

THE ACTION COMPONENT OF STRATEGY

In the words of the old adage, "Actions speak louder than words." Yet many people in management, and even some in public relations, unfortunately believe the myth that communication alone can solve most public relations problems. Typically, however, public relations problems result from something done, not something said. The exception is when the "something said" becomes an event itself, such as when someone in authority or in a prominent position makes a sexist remark, racial slur, or other bigoted comment. Even more problematic is when such a comment appears in official organizational communications.

Acting Responsively and Responsibly

It stands to reason that if something that was done caused the problem, then something must be done to solve the problem. In other words, corrective action is necessary to eliminate the original source of the problem. An example of the need for corrective action is the university that had difficulties attracting freshmen. Investigators discovered that the word was out, "Don't go to State, freshmen can't get classes." Sure enough, freshmen had the lowest priority for registering for classes. Only after the university gave freshman registration priority did the number of freshmen increase significantly.

Another example is the "wild horse problem." The Bureau of Land Management (BLM) runs the Department of the Interior's mandated program to manage the wild horse and wild burro populations on federal lands. Protected under the Wild Horse and Burro Act of 1971, the wild herds grew too large for the range and invaded the grazing land leased to ranchers. The BLM rounded up horses and burros and made them available through the successful "Adopt-a-Horse" program. Because not all horses and burros are desirable to potential adopters, who pay a $125 adoption fee, the BLM waived adoption fees for ranchers who took large numbers of the surplus animals.

Animal-protection protesters charged the BLM with condoning the slaughter of wild horses, "our national heritage," by giving them to ranchers. They alleged that the ranchers shipped the animals directly to slaughterhouses, making a handsome profit in the process. BLM officials disavowed any role in the commercial slaughter of wild horses and burros for pet food but questioned the wisdom of spending $7 million a year to board surplus captured horses at a time when government programs for the poor were being cut. Still the angry protests continued. No amount of communication strategy appeared to ease the problem. When BLM officials recognized that their fee-waiver program was a major contributing factor, the program was canceled. Moreover, beginning in April 1988, ranchers did not take title of adopted horses and burros for 1 year. For that year, even though the rancher was responsible for care and feeding, the animals remained public property. Again, actions spoke louder than words.

The classic case study of responsive and responsible public relations actions, however, remains Johnson & Johnson's handling of the Tylenol crisis (review Exhibit 1.3).

Coordinating Action and Communication

The Tylenol poisoning crisis also illustrates the need for coordinated action and communication: Late in 1982, McNeil Consumer Products, a subsidiary of Johnson & Johnson, was suddenly confronted with a crisis when seven persons on Chicago's West Side died mysteriously. Authorities determined that they had died from cyanide poison that had been inserted in Tylenol capsules. The news spread rapidly over television and the news wires. Panic among consumers, hospitals, doctors, and pharmacists ensued nationwide. The crisis called for an immediate action response supported by communication. The following are the *action components* of the company's response:

1. Alert consumers nationwide, via the media, not to use capsules until the extent of tampering could be determined. (It was unclear at first that the tampering was limited to the Chicago area.)
2. Stop production of Tylenol capsules and halt advertising.
3. Establish liaison with the Chicago police, the FBI, and the Food and Drug Administration.
4. Recall all Tylenol capsules: 31 million bottles with a retail value of more than $100 million dollars.
5. Design and produce tamper-resistant packaging.

6. Return Tylenol capsules to the market with a stepped-up marketing effort to assure users of the product's safety.

Communication strategy supports the action program (Exhibit 12.1): (1) to inform internal and external target publics of the action; (2) to persuade those publics to support and accept the action; and possibly (3) to instruct publics in skills needed to translate intention into action. The following highlights summarize the communication components of Johnson & Johnson's strategy:

1. Publics: Consumers, pharmacists, management and staff of food chains, hospital administrators and staff, doctors, the Food and Drug Administration contacts, FBI contacts, medical press, and general press.
2. Message strategy: Intensive effort to gather facts on production of the lot of capsules in Chicago market. Full cooperation with the Food and Drug Administration. Assurance to alarmed inquirers of the company's determination to solve the mystery and to ensure the purity of its products.
3. Media strategy: Full, candid cooperation with the media to get facts to the public as quickly as possible, including the use of a 30-city press conference

EXHIBIT 12.1

COORDINATING ACTION AND COMMUNICATION

Few corporate management decisions are as difficult as a decision to relocate a company's headquarters. When Southern Railway System and its parent company, Norfolk Southern Corporation, made such a decision, several publics were affected by the decision. The reasons for the move and its ramifications had to be explained as effectively and quickly as possible.

Southern Railway had been headquartered in Washington, DC, since its founding in 1894. Although Atlanta had always been the operational center of the Southern system, the company's top management and up to 700 key officers and support staff were headquartered in Washington.

Southern Railway and Norfolk and Western Railway consolidated under joint ownership of the newly formed Norfolk Southern Corporation. In the first stage of the new partnership, the holding company was established at Norfolk, Virginia; the executive and operating headquarters of the Northern and Western were retained at Roanoke, Virginia; and Southern retained its executive offices in Washington and its operational headquarters in Atlanta.

As implementation of the merger plans unfolded, management determined that the maximum efficiency of operations could be achieved by consolidating Southern's executive and operating headquarters. Atlanta, as the operating heart of this 13-state, 10,000-mile railroad, was the logical site. Thus, the decision was made to close the Washington office and to relocate the personnel either to Norfolk or to Atlanta.

Except for a relatively few personnel who would remain in Washington, all employees would be involved in the relocation, so hundreds of employees and their families would be affected. The first priority of management, then, was to inform employees of the move officially, before they read about it in the paper.

conducted via television satellite. Centralized release of all information. Appearance of Johnson & Johnson chairman on television, including *60 Minutes*.

Action as an Open Systems Response

Public relations action is "socially responsible acts taken by public relations departments or other parts of the organization with your counsel."[4] Action strategy typically includes changes in an organization's policies, procedures, products, services, and behavior. These changes are designed to achieve program objectives and organizational goals, while at the same time responding to the needs and well-being of an organization's publics. In short, corrective actions serve the *mutual interests* of an organization and its publics.

Action strategy results from knowing how an organization's policies, procedures, actions, and other outputs contribute to public relations problems. As pointed out in the situation analysis section of chapter 11, a thorough understanding of the problem situation is essential for designing the action strategy. For example, when the Atlanta Bureau of Police Services (ABPS) tackled the problem of not enough police for public safety and security, it began by

Once the decision to move was final, department heads in the headquarters building were briefed on the decision and then told to advise the personnel in their departments immediately. Everyone used a general letter signed by the president of the parent company as the authoritative source for information about the move. They were told the reasons for the move, were advised that new offices would be constructed in Atlanta to accommodate them, were told that they would be given adequate time to plan an orderly relocation, and were informed that the company offered an extremely generous relocation assistance program.

On the obvious assumption that word of the decision would soon spread, the decision was made to inform key news media in both Washington and Atlanta. The wisdom in this approach, in contrast to saying nothing and then having to handle a "leak" situation, was borne out by universally favorable coverage of the relocation. Not a single negative word appeared in news or editorial coverage.

As word of the pending move spread through the media and other channels, favorable results continued. Southern's public relations department responded to numerous requests for information on the company's traditional relationship with Atlanta and Washington, details on who would move to Atlanta and when, and related questions. All inquiries were answered promptly and thoroughly.

Further evidence of the effectiveness of communicating the move came at a major conference of government, transportation, and business leaders in Atlanta. The mayor of Atlanta gave a resounding official welcome to Southern and told Southern's president, before television cameras and media representatives from around the country, that Atlanta would do everything it could to make the move comfortable and mutually profitable.

"This transition undoubtedly could have been made without a word being uttered," one company public relations officer noted. "But we discovered once again, as we have so many times in the past, that the results are much more positive when you 'talk about it now' rather than have to 'defend it later.' "

studying its own recruiting and training program. Before developing any external recruitment communications, ABPS changed how it operated its recruiting program. First, ABPS expanded the search area from the metropolitan Atlanta area to all Georgia. Second, it staffed an office specifically to handle recruiting. Third, ABPS equipped the office with the computer equipment necessary for expediting applications. These internal changes and the communication campaign resulted in more than 1,800 applicants and a net gain of 80 new officers on the force in one year. Previous attempts at statewide recruiting without the other changes in structure and processing had not reversed the attrition problem.

Action strategy concentrates on adjustment and adaptation *within* the organization. Opportunity to implement such changes, however, requires that both top management and practitioners define public relations as something much more than publicity and persuasive communication. As pointed out by Harold Burson, in its mature form public relations is involved in determining what is done as well as what and how something is said. The case of the Sybron Chemical Inc. provides yet another illustration.

Sixty neighbors of the Birmingham, New Jersey, manufacturer of water purification resins were evacuated following an accidental release of a noxious chemical. A month later, two plant workers were seriously burned during a process accident. These accidents and the resulting publicity only heightened public concerns about odors from the plant, about plant safety, and about the lack of information about plant operations. Neighbors and a U.S. senator called for new state and federal controls. Some in the community demanded that the plant be closed.[5]

With public relations counsel, Sybron devised a strategy to "take immediate, effective and credible action regarding each of the concerns identified by neighbors, local officials and state regulatory officials." The company also decided to break with past practice and begin regularly communicating both what was happening and the results of corrective actions. Action strategy included hiring an independent engineering firm to solve odor and chemical-handling safety problems and to upgrade plant facilities. Communication strategy included forming the Sybron Neighborhood Involvement Council to promote face-to-face communication; issuing a quarterly newspaper, *Sybron Community Update;* holding the first Sybron open house and plant tour; and installing a computerized 24-hour phone system (PINS Hotline) that calls neighbors' homes if there is a problem and allows neighbors to call any time of day for updated information (see Figure 12.1).[6] A follow-up survey of neighbors indicated that nine of ten felt more secure about Sybron as a neighbor and almost all believed that the company had improved communication with its neighbors. A report describes the award-winning program as "the story of how a new commitment to corrective action and communications resulted in a complete turn-around, in just seven months, with state regulators praising Sybron's actions as a model for the entire chemical industry."[7]

"Sybron is certainly a textbook example of how a company can turn neighborhood fear and anger into trust and credibility," according to Christine Foschetti, account executive at Sybron's public relations firm, Holt and

FIGURE 12.1   SYBRON CHEMICAL'S COMMUNITY HOTLINE

Courtesy Environmental Affairs Institute, Edison, NJ.

Ross, Inc. Sybron's management first had to mount an action strategy that included significant odor-reduction efforts and substantial environmental improvements. According to Foschetti, "Without these two very important elements, the company's public outreach program would have been doomed to fail."[8]

Action strategy puts into practice what chapter 7 refers to as the open systems model, or what James Grunig calls "two-way symmetrical" public relations.[9] The first assumption basic to this approach is that change is as likely within the organization as it is on the part of the organization's publics. Another assumption of this approach is that changes result in win-win outcomes, meaning that both sides in an organization–publics relationships can benefit. A third assumption that drives action strategy is suggested by the quote in chapter 7, "Clean up your act, not just your image." If public relations is to have an impact in shaping the mutually beneficial relationships necessary for organizational survival and success, it must participate in developing the action strategy and in coordinating this strategy with the communications that follow.

Action strategy necessarily makes up the main thrust of a program but represents the part of the public relations iceberg that might not show above the surface. Communication, typically the more visible component, serves as the program catalyst to interpret and support the action strategy. Chapter 8 outlines relevant communication theory and concepts that serve as the foundation for this section. What follow are fundamentals and principles for applying the theory to the practice.

Framing the Message

The first principle of framing message content for the communication effort is to know the client's or employer's position and the problem situation intimately. The second principle is to know the needs, interests, and concerns of the target publics. In the words of one practitioner, "Get smart and put yourself in the other party's shoes."[10]

Attempting to establish any single set of surefire rules for framing message content would be disappointing, if not futile. Such rules might appear perfect in principle yet be rendered ineffectual by an unseen characteristic of the audience; for example, a religious belief that bans certain foods. The timing could be bad. A carefully timed announcement of a new stock offering by an oil company was smothered in the news by revelations that it had used corporate funds for political campaigns in the United States and for bribes abroad. The audience could harbor an unspoken prejudice, such as confronts a Democrat campaigning in a Republican precinct. The wording of the message could be such that it does not square with the images in the heads of the audience, or perhaps the audience is not in a listening mood. Regardless of the specific barrier, results from standardized programming are generally frustrating and futile.

Effective communication must be designed for the situation, time, place, and audience. It means careful selection of media and technique. For example, the annual spring migration of college students to Florida's beaches poses health problems for that state, among them the spread of venereal diseases. One year the Florida Health Department gave frisbees carrying messages on how to recognize and prevent venereal diseases to students as they swarmed the Florida beaches. This is targeted communication. So is the campaign against teenagers drinking and driving in Tucson, Arizona: "Driving Drunk Will Put Your Lights Out"—a message framed in the imagery and language of the target public.

Advances in technology and specialized media have created a wealth of possibilities for serving the needs of special audiences. Practitioners would be well advised to think in terms of smaller and more circumscribed patterns of communication as they seek to modify or mobilize opinions. No communication or action, simply because it worked once before in a given situation, can be carted about like a trunk full of clothes and fitted to a new situation. With rare exceptions, the clothes will not fit the second wearer. If nothing else, they will be out of style.

All public relations problems, however, do have people as a common denominator and require communication to bring the people and their viewpoints closer together. This applies whether the programming calls for news releases, institutional advertising, meetings, or any other tool of contact. Continuity is required in communication. So are repetition of a consistent message in simple form, careful selection of time, place, and method, and a variety of media that converge on the audience from several avenues.

Public relations, with its powerful and varied means of selectively disseminating targeted information, suffers from an overcapacity. Simon and Garfunkel sang in "The Sounds of Silence" that our problem is people talking without speaking, people hearing without listening. Likewise, practitioners must define audiences with great precision and must use different strategies and techniques to accomplish different goals. For example, different concerns and different levels of intensity about an issue call for different message strategy.

The following time-tested techniques help reduce the discrepancy between the communicator's position and the audience's attitudes.

1. Use the media most closely identified with the audience's position.
2. Use a communications source that enjoys high credibility for the audience *on the topic of communication.*
3. Play down the differences between the positions in the communication and those of the audience.
4. Seek identification in vocabulary and anecdote with the audience *in an area removed from the issue.*
5. Establish the communicator's position as being the majority opinion, defining the majority from the audience itself.
6. Bring the audience's group identifications into play when those identifications will help develop a positive response. The converse is also true.
7. Modify the message to fit the organization's need.[11]

Framing the message for the media and media gatekeepers also requires attention to news value. Traditional criteria applied by gatekeepers, who see their role as acting on behalf of media audiences, include the following:

1. Impact—the number of people affected, the seriousness of the consequence, the directness of cause and effect, and the immediacy of the effect. This criterion applies not only to news but also to other information.
2. Proximity—the distance between the audience and the problem or issue of concern. This criterion simply suggests that local connections or news angles increase news value.
3. Timeliness—perishability. Like bread, news gets stale. This criterion also explains why journalists and media compete to be first with the news but why print media cannot compete with broadcast media on timeliness. As a result, print media may be more interested in why and how than in when, although daily newspapers remain concerned with the timeliness of information.

4. Prominence—recognizable and well known. Almost by definition, celebrity and celebrities are of interest to large numbers of people; they are newsworthy. Prominence means that journalists and their audiences are interested in the private lives of public organizations and figures.
5. Novelty—the unusual, bizarre, deviant, and offbeat. Some even define news as deviation from the normal. Journalists and editors know that people are attracted by and interested in what is new, unique, and unexpected.
6. Conflict—strikes, fights, disputes, wars, crime, politics, and sports. All too often, conflict is the major ingredient in news, not only because of its appeal to journalists but because of media pandering to public interest in the sensational and uncertain. Conflict situations often have issues that are not clearly defined, uncertainty about what is right or wrong, and oversimplified versions of winners and losers.[12]

Defining news may not be that simple, however. Some contend that news is anything that affects the lives and interests or stimulates the concern and curiosity of a significant number of people. In the final analysis, the distinction between hard news and soft news changes to accommodate audience interests in an ever-expanding range of topics, including science, culture, environment, social change, and education, to name but a few. Day-to-day news selection by gatekeepers, however, may result more from routine, deadline pressures, mechanical requirements, and their perceptions of what other journalists are saying and doing.[13]

Public relations practitioners must frame their messages to make them *newsworthy,* by whatever standard (hence the requirement to know the media and media gatekeepers). Messages also must be *understandable*—uncomplicated, free of jargon, and simple to grasp. They must also be topical or local to take advantage of audience interest in information that is both timely and close to home. Most important, however, is that the message must be *immediately actionable.* In the same way that the action strategy must be mutually beneficial, so must messages. The content should be framed in such a way that the information answers questions, responds to audience interests and concerns, and empowers members of the audience to act on their interests and concerns. The actionable quality deserves special attention.

Journalists systematically tend to shy away from including "mobilizing information" in their news stories. This is the information about identification, location, and instruction or direction audience members would need in order to act on their predisposition. One could speculate that journalists might feel that providing such information would be a departure from their perceived role of objective news reporters. When they include mobilizing information in stories about charities, other community drives, and crises, journalists may see this either as a forgivable departure, given the positive context, or as acceptable professional behavior.[14]

Another useful approach to framing the message is to use the "30-3-30" formula devised by the late author-scholar Clay Schoenfeld.[15] The first number means that many in the audience will give you no more than 30 seconds, no matter how attractive or interesting you make the presentation. You can count on no more than 30 seconds to get your message across, meaning that your key points must be strong, positive, and dominantly displayed. The second number indicates that some will give you up to three minutes, meaning that you can count on bold lines, subheads, illustrations, photo captions, and even highlighted summary statements to carry the message. Thirty-minute audience members will spend the time necessary to get message content, even though the details are reported in small type. Maybe a 3-30-3 formula should replace the optimistic Schoenfeld's 30-3-30 formula when framing most public relations messages.

Finally, framing the message strategy requires attention to four fundamental facts:

1. The audience consists of people. These people live, work, worship, and play in the framework of social institutions in cities, in suburbs, in villages, or on farms. Consequently, each person is subject to many influences, of which the communicator's message is typically only one small source of influence.
2. People tend to read, watch, or listen to communications that present points of view with which they are sympathetic or in which they have a personal stake.
3. Media create their separate communities. For example, those who read *Soldier of Fortune* and *The National Enquirer* are not likely to read *Scientific American* and *Architectural Digest.*
4. Media have a wide variety of effects on individual and collective knowledge, predisposition, and behavior, not all of which are readily measurable. Careful framing must take into account both the intended and unintended effects of message content.

Semantics

Semantics is the science of what words mean. Language is constantly changing, with new words appearing (such as "faxed") and words dropping from use (such as "groovy"). The meanings of words can change (such as "politically correct"). Others take on so many meanings that they become almost meaningless (such as "bottom line" and "strategic planning," according to some in public relations!).

Here we have space only to acknowledge the importance of semantics in public relations. Do not be misled, however; the subject really deserves and gets a great deal of attention from men and women in public relations. For in communicating and interpreting, practitioners live by words and make their living by them. For example, Edward Bernays referred to the "semantic tyranny" represented by the title of what is widely recognized as one of history's greatest special events, "Light's Golden Jubilee," the celebration of the 50th anniversary of Thomas Edison's invention of the incandescent light bulb. There is no escape for communicators from what T. S. Eliot described as "the intolerable wrestle with words and meanings." Practitioners must seek mastery of word meanings.

In the midst of the wrestle with words is the public relations practitioner. Studying the words that leap out of people's mouths, stare up from newspapers, and smile out from a television tube, the practitioner is expected to react and then to be able to tell what those words mean—not what they say, but what they really mean. Then the public relations specialist is expected to combine words and actions that will correct misunderstandings, educate where there is a lack of knowledge, and in general clear up confusion.

Practitioners are constantly making decisions about word meanings, so the basic importance of semantics must not be overlooked. Deciding what the refusal of people to work should be called represents a decision in semantics. Is it a strike, a work stoppage, or an outrage against the people? Cutbacks are referred to as "downsizing" or "rightsizing." Procter & Gamble called its notification that the company was about to cut 13,000 jobs and close 30 factories "the global initiative announcement." Weapons of mass destruction are called "peacekeepers," military invasions are referred to as "police actions," and new taxes are camouflaged as "revenue enhancements." Clearly, there is no one-to-one ratio between a word and its meaning. The same signs and word symbols have different meanings for different people.

In addition, they have two different kinds of meaning: *denotative* and *connotative*. Denotative meaning is the common dictionary meaning, generally accepted by most people with the same language and culture. Connotative meaning is the emotional or evaluative meaning we read into words because of our experience and background. For example, all people will agree that "dog" *denotes* a four-legged, furry, canine animal. For most people, cat *connotes* a friendly, faithful pet and usually awakens nostalgic memories about a childhood pet. To others, however, the word *connotes* a dangerous animal or the cause of dander that causes a severe allergic reaction. Another example is the word "bullfight." North and South Americans fully agree on what the term denotes, but its connotative meaning differs sharply north and south of the U.S.–Mexico border.

Our political language has become an integral part of events and helps shape their meaning. The campaign for national prohibition made *saloon* a dirty word, so today, those who drink do so in "taverns" and "lounges." Incidentally, the Drys were too wise to campaign for "prohibition," a harsh word; they advocated "temperance." Another great coup in semantics was scored in coining the term "life insurance" to describe what could be called more properly "death insurance," but the latter would be harder to sell. A ten-strike in semantics has been the successful effort of bowling promoters to change "bowling alleys" to "bowling lanes" and "bowling centers." "Educational television" became "public television," which has a more popular ring for fundraising. Semantic manipulation is an old art.

Words can excite and inflame. For example, there is evidence that a mistake in translating a message sent by the Japanese government near the end of World War II may have triggered the bombing of Hiroshima and thus ushered in atomic warfare. The word "mokusatsu," used by Japan in response to the U.S. surrender ultimatum, was translated as "ignore" instead of its correct meaning, "withhold comment until a decision has been made." And some years ago, semantic difficulties caused a crisis between the United States and Panama: Panamanians interpreted the English verb "negotiate" as a commitment to negotiate a new treaty, the meaning of the Spanish verb "negociar." The U.S. State Department intended it simply in its noncommittal sense of "to discuss."

Words often become "code words" to convey an unspoken but unmistakable meaning; for instance, "right to life," "law and order," "reverse discrimination," and "ethnic purity of neighborhoods." Even the meaning of commonplace words cannot be taken for granted. For example, one of the authors used the word "fallacy" on an exam, only to find that many students did not know what the word meant.

Public relations people must be able to select and transmit for various audiences words that will be received as kinfolk. Think of the harm that has been done, the confusion created, by legal language. The same is true for the language of doctors, educators, the military, and government. Each has a special jargon not readily understandable to others: legalese, educationese, militarese, and governmentese. And besides jargon there are slang, dialects, slogans, and exaggerations. Practitioners must work with their counterparts in the press, radio, and television and on the platform to help straighten things out for their publics.

Poet Anne Sexton cautioned, "Words, like eggs, must be handled with care; once broken, they are beyond repair." Practitioners must have a flair for picturesque, memorable terms, and a feeling for words.

Symbols

Communication involves more than semantics; in large measure it uses *symbols* and *stereotypes*. The symbol offers a dramatic and direct means of persuasive communication with large numbers of people over long lines of communication. Symbols have been used since the dawn of history to compress and convey complex messages to the multitudes. The Star of David and the Cross of Christ remind us of this. Most people need the shorthand of symbols to deal with whatever is abstract, diffuse, or difficult.

Years ago, Lippmann explained the need met by symbols and stereotypes as "introducing (1) *definiteness* and *distinction* and (2) *consistency* or *stability* of meaning into what otherwise is vague and wavering. . . . We tend to perceive that which we have picked out in the form stereotyped for us by our culture."[16] Here is a current example of Lippmann's point: "Pro-life" is a powerful symbol because it condenses an enormous amount of meaning, information, and experience.

The value and use of a venerated symbol is seen in the British monarchy. The greatly diminished British Commonwealth of Nations today is a free association of independent nations shakily held together, not by legal ties, but by the symbol of the Queen of England. She symbolizes the traditional loyalties, the common interests, the traditional institutional forms held more or less in common, and the family ties.

Symbols play an important role in the public relations and fund-raising programs of health and welfare agencies. Probably the best-known symbol of the kind is the Red Cross, from which that agency takes its name. The Red Cross originated in Switzerland and created its symbol by reversing the white cross and red background of the Swiss flag. The upright sword of the American Cancer Society, chosen in a nationwide poster contest, was created to portray its crusading spirit. Another crusade, that of the National Tuberculosis Association, is symbolized by the Cross of Lorraine, which dates back to the Crusades.

One of the most effective symbols ever created is that of Smokey Bear, used by the U.S. Forest Service, the Association of State Foresters, and the Advertising Council to promote forest-fire prevention. The idea originated in 1944 with a group of foresters and advertising specialists concerned about the need to protect our forests. After experimenting with drawings of deer, squirrels, and other small animals to carry fire-prevention messages, they had the idea of using a bear. A bear—with its humanlike posture, its way of handling itself, and its universal appeal to young and old—seemed ideal to build into a persuasive symbol. (See Figure 12.2.)

FIGURE 12.2   SMOKEY BEAR

The Smokey Bear symbol changed over the years, as did the appeals used in the public service announcements. More than five decades of public awareness campaigns have produced almost universal awareness of Smokey Bear, with 98 percent aided recall in some parts of the country. Surveys typically show that about 95 percent of adults and 85 percent of children recognize Smokey's message, "Only *you* can prevent forest fires." But even though the symbol enjoys widespread recognition, many of the young urban children exposed to Smokey Bear in school programs do not know what to do to prevent forest fires. The bear, however, remains a credible symbol of forest-fire prevention.[17]

Increasingly, for-profit and nonprofit organizations emphasize symbols (designs and logos) to create a public image and instant recognition or to capitalize on widespread public awareness and acceptance. A current example of the latter is the symbol for recycling, which marketers and organizations use to demonstrate their concern for the environment. In fact, another new term—*green*—has entered the language to describe communication and action strategies shaped to demonstrate sensitivity and commitment to protecting the environment.

Surely symbols should be distinct, different, and in character for the institutions using them. However, a changing public climate governed by new and different values can make symbols obsolete or offensive. For example, new public sensitivity for the rights and feelings of minority groups has forced Dartmouth College, Syracuse University, and Stanford University to abandon Indian symbols and names for their athletic teams. The University of Illinois and Florida State University, as well as the Atlanta Braves and Cleveland Indians, face increasing pressure to drop their long-standing Indian symbols and mascots.

Barriers and Stereotypes

Barriers to understanding and to the clarity of messages exist in the communicator and the audience alike. As Lippmann noted, each person lives in the protective shelter of a cocoon of his or her own spinning. This cocoon insulates the individual from the incessant communication babble that is steadily increasing in intensity. There are social barriers, age barriers, language or vocabulary barriers, and political and economic barriers. There is also the race barrier; the barriers and distortions that block communication are seen starkly in the gulf between racial and ethnic groups in the multicultural American society. There is peer pressure exerted within groups, where "reality" is shared and interpreted. There is also the often overlooked barrier of the audience's ability to absorb messages. Finally, there is the constant roar of competition for people's attention in the noisy public arena. Barriers are not the only complications in communication, however.

People have impressions about everything that touches their consciousness. All people live in a world of their own symbols. Public figures, for example, during their lifetimes and afterward, are known partly through a personality created by images fixed in the public imagination. Astronauts, politicians, rock stars, and sports heroes are good examples. Their families and associates know them as people entirely different from their public personalities. People who live on one side of town tend to know people on the other side of town, as well as those in remote cities, in a half-fictional, half-imagined way. The only feeling that people can have about an event they do not experience or a person they do not know is by their own mental image of the event or person, developed from fragmentary, secondary sources.

In communication, nothing raises more problems than the reality that most in mass media audiences have limited access to the facts. With limited access, and with some information tending to confuse as much as it clarifies, people rely heavily on *stereotypes*. Specific and significant impressions become generalities. As Lippmann pointed out, the "pictures in our head" derive mainly from what we see and hear in the mass media. Certainly our impressions of the long-running civil war in Yugoslavia, nuclear tests in India, and riots in Jakarta (Indonesia), as well as our stereotypes of the people in each situation, came from cable and network television, newsmagazines, newspapers, and radio.

Readers looking at a magazine cover picture entitled "Criminal" may pick out two or three sharply defined features. Perhaps they select a low forehead, a squinting eye, a scarred face, or a mouth that curls at the corner. From then on, the impression may be so deeply rooted that readers feel sure that they know the "criminal type" whenever they see it. They can classify everyone, including friends, as to whether or not they are criminal types. Indeed, people have classifications into which they can fit almost everyone they see or hear about.

Such distorted stereotypes pose public relations problems. For example, a newly elected president of the California State Bar announced that she would make addressing negative and distorted public stereotypes of lawyers her highest priority. Unfortunately for lawyers everywhere, however, cartoonists took advantage of her announcement by exploiting stereotypes in a new rash of cartoons portraying lawyers as snakes, vultures, wolves, sharks, and so forth. The media help create new stereotypes by reducing complex people, groups, countries, and situations to their simplest and most general—sometimes distorted—attributes.

Lippmann emphasized the sacrosanct regard that people have for stereotypes as "the core of our personal tradition, the defense of our position in society."

> They may not be a complete picture of the world, but they are a picture of a possible world to which we are adapted. In that world people and things have their well-known places, and do certain expected things. We feel at home there. We fit in. We are members. We know the way around. . . . The stereotypes are, therefore, highly charged with the feelings that are attached to them. They are the fortress of our tradition, and behind its defenses we can continue to feel ourselves safe in the position we occupy.[18]

Stereotypes, then, serve as a defense mechanism against having to exert the effort required to learn about and understand the uniqueness and details of each person, group, and situation. They also form a moral code from which personal standards of behavior are derived. Practitioners must learn to recognize the influence and the presence of symbols and stereotypes in what appear to be the contradictions and contrariness of public opinion. Symbols are used to counter symbols, and stereotypes are used to counter stereotypes.

There is yet another side to stereotypes, however. In the context of a multicultural society, media are trying to be more sensitive and respectful of differences based on age, gender, sexual preference, race, body shape, and ethnicity. Some criticize efforts to purge the language of stereotypes as yielding to the "politically correct language" movement. They say the movement is headed by the kind of "thought police" George Orwell warned us about. Others see eliminating words and phrases that are pejorative stereotypes as a way to promote acceptance of diversity and to make media content more inclusive and less offensive.[19]

To avoid having the words themselves become a public relations problem, practitioners must be sensitive to word choice. A good reference on words to avoid is the *Dictionary of Cautionary Words and Phrases,* published by the University of Missouri, which includes a checklist of offensive words and stereotypes.[20] In the final analysis, language changes carried to extremes can debase the language by substituting euphemisms for accurate and meaningful descriptions. Responding to every charge of "oppression" without care can take away from the real effort to rid language of sexist, racist, and other insensitive stereotypes. Paradoxically, "political correctness" has taken on many different connotations to many different people in many different contexts, robbing the term itself of real meaning.

Putting It All Together in a Campaign

The difficulty of public information campaigns can be clearly seen in the battle to save us from polluted air, polluted water, and chemically dangerous foods. America's pioneer ecologist, Aldo Leopold, thought in his early years that "if the public were told how much harm ensues from unwise land-use, it would mend its ways." In his twilight years, he knew that this conclusion was based on three mistaken assumptions: that the public is listening or can be made to listen; that the public responds, or can be made to respond, to fear of harm; and that ways can be mended without any important change in the public itself.[21]

In a much-quoted article, Hyman and Sheatsley codified the major reasons why many information campaigns fail. They include the following:

1. There exists a hard core of chronic "know-nothings." These people are difficult to reach, no matter what the level or nature of the information.
2. Interested people acquire the most information. Motivation is essential to learning or assimilating knowledge, yet there are large groups in the population who admit that they have little or no interest in public issues.
3. People seek information that is compatible with their prior attitudes and avoid exposure to that which is not compatible.
4. People interpret the same information differently. Selective perception and in-

terpretation of content follows exposure: Persons perceive, absorb, and remember content differently.

5. Information does not necessarily change attitudes. Changes in views or behavior following exposure to a message may be differentially affected by the individual's initial predisposition.[22]

Another researcher, Harold Mendelsohn, countered with an analysis of why information campaigns can succeed.

What little empirical experience we have accumulated from the past suggests that public information campaigns have relatively high success potentials:

1. If they are planned around the assumption that most of the publics to which they will be addressed will be either only mildly interested or not at all interested in what is communicated.
2. If middle-range goals which can be reasonably achieved as a consequence of exposure are set as specific objectives. Frequently it is equally important either to set up or to utilize environmental support systems to help sheer information giving become effective in influencing behavior.
3. If, after middle-range objectives are set, careful consideration is given to delineating specific targets in terms of their demographic and psychological attributes, their life-style, value and belief systems, and mass media habits. Here, it is important not only to determine the scope of prior indifference, but to uncover its roots as well.[23]

That public-information campaigns can succeed has been demonstrated by numerous campaigns against smoking in public places, the highly successful effort by Mothers Against Drunk Drivers (MADD), the Stanford University communication experiments in preventing cardiovascular diseases, and American Cancer Society efforts promoting cancer detection and prevention, to name but a few. The jury is still out on campaigns to prevent HIV infections, to reduce drug abuse, and to promote social tolerance.

One persuasion theorist described the plight of campaign planners this way: The person beginning to design a public communication campaign is like a person lost somewhere in a dense forest of possibilities. He or she can find a way out by following old scout training to keep calm and keep moving in one direction, and sooner or later will reach the clearing; the only real dangers are freezing in place or losing all sense of direction and wandering around in circles. Even when the chosen theory is not optimal for the situation (in that an alternative direction would have led us out more easily), it suffices to lead us out to *terra cognita* with deliberate speed.[24]

Disseminating the Message

Gaining acceptance of an idea or an innovation is more than simply beaming it to an audience through a mass medium or internal publication. To illuminate, communication must be aimed with the precision of a laser beam, not cast in all directions in the manner of a light bulb. Even after many years of research, there is still not definitive evidence of a single model of how ideas are disseminated among people. Elmo Roper, after nearly 30 years of opinion research, formulated a hypothesis that has some value as a guide. His "concentric-circle theory" says that ideas penetrate to the whole public very slowly through a process similar to osmosis. Histories of public campaigns substantiate this. They move out in concentric circles from great thinkers to great disciples to great disseminators to lesser disseminators to the politically active to the politically inert. This hypothesis assumes that American society can be stratified as indicated and emphasizes the importance of using opinion leaders in the public relations process.

The rate of flow in the transmission and acceptance of ideas, however, is governed by many factors other than the characteristics of the people involved. These include Lippmann's "barriers to communication" and George Gallup's "regulators of absorption rate" illustrated in Figure 12.3, pg. 422.

The communication step in the public relations process often requires influencing knowledge, opinions, and actions among sizable and distant groups. The accelerating rate at which innovations are being invented, developed, and spread makes it vital that communicators be able to transfer information to those who need it. Examples include gaining public acceptance of using sunscreen lotions to protect against skin cancer; overcoming fear of technology, such as programming a VCR or paying bills electronically; and getting high-risk publics to get blood pressure checkups. And the rate of adopting new technology is accelerating: "(In 1997) 100 million people logged onto the Internet, up from 40 million the year before. That is faster than the phone, TV, and radio were adopted. When President Clinton took office there were only 50 web sites. Now 65,000 are being added . . . every hour."[25]

Diffusion refers to this process by which new ideas and practices are spread to members of a social system. The U.S. Department of Agriculture has been working at this task longer than most. It learned from experience that getting new ideas accepted involves more than simply discovering a new grain and publicizing it. It took 13 years to gain widespread adoption of hybrid seed corn on America's farms, for example. Out of their long experience and evaluation research, agricultural sociologists have concluded that acceptance goes through five stages:

1. Knowledge. People learn about an innovation and some gain understanding of what it is.
2. Persuasion. Potential adopters develop interest in the innovation. They seek more information and consider its general merits.
3. Decision. Potential adopters decide to adopt or reject the innovation after weighing its merits for their own situation.
4. Implementation. Those willing to try the innovation actually apply it to their situation, usually on a small scale. They are interested in the practice, techniques, and conditions for application.
5. Confirmation. Adoption is either reinforced or the decision to adopt is reversed based on the evaluation.[26]

FIGURE 12.3   COMMUNICATION BARRIERS AND DISSEMINATION

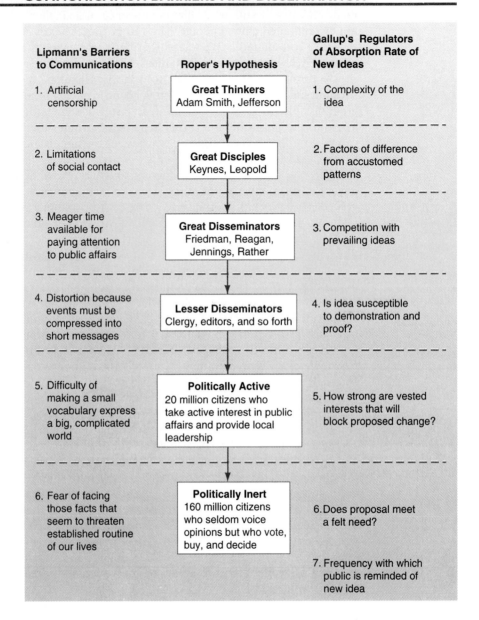

Mass media have their greatest impact and usefulness in creating awareness in the knowledge stage. For farmers, at least, the mass media become less and less influential as the acceptance process advances toward confirmation of the adoption. Interpersonal influence increases with each step. This diffusion model, developed through extensive research among rural families, was supported in subsequent studies in other settings. Chaffee suggests that there are several reasons for this pattern of diffusion:

> The media are comparatively rich in news content, whereas personal associates are likely to have had relevant "consumer" experience. Further, since consumption is partly a matter of defining one's social "self," other persons would be able to offer normative social guides to appropriate consumption patterns that the media cannot. Finally, some matters may not be dealt with by the media in sufficient depth or detail to satisfy personal information needs.[27]

The research conclusions demonstrate that communicating a new idea or practice is a long, tedious task. Different communication tactics are effective at different points and in different ways. The influence of influentials and opinion leaders is great in many situations. It is important for the communicator to know what media and techniques to use at different stages and how to mobilize these influences effectively. In summary, however, effective communication is expensive in research, preparation, attention, and implementation. The cost is higher than is commonly supposed.

Reconsidering the Process

The three elements common to all communication are the source or sender, the message, and the destination or receiver. A communication breakdown can involve one or more of these three elements. Effective communication requires efficiency on the part of all three. The communicator must have *adequate information*. The communicator must have *credibility* in the eyes of the receiver. The communicator must be able to transmit information in codes the receiver can *comprehend*. The communicator must use a channel that will carry the message to the receiver. The message must be within the receiver's *capacity to comprehend* and *relevant* to the receiver's interests or needs. Finally, the message must motivate the receiver's self-interest and cause a *response*.

Wise communicators see receivers not as passive subjects but as selective users of information for their own purposes. Too many public relations programs do not gauge the individual's role in the process. Public relations educator and scholar Doug Newsom says that practitioners should not use "the term 'audiences,' because it implies 'recipients' of messages instead of participants in communication."[28]

Words are symbols. There are words that serve as symbols for real objects—table, chair—thing words. There are words that are symbols of abstract ideas—such as freedom, love—nothing words. Children are taught, for example, that a furry little animal with long ears and a short, fuzzy tail is a "rabbit." Once the word and the little animal are associated, the word will always evoke the image of that creature. Word symbols for real objects are readily understood and agreed upon. This is not so with symbols for abstractions. Abstractions such as "pro-choice" or "pro-life" have no simple or universally accepted referents in the real world of objects. It is difficult for people to agree on an image of "free trade" when they cannot see, touch, hear, taste, or smell it. This difficulty goes right to the heart of the communications problem.

To communicate effectively, the sender's words and symbols must mean the same thing to the receiver that they do to the sender. The word communication is derived from the Latin *communis,* meaning "common." So "communication" means establishing a commonness. A sender can encode a message, and a receiver decode it only in terms of their own experience and knowledge. But if there has been no common experience, then communication becomes virtually impossible. This explains a layperson's inability to understand an Einstein. It explains why—despite the tremendous flow of words to and from China—Americans and Chinese still have little understanding of each other.

Common knowledge and experience provide the connections. The greater the overlap in common interest and common experience, the easier it is to communicate. Many barriers impede achieving this overlap of commonness, but commonness in communication is essential to link people and purpose together in any cooperative system.

Public relations communication provides the climate for an action's acceptance and implementation but is only one element. For example, successful public campaigns against smoking, unsafe sex, drinking and driving, drug use, and careless use of fire in forests must be accompanied by action strategy that changes the problem situation and provides enforcement and social support.

IMPLEMENTING THE STRATEGY

The purpose of this chapter was to introduce some of the major considerations and principles of implementing public relations programs. However, entire books devoted to the topic cannot adequately cover the range of issues and practices related to putting the program in place. The chapter concludes with the venerable seven Cs of public relations communication:

1. Credibility. Communication starts with a climate of belief. This climate is built by performance on the part of the institution, reflecting an earnest desire to serve stakeholders and publics. Receivers must have confidence in the sender and high regard for the source's competence on the subject.
2. Context. A communications program must square with the realities of its environment. Mass media only supplement the words and deeds of daily living. The context must provide for participation and playback. It must confirm, not contradict, the message. Effective communication requires a supportive social environment, one largely set by the news media.
3. Content. The message must have meaning for receivers, and it must be compatible with their value system. It must have relevance to the receivers' situation. In general, people select those items of information that promise them the greatest rewards. The content determines the audience.
4. Clarity. The message must be put in simple terms. Words must mean the same to the receivers as to the sender. Complex issues must be compressed into themes, slogans, or stereotypes that have simplicity and clarity. The

farther a message has to travel, the simpler it must be. An organization must speak with one voice, not many voices.

5. Continuity and consistency. Communication is an unending process. It requires repetition to achieve penetration. Repetition—with variation—contributes to both learning and persuasion. The story must be consistent.

6. Channels. Established channels of communication should be used, channels that receivers use and respect. Creating new ones can be difficult, time-consuming, and expensive. Different channels have different effects and serve effectively in different stages of the diffusion process. Selective channels are called for in reaching target publics. People associate different values with the many channels of communication.

7. Capability of the audience. Communication must take into account the capability of the audience. Communications are most effective when they require the least effort on the part of receivers. This involves factors of availability, habits, reading ability, and prior knowledge.

Communication and action are not the ends, but only the means to ends. The ends of public relations are the outcomes spelled out in program goals and objectives. Assessing the effectiveness of program strategy—the fourth step—is the topic of the next chapter.

NOTES

1. Speech to Raymond Simon Institute for Public Relations, Utica College, Syracuse University, March 5, 1987.

2. Harold Burson, "Beyond 'PR': Redefining the Role of Public Relations," 29th Annual Distinguished Lecture of the Institute for Public Relations Research and Education, Inc., New York, October 2, 1990.

3. Ibid.

4. Norman R. Nager and T. Harrell Allen, *Public Relations Management by Objectives* (Lanham, MD: University Press of America, 1984), 241–42. (Originally published by Longman.)

5. Caron Chess, Michal Tamuz, Alex Saville, and Michael Greenberg, "Reducing Uncertainty and Increasing Credibility: The Case of Sybron Chemicals Inc.," *Industrial Crisis Quarterly* 6, no. 1 (1992): 55–70.

6. PINS Hotline is the registered trademark for the Prompt Inquiry and Notification System of the Environmental Affairs Institute, Inc., Edison, NJ.

7. Public Relations Society of America, "1990 Silver Anvil Winners: Index and Summaries," New York, 1990, 1–2.

8. Christine S. Foschetti, Edison, NJ, correspondence to the authors, July 15, 1993.

9. James E. Grunig, "Communication, Public Relations, and Effective Organizations: An Overview of the Book," in *Excellence in Public Relations and Communication Management,* edited by James E. Grunig (Hillsdale, NJ: Lawrence Erlbaum Associates, 1992), 18–19.

10. A. C. Croft, "Delayed Action Allows Informed Response," *Public Relations Journal* 48, no. 5 (May 1992): 31.

11. Eugene F. Lane, "Applied Behavioral Science," *Public Relations Journal* 23, no. 7 (July 1967): 6.

12. Adapted from Brian S. Brooks, George Kennedy, Daryl R. Moen, and Don Ranly, *News Reporting and Writing,* 3d ed. (New York: St. Martin's Press, 1988).

13. Pamela J. Shoemaker, *Gatekeeping,* Communication Concepts 3 (Newbury Park, CA: Sage Publications, 1991), 50–52.

14. James B. Lemert and Marguerite Gemson Ashman, "Extent of Mobilizing Information in Opinion and News Magazines," *Journalism Quarterly* 60, no. 4 (Winter 1983): 657–62.

15. Clay Schoenfeld, "Thirty Seconds to Live," *Writer's Market,* February 1977, p. 29.

16. Walter Lippmann, *Public Opinion* (New York: Harcourt, Brace and Company, 1922), 81.

17. Smokey's history is summarized in *Public Communication Campaigns,* 2d ed., edited by Ronald E. Rice and Charles K. Atkin (Newbury Park, CA: Sage Publications, 1989), 215–18.

18. Lippmann, *Public Opinion,* 95–96.

19. Natasha Spring, "Freedom of Speech vs. Politically Correct Language," *Communication World* 9, no. 5 (April 1992): 34–38.

20. This useful reference was compiled by the 1989 Multicultural Management Program Fellows at the University of Missouri School of Journalism. It lists derogatory and offensive terms, as well as preferred substitutes.

21. For the story of Leopold's career as an innovator and environmentalist, see Susan Flader, *Thinking Like a Mountain* (Columbia: University of Missouri Press, 1974).

22. Herbert H. Hyman and Paul B. Sheatsley, "Some Reasons Why Information Campaigns Fail," *Public Opinion Quarterly* 11 (1947): 412–23.

23. Harold Mendelsohn, "Why Information Campaigns Can Succeed," *Public Opinion Quarterly* 37 (Spring 1973): 50–61.

24. William J. McGuire, "Theoretical Foundations of Campaigns," in *Public Communication Campaigns,* edited by Rice and Atkin, 65.

25. William M. Daley, Secretary, U.S. Department of Commerce, Washington, DC, April 15, 1998, as quoted in *Collective Destiny* 2, no. 2 (April 1998): 1. *Collective Destiny* is a publication of the Japan–U.S. Telecommunications Research Institute, San Diego State University.

26. Everett M. Rogers, *Diffusion of Innovations,* 3d ed. (New York: Free Press, 1983).

27. Steven H. Chaffee, "The Interpersonal Context of Communication," in *Current Perspectives in Mass Communication Research,* edited by F. Gerald Kline and Phillip J. Tichenor (Beverly Hills, CA: Sage Publications, 1972), 103.

28. Doug Newsom, Texas Christian University, as quoted in *pr reporter* 36, no. 17 (April 26, 1993): 4.

ADDITIONAL SOURCES

Bivins, Thomas. *Handbook for Public Relations Writing,* 3rd ed. Lincolnwood, IL: NTC Business Books, 1996. One of several good how-to books on preparing public relations and publicity materials—writing—based on a strategic plan.

Budd, John F. Jr. *Street Smart Public Relations.* Lakesville, CT: Turtle Publishing Co., 1992. Veteran practitioner's down-to-earth instruction on "how to get things done."

Hunt, Todd, and James E. Grunig. *Public Relations Techniques.* Fort Worth, TX: Harcourt Brace College Publishers, 1994. Adapts authors' theory and principles of managing public relations to program implementation.

Newsom, Doug, and Bob Carrell. *Public Relations Writing: Form and Style,* 3d ed. Belmont, CA: Wadsworth Publishing Company, 1991. Instructs how to prepare and present information in the wide variety of public relations media.

Smith, Alvie L. *Innovative Employee Communication.* Englewood Cliffs, NJ: Prentice-Hall, 1990. Discusses action and communication strategy in the context of employee communication.

Thompson, William. *Targeting the Message: A Receiver-Centered Process for Public Relations Writing.* New York: Longman, 1996. Presents an audience-centered approach to communicating information as an alternative to the too-frequent role as "press agents for our bosses' egos."

Tucker, Kerry, Doris Derelian, and Donna Rouner. *Public Relations Writing: An Issue-Driven Behavioral Approach.* Upper Saddle River, NJ: Prentice-Hall, 1997. Applies state-of-the-art knowledge about anticipating issues and strategic planning to public relations writing.

Wilcox, Dennis L., and Lawrence W. Nolte. *Public Relations Writing and Media Techniques.* New York: Longman, 1997. Addresses a wide range of public relations writing assignments, including advertising, special events, conferences, meetings, and audiovisual presentations.

EVALUATING THE PROGRAM

13

When you can measure what you are speaking about, and express it in numbers, you know something about it. But when you cannot measure it, when you cannot express it in numbers, your knowledge is of a meager and unsatisfactory kind.[1]

—*Lord Kelvin*

In an organizational environment characterized by downsizing and zero-based budgeting, public relations no longer can convincingly argue that the function is justified without evidence of measurable results.[2]

—*Linda Childers Hon*

OBJECTIVES

After studying chapter 13, you should be able to

▼ Define evaluation research.

▼ Discuss how research is used to evaluate the preparation, implementation, and impact phases of public relations programs.

▼ Outline the recommended steps for conducting evaluation research.

▼ Outline the criteria used in evaluating the preparation, implementation, and impact phases of public relations programs.

▼ Use the "benchmarks model" to depict the roles of formative and summative evaluation research in public relations programs.

No topic dominates the practice as does program evaluation—the final step in the process. But not all practitioners "walk the talk," because systematic measurement of program effectiveness lags behind practitioner interest in program evaluation. In the words of Ketchum Public Relations Worldwide's research director, Walter K. Lindenmann,

> By the start of the next century, many of us are convinced that this whole area of endeavor known as PR measurement and evaluation will be widely understood and accepted in our field, rather than being treated as something of a novelty, which has been the case up to now.[3]

Increasingly practitioners are being asked to document measurable results and returns that are commensurate with program costs. Public relations, like other staff and line functions, is being evaluated by how much it contributes to advancing the organization's mission and achieving organizational goals. Executives in all types of organizations, from the largest corporations to the smallest nonprofit groups, ask for evidence of program *impact*—particularly when budgets are reviewed, when new budgets are negotiated, or when organizations are downsized to be more competitive.

THE PUSH FOR MEASURABLE RESULTS

A "results orientation" of top management accounts for much of the increased use of computers to track program progress and of evaluation research to measure impact. Many executives look at unsupported claims with suspicion. More sophisticated use of measurable outcome criteria in public relations objectives (see the "Management by Objectives" section of chapter 11) also makes it possible to measure program impact. Fewer and fewer practitioners get by with the claim that program impact cannot be measured: "It's intangible." The following exchange captures the essence of the problem in taking the position that public relations results are not measurable.

> "Why not?"
> "They're intangible. You can't actually see the results of public relations."
> "Why should I pay you for something that can't be detected—what you call 'intangible results'?"
> "Because public relations is different and can't be held to the same performance standards as other departments."
> "Well, O.K. Here's your money."
> "Where? I don't see any money."
> "Of course not. It can't be detected—it's what you call 'intangible.' "

Surely knowledge, outcomes, predisposition changes, and behaviors can be measured. So what excuse justifies not knowing if the action and communication strategies are making progress toward achieving program objectives? What justifies not documenting how the program worked? What justifies not being able to say whether or not the problem has been solved?

Concurrent with increased interest in evaluation is rapid development of supportive literature. For example, Sage Publications has become the leading publisher of books and journals devoted to the general field of evaluation research. The 1990s began with the publication of two books devoted to using research in public relations programs.[4] *Public Relations Review* has devoted entire issues to the topic.[5] Both the *Review* and *Journal of Public Relations Research* periodically publish scholarly articles related to evaluation research. The February 1993 issue of *Public Relations Journal* features articles on measuring the impact of public relations. Its replacement, *Public Relations Tactics,* as well as *Communication World* and *Public Relations Quarterly,* regularly publish research and evaluation how-to features for practitioners. So lack of available published guidance is not a defense for not using research.

This body of literature serves as the basis for evaluation research courses now taught at many universities and included in a growing number of public relations curriculums. As noted in chapter 5, the Commission on Undergraduate Public Relations Education identified research for planning and evaluation as one of five areas of study in the core curriculum. Among senior practitioners, however, there are many who did not study research methods, and even some who question whether it is necessary. Apparently missing the point that benchmark data ("Where are we now?") are required to evaluate a program, one author advised,

> "Recording a few cogent paragraphs in this area should answer **Question # 1.** Don't spend a lot of ink on this or any other segment of the plan. The measure of merit for effective plans is not weight, but rather precision, conciseness, and elegant simplicity."[6]

Increasingly, however, an increasing number of public relations firms build evaluation research into the services they offer clients. A parallel development, however, is "outsourcing" (the 1990s euphemism for contracting with outside vendors and suppliers) for research services. In fact, most public relations firms do not staff a telephone survey center or keep data-entry specialists on payroll, choosing instead to contract with outside research firms to do most of their data gathering and compilation.

The trend is to contract with specialized research companies providing formative and summative evaluation research services. Miami-based Strategy Research and San Diego–based Market Development Inc. (MDI) illustrate why public relations firms turn to specialized research companies. These are the two largest research companies specializing in Hispanic population research. Former Burson-Marsteller (Chicago) research specialist Roger Sennott manages a staff of full-time MDI professionals and part-time bilingual telephone interviewers. MDI conducts the quarterly Hispanic Poll for 1,250 clients and other users; the quarterly Hispanic Teen Poll, based on a sample of

750 teens in Los Angeles, Miami, Houston, New York, and San Antonio; and the semiannual MDI Mexico Poll, which reports findings from 750 in-home interviews conducted in Mexico City, Guadalajara, and Monterrey. Similar research companies develop databases and expertise in specialized niches based on ethnicity, occupation, geography, demographics, or other categories of interest to clients. Farm Research Institute, based in Urbana, Illinois, for example, provides research results for agricultural companies, associations, agencies, and firms.

Some clients, some line managers, and even some public relations practitioners still do not budget for research or see research as an integral part of the process. Too many are content with the "warm fuzzy feeling they get from counting their media clips," according to many who work in public relations. "If they feel it's working, they don't want to spend the money to get the data," says another. The trend is clear, however, as more are budgeting for research "because top management is asking them to be more accountable," according to Lindenmann. He thinks that there will be more research and evaluation because "students of public relations will see measurement and evaluation techniques built into their curriculums."[7]

An encouraging trend is that research is increasingly vital to firms seeking new business accounts. The ability to document baseline data and results gives firms a competitive edge. In short, good research is fundamental, not an extra. As practitioner Gary Barton, Monsanto Company (St. Louis), put it,

> In general, public relations people are being asked more and more by either their management or their clients to justify the expenditures for a project or the program. For example, after spending $200,000 or whatever for a program, they ask, "Did that change people's minds? Do they think differently now? Are they more aware of the company?" In other words, did it accomplish the objectives you said you were going to accomplish? That is the evaluative use of research at the end of the program. Without research, it is much harder to show results.[8]

EVALUATION RESEARCH PROCESS

The process of evaluating program planning, implementation, and impact is called "evaluation research." Rossi and Freeman use the terms "evaluation research" and "evaluation" interchangeably to represent "the systematic application of social research procedures for assessing the conceptualization, design, implementation, and utility of social intervention programs."[9] They outline the basic questions in evaluation as follows:

Program conceptualization and design
What is the extent and distribution of the target problem and, or, population?
Is the program designed in conformity with intended goals; is there a coherent rationale underlying it; and have chances of successful delivery been maximized?
What are project or existing costs and what is their relation to benefits and effectiveness?

Monitoring and accountability of program implementation
Is the program reaching the specified target population or target area?
Are the intervention efforts being conducted as specified in the program design?
Assessment of program utility: impact and efficiency
Is the program effective in achieving its intended goals?
Can the results of the program be explained by some alternative process that does not include the program?
Is the program having some effects that were not intended?
What are the costs to deliver services and benefits to program participants?
Is the program an efficient use of resources, compared with alternative uses of the resources?[10]

Evaluation research is used to learn what happened and why, not to prove or do something. For example, one organization set up an evaluation project for the sole purpose of justifying the firing of its senior communication officer. In other cases, evaluation research is done to delay or justify decisions or to persuade someone to support or not support something. The major distinction is that true evaluation research is done to gather information objectively, whereas *symbolic* uses are to support positions already held or decisions already made.[11]

Program managers use such "pseudoresearch" for three reasons:

1. Organizational politics: Research is used solely to gain power, justify decisions, or serve as a scapegoat.
2. Service promotion: Pseudoresearch is undertaken to impress clients or prospects that the sponsor is sophisticated, modern, or sincere.
3. Personal satisfaction: Research is done as an ego-bolstering activity to keep up with fads or to demonstrate acquired skills.[12]

In the long haul, these spurious efforts are self-defeating.

Figure 13.1, pg. 434, illustrates the basic steps in the evaluation process, outlined in the following 10 steps:

1. Establish agreement on the uses and purposes of the evaluation. Without such agreement, research often produces volumes of unused and often useless data. Commit to paper the problem, concern, or question that motivates the research effort. Next, detail how research findings will be used. Such statements are doubly important when outside research specialists are hired to avoid buying "canned" or "off-the-shelf" services.
2. Secure organizational commitment to evaluation and make research basic to the program. Evaluation cannot be tacked on as an afterthought. Build research into the entire process, with sufficient resources to make it central to the problem definition, planning and programming, implementation, and evaluation steps.
3. Develop consensus on evaluation research within the department. Even practitioners not eager to trade in their notions of public relations as intangible must be part of the effort. They have to accept the concept of evaluation research long enough to give the process time to work and

FIGURE 13.1   EVALUATION PROCESS

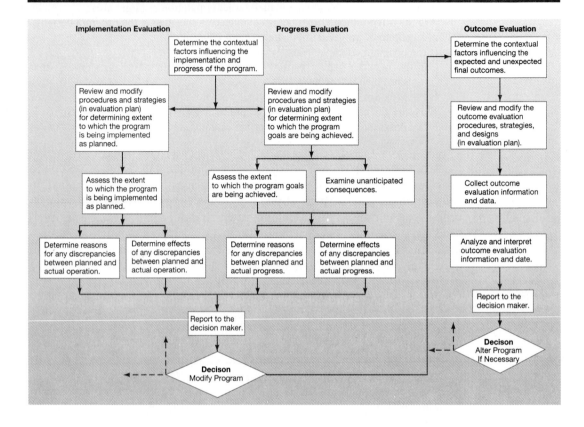

must feel secure that research will not replace completely the lessons and insight gained from experience.

4. Write program objectives in observable and measurable terms. Without measurable outcomes specified in the program objectives, evaluation research cannot be designed to evaluate program impact. If an objective cannot be evaluated, it is not useful. The evaluation imperative forces clarity and precision in the planning process, particularly when writing specific objectives for each of the target publics.

5. Select the most appropriate criteria. Objectives spell out intended outcomes. If increasing awareness of an organization's support of local charities is stated in an objective, for example, then column inches and favorable mentions in the media are inappropriate measures of the knowledge outcomes sought. Identify what changes in knowledge, opinions, attitudes, and behaviors are specified in the objectives before gathering evidence. The same applies when the program seeks to maintain existing levels of desired states. (Review the "Writing Program Objectives" section of chapter 11.)

6. Determine the best way to gather evidence. Surveys are not always the

best way to find out about program impact. Sometimes organizational records contain the evidence needed. In other cases, a field experiment or case study may be the only way to test and evaluate a program. There is no single right way to gather data for evaluations. The method used depends on (1) the questions and purposes motivating the evaluation; (2) the outcome criteria specified in the objectives; and (3) the cost of research resulting from the complexity of the program, setting, or both.

7. Keep complete program records. Program strategies and materials are real-world expressions of practitioners' working theories of cause and effect. Complete documentation helps identify what worked and what did not work. Records help reduce the impact of selective perception and personal bias when reconstructing the interventions and events that contributed to program success or failure.

8. Use evaluation findings. Each cycle of the program process can be more effective than the preceding cycle if the results of evaluation are used to make adjustments. Problem statements and situation analyses should be more detailed and precise with the addition of new evidence from the evaluation. Revised goals and objectives should reflect what was learned. Action and communication strategies can be continued, fine-tuned, or discarded on the basis of knowledge of what did and what did not work.

9. Report evaluation results to management. Develop a procedure for regularly reporting to line and staff managers. Documented results and adjustments based on evidence illustrate that public relations is being managed to contribute to achieving organizational goals. Evaluation reports also help demonstrate the essentiality of the function.

10. Add to professional knowledge. Scientific management of public relations leads to greater understanding of the process and its effects. Most program evaluations tend to be organization- and time-specific, but some findings are cross-situational. For example, findings about how many employees learned about a proposed reorganization from an article may be relevant only to that one article and organization. On the other hand, learning that employees want more information about organizational plans not only provides guidance for future issues of a particular newsletter but may apply in other organizations. Sharing the knowledge gained from relevant research distinguishes the professional practice from the aggregate of technical crafts practiced under the public relations rubric.

The evaluation process is not new; the need has long been recognized. To illustrate, here is what an early publicity specialist, Evart G. Routzahn, told the 1920 National Conference of Social Work:

> After the returns are all in—when the last meeting has been held, the final distribution of printed matter made, and all activities of the immediate effort have been recorded as history—is the time to put yourself and your methods through the third degree . . . with prayerful solicitude that you will be able to untangle the lessons to be applied to the next project.[13]

His counsel has only recently been fully accepted—if not always applied—in public relations, even though its merit has long been obvious.

LEVELS OF PROGRAM EVALUATION

Evaluation means different things to different practitioners. To some it is the "best annual report" award plaque, a letter from the boss or client complimenting the writing and photographs in a new brochure, IABC's Gold Quill Award for publication design, or a PRSA Silver Anvil trophy for a community relations program. To some it is clippings from newspapers around the world. To others the only meaningful evaluations are scientific measures of increased awareness, or changed opinions, attitudes, and behaviors. To those concerned about public policy or social problems, only evidence of economic, political, or social change satisfies their requirements for program evaluation. In fact, these all represent different levels of a complete program evaluation: *preparation, implementation,* and *impact.*

Figure 13.2 shows the stages and levels of program evaluation. The sequence represents typically *necessary,* but not *sufficient,* program elements leading to problem resolution and social change. The most common error in program evaluation is substituting measures from one level for those at another level. This is most clearly illustrated when practitioners use the number of news releases sent, brochures distributed, or meetings held (implementation efforts) to document program effectiveness (impact). Or if asked to document program impact, they substitute publicity placements, in the form of column inches or airtime, for the changes in target publics' knowledge, predisposition, and behavior spelled out in program objectives. Evaluation researchers refer to this as the "substitution game." Somewhat analogously, to create an illusion, magicians talk of "misdirecting" audience attention from what is really happening.

Each stage in program evaluation contributes to increased understanding and adds information for assessing effectiveness. *Preparation evaluation* assesses the quality and adequacy of information and strategic planning. *Implementation evaluation* documents the adequacy of the tactics and effort. *Impact evaluation* provides feedback on the consequences of the program. No evaluation is complete without addressing criteria at each level.

Preparation Criteria and Methods

During a program, practitioners periodically find that vital information was missing from the original situation analysis. Done systematically and recorded, this assessment represents an evaluation of the *adequacy of the background information* used for planning the program. Were key publics missed in the original determination of stakeholder groups? What assumptions about the publics proved to be in error? Did journalists request information that was not readily available in the background packet or fact book? What last-minute crises called for additional research and organization of information? Had all the key actors in the situation been identified? In effect,

FIGURE 13.2   STAGES AND LEVELS FOR EVALUATING PUBLIC RELATIONS PROGRAMS

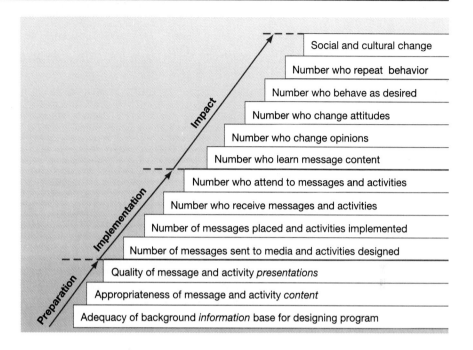

Social and cultural change

Number who repeat behavior

Number who behave as desired

Number who change attitudes

Number who change opinions

Number who learn message content

Number who attend to messages and activities

Number who receive messages and activities

Number of messages placed and activities implemented

Number of messages sent to media and activities designed

Quality of message and activity *presentations*

Appropriateness of message and activity *content*

Adequacy of background *information* base for designing program

Impact

Implementation

Preparation

this part of the evaluation assesses the adequacy of the information-gathering and intelligence steps in the preparation phase of the process.

The second step in evaluation addresses the organization and appropriateness of program and message strategy and tactics. Critical review of what was said and what was done with the advantage of hindsight gives guidance for future program efforts, but only if done with the motivation of constructive criticism. In politics, for example, campaign planners study their candidate's statements in speeches and televised debates in light of media reactions and voter responses in follow-up polls. Did program message content match the problems, objectives, and media? Were communications accurate, timely, and appropriate for the intended publics? Were there adverse reactions to messages or actions? Did the events, corrective actions, and other activities support the program effort? Was enough done? Did the communications capitalize on and complement the action components of the program? Were staff and budget adequate for the task? This phase of the evaluation calls for a review of how well the program matched the demands of the situation.

Content analyses of materials produced, speeches and other presentations, press clipping, and broadcasts also provide evidence for evaluating how closely program efforts match the plan (see Figure 13.3, pg. 438). Practitioners use the results of content analyses of media placements to make changes in how the program is being implemented, as well as for reassessing planned strategy and tactics (preparation). Public relations and research firms are able

FIGURE 13.3   EXAMPLE OF MEDIA CONTENT ANALYSIS IN EVALUATION

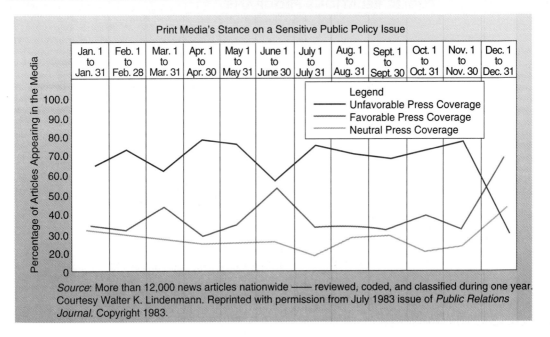

Print Media's Stance on a Sensitive Public Policy Issue

Source: More than 12,000 news articles nationwide ——— reviewed, coded, and classified during one year. Courtesy Walter K. Lindenmann. Reprinted with permission from July 1983 issue of *Public Relations Journal.* Copyright 1983.

to customize content analyses of what is published or aired about clients or issues.

In addition to the usual media names and types, cities, amount of coverage, and nature of coverage, online databases such as ForumOne, NewsSites, and LEXIS-NEXIS make it possible to identify the sources quoted in stories, key message points in the content, the names of journalists or writers, content devoted to other organizations or opposing points of view, and what other subjects the media are reporting. According to Ketchum's Lindenmann, "When we do content analyses for our clients, we build 36 to 40 variables into the computer program."[14] Computer analysis makes it possible to cross-tabulate content by geographic areas, by types of treatment, by audience characteristics, and even by reporters and writers.

Quality of message and other program element presentations constitutes the final step of preparation evaluation. The awards programs of many professional societies and groups employ criteria from this step. Often the "best" annual report, the "most effective" overall program, and even the "outstanding" professional are picked on the basis of style, format, and presentation of program materials. Best graphic design, best use of photographs, or best multimedia presentation are but three of dozens of categories in which awards are given on the basis of production values and judgments of presentation merit. These are the attributes that communication techniques courses and professional workshops emphasize. This step in program evaluation considers the quality of professional performance in light of conventional wisdom and consensus among practitioners as to what is good and bad technique. Presentation quality is not judged by subjective criteria alone, however.

Readability tests are frequently used to assess message preparation objectively. Readability tests, however, take into account only the approximate ease with which printed material can be read and comprehended; they do not consider the content, format, organization, and other elements of writing style. These factors, coupled with an understanding that what writers bring to their writing and readers bring to their reading, all shape the reception and impact of printed words. If used with this perspective in mind, readability tests are useful guides for making copy more readable and for increasing comprehension.

Three commonly used methods for measuring readability include the following:

1. **The Flesch Formula.** Dr. Rudolf Flesch's Readability Score provides an indication of reading difficulty and approximate educational level required to read the material. Calculations require at least two 100-word randomly selected samples of text (or an entire short manuscript).[15]

   A. Count the sentences, words, and syllables (count numbers, abbreviations, symbols, and hyphenated words as single words).

   B. Compute the *average sentence length* by dividing the number of words by the number of sentences.

   C. Compute the *average word length* by dividing the number of syllables by the number of words.

   D. Use these averages in the *Readability Score Formula*. Multiply average sentence length by 1.015. Multiply average word length by 84.6. Subtract the sum of these two numbers from the baseline value of 206.835.

$$Readability\ Score = 206.835 - [(average\ sentence\ length \times 1.015) + (average\ word\ length \times 84.6)]$$

   E. Estimate the relative reading difficulty using Table 13.1. According to

TABLE 13.1	INTERPRETATION OF FLESCH READABILITY SCORE		
	Score	**Readability**	**Grade Level**
	90–100	Very easy	5th
	80–90	Easy	6th
	70–80	Fairly easy	7th
	60–70	Plain English	8th and 9th
	50–60	Fairly difficult	10th to 12th
	30–50	Difficult	College
	0–30	Very difficult	College graduate

Source: Adapted from Rudolph Flesch, *How to Write Plain English: A Book for Lawyers and Consumers* (New York: Harper & Row, 1979), 25–26.

Flesch, "plain English" scores at least 60 and conversational English scores at least 80.

2. **The Gunning Formula.** Robert Gunning's Fog Index measures reading difficulty based on average sentence length and the percentage of words with three or more syllables.[16] The index is based on the number of whole sentences in at least two samples of text containing 100 words. Divide the number of words in the sentences by the number of whole sentences. Next count the number of words with three or more syllables (but not counting capitalized words; those ending in *es, er,* or *ed*; and those that combine simple words, such as "heretofore"). Enter the counts into the following formula.

$$Fog\ Index = 0.04 \times (\text{average number of words per sentence} \\ + \text{number of long words per 100 words})$$

The Fog Index provides an indication of the number of years of education needed to find copy easy to read. (See Table 13.2.)

3. **The Fry Formula.** Edward B. Fry's graph produces results similar to Flesch's Readability Scores.[17] It is also based on sentence length and number of syllables.

A. Start at the beginning of a sentence in each of three randomly selected passages. Count exactly 100 words in each sample passage, including proper nouns, initializations, and numerals. (A word is any group of letters with a space before and after, such as "USDA," "1993," and "&.")

TABLE 13.2

INTERPRETATION OF GUNNING FOG INDEX

Fog Index	Grade Level	
17	College graduate	
16	College senior	
15	College junior	
14	College sophomore	
13	College freshman	
		"Danger line"
12	High school senior	
11	High school junior	
10	High school sophomore	
9	High school freshman	
8	Eighth grader	"Easy-reading range"
7	Seventh grader	
6	Sixth grader	

Source: Adapted from Robert Gunning, *The Technique of Clear Writing,* rev. ed. (New York: McGraw-Hill, 1968), 40.

B. Count the number of sentences in each of the three 100-word samples, estimating the fractions of the last sentences to the nearest tenth.
C. Count the number of syllables in each of the 100-word samples. (A syllable is defined as a phonetic unit. For example, "asked" is one syllable, but "often" is two. For numerals and initializations, count each symbol as a syllable. For example, "USDA" is four syllables, "1993" is four syllables, and "&" is one syllable.)
D. Enter the graph in Table 13.3 using the average sentence length and average number of syllables, putting a dot where the two values on the chart intersect. The dot falls in the area representing the approximate grade level required to find the material easy to read.

Irving Fang's Easy Listening Formula (ELF) provides a comparable measure for estimating the "listenability" of broadcast copy, speeches, and other scripts. In fact, scores correlate highly with Flesch scores ($r = 0.96$). Simply calculate the average number of syllables (above one per word) in sentences.

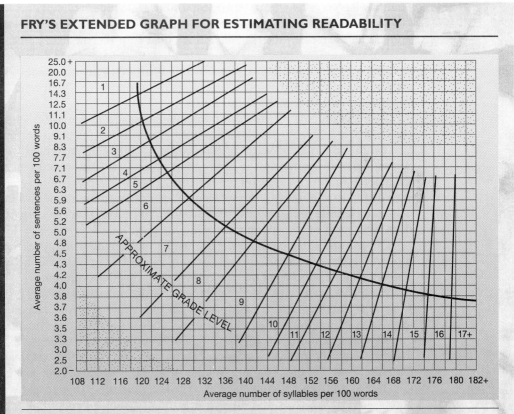

FRY'S EXTENDED GRAPH FOR ESTIMATING READABILITY

Source: Edward Fry, "Fry's Readability Graph: Clarifications, Validity, and Extension to Level 17," *Journal of Reading* 21, no. 3 (December 1977): 149. Used with permission.

Like the Flesch Readability Score, the ELF score represents the approximate grade level required to follow and understand what is being said easily. Fang found that good television news copy averages below 12 on the ELF.[18]

Readability and listenability scores provide only rough indicators of how comprehensible messages are to target publics. Jargon, technical terms, and even dialect may make written material difficult to understand even when the Flesch, Gunning, Fry, or Fang indices indicate otherwise. These measures can help writers gauge the extent to which their copy matches audience needs for easy-to-read-and-understand messages. The measures simply give quantitative and objective indicators useful for monitoring one aspect of writing style.

Clearly, evaluation of the preparation phase of the program includes a mix of subjective and objective assessments of (1) the adequacy of the background research, (2) the organization and content of program materials, and (3) the packaging and presentation of program materials. The next phase of evaluation deals with how effectively the program gets implemented and communications are disseminated to target publics.

Implementation Criteria and Methods

Public relations evaluations are most often done on the implementation phase. This approach typically involves counting the numbers of publications printed; news releases distributed; stories placed in the media; and readers, viewers, or listeners (potential and actual). The ease with which practitioners can amass large numbers of column inches, broadcast minutes, readers, viewers, attendees, and gross impressions probably accounts for widespread use—and misuse—of evaluations at this level.

Whereas records of program implementation are essential for program evaluation, measures at this level cannot be substituted for program impact. Evaluation researchers warn of substituting "countable activities" or recorded effort for achievement of program objectives. This amounts to using the amount of effort and resources expended (means) in place of measures of intended outcomes (ends). Without complete documentation and evaluation of the implementation phase of the program, however, practitioners cannot track what went right or wrong, and why.

Criteria and some methods for evaluating the communication portions of program implementation follow. Analogous evaluations must be done of the action components to complete the assessment of implementation.

The phase begins with keeping records of distribution—number of messages sent. This step is a straightforward documentation of how many letters, news releases, feature stories, publications, public service announcements, and other communications were produced and distributed. It also includes how many speeches, broadcast appearances, audiovisual presentations, and exhibits were used in the program. In other words, this step calls for documenting all the materials and activities produced and distributed. During the program, such records provide evidence that the program is being implemented as planned. Unsatisfactory results identified in subsequent steps may be traced back to the amount of the program directed to specific publics or to the program placement, the next criterion.

Regardless of how much is produced and distributed, the number of messages placed in the media determines whether or not target publics have an opportunity for exposure. Clippings and broadcast logs have long been used to measure how many and what portions of news releases and public service announcements were used by media. Similarly, the number of organizations using a speakers' bureau, audiovisual presentations, and exhibits indicates effectiveness in getting messages placed in the intended channels of communication.

Evaluations at this level sometimes detect fatal flaws in program procedures. Lindenmann reports the case of a client who launched an expensive publicity campaign that produced little use of the materials sent to media. A poll of the media found that the materials were not being used because the right people were not receiving them:

> The press contact list that the client had been using was sorely out of date. Editors and reporters whose names appeared on the list were no longer covering those assignments, had left those newspapers or magazines, or had retired or died. Since the individuals to whom the materials were being sent were no longer at the media at which they were addressed, most of the materials were ending up in the garbage.[19]

Even the most effectively written materials have no chance of impact if they are not available to the intended publics.

Clipping and monitoring services such as Bacon's PR and Media Information Systems (Chicago), Burrelles's Press Clipping Service (Livingston, New Jersey), the Delahaye Group (Portsmouth, New Hampshire), Luce Press Clippings, Inc. (New York), and PR Data Systems, Inc. (Wilton, Connecticut) track national and international print and broadcast media placements for clients. Similar regional and local services in many areas provide documentation of media placements.

Specialized services track publicity placements in selected trade or special-interest print media, help clients monitor crises or other breaking news with same-day customized clipping services, and verify VNR placements on television news programs. One such service that monitors VNR placements, for example, puts an invisible code onto a client's video and then monitors stations to see if any or all of the VNR is aired. The monitor signal decoder is capable of detecting and recording air time and date, station, and exact content aired.[20] CyberScan Internet Clipping Service (Los Angeles) is one of several new companies tracking "hits" and providing "clips" from the World Wide Web. Delahaye Group also monitors the Internet for clients. Increasingly, what is being said in the digital world of cyberspace is being measured, catalogued, and reported to clients.

Services vary in how they operate, but the general procedure calls for the client to provide key words and topics to watch for: organization's name, staff names, products or services, and even similar or competing organizations. Typically, the client also sends its monitoring service copies of news releases and broadcast scripts sent to the media. As noted in the second step in

"Preparation Criteria and Methods," computerization of media placements and coverage makes possible any number of analyses of the quality and quantity of publicity content resulting from program efforts.

Most local organizations maintain their own clipping files and placement records. Interns and entry-level practitioners often find "clipping the media" in their job descriptions. Rather than being a dreaded chore, however, it should be viewed as an opportunity to systematically study content and style preferences of the various media. Maintaining the clipping files also gives beginning practitioners opportunities to practice media surveillance and to learn about issues relevant to their organizations.

Clippings and similar media placement records have gotten a bad name in public relations because too often they are misrepresented as measures of program impact. Used properly, they are important elements of program implementation evaluation.

The next step is determining how many in the target publics received the messages, that is, the number of people potentially exposed to program messages. Care must be taken to separate the *delivered audience* from the *effective audience*. The delivered audience includes all potential readers, viewers, listeners, or those attending. The effective audience represents only those who are in the target publics. Audience size is seldom the major consideration; rather, the makeup of the audience is more important to program evaluation. For example, placement in a prestigious publication not read by the intended target public may make the boss happy but probably contributes little to program success. Practitioners can capitalize on the placement, however, by reprinting the article (with permission) and distributing it themselves to key publics. The expense of such a strategy usually makes placement in appropriate media initially a more cost-efficient practice.

Circulation figures and audience-size data are readily available for most publications and broadcast media. Most newspapers and major magazines belong to the Audit Bureau of Circulation (ABC), which publishes guaranteed circulation figures for member publications. Circulation departments of local newspapers and magazines regularly report the number of paid subscriptions, as well as audience size and characteristics. A. C. Nielson Company and the Arbitron Company report audience estimates for television stations in more than 200 market areas. Arbitron does most of the ratings research for local and network radio. Local television and radio stations often selectively report audience data in their own promotional materials, forcing practitioners to survey all stations in an area to get the complete picture of audience size and demographics.

Traffic Audit Bureau and Simmons Market Research Bureau report audience reach and frequency figures for outdoor advertising, whereas local transportation authorities and commissions provide ridership figures for estimating audience size for transit public service advertising placed inside buses, subways, and trains. Attendance figures for events, meetings, and exhibits are also part of the record used to measure potential exposure to program messages.

Although publicity is not the whole of public relations, it is a large segment of most programs. Astute practitioners have developed tracking systems for evaluating effectiveness in delivering messages to target publics. Ketchum Public Relations uses its own "publicity-tracking model," which it claims goes beyond traditional accounting methods to produce indices of publicity exposure and value (see Figure 13.4). The firm's literature describes the process:

> In planning a publicity campaign to be evaluated . . . the client and agency establish mutually agreed upon standards of performance in two areas in advance of the campaign. First, the number of gross impressions within the target audiences to be achieved. Second, the key messages to be delivered to the target audience. In both cases, the value of the placement is determined by its relations to length, size and media environment.

Calculations of potential audience size produce huge totals that must be interpreted with care. Some evaluation reports boast of literally billions of potential exposures to program messages. Surely few managers and clients are so naive as to think these figures alone indicate program effectiveness. Not unexpectedly, their next question should be, "Of those potentially exposed, how many actually paid attention to the message?"

The number of people who attend to the message, then, constitutes the next criterion in program implementation evaluations. Readership, listenership, and viewership studies measure audience attention to media and messages. Readership studies identify how many read, and what they read, how much they read, as well as who reads and who does not. Studies of broadcast audiences produce similar findings, and researchers and practitioners are developing similar measures of "hits" and other indicators of attention to messages on the Internet.

FIGURE 13.4   PUBLICITY TRACKING REPORT

Placement Type	DMA Target Audience*	Avg. Size/ Length	Avg. Media Units	Publicity Exposure Units	Avg. Impact Factor	Publicity Value Units
NEWSPAPERS	4,552,000	1/9 page	.93	4,233,000	1.26	5,334,000
MAGAZINES	268,000	1/2 page	1.66	455,000	1.47	656,000
TELEVISION, network	95,000	5:10 min	1.93	183,000	.81	149,000
TELEVISION, local	504,000	6:05 min	2.13	1,073,000	1.81	1,946,000
RADIO, local	200,000	10:00 min	2.60	520,000	1.40	728,000
Totals	5,619,000		1.15	6,454,000	1.37	8,813,000

Publicity Exposure Norm* – Orlando DMA 5,960,000
Publicity Exposure Index – 6,464/5,960   1.08
Publicity Value Index – 8,813/5,960   1.48–

The Publicity Exposure Index suggests that the campaign's exposure was 1.08 as good as expected on a Normal* (= 1.00) basis.

The Publicity Value Index suggests that the impact value of the campaign was 1.48 times as good as expected on a Normal* (= 1.00) basis.

The Publicity Exposure Norms are established by estimating the target audiences, (adults 18-49, weighted 60% male, 40% female) exposure of a "good" hypothetical placement schedule.

Courtesy Ketchum Public Relations.

Readership studies of employee publications are commonplace. Weyerhaeuser Corporate Communications tracks *Today* readership (see Figure 13.5) to learn how many employees read each of the stories, their interest in stories, the magazine's readability and appearance, and the perceived balance in how issues are reported. Sometimes readership studies produce surprising results. For example, when Jim McBride surveyed San Diego Kaiser Permanente hospital and clinic employees, he found that fewer than half read anything in the employee newsletter. Readership was high among those who received the publication, but about half of all employees did not receive the newsletter! His findings prompted changes in the method of distribution, not changes in the content, which received high marks from readers. This case illustrates the necessity of evaluating every step in the program implementation process.

The best-known print advertising readership technique is Daniel Starch's recognition method, as now used by Starch INRA Hooper, Inc. Results divide readers into three levels of readership. *Noted readers* simply recall having seen the advertisement. *Associated readers* also remember the name of the advertiser. *Read most readers* say that they read at least 50 percent of the copy and recall enough of the content to support their claim. This method is called "aided recall" because respondents are shown the advertising or other published material and then asked if they recall having read the material. Simmons Market Research Bureau is one of several firms providing magazine and newspaper readership data. Magazine Publishers Association and American Newspaper Publishers Association commission numerous readership studies to track audience characteristics and reading habits.

Radio and television audience research employs four primary methods:

1. Diary. The diary method requires some member (or members) of the household to keep a written record or log of listening or viewing. Recent research findings indicate that this method has a built-in bias, because those who agree to participate may differ significantly from nonrespondents.[21]
2. Meter. The meter method electronically records individual set tuning by frequency or channel and time of day. The information is sent over telephone lines to a central computer. This is the method used by both Nielson and Arbitron in major cities for the "overnight" ratings reported for major television programs. A major problem with this method is that the meter cannot always reliably detect who (if anyone, or how many people) is watching or listening.
3. People meter. Audience measurement companies use sophisticated meters in an attempt to solve the missing-information problem of audimeters and television meters. Each person in a metered home has his or her button to push when watching television. The meter records who in the household is watching what program and feeds the information over telephone lines to the base computer. The people meter also is used in marketing research to report purchasing behavior and then to correlate purchases with television viewing. Not surprisingly, people tire of having to "punch in" and "punch

FIGURE 13.5   **WEYERHAEUSER** *TODAY* **TRACKING REPORT**

Weyerhaeuser *Today* Tracking Report

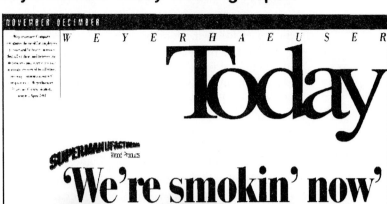

out" and of entering all the other information requested, such as entering for small children too young to manage the technology that goes with living in a metered home. Another problem is that not all television sets in a home are metered, so the people meter yields incomplete reports of household viewing.

4. Telephone interview. The telephone interview method involves calls either during or following a given program to determine audience size and composition. The most common approach is the telephone coincidental survey, meaning that calls are made while the program is running. Answering machines and abusive and high-pressure telemarketers causing nonresponses are making it increasingly difficult to obtain representative samples using this technique.

Combinations of these and other methods are used by audience research firms to measure broadcast audiences for clients. Notice, however, that these, and assessments of print media audiences, are discussed under the *implementation* section of the evaluation process, because they provide no evidence of program effects on target publics. *Impact* is the next level of program evaluation.

Impact Criteria and Methods

As a practitioner once put it, "We must not only seek results, we must be able to measure them." But 83 percent of all organizations responding to a survey marked "no formal review" when asked how often they measure the return on investments made in employee communication.[22] The company report of the survey concluded:

> Communication will no longer be effective simply because it looks good and reads well. It will be effective when it influences action of employees to meet the organization's business objectives and we can demonstrate this influence. . . . We'll have to document our goals and collect data proving that we have met those goals. In short, we will have the same bottom-line accountabilities as other organizational functions.[23]

Impact measurement documents the extent to which the outcomes spelled out in objectives for each target public and the overall program goal were achieved. In chapter 10 the term "benchmark" was used to describe how formative research findings define the problem situation and establish the starting point for the program. *Intermediate* impact assessments monitor progress toward objectives and goals while the program is being implemented. Why wait until the end to find out that the program did not work? Frequent monitoring of progress toward achieving intended outcomes can indicate where changes need to be made. *Summative* impact assessments provide evidence of success or failure in reaching the planned ending point.

The benchmark model in Figure 13.6 illustrates the program evaluation cycle, showing how summative evaluations (Time$_2$) serve as formative evaluations (Time$_1$) for the next program cycle. Here we are limited to discussing

FIGURE 13.6   BENCHMARKS EVALUATION MODEL

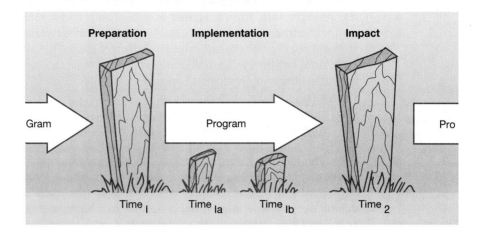

only general guidelines and methods for impact assessments, because intended outcomes are unique to each program. Specific criteria for evaluating program effects should be clearly stated in the objectives that guided program preparation and implementation. For impact evaluation, these same criteria identify both the nature and the magnitude of changes in or maintenance of knowledge, predisposition, and behaviors of internal and external publics. These criteria were chosen because they were viewed as essential steps to achieving the overall program goal (working theory). The first impact assessment deals with what people learned from the program.

The number of people who learn message content is clearly the logical follow-up to measures of how many attended to the message. Most programs seek to communicate information to increase knowledge, awareness, and understanding among internal and external target publics. Increasing knowledge is often critical to increasing their interest or motivation, a sequence leading to taking action. What people know about your organization—regardless of where they got the information—affects how they feel and act and, therefore, the organization's relationships with them. What they do not know may be even more critical: As long as explorers believed that the world was flat, they dared not sail too far toward the horizon. Similarly, what people know or do not know about issues and events may influence opinions and behaviors relevant to organization–public relationships.

The key to evaluating what people learned from a program (or concurrent sources) is to measure the same knowledge, awareness, and understanding variables that were measured before the program began. To determine change, comparisons must be made between at least two comparable measures: by repeating the measures on the same or similar people or by making comparable measures in a control group of similar people not exposed to the program. This same principle applies to all assessments of program impact.

For example, a gas and electric utility evaluates an energy conservation information program designed in part to increase knowledge of how much energy is saved with proper insulation. The research design calls for comparing survey results from a sample of homeowners who received the information ("treatment group") with results from a similar survey of homeowners who did not receive the information ("control group"). An employee communication specialist in a manufacturing organization evaluates a program to increase production employees' awareness of safety procedures by comparing precampaign and postcampaign survey results. Similar research designs are used to assess changes in opinions and attitudes.[24]

The gas and electric utility may also want to know the number of people who change their opinions about the value of home energy conservation efforts. The manufacturer conducting the safety information program could be interested in increasing employee interest in on-the-job safety. The same surveys used to measure changes in knowledge, awareness, and understanding can be used to determine if the programs had an impact on audience predisposition. Different questions would be required, however, because increased knowledge and opinion change are different outcomes, and one can occur without the other. Similarly, changes in opinions that are specific to a particular issue or situation may or may not reflect changes in more basic underlying attitudes.

The number of people who change their attitudes is a higher-order program impact. Attitudes represent broad, cross-situational predisposition. They are less subject to short-term change. They result from a lifetime of reinforcement and experience, so they typically require time and effort to change. And, what you see expressed in a situation may or may not represent the underlying attitude. For example, just because a homeowner holds the *opinion* that adding attic insulation will save on energy bills does not necessarily mean that the person qualifies as a conservationist *attitudinally*. Determining whether or not people hold an attitude about energy conservation requires measuring their predisposition across many energy use issues and situations. (Review the "Orientation" section of chapter 8 for the distinction between opinions and attitudes.)

The number of people who act in the desired fashion—behavioral change—likewise may or may not follow a sequence of knowledge and predisposition changes. Chain-link fences, for example, negate the need for informational and persuasive communications designed to keep all but the most determined people from entering restricted areas. Seldom do public relations programs have such powers, so typically people must be informed and persuaded before behavioral changes occur. Assessments of program impact on behavior include self-reports of behavior through surveys, direct observation of people's actions, and indirect observation through the examination of official records or other "tracks" left by those engaging or not engaging in the behavior.

Surveys sometimes yield unreliable measures of behavior, especially if respondents are asked to report sensitive or socially acceptable actions. Not surprisingly, few employees willingly report that they ignored management policy. Folks tend to claim more viewing of public television programs than detected by other audience measures. Imagine how many students would admit not doing assigned readings on the professor's class survey, or how many taxpayers would mark, "Yes, I cheated on last year's income taxes" on an IRS questionnaire! With validation questions built into the survey, however, many types of behavior can be measured using survey methods.

Examples of direct observation are turnstiles at events, head counts at meetings, tallies of telephone or mail responses, and participant observation. The local Red Cross or blood bank does not need to develop an elaborate measurement technique to determine how many people respond to a call for donations of a rare blood type. Nor does an organization hire a research consultant to learn if protesters stopped picketing in the main lobby.

Indirect methods for observing behavior include a social service agency's records of client appointments, a museum's maintenance records showing where worn floor tiles are most frequently replaced, and library checkout records. By studying these byproducts of behavior, assessments are made about how many people used agency services, which areas or exhibits in the museum are most popular, and how many students checked out assigned public relations reference books. This type of observation technique is called "unobtrusive measures."[25] This approach to assessing impact does not depend on the cooperation of those being observed, and the measurement technique does not contaminate the behavior being observed.

In summary, measures of behavior call for a combination of research skills and ingenuity to get valid evidence for the evaluation and to avoid influencing the behavior of those being observed.

Public relations programs are usually designed to increase the number of people who repeat or sustain the desired behavior. Counts of the number of people who give up smoking on the day of the Great American Smoke Out are not sufficient measures of program success for those wanting to decrease the number of people engaging in this health-threatening habit. As any reformed smoker will attest, success in quitting cannot be determined by checking only once shortly after a quit-smoking program.

Evaluation must include follow-up measures sometimes continuing for months or even years. United Nations family-planning programs are more interested in repeated use of contraceptive methods, not just short-term trials motivated by an educational movie and samples. The same applies to those interested in assessing the impact of safe-sex education programs among at-risk high school and college populations. Evaluating program success in changing long-term behavior calls for an extended period of observation and measurement to document program impact.

At some point in this series of impact levels, the program goal is achieved or the problem solved. Election and referendum results, legislative victories or defeats, and fund balances provide summative indications of the success or failure of political, lobbying, and fund-raising programs, respectively. The program goal spells out the appropriate summative evaluation criteria. It should also be clear that evaluation must extend to this level, because it is possible that some or many of the intermediate impact outcomes may occur without the program goal being achieved.

For example, the goal of an energy conservation program was to reduce total energy consumption. Increased knowledge of cost-saving practices, increased interest in energy conservation, and even changes in energy-use habits do not indicate success or failure in achieving the overall program goal. The utility reported program success this way:

> The average cost of all conservation advertising to provide you with information on how to save energy is about 11 cents per month per customer. An analysis conducted on the actual savings realized by customers through conservation indicates that the savings averaged $10 for each $1 spent on conservation advertising.

The utility's suggestion that the conservation advertising caused the savings illustrates a major problem in program evaluation the tentative nature of cause-and-effect claims. To list but a few alternative explanations for reduced consumption, the drop in energy consumption occurred during a period of escalating energy costs; energy conservation was a topic of many news stories and features in the national and local media; and manufacturers were introducing more energy-efficient appliances. In the uncontrolled environment of most public relations programs, evaluation research only helps answer questions about impact. Definitive answers are elusive, but objectively and systematically gathered evidence certainly beats assertions and strengthens the case for or against claims of program success or failure.

The ultimate summative evaluation of programs and the practice of public relations is their contribution to positive social and cultural change. To complete the range of impact assessments, we conclude with this step. Evaluation at this level is confounded by the passage of time and the existence of other causal factors and is usually left to scholars in sociology and anthropology. Early programs promoted settlement in the West. Health and nutrition education programs have both reduced infant mortality and extended life. Programs that resolved conflicts and built new relationships maintained the dynamic public consensus necessary for meeting human needs. Those in the calling derive their professional motivation and fulfill their social responsibility by being concerned about the impact of their work on society and culture. Both individual practitioners and the practice of public relations will be judged accordingly by future generations.

INTERPRETING AND USING RESULTS OF EVALUATION

In open systems public relations, evaluations are not limited to measures of external change. Implicit to all the evaluation steps discussed in this chapter is that the evaluation criteria refer to both inside and outside the organization. Complete summative evaluation calls for measuring program impact on publics, the organization, and their shared social and cultural environments. The magnitude and complexity of the task probably explains in part why so little evaluation research is done in the closed systems programs that still dominate the practice.

Demonstrating program effects can be a difficult task. Stanford professor

Byron Reeves summarizes the requirements for demonstrating program effects as including the following:

> (1) knowledge of the stimulus material; (2) control of its application; (3) assessment of impact; and (4) understanding of the mechanism or process underlying the effect. In question form: What's having an effect, who's affected, what changes, and when and how does it change?[26]

Evaluation is continuous and central to the process. *Summative research* after the program showing that program effects did or did not occur is of little value. *Formative research* before and during the program provides the information necessary for comparing summative research findings with conditions at the beginning of the program and for making midcourse corrections. Even armed with evidence, however, the practitioner requires care when interpreting and using evaluation results. Three major interpretations are possible when the expected impact is not detected in the evaluations:

1. Even though preparation and implementation were adequate, *the theory behind the program strategy was faulty.* This type of failure is typified by the common notion that "telling our side" will win agreement.
2. If the theory guiding the program was useful, then the absence of impact may be attributed to *program failure: errors made when preparing and, or, implementing the program.*
3. It is also possible that the program succeeded in all respects but that the *evaluation methods did not detect the program impact.* Observations were made on the wrong people, the observations were not valid or used unreliable measures, or the effect was so elusive that it could not be detected using conventional measurement techniques.

In the final analysis, program evaluation involves a great deal of knowledge beyond familiarity with traditional scientific research techniques. Sometimes an in-depth case study in which both qualitative and quantitative data are gathered is the only reasonable approach.[27] The principle in practice is to gather the best available evidence to manage and evaluate public relations programs.

Top management support and acceptance by practitioners are primary among the many structural, process, and organizational factors influencing the utilization of evaluation research in public relations. Following are recommendations for increasing the probability that research will become central to managing public relations:

1. Show how research findings relate to potential users' current concerns, policies, procedures, and practices before discussing long-term applications.
2. Maintain frequent and direct participation of and communication with potential users and other stakeholders throughout the research.
3. Limit reports of research findings to either those with immediate application or those with implications for long-term changes. Save the other type of findings for another report and setting.

4. Report only implications that are logically derived from and supported by the data.
5. Use researchers with established credibility and integrity and avoid using people who might be seen by others as having a vested interest in the results.
6. Use research designs and methods that conform to rigorous scientific standards and technical soundness.
7. Emphasize corroborating information over information that contradicts users' expectations and frames of reference, minimize negative surprises, and avoid early closure on politically sensitive recommendations.
8. Enlist sponsorship of key managers in encouraging serious consideration and use of what was learned from the research.
9. Take the time and effort necessary to persuade potential users to consider and understand the findings and to help them apply what was learned from the research.
10. Conduct the research and use the findings in an ethical and socially responsible manner; respect basic human and civil rights.[28]

Useful program evaluations call for planning from the beginning to the end of their process. Effective program planning and effective program evaluation are inseparable:

> The sins of the program are often visited on the evaluation. When programs are well-conceptualized and developed, with clearly defined goals and consistent methods of work, the lot of evaluation is relatively easy. But when the programs are disorganized, beset with disruptions, ineffectively designed, or poorly managed, the evaluation falls heir to the problems of the setting.[29]

Equally important is viewing research as central to the management of public relations, not seeing it as only the means by which practitioners are held accountable and the worth of their programs is assessed. As the benchmark model suggests, today's evaluation of program impact is tomorrow's baseline for the next program cycle. The late public relations executive Kalman B. Druck vividly made the same point: "I have found that research is too frequently used as an odometer rather than as a speedometer. Research is often used to tell us where we have been, not where we are going."[30]

This chapter concludes on the same point that began these four chapters on the management process: Research initiates, monitors, and concludes the problem-solving process. It is the essential ingredient that makes public relations a management function, as well as a managed function.

NOTES

1. Lord Kelvin, more correctly, First Baron Kelvin, was the British physicist, mathematician, and inventor William Thompson (1824–1907).
2. Linda Childers Hon, "What Have You Done for Me Lately: Exploring Effectiveness in Public Relations," *Journal of Public Relations Research,* 9, no. 1 (1997): 1.

3. Walter K. Lindenmann, "Setting Minimum Standards for Measuring Public Relations Effectiveness," *Public Relations Review* 23, no. 4 (1997): 402.

4. See reviews of Glen M. Broom and David M. Dozier, *Using Research in Public Relations: Applications to Program Management* (Englewood Cliffs, NJ: Prentice-Hall, 1990), and E. W. Brody and Gerald C. Stone, *Public Relations Research* (New York: Praeger Publishers, 1989), in *Public Relations Journal* 47, no. 1 (January 1991): 32–33. See also James Grunig's review of Broom and Dozier's book in *Public Relations Review* 16, no. 2 (Summer 1990): 78–79.

5. *Public Relations Review* 16, no. 2 (Summer 1990), devoted entirely to "Using Research to Plan and Evaluate Public Relations"; *Public Relations Review* 10, no. 2 (Summer 1984), featured articles on "Measuring Public Relations Impact"; and *Public Relations Review* 3, no. 4 (Winter 1977), published papers from the 1977 National Conference on Measuring the Effectiveness of Public Relations held at the University of Maryland and sponsored by AT&T.

6. Alan R. Freitag, "PR Planning Primer: Bite-Sized Morsels Make It Simple," *Public Relations Quarterly* 43, no. 1 (Spring 1998): 15.

7. Quoted by Deborah Hauss in "Setting Benchmarks Leads to Effective Programs," *Public Relations Journal* 49, no. 2 (February 1993): 16.

8. Quoted in Broom and Dozier, *Using Research in Public Relations,* 11.

9. Peter H. Rossi and Howard E. Freeman, *Evaluation: A Systematic Approach,* 5th ed. (Newbury Park, CA: Sage Publications, 1993), 5.

10. Ibid., 34–41. The questions appeared in earlier editions.

11. Broom and Dozier, *Using Research in Public Relations,* 299.

12. Stewart A Smith, "Research and Pseudo-Research in Marketing," *Harvard Business Review* 52, no. 2 (March–April 1974): 73–76.

13. Routzahn (1869–1939) was a social worker and foundation executive, associate director of the Russell Sage Foundation, 1912–1934. He also was the founding chairman of the Social Work Publicity Council, one of the first professional public relations groups. The quotation is from the 1920 National Conference of Social Work proceedings.

14. Quoted in Hauss, "Setting Benchmarks Leads to Effective Programs," 15.

15. Rudolf Flesch, *How to Write Plain English: A Book for Lawyers and Consumers* (New York: Harper & Row, 1979), 23–26.

16. Robert Gunning, *The Technique of Clear Writing,* rev. ed. (New York: McGraw-Hill, 1968), 38–40.

17. Edward Fry, "Fry's Readability Graph: Clarifications, Validity, and Extension to Level 17," *Journal of Reading* 21, no. 3 (December 1977): 242–52.

18. Irving E. Fang, "The 'Easy Listening Formula,' " *Journal of Broadcasting* 11, no. 1 (Winter 1966–67): 63–68.

19. Walter K. Lindenmann, "Dealing with the Major Obstacles to Implementing Public Relations Research," *Public Relations Quarterly* 28, no. 3 (Fall 1983): 12–16.

20. "Hi-Tech VNR Tracking Service Comes of Age," *Public Relations Journal* 47, no. 12 (December 1991): 23, 28.

21. H. Leslie Steeves and Lloyd R. Bostian, "A Comparison of Cooperation Levels of Diary and Questionnaire Respondents," *Journalism Quarterly* 59, no. 4 (Winter 1982): 610–16.

22. "The Changing Role of Today's Communicator," *Communication World* 9, no. 6 (May–June 1992): 39.

23. Ibid., 38.

24. For more information about research designs for evaluating program impact, see chapter 5, "Designing the Research," in Broom and Dozier, *Using Research in Public Relations,* 89–113.

25. Eugene J. Webb, Donald T. Campbell, Richard D. Schwartz, and Lee Sechrest, *Unobtrusive Measures: Nonreactive Research in the Social Sciences* (Chicago: Rand McNally, 1966).

26. Byron Reeves, "Now You See Them, Now You Don't: Demonstrating Effects of Communication Programs," *Public Relations Quarterly* 28, no. 3 (Fall 1983): 17.

27. Robert K. Yin, *Case Study Research: Design and Methods,* rev. ed. (Newbury Park, CA: Sage Publications, 1989).

28. Broom and Dozier, *Using Research in Public Relations,* 302–13.

29. Carol H. Weiss, "Between the Cup and the Lip," *Evaluation* 1, no. 1 (1973): 54.

30. *Arthur W. Page Society Newsletter* 4, no. 1 (April 1988): 4.

ADDITIONAL SOURCES

Broom, Glen M., and David M. Dozier. *Using Research in Public Relations: Applications to Program Management.* Englewood Cliffs, NJ: Prentice-Hall, 1990. Still the most comprehensive introduction to using research in public relations, he said immodestly.

Dozier, David M., with Larissa A. Grunig and James E. Grunig. *Manager's Guide to Excellence in Public Relations and Communication Management.* Mahwah, NJ: Lawrence Erlbaum Associates, 1995. User-friendly source for how the "Excellence Project" findings apply to the practice.

Grunig, James E., ed. *Excellence in Public Relations and Communication Management.* Hillsdale, NJ: Lawrence Erlbaum Associates, 1992. See in particular David M. Dozier and Fred C. Repper, "Evaluation of Public Relations Programs: What the Literature Tells Us about Their Effects," pp. 159–84; and William P. Ehling, "Estimating the Value of Public Relations and Communication to an Organization," pp. 617–38.

Lindenmann, Walter K. *Guide to Public Relations Research.* New York: Ketchum Public Relations, 1993. Seventy-page booklet written by one of the leaders in using research in practice.

Lindenmann, Walter K., et al. *Guidelines and Standards for Measuring PR Effectiveness.* Gainesville, FL: Institute for Public Relations Research and Education, 1997. Admirable attempt to establish criteria and "groundrules" for measuring and evaluating public relations.

Miller, Delbert C. *Handbook of Research Design and Social Measurement,* 5th ed. Newbury Park, CA: Sage Publications, 1991. An encyclopedic presentation of research methods, measurement scales, and references.

Rossi, Peter H., and Howard E. Freeman. *Evaluation: A Systematic Approach,* 5th ed. Newbury Park, CA: Sage Publications, 1993. Essential reading for those engaged in program evaluation.

Smith, Mary John, Contemporary Communication Research Methods. Belmont, CA: Wadsworth Publishing Company, 1988. Addresses how to do communication research in naturalistic settings, combining traditional empiricism with analytical and critical methods of the arts and humanities.

United Way of America. *Measuring Program Outcomes: A Practical Approach.* Alexandria, VA: United Way of America, 1996. A useful guide that lives up to its title.

Wimmer, Roger D., and Joseph R. Dominick. *Mass Media Research: An Introduction,* 5th ed. Belmont, CA: Wadsworth Publishing Company, 1997. Useful research methods reference for understanding and interpreting media research.

BUSINESS AND INDUSTRY

All business in a democratic country begins with public permission and exists by public approval.

—*Arthur W. Page*

OBJECTIVES

After studying chapter 14, you should be able to

▼ Discuss the emergence of corporate social responsibility and the forces that have made this concept of serving the public interest part of corporate philosophy.

▼ Outline the role of public relations in corporate philanthropy.

▼ Describe the financial relations function in publicly held corporations.

▼ Describe the kinds of support public relations practitioners provide to the marketing function.

As America moved toward the 21st century, corporate **CEOs** assessed how their organizations fared during a decade of unparalleled prosperity, at least as measured by the ubiquitous Dow–Jones Industrial Average. As measured by other indicators, however, some observers gave corporate America mixed reviews.

This chapter was written in collaboration with Professor William C. Adams, Fellow, PRSA, Florida International University. Professor Adams has more than two decades of professional experience in corporate public relations at Standard Oil Company–Indiana (now BP Amoco), Phillips Petroleum Company, and ICI Americas Inc.

Downsizing and mergers, for example, continued to alter the corporate landscape. Millions of workers lost their jobs as businesses sought ways to pare overhead and cut costs in order to compete with foreign competition. Some mergers were so vast, so previously unimaginable, that regulatory barriers had to be removed before the megadeals could be consummated. The RJR Nabisco $25 billion buyout during the "decadent decade of greed" in the late 1980s seemed almost quaint in comparison with Citicorp–Travelers' 1998 deal—worth three times as much—and the NationsBank–Bank America merger. SBC (formerly Southwestern Bell), after earlier buying Pacific Telesis (Pac Bell), in 1998 bought Ameritec (old Illinois Bell), forming the largest of the remaining four "Baby Bells." The urge to merger was also an international phenomenon: German industrial giant Daimler-Benz (maker of Mercedes Benz automobiles) bought Chrysler, creating a company with 422,000 employees worldwide. Even the most seasoned financial pros wondered where it would all end.[1]

Lawyers, lobbyists, bankers, and, yes, many stockholders profited greatly from these corporate marriages, and even from divorces, such as when AT&T—the most widely held public company—spun off Lucent Technologies (old Bell Labs) and NCR Corp. (old cash register manufacturer NCR). Some pointed to "downside obstacles": the newly merged companies will handle increased complexity, bureaucracy, and cultural challenges, as well as possible antitrust violations. Others hailed the megadeals for creating "synergies that benefit everyone, including customers who will get greater convenience, easier access, competitive prices, and more services."[2]

Sheer size, however, was not the only problem facing corporate CEOs and their employees as the new millennium beckoned. Companies continued to struggle with balancing effective business practices with environmental and social responsibilities, and shareholder expectations with public interest.

At one extreme, the chairman of Pepsico donated his 1997 million-dollar salary to create scholarships. In contrast, some CEOs took home hefty compensation packages, apparently not tied to either how their companies performed financially or how many of their workers lost their jobs. Xerox, AT&T, Sunbeam, and many other corporate icons slashed hundreds of thousands of jobs in the 1990s. Cuts were justified as necessary for increased profitability and improved shareholder equity. Little wonder that a 1997 Yankelovich Partners survey of senior corporate communications officers found that almost 40 percent reported low company morale.[3]

Even the financially conservative *Wall Street Journal* wrote, "Welcome to the Chief Executive Gravy Train. It overflows with treasure when things go well—and even when they don't."[4]

In this atmosphere of change and uncertainty, public relations professionals working for increasingly cost-conscious companies sought ways to maximize their contributions to the bottom line. "Working harder, working smarter" became the motto as professional journals reflected these concerns in myriad articles on keeping and finding jobs, working more efficiently, cutting costs, and being part of management's goals.

PUBLIC RELATIONS IN THE COMPETITIVE SETTING

Public relations in any organization dependent on profit must be cost-effective and part of the formula for successful competition. Thus, the competitive nature and the profit imperative of business make public relations work extremely demanding. Add to this the increasingly global nature of business (with more foreign ownership of "American" corporations) and its potential clash of cultures, as well as the possibility of a corporate takeover, merger, or acquisition. Now, the "think globally" manifesto proclaimed by many in the 1990s rings true.

The public relations function in business is subject to continuing evaluation—as are marketing, finance, and manufacturing—with the ultimate yardstick being progress toward goals and objectives set by management. Other evaluations of the function are made in terms of "organizational loyalty," being "on the team," and being "in tune with the objectives."

In times of stress, economic downturn, or increased competition, management often increases its concern for the survival of the business and demands greater commitment to organizational goals. The public relations practitioner must be alert to these conditions, must understand that internal dissent and criticism of communication policies may be regarded as disloyal, but must continue to act professionally in the roles defined in part I of this text.

For public relations to survive in business, it must do more than build and maintain relationships with employees and neighbors. Public relations must help business create an environment in which owners or investors are satisfied with the return on their invested capital. This motivation usually means that much of what is called public relations is designed to help the marketing function attract new customers and keep present customers satisfied with products or services. Simply put, public relations must contribute to achieving the profit goal of business in a competitive environment.

The competitive and private nature of the business system and the demands placed on each function make for variety in the role and stature of public relations. Its place in the organization is often determined by top management's concept of the function; hence the ongoing education process some practitioners find necessary in making the function part of the management team and professionalizing the practice.

TITLES IN CORPORATE SETTINGS

Some top business executives simply do not like the term public relations. Many years ago, distaste for the term at IBM led to titles such as "manager, community affairs" and "director, community programs." More recently, IBM's top public relations executive was a "vice president, communications," and there is still nary a title on the organization chart that includes "public relations." Fewer than one-fifth of the Fortune 500 companies use the term "public relations" in the titles of their departments.

On the other hand, a "vice president of public relations" heads the overall function at AT&T, Kaiser Aluminum and Chemical Corporation, and Goodyear Tire and Rubber Company. Enron, Revlon, and the Pillsbury Company call the position "vice president—public relations." Sears changed its "public affairs" department title to "public relations and communications" to more accurately describe its role in the company.

Nonetheless, the trend has been to move away from the "public relations" title at the top corporate level and toward an amalgam of terms such as "vice president, corporate communications" (Motorola, Pacific Gas and Electric Company, Deere and Company, and Baxter International); "vice president, public affairs" (Ford Motor Company, Conoco, and American Express); and "vice president, corporate relations" (VIACOM, ITT Industries, and Manville Corporation). The list of corporate titles includes many other terms and combinations. At Pepsico, for example, there is a "vice president—international public affairs"; Fidelity Investments has a "vice president—communications, public affairs"; and W. R. Grace & Company has a "vice president—communications and investor relations." All these titles cover the public relations management function in the corporate setting.

In some corporations, public relations reports to marketing, personnel, human resources, or even the legal department. In others, it reports directly to the CEO. Each industrial or commercial organization tailors its public relations function to reflect the character and personality of its management, its corporate culture, and its tradition.

One senior public relations executive thinks the field is diminished when executives substitute for the words "public relations" in titles: "How can we reinforce, defend, advance and project the importance and major role of public relations if the leadership . . . doesn't carry the term 'public relations' on its business card, its letterhead and in any public references?"[5]

As ethical standards change and commitments to corporate social responsibility grow, the role of public relations in business has become more clearly defined as helping corporations "do the right thing," as well as say the right thing.

Apparently some in business still agree with a remark attributed to President Calvin Coolidge that "the business of America is business," or even the claim made by a former head of General Motors that what was good for the car maker was "good for America." The 1980s and early 1990s definitely brought about a reassessment of such one-dimensional viewpoints. Companies began to "act green," invest heavily in socially responsible programs, and come under what one major company's CEO called "unprecedented scrutiny" and "unprecedented governmental regulation."[6]

In the past, many business leaders resisted the notion that their corporations should seek to fulfill social responsibilities beyond providing jobs, earning a profit with which to pay investors and underwrite growth, paying taxes, and voluntarily supporting nonprofit health, welfare, and education activities. A number of eminent economists and observers of the social scene agreed with this assessment of the limited role of business.[7]

Although there are holdovers—such as "Chainsaw Al" Dunlap, who cut Sunbeam's workforce in half to create a stock price increase in 1996, only to see prices again tumble in 1998—the number of business leaders who subscribe to the view that business is only for profit and the bottom line is dwindling. With the help of public relations counsel, corporations are targeting their philanthropic contributions, becoming "greener" through environmentally sound products and programs for plant-location communities, and teaming with local agencies and governments to improve schools, employment training programs, and food and shelter programs for the needy. They may take a stance as a "health-conscious company" through AIDS research underwriting; as an arts-oriented company through sponsorships of local, regional, or national programs; or as a company committed to education, with funding, contributions of staff time and equipment to schools and universities, or both.

Years ago, the notion of corporate social responsibility centered around only the stakeholders directly involved with the company: employees, stockholders, customers, and the community. Although the debate over the extent and nature of corporate social responsibility continues today, it has become increasingly clear that public relations practitioners in corporate settings find themselves center stage in helping to formulate policy and programs for carrying out their organizations' social responsibility.

Prelude to the Present: The Uneasy 1960s and 1970s

In the 1960s, business came under scrutiny the likes of which most executives had never experienced. Increased government regulations, investigations by government agencies, and more intense reporting requirements threw the media spotlight on business activities once relegated only to the financial pages.

With insider-trading scandals, conflicts of interest, bribery, price collusion, and illegal political contributions surfacing, the environment was ripe for a new kind of journalism, a new era of muckraking, as it were: "investigative reporting."

Business tried to fight back, but legal defense was time-consuming and costly. Many corporations began to look hard at internal affairs and sought to get their houses in order; the result was the introduction of codes of conduct and early efforts to operate "in the public interest." (See Figure 14.1 for the Caterpillar Inc. code of conduct.) Externally, some businesses maintained a low profile, whereas a few took their cases to the "court of public opinion." Former Mobil Oil public relations executive Herb Schmertz's book *Good-bye to the Low Profile: The Art of Creative Confrontation* outlined and exploited this aggressive reincarnation of the "tell-our-side" approach to public relations.[8] Although some corporate practitioners enjoyed seeing one of their own striking back at the media, others understood that engaging the media in any form of combat—verbal or otherwise—was not wise. As an observer once counseled, "Don't argue with people who buy printer's ink by the barrel." The same counsel applies for those who control broadcast and cable distribution systems.

Still, the 1960s and much of the 1970s was a time of public distrust of business. Public interest groups were on the rise, and many activists spawned during the anti–Vietnam War, antibusiness years on college campuses worked in government, where they had an opportunity to promulgate laws and regulations involving the very companies they sought to restrain. Investigative journalists were not only helping to bring down a corrupt government during the Watergate crisis but were prying open the doors to corporate boardrooms long locked to an inquisitive outside world.

A 1972 Opinion Research Corporation survey found that 60 percent of adults held business in "low esteem," highlighting a growing problem for business. The Washington-based Media Institute published a book about media treatment of business in the 1970s, pointing out that almost half of all media portrayals of business were of illegal activities, and two-thirds of all business leaders in television entertainment programs were shown to be greedy, foolish, or criminal.[9]

For businesses, the problems continued into the 1970s. The Organization of Petroleum Exporting Countries (OPEC) oil embargo of 1973–1974 and the Iranian Revolution of 1978–1979 each disrupted oil prices. Economic shock waves resulting from skyrocketing oil prices produced public frustration and increased media coverage, with the energy industry taking the brunt of the charges. The oil companies, especially, were targeted by Congress through hearings and peered at by the news media as never before. Companies were accused of "perpetrating a hoax, profiteering, withholding supplies, or other devious actions."[10]

Out of this seemingly chaotic public relations environment came several

FIGURE 14.1 CATERPILLAR CODE OF WORLDWIDE BUSINESS CONDUCT AND OPERATING PRINCIPLES

To Caterpillar People:

In 1974, Caterpillar published its first "Code of Worldwide Business Conduct and Operating Principles," a code based on ethical convictions and international business experience dating back to the turn of the century.

This fourth revision of the Code still has the purpose of guiding Caterpillar people in a broad and ethical sense, in all aspects of our worldwide business activities. Experience has demonstrated the practical utility of this document.

The Code isn't an attempt to prescribe actions for every business encounter. And it isn't published out of any doubt about the desire of Caterpillar people to comply with its contents. Rather, we believe that the worldwide reach an complexity of our business—and the fact that ethical conduct isn't always subject to precise definition—argue strongly for our development of standards.

To the extent our actions match these high standards, such can be a source of pride. To the extent they don't, this Code should be a challenge to each of us.

No document issued by Caterpillar is more important than this one. I ask that you give this Code your strong support as you carry out your daily responsibilities.

Donald V. Fites	Issued October 1, 1974
Chairman of the Board	Revised September 1, 1977
	Revised May 1, 1983
	Revised May 1, 1985
	Revised August 1, 1992

(Excerpts from 12-page Code.)

Business Ethics. The company's most valuable asset is a reputation for integrity. If that becomes tarnished, customers, investors, suppliers, employees, and those who sell our products and services will seek affiliation with other, more attractive companies. We intend to hold to a single high standard of integrity everywhere. We will keep our word. We won't promise more than we can reasonably expect to deliver nor will we make commitments we don't intend to keep....

We seek long-lasting relationships—based on integrity—with all whose activities touch upon our own.

Protection of the Environment. Caterpillar's continued competitiveness and leadership in a global marketplace require individual and corporate dedication to a clean and safe environment wherever it conducts business. We will establish, maintain, and follow environmentally responsible policies and practices comply with applicable laws and regulations in both "letter and spirit" and respond openly and promptly to responsible inquiries about environment issues as they relate to Caterpillar and its products.

Public Responsibility. All Caterpillar employees are encouraged to take part in public matters of their individual choice. Further, it is recognized that employee participation in political processes—or in organizations that may be termed "controversial"—can be public service of a high order.

Just as Caterpillar supports the notion of _individual_ participation, it may, to the extent legally permissible, support committees aimed at encouraging political contributions by individuals. The company itself will not normally make political contributions, even where it is legally permissible and common practice....

Overall, it's our intention that Caterpillar's business activities make good social sense—and that Caterpillar's social activities make good business sense.

Courtesy Caterpillar Inc.

organizations dedicated to helping business and the news media meet on common ground, to help each understand the other's jobs. On the one hand there was a need to educate business executives about the role of the journalist and on the other hand there was a need to help educate reporters who might be covering the energy beat for the first time. The Foundation for American Communications and the Media Institute were pioneers in this effort, born during the mid-1970s. Even Harvard University joined in, hosting a series of seminars on "Business and the Media."

Despite these efforts, the 1970s ended with a communication and environmental bang as Three Mile Island became a buzzword for bungled public relations and a suspect nuclear-energy industry. Metropolitan Edison's poor crisis planning and mangled communication efforts earned the company a nation's wrath and exposed a lack of candor and trustworthiness that many Americans, including reporters, had suspected of all of business.[11]

Ironically, the 1970s had seen an almost imperceptible shift by some businesses away from the "traditional" dependence on media to "tell our story" to the use of more "controlled" media (booklets, corporate advertising, speech reprints, and corporate mission statements). Businesses directed more efforts to influencing legislation and its implementation and increased its reliance on trade associations. "Issue management" became a hot buzzword in the corporate setting. Washington, DC, corporate offices saw unprecedented growth in the 1970s, with most major companies having at least one Washington representative. That growth continued virtually unabated during the 1990s.

A corporate credibility gap cast a shadow over many corporations that had operated under the guise of withholding information because of "privacy rights," or fear of "trying a case in public," or simply, "no comment." An economist writing in *The Wall Street Journal* stated the problem simply: "The reason the public is so suspicious is because our large corporations so habitually do engage in clever public relations instead of telling the truth."[12]

New Era of Corporate Social Responsibility: The 1980s

The 1980s introduced a new era of public relations and corporate social responsibility. For example, Johnson & Johnson's classic handling of the Tylenol poisonings in 1983 became a textbook case in how to respond to a crisis (review Exhibit 1.3). Unlike Three Mile Island, Johnson & Johnson responded to all media requests for information and generally fulfilled the company's responsibility to the public interest.

Also early in the decade, Dow Chemical's former chairman outlined some basics of corporate social responsibility:

> The business community's efforts to solving social problems must be integrated with long-term profit growth. If done properly, solving social problems is both good business and good citizenship, for the two goals are wholly compatible.[13]

By the time the 1980s drew to a close, the rest of the chemical industry had caught up with Dow's philosophy and instituted an across-the-industry program of social responsibility. "Responsible Care" is the title of the self-policing code of conduct by which all members of the Chemical Manufacturers Association abide.

Also in the 1980s, churches and universities began scrutinizing their investment portfolios, selling holdings in companies that might conflict with public (and constituency) perceptions of corporate insensitivity to social concerns. Interest groups prodded American companies to pull out of South Africa. A simmering issue for years, it boiled over with a vengeance at corporate annual meetings and on the sidewalks outside corporate headquarters. Companies throughout the world heard the protests, and hundreds of millions of dollars in plants, equipment, and jobs were removed from South Africa in the 1980s. The pros and cons of those actions are still being debated today. In fact, the issue has become localized to the extent that in some states, companies doing any kind of business with South Africa are forbidden to bid on state government contracts.

Even with increased efforts by business to become more socially responsible in the 1980s, public confidence in major institutions, as measured in surveys by the University of Chicago Opinion Research Center, showed that only about 25 percent of Americans expressed a "great deal of confidence" in major corporations, banks, and financial institutions.[14]

Business and industry continued to labor under many government regulations imposed a decade or more earlier because of public and governmental concern about the treatment of the environment, product quality, equal employment, and workplace safety. Public perception was that American corporations were not assuming leadership roles in dealing with social problems and that increased (or continued) regulation was necessary.

News media continued reporting on corporate bribes to foreign government officials, antitrust and product safety violations, cancer-causing drugs and chemicals, and "lemon law" cases involving defective automobiles. All of these further undermined public confidence in business and industry.

When the Reagan administration began deregulating various industries, corporate social responsibility was again tested as airlines, railroads, banks, and savings and loans were given greater freedom to set rates and compete. Although the deregulation debate continues, it became increasingly clear with bank, savings and loan, and airline failures of the late 1980s and early 1990s that simply easing government regulations was not a panacea for social responsibility.

Beginning with the Reagan administration, economic conditions brought about what some termed a "new federalism." Simply put, cuts in federal funds for social, cultural, educational, and welfare programs began to put increased pressure on corporations to carry an even larger share of the financial burden for these activities in their communities. This led to more emphasis on grass-roots lobbying and coalition-building by corporations as they focused increased public relations effort away from Washington and to the heartlands.[15]

Business leaders and public relations practitioners began to take center stage as the times called for a new spirit of volunteerism. Then-President George Bush introduced his "Thousand Points of Light" program to recognize community service. New forms of public–private partnerships created adopt-a-school and adopt-a-highway programs to assist public agencies that had been victims of the budget ax. Private-sector initiatives led the way in addressing social problems, such as caring for the homeless, providing nutrition education and food to pregnant women and their infants, and supporting after-school youth activities.

The professional ethics of business leaders and public relations practitioners, along with the social responsibility of their organizations, began to be scrutinized as never before on a worldwide basis. Union Carbide's Bhopal (India) chemical manufacturing accident, Perrier's tainted bottled water,

Exxon *Valdez*'s oil spill into Alaska's Prince William Sound, Dow Corning's silicone breast implants crisis (and subsequent Chapter 11 filing), and Nike's labor practices and low wages in their Asian plants all became news in every corner of the world. Corporations cannot hide overly generous pay packages for executives from stockholders and consumers. Nor can they ignore environmental damage caused by their processes and products, child-labor abuses in manufacturing plants, or human rights violations in sweatshops paying substandard wages in developing nations. These practices cannot be exported and hidden from instantaneous global news reporting. A skeptical press will put the spotlight on corporate behavior in every corner of the world.

New Roles for Public Relations: The 1990s

Former PRSA president James Fox accurately foresaw three major forces shaping the role of public relations in corporate settings:

> 1) The identification and tracing of issues within corporate staff before legislation is proposed. 2) The formulation of corporate policies and the communication of these policies to modify or forestall restrictive legislation—the management of industry's response to change. 3) The emergence of the CEO as corporate spokesman, . . . and the assumption by chief executives of responsibility for direct involvement in public-policy issues.[16]

As he predicted, issues management began to catch on across all business lines in the late 1980s.

Today, although not an exclusively public relations task, issues management plays a major role in strategic planning in most companies. Lessons learned in corporate America during the 1970s and 1980s make it clear that businesses must actively monitor issues likely to impact their ability to reduce risk, make a profit, serve stakeholders, and operate in the public interest. Yet a panel of experts concluded that public relations has not responded fully to the challenge because

1. The connection to the bottom line is long-term and not well understood.
2. Many issues require organizational changes, not just communication. As a result, practitioners have to move past their traditional communication boundary to develop broader strategy.
3. The profession as a whole has not embraced issues management by defining it as part of public relations and by providing practitioners the training needed to assume the new roles.
4. Issues management is a high-level management function that requires mature judgment, depth of experience, and sophisticated understanding of business, social-political environment, and stakeholders.[17]

Certainly, the concept of the CEO as corporate spokesperson has taken hold in the 1990s, along with unprecedented public interest in the inner workings of business and the private lives of top executives. Increased public interest and scrutiny can be traced to media coverage of what appeared to be outrageous salaries, compensation packages, stock options, and "golden parachutes" for retiring and terminated corporate executives. Interest peaked in 1997 with the $90-million "severance package" given former superagent Michael Ovitz by Disney.[18]

A labor union released data in 1998 that showed the average CEO pay package had increased by 38 percent over the previous year, including DuPont and Nike among a long list of corporations. The union was especially critical of the lucrative golden parachute given a retiring AT&T executive at the same time that workers were losing their jobs and shareholders were pressing for an increased role in setting executive compensation. One highly visible CEO of a publicly traded corporation told CNN news, "I'm not going to discuss my salary with you."[19]

The comment rings hollow amid the seemingly endless stream of industrial accidents, corrupt savings and loans dealings, Wall Street scandals, and defense contractors' fraudulent billings and defective products. It was not a pretty picture for business in the 1990s, but one that apparently stirred public curiosity in the candidacy of H. Ross Perot in the 1992 presidential campaign and the success of the book and HBO movie, *Barbarians at the Gate,* depicting the Wall Street personalities and shenanigans involved in the leveraged buyout of RJR Nabisco.

The following quotations represent the all-too-frequent disparity between how business leaders see themselves and their corporations and they are viewed by skeptical critics:

> We will not sacrifice our reputation with the customer in order to enhance profitability.
>
> *Sears 1997 Annual Report, p. 3*

> I've always believed that where our best interests collide with a corporation's bottom line, our best interests haven't a prayer.
>
> *Syndicated columnist Leonard Pitts,* Miami Herald, *January 22, 1998, p. 1,*
> *Local Section*

Some observers believe that increased public interest has been fueled by the CEOs themselves.[20] More and more CEOs play the spokesperson role in company advertising campaigns, write autobiographies or agree to be the subjects of popular "success-and-power" books, and respond to media requests for interviews, talk-show appearances, and business magazine features. Some CEOs even see themselves as CCOs: the chief communication officers for their corporations. After admitting that others in the organization probably know more about the business side, and some know more about management, one CEO said: "Most importantly, you need to be able to communicate your ideas and thoughts. . . . I think that's why I'm here today and not in some lower position."[21] Many CEOs see explaining company-related issues, such as layoffs, year-end results, and product recalls, as their primary obligation. One CEO said that public relations is "probably in the top five things you must know to run a company."[22]

CEOs also must run their companies in the context of demands for increased social responsibility and public accountability, whether voluntary or imposed by the government. New demands on corporate performance at all levels cast the public relations function as a major player in the process of organizational and social change on a global scale. Clearly, the new century presents even more challenges for corporate public relations professionals helping to merge corporate bottom-line goals with environmentally friendly and socially sound business practices. Continued pressure on profits, downsizing, global competition, new technology, and government regulation will test corporate commitments to social responsibility. But as a corporate CEO wrote,

> The basic goal of private enterprise remains what it has always been—to produce needed goods and services, earn a fair return on investment, and succeed as an economic institution. But the new dimension that must be observed—a new "bottom line" for business, really—is social approval. . . . A successful business organization must possess a moral sense as well as an economic sense.[23]

Recent corporate public interest publications and foundation annual reports reflect a continuing commitment to the "second bottom line," fulfilling social responsibility:

> We believe we have a special responsibility to enhance the quality of life for our customers, employees and community at large. This responsibility goes beyond producing high quality products. It also involves conducting our business in accordance with the highest ethical standards, treating our employees sensitively and fairly, and helping to meet critical community needs. . . . We would not consider ourselves successful as a corporation if we were to fall short as a good corporate citizen.
> *Ralph S. Larsen, Chairman and CEO, Johnson & Johnson*[24]

> The GM Environmental Principles demonstrate our commitment to protecting human health, natural resources, and the global environment. Employees throughout the Corporation recognize and incorporate sound environmental practices into the work they perform and the products they create every day. We view environmental stewardship as both a responsibility to the world around us and a commitment in our business.
> *John F. Smith Jr., Chairman, Chief Executive Officer, and President; and Dennis R. Minano, Vice President, Public Policy and Chief Environmental Officer, General Motors Corporation*[25]

> Our policy is to donate the equivalent of at least 2 percent of our U.S. pretax income to nonprofit organizations. . . . Our giving, like our management style is decentralized. The Sara Lee Foundation makes contributions on behalf of Sara Lee Corporation. In the same way, our divisions—around the country and around the world—work with community agencies to find the best local programs for local needs. Financial aid, food and clothing product donations, and—perhaps most importantly—the personal involvement of our employees are the tangible results of our resolve to make a difference.[26]

Every indicator suggests that nothing had changed this view at the end of the century. In fact, public scrutiny and demands for corporate responsiveness are increasing. What some have called the Big Green Brother—a collection of activist, regulatory, media, and consumer interests—now monitors business and industry to make sure that products and processes are environmentally friendly. "Greenness" and "green marketing" now get top priority when developing any environmental program. According to the *Good Housekeeping* Institute, to be environment-friendly, marketers must address four issues: water conservation, energy conservation, solid waste reduction, and reduction of environmental hazards.[27]

Social Investment Forum, an organization that monitors investments, reports that almost 10 percent of all investments are made on the basis of how green and otherwise socially responsible companies are. The environment is a criterion for 78 percent of "green-minded" and "socially responsible" investors. As the president of an environmental investment counseling firm said, "Quite aside from their responsibility as part of our society, companies who ignore the half-trillion dollars in potential capital that they could be attracting if they weren't polluting do so at their peril."[28]

Examples of corporate greenness include the following:

1. Bayer Corporation's goal to achieve 25 percent reduction by 1998 in overall waste generation from 1993 levels,
2. Procter & Gamble's program to reduce solid waste by using recycled plastic in bottles and by developing more compostable disposable diapers,
3. McDonald's switch from polystyrene foam cups and packaging to more "eco-friendly" materials,
4. Toyota's "Only God and Toyota can make a tree" program to line highways in Japan with trees to reduce carbon dioxide levels, and
5. 3M Company's pioneering "Pollution Prevention Pays" program.

3M's program began in 1975, well before the current green movement, making it the first formally organized corporate effort to control pollution at the source rather than at the end of the production line. It called for reformulating products, modifying manufacturing operations and equipment, and recycling. The program had saved 3M $500 million by mid-1991, garnered widespread public recognition, and earned a PRSA Silver Anvil Award. The updated program goal was to reduce pollution in the year 2000 by 90 percent from 1987 levels.[29]

Clearly, the conflict between corporate America and what some called "eco-freaks" and "tree huggers" that officially began on Earth Day, April 22, 1970, has ended. The environmentalists not only won but made protecting the environment "a core American value." The debate now centers on which policies and practices most effectively achieve the goals of the new environmental ethic.[30]

CORPORATE PHILANTHROPY

The major tactics for expressing and demonstrating corporate social responsibility include mission and value statements, speeches, advertising, and philanthropy—contributing to education, health care, welfare, and the arts. Chapter 12 covers the communication tactics; this chapter addresses corporate philanthropy.

Corporations gave charitable contributions totaling almost $8.5 billion in 1996, or 5.6 percent of all charitable giving ($150.7 billion). Although many top managers willingly participate financially in causes chosen by their corporations, a philosophic debate continues as to whether business has an obligation to "give away" its hard-earned profits to social and cultural programs.

> At the root of this conflict are two warring images of the business organization and its purpose in American society. One sees the corporation as a pivotal institution of democracy with complex responsibilities to a host of constituencies including its employees, customers and the community. The other much more utilitarian view recognizes one primary corporate constituent, the shareholder, and a single purpose, profit-making.[31]

Social responsibility based on "enlightened self-interest" links philanthropy to organizational goals: "Our intent is to tie the grants program to our business and technical interests," according to the executive director of E. I. du Pont de Nemours and Company Committee on Educational Aid.[32] Others define enlightened self-interest as, "You must do well in order to do good." They employ a participative approach, in which employees, customers, and opinion leaders help select which projects receive funds. In this approach, volunteerism, gifts, and services in-kind are often more important than money for building relationships with key publics in communities.[33]

Corporate leaders view philanthropy as a way of giving something back into local communities, improving the quality of life for employees, and practicing corporate citizenship. They give to improve schools because they are experiencing or anticipate problems with low skill levels in the workforce; they give to organizations in the arts, culture, and humanities because it enhances the quality of community life; and they give to hospitals and clinics because the quality of health care helps attract others to the community. Examples include EBSCO Industries Inc. raising $10 million to revive the Alabama Symphony and the Minneapolis-based bank Norwest Corp. providing $300 million in low-interest home mortgages and giving another $16.5 million to Habitat for Humanity International to build 50,000 homes for low-income families.

As the demand for corporate support increases as government support decreases, however, many companies are formulating targeted corporate giving "missions," concentrating on health, environment, education, or even more specific causes. The trend is to focus giving in a particular area to increase giving effectiveness. For example, DuPont Stainmaster Carpet™ provided carpeting for all Ronald McDonald Houses in the United States. These homes provide temporary residence for families of children being treated at nearby hospitals. As Figure 14.2 illustrates, a three-foot-square portrait of Ronald McDonald carved from Stainmaster Carpet provides a permanent reminder (and photo backdrop) of DuPont's philanthropy.

FIGURE 14.2   RONALD MCDONALD PORTRAIT IN CARPET

Courtesy DuPont.

Education has always been a major recipient of corporate philanthropy. Contributions are usually measured in dollar value, although in-kind assistance (facilities and equipment, teaching aids, employees' time in teaching and training, internships, grant and matching gifts made by employees) has grown in recent years. The Council for Aid to Education reports that donations from corporations account for 20 percent ($2.8 billion) of all gifts to higher education. At least 20 endowed chairs and professorships are created annually, prompting one writer to comment, "Some professors' job titles have become the corporate billboards of academe."[34] Not surprising—given the proximity of corporate headquarters to the campuses—the University of Memphis has the FedEx chair of information-management systems; the University of Minnesota, the General Mills chair; Wayne State University, the Kmart chair of marketing; and Stanford University, the Yahoo! chair of information-systems technology.

Corporate executives see an increased need to support public education at all levels as part of their social responsibility. Some have almost made it a corporate mission, as demonstrated by the collaboration led by Phillips Petroleum Company in the Texas Panhandle. Phillips has for decades focused company resources and personnel on aid to education at the secondary and university level. (See Figures 14.3, pg. 472 and 14.4, pg. 473.)

FIGURE 14.3   PHILLIPS PETROLEUM'S VIEW OF CORPORATE PHILANTHROPY

 PHILLIPS PETROLEUM COMPANY
BARTLESVILLE, OKLAHOMA 74004

Phillips Petroleum Company's philanthropic activities are consistent with good corporate citizenship.

Phillips strives to identify and support those charitable organizations which most effectively and efficiently address issues and problems facing our society and which present the best promise for the future. We are especially concerned with education and workforce preparedness, the environment, opportunities for women and minorities, ethics as a lifelong experience and the enhancement of the quality of life through the arts and the humanities.

The majority of the grants approved by Phillips go to organizations in areas where the company has large concentrations of employees and to educational institutions where the company actively recruits. Grants are often in the form of a challenge.

Contributions from Phillips Petroleum Company and Phillips Petroleum Foundation,Inc. are funded through corporate earnings and are a reflection thereof. Funding varies from year to year but Phillips commitment to good corporate citizenship remains constant.

C. J. Silas
Chairman and CEO

PHILLIPS PETROLEUM CONTRIBUTIONS
1988 THROUGH 1992

Courtesy Phillips Petroleum Company.

Often the public relations practitioner plays a key role in corporate philanthropy, sometimes serving as the officer responsible for the function. The public relations role typically includes the following:

1. Staging appropriate events for making a decisive contribution, as in a welfare fund drive or the creation of a scholarship fund
2. Assisting in a charitable campaign or endeavor, with communication-strategy counsel, preparing printed or audiovisual materials, and advertising support or publicity placement
3. Heading a project or campaign or serving as the alternate for a corporate senior official
4. Auditing various community causes to determine where and how a corporation might best be of assistance
5. Guiding, not directing, the participative approach that involves community constituencies in allocating corporate contributions

Corporate philanthropy, once thought of by many as extraordinary generosity, is increasingly viewed as an *obligation* and a necessary component of

FIGURE 14.4   PHILLIPS PETROLEUM'S SUPPORT OF EDUCATION

Courtesy Phillips Petroleum Company.

corporate citizenship. It has also moved to center stage a part of the public relations mission in building relationships with key corporate publics.

CORPORATE FINANCIAL RELATIONS

Economic conditions and a prevailing fast-buck atmosphere have placed financial relations in the forefront of public relations activities. "Benign neglect," one business journalist wrote, "facilitated a wave of takeovers that piled up corporate debt . . . and cost thousands of workers their jobs."[35]

Corporations began to understand who *really* controlled their stock. It was not individual investors anymore but huge, multibillion-dollar retirement funds and pension plans wanting maximum return on their investments. When takeovers were imminent, these money managers tended to eschew loyalty in favor of whoever had the most cash. For a few years, Carl Icahn, T. Boone Pickens, and their like ruled the land, instilling fear and loathing into hundreds of boardrooms across America, providing solid employment for legions of investment bankers, and putting the skills of public relations practitioners to the extreme test.

Investor Relations

Beginning with the first round of takeovers and mergers during the 1980s, investor relations became an integral part of many corporate communications programs. In some corporations, it resulted in the CEO working closely with public relations professionals for the first time. While headlines announced mergers of major national and international corporations, public relations specialists were providing counsel to top management on how to deal with the world's financial press, how to communicate the news to investors within the limits and requirements of government agencies, and how to inform employees about the impact the changes would have on their jobs and lives.

Public relations plays an integral part in most financial relations programs, assisting with analyst presentations, preparing speeches to shareholders, and working with the news media during "road shows" (visits by top corporate officials with analysts and financial editors, often covering many cities in a relatively short period of time; hence, careful planning and coordination is needed).

With large pension plans and investment funds holding more and more shares of corporate stock, individual shareholders often feel powerless. Recent efforts to organize shareholders, ostensibly to give them "more of a voice" in how "their" corporations should be run, what social enterprises should be supported, even what products should and should not be marketed have caught the attention of some boards of directors. For the most part, however, these attempts to put together coalitions of smaller shareholders have little effect on corporate policies, because it is difficult to organize shareholders into common-interest groups with collective voices. Small investors continue to feel awed by the large corporation; their 50, 100, or even 1,000 shares pale in comparison with the huge blocks of stock bought by investment funds and trusts. Their only contact with management is through printed materials, such as quarterly and annual reports, company publications, and the news media. Small investors feel helpless; to some management, they may even seem apathetic. Meanwhile, many heads of large investment trusts meet face-to-face with corporate executives and boards of directors, even demanding the appointment of new directors or the replacement of CEOs. The financial public relations practitioner must be aware of these conditions and work closely with top management to address shareholder concerns.

Much of financial relations is governed by law, as described in chapter 6, by SEC rules and regulations, by stock-exchange requirements, and by management attitudes toward disclosure. Implementation of policies and financial relations plans fall largely to financial officers with advice and support from the public relations staff or specialized outside counsel.

The usual assignments given to public relations in the financial arena include the following:

1. Measuring opinions toward the company, the industry, or free enterprise, held by shareholders, financial analysts, federal agency executives, and legislators
2. Recommending communication strategy, particularly with respect to corporate goals
3. Assisting with preparation of financial literature, such as letters to new stockholders, interim and annual reports, dividend enclosures, and information for brokerage-firm research reports
4. Making arrangements and preparing informational materials for financial meetings, facility tours, and presentations for investor groups, analysts, and the financial media
5. Writing financial news releases and handling inquiries from financial media

A company's first contact with new shareholders is extremely important. The public relations practitioner can work with management to create a *letter of welcome,* enclosing recent financial reports and booklets or brochures about the company. Likewise, there is correspondence from investors. Often investors request information about products, sales, research, stock prices, number of shares owned, or the company's stand on social, political, or ethical issues. These letter exchanges with stockholders can function as a useful two-way communications tool. Some top corporate executives handle selected responses personally.

Annual Reports

The keystone of any financial relations program is the *annual report,* a window, in effect, through which varied constituents view the company and its operations. Corporations use different approaches to the annual report:

> To some corporate chieftains, each annual accounting to shareholders is another chance to put their personal stamp on a completed document; to engage readers in their hopes and plans for improving profits, products, people's lives and even peace in the global economy. Some just give the job to the lawyers.[36]

In some companies, the annual report is the most used external communications tool, sent to a wide range of publics, from employees to analysts, educators, and business media. This tool has evolved to a high degree of technical and graphic excellence, due in a large part to its public relations objectives for so many different publics. In the early 1990s, however, reflecting tighter economic times, many companies took a close look at the expenses connected with producing the annual report and issued slightly less glossy and expensive models. "Some companies cut back from 6-color reports to 2-color reports, pruned mailing lists and eliminated photographs altogether."[37] Others cut other departmental budgets to maintain or increase the annual report budget.

The bullish stock markets and increased competition for investors' dollars changed that—dramatically. Slick, artfully designed, graphically hip, die-cuts, inserts, and other eye-catching devices are again in vogue. Some corporations issue their annual reports on CDs and on-line through the Web site. For its 1997 annual report, for example, typically staid IBM decided one size did not fit all, so it split the 1.6-million-copy press run: one version's cover featured a black-and-white photograph of a female IBM employee; the other a male employee. Some companies produce an expensive "marketing" version of the annual report but send shareholders a no-frills version to impress them with management's concern about controlling costs.

The annual report does more than merely present financial results from the previous year, information reported on the 10K form, as required by the SEC (review the chapter 6 section on disclosure). Some reports also discuss the company's impact on the economy of plant cities, reflect on the firm's international scope, show concern for social problems, and indicate ways in which environmental issues are being addressed. Others may convey management's position on various public issues crucial to the company's well-being. Overall, today's annual report places increased emphasis on the role of the modern corporation in society.

Since the early 1980s, some companies have produced supplemental annual public interest and social responsibility reports detailing environmental activities; programs to meet community and employee needs; and support for the arts, health, and welfare, and other social quality-of-life concerns. The reports often are as well produced and as costly as the financial annual report (see examples in Figure 14.5).

In some large corporations, the annual report is the primary responsibility of a specialized public relations professional working within an internal communications division or as an expert counsel in an outside firm. In either case, this specialist maintains close contact with company financial executives. For most of those charged with producing the annual report, it is at least a half-time job for up to 6 months each year.[38] It can be a frustrating, politically charged task, requiring excellent writing (and editing) skills, an understanding of corporate finance, and the ability to work with top management in all lines of business. Not surprisingly, investor relations is the highest-paid specialty in public relations, with a median salary of almost $72,500 (see Table 2.3 in chapter 2).

Economic conditions and management direction dictate the content, graphics, and style of annual reports. And although there are no tried-and-true formulas, effective annual reports contain all or most of the following:

1. A distinctive cover to attract interest and reflect corporate character
2. An inviting design that helps the reader get the main message points easily and quickly by scanning the report
3. A table of contents or highlights

FIGURE 14.5   SPECIAL AND ANNUAL REPORTS

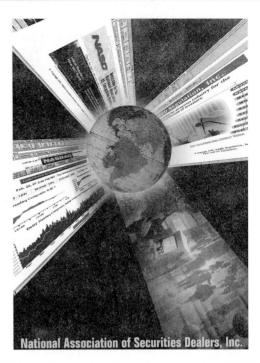

Courtesy Northwestern Mutual; © 1997 National Association of Securities Dealers, Inc. (NASD). Reprinted with permission from NASD.

4. Identification of members of the board of directors and top corporate officers
5. A statement or letter from the CEO, generally summarizing the past year's events and emphasizing goals for the future
6. Consolidated balance statements of earnings, shareholders' interest, and operating cash flows for the year
7. Financial highlights and comparisons with at least the previous year, but often with the past 5 to 10 years
8. Auditor's statement of independence and adherence to accepted accounting principles

In addition, public relations practitioners often create communications to be attached to the reports, targeting financial news media, analysts, educators, and other constituents. These take the form of news releases, personalized letters, or fact sheets detailing highlights of the report for specific audiences.

Annual Meetings

Another important component of investor relations is the annual meeting. Largely a ritual prescribed and governed by SEC regulation, the annual meeting symbolizes corporate democracy in action. Although these yearly gatherings (usually held at corporate headquarters or at a venue in the headquarters city) provide opportunity for face-to-face contact, it is often only those who live nearby or who represent huge blocks of shareholders who take the time and effort, and who can afford the time and expense, to attend. Therefore, postmeeting communications have become increasingly important if all shareholders are to be reached.

In conjunction with annual meetings, the public relations department typically supports the event by

1. Helping with physical arrangements
2. Creating handouts and other on-site communications
3. Assisting with tours and souvenirs
4. Accommodating the news media, including arrangements for computers, telephones and modems, fax machines, photo opportunities, and postmeeting interviews
5. Generating publicity support
6. Preparing question-and-answer sheets for top executives in anticipation of shareholder questions

For the last task, practitioners are often charged with anticipating the tough questions likely to be asked of the CEO and other company officials during and after the meeting. Many an annual meeting has come to a halt by shareholders seeking simple answers to extremely difficult questions or asking embarrassing questions about company operations, disappointing earnings, executive compensations and perks, or alleged misdeeds by top executives. Management must be ready to respond satisfactorily not only to shareholders but to news media covering the event as well. Some executives rehearse their responses by having the public relations staff role play audience members or reporters asking the tough questions.

CONSUMER AFFAIRS AND THE "MARKETING MIX"

Public relations has long been an essential supplement to the marketing effort, particularly in consumer product and services companies. In fact, for many counselors and staff professionals, participation in the "marketing mix" is their bread and butter; it pays the bills. As one practitioner noted, "By being involved early and regularly with the client marketing functions, public relations can help assure totally integrated, strategically focused and cost-effective marketing communications."[39]

According to integrated marketing communication specialist Thomas Harris, public relations support for marketing includes the following:

1. Building marketplace excitement before advertising breaks (announcing that VW was bringing back the Beetle)
2. Driving the communication program when there is not advertising (news

that Crayola was "retiring" some colors and replacing them with eight new "child-tested" colors)

3. Making advertising news when there is no product news (announcing a new advertising creative approach to be introduced during the Super Bowl)
4. Bringing advertising to life (touring Oscar Mayer's "Wiener Mobile"; "Morris," the cat with nine lives; California's "Dancing Raisins"; and "Tony the Tiger")
5. Extending promotion programs (establishing follow-up events and other outreach efforts tied to marketing promotions, such as Ralston Purina's "Big Cat Survival Fund" donations and publicity support for the National Zoological Association)
6. Building personal relationships with customers (soliciting recipes from bakers competing for the Pillsbury Bake-Off grand prize)
7. Influencing the influentials (sponsoring events and providing information targeting opinion leaders)
8. Communicating new product benefits (reporting newsworthy uses and discoveries about product effects, such as the link between aspirin use and the reduced risk of heart attack and stroke
9. Demonstrating social responsibility and building consumer trust (linking corporations and their brands with consumers' causes and concerns)
10. Defending products at risk (responding to critics or false claims, such as a man's claim that he had found a syringe in a can of Diet Pepsi)[40]

The dramatic growth of public relations in the marketing mix is documented by a survey of 243 marketing executives, more than one-third of whom claimed to have spent more than 20 percent of their marketing budgets on public relations.[41] The ten activities listed above clearly demonstrate that most of what is called "public relations" or "marketing public relations" is what has been referred to for years as "publicity."

Whatever the activity, practitioners play important support roles in the marketing mix, promoting the sale of products and services while helping to ensure more attention to truth and accuracy of claims. Public relations' expanded role includes creating and managing communication projects and vehicles for product-problem alerts and recalls, consumer education programs, and consumer access programs linking them to information and resources in corporations from which they buy products and services. But most important, corporations have seemingly become obsessed with satisfying customers by improving the quality of products and services, again expanding public relations involvement.

QUEST FOR QUALITY

Business and industry got a wake-up call during the 1980s: Produce high-quality, reliable products at a reasonable price or consumers will find somebody else, often in another country, who will. Corporations worldwide mounted programs under the banners of "total quality management" (TQM) and "ISO 9000." In a bit of semantic tyranny, TQM became the hot buzzword of the 1990s: Who could be against creating quality? Companies stopped buying from suppliers that did not meet ISO 9000 standards. Quality is not a passing fad. It is an international revolution.

TQM means near-zero defects in every task performed in the production and delivery of products and services, with total customer satisfaction as the goal. At Motorola, for example, the goal was to reach "Six Sigma." Six Sigma stood for six standard deviations from the usual result, or "a defect rate of 3.4 parts per million for each and every process step or procedure. That's 99.9997 percent perfect."[42]

Motorola developed a course called "Six Steps to Six Sigma" to introduce TQM to all its employees. The six steps included the following:

1. Identify the product you create or the service you provide. In other words, answer the question, "What is my mission?"
2. Identify the person who actually pays for the products and services that the company produces.
3. Identify what you need in order to provide a product or service that satisfies the customer.
4. Identify the process for doing your work. In other words, break down operations into steps and tasks, chart the flow of work from supplier to customer, spot tasks that are prone to error, and measure the defect rate and cycle time.
5. Redefine the process so that it is mistake-proof and so that wasted effort is eliminated. If a task adds no value, throw it out.
6. Ensure continuous improvement by measuring, analyzing, and controlling the process.[43]

TQM is not just an internal matter either:

> For example, soon after Motorola won the Malcolm Baldrige National Quality Award in 1988, its thousands of suppliers were asked to pledge that they, too, would apply for the award within five years. Those refusing to sign the pledge were dropped from the rolls of qualified suppliers unless they did not qualify as an applicant due to size or other exclusions, or there were some extenuating circumstances.[44]

TQM dominated U.S. business and industry during the late 1980s and early 1990s, but ISO 9000 became a worldwide movement. The International Association for Standardization (ISO) published a set of five standards used to document, implement, and demonstrate quality management and assurance in 1987. Since then, more than 110 countries have adopted the standards. Worldwide, companies are certified on one of the ISO 9000 standards, meaning that an independent third party has conducted an on-site audit of company operations against ISO standards.[45]

ISO 9000 was originally designed to be a voluntary guide for ensuring quality products and services, but it has become an imperative in the competitive marketplace. According to one consultant, "Industry wails about government imposing regulations, and here we are imposing them on ourselves." For some companies doing business abroad, ISO 9000 has become an informal requirement. A certified ISO assessor says, "There's a fear of being shut out. They're told they must get certified if they want to export to Europe, but that is stretching the truth." But meeting ISO 9000 standards is a requirement for doing business with an increasing number of European Community companies, many of which refuse to buy or accept bids from suppliers (including public relations firms) who do not.

Yet another quality movement holds manufacturers and their products accountable on 15 environmental standards—ISO 14000. The voluntary standards were first introduced in Europe to serve the function the Environmental Protection Agency plays in the United States. Standards include criteria for assessing manufacturers' processes for managing, measuring, improving, and communicating the environmental impact of their operations. Separate sets of criteria focus on organization, management, manufacturing processes, products, and terms and definitions of all environment-related standards.

Although ISO 9000 and ISO 14000 both require top-down management commitment, information management, training, corrective action, management review, and continual improvement, many think that ISO 14000 will affect more companies than will ISO 9000: "Unlike ISO 9000, the ISO 14000 standards will have significant legal implications and a broader stakeholder base."[46]

The TQM, ISO 9000, and ISO 14000 revolutions demonstrate a worldwide commitment to quality and the environment motivated by serving the public interest, but some have suggested that the focus on customer satisfaction and employee participation is "simply a dramatic return to the basics."[47] The critical role that communication plays in the quest for quality puts public relations square in the middle of this revolution, even if it is simply a glorified return to the basics of good business.

CORPORATE PRACTICE AS THE MODEL

It is in business and industry that the public relations function is most often held up for public scrutiny and evaluation. Individual practitioners and the profession as a whole are often judged on the basis of how those in business and industry discharge their duties and fulfill their social responsibility.

Corporate practitioners must assume an even greater share of the burden in anticipating long-term consequences of their companies' policies, balanced with professional crisis planning and response to social concerns. Public relations executives must counsel management that the public interest and corporate interest converge in the long run and that this approach to corporate social responsibility must take precedence over—or at least balance—concerns about immediate profit and loss. Such an approach is spelled out in Ciba-Geigy Canada Ltd.'s vision statement on social responsibility:

Ciba-Geigy is open and trustworthy towards society. Through our business activities we wish to make a worthwhile contribution to the solution of global issues and to the progress of mankind.

We recognize our responsibility when turning new discoveries in science and technology into commercial reality; we carefully evaluate benefits and risks in all our activities, processes and products.[48]

Tim Traverse-Healy, longtime public relations leader in Europe, sees public relations as an essential part of corporations operating in the social responsibility model:

A company will see nothing unusual in being quizzed and in responding fully and quickly on matters such as, its employment record and practices; its environmental policies; the quality of its products; the safety of its products; and the effectiveness of its services. Discussion and debate will be encouraged, rather than feared; sought rather than avoided. One measure of a corporation's social acceptance will be the professionalism of its two-way communications and the degree of genuine dialogue it encourages and entertains.[49]

NOTES

1. See, for example, Ron Chernow, "The Birth of a Bureaucratic Mastodon?" *The Wall Street Journal,* April 9, 1998; and Gregg Fields, "In era of the supermerger, rules have changed," *Miami Herald,* April 8, 1998, p. 1.
2. Fields, *Miami Herald,* p. 1.
3. "The State of Corporate Communications," Corporate Reputation Watch, Yankelovich Partners, October 1997.
4. Joann S. Lublin, "Pay for No Performance," *The Wall Street Journal Reports,* April 9, 1998, p. R1.
5. "Edelman Sees Field Diminished by Not Using Term PR," *pr reporter,* October 13, 1997, p. 2.
6. C. J. Silas, "The Environment: Playing to Win," *Public Relations Journal* 46, no. 1 (January 1990): 10. Silas is chairman and CEO of Phillips Petroleum Company.
7. Most notable among those holding the "business-for-business" view are economist Milton Friedman and Wall Street commentator Louis Rukeyser.
8. Herbert Schmertz (with William Novak), *Good-bye to the Low Profile: The Art of Creative Confrontation* (Boston: Little, Brown, 1986).
9. *Crooks, Conmen, and Clowns: Businessmen in TV Entertainment* (Washington, DC: Media Institute, 1981).
10. Leonard J. Theberge, ed., *TV Coverage of the Oil Crises: How Well Was the Public Served?* I (Washington, DC: Media Institute, 1982); p. xii. Three-booklet series of quantitative and qualitative analyses and commentary.
11. See Richard C. Hyde, "Three Mile Island: PR's Balaklava," *Public Relations Journal* 35, no. 6 (June 1979): 10–14.
12. Irving Kristol, "The Credibility of Corporations," *The Wall Street Journal,* January 17, 1974.
13. As quoted by Donald R. Stephenson, "Internal PR Efforts Further Corporate Responsibility: A Report from Dow Canada," *Public Relations Quarterly* 28, no. 2 (Summer 1983): 7–10.

14. Seymour Martin Lipset and William Schneider, "The Decline of Confidence in American Institutions," *Political Science Quarterly* 98 (Fall 1983): 379–402, or the same authors' book, *The Confidence Gap: Business, Labor, and Government in the Public Mind* (New York: Free Press, 1983).

15. Seymour Martin Lipset and William Schneider, "The Decline of Confidence in American Institutions," *Political Science Quarterly* 98 (Fall 1983): 379–402, or the same authors' book, *The Confidence Gap: Business, Labor, and Government in the Public Mind* (New York: Free Press, 1983).

16. James F. Fox, "The Politicizing of the Chief Executive," *Public Relations Journal* 38, no. 8 (August 1982): 23.

17. Adapted from summary report of the "Public Relations Colloquium 1992—Issues Management," held January 20–21, 1992, at Northwestern University, cosponsored by San Diego public relations firm Nuffer, Smith, Tucker, Inc., and San Diego State University.

18. Allan Sloan, "No Hits, Lots of Errors," *Newsweek,* July 28, 1997, p. 50. Sloan, *Newsweek*'s Wall Street editor, criticizes the Disney-Ovitz deal, as well as the AT&T contract with former CEO John Walter.

19. Cable News Network report, April 12, 1998.

20. J. David Pincus, Robert E. Rayfield, and Michael D. Cozzens, "The Chief Executive Officer's Internal Communication Role: A Benchmark Program of Research," *Public Relations Research Annual* 3 (1991): 1, 5.

21. Quote from J. David Pincus, Robert E. Rayfield, and J. Nicholas DeBonis, "Transforming CEOs into Chief Communications Officers," *Public Relations Journal* 47, no. 11 (November 1991): 24.

22. "Engineering an Image Turnaround," *The Public Relations Strategist* 4, no. 1 (Spring 1998): 10. See also Miles Martel, "Last Word: Communication Leadership," *The Public Relations Strategist* 4, no. 2 (Summer 1998): 40.

23. Thornton F. Bradshaw, then president of Atlantic Richfield Company, in the introduction to *Participation III: Atlantic Richfield and Society,* edited by Nita B. Whaley (Los Angeles: Atlantic Richfield Company, undated).

24. From interview printed in *Social Responsibility in Action Worldwide* (New Brunswick, NJ: Johnson & Johnson, undated).

25. Quote from Smith and Minano's introduction to *General Motors Environmental, Health and Safety Report* (Detroit: General Motors Corporation, October 1997).

26. *Sara Lee Foundation Programs and Application Procedures* (Chicago: Sara Lee Corporation, undated).

27. Susan Schaefer Vandervoort, "Big 'Green Brother' Is Watching: New Directions in Environmental Public Affairs Challenge Business," *Public Relations Journal* 47, no. 4 (April 1991): 14–19, 26.

28. "Investing in the Environment: Options Appeal to Green-Minded Investors," *CALPIRG Citizen Agenda* 7, no. 4 (Spring 1991): 6. CALPIRG is the California Public Interest Research Group, a consumer and environmental activist organization.

29. Lowell F. Ludford, "3P Program Pays Off in Cost Savings of $500 Million for 3M," *Public Relations Journal* 47, no. 4 (April 1991): 20–21.

30. A. Joseph LaCovey, "Business Changes Its Ways," *Public Relations Journal* 47, no. 4 (April 1991): 23.

31. Andrea Gabor, "Hard Work and Common Sense," *Los Angeles Times* (Book Review section), February 8, 1998, p. 5.

32. Julie L. Nicklin, "Charitable Giving Rises 6.4%; Education Gets $14 Billion," *Chronicle of Higher Education* 39, no. 38 (May 26, 1993): 25, 27.

33. For another view, see David Martinson, "Enlightened Self-Interest Fails as an Ethical Baseline in Public Relations," *Journal of Mass Media Ethics* 9, no 2 (1994): 100–108, or Martinson, "Ethical Public Relations Practitioners Must Not Ignore Public Interest," *Journal of Mass Media Ethics* 10, no. 4 (1995): 210–222.

34. Julianne Basinger, "Increase in Number of Chairs Endowed by Corporations Prompts New Concerns," *Chronicle of Higher Education,* April 24, 1998, p. 51.

35. Dan Cordtz, "American Business: The Golden Century," *Financial World* 160, no. 13 (June 25, 1991): 54.

36. Pamela S. Leven, "Do You Know Where Your Annual Report Is? *Ambassador* (TWA in-flight magazine), February 1998, p. 33.

37. Adam Shell, "Communicating in Tough Times," *Public Relations Journal* 48, no. 8 (August 1992): 23.

38. Robert K. Otterbourg, "Managing the Annual Report," *Public Relations Journal* 48, no. 8 (August 1992): 24.

39. Anthony J. Tortorici, "Maximizing Marketing Communication through Horizontal and Vertical Orchestration," *Public Relations Quarterly* 36, no. 1 (Spring 1991): 20.

40. Adapted from Thomas L. Harris, "Integrated Marketing Public Relations," in *The Handbook of Strategic Public Relations and Integrated Communications,* ed. Clark L. Caywood (New York: McGraw-Hill, 1997): 94–103.

41. Ibid., p. 91.

42. Charles A. Sengstock Jr., "The Quality Issue in Public Relations." Paper presented to the Arthur W. Page Society Meeting, Northwestern University, Evanston, IL, May 31, 1991.

43. Ibid. Adapted with permission of the author.

44. Charles A. Sengstock Jr., "Pursuing the Not-So-Elusive Goal of Perfection," *Public Relations Journal* 47, no. 8 (August 1991): 22.

45. Navin S. Dedhia, "The Basics of ISO 9000," *Quality Digest* 15, no. 10 (October 1995): 52–54.

46. Caroline G. Hemenway, "10 Things You Should Know about ISO 14000," *Quality Digest* 15, no. 10 (October 1995): 51.

47. Dan Koger and Greg Brower, "If Total Quality Seems Like a Revolution, That's Because It Is," *Communication World* 9, no. 10 (October 1992): 21.

48. Léon Jacobs, "President's Letter—Social Responsibility: How We All Make a Difference! *Chimo 72: Social Responsibility* (Summer 1995), p. 4. Publication of the Corporate Relations Department, Ciba-Geigy Canada Ltd., Mississauga, Ontario.

49. Tim Traverse-Healy, O.B.E., "Riding Point." Hall of Fame Award Lecture presented to the Arthur W. Page Society Annual Meeting, Orlando, FL, September 16, 1990.

ADDITIONAL SOURCES

Bollier, David, and Norman Lear. *Aiming Higher: 25 Stories of How Companies Prosper by Combining Sound Management and Social Vision.* New York: American Management Association, 1997.

Buchholz, Rogene A. *Principles of Environmental Management: The Greening of Business.* Englewood Cliffs, NJ: Prentice-Hall, 1993. Traces growth of environmentalism, environmental public policy and regulation, and strategies for managing environmental issues.

Budd, John F. Jr. *Street Smart Public Relations.* Lakesville, CT: Turtle Publishing

Company, 1992. Recounts lessons learned by a respected corporate practitioner and counselor.

Caywood, Clark L., ed. *The Handbook of Strategic Public Relations and Integrated Communications.* New York: McGraw-Hill, 1997. Loosely merges 37 chapters written by public relations and marketing professionals and scholars under "integrated marketing communications" rubric.

Ewen, Stuart. *PR! A Social History of Spin.* New York: Basic Books, 1996. Provides unflattering critique of public relations in the service of corporations, "revealing disturbing trends that have persisted to the present day" (from dust cover).

Harris, Thomas L. *The Marketer's Guide to Public Relations: How Today's Top Companies Are Using the New Public Relations to Gain a Competitive Edge.* New York: John Wiley and Sons, 1991. Defines "marketing public relations" as "programs to encourage purchase and consumer satisfaction," or, more precisely, "marketing."

Harrison, E. Bruce. *Going Green: How to Communicate Your Company's Environmental Commitment.* Homewood, IL: Business One Irwin, 1993. Outlines a participative approach to building "sustainable communications" with core environmental constituencies; "green listening."

Paradis, Gerard W., Fen Small, and Information Mapping's Team ISO. *Demystifying ISO 9000.* Reading, MA: Addison-Wesley Publishing Company, 1996. Outlines basic concepts and benefits of having ISO 9000 certification.

Thompson, Louis Jr. "The Fight for Good Governance." *Harvard Business Review* 71, no. 1 (January–February 1993): 76–83. Discusses the expanded role of boards of directors in investor relations, reforms in how directors relate to CEOs, and the push for greater accountability.

Young, Davis. *Building Your Company's Good Name.* New York: American Management Association, 1996. Builds case for building and protecting a company's key asset—its reputation.

GOVERNMENT AND POLITICS

15

A popular government without popular information or a means of acquiring it, is but a prologue to a farce or tragedy, or perhaps both.
—*James Madison*

OBJECTIVES

After studying chapter 15, you should be able to

▼ List the three major goals of government public relations
programs.

▼ List and discuss the two major barriers to effective public
relations in government.

▼ Identify the major aspects of government–media relationships.

▼ Describe the role of public relations in the military.

Government public relations specialists play a variety of roles. The
diversity of goals and activities in government is greater than in any
other area of public relations practice. One public affairs specialist tries
to explain how the Internal Revenue Service will become more user
friendly, whereas another conducts a campaign to recruit pregnant
women to WIC (Women, Infants, and Children) nutrition education
classes. Whereas one practitioner publicizes the introduction of a new

This chapter was written in collaboration with Mark S. Cox, APR, Director of Public Communications,
City of Chesapeake, Virginia.

commemorative postage stamp, another promotes youth basketball at the local community center. As one practitioner seeks to gain public compliance with the mandatory use of child safety seats in cars, another attempts to interpret national public opinion to assist in domestic policy formulation. Yet another practitioner may publicly defend controversial art created with taxpayers' money, whereas another explains troop movements or explains why an aircraft crashed while on a training mission.

THE ROLE OF PUBLIC RELATIONS IN GOVERNMENT

Government touches every aspect of society, and virtually every facet of government is closely tied to and reliant upon public relations. In a very real sense, the purpose of democracy itself closely matches the purpose of public relations. Successful democratic government maintains responsive relationships with constituents, based on mutual understanding and two-way communication. Government in the United States is structured upon principles that mandate effective public relations, with public apathy and ignorance its greatest enemies.

Without an informed and active citizenry, elected and appointed officials may lose touch with the true needs and interests of their constituents. Programs costing millions of dollars may be undertaken to address public needs that have been overestimated, while more pressing needs remain hidden. Special-interest politics may dominate decision making. Citizen discontent may linger just under the surface, then suddenly appear and be fueled by simplistic rhetoric in place of a deeper understanding of issues.

The problems and pressures of society increasingly strain the machinery of government. Government is intended to provide services that would otherwise be impractical for individuals to provide, such as police and fire protection, wildlife preserves, national defense, transportation systems, justice systems, social programs, and national museums. These programs, although administered by government officials, are responses to needs originating with ordinary citizens. As the needs of society have expanded in scope and complexity, government at all levels has also grown. Now some see government as no longer an extension of the people but as rather an adversary or "big brother." A labyrinth of bureaus, offices, departments, agencies, divisions, authorities, commissions, councils, boards, and committees has developed. Millions of tons of forms and reports are generated annually, most containing technical terms and jargon that inhibit many citizens' understanding and confidence in working with government effectively.

Much of the expansion of government can be attributed to two basic trends in America. First, increased population, social movements, business and economic activity, and technology have created new problems and issues that require regulatory attention. A few examples include the actions of the

Federal Communications Commission, Food and Drug Administration, Immigration and Naturalization Service, Federal Trade Commission, Department of Transportation, state health departments, local zoning boards, and many other agencies created to address the increasing complexities of modern society.

Second, U.S. citizens have increasingly grown to expect more from all levels of government. What may start as an offhanded remark such as, "There ought to be a law against that!" often leads not just to new regulations but to agencies set up to ensure that the new laws are obeyed. In the simpler times of our agrarian past, neighbors often worked together to build community projects, families were extended to include elderly grandparents, and food was grown locally. Today government is viewed more than ever as the primary mechanism to address injustices and inequities in virtually all human activities, from the bedroom to outer space.

As a result, government at all levels has grown to heretofore unimagined proportions. In state and local government, the growth rate for the number of employees has increased faster than the rate of population growth. New York City has close to 400,000 city government employees. In recent years, cities such as Washington, DC, have increased the number of government employees while the population actually decreased. Reporting on the "shrink-proof bureaucracy," journalist Jonathan Walters concluded that the number of employees is only one aspect of the problem of dealing with government:

> A further complication is the intricate system of job classification within civil service. New York State has 7,300 different job categories for its 285,000 state employees. Iowa has 1,254 different job titles for 44,000 employees; of those job titles, 364 apply to positions held by one individual. Under Florida's current civil service system, there are 23 categories of administrative assistant, none interchangeable.[1]

As government becomes more complex and ubiquitous, the challenge of maintaining citizen involvement and ensuring that government is responsive to societal needs becomes more difficult. Elected officials often claim credit for their election on their ability to keep a finger on the pulse of constituents. However, because of the sheer magnitude and complexity of the job, much of that responsibility falls to government public relations specialists.

The complexity of public relations work is very apparent in local government. This level is closest to its constituents, both in the services it provides and in the accessibility of elected and appointed officials. Moreover, the growing influence of neighborhood-level activist groups places a unique burden on local government management.

> Although the neighborhood associations are infrequently direct initiators of new agenda items, they play an important secondary role in creating a policy-making environment that will be hospitable to some kinds of proposals and unkind to others. They incrementally alter agendas, force initiators to anticipate their preferences, and play a vital role in the planning process at both the neighborhood and citywide levels.[2]

Increases in the level of public involvement in government can be found at the national level as well. For example, at its annual conference in 1998, the International Association for Public Participation reported a growing membership of over 1,000 persons in seventeen different countries. The goal of the organization is to involve the public in government and industry decisions that affect their lives. Conferences have taken place every year since 1992, alternating between U.S. and Canadian locales. The group also maintains a semiannual journal, Web site, and several local chapters.

Another example is the Center for Living Democracy. The organization maintains the American News Service which disseminates information to national news media in the hope of providing what the group's leaders believe is a more accurate perspective of what the ordinary citizen thinks about current governmental activities and programs.

Government public relations activities, many embraced by terms such as *public affairs, public information,* and *public communication,* have developed as a political and administrative response to achieve various organizational goals. They are a key component of the administrative system, specifically designed to bridge the gap between popular and bureaucratic government. The number of people employed as government public relations practitioners is difficult to pinpoint because of varying job titles and the reluctance of some government agencies to acknowledge the function's existence. Too often this vital part of the government process is referred to as "just PR," "publicity budgets," "propaganda machines," or "spin doctors."

The National Association of Government Communicators estimates that there are about 40,000 government communicators in the United States at all levels of government.[3] In Washington, DC, alone, *CBS News* identified almost 11,000 public affairs specialists working in federal agencies.[4] However, difficult economic conditions often affect the size of public relations staffs. The recession of the early 1990s brought with it government cutbacks in many areas, including government public relations. In Georgia in 1991, 29 of the 40 communication specialists in the state's Cooperative Extension Service lost their jobs, and the Arizona State Extension Service eliminated its entire communication staff. Other similar instances showed that government policy makers often view public relations as a soft service that can be cut more easily than the core services such as police protection, road building, and human services. In response, National Association of Government Communicators President Russell Forte wrote to the governors of every state emphasizing the importance of maintaining the public information function in government:

> When we cut back on communication offices and staff, we dilute the ability to provide the flow of information Americans need to make basic decisions for this country. In the end, the public does make the basic decisions that guide our governments. With inadequate information, those decisions are sometimes off target, wasteful and disruptive.[5]

Often, but certainly not always, government public relations programs deal with one-way communication directed to constituents. However, when viewed this way by policy makers, whether in government or in the private sector, the perceived impact of cutting public relations budgets is reduced to making publics themselves more responsible for obtaining information about the organization. When budgets get tight, this is a regrettable but acceptable consequence for many government leaders. For example, a California legislator apparently was serious when he proposed in 1993 a bill that would have eliminated all public affairs and public information specialists in state government "to eliminate waste." However, even when the full benefit of public relations is not realized and the function is seen as only public information, it nevertheless serves a vital function in government. In *Communicating for Results in Government,* James L. Garnett discussed the importance of straightforward communication with citizens:

> Whether a government job is primarily managerial or technical, involves preparing budgets or analyzing educational progress, or is routine or nonroutine, effective communication is crucial to solid performance. Yet communication is not important for its own sake. As with planning, budgeting, program evaluation, and other managerial tools, communication is important because it affects people's control over government. It influences employee morale and productivity and permeates all facets of government. Because government decisions and actions often affect more people and with greater consequences, communicating in government tends to be more important and often more difficult than communicating in business.[6]

Specific public relations objectives will vary from agency to agency, but the basic justification for government public relations rests on two fundamental premises: (1) that a democratic government must report its activities to the citizens, and (2) that effective government administration requires active citizen participation and support. Even the staunchest critics of "government propaganda" concede that the first justification is a valid one. However, effective government administration is sometimes construed by critics to mean protection of the bureaucracy at all costs.

Overall goals for government public relations programs, regardless of the level of government, have at least three things in common:

1. Informing constituents about the activities of the government agency;
2. Ensuring active cooperation in government programs (for example, voting, curbside recycling), as well as compliance in regulatory programs (for example, mandatory seat belt use, antismoking ordinances); and
3. Fostering citizen support for established policies and programs (for example, foreign aid, welfare). (See Figure 15.1 for examples of program materials.)

MAINTAINING AN INFORMED CITIZENRY

The primary job of government public relations practitioners is to inform. A multitude of other roles and responsibilities are assigned to specific government practitioners, many of enormous importance and scope, but ensuring

FIGURE 15.1   EXAMPLES OF CITY PUBLIC RELATIONS MATERIALS

Courtesy City of Chesapeake, VA.

the constant flow of information to persons outside and inside government is generally speaking the top priority. The information task is global, because the need to inform extends well beyond U.S. borders.

United States Information Agency (USIA)

The United States Information Agency coordinates America's informational and educational efforts in more than 200 locations in more than 140 countries. It also interprets public opinion overseas and provides analysis and feedback to the federal government. USIA, an independent foreign affairs agency within the executive branch, reports directly to the president. It is perhaps best known for its radio broadcast network, Voice of America (VOA), which began in World War II and was responsible for providing information to American troops and citizens in war areas. In addition, USIA operates Worldnet, a 24-hour satellite television service, and various other programs and services.

All nonmilitary broadcast services of the federal government were consolidated under the International Broadcasting Bureau by the 1994 International Broadcasting Act. The bureau is composed of the VOA, Worldnet and other similar services.

Overseas, USIA is known as the United States Information Service, or USIS. In American embassies, the chief USIS officials are the public affairs officers. They advise ambassadors and other diplomats on relevant public relations issues affecting U.S. interests and policy and on embassy operations and relationships within host countries. President Jimmy Carter said that the USIA role is to "build two-way bridges of understanding between our people and the other peoples of the world."

A vital responsibility of USIA is to correct information or to counter adverse propaganda that might have a detrimental effect on the United States. For example, in the early 1980s, USIA had to respond aggressively to a story planted by the Nigerian press claiming that the United States was developing a weapon that would kill Blacks but not Whites.[7]

Since World War II, the United States has been concerned with the problems of international communication, particularly in getting the people of other nations to understand America's foreign policy motives and goals. USIA has the responsibility of presenting to the world "a full and fair picture" of the United States. America's overseas public relations program has had two main goals: (1) countering divisive propaganda disseminated by hostile nations and fostering in other countries a fuller and friendlier understanding of American policies and (2) making technical knowledge available to assist developing countries.

More than once the agency has been subjected to philosophical debates concerning its role overseas in advancing foreign policy objectives that resulted in reorganization and restructuring. The agency often suffers from a split personality as it attempts to maintain credibility abroad through objective reporting while dealing with domestic political demands to disseminate persuasive or even biased, unbalanced information. The philosophy of the organization is best summarized in the Voice of America charter written into Public Law 94-350 and signed by President Gerald Ford in July 1976:

1. VOA news will be accurate, objective, and comprehensive.

2. VOA will present a balanced and comprehensive projection of significant American thought and institutions.
3. VOA will present the policies of the United States clearly and effectively.[8]

Although the Voice of America is best known by its history of worldwide radio broadcasts, in 1996 the agency began simulcasting radio and television programs. Broadcasts are disseminated in more than 50 different languages and reach millions of viewers and listeners in every part of the globe.

To achieve its purposes, USIA uses personal contact, the Internet, print media, radio, television, film, libraries, books, the arts, and exhibits to communicate the U.S. message abroad. To facilitate two-way communication, agency programs include cultural and educational exchanges of scholars, journalists, students, and cultural groups around the world.

Citizen Participation in Government

An important but often overlooked responsibility of government practitioners is soliciting and motivating involvement of citizens in government, including decision-making processes. Often the major obstacle is internal, because elected officials and administrators may be reluctant to have their carefully formulated plans altered by the multitude of interests and viewpoints citizen involvement inevitably generates. Writing in *Policy Studies Review,* Mary Kweit and Robert Kweit discussed the trade-offs inherent in encouraging citizen input:

> In the ideal bureaucracy there is no place for citizen participation. Citizens lack the technical expertise, are unfamiliar with bureaucratic routines, and are emotionally involved in issues rather than being detached and rational. Citizens are outside the hierarchy and therefore hard to control. As a consequence, participation may increase the time needed to reach decisions as well as the level of conflict.[9]

Public involvement typically slows and complicates the process, but it nonetheless increases government responsiveness. Forrest M. Landon, executive director of the Virginia Coalition for Open Government, counsels government administrators:

> Watching somebody make laws isn't always pretty. But give citizens an opportunity for timely input in crucial stages of lawmaking, and government effectively starts working for them. It works that way for savvy influence-peddlers, lobbyists and special interests; it needs to work that way for all.[10]

Scientific surveys of citizens are increasingly used in government. Politicians, especially those running for national office, have long relied on the Roper and Gallup polls, as well as privately commissioned surveys, for guidance in formulating campaign strategies. More recently citizen surveys have been used for identifying priorities for government. In addition, surveys are being used as the bottom line for government, whereby citizens' ratings of various services are the barometer of organizational success. In some cases, citizens' ratings have been directly tied to employees' performance and their salary increases.

When used to set goals and priorities, citizen surveys prove to be an equalizer against well-funded special interests and lobbying groups. "The greatest strength of citizen surveys is that they have the potential to sample the viewpoints of all citizens—not simply those who choose to participate."[11] Conducting surveys of citizens can prove counterproductive when they are not properly administered. For example, surveys that ask citizens to answer questions on subjects they have little or no knowledge about, such as how best to design a major highway or how to solve complex financial problems facing government, can have negative results.

> A second serious problem with citizen surveys is that they can have some serious political repercussions. The public may express a negative view of whatever services are dutifully provided. Pressures may develop to enact whatever recommendations the public might suggest. And then, apart from the issues of effectiveness and political advisability, there is always the issue of cost. With budgets getting ever tighter, a citizen survey might easily seem like an unnecessary frill. The costs could be particularly onerous to small governments.[12]

Surveys also provide only a snapshot in time of public opinion. This is clearly evident prior to nearly every presidential election, when polls show drastic changes in voters' preferences in response to events such as national conventions and domestic or international crises. Surveys take on greater credibility the more often they are repeated, allowing trends to be charted and previous findings to be validated.

Increasing involvement in programs and activities leads many government practitioners to use other tools and tactics often identical to those of private public relations and advertising firms. Many of these efforts go beyond mere increased communications efforts.

For example, the City of Springfield, Missouri, invested millions of dollars in a renovation project for its 1930s-era city hall that emphasized citizen-customer service, convenience, and comfort. The renovation was accompanied by a system of touch-screen kiosks throughout the community which guides citizens through the maze of local government.

> Today, there is a one-stop approach to working with every department of the city, now that first-floor offices are easily accessible to the public and a reception station offers help and directions quickly. Departments most commonly used by citizens are all on the ground floor.[13]

BARRIERS TO EFFECTIVE GOVERNMENT PUBLIC RELATIONS

Public relations practitioners in government shape much of the meaningful dialogue necessary to make democracy work. Their work carries with it a civic obligation to serve as intermediaries between elected officials and staff and their citizen constituencies. Yet the work of building and maintaining government and citizen relationships is hampered by two major factors: public apathy and legislative hostility.

Public Apathy

Unlike most business operations, government practitioners usually cannot target small segments of broad publics to achieve desired results and ignore the rest of the people. An automobile manufacturer, for example, may be satisfied with achieving success with 10 or 20 percent of the car-buying adults in the country. Government seeks to serve all taxpayers, or at least as great a portion as possible. This is an extremely difficult task, made nearly impossible because of the lack of interest among many citizens. Figure 15.2 illustrates how one city tried to spark interest in its recycling program.

Public apathy is an indisputable fact of public life. The percentage of eligible voters who participate in major national elections is invariably low, and the percentage of those voting in state and local elections is even lower. Even in large and midsize cities, candidates are often elected by slim margins. Only 50 percent of adult Americans voted in the 1988 presidential election, and only 36 percent voted in the 1990 elections. One writer said that public apathy is a "ground swell" among Americans:

> The hard fact is that most Americans are contemptuous of politicians and cynical about the motives of government and business. The U.S. now ranks 23rd in voter participation among Western democracies, and the share of adults who vote in presidential elections has dropped 20 percent since 1960.[14]

Voter turnout did rise slightly in the 1992 presidential election, to just over 55 percent. Voter interest often increases when there are major issues that move voters emotionally or affect them financially. In 1992, voter participation increased because of a severe economic recession, increasing discontent with government gridlock, and the emergence of H. Ross Perot as a national political figure. Political author Ruy A. Teixeira was cautiously optimistic about any trend toward increased voter turnout:

> Thus, while we should take heart from the 1992 election results—turnout can go up, not just down—much remains to be done. Absent a combination of substantial registration and political reforms, turnout is unlikely to rise much above its level in 1992 and may even fall again.[15]

As Teixeira predicted, the percentage of voters going to the polls in the 1996 presidential election once again fell below 50 percent.

City councils, county boards of supervisors, citizen advisory boards, and commissions all struggle with apathy each time a public hearing is scheduled, frequently cutting meetings short when few, if any, citizens show up to voice an opinion. Local government agencies that appoint citizens to serve on advisory boards often have woefully few candidates from which to choose.

Lack of interest and a basic knowledge of government is not new, however. The *New York Times* reported in 1989 that Americans' "factual knowl-

FIGURE 15.2   "RALPHY RECYCLER" PROGRAM MATERIALS

Courtesy June McPartland, APR, City of Hampton, VA.

edge about civics and politics has improved only marginally in the past 40 years, and many Americans still lack basic knowledge of the country's political system."[16] This conclusion was based on the results of a survey conducted in 1989 by the Survey Research Laboratory of Virginia Commonwealth University that found, among other things, that only 25 percent of those surveyed could name the two U.S. senators representing their state and only 46 percent knew that the first ten amendments to the Constitution are called the Bill of Rights.[17]

Despite its unique role and responsibilities in the American system of checks and balances, the explosion of news media, talk shows, public affairs programs, and special-interest publications has done little to make Americans better informed about government. Commenting on the performance of the broadcast media during political campaigns, Bernard Shaw, anchor of Cable News Network, refused to blame the media for the lack of interest among citizens:

> The juice of a democracy is information, and that is what we [the news media] are about. One of the reasons journalists do not point out what we do, especially what we do successfully—we all have PR departments that specialize in that—is we feel that it is self-serving. We feel we are there to serve the people. I would like to turn the mirror around and say that just as we have a responsibility in our democracy, the American people have a responsibility. And when you consider that at least 73 to 75 percent get our information from television, we know instantly that most Americans are underinformed.[18]

Lydia Bjornlund, citizenship education coordinator for the International City Management Association, stated,

> Government leaders are aware of the frustrations of dealing with an apathetic and poorly educated citizenry. Many have been confronted by irate citizens who do not understand the issue, the problem, the reasons behind unpopular decisions. Officials at one level of government are blamed for policies enacted at another. Citizens vote down government proposals in referenda because they do not understand the proposed actions or the alternatives. And, too often, citizens are shaken from their apathy only when a problem directly affects them.[19]

Contributing to public apathy are citizen frustration and a general sense of impotence toward government at all levels. Correct or not, the popular perception of government is one of gridlock, a maze of red tape, special interests, corruption, ineptitude, and partisan politics. A law degree is virtually a prerequisite for elected officials at the federal and state levels. The system has grown too complicated for most citizens either to understand or to gain access to services easily. Simply adding a room or a back porch to a home often requires the help of an architect or development consultant to ensure that proper permits are acquired and that no environmental regulations are violated.

Paying taxes, especially to the federal government, creates citizen hostility that spills over into other areas of government not related to the collection of taxes. Despite the annual rhetoric calling for simplifying the filing of personal income tax forms, millions of Americans still must seek the assistance of accountants and tax-preparation experts. Beginning in late 1997, the public outcry reached a peak when the Internal Revenue Service became a target of public and legislative scrutiny because of charges of intimidation, invasion of privacy, and favoritism. In Senate hearings "hooded witnesses told horror stories about IRS abuse, and the agency was depicted as a heartless cell snatching money and property from regular working folks."[20]

Facing citizen hostility is not unusual for many government agencies, even when they are simply performing their most basic responsibilities. The industry newsletter "Public Relations Tactics" chronicled in 1998 the challenges faced by wildlife park management officials in controlling the growing deer population. Officials were forced to face realities such as the more than 100 drivers who died in 1997 in automobile accidents caused by deer; the deer population in Gettysburg National Military Park is about 12 times what the forest can reasonably maintain; deer also contribute to the spread of Lyme disease and cause damage to crops and grazing lands. Despite what many believe are humane actions to control the deer population, deer management opponents were effective at promoting their cause.

At Seneca Creek State Park in Virginia, protesters attracted news cameras with a religious rite to "bless" the deer before a controlled hunt. While hunters in Groton, Connecticut, were bagging 226 deer in Bluff Point State Park, police were arresting eight protesters who tried to disrupt the hunt. It was "David and Goliath" made for television, only this time Goliath carried the weapons.[21]

Legislative Hostility to the Function

The public relations function has been established longer in government than in any other field of practice, yet it has never been totally effective or given the respect enjoyed by practitioners in the private sector. In government, as in other organizational settings, public relations is a legitimate management function that helps make agencies, departments, and other public entities responsive to the citizens they were created to serve. However, government practitioners often face more hostility and suspicion than do other practitioners. This hostility stems from four fundamental and long-standing conflicts embedded in our democratic government:

1. The continuing struggle between the press, fighting for "the people's right to know," and the officials of government, who insist upon discretion in certain sensitive areas of the public business.
2. The unrelenting struggle for the balance of power between the legislative and executive branches of government. This contest is present whether it is between mayor and council, governor and legislature, or president and Congress.
3. The continuing struggle for power between the major political parties. The "out" party fears the power of an army of "propagandists" in keeping the "ins" in and the "outs" out.

4. The protests of industries, institutions, and other vested interests when threatened by proposed legislation or government regulation. They often disparage the use of public funds and government machinery to carry the day against them.

Beyond these conflicts is the inevitable association of government information programs with the word "propaganda." Americans have long been deeply suspicious of anything with that label, particularly because this powerful technique has been used in other countries to gain and hold despotic control. Thus, public suspicion of information as "nothing but propaganda" is especially strong when the information comes from the government. This is reflected in a fear that government communication could become little more than tax-supported propaganda designed to persuade taxpayers to spend even more tax dollars.

Also involved in this opposition is the double standard that many citizens have for government and for private enterprise. The public generally accepts the propriety of business publicizing and advertising even though the customer pays for it. On the other hand, many people regard government information work as a waste of tax dollars; they see no need for government to sell itself or its products and services. There is no way of telling just how deep-seated and widespread this citizen attitude is, but some politicians think that they win votes when they flay "government propaganda."

The public relations function in government has been handicapped by the opposition of legislators, which prevents maximum effectiveness and accurate accounting of the function's cost and performance. Attacks on public relations by legislators are less frequent than those by the press but perhaps more damaging.

Legislative opposition is often stimulated by other sources of hostility. At the turn of the nineteenth century, the Roosevelt-Pinchot campaign for land conservation sparked congressional reaction, thanks in large part to the efforts of spokespersons of lumber interests, mine operators, and cattle grazers who had been exploiting the nation's public lands. Congressman Franklin Mondell of Wyoming, spokesman for sheep and cattle ranchers, won adoption in 1908 of an amendment to the agricultural appropriation bill dealing with the Forest Service, which read:

> That no part of this appropriation shall be paid or used for the purpose of paying for in whole or in part the preparation of any newspaper or magazine articles.[22]

Thus, the first effective use of public relations to promote acceptance of an administration's policies brought congressional restriction of the function in the executive branch.

Congressional ire next erupted in 1910, when Joseph T. Robinson, representative from Arkansas, demanded an investigation of the Census Bureau for employing a special agent at $8 per day in 1909. The agent was to explain to the public the purpose of the 1910 census. Census Bureau Director E. Dana Durand insisted that it was essential, if the census was to be complete, that all citizens and aliens be reached—through newspapers, the foreign-language press, and agricultural weeklies—and be assured that their replies would not be used for taxation purposes. The committee, after hearing this, tacitly approved.

By 1912 the number of "publicity agents" employed by executive departments was growing, and some campaigns were not beyond reproach. In May 1912, Congressman John Nelson of Wisconsin gained passage of a House resolution to investigate meat inspection in the Department of Agriculture's Bureau of Animal Industry. Early in the hearings, Nelson was angered by a circular criticizing the resolution and defending the department; the pamphlet had been published before the hearings opened. He charged that the department was using publicity to discredit one of its accusers, and he introduced a House resolution to investigate "the expenditure of public moneys for press bureaus, postage, stationery, and employees by the Department of Agriculture and by other departments; and that said committee be directed to make recommendations to the House as to what steps are necessary to protect public funds from newspaper exploitations."[23] The resolution did not pass.

A year later the Civil Service Commission advertised for "a press agent to help boom the good roads movement" in the Office of Public Roads. The circular called for a "publicity expert" whose "affiliations with newspaper publishers and writers is extensive enough to secure publication of items prepared by him." The circular prompted Representative Frederick H. Gillett to offer an amendment to an appropriations bill specifying that no money could be spent for publicity unless specifically authorized by Congress. It passed.

The 1913 Gillett Amendment remains embedded in law and the source of much confusion. As one government public affairs officer explained, "The amendment does not prohibit the use of publicity; it merely states that such funds be clearly identified." He went on to say that the 1913 amendment continues to intimidate those who work in government public relations.[24]

The Gillett Amendment is only one of six restrictions on the function that have been written into U.S. codes. These laws cloud and confuse the practice in the federal government:

1. Amendment (by Rep. Gillett) to Interstate Commerce Commission appropriations bill passed October 22, 1913, forbids spending for "publicity experts" any part of an appropriation unless that money is specifically appropriated by Congress [Ch. 32, § 1, 38 Stat. 212 (1913)].
2. The "gag law" of July 11, 1919, prohibits using any part of an appropriation for services, messages, or publications designed to influence any member of Congress in his or her attitude toward legislation or appropriations [18, U.S.C. (1919)].
3. Another law passed in 1919, but not strictly enforced until 1936, requires that all duplicating of material must be done by the Government Printing Office, or at least farmed back to the department for reproduction by the GPO [44, U.S.C. § 501 (1919)].
4. Title 5, Section 3107, U.S.C. 54 (Sept. 6, 1966), of the United States Code restated the 1913 Gillett Amendment prohibition against hiring publicists "in positive form," clearly stating that "appropriated funds may not be

used to pay a publicity expert unless specifically appropriated for that purpose" [Pub. L. No. 89-554, § 3107, 80 Stat. 416 (1966)].

5. No part of any appropriation contained in Public Law 92-351 (enacted July 13, 1972) or any other act, or of the funds available for expenditure by a corporation or agency, shall be used for publicity or propaganda purposes designed to support or defeat legislation pending before the Congress [Pub. L. No. 92-351, § 608a (1972)].

6. No part of any appropriation contained in Public Law 93-50 (enacted July 1, 1973) or any other act, or of the funds available for expenditure by any corporation or agency, shall be used, other than for normal and recognized executive-legislative relationships, for publicity or propaganda purposes, for the preparation, distribution, or use of any kit, pamphlet, booklet, publication, radio, television, or film presentation designed to support or defeat legislation pending before the Congress, except for the presentation to Congress itself [Pub. L. No. 93-50, § 305, (1973)].[25]

Legislative opposition to the function at all levels has led to legal restrictions, circumvention of budgetary procedures, and wasteful practices designed to conceal legitimate government functioning. Legislative hostility and self-serving posturing by elected and appointed officials also causes many competent professionals to shy away from government service.

GOVERNMENT–MEDIA RELATIONS

Since the very beginning of American government, the First Amendment to the Constitution has guaranteed freedom of the press. This freedom was vital to the founders of the new nation, so much so that Thomas Jefferson said, "Were it left to me to decide whether we should have a government without newspapers or newspapers without government, I should not hesitate a moment to prefer the latter."

Media Access to Government

In more recent times, the constitutional freedoms guaranteed to the press have been expanded and clarified. Access to government information, in addition to the freedom to speak out or write freely about government, has been codified in freedom of information legislation, or "sunshine laws." Except for well-defined areas, such as national security, litigation, certain personnel records, and so forth, virtually every piece of information maintained by government is open to inspection by the press, and by the public for that matter. In most cases, a reporter can demand to see unfinished drafts of reports and handwritten notes if the reporter has specific knowledge of these and can request them with adequate specificity.

The right of access to government information and meetings is of paramount importance. Beyond just informing citizens about the official actions of government, the indispensable role of the press as the watchdog of government helps guarantee accountability, reduce corruption, and crystallize public issues and opinions, and it places the press in the position of being the citizen's representative in the broad system of checks and balances. Almost by definition, government–press relationships are adversarial. Government frequently argues that any large organization is more effective if it has a degree of privacy in formulating strategies. For example, in labor and contract negotiations or the purchase of land, privacy is needed to avoid giving the other side, who is often exempt from freedom of information laws, an unfair advantage. The press counters that the public's business should be conducted in the open to ensure that all activities are conducted ethically and in the public interest.

Many attribute the strained relations between reporters and government officials to events surrounding the Watergate scandal of the mid-1970s. President Richard Nixon was openly hostile to reporters and made it as difficult as possible for them to obtain information about his administration. Others argue that *Washington Post* reporters Bob Woodward and Carl Bernstein, who were in large part responsible for the resignation of Nixon, marked a drastic change in journalism's approach to government reporting. Several government officials were exposed as ruthless, Machiavellian, and at times, liars. Although the Justice Department and the FBI were responsible for uncovering most of the information about the break-in of the National Democratic Party's headquarters, the news media affirmed their role as the guardian of the public trust.

Years later, the historic events referred to as Watergate serve as a reminder and a model to reporters of what might be lurking behind the doors of city halls, state capitols, and the halls of Washington. The ultimate effect of the Watergate scandal is still debated, and in the last few decades Watergate is only one of the many factors affecting the press's and the public's perception of government. Michael Schudson observed in the *Columbia Journalism Review:*

> Did Watergate lead to an increase in investigative reporting? This depends on what investigative reporting is. Of course, Watergate was not the beginning of the adversarial relationship between the government and the Washington press corps. The key event was Vietnam, not Watergate, and the "credibility gap" that drew the press toward deep distrust of government voices first came to a head in Johnson's administration, not Nixon's.[26]

Competition among news organizations has intensified, and many seem to be searching for the next Watergate or Whitewater scandal. From city halls to Capitol Hill, reporters and government communicators today continue to work together in a volatile environment of caution and, in many cases, mutual distrust about each other's motives and tactics. Journalists criticize public officials for not being candid and honest in public statements; government officials point to the press's habit of looking only for what government is doing wrong, and they condemn reporters for their lack of knowledge in the areas they cover and for their lack of simple objectivity. Christopher Lasch, writing in the *Gannett Center Journal,* counters that the press is, in fact, too unbiased in government coverage:

> The job of the press is to encourage debate, not to supply the public with information. But as things now stand the press generates information in abundance, and nobody pays any attention. It is no secret that the public knows less about

public affairs than it used to know. Millions of Americans cannot begin to tell you what is in the Bill of Rights, what Congress does, what the Constitution says about the powers of the presidency, how the party system emerged or how it operates. A sizable majority, according to a recent survey, believe that Israel is an Arab nation. . . . But since the public no longer participates in debates on national issues, it has no reason to be better informed.[27]

The idea of the news media having responsibilities beyond simply providing the facts and offering a few editorial columns is becoming more accepted. Sometimes labeled "public journalism" or "civic journalism," a more activist form of news coverage is being used by a growing number of media covering government agencies and programs.

Editors at the *Spokesman-Review* in Spokane, Washington, and the *Virginian-Pilot* in Norfolk, Virginia, are examples of news media unabashedly seeking to affect the agenda of political and governmental discourse. The editors have convened public forums in the communities to discuss the same issues being discussed by legislative bodies, have sought out nonjournalists to write columns, and have generally attempted to increase the number of options and entities involved in government decision making. Christopher Conte, in *Governing Magazine,* described the emergence of this new strain of journalism:

> "Public" or "civic" journalism, as it is called, seeks to restore grassroots democracy to America—and in the process recapture a vanishing audience for the news business. To that end, newspapers and television stations all around the country are convening public forums, pounding the pavement to seek out the views of ordinary citizens, giving readers more of a voice in news and editorial pages, and actively enlisting citizens in a search for solutions to society's problems. "We aim," explains Tom Warhover, the *Virginian-Pilot*'s regional editor, "to put the 'participatory' back in 'participatory democracy.' "[28]

The new role taken on by these news organizations is not without critics. Many government officials condemn the effort as ignorant of the basic principles of representative government. Many assert that American democracy is founded on the idea that most ordinary citizens—who do not have the time, expertise or interest to fully research and understand complex and numerous issues facing governments—elect persons they trust to conduct the public's business. Reaching consensus, they argue, is already a difficult, arduous process already criticized for its snail-like pace. Injecting additional entities with tremendous publicity powers but no legal accountability is counterproductive. Likewise, many journalists are fearful that by becoming news makers themselves, reporters and editors may lose the objectivity, independence, and courage to report on public issues.[29]

Government Dependence on Media

The relationship between journalists and government is simultaneously an unquestioned necessity and an obstacle to government communication with citizens. A shortage of media attention is rare, but it usually comes when government agencies want it least. Mark Hughes, public information officer for the city of Phoenix, describes media attention as unrelenting: "We get shelled on a daily basis. We have four full-time reporters who spend eight hours a day trying to catch us screwing up."[30] But when government needs to just "get the word out" on routine issues, the news media are often only mildly interested.

The standards used by reporters and government communicators to define news are usually quite different. It is not surprising that much information considered by individual agencies to be of vital importance gets lost in the mountains of information generated by public relations staffs. Anne Groer, Washington-based national correspondent for the *Orlando Sentinel,* described the challenge of sorting through the barrage of publicity from just one government agency:

> NASA led the hypesters with seven faxes, including three concerning personnel changes that I, personally, would have combined into one—except that I am not a government information specialist wedded to the notion that every GS-Whatever deserves his/her own release. . . . The one truly useful release announced an April 13 press conference to unveil a report from NASA's Aerospace Safety Advisory Panel, created after the horrific 1986 Challenger disaster. My colleague, Chris Reidy, covered the story, which went out on the *Chicago Tribune–Knight Ridder* wire and was picked up by several papers, including the *Washington Post.*[31]

In just five days, Groer had collected 228 pieces of printed matter weighing more than 16 pounds:

> How many daily stories sprang directly from that pile? One. How many long-range ideas or follow-up calls? Perhaps three. How many pieces would we normally have saved for more than a day or two? Maybe 20 out of the 228 pieces (which, for all I know, is a terrific ratio).[32]

Despite the difficulties, government relies heavily on the press to pass on important information. And regardless of its use of brochures, speakers' bureaus, cable television, and many other methods of disseminating information, government's communication vehicles will never match the effectiveness of the privately owned mass media. Perhaps more important, the power of the press to set the agenda for public debate, although often underemphasized by reporters and editors, is unmistakable. "Everyone in politics turns to the press, if only to manipulate it or deflect it," asserts William Greider, former assistant managing editor of the *Washington Post.*[33]

> What matters to the press matters perforce to politicians. What the press ignores, the politicians may safely ignore too. What the newspapers tell people, whether it is true or false or cockeyed, is what everyone else must react to, since alternative channels of political information are now weak or nonexistent for most Americans.[34]

The news media do not have the resources to cover all that is the public's business in government. First, there are not enough journalists on all the news media payrolls to adequately track all the developments in the many agencies and activities at all levels of government. Second, there is a dominant set of news values that prefers and rewards the negative, controversial, and sensational aspects of government. Critics condemn the media for "elections by sound bites" and for an overemphasis of issues not relevant to the performance of government.

> Because government is seen as the "public's business," citizens as individuals or organized in interest groups justifiably deem it their right to know what government does. News media correspondingly consider it their duty to report on virtually every facet of government judged to be newsworthy because it involves politics, scandal, tax dollars, or simply the public interest. For these reasons, the decisions, thoughts, and even the life-styles of public officials and administrators are far more likely to receive public scrutiny than is the case for their business sector counterparts, Donald Trump notwithstanding.[35]

Media Reporting on Government

The news media are grappling with the task of reporting government activities under the heavy hand of news values fashioned in frontier days and with too few reporters. In days gone by, news of government was a relatively simple matter of personalities, oratorical political campaigns, trust busting, and the like. It was entirely different from reporting government finance, world affairs, nuclear energy, mental health, space travel, controversies over issues affecting equal opportunity, the environment, and other complex subject matters. Interpreting the complexities of government requires trained specialists and often takes more time than news media deadlines permit. Hence, government public relations specialists play an essential role in working with journalists to communicate with citizens.

Much progress has been made by the media in government reporting. But the need for government to strengthen and supplement today's reporting by the media is greater than ever. Problems in the media coverage of federal government are not always the fault of either the media or individual journalists. Rather, shortcomings in coverage are due to the magnitude of the task, and the size of the job is staggering. Washington dominates the nation's news system. News organizations, write Grossman and Kumar, "have become one of the principal forces on the national political scene, influencing the other major forces—the President, Congress, the bureaucracy, the parties, and the pressure groups—and in turn being influenced by them."[36]

Many in government do not think that the media measure up to their task. David Brown asserted,

> On the reportorial side, I find the media have become society's follower, not leader. The media lack understanding of the complexity of government and dwell on exceptions, which all too often disguise the rule. The media tend to judge the nation's capital by the White House, The Congress, the State Department, and the Defense Department. These are but four of the some 200 Federal entities in Washington.[37]

Washington's dominance of government reporting often comes at the expense of state and local governments, thus making the job of state and municipal practitioners more difficult. Stephen Hess, an astute student of Washington journalism, observed, "Given the limits to the size of news holes, a rise in Washington stories presages a decline in news of municipal and state governments, most often the latter."[38]

The type and quality of the news media's reporting of government activities reached a new level in the late 1990s. Public officials—especially those holding elected offices—have always been accustomed to living "life in the fishbowl." One writer said that things previously considered private are now potential stories:

> As for the private lives of public officials, adultery, drug dependency, abortion, mental health and sexual preferences are all potential news material. There are no longer any skeletons too personal to remain in the closet.[39]

At no time in history had this point come through so clearly as it did during the news coverage of the Clinton administration. Allegations of past marijuana use, draft dodging, questionable real estate dealings, and other issues early in the Clinton presidency served as merely a warm-up for what was to follow, ultimately leading all the way to impeachment by the House of Representatives and trial in the Senate. The issues centered not on the job performance of the President but on his purported liaisons with a variety of women close to the White House and his comments regarding the accuracy of those allegations. All of this came at a time when the country was at peace, the economy was strong, and the President's approval ratings in the national polls remained near historic high levels.

Instead of reporting on the President's relationships with foreign heads of state, every major news organization repeatedly led with stories about Clinton's affairs with former government employees such as Paula Jones and Gennifer Flowers and White House intern Monica Lewinsky. Many questioned the role of the press in making activities that had once been considered too sensitive—and perhaps too insignificant—the dominant issue in the nation's headlines.

The emphasis on sex and scandal in government reporting has received a great amount of criticism from various sources. However, public officials and government public relations practitioners should be prepared for the trend to become the standard.

Why is it unlikely to go away? For one thing, the proliferation of television news and information programming has spawned saturation coverage which, to fill time, nourishes itself on speculation, rumor, and the opinions of a staggering array of "reliable" sources and "experts."

For another, investigations and preparation for trial in civil and criminal cases can take years, during which there may be other parties involved with vested interests to keep the story on the front page, that is, litigation journalism.[40]

The American public's view of and relationship with the military changed dramatically in the 1990s, threatening to weaken recruitment efforts and legislative support. Although the end of the cold war offered renewed hope for a peaceful world, many internal issues facing the military made front-page news as well as lead stories for tabloid television programs. Some of the most noteworthy had little to do with national defense, security, nuclear weapons, or similar topics. Instead, the focus of many administrative and news media investigations was often on the sexual activities of members of the armed forces, from the lowest to the highest ranks.

Homosexuals in the military stirred considerable debate concerning the appropriateness of the don't ask–don't tell rule, which was an attempt to avoid discharging otherwise capable military personnel because of their sexual preferences. Perhaps posing a greater threat to the military's overall reputation was a series of scandalous episodes that brought into question the military establishment's moral character. In 1991, sexual misconduct at the Navy's Tailhook convention in Las Vegas captured the attention of the nation and led to the resignations of Rear Admiral Duvall M. Williams Jr. and Rear Admiral John E. Gordon. In 1997 it came to light that military trainers at the Army's Aberdeen Proving Ground had coerced female recruits into having sex. Soon after this, the base moved to address concerns and opened a hot line to allow complaints about sexual abuses to be logged anonymously. The result of one of the tips was that the commander of the facility, Major General John Longhouse, was forced to retire after confirming that he had committed adultery five years earlier. That same year, Rear Admiral R. M. Mitchell Jr. was relieved of duty as commander of the Navy's supply system because of allegations that he had repeatedly propositioned one of his subordinates and created a work environment hostile to women. Also in 1997, Air Force General Joseph W. Ralston lost his opportunity to become the chairman of the Joint Chiefs of Staff because of allegations of an adulterous affair more than 10 years earlier.

Public relations activities were central to the case of Air Force Lieutenant Kelly Flinn. In 1995, Flinn was publicized by the Air Force as the first female B-52 pilot. A year later, she became the target of an investigation by the service that alleged adultery, lying to superiors, and conduct unbecoming an officer. Flinn went on the offensive, retaining a public relations agency and appearing on nationally televised news programs to tell her side of the story. Flinn ultimately resigned, but the military's handling of the case caused many public relations professionals to question the service's strategy. John Elsasser, editor-in-chief of *Public Relations Tactics,* observed,

> A sexy story like this was sure to cause a sensation. The Air Force may have wanted to make an example of Flinn, but it backfired, perpetuating the stereotype of a male-dominated military. This was an issue better left handled on the inside and not on *Hard Copy.*[41]

The actions of the military have long been covered by news reporters in times of both peace and war. For just as long, military leaders have attempted to limit the flow of information that could potentially benefit their adversaries. The conflict between reporters and the military can be traced at least as far back as the Civil War.

During the Civil War, the horrors of war were vividly brought to the folks back home. Mathew Brady and his assistant Alexander Gardner documented major battles throughout the war. Brady's black wagon, which served as his darkroom, became a dreaded sight on the battlefield. Brady seemed to know where the action would be the heaviest, and soldiers soon learned that when Brady's wagon came on the scene, heavy fighting would likely follow. Brady took more than 3,500 photographs of the war, and these had a profound impact on the civilian population of the day and on the way that war in general was perceived.[42]

By the Vietnam War, same-day coverage had become the norm. The American people not only saw the consequences of war but could witness much of the actual fighting. As the popularity of the war decreased among many Americans at home, the pictures of burning villages and body bags fueled the growing antiwar sentiment. Extensive coverage of antiwar demonstrations on college campuses contributed to public distrust of U.S. involvement in the affairs of Southeast Asia and the escalating military actions. Military leaders who had once criticized the press for revealing potentially sensitive information faced a new, more complex problem. News coverage was influencing public opinion against them, and many in the military viewed the media as adversaries set on undermining the entire war effort.

> Since Vietnam, when the military thought its conduct of the war had been impaired by negative media coverage, people in the Pentagon had been simmering, planning and talking. In sessions there and in the war and naval colleges, the issue of "handling" the media was widely discussed and carefully understood. While the military assessment of the media's role in Vietnam and other wars may have been wrong—some of the most critical reporters in Vietnam, for example, were hawks, not doves—there was nonetheless a determination to be ready for the next war not only in strictly military terms but also in terms of public opinion.[43]

In subsequent years, the military has placed much greater emphasis on preparing for dealing with the media in times of war. During the brief Grenada conflict in 1983, reporters were not allowed to cover the invasion as it began. Although members of the news media were highly critical of the military, national polls showed that most Americans did not share their outrage.

The news media's reporting of the Persian Gulf conflict in early 1991 was unlike anything previously experienced. According to H. J. (Jerry) Dalton Jr., corporate public relations specialist and former Air Force brigadier general in charge of Air Force public affairs, "We are witnessing for the first time the phenomenon of live TV coverage of a war. The problem is that there's absolutely no time to put the report in perspective and explain how it fits into the big picture."[44]

So immediate was the coverage that military leaders on both sides, including Iraqi leader Saddam Hussein, relied heavily on news reports—particularly that of Cable News Network (CNN)—to follow initial military activities as they occurred. And unlike in previous military engagements, the military was well prepared for the onslaught of reporters, perhaps too well prepared, according to some reporters. Then Department of Defense Assistant Secretary for Public Affairs Pete Williams became a regular on the evening news, because he was often the only authoritative source on events in the Persian Gulf.

In 1992, 20 news organizations, including the Associated Press, the *Washington Post,* and CNN, proposed to the Pentagon a set of principles for wartime news coverage. The principles provided that public affairs officers should act as liaisons but should not interfere with the reporting process, journalists would be allowed to ride on military vehicles and aircraft whenever possible, and journalists would make every effort to assign experienced reporters to cover combat operations. Although many in government endorsed the principles, the Pentagon insisted on retaining the right to review battlefield reports prior to their publication or release to reporting pools.[45]

Since the end of World War II, a key component of U.S. military policy has been based on the precept that a high state of military readiness is an ef-

FIGURE 15.3   MACNELLY CARTOON OF CNN PERSIAN GULF WAR COVERAGE

© Tribune Media Services, Inc. All Rights Reserved. Reprinted with permission.

EXHIBIT 15.1

PUBLIC RELATIONS, NAVY STYLE

Military public relations is no different from any other public relations, just our product is different. We use the same tools, we compete for the same news space, and we approach public relations problems in the same way as practitioners in the private sector do. The basic process is the same: research, planning, implementation, and evaluation.

There is a greater emphasis on internal audiences in the military. There is also a more complex organizational structure to deal with in the military, and more people are usually involved in addressing public relations issues. Often our activities are scrutinized by local, national, and international news organizations. The result is that doing public relations work in the military is often more demanding than in the private sector.

Today's environment requires a high degree of professionalism among military public affairs officers, including high ethical standards as well as a solid educational foundation. When I first entered the Navy, there were many excellent public affairs officers doing their jobs very effectively. However, most of them were former news reporters who had no formal public affairs training. The demands of the field today require professionals specifically trained in military public affairs. The Navy has tremendous respect for public relations as a discipline, and it takes a strong, aggressive approach to public affairs issues.

The military attracts more media attention than most other organizations. There are more military reporters than ever before, and many—if not most—had very little experience with military operations when they first come to us. It requires a constant educational process. During Vietnam and the Persian Gulf War, Americans had a war in their living rooms. Coverage of a crisis is virtually instantaneous. We have to be well prepared, and we have to act and react very quickly.

The primary goals of Navy public affairs are (1) keeping the American public informed about Navy operations in a timely, complete, and accurate fashion; (2) coordinating Navy participation in special events and community affairs; and (3) supervising the Navy's internal communications activities. In addition, every public affairs officer—from the Chief of Information to the information officer on a ship—is constantly a part of the decision-making process. He or she is an indispensable member of the leadership team. When important decisions are made in the Navy, the public relations ramifications of those decisions are carefully considered in advance.

—Rear Admiral Kendell Pease, Former Chief of Information, Department of the Navy (Retired).

fective deterrent to war, but only if that readiness is communicated to the rest of the world. To that end, an increasingly professional cadre of public relations specialists serves in every branch of the military, usually under the title of "public affairs" (see Exhibit 15.1.) Many of the enlisted "journalists" and public affairs officers trained for their public relations roles at the Defense Information School, Fort George G. Meade, in Maryland, or at universities offering undergraduate and graduate curricula in public relations and journalism.

The 1990s brought significant changes to the way many government agencies integrate their activities into society. These new developments may have altered some of the basic philosophies of government for a long time to come. They included the following:

1. Economic conditions and greater taxpayer scrutiny caused nearly every government entity to tighten its belt.
2. Government entities at all levels grew increasingly aware of the need to compete with other government agencies in the public and political arenas for scarce funding resources.
3. There was a growing attitude among many observers that government should be run like a business, not a nonprofit charitable organization with unlimited resources. This concept was effectively popularized during the presidential campaigns of Texas businessman and unsuccessful presidential candidate H. Ross Perot.
4. Perhaps the most widely read book ever on the subject of government management was published: *Reinventing Government: How the Entrepreneurial Spirit Is Transforming the Public Sector,* by David Osborne and Ted Gaebler.

Osborne and Gaebler said that government needs to go back to square one, evaluate its basic goals, and establish concrete, achievable objectives. The cornerstone of their approach was effectively integrating government management with the real needs of constituents, and the authors asserted that much could be accomplished toward improving government's image among citizens through one-to-one contact. "The greatest irritant most people experience in their dealings with government is the arrogance of the bureaucracy. People today expect to be valued as customers—even by government."[46]

Osborne and Gaebler point out that unlike businesses, however, most public agencies do not get their funds from their clients or customers. Rather, funding decisions are made by city councils, legislatures, or elected boards. Agency heads therefore aim to please these bodies, not those they are designed to serve. Besides, their clients—unless they move to another city or state—have little choice for the services provided by government. Most businesses, on the other hand, must remain competitive and attempt to please their customers just to stay in business.[47]

Some see inherent similarities, but important differences, between government and business. According to the chief executive officer of Eugene, Oregon, Mike Gleason,

> First, these businesses are *owned by their customers.* Second, to that end, they must be operated in the light of day and in a democratic fashion. Third, in addition to producing products and services, as any private corporation would, they have major responsibilities regarding legislation.[48]

In several other aspects, government operates in a competitive, businesslike environment, and public relations plays a key role. Many government activities are being funded by corporate sponsorships, and public–private partnerships are favored by politicians and taxpayers alike. States and cities launch massive promotional campaigns to attract tourists and conventions. Tourism is a relatively clean industry that brings millions of dollars into communities. These dollars support local businesses, which in turn pay more taxes and keep the general tax rates down for residents. For many communities, tourism is the key source of revenue. State and local governments also compete to attract new industry through advertising, participation in international trade shows, and tax incentives, thereby creating more jobs and opportunities for their residents and diversifying their tax base.

PUBLIC RELATIONS IN POLITICS

For as long as there have been leaders in society, there has been a love–hate relationship between the governed and those who govern. The politician—impossible to accurately stereotype—often spends a large percentage of his career dedicated to serving his fellow citizens only to be crudely thrown out of office when the political environment or the local newspaper editorial policies change. At the same time, another politician may lack high ethical standards, or even may be guilty of serious crimes, and yet be returned to office when reelection time comes. Such was the case with Washington, DC, Mayor Marion Barry, who was videotaped by police using illegal narcotics yet returned as mayor of the nation's capital.

The challenge to lead and to serve in the midst of constant conflict is a difficult one for any political figure or organization.

> Today, many Americans feel angry toward their government institutions and alienated from governance and policy making. The signs of this major lack of connection between citizens and their government are clear: fewer citizens are voting in elections at all levels of government; public debate is often uncivil, derogatory, and confrontational as a "we-they" mentality sets the tone for city council meetings, public hearings, and other open forums; and public opinion polls indicate that more than 75 percent of Americans have little or no confidence in their local governments to resolve problems, with even larger percentages having no confidence in their state or the federal government to resolve those issues that affect their lives.[49]

Cynicism about public relations in government is greatest when associated with elected officials, or "politicians." Within an environment of skepticism, many view communication from elected officials as mere propaganda. Often many wonder whether the work of government is at its roots purely politics and running for reelection.

For example, members of Congress use their franking privileges (free mailing) to communicate to their constituents back home. However, as one newspaper report illustrates, such communication can be an easy target for critics:

> You know that chatty newsletter your local congressman mails you? The one that leaves a lingering impression of how hard-working your federal representative has been over the past few months? Well, read it carefully, because you're paying for it. . . . Last year, the 435 members of the House of Representatives spent $44 million on such mailings, says the National Taxpayer's Union. That's enough to buy 44 million school lunches for poor children. And it was all at taxpayers' expense.[50]

Voters decided in California in 1988 that many elected officials were taking advantage of their agencies' publications to gain recognition and popularity. Proposition 73 was aimed at limiting campaign contributions as well as prohibiting elected officials from using public funds to gain political advantage. Included in the new law was a provision that prohibited government agencies from mailing newsletters and other mass-produced publications if the publication included "the name, office, photograph, or other reference to an elected officer affiliated with the agency which produces or sends the mailing." The California Fair Political Practices Commission, the agency responsible for enforcement, later clarified the law to prohibit any publication that "features" an elected official. This includes—by the Commission's definition—material that "singles out the elected officer by the manner of display of his or her name or office in the layout of the document, such as by headlines, captions, type size, typeface, or type color."[51] Elected officials' photographs and signatures were also prohibited.

Leaders in both government and business share a concern about political interference:

> Government agencies are also more likely to experience intervention from political party officials, legislators, public interest groups, and other political actors than are typical business firms. While politics tends to be underrated as a force in business, it can hardly be overrated as the dominant driving force in government agencies.[52]

In fact, politics and government cannot be separated. Likewise, the role of public relations in politics and government is inextricably interrelated. At no level of government is public relations more important than in our cities, where government provides schools, fire and police protection, safe streets and public transportation, recreation facilities and programs, housing, and a host of other vital services. Yet even with cities in crisis, public relations has been slow to develop and is often the target of tax protesters and politicians looking for easy targets to exploit.

As the practice in government matures and becomes more professional, however, it has demonstrated its ability to make government more responsive to citizens' needs and concerns, gain acceptance of necessary programs, and make services widely available to those who need them. In short, the public relations function in government is increasingly recognized as an essential element of effective government.

NOTES

1. Jonathan Walters, "The Shrink-Proof Bureaucracy," *Governing* 5, no. 6 (March 1992): 36.

2. Jeffrey M. Berry, Kent E. Portney, and Ken Thomson, *The Rebirth of Urban Democracy* (Washington, DC: Brookings Institution, 1993): 113.

3. Robin Pan-Lener, "There's Room to Grow," *Government Communications* (publication of the National Association of Government Communicators), March 1992, p. 3.

4. "CBS Evening News," September 7, 1993, in a report by Erik Engberg in which he referred to the "Flack Attack" in the nation's capital.

5. Russell Forte, "More Communicators Get the Ax," *The Communicator* (October–November 1991): 3.

6. James L. Garnett, *Communicating for Results in Government* (San Francisco: Jossey-Bass, 1992): 14.

7. Clinton L. Doggett and Lois T. Doggett, *U.S. Information Agency* (New York: Chelsea House Publishers, 1989): 25.

8. Robin Grey, "Inside the Voice of America. Government Radio Has Gone to War—with the Soviets and with Itself," *Columbia Journalism Review* 21 (May/June 1982): 26.

9. Mary Grisez Kweit and Robert W. Kweit, "The Politics of Policy Analysis: The Role of Citizen Participation in Analytic Decision Making," *Policy Studies Review* 3, no. 2 (February 1984): 32.

10. Forrest M. Landon, "The Freedom of Information Act: Too Far—or Not Far Enough?" *University of Virginia Newsletter* 72, no. 5, (August 1996): 3.

11. Gregory Streib, "Dusting Off a Forgotten Management Tool: The Citizen Survey," *Public Management* 72, no. 7 (August 1990): 17.

12. Ibid., 18.

13. George Freeman, "Springfield's New Take on City Hall," *Public Management* 78, no. 6 (June 1996): 14.

14. Mark D. Uebling, "All-American Apathy," *American Demographics* 13, no. 11 (November 1991): 30.

15. Ruy A. Teixeira, "Turnout in the 1992 Election," *Brookings Review* 11, no. 2 (Spring 1993): 47.

16. Michael R. Kagay, "Public's Knowledge of Civics Rises Only a Bit," *New York Times*, May 28, 1989, p. 31.

17. Ibid.

18. Bernard Shaw, comments made during "The Press and Politics," Joan Shorenstein Barone Center, New York, July 12, 1992.

19. Lydia Bjornlund, "Citizen Education," *Management Information Service Report* 23, no. 6 (June 1991): 2.

20. Keith Elliot Greenberg, "A Taxing Challenge: The IRS Works to Improve Its Image," *Public Relations Tactics* 5, no. 2 (February 1998): 27.

21. William E. Sledzik, APR, "Killing Bambi: The deer population explosion challenges public officials and PR pros," *Public Relations Tactics* 5, no. 3 (March 1998): 13.

22. *Congressional Record*, 60th Congress, House Rules Committee, 1st sess., 1908, vol. 42, p. 4137. Historical data provided by Felice Michaels Levin.

23. U.S. Congress, House Rules Committee, *Hearing on H. Res 545 Department Press Agents*, 62nd Cong. 2d sess., 1912, pp. 3–4.

24. David H. Brown, "Government Public Affairs—Its Own Worst Enemy," *Public Relations Quarterly* 26 (Spring 1981): 4.

25. For debate on this measure, see *Congressional Record*, May 31, 1973, S10129–31.

26. Michael Schudson, "Watergate: A Study in Mythology," *Columbia Journalism Review* 31, no. 1 (May–June 1992): 32.

27. Christopher Lasch, "Journalism, Publicity, and the Lost Art of Argument," *Gannett Center Journal* 4, no. 2 (Spring 1990): 1–2.

28. Christopher Conte, "Angels in the Newsroom," *Governing* 9, no. 11, (August 1996): 20.

29. Ibid., 20.

30. Comments from workshop at PRSA 1991 national convention, "Handling Issues, Crises, and Emergencies in Local Government," quoted in "At City Hall, Every Day's a Crisis," *Public Relations Journal* 48, no. 2 (February 1992): 7.

31. Anne Groer, "Paper Madness in Washington," *Gannett Center Journal* 4, no. 2 (Spring 1990): 72.

32. Ibid., 80.

33. William Greider, *Who Will Tell the People: The Betrayal of American Democracy* (New York: Simon and Schuster, 1992): 299.

34. Ibid., 287.

35. Garnett, *Communicating for Results,* 17.

36. Michael Baruch Grossman and Martha Joynt Kumar, *Portraying the President* (Baltimore: Johns Hopkins University Press, 1981), p. 16. An insightful analysis of the relationship of political leadership and the power of the media.

37. David Brown, in a speech to American Business Communicators Association, San Diego, CA, December 30, 1976.

38. Stephen Hess, *The Washington Reporters* (Washington, DC: Brookings Institution, 1981), 133. Also see David Morgan, *The Capital Press Corps: Newsmen and the Governing of New York State* (Westport, CT: Greenwood Press, 1978).

39. Judy Leon, "The News Business: It's Not What It Used To Be and Neither Is Your Job," *Government Communications,* December 1991, p. 15.

40. Carole Gorney, APR, "The Clinton Crisis: Public Relations vs. Legal Advice," *Public Relations Strategist* 4, no. 1 (Spring 1998): 14–15.

41. John Elsasser, "Kellygate," *Public Relations Tactics* 4, no. 8 (August 1997): 26.

42. Edwin Emery, *The Press and Americans: An Interpretive History of the Mass Media* (Englewood Cliffs, NJ: Prentice-Hall, 1972): 239.

43. Everette E. Dennis, "The Media at War: The Press and the Persian Gulf Conflict," conference report edited by Craig LaMay, Martha FitzSimon, and Jeanne Sahadi, Gannett Foundation Media Center, New York City, June 1991, p. 1.

44. Adam Shell, ed., "Military PIOs Direct 'Theater' of War," *Public Relations Journal* 47, no. 3 (March 1991): 9.

45. "Wartime News Coverage Guidelines Are Okayed," *O'Dwyer's Washington Report* 2, no. 10 (June 8, 1992): 4.

46. David Osborne and Ted Gaebler, *Reinventing Government: How the Entrepreneurial Spirit Is Transforming the Public Sector* (Reading, MA: Addison-Wesley Publishing Company, 1992), 167.

47. Ibid., 166–67.

48. Mike Gleason, "The Business of Government: Serving the Customer," *Nation's Cities Weekly* 15, no. 10 (March 9, 1992): 3.

49. Mary L. Walsh, *Building Citizen Involvement: Strategies for Local Government* (Washington, DC: International City/County Management Association, 1997): 1.

50. Alex Marshall, "Big Spender: Pickett's Mailings Cost $205,000," *Virginian-Pilot,* April 1, 1992, p. D1.

51. Information supplied by the League of California Cities in March 1990 letter to California city managers. Also see California Government Code Sections 82041.5 and 89001.

52. Garnett, *Communicating for Results,* 16.

Books, John W., and Charles L. Prysby. *Political Behavior and the Local Context.* New York: Praeger, 1991. Scholarly review of research on politics, political information, and people in neighborhoods, counties, communities, and regions.

Brody, Richard A. *Assessing the President: The Media, Elite Opinion, and Public Support.* Stanford, CA: Stanford University Press, 1991. Correlates the results of public opinion polls on approval of the president with the cumulative effect of news coverage; the number of "good-results" stories versus the number of "bad-results" stories.

Kotler, Philip, Donald Haider, and Irving Rein. *Marketing Places: Building a Future for Cities, States, and Nations.* New York: Free Press/Macmillan, 1993. Suggests that there is hope for places in crisis through strategic marketing approaches to economic renewal.

Nelson, Dale W. *Who Speaks for the President? The White House Press Secretary from Cleveland to Clinton.* Syracuse, NY: Syracuse University Press, 1998. Former White House reporter traces the presidential press secretary's role from 1890 through the Clinton administration.

Pedersen, Wesley, ed. *Leveraging State Government Relations.* Washington, DC: Public Affairs Council, 1990. Fifth in a series of handbooks published by the Public Affairs Council, this edition outlines the history of the public relations function in state government, organization and management of the function, dealings with elected officials and lobbyists, and grassroots participation.

Pfau, Michael, and Henry C. Kenski. *Attack Politics: Strategy and Defense.* New York: Praeger, 1990. Details how attack ads were used in political campaigns in the 1980s, as well as the results of two studies testing "inoculation" strategy to counter advertising messages that emphasized candidates' weaknesses.

Yankelovich, Daniel. *Coming to Public Judgment: Making Democracy Work in a Complex World.* Syracuse, NY: Syracuse University Press, 1991. One of the leaders in public opinion polling discusses problems in how opinion polls are conducted and used, defines different levels of public opinion, and outlines steps for achieving resolution of issues in public debate.

NONPROFIT ORGANIZATIONS, HEALTH CARE, AND EDUCATION

In the United States, this sector accounts for over half of the hospital beds, half of the colleges and universities, most of the social services, and almost all of the cultural activity.[1]

—*Lester M. Salamon and Helmut K. Anheier*
in **Defining the Nonprofit Sector**

OBJECTIVES

After studying chapter 16, you should be able to

▼ Describe the role of public relations in the nonprofit sector.

▼ Outline some of the major changes affecting nonprofit organizations, health care, and education.

▼ List and briefly discuss major changes in recent public relations practice in nonprofit organizations.

▼ Discuss the changing role of public relations in health care organizations—especially hospitals.

▼ Identify intensified *competition* for donations and increasing demands for *accountability* as driving forces in many nonprofit organizations' public relations efforts.

This chapter was written in collaboration with Stephanie Casenza, APR, Communications Officer, Alliance Healthcare Foundation, San Diego, California. She was the manager of corporate public relations for a major, nonprofit health care organization that attempted a for-profit joint venture with an international for-profit corporation. She has held similar management positions with a regional blood bank and with public relations firms serving both corporate and nonprofit clients.

More so in the United States than in any other country, an array of voluntary nonprofit organizations provides many of the social, educational, cultural, and welfare services vital to society. In effect, the nonprofit sector fills the gaps in meeting the needs of society left unattended by the other two sectors—for-profit corporations and government agencies. Recognition of the role and importance of nonprofit organizations in society highlights the need for effective public relations in the "third sector."

THE THIRD SECTOR

Nonprofit organizations did not always play such a large and significant role in society. There were only 12,500 charitable tax-exempt organizations not affiliated with churches in 1940, and only 32,000 in 1950. In the United States, there are approximately 750,000 "public-serving" nonprofit organizations, with rapid expansion in the 1980s and 1990s. Add to that total almost 400,000 "member-serving" nonprofit organizations, such as business and professional associations and societies, social and fraternal organizations, and cooperatives. The nonprofit sector in the United States represents expenditures of more than $350 billion (6.3 percent of gross domestic product) and more than 7.1 million full-time equivalent employees (6.9 percent of total employment).[2]

Defining Nonprofit Organizations

Nonprofit organizations exist as a special category of organizations in the tax code in recognition that society is "delegating public tasks to private groups."[3] A definition of the nonprofit sector that can be applied in many countries includes five distinguishing features of such organizations:

1. *Organized.* In short, there is some institutionalized entity, meaning that the organization has a charter, regular meetings, officers, rules, or other indicators of relative permanence.
2. *Private.* Nonprofit organizations are institutionally separate from government, meaning that they are not agencies of or controlled by government, even if they receive government funding.
3. *Nonprofit distributing.* Unlike other organizations in the private sector, nonprofit organizations are not attempting to generate profits for the owners or directors, meaning that excess revenues must be spent to achieve the organization's mission. This does not mean that nonprofit organizations cannot make a profit. Rather, it means that distributing the profits to those who manage or direct the enterprise is prohibited, hence the term "not-for-profit."

4. *Self-governing.* Nonprofit organizations govern themselves and control their activities, meaning that they set their own procedures and are independent of external control. They have their own boards of directors and provide opportunities for citizen involvement without government control or direction. Because of this characteristic, some refer to nonprofit organizations as the "independent sector."

5. *Voluntary.* At a minimum, there must be some voluntary participation in either the management of the organization or in the conduct of its program, meaning that there is some aspect of charitable contribution involved. The terms "charitable organizations" and "voluntary organizations" derive from this characteristic of nonprofit organizations.[4]

And although debate continues over whether or not the wide variety of charitable tax-exempt organizations truly represents a category that can be meaningfully defined, there is little question about the interdependence of government and the nonprofit sector.

For example, then President George Bush asked Congress for $425 million to support his "Points of Light Initiative" to help fight drug abuse, illiteracy, homelessness, and other critical social problems. The program's objective was to recognize and promote volunteer public service as part of every individual, group, and organization's life and work. President Bush recognized that nonprofit organizations are essential to the quality of life and in some instances the very survival of many citizens. The Clinton administration has continued to emphasize the essential role of nonprofit organizations in "building a bridge to the twenty-first century." Indeed, volunteers and philanthropic donations are the only sources of support for many social, health, cultural, and arts programs.

Voluntarism and Philanthropy

In many nonprofit organizations, volunteers mean the difference between providing services and closing down the organization. Almost 40 million people volunteer (work without pay) each year. More than one million organizations in the United States are recognized by the Internal Revenue Service as tax-exempt or nonprofit organizations. This figure includes private foundations reporting annual revenues of $20 billion and a broad range of nonprofit organizations raising more than $300 billion annually. Despite these impressive numbers, however, the number of volunteers and donated dollars are seldom enough to meet the increased demand for nonprofit organizations' services. Public relations, therefore, has become more critical in the nonprofit sector as a turbulent economic, social, and political climate presents new challenges with each passing year.

Across the country, state and local governments have struggled for more than a decade with budget deficits as demand for services has outpaced revenues. Localities, both large and small, slashed budgets and increased taxes and user fees. Government cutbacks to deal with these deficits meant fewer staff and reduced resources for social services. At the same time, corporate philanthropic contributions remained about level, reflecting the economic uncertainties of the 1990s. Corporate donations actually declined, after adjusting for inflation. Individuals, on the other hand, increased their giving during the same period, possibly reflecting the bullish stock market of the mid- to late 1990s. Total charitable giving totaled almost $150 billion annually (see Figure 16.1 for how much each nonprofit segment received).[5]

Changing Climate

The nonprofit sector operates within a climate of change:

1. Shifting responsibility for public service and assistance from government programs to voluntary organizations
2. Increasing competition among charitable groups for financial, in-kind (goods and services), and volunteer support
3. Growing public concern about the credibility and accountability of tax-exempt organizations
4. Increasing cost and difficulty in raising funds
5. Lessening of community ties on the part of corporate leaders and professional staff, who tend to move frequently for career advancement
6. Growth of cause marketing in the corporate sector

Charitable agencies within the nonprofit sector are still reeling from exposés in the early 1990s of six-figure executive salaries and charges of financial mismanagement and lavish spending. Figure 16.2 illustrates one organization's rebuttal. Ethics and accountability dominate hallway discussions, staff meetings, and convention programs. Headlines about former United Way of America president William Aramony's $360,000 annual salary and lavish lifestyle and a spate of follow-up stories reporting that top executives in many nonprofit organizations make $100,000-plus salaries erode public trust of many

FIGURE 16.1   CHARITABLE GIFTS

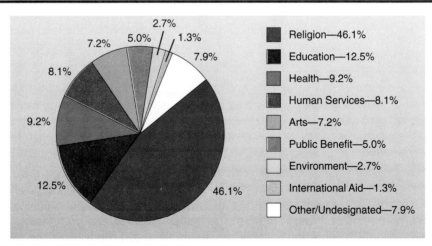

Source: *The Chronicle of Philanthropy,* June 12, 1998.

FIGURE 16.2   **AMERICAN HEART ASSOCIATION CONTRIBUTION
SOLICITATION INSERT**

76% of every dollar we spend goes
directly towards research, education and
community service programs.

American Heart Association
California Affili

To reduce administrative costs, all gifts are
processed at a central facility. Rest assured
your contribution supports research and
programs in your local area. For more
information, please call your local American
Heart Association. Thank you.

American Heart Association

Courtesy American Heart Association.

charities. Reform-minded critics call for more effective policing of charitable
fund-raising and fuller disclosure of how nonprofit organizations spend their
funds. Individual donors are better consumers and ask more questions about
how their philanthropic dollars will be utilized. Public relations is charged
with both helping rebuild credibility and maintaining or trying to restore public confidence in the many charitable agencies and voluntary groups that
serve the needs of so many.

When the Clinton administration put health care reform at the top of the list of national domestic policy issues in 1992, health care reform became the hottest topic of national debate. The attention resulted in increased scrutiny of health care costs and calls for increased accountability within the health care delivery system. Headlines and lead stories on the evening news kept health care at or near the top of the public agenda. Debates covered why health care costs so much; who will pay; who will be covered; what care will be available; and what the roles are of government, health insurance companies, health maintenance organizations (HMOs), private hospitals, doctors, nurses, psychologists, and other caregivers such as midwives and nurse practitioners. Talk shows featured politicians, executives of public health agencies, hospital administrators, doctors, insurance company executives, and representatives from a long list of special interest groups and associations. Public relations played a central role in shaping both the national agenda and health care reform.

Education reform closely follows health care reform on the public agenda, with questions about cost and quality also dominating public discussion and debate. Public concern and controversy almost caused a major change in California's educational system and public policy. For example, California voters defeated an education vouchers initiative that would have allowed parents to transfer tax dollars from public schools to qualifying private schools by using state-funded vouchers. Each child would qualify for a voucher, regardless of financial need. Parents would have the right to cash the vouchers at the school of their choice—public or private. Proponents said that ineffective, administratively bloated public schools would have to shape up in order to successfully compete for state funds in the new educational marketplace. Voucher critics said that the initiative would deplete an already financially strapped system and lead to state subsidies of segregated, elitist private schools. Even though the ballot initiative failed, it spurred a serious reassessment of the education system and served as a wake-up call for public schools across the country. Education administrators invited public relations specialists to join the management team and work more closely with the executive offices of school districts, colleges and universities, and educational associations. Educational reform was a real threat, or opportunity, depending upon the views of top administrators in school systems.

In short, following a historic pattern, public relations is often added, expanded, and elevated in stature when organizations are confronted by outside forces, threatened with funding cuts or outright elimination, or otherwise pressured to change or reform. The nonprofit sector faces all these crises in an environment of increasing competition for donations, diminishing government subsidies, and increasing demand for services.

As social and economic conditions require and the need for public support grows, public relations helps create the public policy environment, volunteer participation, and philanthropic support crucial to the survival of charitable organizations. (See Figure 16.3.) In other words, in the nonprofit sector public relations establishes and maintains the relationships necessary to secure the organizational autonomy and resources needed to achieve the organizations' humanitarian missions.

FIGURE 16.3   EXAMPLES OF SMALL COMMUNITY HOSPITAL
              PUBLIC RELATIONS

Courtesy Utlaut Health Services, Inc., Greenville, IL.

ROLE OF PUBLIC RELATIONS IN NONPROFIT ORGANIZATIONS

Nonprofit organizations in different fields approach public relations programming with diverse tactics, but promoting public service and building public trust are common to all. Health care agencies, social welfare organizations, churches, educational institutions, and fine and performing arts groups all depend upon public support (see Exhibit 16.1 for principles of fund raising). All are also caught in the conflicting crosscurrents of social, political, and economic trends that require increasingly sophisticated managerial and public relations efforts. In this era of intensive media scrutiny, there can be neither the intent nor the appearance of "putting something past the public" or "getting the public off our backs."

EXHIBIT 16.1

PRINCIPLES OF FUND RAISING

Preparation

1. The five essentials of a successful campaign are a strong case, effective leadership, conscientious workers, prospects willing and able to give, and sufficient funds to finance the campaign. These five essentials should be weighed with scrupulous care before outlining a strategic plan.
2. Committee work and publicity work should be mapped out in advance. The coordination of these two lines of activity, all designed toward bringing a trained and enthusiastic worker face to face with sympathetic and well-informed prospects, is fundamental to the success of any fund-raising effort.
3. The cost of a campaign, within reasonable limits, should be estimated in advance.
4. All campaign activities should be given a time limit. Deadlines provide the only insurance for proper coordination of committee work, publicity, and canvassing.

Committee Work

1. The originating group, whether a committee or a board of directors, should be a representative body.
2. The necessity for strong leadership is inversely proportional to the strength of the appeal.
3. The effectiveness of the group is conditioned by the degree to which individuals will accept responsibility.
4. The activity of the originating group determines the activity of all subordinate groups: The originating group is the inevitable yardstick, both for giving and for working.
5. Committees are better at critiquing than creating. Before asking any group for ideas on a plan of action or for suggestions on a list of prospects, give each member of the group a copy of the plan.

In fact, public relations in most nonprofit agencies aims to

1. Gain acceptance of an organization's mission
2. Develop channels of communication with those an organization serves
3. Create and maintain a favorable climate for fund raising
4. Support the development and maintenance of public policy that is favorable to an organization's mission
5. Inform and motivate key organizational constituents (such as employees, volunteers, and trustees) to dedicate themselves and work productively in support of an organization's mission, goals, and objectives

Even though these missions are common to most nonprofit organizations, the tactical approach and level of sophistication of public relations practice differ greatly. For example, compared with other nonprofit organizations, hospitals typically invest relatively more in public relations and associated programs such as marketing and development. In recent years, many nonprofit hospitals converted to for-profit corporations or sought affiliations with other

PRINCIPLES OF FUND RAISING

Publicity

1. The case must be bigger than the institution. The first objective of publicity is to sell the idea; the second objective is to sell the means of its accomplishment.
2. Publicity materials should appeal both to the emotions and to the intellect.
3. Publicity must have continuity, with all of the elements of a campaign tied together with a theme of common appeal.
4. Publicity should proceed from the general to the specific. Interest in an idea proceeds from an appeal of general application.
5. Cheap publicity is expensive. Quality in publicity efforts pays dividends.
6. Publicity should be positive and not negative. Effective publicity always plays up elements of strength.

Campaign Operation

1. A campaign should not only solve immediate financial needs but should lay a firm foundation for the future campaigns.
2. Solicitation should proceed in six steps: listing, rating, assignments, cultivation, canvassing, and follow-up.
3. Effective canvassing answers five questions: why, where, who, what, and how.
4. Campaigns should periodically reach a climax. The climax is essential in arousing and maintaining interest in the campaign.
5. All canvassing, even for special gifts, should be conducted in an atmosphere of universality. Prospects typically ask, "What are others doing?"
6. Campaigns should be conducted under a steady and constant pressure and sense of urgency.
7. The time spent on a campaign varies directly with the size of the goal and inversely with the popularity of the appeal.
8. The direct appeal for help should be made when the interest is at its peak.
9. Ask for ideas, not for money. The canvasser should first interest prospects in an idea.
10. There are four tests of the effectiveness of campaign operations: quality, quantity, cost, and time.
11. Campaign impact is judged by success or failure in achieving the campaign objectives and the overall goal.

hospitals or health care organizations. These new hospitals and organizations often take an integrated approach to public relations and marketing similar to and every bit as sophisticated as that found in other corporate settings, setting a standard that other hospitals are compelled to match in order to survive.

In contrast, many social welfare agencies have neither the financial resources nor the depth of expertise necessary to mount sophisticated public relations or marketing efforts. Some nonprofit organizations must rely on inexperienced practitioners or even nonprofessional volunteers to conduct their public relations programs.

Thus, public relations practice in nonprofit institutions encompasses a wide variety of approaches and services. At one extreme is a lone practitioner implementing a simple, unstructured publicity campaign. The other end of the spectrum is a large professional, management-level department following a research-based strategic plan with adequate funding and the support of outside consultants. The practice in nonprofit organizations continues to grow, reflecting growth in the charitable nonprofit sector as it seeks to reduce dependence upon government, which at all levels is seeking to reduce taxes, pay off public debt, and respond to new social needs.

The changed climate of the 1990s, however, led to profound changes in how public relations is practiced in nonprofit organizations:

1. Marketing concepts and management by objectives have emerged as important parts of communication strategy.
2. Technology has extended communications selectivity and reach, but in some instances, such as electronic ministries, has raised questions about ethics, privacy, and legitimacy.
3. Paid advertising has emerged as a major controlled communications tactic for nonprofit organizations, particularly for the health care industry.
4. Nonprofit sector leaders (boards of directors or trustees and program managers) have raised the standards and stepped up pressure to engage professional public relations assistance.
5. The need to build coalitions in communities and to empower those being served call for different skills from those learned in traditional public relations curricula.

These changes derive from the realities of financing the third sector. Nonprofit organizations generate revenue from three major sources: *Private charitable giving* (gifts from individuals, corporations, and foundations), *government support or payments* (grants and contracts or reimbursements for services), and *private fees and payments* (proceeds from the sale of services or products to the consumer). Unlike the widely held misconception that "charity" is the main source of revenue, nonprofit organizations in the United States generate 52 percent of their revenue from private fees and payment. In Japan, 60 percent of nonprofit organizations' revenues come from the sale of services and products in the form of fees and payments, 57 percent in Hungary, 53 percent in Italy, and 48 percent in Great Britain. Government sources account for only 30 percent of nonprofit revenues in the United States, but 68 percent in Germany, 60 percent in France, 43 percent in Italy, and 40 percent in Great Britain. Private charitable giving contributes only 19 percent of all nonprofit revenues in the United States, 20 percent in Hungary, 12 percent in Great Britain, 7 percent in France, 4 percent in Germany, and only 1 percent in Japan.[6]

These data help explain the nature of fund-raising approaches used by nonprofit organizations. The most obvious conclusion is that fees and payments from those served are the major source of nonprofit funds in the seven countries listed above, representing 47 percent of total revenue. Not surprisingly, public relations and marketing play major roles in the life of nonprofit organizations, just as they do in the for-profit sector. Government funds are the second major source of revenue across nonprofit organizations in the seven countries, totaling 43 percent. That leaves only 10 percent of total revenue for nonprofit organizations being raised through private charitable giving, meaning that the third sector represents an independent mechanism through which charity, fees and payments by users, and government funds are merged to meet the social, cultural, educational, and health care needs of society.

FOUNDATIONS

Private and community grant-making foundations are part of the growing nonprofit sector. Foundations are often the mechanism for linking single sources of funds to other nonprofit organizations seeking funding. *Company-sponsored* foundations either have an endowment established by a for-profit corporation or receive annual contributions from that corporation or both. *Independent* foundations are those established when an individual, family, or group contributes a significant sum to achieve a goal. *Community* foundations receive gifts from many different donors who are interested in funding programs in their own community.

The Foundation Directory defines a foundation as

> A nongovernmental, nonprofit organization with its own funds (usually from a single source, either an individual, family, or corporation) and program managed by its own trustees and directors that was established to maintain or aid educational, social, charitable, religious, or other activities serving the common welfare, primarily by making grants to other nonprofit organizations.[7]

The directory lists the 7,960 foundations that either have at least $2 million in assets or award at least $200,000 in grants annually, but this total represents fewer than one-fifth of all grant-making foundations in the United States. The larger foundations, however, held 87 percent of the $207 billion in total foundation assets and awarded $11 billion in grants, or about 90 percent of all foundation giving.[8] The Lily Endowment in Indianapolis became the largest U.S. foundation in 1996, with total assets of almost $13 billion, following the rise in the value of its endowment of stock in pharmaceutical giant Eli Lilly and Company. The Ford Foundation, which had been the largest foundation for more than 30 years, now ranks second, with almost $10 billion, with the David and Lucile Packard Foundation third, with approximately $9 billion in assets. To comply with federal law, foundations must distribute at least 5 percent of their investment assets annually, making foundations one of the major sources of grants to other nonprofit organizations.[9]

HEALTH CARE

Almost a decade ago, Pennsylvania college professor and Democratic state official Harris Wolford scored a stunning U.S. Senate victory over his White House–endorsed opponent by making health care reform the centerpiece of his campaign. The election demonstrated how hospitals and health care agencies, nonprofit and for-profit alike, are caught in the vise of rising public expectations and demands on one side and with escalating costs, limited access, and stiff competition on the other. In addition to concerns about quality and cost of health care, some are beginning to raise questions about the nonprofit status of some hospitals: "The ultimate question is should these institutions [nonprofit hospitals] continue as tax-exempt entities. And it's being raised more than ever before."[10]

Health care became *the issue* of the 1990s when President Clinton appointed First Lady Hillary Rodham Clinton to head his administration's effort to reform national health care policy and delivery systems. After several earlier efforts to put health care reform on the public agenda, the public opinion climate now agreed with what labor, business leaders, academicians, and others had long been diagnosing—health care was in a "code blue" (emergency or crisis) situation.

Health Care in Crisis

Driving this ascendancy to public attention were two increasingly critical problems: cost and access. The cost of health care has grown ever more burdensome. In the early 1960s, the United States spent no more than 5 percent of its economic resources on health care. By the early 1990s, health care costs almost tripled as a percentage of the nation's total spending. Health care costs almost twice as much in the United States as in Germany and Japan, with an average of $1,200 of the cost of an American-made car traced to health insurance premiums to cover workers and pensioners. Some economists have predicted that the percentage of national spending on health care could reach 20 percent without major reform. In the meantime, approximately 37 million U.S. citizens, including almost 10 million children (one in seven), are not covered by health insurance of any kind.[11] Individual insurance premiums costing at least $5,000 per year put coverage out of reach for most not covered at work. Layoffs and shifts to part-time, per diem, and temporary employment arrangements also have increased the number of uninsured. These disenfranchised Americans are joining business and labor leaders (who represent the mechanism that funds those who are insured) in demanding that hospitals, physicians, and other health care providers explain why the system is not serving so many people. The Secretary of the U.S. Department of Health and Human Services Donna E. Shalala says the crisis represents a "crossroads in the history of our health-care system":

> It is a modern-day tragedy that in the next two years *one of four* Americans will lose the health insurance that he or she has today. It is an American tragedy that *85 percent* of the uninsured come from working families. It is an American tragedy that one-year-old children are less likely to have two shots of polio vaccine than children of the same age in *eighty-eight* other countries. It is an American tragedy that our senior citizens should now face the terrible choice of whether to purchase prescription drugs or food.[12]

Public Relations as Marketing

The hospital industry is increasingly embroiled in public policy debates and aggressively pursuing patients. Decreasing reimbursement from third-party payers (insurance, health maintenance organizations, and the government) and the advent of managed care drastically impact both the way hospitals deliver care and their finances. Metropolitan areas, especially those in which managed care is prevalent, often have too many hospitals and beds, too many physician specialists, and duplication of services and programs. Although these factors have led to mergers, acquisitions, and affiliations among hospitals and health care organizations, they also have fueled aggressive public relations and marketing campaigns that have attracted new business—and criticism. Some longtime health care professionals believe the increased emphasis on marketing and public relations has driven up administrative costs, thus driving up the cost of health care to consumers.

Competition for consumers' favor creates another challenge, in that some consumers feel they must choose a *hospital or health care organization* rather than the *physician* they want for their care. Still, the majority of people still choose their health care provider (hospital, health care organization) on the basis of their physician of choice. However, if their physicians are affiliated with several hospitals, then individuals make the choice on the basis of their perceptions of the quality of medical and staff care and the hospital's reputation, along with location.[13] Competition has intensified as health care must find ways to reduce costs, maintain or increase the quality of care, and also maintain or increase market share. As traditional nonprofit community-based hospitals are absorbed by or affiliate with corporate hospital chains, operated to return a profit to investors or bondholders, these issues further intensify.

Harvard Medical School professor and former editor of the *New England Journal of Medicine* Arnold S. Relman, M.D., refers to the commercialized system of health care as the "medical-industrial complex."[14] Dr. Relman estimates that at least one-third of all nonpublic health care facilities are investor-owned businesses. These include nursing homes, psychiatric hospitals, and clinics. Two of three HMOs operate as investor-owned health care businesses. These commercial enterprises compete with traditional acute-care general hospitals that "originally were philanthropic social institutions with the primary mission of serving the health-care needs of their communities."[15] Now, as a "matter of survival," even a community hospital with more than 100 years of history must "position itself in a very competitive health care market" to assure "making a fair return" on services by addressing "prospective customers."[16] Public relations in many hospital settings has assumed a marketing or "integrated marketing communication" orientation similar to that in business and industry.

An excess of hospital beds in most large cities forces hospitals to compete to keep beds occupied, or as one practitioner put it, albeit crudely, "To put butts in beds." Some hospitals have moved to "delicense," or close beds, as fewer beds are needed and patients' length of stay decreases. This has occurred in part because of improved medical practices and technology, but also because of the policies of managed care organizations, such as HMOs.

Many for-profit hospital chains as well as nonprofit hospital groups have formed multihospital systems. These new chains and merged systems are organized to combine management know-how and financial strength. As hospitals become more competitive and businesslike, however, much of the old goodwill from the time they were viewed as a paternalistic cottage industry has waned. Under the new customer-centered or patient-focused approach to patient care, hospitals are now expected to be more responsive to their market wants and needs. The emphasis on marketing in health care is pervasive:

1. Marketing is defined as identifying the wants and needs of a hospital's constituents and guiding the organization toward effectively satisfying those wants and needs. It includes a diagnosis of the environment using tools and techniques founded in behavioral and social science research.
2. Hospital marketing differs from marketing in most other business and industry for three reasons: (1) generally the payer for health services—an insurance company—has limited control over the purchase or cost of service (in some situations they can limit the amount of reimbursement for a service or they can deny or limit access to a service); (2) selection of the hospital and the decision to order services generally are not made by the consumer but rather by a supplier, usually a physician; and (3) the services rendered can be painful and unpleasant, clearly making a distinction between wants and needs.
3. Health care professions and the insurance industry play important roles as intermediaries in dealing with the consumers of health care. Consequently, a growing number of public relations practitioners work for the American Medical Association, the American Nursing Association, Blue Cross, Health Maintenance Organizations (HMOs), Preferred Provider Organizations (PPOs), and similar groups at the national, state, and local levels.
4. Prospective customers do not have to be sold on their need for hospitals, doctors, and nurses. They want assurance of ready access to them when they need them. They worry most about financing their health care needs. Unless the financial concern is addressed, other issues matter little.

In the final analysis, however, hospitals need both marketing and public relations, because the two seek to achieve different essential outcomes:

> The careful analysis and planning, demand forecasting, feasibility analysis, and input given to pricing, access, channeling (distribution), and product design, which marketing provides, are essential in this era when the financial risks are great and the competition is intense. And . . . hospitals, which are considered community resources regardless of their ownership and are held very accountable to the public for their decisions, increasingly must balance price and quality, sound communication and issues management are needed.[17]

Role of the News Media

Media coverage of health care increased sharply after the 1992 presidential election. One study found an increase in the number of published stories of more than 46 percent in the first quarter of 1993, with the tone of coverage having shifted from positive to slightly negative.[18] With increased media scrutiny and a more critical treatment of health care issues, practitioners in health care face unprecedented challenges, according to Bruce Vladeck, president of the United Hospital Fund: "Of all the tasks of leadership in healthcare organizations, maintaining communications between the organization and its communities is perhaps the most important."[19]

Even though personal contact and publications distributed to patients and others who have contact with the hospital are the most effective methods for reaching community publics, the mass media play an important role in setting the health care agenda and in conveying messages about individual hospitals and health care issues. Just as in other settings, honesty, access, and responsiveness are the keys to good media relations in a hospital or health care setting. Most hospitals have an authorized spokesperson on call 24 hours a day to answer inquiries from the media. Hospital administrators who maintain cooperative relationships with the press typically have greater community access through media.

The public relations officer also must prepare medical personnel for press interviews and provide adequate background information to reporters. Health care is a complicated technical beat that often needs a human interest angle to make it compelling to the media and the public. Time spent orienting and educating reporters, as well as providing them with physicians and patients to interview, is a good investment. A well-informed reporter increases the likelihood of accurate, complete, and fair media coverage of complex health care issues increasingly in public debate.

Another area of news media interest—patient information—requires special attention. Simply put, there is often a gap between what health care professionals can reveal about patients and what the press wants for publication about personal injuries and illnesses, especially when the patients are minors, celebrities, or otherwise in the news. Press demands for news and "the public's right to know" collide with laws protecting an individual's privacy, the medical profession's code of ethics, and the confidential relationship between doctor and patient. In part to respond to this conflict, medical societies and hospitals have devised Confidentiality of Medical Information codes outlining the principles guiding both the press and hospital staff when dealing with news about patients:

1. To safeguard the private rights of the individual, so that no hospital patient will be caused unnecessary embarrassment or discomfort, or be made the object of scorn or ridicule
2. To report the news accurately, authoritatively, and promptly
3. To cooperate sincerely, in all relationships

Unless there is a written request by the patient to the contrary, the guidelines typically allow hospitals to release name, age, sex, general description of treatment, reason for treatment, and general condition of the patient. Medical information protected by the confidentiality guidelines includes the patient's medical history, mental or physical condition, and details of treatment. The guidelines also recommend that every hospital should have a designated person or staff available to the media on a 24-hour basis.

But care must be taken even when following the guidelines. In the era of tabloid journalism and increased litigation, hospitals and other health care organizations find themselves the target of patient charges. The legal and ethical considerations limit how health care organizations can respond in the media. Again, however, any response must take into account the press's obligation to report medical news adequately and accurately and health care organizations' obligation to serve as a cooperative news source while protecting the right to privacy and professional reputations of those both inside and outside the organization. Exhibit 16.2 outlines one public relations practitioner's advice for when patients take complaints to the media.

No longer a low-profile, low-status function, public relations in health care has moved into the management function. In the debate over health care reform, Steven V. Seekins, a vice president of the American Medical Association and an accredited member of PRSA, identifies an increasingly important role for practitioners in health care settings: "To make public relations indispensable to senior management, practitioners must stake out issues management as an area of expertise."[20] No doubt the complex and hotly contested public debate on how to make quality health care both affordable and available to all those in need will continue for years. All parties in the debate will call on public relations practitioners to help set the agenda and to contribute constructively to shaping public policy in health care.

SOCIAL WELFARE

The work of social welfare agencies is society's response to the consequences of its social disorganization. These agencies are an outgrowth of the conflicts and maladjustment produced by America's high-speed, urbanized living and of the recognition that not everybody has equal access to or the resources to acquire services. In order to gain support for their programs, such agencies must convince their many constituencies collectively and individually that the agencies are "doing for others what I would like to do if I could."[21]

Federal and state government spending on social welfare programs totals more than $800 billion annually. In many communities, government spending on social welfare programs is being cut in response to budget deficits, shifting the burden to community nonprofit agencies. Apart from Medicaid, where spending keeps rising, poor people are especially vulnerable. Governors are using the current fiscal crisis to work their versions of welfare reform. For example, when Ohio faced a $1.5 billion revenue shortfall, Governor George Voinovich suggested turning over welfare support for able-bodied adults to local governments and cutting the program by $50 million. Michigan's Governor John Engler wanted to cut benefits to families whose children drop out of school. He also ended general assistance to some 100,000 people who he said were able to go out and find work.

Charitable contributions to the "human services, public, and society benefit" categories of nonprofit groups and causes totaled $17 billion in 1992.[22] Although individual philanthropic giving continues to increase slightly each year, funding for social service agencies has not kept pace with community needs. "In addition, current frictions between publics splintering along demographic and ethnic lines tend to adversely affect agencies which depend on gifts and volunteers."[23]

Social agencies are hard hit during economic recessions. Yet the demand for their services multiplies in hard times even as sources of funds shrink.

EXHIBIT 16.2

WHEN PATIENTS TAKE COMPLAINTS TO THE MEDIA

Vicki Hoffman Beck
Health Communication Specialist
Office of Communication, Office
  of the Director
Center for Disease Control and Prevention
Atlanta, GA

Confidentiality of a patient's medical record is a right that is guaranteed by law. As public relations practitioners who work in health care and research settings know, it is our responsibility to guard this right and to use appropriate guidelines and consents when we release condition reports on accident victims, or when we pitch patient stories to illustrate the excellent care our organizations provide.

But there are also instances when patient confidentiality can be a sticky issue. This can occur when a patient or volunteer for medical research alleges ill treatment and takes the story to the media. If the story is compelling and the reporter or producer pursues it, what can the institution say in its defense? If the patient has filed or threatened a law suit, should you avoid talking to the media altogether?

Media response is complicated because confidentiality laws prohibit the health care organization from talking about a case even when the patient talks about the case in the media and charges malpractice, wrongdoing, or misconduct. Unless the patient is willing to sign a release, the public relations practitioner may not reveal any details about the case.

The situation poses an interesting public relations challenge. Although specific information which would undoubtedly help to explain the situation cannot be divulged, we can still reinforce openness and concern by providing more general information and effective spokespersons in a timely and responsive manner.

Initial communications can diminish the impact of negative allegations when a high-level spokesperson comes forward to reassure the public that the organization cares about the well-being of all patients and that they are looking into the charges.

Also, since general information about medical treatment and programs can be easily distorted and confused, it is critical to provide accurate information to reporters, in the form of fact sheets and backgrounders. To keep the rumor mill at a minimum, similar materials may be distributed to patients, staff, and outside audiences who may be affected by the adverse publicity.

When the charges have little or no merit, and media interest remains intense, the public relations practitioner may need to recommend additional strategies. For example, an internal- or external-conducted investigation could help to demonstrate due concern and ultimately alleviate the appearance of guilt. Meeting with key leadership in health care advocacy, research, and government could also broaden support and media focus.

During the critical period of media scrutiny, when there is great temptation to pull back and bury our heads, we must always remember our obligation to represent the public's concerns among administrative, legal, clinical, and research leadership in our organization. If media response is based on litigious or other administrative concerns, without due concern for public trust, the ultimate loss of public faith in the organization could be far greater than any courtroom defeat.

(Written when Beck was Assistant Director of Communication, UCLA Center for Health Sciences.)

Public and private agencies represent a less-than-adequate response to social welfare needs and pose public relations problems of awesome complexity. At the very times of greatest need, citizens are hounded by demands for funds from a seemingly multiplying number of causes and agencies. At the same time, citizens see their tax bills increase to pay for some of the same services through government agencies. More effective two-way communication with all constituencies will be required in order to build and maintain the relationships needed to achieve public-interest goals through nonprofit social service agencies. Figure 16.4 shows the "United Way Wheel," graphically illustrating the components of United Way of America's public relations effort.

It is from the upper- and middle-income groups that donor-supported agencies must get the bulk of their budgets. It is in the middle-income group that a strong sense of responsibility must be built. The alternative is to transfer the burden to government; then all will pay, through compulsory contributions in the form of taxes. The donor-supported, volunteer-dependent agency, however, has an important innovative function that must be maintained. Leaders of these agencies must strive even harder to muster public support through public relations, support that will endure in good times or bad.

FIGURE 16.4   UNITED WAY WHEEL

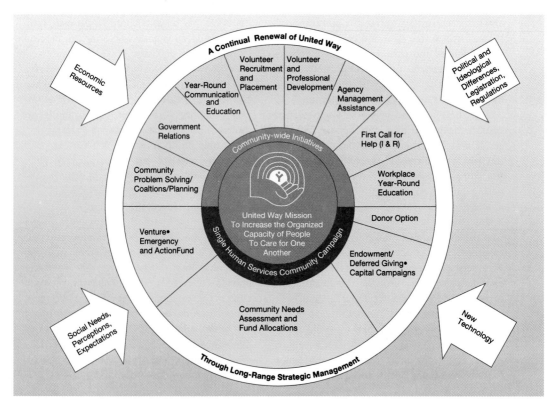

Courtesy United Way of America.

A welfare agency starts out in an enviable position. Its sole reason for existence is to help people. Yet the public is ambivalent in its attitude toward welfare. The term "welfare" has come to have a pejorative ring. Poll after poll shows public opinion deeply antagonistic to the concept of public welfare but strongly supportive of what welfare programs do.

Part of the difficulty results because social agencies often deal with intangibles. The United Way has widely proclaimed, "Thanks to you, it works for all of us," but still many people regard these agencies as existing for the "other fellow." Some in need shun the services provided by social agencies because "it's charity." Many who could use these services simply do not know of their availability. Potential supporters often will not find concrete illustrations of tangible benefits to individual citizens in agency publications and presentations because of the confidential relationship that must exist between agency and client.

Welfare agencies must link their programs tightly to educating the public to accept enlightened social concepts in fields such as poverty, mental health, crime and correction, child welfare, problems of aging, and drug addiction. Planned, consistent programs are required to break the barriers of public apathy, superstition, and the deadweight of indifference on these fronts.

Among the difficult problems facing health and welfare agencies is that of building a communication bridge among ethnic communities and between the inner city and the outer city. Traditional "come-and-get-it" services and communication messages fail to reach many in need because of cultural and language differences, limited access to information, and low levels of education. The public relations challenges are to make communication and programs more effective through greater empowerment and involvement of inner-city residents in the affairs of social agencies.

EDUCATION

Education touches the lives of virtually every citizen. It employs 3.1 million teachers and administrators. Federal, state, and local government spend almost $300 billion dollars a year for elementary and high school education and higher education. According to the U.S. Census Bureau, state governments pay the greatest share, about 55 percent.

Surveys repeatedly show that education ranks among the most valued symbols in American life. In fact, many Americans expect too much from education, presuming it to be the panacea for all the ills that beset the nation. Yet with all these high expectations, Americans remain ambivalent toward education.

Accountability

Growing public dissatisfaction with the performance and cost of schools has led to widespread demands for more accountability. Demands for accountability have moved far beyond student achievement scores to include calls for teacher competency tests and the institution of merit-based incentive pay.

Tenure is under siege at every level of education. And both taxpayers and legislators reject the notion that schools and universities will improve if given more funds. Educators' and their institutions' responses to these new and stricter demands for accountability will require greater attention and more adequate information programs for most school systems.

Accountability requires keeping good records and making actions public. An "accountable school" is one that (1) discloses its activities, (2) makes good on its promises, (3) assigns staff responsibility for each area of public concern, and (4) monitors its teaching and learning.[24] Accountability also includes gathering evidence to document progress on meeting public expectations and using research to explain both strengths and weaknesses. The demand for accountability in education is a relatively recent development:

> Whereas business for years has been the bad guy in terms of the public's acceptance of the credibility of its actions, education and the nonprofit organizations have been ranked with apple pie and motherhood. That's no longer true. We, too, are now expected to be efficient, productive, purposeful and accountable in our work.[25]

Basic to effective public relations in any setting is performance that the public deems satisfactory. Central to the difficult task facing public education officials is widespread concern that the money American taxpayers have spent on their schools and universities has not been effectively used. The progress of any educational system depends, in the final analysis, on public support.

Public Relations for Public Schools

The major general objectives of public relations for public schools include the following:

1. Increasing awareness of education and heading off misinformation and rumor
2. Building the public support necessary to obtain adequate funds
3. Gaining public acceptance and cooperation in making educational changes
4. Building amicable working relationships with news executives and reporters

Public relations for education is expanding in scope, concept, and utilization. It has taken on increased importance as officials try to persuade taxpayers to raise school levies to cope with inflation, or to pass bond issues for new buildings because of shifting enrollment patterns. In fact, most school public relations practitioners regard the financing of public education as the issue that will present the greatest communications problem during the next several years.

For example, when the Dayton, Ohio, Board of Education voted to put a tax levy on the ballot, it took an all-out campaign focused on positives to win voter support. Based on research findings showing that voters were reluctant to vote for higher taxes but were concerned about economic issues, the strategy focused on the positive outcomes of the proposed education tax: (1) how schools attract jobs and provide qualified workers, (2) the link between good schools and stable property values, (3) the contribution schools make to order and discipline, and (4) how good Dayton schools are and their prospects for getting better. The systems public information officer, Jill Moberley, said,

> Key to success was that we did our research and targeted our messages. Also our superintendent was up front, available to answer voters' questions, doing door-to-door literature drops and talking one-on-one with people in neighborhoods. We made it personal. And we're continuing to tell our story, after the campaign. It's important to apprise people of how dollars are being spent, what changes are occurring and how schools are benefiting the community.[26]

Other major issues include a return to the "basics," discipline, religion and the theory of creation, violence and weapons, substance abuse, sex education, pupil achievement, parental concern and participation, teacher competence and performance, negotiations with teachers' unions, and students' right of free expression.

Essential aspects of a school–community relations program designed to anticipate, avoid, and respond to these problems include the following:

1. Commitment to public partnership on the part of school boards, administrators, and teachers
2. Competence in the school–community relations staff
3. Centralization of community relations policy making
4. Free-flowing communication from and to publics—up, down, and across
5. Coordination of all efforts to ensure accomplishment of predetermined goals

The relationships between educational institutions and the people are many, diverse, and complex. Key internal and external publics for public school public relations include the following:

1. **Parents play a key role in the educational process and in building support for adequate budgets.** A strong parent association also serves as a buffer against extremist groups. Good relationships with parents start with frequent, frank communication between teachers and parents. Communication means conferences, encouragement of parents' observation of normal classroom situations, special programs for parents, and home visits by the teachers to help resolve students' problems.
2. **School staff, from principal and teacher to bus driver, custodian, and school nurse, must be brought into a public relations program.** Teachers in their day-to-day activities are in a position to relate effectively to students, parents, and others. As a result, they are able to provide valuable feedback to administrators and those responsible for the curriculum and other programs. Many superintendents have found it desirable to organize advisory

FIGURE 16.5   SCHOOL PUBLIC INFORMATION LITERATURE

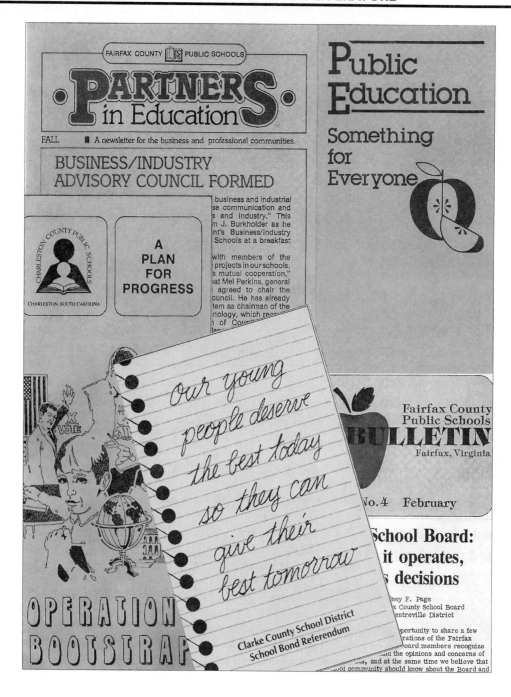

councils that include representatives from all categories of employees (teacher advisory council, food-service advisory council, and so on). Increasingly superintendents are also using employee newsletters for keeping staff informed about the school system.

3. **Students represent what may be the school system's most important public.** Public relations truly starts in the classroom. In public-opinion surveys, parents say they rely most on their children for information about the schools. School executives should determine students' views of their school experiences, see that pupils are well informed about policies, make sure that courses satisfy their needs and challenge their abilities, arrange that individual attention is provided for those who need it, and create an overall atmosphere that engenders pupil and parent pride in the school.

4. **Business community–school partnerships take many forms.** These include adopt-a-school programs, resource sharing for professional training of staffs, consultation in management and technology to improve school system effectiveness and to promote innovation, and advocacy with state and local governments to increase support of public schools. School systems recognize the necessity for assistance and support from business and industry. Likewise, business–industry communities recognize that they have a high stake in the public schools.

5. **Community groups include many groups: parents, taxpayers, and other citizens concerned about "what our schools ought to be teaching."** These groups can be reached through Parent–Teacher Associations, press, service clubs, church groups, and in countless other ways. Periodic surveys of parents and community groups provide benchmarks for evaluation of the system's public standing but also, and more important, provide feedback that improves education.

6. **Local news media are key to informing the public of what schools are doing and with what they contend in doing it.** This requires continuous reporting, so schools must take the initiative with a planned information program directed by a trained practitioner. Most local news media have neither the staff resources nor the expertise to adequately cover public education. The press typically covers administrative changes, school conflicts, and school sports but will not assign reporters to the more time-consuming assignments to cover topics such as curriculum changes and educational policies. Thus, school systems must, in their own self-interest, provide broad, constructive coverage of education at the local level.

   Cable television can provide almost unlimited opportunity for communicating with the community publics: school–community bulletin boards, board meetings and public hearings, student and school system news programs, fine arts and other cultural events, athletic contests, school closing and crisis announcements, and school leader interviews and panel programs.

7. **Board of education members act as intermediaries between school publics and the professional administrators.** It is essential that board members agree on an adequate statement of public relations policy. The board must

serve its function of interpreting the community to the school staff and, in turn, interpreting staff ideas and policies to the community.

Nationally, advances are being spearheaded by the National School Public Relations Association, whose membership includes most school practitioners, as well as many school administrators. Other national educational organizations include the National School Boards Association, the American Association of School Administrators, the National Association of Elementary School Principals, the National Association of Secondary School Principals, and two major teachers' unions—the National Education Association and the American Federation of Teachers.

Higher Education

Each year American society invests about $160 billion in higher education, with almost half coming from federal, state, and local governments. An analysis of the return on Massachusetts taxpayers' investments in higher education at the University of Massachusetts at Boston conservatively concluded that "for every $1 the state spends on the university, it will receive $1.57 in return."[27] The total state subsidy for a student's four-year program was estimated to be $13,253 for the 1991 entering class. The average expected return in income and sales-tax revenues above the average of what high school graduates contribute, after excluding the 11 percent of undergraduates and 18 percent of graduate students who leave the state after graduation, will total $20,832.[28]

Sectors of society with greater political clout and more sophisticated lobbying techniques than those possessed by higher education compete for funding from state governments. As a result, in recent years many states have not increased higher education budgets in proportion to increased costs and increased demands for classes, research, and off-campus services. In too many states, an increasing share of the cost is being covered by increases in student tuition and fees, raising concerns about access and equal opportunity in tough economic times. Surely many qualified young people are excluded from the benefits of higher education because of the escalating cost of college.

Higher education faces four continuing problems:

1. Financial support is insufficient and precarious as other public institutions' roles in society are expanded.
2. Competition for qualified students is spirited and costly.
3. Constraints and regulations that make university administration difficult and costly are imposed by agencies of the federal government.
4. Academic freedom and tenure are challenged by both internal and external stakeholders.

Additionally, just as in other organizations, taxpayers are demanding more accountability by state colleges and universities for how tax dollars are spent. According to Roger Williams, assistant vice president and executive director of university relations, Pennsylvania State University, University Park,

We had a nice, protected status until the late 1980s, when a series of unrelated incidents from misreporting the use of government funds to scientific fraud, animal welfare, and so-called tuition price-fixing began to undermine public confidence in higher education. Now we have to begin work on the long road back toward (regaining) public trust.[29]

This demand for accountability underscores the need to provide feedback from students, faculty, townspeople, taxpayers, and other constituent–claimant publics. Stakeholders want to know what higher education institutions are doing to keep costs under control and to eliminate wasteful programs. At the same time, taxpayers also demand that colleges and universities maintain quality and remain accessible to an increasingly diverse population. Higher education must "meet these issues head on," according to Gail Raiman, vice president for public affairs, National Association of Independent Colleges and Universities:

Just as the media are being more aggressive in covering education, we must be more aggressive in educating the public and opinion leaders. We need to use clear language, not academic jargon. We have to go to these opinion leaders instead of waiting for them to come to us.[30]

The ingredients of a system of accountability include the following:

1. A clear mission statement, including goals and an ordering of priorities
2. Allocation of resources toward maximum return in relation to goals
3. Cost and benefit analysis, including allocation of costs and benefits to each institution and to programs within institutions
4. Evaluation of actual results
5. Reporting on the evaluation to governing boards, to sources of financial support—including constituents throughout the region served—and to the faculty and administrative staff

Responding to demands for accountability has a long history of public relations in higher education. Institutions of higher learning were among the first to seek public favor on a systematic basis. The University of Michigan led the way when it established a publicity office in 1897. Increased competition for funds and students forced private institutions to counter with similar programs. As classical education gave way to curricula responsive to the needs of the 20th century, as the demand for extension and research grew, and as the need for money increased sharply, college administrators turned to the use of publicity and ultimately to public relations.

The 1974 merger of two associations, the American College Public Relations Association and the American Alumni Council, brought together public relations practitioners working in alumni relations, fund-raising, government relations, publications and periodicals, and student recruitment, as well as administrators. The merger formed the Washington, DC–based Council for Advancement and Support of Education (CASE). The goals of the organization are to build public understanding of higher education, step up the level of alumni involvement and support, improve educational government relations, strengthen communication with campus internal and external audiences, and increase private financial support for education. Membership includes approximately 14,000 individuals representing 3,200 colleges, universities, independent elementary and secondary schools, and other educational organizations such as museums and teaching hospitals.

To maintain quality and access in the face of declining state support, public institutions of higher education must look to private sources for an increasing portion of their financial support. Florida, like many states, relies on nonstate sources to fund higher education. According to the top budget and finance officer of the State University System of Florida, "The only way our universities could become outstanding institutions was to rely on external support."[31] Adapting a practice used by many private nonprofit organizations, some states have passed laws promising public funds to match some private donations to public universities and colleges.

State universities and colleges must actively compete with private universities and colleges for donor dollars. For example, the University of Michigan recently completed a $1 billion capital campaign, including more than $800 million in gifts and pledges and more than $200 million in bequests, more than a year ahead of the target date. The total is the most ever raised by a public university in a fund-raising drive. Overlapping by several years with the Michigan campaign, Harvard University's seven-year campaign raised almost double the Michigan total. These high-profile fund-raising campaigns also can complicate smaller institutions' attempts to attract donors. That happened in Michigan when some donors told Kalamazoo College they could not contribute because they had made commitments to the University of Michigan.[32]

Caught in the vise of rising costs and rising public demands on one side and declining government support and increased competition for private donations on the other, colleges face public relations tasks unparalleled in the history of higher education. Therefore one of the primary goals of public relations in higher education is improving the climate for fund-raising.

To achieve public relations goals in higher education, programs typically target the following key publics:

1. **Students.** Students are both a university's most important public and its most important public relations representatives—first as students and later as alumni. Student opinion and conduct are powerful factors in determining public perceptions of higher education. A university must develop enthusiastic, responsible students to act as goodwill ambassadors.

   Fundamental to effective student relationships is maintaining—regardless of the institution's size—free-flowing communication between administrators and students. Likewise, students who have good teachers, who are given wise counsel, and who receive helpful individual attention generally become loyal alumni.

To bring quality and diversity to their student bodies, most colleges and universities now have special recruitment programs for National Merit Scholars, National Achievement Scholars, and minority students. These programs, usually directed by full-time staff in admissions, require strong public relations backup to achieve quality and diversity goals.

2. **Faculty and staff.** Faculty and staff are important internal publics because of their critical roles in education and governance, and their role as representatives of the university to external constituencies. Yet some faculty members remain aloof, many merely indifferent, and a few plainly hostile to assuming any role or responsibility in effectively representing the university to external groups and the media. Internally, faculty and staff insist on having a voice in policy making. If their participation is to be informed and meaningful, they must be kept informed by the administration and empowered to participate in determining the mission, values, and governance of the university.

Unions and collective bargaining have changed the nature of faculty–administration and staff–administration relationships on many campuses. As a result, some campus public relations offices also must deal with the press during labor negotiations, following the same legal guidelines outlined in chapter 6.

3. **Alumni.** Alumni contributions are the single most important source of voluntary support in higher education. It is no surprise, then, that colleges and universities strive to gain loyalty, interest, and counsel from their alumni. Win those, and the dollars will follow. The director of alumni relations makes sure that alumni are appreciated rather than exploited, cultivated rather than coerced, fully informed rather than fed a party line, and above all interested in and organized for more than money making (see job description in Figure 16.6). The alumni association must be kept harnessed to its basic objective—supporting the alma mater through organized effort.

Liberal arts colleges receive more than 10 percent of their total annual revenues from alumni giving, whereas for all colleges and universities the average is almost 6 percent. Larger institutions get more total dollars from alumni, but smaller institutions average about 25 percent more per alumnus. The inverse relationship between the size of the university and the average amount contributed by each alumnus suggests that large colleges and universities must take steps to establish a strong feeling of affinity between students and the institution. Private institutions do not receive more from their alumni than do public institutions of comparable size, scope, and perceived quality.

Just as in other settings, relationships begin to be formed at the time of first contact. "Given the importance of graduates' pride in their alma maters, a fund-raising strategy should begin at the time students are enrolled."[33] Too many institutions wait until graduation to begin building good alumni relations.

4. **Community groups and business leaders.** The "town-gown" relationship has always been a set of complex and symbiotic relationships. Colleges and universities lag behind industry in recognizing the importance of good

FIGURE 16.6   ALUMNI RELATIONS JOB DESCRIPTION

THE STATE UNIVERSITY OF NEW JERSEY

RUTGERS

ASSISTANT VICE PRESIDENT
OF ALUMNI RELATIONS

Rutgers, The State University of New Jersey, invites applications and nominations for the position of University Assistant Vice President of Alumni Relations with responsibilities for planning, directing, and coordinating a comprehensive program of activities and communications designed to inform and engage alumni worldwide on behalf of the University. In this capacity, the Assistant Vice President serves as the principal liaison between the alumni, faculty, administration, students, and the Rutgers University Foundation. The Assistant Vice President will also work with the leadership of the Alumni Federation, as well as a growing number of school-based alumni associations and regional alumni clubs to develop programs and services that will both advance the University's goals and objectives and encourage alumni support. The Assistant Vice President shall also have editorial responsibility for the 24-page alumni supplement in RUTGERS MAGAZINE, the University's quartely magazine for alumni and friends.

Founded in 1766, Rutgers today has campuses in New Brunswick, Camden and Newark and has an enrollment of 49,000 students in 26 degree-granting units. The University has an alumni population of 225,000 graduates and graduates 10,000 students each year. Rutgers is a member institution of the Association of American Universities and is linked through athletics to the Big East and Atlantic 10 Conferences.

The Assistant Vice President reports to the President of the Rutgers University Foundation, the University's chief development and alumni relations officer. Candidates for the position must have senior-level management experience in alumni relations or some other advancement area. The position requires strong organizational and interpersonal skills and an ability to write and speak effectively on behalf of the University. Knowledge of computer records systems and standard management and accounting practices is desirable.

Rutgers, The State University of New Jersey, is an Equal Opportunity, Affirmative Action Employer.

Interested candidates are invited to contact Bruce D. Newman, President, Rutgers University Foundation, Winants Hall, 7 College Avenue, New Brunswick, New Jersey 08901-1261.

Courtesy Rutgers University.

community relations. Because state funding does not keep pace with increased costs on campuses, however, many colleges and universities are turning to the business sector to build new, mutually beneficial relationships. Support can be won by giving citizens a voice and a sympathetic hearing through consultation on campus matters directly affecting the community, such as campus expansion and building projects that have direct impact on traffic, property values, and ambiance in nearby neighborhoods.

The tax-exempt status of educational institutions may appear as a sign of partiality or bias in favor of the campus. Municipalities, however, are increasingly hard-pressed to find adequate revenues to pay for expanding demand for services from all parts of the community, including the campus. When metropolitan campuses must expand in already built-up areas, the growth ultimately greatly benefits the community. In the short term, however, campus expansion means removal of property from the tax rolls and, hence, reduced revenues to the campus host community. A public relations task is to remind townspeople and business leaders that the campus has a major economic impact in addition to the obvious cultural, intellectual, and sports contributions to community life.

5. **Government.** Building understanding and support in federal and state executive branches and agencies—mainly in departments of education and legislative bodies—as well as in the voter public are major public relations assignments in higher education. Many universities and state systems now retain full-time or part-time public relations officers in Washington and in their respective state capitals. These representatives work as lobbyists for higher education and their universities—primarily monitoring and reporting government actions related to education and providing governmental officials information to help build their case for higher education. Their concerns include funding for higher education, legislative and executive interference and regulation, and other public policy that affects higher education stakeholders.

7. **Media.** Building good media relations is an investment that pays off over the long term but can be destroyed in an instant, as pointed out in chapter 9. Centralizing and coordinating the news flow from the campus is an almost impossible task. A college or university speaks with many voices—the public information office, the student newspaper and radio station, publicity-seeking professors, and campus sources with whom reporters have developed special relationships. The most frequent sources of news are college presidents, other administrators, athletic directors and coaches, and professors.

   Colleges also are the center of youthful and vocal discontent; sometimes focused on legitimate complaints about the deficiencies of the institution and at other times used as a convenient tactic for assault upon the general society. Student grievances and campus protests attract news coverage, often offering enticing video for the evening news. Public opinion is influenced by the news media spotlighting protests but neglecting quiet academic achievement. The job of public relations is to help balance media coverage by giving reporters examples of achievements and contributions to the community.

8. **Parents and others.** Parents represent a ready-made nucleus of support. They have a vital stake in the institution and thus can be welded into an effective group of allies. Other publics include prospective students, parents of prospective students, present and prospective major donors, opinion leaders, philanthropic foundations, sister educational institutions, the armed forces, and various agencies of the federal government—particularly those with research programs. The public relations challenge is to build and maintain mutually beneficial relationships with each of the higher education stakeholder groups.

College Presidents' Public Relations Role

College and university presidents must lead—not direct—faculties, staff, students, and governing boards. Leaders in higher education are caught in the crunch of conflicting values and demands from stakeholder–constituent publics. To thread their way through these conflicts, presidents must be effective communicators and mediators. In fact, they spend as much time practicing public relations as they do on the other aspects of administering their institutions:

> Thirty-nine percent of the presidents said they spent between 21 percent and 40 percent of their time over the past year on public relations. Twenty-seven percent said they devoted 41 percent to 60 percent of their time to public relations. Only 10 percent said they spent more than 60 percent of their time on public relations activities.[34]

Almost a third of the presidents said they met more frequently with their public relations officers than with any other member of the management team.[35]

The president gives the university a face, a personality, a presence in the larger community. A strong president brings prestige, stature, and public confidence. Given the many demands made on institutions of higher learning—to do more and better with less public funds—the president's role in public relations is more important than ever before. The president is the key to establishing the relationships and public support needed to fulfill higher education's mission in the new global society. As one former president said, "The president is the one best able to sell the entire institution."[36] Of course the president works closely with the university's top public relations officer, sometimes referred to as the "development officer" or "advancement officer." Development officers also typically place the major responsibility on the president, as "both the principal author of the vision and, as the university's chief advocate, the ultimate asker for big money."[37] But as fund-raising has increased in importance on campuses, development officers have gained staff and resources, as well as position and stature in management: "Today the chief development officer often helps articulate the institution's purposes and creates a strategic plan to achieve those ends."[38]

CHURCHES AND OTHER NONPROFIT ORGANIZATIONS

Space does not allow detailed analysis of all nonprofit settings. Brief descriptions of some of the issues and pressures on churches, libraries, museums, and arts groups will illustrate how the practice of public relations is both as complex and as essential in these settings as in other nonprofit settings. Finding support for nonprofit organizations, see Figure 16.7, is one aspect in which public relations plays a large role.

Religion and spirituality appear to be enjoying a revival in America. Findings from a Pew Research Center poll indicate that 71 percent of Ameri-

Meet J. Robert Anderson, philanthropist.

He's not a millionaire. In fact, he's not even rich. But he gives.

Most of the giving in this country doesn't come from the wealthy. Almost half of it comes from people who earn less than $20,000 a year. Everyday, ordinary people. Like the guy down the street. Or your next-door neighbor. Or 100 million others who, every year, give unselfishly just to help people.

And while those who give may sometimes go unnoticed, their contributions don't. Because in this country, when a lot of people give, it adds up to a lot.

It helps fund important research. It helps run community church programs. It helps support local charities.

It helps people out.

There are so many things in this country that could use your hand. Your time, your tal-

ents, your money. What you give isn't so important. That you do give is. Because you don't have to

be rich to be a philanthropist. You just have to care.

A Public Service of This Publication & The Advertising Council

From the Advertising Council.

cans believe in God and that 53 percent think prayer is important in their daily life. Both figures represent increases of more than 10 percent during the past decade. Additionally, *Touched by an Angel* enjoyed a long run as one of television's top-rated shows, and bookstores sold millions of books on angels, miracles, and spirituality.[39]

Even in good times, however, the church is not immune to public relations crises. Few Seventh-day Adventists church members among the seven million worldwide had ever heard of cult leader David Koresh and the group in Waco, Texas, that called themselves "Branch Davidian Seventh-day Adventists" until that fateful day, February 28, 1993. Suddenly television satellites around the globe carried the horrifying pictures of a botched U.S. Treasury Department Bureau of Tobacco and Firearms raid and the subsequent fire that killed men, women, and children. It was the beginning of a crisis for Seventh-day Adventist public relations departments across the nation.[40]

Episcopalians see the New Age movement as a threat to religion, Catholic priests are charged with sexual misconduct, and some television evangelists and faith healers are exposed as lavish spenders and frauds. Polls conducted by the Gallup Organization for the National Catholic Evangelization Association show that the percentage of Americans who identify themselves as members of a church or synagogue is the lowest—65 percent—since Gallup Poll began tracking membership in 1937. The National Conference of Catholic Bishops broke tradition in 1990 and retained Hill & Knowlton, then the nation's biggest public relations firm, and former President Ronald Reagan's pollster, The Wirthlin Group, to help design a counterattack against growing public support for abortion.

On top of such crises and activism, churches face increased competition for volunteer commitment and dollars. Slightly less than half the nation's population are regular churchgoers. Declining participation and the financial squeeze have underlined the importance of public relations to many church leaders, but churches face some unique obstacles:

1. The intangible nature of many religious activities
2. The sacred nature of many activities, which demands a dignified approach
3. The problem of showing the practical worth of religious values
4. The difficulty of finding which level to project ideas on so they will appeal to many

Organized religion has not escaped the vortex of change, crisis, and confrontation, so it has become top news. Whereas the church has long been comfortable using the media in the cause of religion, it is not experienced or comfortable in the spotlight of the evening news and tabloid exposés. As a major force in society and social change, however, the church cannot avoid the spotlight. Increased media attention and a whole range of other relationship problems suggest an important and growing role for public relations in the church and synagogue.

Although apparently much less controversial by their very nature and missions, libraries, museums, and arts groups compete for public support in the form of volunteers, donations, and public funding. Many of these important institutions, which contribute so much to the quality of American life, live in a financial straitjacket that does not permit adequate funding for either their programs or professional public relations assistance.

Most public libraries in major cities have public relations departments, usually called public information departments. But in smaller cities and suburbs, the public libraries may have very small staffs that do not include public relations expertise. At best, these libraries may take advantage of volunteer support and special events like National Library Week to achieve limited public relations objectives. To provide effective public relations support to its many small libraries, Wisconsin established the Coordinated Library Information Program, which provides the counsel of a public relations specialist to libraries in that state.

Like libraries, arts groups in this nation are faced with a constant battle to keep the financial wolf from the door. In recent years both foundations and the government have cut support of cultural institutions and museums. The early 1990s recession made many question the relevance of arts and cultural organizations: "When families begin to choose tangibles over intangibles in their budgets, relevance becomes increasingly important when planning activities, fund raising and launching drives for new members."[41]

Always confronted with the challenges of attracting individual volunteers and donations, and funding from other public and private sources, nonprofit organizations rely more on good public relations than any other sector in society. The recession has only made this sector more vulnerable, because the base of support has diminished while the need has expanded. Without effective public relations, many of these organizations will not survive the recession and what many see as a permanently downsized economy. Without these organizations, many needs not now addressed by either business and industry or government will go unmet. At stake are the very existence of some nonprofit organizations and the continuing vitality of the "third sector."

NOTES

1. Lester M. Salamon and Helmet K. Anheier, "Toward a Common Definition," in *Defining the Nonprofit Sector: A Cross-National Analysis,* ed. Lester M. Salamon and Helmet K. Anheier (Manchester, UK: Manchester University Press, 1997), p. 3.
2. Lester M. Salamon and Helmet K. Anheier, *The Emerging Nonprofit Sector: An Overview* (Manchester, UK: Manchester University Press, 1996), pp. 33–42.
3. Peter Dobkin Hall, *Inventing the Nonprofit Sector and Other Essays on Philanthropy, Voluntarism, and Nonprofit Organizations* (Baltimore, MD: Johns Hopkins University Press, 1992), pp. 13, 14, and 82.
4. Adopted from Salamon and Anheier, "Toward a Common Definition," pp. 33–34, 291–92.
5. Susan Gray, "Charitable Giving Rose 7.3% in 1996; Health and Arts Groups Were Biggest Winners," *The Chronicle of Philanthropy,* (June 12, 1998), on-line version.
6. Salamon and Anheier, *The Emerging Nonprofit Sector,* p. 66
7. Michael N. Tuller and Gina Marie Cantarella, eds., *The Foundation Directory— 1997 Edition* (New York: The Foundation Center, 1997), p. vii.
8. Ibid.
9. Marina Dundjerski and Holly Hall, "Lilly Now No. 1 Among Foundations," *The Chronicle of Philanthropy,* January 29, 1998. From *Chronicle* web site: **www.philanthropy.com/update.dir/givingusa.htm** (9 March 1998).
10. Internal Revenue Service official Marcus Owens, as quoted by Monica Langley, "Really Operating: Nonprofit Hospitals Sometimes Are That in Little but Name," *The Wall Street Journal,* July 14, 1997, p. A1.
11. Marilyn M. Friedman, *Family Nursing: Research, Theory and Practice,* 4th ed.

(Stamford, CT: Appleton & Lange, 1998), p. 410, and *The State of America's Children: Yearbook 1997* (Washington, DC: Children's Defense Fund, 1997), p. 21.

12. Donna E. Shalala, "The Future of Health-Care Reform in America," *National Forum* 53, no. 3 (Summer 1993): 10.

13. "How is a Hospital Selected?" *pr reporter* 36, no. 24 (June 24, 1993): 2.

14. Arnold S. Relman, "What Market Values Are Doing to Medicine," *National Forum* 53, no. 3 (Summer 1993): 18.

15. Ibid., p. 19.

16. Susan L. Fry, "Century-Old Hospital Complex Repositioned as Medical Center," *Public Relations Journal* 47, no. 8 (August 1991): 13.

17. Rebecca H. Christian, "A Personal Look at the Marketing/PR Evolution," *Hospital Marketing and Public Relations* 15, no. 4 (July–August 1989): 6.

18. "Media Coverage of Health Care Rebounds," *Issue Scan* 3, no. 1 (First Quarter 1993): 1. *Issue Scan* is a quarterly media report on health care issues and trends published by S.D. Searle & Co., a pharmaceuticals manufacturer.

19. Quoted by David Kirk in "Briefings: Hospital Research Targets 'Key Leaders,' " *Public Relations Journal* 49, no. 3 (March 1993): 12.

20. Steven V. Seekins, "Forecast 1993: System Reform Looms," *Public Relations Journal* 49, no. 1 (January 1993): 21.

21. Richard T. McCartney, "Forecast 1992: Gain Community Support," *Public Relations Journal* 48, no. 1 (January 1992): 24.

22. Julie L. Nicklin, "Charitable Giving Rises 6.4%; Education Gets $14-Billion," *The Chronicle of Higher Education* 39, no. 38 (May 26, 1993): A25 and A27. See *Giving USA,* published annually by the American Association of Fund-Raising Counsel Trust for Philanthropy (New York) for detailed description of philanthropic giving each year.

23. McCartney, "Gain Community Support," p. 24.

24. Robert E. Stake, "School Accountability Laws," *Journal of Education Evaluation* 4 (February 1973).

25. Karen L. Cedzo, "Forecast 1993: Increased Scrutiny of Nonprofits Ups Stakes," *Public Relations Journal* 49, no. 1 (January 1993): 18.

26. "School Case Shows How Tough Selling Tax Hikes Is Today," *pr reporter* 36, no. 29 (July 26, 1993): 1, 2.

27. Barry Bluestone, "States May Be Making a Healthy Profit on Their Public Colleges and Universities," *The Chronicle of Higher Education* 40, no. 7 (October 6, 1993): A52.

28. Ibid.

29. Judith R. Phair, "1992 Education Report Card," *Public Relations Journal* 48, no. 2 (February 1992): 22.

30. Ibid., p. 23.

31. Peter Schmidt, "More States Use Matching Grants to Encourage Giving to Public Colleges," *The Chronicle of Higher Education* (December 5, 1997): A44.

32. Mary Geraghty, "A Year Ahead of Schedule, Michigan Raises $1-Billion, a Record for a Public University," *The Chronicle of Higher Education* (May 31, 1996): A26.

33. Robert A. Baade and Jeffrey O. Sundberg, "Identifying the Factors That Stimulate Alumni Giving," *The Chronicle of Higher Education* 40, no. 6 (September 29, 1993): B1, B2.

34. "Briefings: Campus CEOs Say Public Relations' Role Will Increase," *Public Relations Journal* 47, no. 8 (August 1991): 12.

35. " 'In' Box," *The Chronicle of Higher Education* 37, no. 47 (August 7, 1991): A9. For the complete report, see Commission on Institutional Relations, *Survey of*

College and University Presidents' Perceptions of the Public Relations Function (Washington, DC: Council for Advancement and Support of Education, 1991).

36. Michael J. Worth and James W. Asp II, *The Development Officer in Higher Education: Toward an Understanding of the Role.* ASHE-ERIC Higher Education Report No. 4. (Washington, DC: George Washington University, Graduate School of Education and Human Development, 1994), p. 54.

37. Ibid.

38. Worth and Asp, "Salesperson, Catalyst, Manager, Leader," *Currents,* February 1996, p. 26.

39. Associated Press, "Americans' Belief in God Grows," *San Diego Union-Tribune,* 22 December 1997, p. A–8.

40. Marilyn Thomsen, "Briefings: Church Distances Its Name from Waco Cult," *Public Relations Journal* 49, no. 8 (August 1993): 10, 12.

41. Robert H. Woodroof, "Forecast 1992: Find a Niche That's Relevant," *Public Relations Journal* 48, no. 1 (January 1992): 20.

ADDITIONAL SOURCES

Cutlip, Scott M. *Fundraising in the United States.* New Brunswick, NJ: Transaction Publishers, 1990. Reprint of 1965 classic history of how fund-raising evolved to become big business, its early pioneers, and campaigns that had a major impact on society.

Kelly, Kathleen S. *Effective Fund-Raising Management.* Mahwah, NJ: Lawrence Erlbaum Associates, 1997. First textbook to cover history, principles, theory, and process of contemporary fund-raising as a specialized public relations practice.

Kelly, Kathleen S. *Fund Raising and Public Relations: A Critical Analysis.* Hillsdale, NJ: Lawrence Erlbaum Associates, 1991. Argues that fund-raising should be a part of the larger public relations function in charitable, educational, and other nonprofit organizations, with the main purpose being to give these organizations the autonomy they need to achieve goals.

Kotler, Philip, and Alan R. Andreasen. *Strategic Marketing for Nonprofit Organizations,* 5th ed. Englewood Cliffs, NJ: Prentice-Hall, 1996. Outlines application of marketing principles and practices to building interest in programs offered by churches, government agencies, schools, health care organizations, and fine and performing arts groups.

Maibach, Edward, and Roxanne Louiselle Parrott, eds. *Designing Health Messages: Approaches from Communication Theory and Public Health Practice.* Thousand Oaks, CA: Sage Publications, 1995. Contributing authors synthesize communication and health behavior change theory and research findings from AIDS, cancer, and other health promotion campaigns.

TRADE ASSOCIATIONS, PROFESSIONAL SOCIETIES, AND LABOR UNIONS

The concept of a business or professional association is a highly civilized one. It calls for what people do least well, subordinating their self interest to the betterment of all. And when members of the group are competitors, it seems an unnatural alliance that won't work. Yet it does, as the proliferation of associations has demonstrated.

—*Howard Penn Hudson*

OBJECTIVES

After studying chapter 17, you should be able to

▼ Outline the three major purposes of associations, professional societies, and labor unions.

▼ List the major public relations activities of associations and professional societies.

▼ Describe the major purposes of public relations in the labor movement.

Trade associations, professional societies, and labor unions exist to advance the interests of their members. They do so in three ways: They provide information and services to members, they promote high standards of self-discipline, and they present the members' case to important publics and to government bodies at various levels. "Driven by the knowledge that they can achieve more through group efforts than they can individually, Americans have made associations one of the most powerful forces in the United States today."[1]

TYPES OF ASSOCIATIONS

Professional associations and *professional societies* typically represent individuals engaged in similar work based on common educational preparation or specialized knowledge. Examples include the American Nurses' Association, the American Bar Association, and the Public Relations Society of America. There are an estimated 2,500 such professional associations and learned societies.[2] *Cause groups* and *special-interest groups* function as associations of individuals with a common interest or goal. Examples include the National Audubon Society and the American Automobile Association, the nation's largest association, with more than 34 million members.[3]

Membership in the more than 3,500 *trade associations* includes companies, firms, or other organizations engaged in similar activities. Business competitors associate in order to organize and implement mutual-assistance efforts and to expand or protect their industry. Examples include the American Automobile Manufacturers Association, with only three members, and the National Automobile Dealers Association, with approximately 19,000 members.

Producer associations and *commodity boards,* such as the National Dairy Promotion and Research Board, the National Livestock and Meat Board, and the Illinois Pork Producers Association, represent the interests of their members and promote consumption of their commodities.

Members of *federations*—also referred to as councils or institutes—typically include other associations. Examples are the Federation of National Associations, the National Cotton Council of America, and the Transportation Institute.

Organized labor has a similar structure in that approximately 165 national *labor unions* represent individual workers. Examples include the television and movie stars in the Screen Actors Guild and the Communication Workers of America. *Federations* of labor unions, such as the Teamsters and the American Federation of Labor and Congress of Industrial Organizations (AFL-CIO), represent many different occupational, trade, and craft unions. AFL-CIO, for example, includes 78 different unions with more than 13 million members. It was formed in 1955, when two labor federations—the Congress of Industrial Organizations and the American Federation of Labor—merged under the leadership of the late George Meany.

ASSOCIATIONS AND SOCIETIES

Associations and societies have proliferated. Gale Research's *Encyclopedia of Associations,* CD-ROMs, and on-line services indexes more than 144,000 national, international, regional, state, and local associations.[4] The American

Society of Association Executives (ASAE) estimates that there are approximately 2,500 business and professional associates headquartered in the Washington, DC, area alone, making associations the third-largest industry in the nation's capital, after government and tourism. Almost 1,800 associations are based in the New York City area and 1,550 in the Chicago area. Associations nationwide employ more than 500,000 people—almost 27,000 work for the YMCA and 18,000 for the United Services Automobile Association. Seventy percent employ at least one lobbyist, 32 percent have political action committees (PACs), 91 percent hold annual conventions, and 83 percent conduct educational seminars apart from national conventions.

According to 1998 ASAE member records, approximately 80 percent of its member associations have staffs of 20 or fewer.[5] In contrast, the American Medical Association has a staff of approximately 1,000 in its Chicago headquarters, 35 in the Washington, DC, office, and 12 in a New York office. There are 33 on the public relations staff in Chicago and two each in the Washington and New York offices.[6] The 296,000-member American Institute of Certified Public Accountants has a staff of 700 in its New Jersey headquarters and 75 in Washington, DC. The vice president of communications supervises a staff of 10 professionals with a budget of more than $5 million.[7] Association chief executive officers earn average annual salaries of almost $117,000, and public relations officers average more than $63,000.[8]

The number of members is not the only basis for influence and power. Some associations have small but mighty memberships. The Aluminum Association, for example, has only 84 members, but each is a corporation. The same applies to the American Tobacco Institute, which represents a relatively small number of corporations but is one of the most powerful associations in the United States. The powerful American Medical Association represents almost 300,000 dues-paying physician members. And what some call the most powerful association in the United States, the American Association of Retired Persons (AARP), represents more than 32 million members aged 50 and older and 4,000 local chapters. AARP's membership and influence no doubt will continue to grow because it represents the interests of the fastest-growing segment of U.S. society.

At the state level, the California Milk Advisory Board promotes consumption of dairy products. Another statewide dairy association, the Dairy Council of California (DCC), conducts nutrition education programs financed by more than 2,000 California producers and more than 100 handlers of milk and milk products. In 1992, DCC had a budget of more than $4 million, five offices, 30 professionals working in nutrition education, and the services of the San Diego public relations firm of Nuffer, Smith, Tucker, Inc. Their educational programs are presented in secondary school classrooms and directed to the medical and nutrition communities.

The resources dairy associations are able to direct to such activities illustrates the power of producer groups: Congress mandated that dairy farmers nationally contribute a 15-cent checkoff on every 100 pounds of milk produced to promote dairy products. Five cents of the checkoff goes to the National Dairy Promotion and Research Board, 5 cents goes to state or regional promotion organizations, and the remaining 5 cents (sometimes referred to as the middle nickel) can go to either the national or state organization, depending on which one individual diary farmers designate. When 93 percent of the Wisconsin dairy farmers casting ballots in a referendum voted in favor of directing the discretionary 5 cents to the Wisconsin Milk Marketing Board (WMMB), $10 million was added to the WMWB budget for promoting dairy products, consumer and trade relations, and nutrition education programs in Wisconsin.[9]

The Problem of Serving Many Masters

In contrast to corporations and many other organizations with relatively monolithic interests and hierarchical structures, associations typically serve a variety of membership interests. Association staffs must attempt to meet membership demands and serve their interests externally but often must do so with little centralized power and authority to act. Difficulties that corporations have in marshaling employees or gaining public support pale by comparison with the task of associations seeking to satisfy a diversity of members and sometimes competing factions. Differences within an association's membership can result from regional influences; narrow concerns particular to specialties within the broad membership; and varying political, ethnic, or proprietary interests. The challenge for public relations is to find the common ground and unifying positions that best represent member interests.

A corporation's management can decide with comparative ease whether—and the degree to which—corporate interests are affected by high or low tariffs, a change in public policy, a new regulation, a strike in the coal industry, or a change of administration in Washington. But such decisions are much more complex for an association's executives and elected officials. The views of all members, and perhaps an evaluation of which ones count most, must somehow be synthesized, represented, and weighed in decisions. This can be a lengthy process. This problem is reflected in a statement of policy of the National Council of Farmer Cooperatives:

> We recognize the wide divergence of political opinion among our employees, member cooperative personnel, and farmer-owners. It would be inappropriate for us to express a partisan viewpoint. Therefore, we will support nonpartisan programs, as far as is practicable, and will encourage employee participation in partisan programs of their choosing.

Thus, associations are by nature limited to areas of action in which there is an obvious, predetermined unanimity of opinion or a substantial majority in support of any initiatives taken on behalf of membership.

Many times this characteristic of associations does not present a problem, particularly when the greater public interest is involved. For example, when cyanide-laced Tylenol capsules caused seven deaths in Chicago, an association that represents many competing manufacturers—the Nonprescription Drug Manufacturers (NDM)—took the lead for the industry as a whole. NDM representatives met with Food and Drug Administration staff to investigate ways to improve packaging and to develop federal legislation to require safer packaging. The association also launched an education campaign to teach consumers how to protect themselves from product tampering.

The Electronics Industries Association project to develop common standards for equipping television sets with captioning devices for the hearing impaired is another example of competitors cooperating and collaborating through an association. A group of engineers who worked for competing television manufacturers worked together to respond to the requirements of the Americans with Disabilities Act. As a result, every television set sold is equipped with a captioning device.

Era of Change and Gain

Providing noncontroversial services to members continues as the primary mission of associations, but the element of public advocacy is growing. The need first became evident in the 1960s with the passage of many regulatory laws. Legislators began to respond to growing public concerns about civil rights, workplace and public safety, the environment, and social responsibility. The wave of government regulations and consumer activism spurred even more rapid change during the 1970s. A climate of growth, competition, and deregulation encouraged even bolder advocacy in the 1980s. The 1990s brought technological advances, workplace diversity, economic restructuring, and globalization of markets and competition.

Members demand that their associations more aggressively counter government intervention in the natural forces of commerce and competition and more persuasively advocate their positions to other publics. Regulatory agency officials might counter by saying that there has been too little self-discipline and social responsibility within the trades and professions. Some stakeholders see too little responsiveness by association members to public interest and call for increased government regulation. Others assert that self-policing and member education reduce the need for government oversight.

Whatever the rationale, the crunch of controversy seems to have left little choice for associations preparing for the 21st century. The mounting tide of social and environmental concerns, protests, boycotts, and litigation simply cannot be treated as routine business, exceptions, or nuisances. Response will not wait for an association consensus to develop. Nor would adversaries accept silence. Making matters worse, some situations are unexpected. Some involve only a few members. Some have implications far beyond the scope of the association's franchise. Many associations learned from bitter experience that an aggressive public relations program is a better investment than waiting until the situation calls for a "legislative fire-fighting operation."[10]

Another lesson from experience is that the reputation and effectiveness of an association or society often depend on the public actions of individual members. Individual members taking a posture that is purely defensive, defiant, or protective serves neither the public interest nor the ultimate collective goals of association members. As a result, associations and professional societies have been increasingly willing to serve as advocates and media contacts rather than leaving such actions and responses to individual members.

Not all associations and societies have had to assume an aggressive stance, however. The degree of advocacy and public response to criticism or protest usually reflects the example set by those members who dominate a given association. As a generalization, however, more and more industrial and professional leaders are speaking up in efforts to shape public opinion when their interests are at issue. Public relations staffers in associations and societies have been following suit. Additionally, the increasing number of PACs and political education campaigns make these organizations important power groups in the political process.

Growing Importance of Public Relations

With such heavy stakes riding on effective communications and strategy in a climate of public skepticism and opposing advocacies, public relations counsel and skill assume major importance. Association public relations practitioners design and implement programs to serve the following needs:

1. To provide members with helpful information (see Figure 17.1 for examples of association publications)
2. To expand the association itself by recruiting new members
3. To harmonize member viewpoints by promoting positive positions
4. To promote the industry or profession
5. To influence government legislation and regulation
6. To improve products and services collectively
7. To gain popular support and combat adverse publicity
8. To train recruits and provide programs of continuing education for all members
9. To contribute to social progress by sponsoring public service programs
10. To promote acceptable public behavior among members in order to gain public credit and stave off government regulation

To achieve these purposes, public relations practitioners in associations are playing increasingly important roles in dealing with issues in the news that affect their members. For example, when health care reform dominated public debate, the American Medical Association public information staff responded to more than 1,100 calls a month, with about 75 percent of the calls from reporters:

> Associations have an advantage when it comes to dealing with the news media and other audiences. To the media and other publics, associations often have more credibility than individual companies or public relations firms because, correctly or not, they are perceived as less self-serving.[11]

Former ASAE president R. William Taylor, CAE, explained the importance of public relations in associations when government, media, and citizens view with skepticism what they perceive to be "special interests":

> Each of us has some interest that is special to us, whether it be a farmer con-

FIGURE 17.1   EXAMPLES OF ASSOCIATION PUBLICATIONS

Courtesy American Society of Association Executives.

cerned about his business, a manufacturer interested in marketing his product, or a teacher worried about salary and benefits. Each of these people can work through their association to make sure his or her interests are protected. Effective public relations combined with government relations will ensure that the correct message is expressed and the members' needs have been addressed. This is where good public relations can combat the image that "special interest" is bad.[12]

Ironically, ASAE did not have a public relations department until 1982. It was formed after Hill & Knowlton, its public relations firm, conducted an audit, and an ASAE Foundation study of association members found that public relations was one of the lowest rated among a list of functions performed by their respective associations.

Association public relations plays major roles because both internal service programs for members and external advocacy functions call for communication support and sound public relations counsel. In fact, the major goals of associations parallel those of public relations: to establish and maintain mutually beneficial relationships among internal publics and between the membership collectively and their many external publics. (Exhibit 17.1, pg. 562, provides some examples.)

EXHIBIT 17.1

ASSOCIATION PUBLIC SERVICE PROGRAMS

The following examples were selected from "Summit Award" winners of the 1996 and 1997 "Associations Advance America" Awards Program, American Society of Association Executives, Washington, DC.

The *Atlanta (Georgia) Chamber of Commerce* teamed with former President Jimmy Carter's Atlanta Project and six major financial institutions to launch the "Entrepreneurial Development Loan Fund." The fund has loaned more than $4 million to 65 minority businesses in Atlanta's most economically depressed neighborhoods, creating more than 550 jobs.

The *Oklahoma association community*— nurses, physical therapists, veterinarians, psychologists, engineers, insurance agents, and many others—provided rescue and relief within hours after the April 19, 1995, bombing of the Alfred P. Murrah Federal Building in downtown Oklahoma City. Members of several food-related associations setting up a convention nearby switched to helping feed and house rescue workers and victims.

The *American Academy of Dermatology* (Schaumburg, IL) created the Melanoma and Skin Cancer Detection and Prevention Campaign to increase public awareness of melanoma and skin cancer and to promote regular self-exams. An extensive media campaign complemented a free national skin cancer screening program with more than 3,000 dermatologists participating.

The *California Veterinary Medical Association* (Sacramento, CA) formed the Disaster Response Program to provide emergency rescue, treatment, and sheltering of displaced animals during disasters. Volunteer veterinarians worked alongside other disaster response agencies during the 1997 floods to rescue, shelter, and treat more than 2,500 pets and livestock.

The *Dairy Council, Inc.* (Southampton, PA) partnered with a children's theatrical company to create and tour "The Marvelous Machine" elementary school assembly project to educate children about proper nutrition and regular physical activity. More than 80,500 students in three states participated.

The *National Science Teachers Association* (Arlington, VA) created "Building a Presence for Science" to provide a copy of the National Science Education Standards to every school in the United States by 2000. A network of advocates works with teachers in every school to familiarize them with program guidelines and support systems.

The *American Medical Association Alliance* (Chicago, IL) sponsors the "SAVE-A-Shelter" program in hundreds of localities which helps physicians and their spouses adopt shelters, transition homes, rape crisis centers, and other community resources for abused women and children. Projects include training physicians in diagnosing abuse, teaching children conflict resolution skills, and providing women with career counseling.

The Nature of Programming

Much of what associations and societies do in the name of public relations follows an annual cycle: seeking new members, making reports to them, and holding conferences. Most associations engage in some of or all of the following:

1. Preparing and disseminating technical and educational publications, videos, and other public information materials

2. Sponsoring conventions and meetings, instructional seminars, and exhibitions
3. Handling government contacts and interpreting to members the legislative and administrative actions of government agencies
4. Compiling and publishing relevant statistics
5. Preparing and distributing news, information, and public service announcements to the media
6. Planning and implementing public service activities (see Exhibit 17.1 for examples of association public service programs)
7. Establishing and enforcing codes of ethics and standards of performance
8. Disseminating governmental and other standards to members
9. Conducting cooperative research: scientific, social, and economic
10. Placing institutional and product advertising on behalf of an entire industry, profession, or business endeavor; or in furtherance of such matters as public health, safety, or welfare (see Figure 17.2 for example of American Medical Association advocacy advertising)
11. Promoting good employee relations, accident prevention, and cooperation within an industry, profession, or other special-interest membership
12. Maintaining Internet and Intranet sites serving current information needs of members and external stakeholders

The public of first importance is members, with public officials second, the voting public third, and consumers or customers fourth. Trade associations typically rank consumers higher in the list. By design, associations facilitate the exchange of information among members and externally to publics who are affected by, involved with, or have an impact on members' activities. Nine out of ten associations conduct educational programs for both their members and external publics. The American Chamber of Commerce Executives (ACCE), the national association of chamber management professionals based in Alexandria, Virginia, for example, lists more than 100 books and other reference publications available to members. ACCE also offers members access to a comprehensive electronic database, ChamberNet, via the Internet (www.chambernet.org/). Members can access information about chamber management, membership databases, case studies, abstracts of chamber-related articles published in national and regional periodals, and other commercial information services. (See Figure 17.3.)

Trends include growing emphasis on public affairs and advocacy communication directed to external constituents and on the use of communication technology to meet the information needs of members. After interviewing a panel of technology consultants, the editor of ACCE's monthly journal to members, *Chamber Executive,* concluded that "providing information transcends all chamber functions and the future simply holds more of the same."[13] The panel of technology experts' observations about chambers apply to all associations:

> Chambers will have to become more information-driven if they want to impact legislation, do economic development, educate folks. Traditional (chambers of commerce) have been in the middle, moving information. Now there are so many sources of information that chambers must figure out how to tie-in, how to be-

FIGURE 17.2   AMERICAN MEDICAL ASSOCIATION ADVERTISEMENT

How do you improve on America's High Quality Health Care?

You Share it.

By making it accessible to all.

At its best, the U.S. medical system delivers the highest quality health care in the world. Advances in medicine have strengthened lives, lengthened lives and saved the lives of countless Americans. And for the 87% who have health care coverage, the system is working.

But we can do better.

Because, despite the overwhelming success of our medical system, 33 million uninsured Americans lack regular access to affordable health care, even though physicians donate an estimated $6 billion in free services each year.

That's why the American Medical Association and physicians across the country are finding ways to improve today's

health care system, through a proposal called Health Access America.

A proposal that endorses quality health care for all Americans, regardless of income or health status, by making it more accessible and affordable. And by expanding publicly-funded health care for the needy.

A proposal that requires employer coverage for all workers and their families, and provides tax incentives to encourage small businesses to offer health insurance to their employees.

A proposal that gives Americans an active role in selecting their own health care coverage, preserving their freedom of choice.

A proposal that reforms our Medicare program so every American is assured benefits following retirement.

Yes, change is needed. And America's physicians are ready to lead the way. The AMA recognizes that reform won't come quickly. That's why we're committed to working with government and other health care providers for as long as it takes to make this system work for everyone.

How can you improve on America's quality health care? Talk to your doctor about the issues. Share your views with others. And, for more information about our proposal, contact: Health Access America in care of The American Medical Association, 535 N. Dearborn Street, Chicago, IL, 60610.

Health Access America

The AMA proposal to improve access to affordable, quality health care.

The American Medical Association
on behalf of America's physicians.

Courtesy American Medical Association.

come a leading source of information and deliver that information faster, cheaper, easier. Otherwise, chambers will be usurped by technology.[14]

LABOR UNIONS

Organized labor unions, with a total membership of about 16 million, represent only about one of every seven of the nation's wage earners and salaried employees. The percentage of workers who belong to unions has been declining for more than 50 years. (See Table 17.1.) In 1983, for example, one of every five employed workers belonged to a union (20.1 percent), significantly

FIGURE 17.3   CHAMBERNET SEARCH MENUS

Courtesy American Chamber of Commerce Executives.

TABLE 17.1

UNION AFFILIATION

	Percentage of Union Members		
	1987[a]	1992[b]	1997[c]
All employed workers	17.0	15.8	14.1
Employed *men*	20.9	18.7	16.3
Employed *women*	12.6	12.7	11.6
Full-time workers	19.4	17.8	15.6
Part-time workers	6.7	7.2	7.0
Government workers	36.0	36.7	37.2
Manufacturing workers	23.2	19.7	16.3
Service workers	14.1	13.9	13.2
Total number employed workers (16+ yrs.)	99,303,000	103,688,000	114,533,000
Total union members	16,913,000	16,390,000	16,110,000

[a] *Employment and Earnings* 35, no. 1 (January, 1988): 222–23.
[b] *Employment and Earnings* 40, no. 1 (January, 1993): 238–39.
[c] *Employment and Earnings* 45, no. 1 (January, 1998): 215, 217.

lower than in 1945, when about one in three workers was a union member (35.5 percent).[15]

Despite the decline in membership, organized labor still symbolizes and speaks for working men and women in the United States. According to Lynn Williams, president of the United Steel Workers of America (USWA), suggestions that the labor movement is dead are exaggerated:

> The figures on unionization rates in the private sector are quite misleading. . . . When you look at the Northeastern states, such as New York and Pennsylvania, the percentage of the unionized work force is quite respectable by world standards. It's not the 90 percent-plus figure of Sweden or the 50 percent-plus of Germany or even the 40 percent figure of Canada. But at 34 percent, it's quite respectable.[16]

The American labor movement is credited with helping bring about many of the changes and legislation in civil rights, health, education, and employee rights that have occurred since the death of President Franklin Roosevelt. Labor's clout has diminished in recent years, however, as a result of changes in the workforce, a series of judicial rulings supportive of management, and declining public support of labor unions. The critical turning point may have occurred in 1981, when President Ronald Reagan ordered the firing of striking air traffic controllers, effectively breaking their union, the Professional Air Traffic Controllers Organization (PATCO).[17] Since that time, employers have used various tactics to counter powerful unions, including filing for protection under the bankruptcy laws, using company lockouts of striking workers, slashing payrolls or outsourcing to nonunion vendors, closing domestic plants and contracting with low-wage suppliers abroad, and following through on threats to replace striking workers.

The power of labor's voice in shaping national public opinion and policy goes far beyond what might be suggested by its modest numerical share of the popular electorate, however. One reason is that the movement's specific and deeply held convictions hold strong attraction for adherents. In the words of an early 1900s union organizer who was sentenced to be executed, "Don't mourn, organize."[18] Strong convictions get translated into cash that is dispersed to selected candidates by organized labor's powerful PACs. Even that power is being threatened by new and proposed state laws restricting the use of union dues for political purposes. For example, California Proposition 226 (passed in June 1998) requires unions to obtain a member's written permission before it can use any portion of that member's dues to support political candidates. Given labor unions' traditionally strong financial support of Democratic candidates, Republican leaders typically back such efforts to limit union involvement in politics.

Another reason unions remain powerful is that union leadership traditionally has been able to leverage concessions for members because of leadership's ability to deliver a majority of their members' votes as a bloc in local, state, and national elections. Even this traditional voting bloc power was threatened after the PATCO case. PATCO had broken ranks and joined the Teamsters in supporting Reagan over Jimmy Carter in 1980. In the 1992 and 1996 presidential elections, however, some credited union support with having made the difference in President Bill Clinton's bids for the White House.

The Role of Public Relations

In pursuing their stated goals, unions and their leadership share in the burden of responsibility for the health of the economy. When globalization forced a restructuring of the economy in the 1990s, it followed that there had to be changes in labor's role. Understandably, public relations took on added emphasis as labor's political, educational, and community involvement has increased, adding new roles to its traditional role in labor–management relations. The skills of public relations specialists and others have been augmented and honed to meet the needs of expanded, more sophisticated programs. Indicative of this trend, most unions now have a "public relations director" rather than a "publications director" who simply responds to news media inquiries between putting out union newsletters and other publications directed to members.

Awareness of the need to be more responsive constitutes a major change for the labor movement from the early days of George Meany, who served as the first president when the American Federation of Labor merged with the Congress of Industrial Organziations (AFL-CIO) in 1955. Meany's early notions of dealing with the media reportedly included the directive, "Kick the damn reporters down the stairs." For much of the mid-1950s until the 1970s, no group in American society had a more identifiable, outspoken, and unquestioned spokesperson than labor's Meany. He strongly backed the Vietnam War, provided lukewarm support for Democratic Senator George McGovern's presidential candidacy, and led the AFL-CIO call for President Richard Nixon's impeachment. For 25 years, he was the chief public relations spokesman for labor.

Labor's primary public relations orientation remains to print media, both within and outside the labor movement. Labor public relations uses press contacts, preparation and distribution of materials on specific subjects, television spots (see Figure 17.4), and interviews and press conferences to get labor's point of view across. Of increasing importance are the estimated 5,000 union publications on the national and local level. Many of these have improved their format and writing quality and toned down their rhetoric, often publishing articles from the International Labor Press Association about issues affecting the labor movement.

The Problem of Strikes

Labor has had its problems in developing and sustaining a broad base of sympathetic support from the nonunion lay public. This results, in part, from strikes—the strategic use of work stoppages to gain concessions from employers. Stoppages are typically timed for maximum inconvenience, thereby exerting the greatest pressure for settlement on the employer.

The effect of a strike, however, can extend well beyond employers, as many learned after the biggest strike in the history of professional sports—the 232-day strike of major league baseball in 1994–95. Fans were not pleased with the cancellation of postseason play and with the strike-shortened season in which several players were on track to break major league records. Team owners suffered through a 20-percent drop in attendance the first year after the strike. The average salary for players dropped by about 5 percent the year after the strike, "as financially straitened clubs dug deeply into the minor leagues for cheaper talent and many veterans were released or took sizable pay cuts."[19]

Despite the inconveniences and costs involved, the strike weapon is considered essential to labor's success. It is visible, in contrast to management's policies and reactions. It also takes advantage of management's need not to appear to be bullying workers and not to portray employees as enemies. Media coverage tends to feature picket lines, angry strikers, and vocal labor leaders. Management, on the other hand, is somewhat restricted by law as to what they can say and do. (Review the section in chapter 6 on the National Labor Act of 1935 and the Taft-Hartley Act of 1947.)

Explaining public inconveniences caused by strikes is part of the role public relations plays in organized labor. But it is a story that has had to be told less frequently: The number of major work stoppages and idleness in the 1990s was at its lowest levels since record keeping began in 1947. There were 38 work stoppages and almost five million days of idleness in 1996. A total of 275,000 workers were involved in major stoppages involving 1,000 or more workers.[20]

When I began working as a young man the
government had just started Social Security.

Part of every worker's paycheck would be matched
by the boss and sent to the government. When we
retired, we'd get enough of our money back to help
us get by.

It was sort of a contract between working people and
the government.

Now the administration wants to cut out some of the
benefits you'd get at 65. And at 62 they want to cut
your benefits . . . from 80% to 55%.

Courtesy American Federation of State, County, and Municipal Employees.

The Teamsters's strike of United Parcel Service of America (UPS) in 1997 reminded managers that unions still wield the power to shut down companies and other organizations. The UPS–Teamsters contract covering 185,000 workers expired at midnight July 31, 1997. Then teamsters president Ron Carey announced a strike when nogotiations ended on August 4. A tentative agreement was reached two weeks later, following a union public relations victory around the slogan, "Part-time America doesn't work." The strike cost UPS more than $600 million in lost business, plus undetermined additional costs of trying to win back customers that found alternative delivery services during the strike. It also forced the board of directors to reduce the company's stock price for the first time in the 90-year-old company's history. When the strike ended, customer comments illustrated the importance of building relationships:

> As UPS tries to win back customers, among its biggest allies, ironically, may be the former striking employees themselves. Over the years, UPS drivers have become ambassadors for Big Brown. . . . (A receptionist) said she has missed seeing the UPS man who picks up and drops off packages twice a day. "I'm so used to seeing him," she said. . . . Yesterday, after the UPS man stopped by, she said: "He was kind of rushing, but it was very nice to see him again."[21]

In contrast, the United Auto Workers's seven-year strike of Caterpillar Inc. ended in March 1998 without resolving some of the major issues—a two-tiered wage structure and overtime pay limits. The company prospered during the long strike, fired union members who would not cross picket lines, and hired replacement workers. Although the new six-year contract gives raises and job security to workers and reinstates fired union members, it clearly did not represent a victory for workers who had missed years of paychecks. Nor was it a victory in the court of public opinion during years when tens of thousands of workers were being laid off, displaced, and underpaid.

In a typical year, contract negotiations involve almost three million workers under 700 major collective bargaining agreements (those covering 1,000 or more workers).[22] On the surface, it would be easy to advise unions not to go on strike because of the impact on public opinion and relations with management. The primary obligation of unions, however, is to meet the needs of the people they represent. Strategic public relations in the labor movement often calls for leveraging labor's position of power in ways that will not be universally popular but that will achieve labor's goals for members.

The need for unions is as valid today as in the past, according to USWA President Williams:

> All across the United States, one sees that workers need to have their economic interests represented in order to be able to bargain with their employers to ensure that they receive the best wages and working conditions. Look at what has happened . . . the decline in real wages, barely maintainable family incomes despite the fact that both partners now work as a rule, the increase in temporary workers and companies contracting out.[23]

The Challenge for Labor

The challenges of public relations in the labor movement are basically the same as in all other settings: to establish and maintain mutually beneficial relationships with those upon whom success or failure depends. It is labor's position that its success should be measured not on a barometer of public opinion of its "image" but on results. Similarly, labor public relations efforts should be measured by the quality and persuasiveness of the information presented to union members and to other publics on important issues rather than on image-building advertising campaigns that ignore a union's inescapable responsibility to its members.

Members of the workforce in the 21st century will be largely younger than members today, female, and multicultural. Therefore, the greatest challenge facing the largely older, male, and white union leadership is not unlike the challenge facing leaders in other institutions: Labor must attract the next generation of leaders from females and people of color. To that end, in 1996 AFL-CIO President John Sweeney began "Union Summer," attracting more than 1,000 volunteers primarily from college campuses to work in the union movement—walking picket lines, demonstrating against unfair labor practices, knocking on doors to organize workers, and pressuring stores to stop buying goods made in sweatshops. The summer program reflects Sweeney's position on the state of the union movement—"Organize or Die."[24]

The AFL-CIO Organizing Institute also began an annual 6-month internship program that prepares young, potential leaders for careers as union organizers. The program goal is to place new organizers, with diversity in the leadership ranks as a priority. Seventy percent of the interns have been female or people from underrepresented groups.[25] In the final analysis, the labor movement is also a social movement in a changing environment.

Whereas the UPS strike demonstrates that union work stoppages can still be a powerful weapon for leveraging collective bargaining demands, the long and generally unsuccessful Caterpillar strike reminds that the Industrial Revolution—which gave rise to labor unions—has given way to the Information Age, changing the rules for unions. According to futurist David Pearce Snyder,

> We in America are reinventing our corporations, reinventing government, reinventing labor relations, reinventing health care and public education. We are reinventing all of our great institutions, and when we are all done, we will have reinvented America. The other industrial nations are beginning to reinvent themselves as well. Eventually, the whole world will be reinvented.[26]

In labor unions, as in all other organizational settings, public relations will play a central role as organizations reinvent themselves and their relationships with publics during the 21st century. Change, in the final analysis, drives the public relations management function.

NOTES

1. Christine Maurer and Tara E. Sheets, eds., *Encylopedia of Associations,* 33rd ed., vol. 1 (Detroit: Gale Research, 1998), vii.
2. Buck Downs et al., eds., *National Trade and Professional Associations of the United States,* 33rd ed. (New York: Columbia Books, 1998), 6.
3. "Associations in a Nutshell," fact sheet published by the American Society of Association Executives, Washington, DC, March 29, 1998. Current information available on-line at www.asaenet.org.
4. *Encyclopedia of Associations,* 33rd ed., vols. 1 and 2 (Detroit: Gale Research, 1998). Association listings also available by CD-ROM and on-line (**www.gale.com**).
5. Personal communication from Lorri Lee Ragan, APR, Director of Public Relations, American Society of Association Executives, April 3, 1998. Lee helped update this chapter by providing useful suggestions, data, examples, and illustrations.
6. Personal communication from Thomas G. Toftey, Director of Corporate Relations, American Medical Association, Chicago, October 26, 1993.
7. *Jack O'Dwyer's Newsletter* 23, no. 24 (June 13, 1990): 1.
8. Salary figures from *Association Executive Compensation Study,* 10th ed. (Washington, DC: American Society of Association Executives, January 1996), xiii.
9. From "Wisconsin Milk Marketing Board 'Middle Nickel,' " unpublished 1993 case study, Morgan and Myers (public relations firm), Jefferson, WI.
10. Helen Frank Bensimon and Patricia A. Walker, "Associations Gain Prestige and Visibility by Serving as Expert Resources for Media," *Public Relations Journal* 48, no. 2 (February 1992): 16.
11. Ibid., 16.
12. R. William Taylor, in speech to the International Convention Center Conference, October 29, 1993, San Antonio, TX.
13. "Changing Technology—How Can We Keep Up?" *Chamber Executive* 20, no. 9 (September 1993): 1.
14. Ibid. Quote from Mike Herron, president, Humanomics, Sandy, OR.
15. Data on union affiliation found in the January issues of *Employment and Earnings,* published monthly by the U.S. Department of Labor, Bureau of Labor Statistics, Washington, DC.
16. Ibid., 116.
17. Mark Shields, "What PATCO Did to Labor," *Washington Post National Weekly Edition,* January 2, 1984, p. 26.
18. John Hill, as quoted by Barbara Presley Noble, "Organizing the Future," *Harvard Business Review* 71, no. 4 (July–August 1993): 124.
19. Paul D. Staudohar, "The Baseball Strike of 1994–95," *Monthly Labor Review* 120, no. 3 (March 1997): 21, 26–27.
20. *Monthly Labor Review* 121, no. 1 (January 1998): Table 26.
21. "UPS Cuts Its Stock Price in Aftermath of Strike," *Wall Street Journal,* August 21, 1997, p. A16.
22. Lisa M. Williamson, "Collective Bargaining in 1993: Jobs Are the Issue," *Monthly Labor Review* 116, no. 1 (January 1993): 3.
23. Noble, "Reinventing Labor," 121.
24. Margot Hornblower, "Labor's Youth Brigade," *Time,* July 15, 1996, pp. 44–45.
25. Noble, "Organizing the Future," 124.
26. David Pearce Snyder, "The Revolution in the Workplace: What's Happening to Our Jobs?" *The Futurist* 30, no. 2 (March–April 1996): 13.

ADDITIONAL SOURCES

"Association Public Relations," special issue of *Public Relations Quarterly* 37, no. 1 (Spring 1992). Features a collection of articles on professional, ethical, legal, and management issues in association public relations.

Ballot, Michael. *Labor-Management Relations in a Changing Environment.* New York: John Wiley and Sons, 1992. Covers the broad field of industrial relations, including the changing relationship between unions and employers, the future of organized labor, and public sector unionization.

Dunlop, John T. *Industrial Relations Systems,* rev. ed. Boston: Harvard Business School Press, 1993. Presents a general theory of industrial relations, outlining the formal and informal ways management organizations, workers, and government agencies are organized.

Godfried, Nathan. *WCFL: Chicago's Voice of Labor, 1926–78.* Champaign: University of Illinois Press, 1997. Traces Chicago Federation of Labor's attempt to create a "voice of labor" by establishing Chicago radio station WCFL.

Heckscher, Charles C. *The New Unionism,* rev. ed. Ithaca, NY: ILR Press, 1996. Argues that the displacement of manufacturing and production line jobs by white-collar and service-sector jobs is eroding the influence of traditional unions slow to change from their 19th-century origins.

Henson, Keven D. *Just a Temp.* Philadelphia: Temple University Press, 1996. Presents history of rapidly expanding business of temporary help supply firms, portrays who temporary workers are and what they do, and suggests policy changes to improve working conditions for temporary workers.

Masters, Marick F. *Unions at the Crossroads: Strategic Membership, Financial, and Political Perspectives.* Westport, CT: Quorum Books, 1997. Analyzes "institutional health" of the 28 unions in the United States with 80 percent of all union members and control over two-thirds of all union wealth.

Robinson, Archie. *George Meany and His Times: A Biography.* New York: Simon and Schuster, 1981. Details the life and personality of the man who shaped the American labor movement and the political events and social changes during his 63 years in labor unions.

Tilly, Chris. *Half a Job: Bad and Good Part-Time Jobs in a Changing Labor Market.* Philadelphia: Temple University Press, 1996. Explores why part-time employment has increased, where part-time jobs exist, and how organizations choose to use part-time instead of full-time workers.

INDEX

Arnold, Gen. H. H., 131
Arnold, Jim, 76–77
Arthur W. Page Society, 127, 163, *164*
Arts groups, 551
Arvida Corp., 206
ASAE (American Society of Association Executives), 557, 560–61
Associated Advertising Clubs of the World, 128
Associated Press (AP), 309–10
Association for Education in Journalism and Mass Communication, 134
Association of American College News Bureaus, 129
Associations and societies, 556–64, 565
Asymmetric digital subscriber line (ADSL), 322–23
AT&T
    and Arthur W. Page Society, 163
    break-up of Bell System, 240
    employment of PR practitioners, 32
    history of public relations, 113, 116, 120, 127
Attention considerations in communication, 251
Audience considerations, 257–58, 260–63, 444 (*see also* Publics)
Audit Bureau of Circulation (ABC), 444
Ayer, N. W., 113, 120

B

"Backgrounders," reprinted, 295
Baer, George F., 117
Baker, Joseph Varney, 130
Baker, Ray Stannard, 114
Baker v. *Daly,* 157
Bank Marketing Association, 128
Barkelew, Ann H., 351
Barlow, Walter, 345
Barnum, Phineas Taylor ("P. T."), 106–7
Barriers to communication, 417–19, *422,* 495, 497–502
Barry, David S., 118
Baxter, Leone, 130
Beckley, John, 107
Beeman, Alice L., 129
Bell, Eugene C. and Sue H., 240–41
Bell Telephone System, 105, 240 (*see also* AT&T)
Benchmark 1997 survey, 79
Benton & Bowles, 84
Bentsen, Lloyd, 20
Bernays, Edward L.
    career development, 123, 124
    definition of public relations, 3
    on history of public relations, 112
    on licensing and accreditation, 150, 155–56, 157
    role of PR in democracy, 244
    on semantics of message, 413
Bhopal chemical manufacturing incident, 465
Biddle, Nicholas, 102, 105–6

Bjornlund, Lydia, 498
Blackmun, Harry, 183
Black Public Relations Society, 163
Bleyer, Willard G., 121
Block, Edward M., 96, 372
Blythe, Richard, 125
Body of knowledge, importance of profession's, 152–55 (*see also* Research, public relations)
Boeing Company, 67
Boesky, Ivan, 210
Boorstin, Daniel, 148
Boulware, Lemuel R., 205
Bradlee, Ben, 325
Brennan, William J., 193
Bridge, C. A., 116
Brisbane, Arthur, 117
Broadcast media, 193–95, 315–23, 493
Brodeur Porter Novelli, 81
Brown, David, 506
Bruno, Harry A., 125
Bruno Magli, 14
Bryan, William Jennings, 108
Buckley, Walter, 236, 243
Buckley v. *Valeo,* 186, 188
Budgeting, and planning process, 394–96
Bulletin boards, organizational, 295–96
Burger, Chester, 87, 241, 330
Burger, Warren, 193
Burson, Harold, 83, 408
Burson-Marsteller, 31–32, 81, 83, 84, 92
Bush, George, 194
Business
    government as, 512–13
    public perceptions over time, 460–69
Byoir, Carl, 122, 123

C

Cable television, 322–23
Calhoun, John C., 105
Call-in telephone lines, 356–57
Campaign, public relations, 419–20
Campaigning, political. (*See* Political considerations)
Canadian Public Relations Society (CPRS), 47–48, 161
Cantor, Bill, 52, 54–55
Carey, Ron, 570
Carl Byoir & Associates, 191
Carlzon, Jan, 224
Carnation Company, 210
CASE (Council for the Advancement and Support of Education), 129, 543–44
Caterpillar, Inc., 570, 571
Catholic Church, ancient public relations, 102
CCTV (closed circuit television), 301–2
Celler, Emanuel, 191

Strategy Research, 431
Strikes, labor, 568, 570
Structure vs. process in systems theory, 234
Student organizations, 165
Subsystems, 231–33
Success, requirements for, practitioners of public relations, 52–53
Sumner Rider & Associates, 83
Supplemental publications, 293
Supportive-disposal subsystems, 233
Suprasystems, 231–33
Supreme Court, U.S.
    on First Amendment issues, 181–84, 186
    on labor relations, 204
    licensing issue, 157
    on lobbying, 189, 190–91
    on media access issues, 192–93
    on referenda issues, 187–88
Surles, Alexander, 131
Surveys, 362–64
Sweeney, John, 571
Swift, Paul, 293
Sybron Chemical Inc., 408–9
Symbols and stereotypes, 415–17
Systems perspective on organizations, 228–33

T

Tactics vs. strategy, 377–78
Taft-Hartley Act, 185, 204
Tandem Computers, Inc., 12
Tarbell, Ida, 113
Task Force on the Stature and Role of Public Relations, 66
Taylor, R. William, 560–61
Technician vs. managerial roles, 45–48
Technology issues, 287, 296, 299–304, 322–23
Teixeira, Ruy A., 497
"Telecommunities," 226
Teleconferencing, 299–301
Telephone lines, 356–59
Television, 301–2, 317–23
Texaco, 63–64
Texas Beef Group, 239
Texas Gulf Sulphur, 210
Third sector. (*See* Nonprofit organizations)
30-3-30 formula, 412–13
Thomas R. Shipp and Co., 116
Three Mile Island, 463
Time v. *Hill,* 157
Time Warner, 34
TIRC (Tobacco Industry Research Committee), 125–26
Titles and reporting relationships, 23–24, 72–74, *75,* 460
Tobacco Industry Research Committee (TIRC), 125–26

Toffler, Alvin, 221
Top management role in public relations, 63–65, 453–54, 467–68
Tornillo, Pat, 192
Toshiba Corp., 12
Total quality management (TQM), 480
Towers, Perrin, Forster and Crosby, 289
TQM, (total quality management), 480
Trade associations, 556
Trademarks, 203
Trade names, 203
Trading of securities, 207–9
Traffic Audit Bureau, 444
Traverse-Healy, Tim, 482
Trinity Episcopal Church of New York City, 121
Trust, importance in PR, 145
TWA, 63, 64
Two-way communication, 3–4
Tylenol crisis, 26, 63, 301, 464
Tyler, Bessie, 127

U

Uhlman v. *Sherman,* 192
Union Carbide, 465
United Airlines, 67
United Auto Workers, 570
United Nations, 162
United Parcel Service (UPS), 570, 571
United Press International (UPI), 309
United States, origins of public relations in, 102–6
United Way of America, 232, 536–37
Universal Accreditation, 158
Universal Press Syndicate, 312
Universities and colleges
    and excess overhead charges, 78
    historical development of public relations, 121, 124, 129, 150–51
    PR for, 542–47
University Bureau of Publicity, 121
University of Chicago, 121
University of Illinois, 150
University of Pennsylvania, 121
University of Stirling in Scotland, 151
University of Wisconsin, 121
University of Wisconsin Press, 154
UPI (United Press International), 309
UPS (United Parcel Service), 570, 571
Upward vs. downward communication, 289
U.S. Air Force, 78
U.S. Army Air Corps, 131
U.S. Department of Labor, 30, 32
U.S. Information Agency (USIA), 31, 131, 133, 493–94
U.S. Information Service (USIS), 493
U.S. Marine Corps, 121
U.S. Navy, 131
U.S. Office of Personnel Management, 31